EVIDENCE

by
Steven Emanuel

Harvard Law School, J.D. 1976

Second Edition
with the assistance of

Renee Samuelson

William Mitchell College of Law, J.D. 1988

emanuel law outlines,inc.

Evidence, Second Edition, Copyright © 1991 by Steven L. Emanuel
Emanuel Law Outlines, Inc. • 1865 Palmer Avenue • Larchmont, NY 10538

Dedication

In memory of my father-in-law
Herman Mandel

Abbreviations Used in Text

FRE — *Federal Rules of Evidence*

G&N — Green and Nesson, *Problems, Cases, and Materials on Evidence* (1983)

Imwinkelried — Edward Imwinkelried, *Evidentiary Foundations* (2nd Ed. 1989)

K&W — Kaplan and Waltz, *Cases and Materials on Evidence* (6th Ed. 1987 with 1990 Supplement)

L&S — Lempert and Saltzburg, *A Modern Approach to Evidence*, (2nd Ed. 1983)

Lilly — Graham Lilly, *An Introduction to the Law of Evidence* (2nd Ed. 1987)

M — Cleary *et al*, *McCormick on Evidence* (3rd Ed. 1984)

S&R — Saltzburg and Redden, *Federal Rules of Evidence Manual* (4th Ed. 1986)

W,M,A&B — Weinstein, Mansfield, Abrams and Berger, *Cases and Materials on Evidence* (8th Ed. 1988 with 1990 Supplement)

W&B — Weinstein and Berger, *Weinstein's Evidence* (1986)

ACKNOWLEDGEMENT

The diagrams on Pages 118, 122, 123 and 124 of this Outline and the chart on Page 445 were adapted in part from Lempert and Saltzburg, *A Modern Approach To Evidence*; permission by West Publishing Co. to adapt them is gratefully acknowledged.

TABLE OF CONTENTS

CAPSULE SUMMARY .... C-1.

BASIC CONCEPTS

I. FIRST PRINCIPLES .... 1.

    A. Only admissible evidence usable .... 1.

    B. Roles of judge and jury................................. 1.

    C. The Federal Rules .... 1.

II. ORGANIZATION OF THE TRIAL .... 2.

    A. Flow of the case .... 2.

    B. Examination of witnesses .... 3.

        1. Four stages .... 3.

        2. Sequestration of witnesses .... 3.

III. MAKING AND RESPONDING TO OBJECTIONS .... 4.

    A. Making objections .... 4.

    B. Time for objection .... 4.

    C. General vs. specific objections .... 4.

        1. Effect of specificity on appeal .... 4.

    D. Taking of "exceptions" .... 5.

    E. Offer of proof .... 6.

    F. The "plain error" and "harmless error" doctrines .... 7.

IV. COMPETENCY .... 7.

    A. Meaning.. 7.

    B. Common-law approach .... 7.

    C. Modern approach .... 7.

        1. Federal Rules .... 7.

        2. Dead Man's Statutes .... 8.

RELEVANCE

I. RELEVANCE GENERALLY .... 10.

    A. All relevant evidence admitted......................... 10.

    B. Two aspects of relevance .... 10.

        1. Probative relationship .... 10.

        2. Materiality .... 10.

    C. "Direct" vs. "circumstantial" evidence .... 11.

        1. Consequence of distinction .... 11.

II. PROBATIVE VALUE .... 11.

    A. Problem generally .... 11.

    B. Chain of inference .... 12.

III. PREJUDICE, CONFUSION, AND WASTE OF TIME .... 14.

    A. "Counterweights" to relevance......................... 14.

    B. Prejudice .... 14.

    C. Confusion .... 15.

    D. Waste of time .... 15.

    E. No "unfair surprise" .... 15.

    F. Standard for appellate review .... 15.

CIRCUMSTANTIAL PROOF: SPECIAL PROBLEMS

I. CHARACTER EVIDENCE IN GENERAL . . . . 17.
    A. Nature of the problem . . . . 17.
        1. Countervailing considerations . . . . 17.
        2. General rule . . . . 18.
        3. Distinctions . . . . 18.

II. CHARACTER IN ISSUE . . . . 19.
    A. General rule . . . . 19.
    B. Type of evidence . . . . 19.

III. CHARACTER AS CIRCUMSTANTIAL EVIDENCE -- GENERALLY . . 20.

**IV. USE OF CIRCUMSTANTIAL CHARACTER EVIDENCE
     IN CIVIL CASES** . . . . 20.
    A. General rule . . . . 20.
    B. Character for care . . . . 20.
    C. Quasi-criminal acts alleged . . . . 21.
        1. Minority view . . . . 21.
        2. Majority view . . . . 21.

V. OTHER CRIMES AS EVIDENCE IN CRIMINAL CASES . . . . 22.
    A. General principle . . . . 22.
    B. Proof of element of crime . . . . 23.
        1. Admissible . . . . 23.
        2. No catalogue . . . . 24.
    C. Context . . . . 24.
    D. Larger plan . . . . 24.
    E. Preparation . . . . 25.
    F. "Signature" or modus operandi . . . . 25.
    G. Intent . . . . 26.
        1. Rebutting an innocent explanation . . . . 26.
        2. Requirement of similarity . . . . 26.
        3. Degree of similarity . . . . 26.
    H. Abnormal sex . . . . 28.
        1. Same victim . . . . 28.
        2. Different victim . . . . 28.
    I. Knowledge . . . . 29.
    J. Motive . . . . 29.
    K. Opportunity . . . . 30.
    L. Identity . . . . 30.
    M. Impeachment . . . . 31.
    N. Other exceptions . . . . 31.
    O. Other issues . . . . 32.
        1. Degree of certainty . . . . 32.
        2. Genuine controversy . . . . 34.
        3. Subsequent acts . . . . 34.

VI. EVIDENCE OF CRIMINAL DEFENDANT'S GOOD CHARACTER . . . 36.
    A. General rule . . . . 36.
    B. Method of proof . . . . 37.
    C. Rebuttal by prosecution . . . . 38.
        1. Character "in issue" . . . . 38.

    2. Cross-examination of defendant's witness . . . . 38.

VII. **CHARACTER OF VICTIM, ESPECIALLY IN CASES OF ASSAULT, MURDER, AND RAPE** . . . . 40.

   A. Problem generally . . . . 40.
   B. Murder and assault victims . . . . 41.
      1. Knowledge unnecessary . . . . 41.
      2. Type of evidence . . . . 41.
      3. Rebuttal by prosecution . . . . 42.
   C. Rape . . . . 43.
      1. Rape Shield laws . . . . 44.
      2. Federal Rape Shield law . . . . 44.

VIII. **HABIT AND CUSTOM** . . . . 47.
   A. General rule . . . . 47.
   B. Distinction between habit and character . . . . 48.
   C. Minority rule . . . . 48.
   D. Federal rule . . . . 49.
   E. Business practice . . . . 50.

IX. **SIMILAR HAPPENINGS** . . . . 50.
   A. General problem . . . . 50.
   B. Similar accidents and injuries . . . . 51.
      1. Evidence of past safety . . . . 52.
   C. Other kinds of events . . . . 52.
      1. Contracts . . . . 52.
      2. Criminal allegations . . . . 54.
      3. Prior claims by same plaintiff . . . . 54.
      4. Accident proneness . . . . 54.

X. **SUBSEQUENT REMEDIAL MEASURES** . . . . 55.
   A. Problem generally . . . . 55.
   B. Permissible purposes . . . . 56.
      1. Typical issues . . . . 56.
      2. Federal Rule . . . . 57.
      3. Must be controverted . . . . 57.
   C. Third persons . . . . 58.
   D. Product liability . . . . 58.

XI. **LIABILITY INSURANCE** . . . . 59.

XII. **COMPROMISES AND OFFERS TO PLEAD GUILTY; OFFERS TO PAY MEDICAL EXPENSES** . . . . 60.

   A. Compromises . . . . 60.
      1. Actual dispute required . . . . 60.
      2. What is excluded . . . . 61.
      3. Other purposes . . . . 62.
      4. Completed compromises . . . . 63.
   B. Guilty pleas . . . . 64.
      1. Offer of plea . . . . 64.
      2. Withdrawn plea . . . . 65.
      3. Impeachment . . . . 65.
   C. Payment of medical expenses . . . . 65.

EXAMINATION AND IMPEACHMENT OF WITNESSES

I. DIRECT EXAMINATION . . . . 66.
    A. Definition of direct examination . . . . 66.
    B. Free narrative vs. specific questions . . . . 66.
    C. Leading questions . . . . 67.
        1. Definition of leading . . . . 67.
        2. Exceptions . . . . 68.
    D. Impeachment of own witness . . . . 69.

II. CROSS-EXAMINATION . . . . 69.
    A. Nature of cross-examination . . . . 69.
    B. Leading questions allowed . . . . 70.
    C. Scope of Cross . . . . 70.
        1. "Restrictive" majority rule . . . . 70.
        2. Traditional "wide open" rule . . . . 72.
        3. Middle ground . . . . 72.
    D. Art of cross-examination . . . . 72.

III. REDIRECT AND RECROSS . . . . 73.
    A. Redirect . . . . 73.
        1. Scope . . . . 73.
        2. Discretion of judge . . . . 74.
    B. Recross . . . . 74.

IV. REFRESHING RECOLLECTION AND OTHER TECHNIQUES . . . . . 74.
    A. Refreshing the witness' recollection . . . . 74.
        1. Traditional rule . . . . 75.
        2. Danger . . . . 75.
        3. Document consulted before trial . . . . 75.
    B. Argumentative and misleading questions . . . . 76.

V. EXAMINATION BY THE COURT . . . . 76.
    A. General rule . . . . 76.
        1. Witness called by judge . . . . 76.
        2. Judge's discretion . . . . 77.
        3. Questioning by judge . . . . 77.

VI. IMPEACHMENT--GENERALLY . . . . 77.
    A. Meaning of "impeachment" . . . . 77.
    B. Five types . . . . 77.
    C. Impeaching one's own witness . . . . 78.
        1. Rationale . . . . 78.
        2. Exceptions to common-law rule . . . . 79.
        3. Modern and Federal rule . . . . 80.
        4. Leading questions . . . . 80.

VII. IMPEACHMENT BY PRIOR CRIMINAL CONVICTIONS . . . . . . 80.
    A. Problem generally . . . . 80.
    B. Common-law approach . . . . 81.
    C. Federal Rules . . . . 81.
        1. Criminal defendant as witness . . . . 81.
        2. Definition of *crimen falsi* . . . . 82.
        3. No discretion . . . . 82.

    4. Similar prior felonies . . . . 82.
    5. Balancing . . . . 83.
    6. Witnesses other than an accused . . . . 84.
    7. Time limit . . . . 84.
    8. *In limine* motions . . . . 85.
    9. Pardon . . . . 86.
   10. Juvenile adjudications . . . . 86.
   11. Appeals . . . . 86.
   12. *Nolo contendere* pleas . . . . 87.

VIII. IMPEACHMENT BY PRIOR BAD ACTS . . . . 87.
IX. IMPEACHMENT BY OPINION AND REPUTATION

     REGARDING CHARACTER . . . . 91.
  A. Issue generally . . . . 91.
    1. Distinguished from substantive evidence . . . . . . 91.
  B. Common-law rule . . . . 91.
    1. Reputation . . . . 91.
    2. General character not allowed . . . . 91.
    3. Opinion . . . . 92.
    4. Opening the issue . . . . 92.
    5. Proof that others have disbelieved witness . . . . . 92.
  C. Federal Rule . . . . 92.

X. IMPEACHMENT BY PRIOR INCONSISTENT STATEMENTS . . . . 93.
  A. General rule . . . . 94.
    1. Limits . . . . 94.
    2. Parties not covered . . . . 94.
  B. Foundation requirement . . . . 95.
    1. Common law . . . . 95.
    2. Federal rule . . . . 96.
    3. Writing . . . . 96.
  C. Extrinsic evidence . . . . 97.
    1. Limits . . . . 97.
    2. Federal Rule . . . . 98.
    3. Use for substantive purposes . . . . 98.

XI. IMPEACHMENT FOR BIAS . . . . 98.
  A. Types of bias . . . . 98.
    1. Friendly feeling . . . . 99.
    2. Hostility . . . . 99.
    3. Self-interest . . . . 99.
    4. Membership in group . . . . 99.
  C. Foundation . . . . 99.
    1. Extrinsic evidence . . . . 99.
    2. Federal Rules . . . . 100.
    3. Bias never collateral . . . . 100.
  D. Confrontation Clause rights in criminal cases . . . . 100.
    1. Sexual history of rape victim . . . . 100.

XII. IMPEACHMENT BY SENSORY OR MENTAL DEFECTS . . . . 101.
  A. General Rule . . . . 101.
    1. Sensory defect . . . . 101.
    2. Mental defect . . . . 101.
    3. Drugs and alcohol . . . . 101.

4. Psychiatric testimony . . . . 101.

XIII. **IMPEACHMENT BY CONTRADICTION; THE "COLLATERAL ISSUE" RULE** . . . . 102.
   A. General theory of contradiction . . . . 102.
   B. "Collateral issue" rule . . . . 102.
      1. The *Oswalt* case as illustration . . . . 102.
      2. Solely for contradiction . . . . 103.
      3. Rationale . . . . 103.
      4. Various contexts for rule . . . . 103.
      5. Fact about which no honest mistake possible . . . . 105.
      6. Federal approach . . . . 105.

XIV. **RELIGIOUS BELIEFS** . . . . 105.

XV. **REHABILITATING THE IMPEACHED WITNESS** . . . . 106.
   A. General rules . . . . 106.
      1. No bolstering . . . . 106.
      2. Exceptions . . . . 106.
   B. Rehabilitation . . . . 107.
   C. Must meet the attack . . . . 107.
      1. Two categories . . . . 107.
      2. Good character . . . . 107.
      3. Prior consistent statement . . . . 108.

XVI. **SOME SPECIAL TECHNIQUES FOR DEVELOPING OR EVALUATING TESTIMONY** . . . . 110.
   A. Scope . . . . 110.
   B. Psychiatric testimony . . . . 110.
      1. Sex cases . . . . 111.
      2. Other cases . . . . 111.
   C. Hypnosis and truth serum . . . . 112.
      1. Statement made under influence . . . . 112.
      2. Testimony at trial . . . . 112.
      3. Criminal defendant's right to testify . . . . 113.
   D. Lie detector tests . . . . 114.

HEARSAY

I. **INTRODUCTION** . . . . 117.
   A. Nature of hearsay . . . . 117.
      1. Basic definition . . . . 117.
      2. Written hearsay . . . . 117.
   B. Truth of matter asserted . . . . 117.
   C. Dangers of hearsay . . . . 118.
      1. The four dangers . . . . 118.
      2. Tribe's triangle . . . . 118.
   D. Dangers of out-of-court declaration . . . . 119.
      1. Explanation . . . . 119.
      2. Mistakes in transmittal . . . . 121.
      3. Cross-examination . . . . 121.

II. **THE DEFINITION OF HEARSAY** . . . . 121.
   A. The problem generally . . . . 121.

1. Common-law definition . . . . 122.
2. Federal Rule's definition . . . . 125.
B. Statement made "out of court" . . . . 126.
C. "Truth of matter asserted" . . . . 127.
1. Significance of assertions for truth . . . . 127.
2. Verbal acts . . . . 128.
3. Verbal parts of acts . . . . 128.
4. Effect on hearer or reader . . . . 129.
5. Declarant's state of mind . . . . 131.
6. Reputation . . . . 134.
7. Opinion surveys . . . . 134.
8. Impeachment . . . . 135.
D. Statements and conduct . . . . 135.
1. Assertive conduct . . . . 135.
2. Silence . . . . 136.
3. Non-assertive conduct . . . . 138.
4. Assertions not offered to prove truth of matter asserted . . . . 141.
E. Other hearsay problems . . . . 143.
1. Lack of first-hand knowledge . . . . 143.
2. "Not offered in presence of party" . . . . 145.
3. Multiple hearsay . . . . 145.
4. "Statements" by machines or animals . . . . 146.

EXCEPTIONS TO THE HEARSAY RULE

I. INTRODUCTION . . . . 149.
   A. Availability of declarant . . . . 149.
   B. Confrontation Clause of Constitution . . . . 149.
II. ADMISSIONS . . . . 149.
   A. Admissions made by party-opponent . . . . 149.
   B. General rule . . . . 150.
      1. Rationale . . . . 150.
      2. Distinguish from declaration against interest . . . . 150.
      3. May be contradicted in court . . . . 151.
      4. Can be opinion or conclusion . . . . 151.
      5. Federal Rule . . . . 152.
   C. Personal admission . . . . 152.
      1. Representative capacity . . . . 152.
      2. Pleadings . . . . 153.
      3. Conduct as admission . . . . 154.
      4. Admissions in criminal case . . . . 154.
   D. Adoptive admissions . . . . 155.
      1. Test for adoption . . . . 155.
      2. Real acquiescence . . . . 155.
      3. Silence . . . . 156.
   E. Representative admissions . . . . 158.
      1. Explicitly authorized admission . . . . 158.
      2. Vicarious admissions by agents . . . . 159.
      3. Other exceptions . . . . 161.
   F. Co-conspirators . . . . 161.
      1. Partners . . . . 161.
      2. General rule . . . . 162.

3. Requirements for exception . . . . 164.
4. "In furtherance" requirement . . . . 165.
5. No need to be charged with conspiracy . . . . 166.
6. Procedure . . . . 166.
G. **Privity** . . . . 167.

III. **AVAILABILITY IMMATERIAL - GENERALLY** . . . . 168.
A. **Rationale** . . . . 168.
B. **Exceptions** . . . . 168.

IV. **SPONTANEOUS, EXCITED, OR CONTEMPORANEOUS
UTTERANCES (INCLUDING STATEMENTS ABOUT
PHYSICAL OR MENTAL CONDITION)** . . . . 168.
A. **General Principle** . . . . 168.
B. **Statements of physical condition** . . . . 168.
1. Statements to laypersons . . . . 169.
2. Statements to treating physician . . . . 170.
3. Statements to third persons . . . . 171.
4. Physician who does not treat but testifies . . . . 171.
C. **Statements about the declarant's mental state** . . . . . . 172.
1. State of mind directly in issue . . . . 172.
2. Proof of subsequent act . . . . 175.
3. Cooperation of other . . . . 177.
4. Proof of prior acts . . . . 180.
D. **Excited utterances** . . . . 184.
1. Federal codification . . . . 184.
2. Sufficiently startling . . . . 185.
3. Time factor . . . . 185.
4. Reference to exciting event . . . . 186.
E. **Present sense impressions** . . . . 187.
1. *Houston Oxygen* case . . . . 187.
2. Immediacy . . . . 188.
3. No corroboration required . . . . 188.

V. **PAST RECOLLECTION RECORDED** . . . . 189.
A. **Requirements for the rule** . . . . 189.
1. First-hand knowledge . . . . 190.
2. Made when fresh in memory . . . . 190.
3. Impaired recollection . . . . 190.
4. Accuracy when written . . . . 191.
B. **Other considerations** . . . . 191.
1. Not always admissible as evidence . . . . 191.
2. Distinguished from present recollection refreshed . . . . . . 192.

VI. **BUSINESS RECORDS** . . . . 193.
A. **History** . . . . 193.
1. Two historical exceptions . . . . 193.
2. Federal Rule . . . . 194.
B. **Definition of "business"** . . . . 194.
C. **Person who originally supplies information** . . . . 194.
1. First-hand information . . . . 195.
2. Requirement of business duty . . . . 195.
D. **Made in "regular course of business"** . . . . 196.
1. *Palmer* case . . . . 196.

      2. Modern view . . . . 196.
      3. Police reports and records . . . . 197.
  E. Opinions . . . . 197.
  F. Trustworthiness . . . . 198.
  G. Absence of Entry . . . . 198.
  H. Oral Report . . . . 199.
  I. Proving the record . . . . 200.
      1. Who must be called . . . . 200.
  J. Special situations . . . . 200.
      1. Hospital records . . . . 200.
      2. Computer printouts . . . . 202.

VII. PUBLIC RECORDS AND REPORTS . . . . 204.
  A. Common-law rule . . . . 204.
      1. Self-authenticating . . . . 204.
      2. Not-necessarily open to public . . . . 204.
      3. Evaluative reports . . . . 205.
  B. Federal Rule . . . . 205.
  C. Three Categories . . . . 205.
      1. Activities of the office . . . . 205.
      2. Matters observed under duty . . . . 206.
      3. Investigative reports . . . . 206.
  D. Criminal cases . . . . 207.
      1. Federal language . . . . 207.
      2. Accused's use of subsection(B) . . . . 207.
      3. "Other law enforcement personnel" . . . . 207.
      4. Routine observations . . . . 208.
      5. Use of "business records" or other rules . . . . 208.
  E. Other issues . . . . 210.
      1. "Factual" versus "evaluative" . . . . 210.
      2. Trustworthiness . . . . 211.
      3. Multiple hearsay . . . . 212.

VIII. MISCELLANEOUS EXCEPTIONS -- AVAILABILITY

IMMATERIAL . . . . 214.
  A. Learned writings and commercial publications . . . . . . 214.
      1. Common law . . . . 214.
      2. Federal Rule . . . . 215.
      3. Commercial publications . . . . 216.
  B. Ancient documents and documents relating to property . . . . . . 216.
      1. Ancient documents . . . . 217.
      2. Newer title documents . . . . 218.
  C. Reputation . . . . 218.
      1. Personal or family history . . . . 218.
      2. Boundaries and general historical facts . . . . 219.
      3. Reputation for character . . . . 219.
  D. Miscellaneous public and quasi-public records . . . . 219.
      1. Vital statistics . . . . 219.
      2. Marriage certificates . . . . 220.
      3. Vital statistics kept by religious organizations . . . . 220.
      4. Absence of public record . . . . 221.
      5. Previous felony convictions . . . . 221.

IX. UNAVAILABILITY REQUIRED -- GENERALLY . . . . 222.
    A. Introduction . . . . 222.
        1. Not necessarily less reliable . . . . 222.
        2. Four main exceptions . . . . 222.
    B. Meaning of "unavailable" . . . . 223.
        1. Federal rule . . . . 223.
        2. States generally follow . . . . 223.
        3. Constitutional problems . . . . 224.

X. FORMER TESTIMONY . . . . 225.
    A. In general . . . . 225.
    B. Opportunity for cross-examination . . . . 225.
        1. Actual examination not required . . . . 226.
        2. Direct examination . . . . 226.
    C. Identity of issues . . . . 227.
        1. "Substantial identity" . . . . 227.
        2. Federal Rule . . . . 227.
        3. Different contexts . . . . 227.
    D. Identity of parties . . . . 228.
        1. Applies only to opponent . . . . 228.
        2. Similar party in interest . . . . 228.
        3. Criminal cases . . . . 230.

XI. DYING DECLARATIONS . . . . 231.
    A. General rule . . . . 231.
    B. Requirements . . . . 231.
        1. Awareness of imminent death . . . . 231.
        2. Actual death . . . . 232.
        3. Homicide . . . . 232.
        4. Declarant must be victim . . . . 232.
        5. Must relate to circumstances of killing . . . . 233.
    C. Miscellaneous . . . . 233.
        1. Usable on accused's behalf . . . . 233.
        2. First-hand knowledge . . . . 233.
        3. Opinions . . . . 233.
        4. Belief in God not required . . . . 233.
        5. Preliminary fact questions . . . . 234.

XII. DECLARATIONS AGAINST INTEREST . . . . 234.
    A. Generally . . . . 234.
        1. Distinguished from admissions . . . . 235.
        2. Federal Rule . . . . 235.
    B. Meaning of "against interest" . . . . 236.
        1. When made . . . . 236.
        2. Pecuniary interest . . . . 236.
        3. Penal interest . . . . 237.
        4. Collateral statements . . . . 240.
        5. Factual background . . . . 241.
    C. Constitutional issues . . . . 242.
        1. Use by prosecution . . . . 242.
        2. Use by accused . . . . 242.

XIII. STATEMENTS OF PEDIGREE . . . . 243.
    A. In general . . . . 243.

B. Family relationship . . . . 244.
C. Before controversy . . . . 244.
D. Relation to reputation evidence . . . . 245.

XIV. PRIOR STATEMENTS OF AVAILABLE WITNESS . . . . 245.
A. In general . . . . 245.
B. Prior inconsistent statements . . . . 248.
   1. Federal Rules compromise . . . . 252.
   2. Statements remembered but repudiated . . . . 253.
   3. Prior statement denied . . . . 253.
   4. Prior statement adopted but underlying facts not remembered . . 254.
   5. Prior statement eventually adopted by witness . . . . 255.
C. Prior consistent statements . . . . 255.
D. Prior identification . . . . 255.

XV. THE RESIDUAL ("CATCH ALL") EXCEPTION . . . . 257.
A. Generally . . . . 257.
B. Federal Rule . . . . 258.
   1. Five requirements . . . . 259.
   2. How used . . . . 260.
   3. Grand jury testimony . . . . 261.
C. Circumstantial guarantees of trustworthiness . . . . 261.
   1. "Average" of other exceptions . . . . 261.
   2. Factors bearing on declarant . . . . 261.
   3. Corroboration by other evidence . . . . 262.
   4. Other post-declaration factors . . . . 264.
D. Near-miss problem . . . . 264.
   1. Grand jury testimony . . . . 265.
E. Notice . . . . 265.

XVI. THE FUTURE OF HEARSAY . . . . 266.
A. Generally . . . . 266.
B. The future of hearsay . . . . 268.

CONFRONTATION AND COMPULSORY PROCESS

I. INTRODUCTION . . . . 269.
A. Constitutional limits . . . . 269.
   1. Confrontation clause . . . . 269.
   2. Compulsory process . . . . 269.

II. CONFRONTATION -- GENERAL THEORY . . . . 270.
A. History . . . . 270.
B. Declarant produced at trial . . . . 270.
   1. Evasive witness . . . . 271.
C. Preference for live testimony . . . . 271.
   1. Observation of demeanor . . . . 271.
   2. Unavailability required . . . . 272.
   3. Not to be taken literally . . . . 272.
D. "Indicia of reliability" . . . . 273.
   1. Traditional exception . . . . 273.
   2. Particularized facts . . . . 273.
   3. What exceptions are "firmly rooted" . . . . 275.
   4. Opportunity to cross-examine . . . . 275.

     5. Criticism of *Roberts'* two-step test .... 276.

  E. Right to confront testifying witness .... 276.

     1. Right to be face-to-face with W .... 278.

III. CONFRONTATION -- SPECIFIC CONTEXTS .... 279.

  A. W present and available for cross-examination .... 279.

     1. Effective cross-examination........................ 279.

     2. Denies recollection of underlying event .... 279.

     3. Denies underlying event .... 280.

     4. Identification of person .... 280.

  B. Co-conspirator's statement in furtherance of conspiracy ...... 281.

     1. Unavailability unimportant .... 281.

     2. Indicia of reliability .... 281.

  C. Declarant's availability immaterial .... 281.

  D. Declarant unavailable............................. 282.

     1. General rule .... 282.

     2. Former testimony .... 282.

     3. Dying declaration .... 282.

     4. Statement against interest .... 282.

     5. Meaning of "unavailable" .... 282.

  E. Co-defendant's statement .... 283.

IV. COMPULSORY PROCESS .... 284.

  A. General meaning .... 284.

  B. State rules restricting evidence .... 285.

     1. Ban on accomplice's testimony .... 285.

     2. Restrictive hearsay rule .... 285.

  C. Equality principle .... 286.

  D. Due Process .... 287.

PRIVILEGES

I. PRIVILEGES GENERALLY .... 288.

  A. Introduction.................................. 288.

     1. Rationale................................. 288.

     2. List of major privileges .... 289.

  B. Where applicable .... 290.

  C. Who may assert .... 290.

  D. Risk of eavesdropping .... 290.

     1. Older view................................ 291.

     2. Modern view .... 291.

  E. Sources of Privilege .... 291.

     1. State development .... 291.

     2. Federal courts.............................. 291.

II. THE ATTORNEY-CLIENT PRIVILEGE .... 292.

  A. Introduction.................................. 292.

  B. Rationale.................................... 294.

  C. The professional relationship .... 296.

     1. No retainer needed .... 296.

     2. Non-legal advice .... 296.

     3. Reasonable belief .... 296.

     4. Client holds the privilege .... 296.

   D. **Confidential communications** . . . . 296.
      1. Client-to-lawyer communication . . . . 297.
      2. Lawyer-to-client communication . . . . 297.
      3. Information from third parties . . . . 297.
      4. Tangible evidence and documents . . . . 298.
      5. Miscellaneous issues . . . . 298.
  E. **Fact of employment; client's identity** . . . . 300.
  F. **Physical evidence and documents** . . . . 301.
      1. Cannot assist ongoing fraud . . . . 301.
      2. Concealment of evidence . . . . 301.
      3. Evidence of source . . . . 304.
      4. Information from third parties . . . . 305.
      5. Writings . . . . 306.
  G. **Corporate clients** . . . . 307.
      1. Who may communicate . . . . 307.
      2. Must concern employee's employment . . . . 309.
      3. Reports and other routine communications . . . . 309.
      4. Potential for abuse . . . . 309.
  H. **Exceptions to privilege** . . . . 310.
      1. Crime or fraud . . . . 310.
      2. Through same deceased client . . . . 311.
      3. Attorney-client dispute . . . . 311.
      4. Joint clients . . . . 311.
  I. **Other constraints and ethical issues** . . . . 312.
      1. Code of Professional Responsibility . . . . 312.
      2. Work product immunity . . . . 313.
      3. Perjury on the stand and the right to counsel . . . . 314.

III. **PHYSICIAN-PATIENT PRIVILEGE** . . . . 315.
  A. **Generally** . . . . 315.
  B. **Special issues** . . . . 316.
      1. Relationship . . . . 316.
      2. Confidentiality . . . . 317.
      3. Who holds privilege . . . . 317.
      4. Waiver . . . . 317.
      5. "Public safety" . . . . 320.

IV. **THE PRIVILEGE AGAINST SELF-INCRIMINATION** . . . . 320.
  A. **Introduction** . . . . 320.
      1. Two branches . . . . 320.
      2. Constitutional language . . . . 322.
  B. **General rules** . . . . 323.
      1. Who may assert . . . . 323.
      2. Proceedings where applicable . . . . 324.
      3. Information must be "testimonial" . . . . 325.
      4. Testimony must be "compulsory" . . . . 325.
      5. Must be incriminatory . . . . 326.
  C. **Procedure for invoking** . . . . 326.
      1. Criminal defendant . . . . 326.
      2. Non-defendant witness . . . . 326.
  D. **Waiver** . . . . 327.
      1. Criminal defendant . . . . 327.
      2. Witness . . . . 329.

E. Documentary evidence . . . . 330.
    1. Contents . . . . 331.
    2. Production . . . . 331.
    3. The "required records" exception . . . . 332.
    4. Other kinds of production . . . . 333.
    5. Consent to production by another . . . . 333.
F. Inferences and comment . . . . 333.
    1. "No comment" rule . . . . 334.
    2. Right to instruction . . . . 334.
    3. Silence at other proceedings . . . . 334.
    4. Civil suits . . . . 335.
G. Immunity . . . . 336.
    1. "Transactional" vs. "use" immunity . . . . 336.
    2. Use immunity sufficient . . . . 336.
    3. Defense witness immunity . . . . 337.
H. Prosecutorial discovery . . . . 338.

V. THE MARITAL PRIVILEGE . . . . 339.
A. Two privileges . . . . 339.
    1. Nature of the two provisions . . . . 339.
    2. Rationale . . . . 340.
    3. Distinctions . . . . 340.
B. Adverse testimony privilege . . . . 342.
    1. Who holds . . . . 342.
    2. Criminal vs. civil . . . . 343.
    3. "Testimony" required . . . . 343.
    4. Divorce . . . . 343.
C. Confidential communications . . . . 343.
    1. Where applied . . . . 343.
    2. Who holds . . . . 344.
    3. "Communication" required . . . . 344.
    4. Confidentiality . . . . 344.
    5. Marital status . . . . 344.
    6. Exceptions . . . . 345.

VI. MISCELLANEOUS PRIVILEGES . . . . 345.
A. Priest-penitent privilege . . . . 345.
B. Journalist's privilege . . . . 346.
    1. Constitutional argument . . . . 346.
    2. Conflict between privilege and defendant's rights . . . . . . 347.
C. Government information . . . . 348.
    1. Government secrets generally . . . . 348.
    2. Military and diplomatic secrets . . . . 348.
    3. Other government information . . . . 349.
    4. Procedures and consequences . . . . 350.
    5. Government informers . . . . 351.
    6. Required reports and returns . . . . 353.
D. Trade secrets . . . . 354.
    1. Qualified privilege . . . . 354.
    2. Protective order . . . . 354.
E. Newly-emerging privileges . . . . 354.
    1. Parent-child communications . . . . 354.
    2. Other professional-client relationships . . . . 355.

      3. Academic researchers .... 355.
  F. **Exclusionary rule** .... 355.

REAL AND DEMONSTRATIVE EVIDENCE, INCLUDING WRITINGS

I. **INTRODUCTION** .... 356.
  A. **Real and demonstrative evidence** .... 356.
  B. **Direct vs. circumstantial** .... 358.

II. **Authentication** .... 359.
  A. **Authentication generally** .... 359.
  B. **Method of authentication** .... 360.
      1. Real evidence .... 360.
      2. Demonstrative evidence .... 362.
      3. Federal Rules .... 362.
      4. Judge-jury allocation .... 364.
  C. **Authentication of writings and other recorded communications** .... 364.
      1. Authorship .... 365.
      2. No presumption of authenticity .... 365.
      3. Direct testimony .... 365.
      4. Distinctive characteristics .... 366.
      5. Signature and other handwriting .... 366.
      6. Reply letters and telegrams .... 367.
      7. Telephone conversations .... 367.
      8. Sound recordings .... 369.
      9. Attesting witnesses .... 369.
      10. Ancient documents .... 370.
  D. **Self-authentication** .... 371.
      1. State statutes .... 371.
      2. Federal Rules .... 371.
      3. Attack on genuineness .... 372.
  E. **Ways of avoiding authentication** .... 372.
      1. Request for admission .... 372.
      2. Stipulation .... 372.

III. **OTHER FOUNDATION REQUIREMENTS AND OBJECTIONS** .... 372.
  A. **Mere relevance not enough** .... 372.
      1. Chain of custody .... 373.
      2. Condition unchanged .... 373.
  B. **Demonstrative evidence** .... 374.
      1. "Essential" vs. merely useful .... 374.
      2. Not a fair representation .... 374.
  C. **Undue prejudice** .... 375.
      1. Gruesome photos .... 375.
      2. "Day in the life" films .... 375.
      3. Bodily demonstration .... 375.

IV. **THE "BEST EVIDENCE RULE" FOR RECORDED COMMUNICATIONS** .... 375.
  A. **Best Evidence Rule generally** .... 375.
      1. Only writings and equivalents .... 376.

2. Federal Rules .... 377.

B. What is a "writing" or other recorded communication .... 377.
    1. Short inscription .... 377.
    2. Photographic evidence .... 378.
    3. Sound recordings .... 378.

C. What constitutes "proving the terms" .... 378.
    1. Existence, execution, etc. .... 378.
    2. Incidental record .... 379.
    3. Contract deed, or other key document .... 381.

D. Collateral writings .... 381.

E. Which is the "original" .... 381.
    1. Not necessarily earliest .... 382.
    2. Duplication of originals .... 382.
    3. Original destroyed .... 382.

F. Reproductions .... 383.
    1. Common law .... 383.
    2. Photocopying and other modern techniques .... 383.
    3. Federal Rules .... 384.

G. Excuses for non-production .... 384.
    1. Loss or destruction .... 385.
    2. Inconvenience .... 385.
    3. Possession by third person .... 385.
    4. Original in opponent's possession .... 386.
    5. Public records .... 386.

H. Summaries .... 386.

I. Admission by adversary .... 387.
    1. Written admission or transcript .... 387.
    2. Oral admission .... 387.
    3. Federal Rules .... 387.

J. Preferences among secondary evidence .... 388.
K. Judge-jury allocation .... 388.

V. SPECIAL TYPES OF REAL AND DEMONSTRATIVE EVIDENCE ... 389.

A. Pictorial evidence .... 389.
    1. Authentication of pictures .... 389.
    2. Movies .... 391.

B. Computer print-outs .... 391.
    1. Authentication .... 391.
    2. Best Evidence rule .... 391.

C. Maps models, diagrams, and summaries .... 392.
    1. Authentication .... 392.
    2. Generally admissible .... 392.
    3. Charts and summaries .... 392.

D. Views .... 393.
    1. Discretion of judge .... 393.
    2. Presence of judge .... 393.
    3. Defendant's right to be present .... 393.
    4. Evidentiary status of view .... 394.

E. Demonstrations and experiments .... 394.
F. Exhibits in the jury room .... 396.
    1. Tangible evidence including writings .... 396.
    2. Substitute for testimony .... 396.

OPINIONS, EXPERTS AND SCIENTIFIC EVIDENCE

I. FIRST-HAND KNOWLEDGE AND LAY OPINIONS . . . . 397.

  A. First-hand knowledge required . . . . 397.

    1. Distinguished from hearsay . . . . 397.

    2. Experts . . . . 397.

    3. Federal Rules . . . . 397.

  B. Lay opinions . . . . 398.

    1. Traditional formulation . . . . 398.

    2. Exception for "short-hand renditions" . . . . 398.

    3. Modern view . . . . 399.

    4. Federal Rule . . . . 399.

    5. Specifics still preferable . . . . 400.

    6. Expert opinions . . . . 400.

  C. Opinion on "ultimate issue" . . . . 400.

II. EXPERT WITNESS . . . . 402.

  A. Reasons for using experts . . . . 402.

    1. Opinions . . . . 402.

    2. Statements of fact . . . . 403.

  B. When expert testimony allowed . . . . 403.

    1. Qualifications . . . . 403.

    2. Subject matter . . . . 404.

    3. Role of trial judge . . . . 405.

  C. Basis for expert's opinion . . . . 405.

    1. Personal knowledge . . . . 405.

    2. Observation of prior evidence . . . . 406.

    3. Hypothetical questions . . . . 406.

    4. Otherwise inadmissible evidence . . . . 406.

    5. Mandatory disclosure to jury . . . . 408.

  D. The hypothetical question . . . . 408.

    1. General technique . . . . 409.

    2. Evidentiary basis required . . . . 409.

    3. Advantage of hypothetical . . . . 410.

    4. Federal approach . . . . 410.

  E. Procedural issues . . . . 411.

    1. Cross-examination . . . . 411.

    2. Court-appointed experts . . . . 412.

    3. Discovery . . . . 413.

    4. Calling at trial . . . . 414.

III. SCIENTIFIC EVIDENCE — THE *FRYE* STANDARD . . . . 414.

  A. Special rule for scientific evidence . . . . 414.

    1. *Frye* case . . . . 414.

    2. Spotty adherence . . . . 414.

    3. Federal Rules . . . . 415.

IV. SCIENTIFIC EVIDENCE AND EXPERTISE —

    PARTICULAR TYPES . . . . 416.

  A. Probabilities . . . . 416.

    1. Foundation . . . . 416.

    2. Modern trend . . . . 418.

B. **Speed detection** . . . . 419.
    1. Radar . . . . 419.
    2. VASCAR . . . . 420.
C. **Intoxication** . . . . 420.
    1. Breathalyzer . . . . 420.
D. **Voice prints** . . . . 420.
E. **Blood tests and other biological tests** . . . . 421.
F. **Neutron Activation Analysis** . . . . 421.
G. **Psychology and psychiatry** . . . . 422.
    1. Mental condition of defendant . . . . 422.
    2. Reliability of eyewitness testimony . . . . 423.
    3. Lie detectors, truth serums, and hypnosis . . . . 425.

BURDENS OF PROOF, PRESUMPTIONS AND OTHER PROCEDURAL ISSUES

I. **BURDENS OF PROOF** . . . . 427.
A. **Two burdens** . . . . 427.
    1. Burden of production . . . . 427.
    2. Burden of persuasion . . . . 427.
    3. One burden shifts, other does not . . . . 427.
B. **Allocating the burdens in civil cases** . . . . 431.
    1. Usually on plaintiff . . . . 431.
    2. Pleading burden . . . . 431.
    3. Substantive law . . . . 431.
    4. Factors . . . . 432.
C. **Allocation of burdens of proof in criminal cases** . . . . . . 433.
    1. Element distinguished from affirmative defense . . . . 433.
    2. Production burden . . . . 434.
    3. Burden of persuasion . . . . 434.
D. **Satisfying the burden of production** . . . . 436.
    1. Civil case . . . . 437.
    2. Criminal case . . . . 438.
E. **Satisfying the burden of persuasion** . . . . 439.
    1. Civil case . . . . 439.
    2. Criminal case . . . . 440.

II. **Presumptions** . . . . 441.
A. **Presumptions generally** . . . . 441.
    1. Four meanings . . . . 441.
    2. Presumptions are rebuttable . . . . 443.
    3. Reasons for creating . . . . 443.
B. **Effect of presumption in civil cases** . . . . 443.
    1. Debate between Thayer and Morgan . . . . 443.
    2. Defense of "bursting bubble" view . . . . 444.
    3. Federal Rules . . . . 446.
    4. Conflicting presumptions . . . . 447.
    5. Constitutional questions . . . . 448.
C. **Effect in criminal cases** . . . . 449.
    1. Terminology . . . . 449.
    2. Constitutionality . . . . 450.
D. **Choice of law** . . . . 452.

1. "Tactical" presumptions . . . . 453.

III. **JUDGE-JURY ALLOCATION** . . . . 453.

   A. **Issues of law** . . . . 454.

   B. **Issues of fact** . . . . 454.

      1. Competence . . . . 454.

      2. Relevance . . . . 455.

      3. Presence of jury . . . . 457.

   D. **Instructions** . . . . 457.

      1. Limiting instructions . . . . 457.

      2. Cautionary instruction . . . . 458.

   E. **Summary and comment** . . . . 458.

   F. **Nonjury trials** . . . . 458.

IV. **APPEALS AND THE "HARMLESS ERROR" DOCTRINE** . . . . 459.

   A. **"Harmless error" generally** . . . . 459.

   B. **Sufficiency of evidence** . . . . 461.

JUDICIAL NOTICE

I. **JUDICIAL NOTICE GENERALLY** . . . . 463.

   A. **Function** . . . . 463.

      1. Correction after close of evidence or on appeal . . . . 463.

   B. **Two types of facts** . . . . 463.

      1. Adjudicative facts . . . . 463.

      2. Legislative facts . . . . 463.

   C. **Judicial notice of law** . . . . 464.

   D. **Federal Rules** . . . . 464.

II. **ADJUDICATIVE FACTS** . . . . 465.

   A. **Definition** . . . . 465.

   B. **Common knowledge** . . . . 465.

   C. **Certain verification** . . . . 466.

      1. Scientific tests and principles . . . . 466.

      2. Court records . . . . 466.

   D. **Jury's right to disregard** . . . . 466.

      1. Civil . . . . 467.

      2. Criminal . . . . 467.

   E. **Procedure** . . . . 468.

      1. Advance notice to parties . . . . 468.

      2. Contradictory evidence . . . . 468.

      3. When taken . . . . 469.

III. **LEGISLATIVE FACTS** . . . . 469.

   A. **Notice of legislative facts** . . . . 469.

      1. Types of legislative facts . . . . 469.

   B. **Not usually codified** . . . . 470.

   C. **Binding on jury even in criminal cases** . . . . 471.

IV. **NOTICE OF LAW** . . . . 471.

   A. **Notice of law generally** . . . . 471.

   B. **Domestic law** . . . . 472.

   C. **Law of sister states** . . . . 472.

   D. **Law of other countries** . . . . 472.

EXAM QUESTIONS AND ANSWERS .... 473.

TABLE OF CASES .... 508.

TABLE OF REFERENCES TO THE FEDERAL RULES OF EVIDENCE .... 511.

SUBJECT-MATTER INDEX .... 513.

CAPSULE SUMMARY

This Capsule Summary is intended for review at the end of the semester.
Reading it is not a substitute for mastering the material in the main
outline. Numbers in brackets refer to the pages in the main outline
where the topic is discussed.

BASIC CONCEPTS

I. KINDS OF EVIDENCE

A. Direct versus circumstantial [11]

1. **Direct evidence:** Direct evidence is evidence which, if believed, automatically resolves the issue. (*Example:* W says, "I saw D strangle V." This is direct evidence on whether D strangled V.)

2. **Circumstantial:** Circumstantial evidence is evidence which, even if believed, does not resolve the issue unless *additional reasoning* is used. (*Example:* W says, "I saw D running from the place where V's body was found, and I found a stocking in D's pocket." This is only circumstantial evidence of whether D strangled V.)

3. **Probative value:** The probative value of direct evidence is not necessarily higher than circumstantial evidence, but it will sometimes be more readily admitted by judge.

B. Testimonial versus real and demonstrative: [356]

1. **Testimonial:** Testimonial evidence arises when W makes assertions in court. The fact-finder must rely on W's interpretation of W's sensory data, W's memory, etc.

2. **Real and demonstrative:** Real evidence is a thing involved in the underlying event (e.g., a weapon, document, or other tangible item). Demonstrative evidence is a tangible item that illustrates some material proposition (e.g., a map, chart, summary). The fact-finder may interpret either real or demonstrative evidence by use of its own senses, without intervening sensing and interpreting by a witness.

II. CONDITIONS FOR ADMITTING EVIDENCE

A. Relevant: Only *relevant* evidence may be admitted. (FRE 402) [10-16]

1. **Definition:** Evidence is "relevant" if it has "any tendency to make the existence of [a material] fact . . . more probable or less probable than it would be without the evidence." (FRE 401)

   a. **"Brick is not wall":** The piece of evidence need not make a material fact more probable than not; it must merely increase the probability (even by a small amount) that the material fact is so. "A brick is not a wall," and the piece of evidence merely has to be one brick in the wall establishing a particular fact.

2. **Exclusion:** Even relevant evidence may be excluded if its *probative value* is *substantially outweighed* by the danger of: (1) *unfair prejudice*; (2) confusion of the issues; (3) misleading of the jury; or (4) considerations of undue delay, waste of time, or needless presentation of cumulative evidence. (FRE 403)

B. Offering testimonial evidence

    1. Lay (i.e., non-expert) witness:

        a. W must take *oath*, i.e., solemnly promise to testify truthfully. (FRE 603)

        b. W must testify from *personal knowledge*. (FRE 602)

        c. W must preferably state *facts* rather than *opinions*. At common law this rule is sometimes stated as a firm requirement (although often loosely enforced). Under FRE 701, W may give an opinion if it is: (1) rationally based on his own perceptions; and (2) helpful to the fact-finder.

        d. At common law, W must be *competent*, and many groups of witnesses are deemed not to be (e.g., atheists, felons, interested parties). Under Federal Rules (and by statute in most states), nearly everyone with first-hand knowledge is competent. See, e.g., FRE 601: *everyone* is competent (except for judges and jurors, made incompetent by Rules 605 and 606 respectively). (But the federal court must generally honor a state rule of competency in diversity cases.)

    2. Experts: Same rules apply to experts as to lay witnesses, except:

        a. The expert may give *opinion* if this will be helpful to trier (FRE 702).

        b. The expert's opinion need not be based on his personal knowledge — it may be based on information supplied by others. At common law, this is usually done by the hypothetical question. Under Federal Rules, it may be done either by the hypothetical or by out-of-court statements made to the expert (even inadmissible evidence); FRE 703. Under FRE 705, facts relied on by the expert need not be disclosed except under cross-examination or as required by court.

        c. Qualification: Expert may be qualified by reason of "knowledge, skill, experience, training, or otherwise" (FRE 702), so formal academic training is not necessary.

    3. Ultimate issues: At common law, opinions on "*ultimate*" issues are usually barred. But under FRE 704, even such opinions are allowed (except when they relate to the mental state of a criminal defendant).

C. Offering real and demonstrative evidence: See p. 49 of this Capsule Summary.

D. Making and responding to objections: [4-7]

    1. Making objections:

        a. Not automatic: Evidence will not be excluded unless the opponent makes an *objection*. FRE 103(a)(1).

        b. Timely: The objection must be *timely* (usually before the witness can answer the question). FRE 103(a)(1).

        c. Specific: The objection must be *specific* enough to explain to the trial judge and the appeals court the basis for it. *Id.*

        d. Taking of exceptions: At common law, the opponent whose objection is denied must "*take exception*" in order to preserve the objection for appeal. In most states today, and under the Federal Rules, exceptions are no longer necessary.

    2. Responding to objection: If judge sustains objection, the proponent must usually make an "*offer of proof*" in order to preserve his right to argue on appeal that the evidence should have been admitted. That is, proponent must make it clear to the court (either by the lawyer's own explanation of what the evidence would be, or by questions and answers to the witness outside the jury's presence) what the evidence would be. FRE 103(a)(2).

CIRCUMSTANTIAL PROOF: SPECIAL PROBLEMS

I. RELEVANT EVIDENCE SOMETIMES EXCLUDED

A. Possible exclusion: Normally, all relevant evidence is admissible. (FRE 402) But even relevant evidence may be excluded if its probative value is "substantially outweighed by the dangers of unfair prejudice, confusion of the issues, or misleading the jury. . . ." (FRE 403) Special rules govern certain types of circumstantial evidence which have been found over the years to be so misleading or so prejudicial that they should be categorically excluded without a case-by-case balancing of probative value against prejudice. [10, 14-16]

II. CHARACTER EVIDENCE

A. General rule: Evidence of person's character is, in general, ***not admissible to prove that he "acted in conformity therewith on a particular occasion."*** FRE 404(a). (*Example:* In a civil suit from an auto accident, P cannot show that D has the general character trait of carelessness, or even that D is a generally careless driver, to suggest that D probably acted carelessly in the particular accident under litigation.) [17-19]

B. Character in issue: [19-20]

   1. Essential element: A person's general character, or his particular character trait, is admissible if it is an ***essential element*** of the case. (*Example:* P says that D has libeled him by calling him a liar. D may introduce evidence of P's character for untruthfulness, since that character trait is an essential element of D's defense that his statement was true.)

   2. Types of evidence: When character is directly in issue, all three types of character evidence (specific acts, W's opinion, or the subject's reputation) are admissible.

B. Circumstantial evidence in civil cases: In civil cases, circumstantial evidence of character is generally inadmissible. [20-22]

   1. Quasi-criminal acts: A few courts allow one who is charged in a civil case with conduct that would also be a crime to rebut this charge by presenting circumstantial evidence of his good character. But most courts, and the Federal Rules, do not.

C. Other-crimes evidence in criminal cases: [22-36]

   1. General rule: The prosecutor may ***not*** introduce evidence of ***other crimes*** committed by D for the purpose of proving that because D is a person of criminal character, he probably committed the crime with which he is charged.

   2. Proof of elements: But other crimes by D may be admitted if this is done not to show D's general criminal disposition, but to establish circumstantially ***some element of the crime charged.*** Here are some common elements that may be circumstantially proved by other crimes that D has committed:

   a. Signature: If the perpetrator's ***identity*** is in doubt, proof that D has committed prior crimes that are so similar in method that they constitute his ***"signature,"*** and thus identify him as the perpetrator of the crime charged, may be proved.

   b. Intent: Other crimes may be used to prove that D had the particular ***intent*** required for the crime charged. Generally, this is done to rebut D's contention that he did the act charged ***innocently*** or ***unknowingly***. (*Example:* D, a mailman, is charged with stealing a coin from the mails; the prosecution is allowed to show that D also unlawfully possessed credit cards taken from the mails, in order to rebut D's argument that the coin accidentally fell out of an envelope and he planned to return it. *U.S. v. Beechum.*)

    c. Motive: Other crimes may be used to establish the defendant's ***motive*** for the crime charged. (*Example:* D is charged with car theft; prosecution may show that D had previously escaped from jail, and thus had a motive to steal the car.)

    d. Identity: Other crimes may be used to show that D was really the perpetrator, if he disputes this. For instance, the prosecution may be allowed to show that D committed other crimes, and that the other crimes and the crime charged are part of a ***common plan or scheme***. (*Example:* D is charged with embezzling from his employer; he claims that someone else did the embezzling. The prosecution will be allowed to show that D embezzled from three prior employers, since this demonstrates that D was probably acting as part of a general scheme to steal from each of his employers.)

3. Other aspects of other-crimes evidence:

    a. No conviction: The other crimes need not have led to a conviction. Many state courts require that the evidence of the defendant's guilt of the other crime be "clear and convincing" or "substantial." But in federal courts, it does not even have to be by a preponderance of the evidence. (*Huddleston.*)

    b. Acquittal: The fact that the defendant was ***acquitted*** of the other crime will be a factor in determining whether there is "substantial" evidence of his guilt (in courts requiring this). But most courts will probably not automatically exclude the evidence of the other crime merely because of the acquittal. (*Example:* D is charged with murdering her child. Evidence that four of her other children died of unnatural causes will probably be allowed because of its strong tendency to prove that the death currently charged was not accidental, even though D was acquitted of similar charges as to the first death, when no cumulative evidence was available.)

    c. Balancing: Even where other crimes by D circumstantially establish an element of the present charge, the judge must still balance probative value against prejudice, and must exclude if the latter substantially outweighs the former. (FRE 403)

D. Evidence of criminal defendant's good character: [36-40]

1. Allowed: Evidence by a criminal defendant that he has a ***good general character*** is ***allowed*** by all courts. Evidence that he possesses a narrow favorable trait is allowed, but only if it is ***relevant*** to the crime charged. (*Example:* D is charged with murder. He will be allowed to show that he has the general character of being law abiding. He will also be permitted to show the narrower trait of being peaceable. But he will not be allowed to show the narrow trait of being truthful, since this is not relevant to the murder charge.)

2. Method of proof:

    a. Common law: At common law, proof of good character must be made by ***reputation*** evidence only (not by the character witness' opinion, or by proof of specific acts showing good character).

    b. Federal: FRE 405(a) allows not only reputation evidence but also the character witness' own ***opinion*** as to D's good character. (But not even the Federal Rules allow proof of ***specific incidents*** showing D's good character.)

3. Rebuttal by prosecution: If D puts on proof of his good character, the prosecution may ***rebut*** this evidence:

    a. Own witnesses: The prosecution may do this by putting on its own witnesses to say that D's character is bad.

    b. **Cross-examination:** The prosecution may cross-examine D's character witness to show that D's character is not really good. The prosecutor may even do this by asking the witness about **specific instances** of bad conduct by D, provided that: (i) the prosecutor has a **good faith basis** for believing that D really committed the specific bad act; and (ii) the specific bad act is **relevant** to the **specific character trait** testified to by the witness (so if W testified that D was honest, the prosecutor could not ask about specific bad acts showing D's character for violence). Even an arrest that did not lead to a conviction may be brought up in cross-examination, if relevant to the character trait in question.

    c. **No extrinsic evidence:** The prosecutor's ability to show specific bad acts is limited to cross-examination. He may not put on extrinsic evidence (e.g., other witnesses) to prove that the specific acts took place, if the character witness denied that they did. Conversely, the defendant may not put on other witnesses to show that the specific act referred to by the prosecutor on cross-examination never took place.

E. Character of victim: [40-47]

    1. V's violent character: The defendant in a homicide or assault case who claims that the victim was the first aggressor, may in all courts introduce evidence that the **victim** had a **violent character.** This is true even if D cannot show that he was aware of the victim's violent character at the time of the assault or murder. This character evidence must generally be in the form of reputation or opinion evidence; most states (and the Federal Rules) prohibit evidence of **specific past acts** of violence by the victim.

    2. Federal Rules: FRE 404(a)(2) allows not only proof of a murder or assault victim's violent character, but any "evidence of a pertinent trait of character of the victim of the crime offered by an accused. . . ." (But this is very limited in rape cases, discussed below.)

    3. Rebuttal by prosecution: Once the defendant introduces evidence of the victim's character for violence, the prosecution may then **rebut** this evidence by showing the victim's **peaceable** character. The Federal Rules expand this right of rebuttal; if the defendant claims that the victim was the first aggressor (even though the defendant does not put in proof of the victim's general character for violence), the prosecution may put in evidence of the victim's peaceable character. FRE 404(a)(2).

    4. Rape: At common law, the defendant in a **rape or sexual assault** case could usually show the victim's character for **unchastity,** to show that the victim **consented** on this particular occasion. But nearly all states have now enacted rape shield statutes to restrict evidence of the victim's past sexual conduct. FRE 412 completely disallows reputation or opinion evidence concerning the victim's past sexual behavior. FRE 412 also prohibits evidence of specific acts concerning the victim's past sexual behavior in most situations; for instance, D is never allowed to offer evidence of V's past sexual behavior with **persons other than himself** if offered on the issue of whether there was consent.

III. HABIT AND CUSTOM

A. Generally allowable: Evidence of a person's **habit** is admissible to show that he followed this habit on a particular occasion. "Habits" are more specific, and tied to narrower facts, than are "character traits" (generally disallowed as circumstantial evidence that the character trait was followed on a particular occasion). (*Example:* If V is killed when his car is hit on the railroad tracks, his estate will be allowed to show that he had the habit of stopping and looking carefully before crossing those tracks every day. But his general character trait for carefulness would not be admissible to show that he probably behaved carefully at the time of the fatal crossing.) [47]

    1. Minority: A minority of courts refuse to allow habit evidence at all, and another minority allow it only when there are no eyewitnesses available to testify about what really happened on the particular occasion.

B. Federal Rules: FRE 406 follows the majority rule, by providing that "evidence of the habit of a person or of the routine practice of an organization, . . . regardless of the presence of eyewitnesses, is relevant to prove that the conduct of the person or organization on a particular occasion was in conformity with the habit or routine practice." [49]

C. Business practices: All courts allow evidence of the *routine practice* of an *organization*, to show that that practice was followed on a particular occasion. (*Example:* A business may prove that a particular letter was mailed by showing that it was the organization's routine practice to mail all letters placed in any worker's "outgoing mail" box, and that the letter in question was placed in such a box.) [50]

IV. SIMILAR HAPPENINGS

A. General rule: Evidence that similar happenings have occurred in the past (offered to prove that the event in question really happened) is generally *allowed*. However, the proponent must show that there is *substantial similarity* between the past similar happening and the event under litigation. [50-55]

    1. Accidents and injuries: Thus evidence of past similar injuries or accidents will often be admitted to show that the same kind of mishap occurred in the present case, or to show that the defendant was negligent in not fixing the problem after the prior mishaps. But the plaintiff will have to show that the conditions were the same in the prior and present situations.

    2. Past safety: Conversely, the defendant will usually be allowed to show due care or the absence of a defect, by showing that there have *not* been similar accidents in the past.

V. SUBSEQUENT REMEDIAL MEASURES

A. General rule: Courts generally *do not allow* evidence that a party has merely taken *subsequent remedial measures*, when offered to show that the party was negligent, or was conscious of being at fault. (*Example:* P trips on D's sidewalk; P may not show that just after the fall, D repaved the sidewalk and thus conceded the sidewalk's dangerousness.) [55-56]

    1. Federal Rules: FRE 407 follows this rule: subsequent remedial measures may not be admitted to prove negligence or culpable conduct in connection with an event.

B. Other purposes: But subsequent remedial measures may be shown to prove elements other than culpability or negligence. For instance, such measures may be used to rebut the defendant's claim that there was no safer way to handle the situation. Or, if the defendant claims that he did not own or control property involved in an accident, the fact that he subsequently repaired the property may be shown to rebut this assertion. [56-58]

C. Product liability: Courts are split on whether the plaintiff in a *product liability* suit may show subsequent redesign to prove that the product was initially defective. The trend is probably to *allow* such evidence. [58-59]

VI. LIABILITY INSURANCE

A. General rule: Evidence that person carried or did not carry *liability insurance* is *never* admissible on the issue of whether he acted negligently. See FRE 411. (But evidence of the existence or non-existence of liability insurance is admissible for purposes other than proving negligence. For instance, the fact that W, a witness for D in a tort suit, works for D's liability insurance company, could be admitted to show bias on W's part.) [59-60]

VII. SETTLEMENTS AND PLEA BARGAINS

A. Settlements: The fact that a party has offered to *settle* a claim may *not* be admitted on the issue of the claim's validity. See FRE 408. [60-63]

   1. Collateral admissions of fact: *Admissions of fact* made during the course of settlement negotiations are generally admissible at common law, but not admissible under FRE 408. (*Example:* "I was drunk when I ran over you, so I'll pay you $5,000 in damages," would be admissible at common law to prove D's drunkenness, but not admissible under FRE 408.)

   2. Other purposes: But settlement offers may be admissible to prove issues other than liability. (*Example:* If W testifies on behalf of D in a civil suit, the fact that W received money from D in settlement for a related claim may be admitted to show that W is biased in favor of D and against P.)

B. Guilty pleas: [64-65]

   1. Defendant's offer to plead: The fact that the defendant has offered to *plead guilty* (and the offer has been rejected by the prosecutor) may *not* be shown to prove that D is guilty or is conscious of his guilt. FRE 410(4) excludes not only the offer to plead guilty but any other statement made in the course of plea discussions with the prosecutor, from being used against the defendant.

   2. Withdrawn plea: Similarly, the fact that D made a guilty plea and then later *withdrew it* may not be admitted against D in the ultimate trial.

C. Offer to pay medical expenses: The fact that a party has paid the *medical expenses* of an injured person is not admissible to show that party's liability for the accident that caused the injury. See FRE 409. But only the fact of payment, not related admissions of fact, are excluded. (*Example:* D says to P, "I'm paying your medical expenses because if I hadn't been drunk that night, I wouldn't have hit you." This may be admitted to show D's drunkenness but not to show that D paid the expenses.) [65]

EXAMINATION AND IMPEACHMENT OF WITNESSES

I. FLOW OF EXAMINATION

A. Four stages: The examination of a witness goes through up to four stages: [3]

   1. Direct: First, the party who called the witness engages in the *direct* examination.

   2. Cross: After the calling side has finished the direct exam, the other side may *cross-examine* the witness.

   3. Re-direct: The calling side then has the opportunity to conduct *re-direct* examination.

   4. Re-cross: Finally, the cross-examining side gets a brief opportunity to conduct *re-cross*.

II. DIRECT EXAMINATION

A. Leading questions: Generally, the examiner *may not ask leading questions* on direct. [67-69]

   1. Definition: A leading question is one that *suggests to the witness the answer desired by the questioner*. (*Example:* Auto negligence suit by P against D. Question by P's lawyer to P: "Was D driving faster than the speed limit at the time he hit you?" This is leading, since

CAPSULE SUMMARY

it suggests that the questioner desires a "yes" answer.)

      2. Hostile witness: Leading questions are allowed on direct if the witness is **"hostile."** The **opposing party** will almost always be deemed hostile; so will a witness who is shown to be biased against the calling side, as well as a witness whose demeanor on the stand shows hostility to the calling side.

III. CROSS-EXAMINATION

    A. Leading questions: Leading questions are usually **permitted** during cross-examination. (FRE 611(c)) [70]

      1. Exception: But if the witness is biased in favor of the cross-examiner (e.g., one party is called by the other and then "cross"-examined by his own lawyer), leading questions are not allowed.

    B. Scope: The majority (and federal) rule is that cross is **limited** to the **matters testified to on the direct examination.** (FRE 611(b)) [70-72]

    C. Credibility: The witness' **credibility** may always be attacked on cross-examination. [71]

IV. RE-DIRECT AND RE-CROSS

    A. Re-direct: Re-direct is limited to those aspects of the witness' testimony that were **first brought out during cross**. [73-74]

    B. Re-cross: Similarly, re-cross is limited to matters newly brought up on the re-direct. [74]

V. REFRESHING RECOLLECTION AND OTHER TECHNIQUES

    A. Refreshing recollection [74-76]

      1. General rule: If the witness' memory on a subject is hazy, **any item** (picture, document, weapon, etc.) may be shown to the witness to refresh his recollection. This is the technique of **"present recollection refreshed."**

      2. Not evidence: The item shown to the witness is **not evidence** at all; it is merely a stimulus to produce evidence in the form of testimony from the witness.

      3. Abuse: If the item shown to the witness is a **document**, and the trial judge concludes that the witness is really reading the document on the stand instead of testifying from his now-refreshed recollection, he may order the testimony stricken.

      4. Cross-examination: The cross-examiner may examine the document or other item shown to the witness, and test whether the witness really has an independent recollection.

      5. Documents seen before trial: If a document has been consulted by the witness **before he took the stand**, the Federal Rules give the trial court discretion to order that the document be shown to the other side, if "necessary in the interests of justice." (FRE 612)

    B. Argumentative and misleading questions: A question will be stricken if it is either argumentative or misleading: [76]

      1. Argumentative: An **argumentative** question is one which tries to get the witness to agree with counsel's interpretation of the evidence. It is more common on cross than on direct, and usually has an element of badgering the witness.

      2. Misleading: A **misleading** question is one that assumes as true a fact that is either **not in evidence** or is in dispute. It usually has a "trick" aspect. (*Example:* "When did you stop beating your wife," will be misleading if there is no or disputed evidence of wife-beating, since any answer by W will be an implicit admission that he has beaten her.)

VI. EXAMINATION BY COURT

A. **General rule:** The trial judge may call his own witnesses, and may question any witness (whether called by the judge or by a party). (FRE 614(a) and (b)) [76-77]

VII. IMPEACHMENT — GENERALLY

A. **Five types:** There are five main ways of *impeaching* a witness, i.e., of destroying the witness' credibility: (1) by attacking W's general character (e.g., by showing past crimes, past bad acts, or bad reputation); (2) by showing a prior inconsistent statement by W; (3) by showing that W is biased; (4) by showing that W has a sensory or mental defect; and (5) by other evidence (e.g., a second witness' testimony) that contradicts W's testimony. [77-78]

B. **Impeaching one's own witness:** [78-80]

    1. **Common law:** At common law, *a party may not impeach his own witness*. That is, impeachment is generally *not allowed on direct examination*.

        a. **Exceptions:** But this common-law rule has several exceptions. Impeachment on direct is allowed if: (1) W's unfavorable testimony comes as a genuine surprise to the direct examiner (who may then show prior inconsistent statements by W); or (2) W is an adverse party or a hostile witness.

    2. **Modern and Federal Rule:** Many states, and the Federal Rules, have now completely *abandoned* the common law rule prohibiting impeachment of one's own witness. See, e.g., FRE 607 ("The credibility of a witness may be attacked by any party, including the party calling the witness.") Also, a criminal defendant may have the right under the Sixth Amendment's Confrontation Clause to impeach a witness he has called.

VIII. IMPEACHMENT BY PRIOR CRIMINAL CONVICTION

A. **Common-law rule:** At common law, two types of prior convictions may be used to impeach W's credibility: [81]

    1. *Any felony* conviction;

    2. A *misdemeanor* conviction, but only if the crime involved *dishonesty* or a *false statement*.

B. **Federal Rule:** The Federal Rules make it slightly harder to use prior convictions to impeach the witness. Under FRE 609(a): [81-87]

    1. **Crimen falsi:** If the crime involved *dishonesty or false statement* ("*crimen falsi*"), *it may always be used to impeach W,* regardless of whether it was a misdemeanor or a felony, and regardless of the degree of prejudice to W (who will usually be the defendant in a criminal proceeding). (The judge may not even exclude the evidence under FRE 403, which normally allows exclusion of evidence whose probative value is substantially outweighed by the danger of unfair prejudice.)

    2. **Felony:** If the crime was a *felony* not involving dishonesty or false statement, it may be used only if the court "determines that the probative value of admitting this evidence outweighs its prejudicial effect to the accused."

        a. **Witnesses other than an accused:** The above rule applies only when the witness is a *criminal defendant*. If the witness is *not* a criminal defendant (e.g., a prosecution witness, a witness for a criminal defendant, or any witness in a civil case), the witness gets no special protection against impeachment. Instead, FRE 403 applies, allowing a prior conviction to be excluded only if the person opposing its introduction shows that the conviction's probative value is "substantially outweighed by the danger of unfair prejudice. . . ."

3. **Other misdemeanors:** If the crime was a misdemeanor not involving dishonesty or false statement, it may not be used for impeachment at all.

4. **Old convictions:** If more than 10 years have elapsed from both the conviction and the prison term for that conviction, the conviction may not be used for impeachment unless the court determines that there are "specific facts and circumstances" that make the probative value of the conviction substantially outweigh its prejudicial effect. FRE 609(b). This makes it much harder to get more-than-10-year-old convictions into evidence.

5. *In limine* **motions:** D may, before taking the stand, ask the trial court to rule *in limine* whether a particular conviction will be allowed to impeach him. If the ruling goes against D, D can then elect not to take the stand. (But if he doesn't take the stand, the *in limine* ruling will not be reviewed on appeal, at least in federal courts.)

6. **Ineligible convictions:** Certain types of convictions are excluded by special rules: If W was ***pardoned***, based on a finding of ***innocence***, the conviction may never be used. (If the pardon was because W was rehabilitated, it may be used for impeachment only if W has been convicted of a subsequent felony.) A *"juvenile adjudication"* of D may not be used to impeach him. FRE 609(c), (d).

IX. IMPEACHMENT BY PRIOR BAD ACTS

A. **Common law:** [87-88]

1. **Generally allowed:** Most common-law courts allow the cross-examiner to bring out the fact that the witness has committed ***prior bad acts***, even though these have not led to a criminal conviction. (E.g., "Isn't it true that you lied on your job application by falsely stating that you had never used drugs?")

2. **No extrinsic evidence:** However, the prior bad acts ***must*** be introduced solely through the cross-examination, ***not*** through ***extrinsic evidence***. (*Example:* If W denies having lied on a job application, the cross-examiner cannot call a different witness to prove that the lie occurred.)

3. **Good-faith basis:** Before the prosecutor may ask a witness about a prior specific bad act, he must have a ***good faith basis*** for believing that the witness really committed the act.

D. **Federal Rule:** The Federal Rules basically follow the common-law approach to prior bad act impeachment. (FRE 608(b)) [88-91]

1. **Probative of truthfulness:** However, only prior bad acts that are ***probative of truthfulness*** may be asked about. (*Example:* A prior act of lying on a job application or embezzling from an employer could be asked about, but the fact that W killed his wife and was never tried could not be, because this act does not make it more likely than it would otherwise be that W is now lying.)

2. **No extrinsic evidence:** As at common law, any prior bad act must be shown only through cross-examination, not through extrinsic evidence.

3. **Discretion of court:** All questions about prior bad acts are in the ***discretion of the court***. The extent to which the questioner has a good faith basis for believing W really committed the act will, of course, be one factor the court normally considers.

X. IMPEACHMENT BY OPINION AND REPUTATION REGARDING CHARACTER

A. **Common law:** [91-92]

1. **Allowed at common law:** Common law allows W1's credibility to be impeached by testimony from W2 that W1 has a ***bad reputation for truthfulness***.

2. **Opening issue:** As soon as a criminal defendant takes the stand, he opens himself up to this kind of evidence, even if he does not affirmatively state that he is a truthful person.

3. **Opinions:** W2 must say that W1 has a bad reputation for truthfulness; W2 may not state his own *opinion* that W1 is untruthful. Nor may W2 describe *specific instances* of conduct by W1 that led to his bad reputation for truthfulness.

4. **General bad character:** W2 must talk only about W1's reputation for truthfulness, not W1's reputation for general bad character.

B. **Federal Rules:** FRE 608(a) basically follows the common law, except that W2 may state his *opinion* that W1 is a liar (as well as stating that W1 has a reputation for being a liar). Here, too, no specific instances of untruthfulness by W1 are allowed. [92-93]

XI. IMPEACHMENT BY PRIOR INCONSISTENT STATEMENT

A. **General rule:** W's credibility may generally be impeached by showing that he has made a *prior inconsistent statement.* [94-95]

B. **Foundation:** But before W's prior inconsistent statement may be admitted to impeach him, a *foundation* must be laid. [95-97]

1. **Common law:** At common law, the foundation requirement is rigid: W must be told the substance of the alleged statement, the time, the place, and the person to whom it was made. He must then be given a chance to deny having made the statement, or to explain away the inconsistency. Only after all this may the prior inconsistent statement be introduced into evidence.

2. **Federal Rule:** The Federal Rules liberalize the foundation requirement: W must still be given a chance to explain or deny the prior inconsistent statement, but this opportunity does not have to be given to him until *after* the statement has been proved (e.g., by testimony from W2 that W1 made the prior inconsistent statement).

3. **Writing:** If the prior inconsistent statement is *written*, the common-law rule is that the writing must be shown to the witness before it is admitted. But FRE 613(a) relaxes this requirement, too: the examiner may first get W to deny having made the prior statement, and then admit it into evidence.

C. **Extrinsic evidence:** Special rules limit the questioner's ability to prove that W made a prior inconsistent statement by *"extrinsic"* evidence, i.e., by evidence other than W's admitting that he did so (e.g., testimony by W2 or admission of a copy of W's prior written statement). Such extrinsic proof can only be made where two requirements are satisfied: [97-98]

1. **Collateral:** First, at common law extrinsic proof of the prior inconsistent statement is *not* allowed if the statement involved only *"collateral"* matters. Thus the statement must relate to a material issue in the case, or to some other fact that could be proved even if there were no claim that W had contradicted himself (e.g., W's prior statement showing bias could be introduced to contradict his trial testimony that he is unbiased, since extrinsic evidence could be used to show W's bias even if W did not deny the bias). Nothing in the Federal Rules expressly bars extrinsic proof of a prior inconsistent statement on a collateral matter (though the trial judge could keep such testimony out under FRE 403's balancing test).

2. **Material:** Also, extrinsic evidence of the prior inconsistent statement is allowed only if the inconsistency between the prior statement and the trial testimony is *material* (i.e., the variation is great enough to cast doubts on the veracity of W's present testimony).

XII.   IMPEACHMENT FOR BIAS

A.   Generally allowed: All courts allow proof that the witness is *biased.* W may be shown to be biased in favor of a party (e.g., W and P are friends or relatives), or biased against a party (e.g., W and D were once involved in litigation). W's *interest in the outcome* may be also shown as a form of bias (e.g., if W is an expert, the fact that he is being paid a fee for his testimony is generally allowed as showing that he has an interest in having the case decided in favor of the party retaining him). [98-99]

B.   Extrinsic evidence: Bias may be shown by use of *extrinsic evidence.* However, most courts require a foundation before extrinsic evidence may be used for this purpose: the examiner must ask W about the alleged bias, and only if W denies it may the extrinsic evidence (e.g., testimony by another person that W is biased) be presented. [99-100]

XIII.   IMPEACHMENT BY SENSORY OR MENTAL DEFECT

A.   Generally allowed: W may be impeached by showing that his capacity to *observe, remember,* or *narrate* events correctly has been impaired. (*Example:* W may be shown to have such poor eyesight that he couldn't have seen what he claims to have seen.) [101]

B.   Alcohol and drugs:

   1.   Use during event: W may be impeached by showing that he was *drunk* or *high on drugs* at the time of the events he claims to have witnessed.

   2.   Addiction: Courts are split on whether W may be shown to be a *habitual* or addicted user of alcohol and drugs — many courts will not allow this if there is no showing that W was drunk or high at the time of the events in question.

XIV.   IMPEACHMENT BY CONTRADICTION; THE "COLLATERAL ISSUE" RULE

A.   Showing of contradiction allowed: W1 may be impeached by presenting W2, who contradicts W1 on some point. (*Example:* W1 says that perpetrator of robbery had red hair; defense can put on W2 to testify that robber had brown hair — this not only is evidence of a material fact, but also impeaches W1.) [102]

B.   Collateral issue rule: However, the right to put on a second witness to impeach the first by contradicting him, is limited by the *"collateral issue"* rule, at least at common law. By this rule, certain types of testimony by W2 are deemed to be of such collateral interest to the case that they will not be allowed if their sole purpose is to contradict W1. [102-105]

   1.   Disallowed: Thus, W2 may not testify as to: (1) prior bad acts by W1 that did not lead to a conviction; (2) prior inconsistent statements made by W1 that do not relate to a material fact in the case; or (3) things said by W1 in his testimony which according to W2 are not true, unless these facts are material to the case.

   2.   Allowed: On the other hand, testimony by W2 will not be deemed to be collateral, and will thus be allowed, as to the following subjects: (1) prior criminal convictions by W1; (2) W1's bad character for truthfulness; (3) W1's bias; or (4) W1's sensory or mental defect that prevents W1 from observing, remembering or narrating events correctly.

   3.   Federal Rule: The Federal Rules do not contain any explicit "collateral issue" rule. However, the trial judge can apply the policies behind the rule by using FRE 403's balancing test (evidence excludible where its probative value is substantially outweighed by confusion, prejudice, or waste of time).

XV. RELIGIOUS BELIEFS

A. General rule: Most courts do not allow W to be impeached by a showing that he does not believe in God. Impeachment based on religious beliefs is also barred by FRE 610. [105-06]

XVI. REHABILITATING IMPEACHED WITNESS

A. No bolstering: A lawyer may not offer evidence *supporting his witness' credibility*, unless that credibility has first been *attacked* by the other side. This is known as the rule against *"bolstering one's witness"*. (*Example:* On direct, W tells a story favorable to P. P's lawyer will not be permitted to bring out on direct the fact that prior to the trial, W told the same story to the police — W's credibility has not yet been attacked, so it may not be bolstered by a showing that W made a prior consistent statement.) [106]

    1. Prior identification: However, the "no bolstering" rule does not apply where W has made a prior out-of-court *identification* — most courts allow this to be brought out as part of the direct examination of W.

    2. Prompt complaint: Similarly, in *rape* cases most courts allow the victim to in effect bolster her own testimony by stating that she made a *prompt complaint* to the police immediately following the crime.

B. Rehabilitation: Apart from these exceptions, W's credibility may be supported only to rehabilitate it, i.e., only to repair the damage done by the *other side's attack* on that credibility. [107-110]

    1. Meet attack: The rehabilitating evidence must *"meet the attack."* That is, it must support W's credibility in the same respect as that in which the credibility has been attacked by the other side. (*Example:* P attacks W as being biased because he is D's son. D may rehabilitate W's credibility by showing evidence of non-bias. But D may not rehabilitate W by showing W's good reputation for truthfulness, or W's prior out-of-court statements that are consistent with his trial testimony — D's attempts at rehabilitation do not respond directly to the charge of bias.)

    2. Good character: If W's credibility is attacked by evidence tending to show that he is generally untruthful, the proponent may show that W has a good character for truthfulness. Thus evidence of W's *good character for truthfulness* may be used to rebut evidence that: (1) W has a *bad reputation* for truthfulness; (2) that W2 has a *bad opinion* of W's truthfulness; (3) that W has been *convicted* of a crime; or (4) that W has committed a *prior bad act*; and perhaps (5) that W has been subjected to a slashing *cross-examination* by the opponent, implying or stating that W is a *liar*.

        a. Attack on present testimony: But if the attack on W has merely been to show that his testimony in the present case is inaccurate, W's credibility may not be rehabilitated by a showing of his general good character for truthfulness. Thus good character evidence will not be allowed to rebut evidence that: (1) W is *biased* because he is related to the other party; (2) W has given *erroneous testimony* in this case, perhaps through honest mistake.

        b. Prior inconsistent statement: If W has been attacked by a showing that he made a *prior inconsistent statement*, the courts are split. Most treat this as an implicit attack on W's general credibility, and thus allow him to be rehabilitated by a showing of good general character for truthfulness.

    3. Prior consistent statement: The fact that W has made a *prior consistent statement* (i.e., an out-of-court statement that matches his trial testimony) may be used only to rebut an express or implied charge that W's trial testimony is a *recent fabrication* or the product of *improper influence or motive*. This is the common-law rule, and is also carried out by FRE 801(d)(1)(B).

a. **Attack on general character:** Thus if W is attacked by showing his *prior criminal convictions*, *prior bad acts*, or his general *bad reputation* for veracity, his credibility may *not* be rehabilitated by a showing that he made prior consistent statements.

b. **Prior inconsistent statement:** The opponent's showing that W has made a prior *inconsistent* statement will not, by itself, entitle the proponent to show that W has also made a prior consistent statement. The proponent must demonstrate that the adversary's use of the prior inconsistent statement amounts to an express or implied claim that W has recently made up his trial testimony, or is lying because of improper influence or ulterior motives. (Thus if the showing of the prior inconsistent statement can reasonably be interpreted as suggesting that W is merely honestly mistaken, W cannot be rehabilitated by the prior consistent statement.)

c. **Before motive arose:** At common law, the proponent who wants to use a prior consistent statement must usually show that the prior statement was made *before* the alleged motive to fabricate or improper influence arose. (But this is not explicitly required by the Federal Rules.)

XVII. SPECIAL TECHNIQUES FOR DEVELOPING OR EVALUATING TESTIMONY

A. Psychiatric testimony: The trial judge has discretion to allow psychiatric expert testimony to show that W's accuracy is doubtful because of some mental illness or defect. For instance, the judge might appoint a psychiatrist to give expert testimony as to whether V's mental illness may have caused her to imagine a rape, or to have falsified the surrounding details. But judges will generally order a party or witness to undergo psychiatric examination for purposes of evaluating credibility only if there are *compelling reasons* to do so. [110-12]

B. Hypnosis and truth serum: [112-14]

1. **Statement made under influence:** Statements made under the influence of hypnosis or truth serum are almost always *rejected*.

2. **Testimony at trial:** Live testimony by W about an event, his recall of which has been refreshed through hypnosis or truth serum, is also usually *rejected*. But a minority of courts allow hypnosis-influenced testimony if stringent safeguards have been followed (e.g., a video tape was made of the hypnosis session).

   a. **Criminal defendant's right to testify:** Where the hypnotized witness is a *criminal defendant*, the court's right to reject hypnotically-refreshed testimony is limited by the defendant's constitutional right to *testify in his own defense*. [*Rock v. Arkansas*]

C. Lie detectors: [114-16]

1. **General rule:** Nearly all courts reject lie detector evidence when offered on the issue of whether the statements made by the subject during the test are true.

2. **Stipulation:** A substantial minority of courts allow lie detector results where both parties have *stipulated* before the test that the results may be admitted.

HEARSAY

I. DEFINITION

A. Simple definition: Hearsay is *"a statement or assertive conduct which was made or occurred out of court and is offered in court to prove the truth of the matter asserted."*

(*Example:* V says, "D tried to poison me last night." This is hearsay if offered to show that D really tried to kill V last night, since it is an out-of-court statement offered to prove the truth of the matter asserted.) [117]

   1. **Writing:** Hearsay may be ***written*** as well as oral. (*Example:* A letter written by V to her mother, "D tried to kill me last night," would be hearsay if offered to prove that D really did this, just as would V's oral statement to her mother to the same effect.)

B. **Four dangers:** The use of hearsay testimony presents four main dangers: (1) ***ambiguity***; (2) ***insincerity***; (3) ***incorrect memory***; and (4) ***inaccurate perception***. All of these relate to the fact that the person making the out-of-court statement (the declarant) is not available for cross-examination. [118, 119-21]

C. **Triangle:** In terms of the following "testimonial triangle," O's statement will only be hearsay if the trier of fact is asked to travel from point A to point B to point C (i.e., the fact-finder must be asked to determine that the declarant truly held the belief which his declaration suggests he held — point B — and also that declarant's belief accurately reflects reality — point C). [118]

Figure C-1

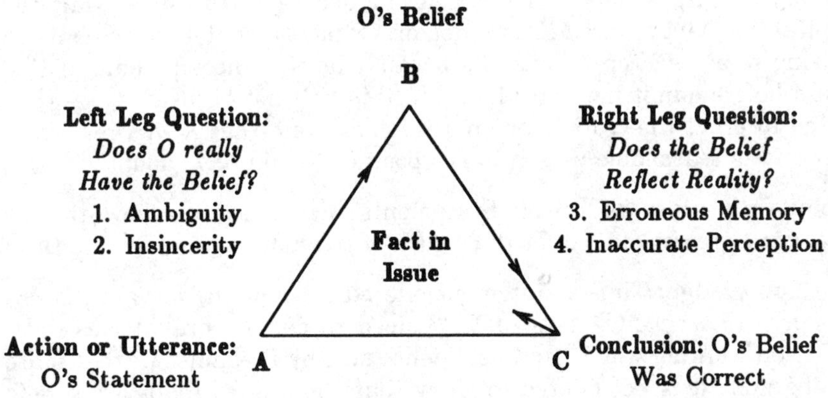

O's Belief

B

Left Leg Question:
*Does O really
Have the Belief?*
1. Ambiguity
2. Insincerity

**Fact in
Issue**

Right Leg Question:
*Does the Belief
Reflect Reality?*
3. Erroneous Memory
4. Inaccurate Perception

Action or Utterance:
O's Statement

A

C

Conclusion: O's Belief
Was Correct

Example: O is prosecuted for robbery; he claims that he was captured and forced to take part in the robbery. He offers a note he wrote to his wife during the captivity, "If I don't take part in the robbery, they'll kill me." The fact-finder is asked to travel from point A to point B (i.e., to determine whether O really believed his statement), but not to travel from point B to point C (i.e., to determine whether O's belief accorded with reality). Since the fact-finder is not asked to travel all the way around the triangle, O's statement is not hearsay.

II. SPECIAL ISSUES

A. **"Out of court" statement:** An out-of-court statement is any statement except one made "by a witness during the trial while testifying before the trier of fact." Therefore, the following will be out-of-court statements (and thus might be hearsay): [126-27]

   1. Any oral or written statement by someone other than the at-trial witness; and

   2. A prior statement by the at-trial witness, where the prior statement was not made in the present trial before the trier of fact. Therefore, W's prior statement made in a ***deposition*** or at an ***earlier trial***, or even W's statement made in the judge's chambers during the present trial, are all "out of court" and so may be hearsay.

B. **"Truth of matter asserted":** Here are some uses to which a statement may be put that do ***not*** constitute offering the statement for the "truth of the matter asserted": [127-35]

   1. **Verbal acts:** The statement is a "verbal act," i.e., an operative fact that gives rise to legal consequences. (*Example:* O says to W (a vice officer), "If you pay me $5 I will have sex with you." If O is prosecuted for solicitation, her statement will not be hearsay because it is not offered to show its truth (that O would really have had sex with W had he paid her $5); rather, the crime of solicitation is defined so as to make an offer to have sex for money an act with legal consequences.)

      a. **Verbal parts of act:** Similarly, a ***"verbal part of the act"***, i.e., words that accompany an ambiguous physical act, is not offered for truth and thus is not hearsay. (*Example:* O gives X money, saying, "This will repay you for the money you lent me last year." If offered by X in defense of a bribery charge, this will be non-hearsay because the words that accompanied the payment give the payment its particular legal effect — loan repayment.)

   2. **Effect on hearer/reader:** A statement offered to show its effect on the ***listener*** or ***reader*** will generally not be hearsay. Thus if a statement is offered to show that the listener or reader was ***put on notice***, had certain ***knowledge***, had a certain ***emotion***, or behaved ***reasonably*** or unreasonably, this will not be hearsay. (*Example:* Malpractice suit against D, a hospital, for having hired X as a doctor. P offers written statements by two other hospitals refusing to allow X on their staffs because he was incompetent. If P shows that D saw the letters before admitting X to the staff, this will not be hearsay — the letters are not being offered to prove the truth of the matters asserted (that X was really incompetent), merely to show that a reasonable person in D's position would have doubted X's competence.)

   3. **Declarant's state of mind:** Statements introduced to show the ***state of mind*** of the ***declarant*** are not offered for the "truth of the matter asserted" and thus are not hearsay.

      a. **Knowledge:** Thus a statement offered to show the declarant's ***knowledge*** is not hearsay. (*Example:* D says to X, "I need to get my brakes checked because they haven't been working well." In a negligence suit by P against D, that statement is not hearsay, because it is not offered to show that the brakes really were defective, merely that D had knowledge that the brakes might be defective.)

      b. **Other mental state:** Statements offered to show the declarant's ***sanity*** or ***emotion*** (e.g., fear) are similarly not offered for truth and thus are not hearsay. (Also, there is an exception for "statements evidencing states of mind").

   4. **Reputation:** Statements about a person's ***reputation*** may not be hearsay. (*Example:* Libel action; W testifies at trial, "O told me that P has a reputation for thievery." If offered to show that O's statement caused this false reputation of P, this will not be hearsay — it is not offered to prove that P is really a thief, merely to prove that P has been given a false reputation for thievery.)

   5. **Impeachment:** If W makes a statement at trial, use of a prior inconsistent statement made out of court by W will not be hearsay when used to ***impeach*** W's present testimony — what is being shown is not that the prior out-of-court statement was truthful, but that the conflict between the two statements raises questions about W's credibility.

C. **"Statement" and conduct:** The hearsay rule applies only to "statements." An oral or written assertion is obviously a statement. But certain types of ***conduct*** may also be statements: [135-43]

   1. **Assertive conduct:** ***Assertive conduct*** is treated as if it were a "statement," so that it can be hearsay. (*Example:* O pulls D's mug shot out of a collection of photos; since by this act O intends to assert, "That's the perpetrator," this act will be hearsay if offered on the issue of whether D was the perpetrator.)

2. **Silence:** A person's *silence* will be treated as a "statement," and thus possibly hearsay, only if it is *intended* by the person as an assertion.

    a. **Absence of complaints:** The fact that one or more people have *not made complaints* about a situation will *not* usually be treated as the equivalent of a statement by them that there is nothing to complain about. Therefore, absence of prior complaints can usually be admitted without hearsay problems.

    b. **Silence in face of accusation:** But a person's silence in the face of an *accusation against him*, where the silence is offered to show that the accusation was true, usually will be held to be intended as an assertion, and thus hearsay. (But the hearsay exception for admissions will usually apply anyway.)

3. **Non-assertive conduct:** Conduct that is *not intended as an assertion* will *never* be hearsay, under the modern and Federal Rules. (This reverses the earlier common-law rule of *Wright v. Doe.*)

    a. **Non-assertive verbal conduct:** Even a verbal statement will not be hearsay if it is not intended as an assertion. (*Example:* D is charged with running a bookmaking operation out of his premises. W testifies that he answered D's phone, and the caller on the other end said, "Secretariat to place in the third." Caller's statement will not be hearsay, because even though it was verbal, the caller did not intend to assert, "I am talking to a betting parlor," or anything else.)

    b. **Non-verbal conduct:** Similarly, non-verbal conduct that is not intended as an assertion will not give rise to hearsay. (*Example:* O, while walking down the street, suddenly puts up his umbrella. If this act is introduced to show that it was raining, it will not be hearsay — O was not intending to assert to anyone, "It's raining.")

4. **Assertions not offered to prove truth of matter asserted:** If an assertion is offered to prove another assertion that is *implied by* (or can be inferred from) the former, there is a hearsay problem only if the person making the assertion was thinking about the proposition now sought to be proved. (*Example:* O writes to T, "Cousin, the weather is wonderful in America and you would like it here." This assertion would not be hearsay if offered to establish that O thought T was sane, since it is unlikely that O was consciously thinking to himself when he wrote this letter, "T is sane." On the other hand, if O wrote to T, "As of your last letter, you seemed to be of sound mind," this would be hearsay even if offered as circumstantial proof that at some later date, T was still sane — O was thinking about the very issue now sought to be proved, T's sanity.)

D. **Multiple hearsay:** If one out-of-court declaration quotes or paraphrases another out-of-court declaration, there is a problem of *"multiple hearsay."* The evidence is inadmissible if *any* of the declarations is hearsay not falling within an exception. (*Example:* W, an investigator, writes a report saying, "D told me that at the time of the crash, he was travelling at 65 mph." If this report is offered by P to show that D was indeed travelling at 65 mph, there are two levels of hearsay: D's original oral statement and W's out-of-court written paraphrase of it. But each would probably fall within an exception — D's original statement as an admission, and W's report under the business records rule. Therefore, the report could come into evidence.) [145-46]

HEARSAY EXCEPTIONS

I. ADMISSIONS

A. **General rule:** "Admissions" receive an exceptions from the hearsay rule. That is, *a party's words or acts may be offered as evidence against him,* even though these would be inadmissible hearsay if said or done by someone other than a party. (Under the Federal Rules, an admission is simply not hearsay at all. See FRE 801(d)(2). At common law, admissions are hearsay, but receive an exception.) [150-52]

1. **Distinguished from declaration against interest:** Be sure to distinguish admissions from declarations against interest. Unlike a declaration against interest, an admission need not be against the declarant's interest at the time it is made; thus even a statement that seems neutral or self-serving at the time it is made may be introduced against the party who made it.

2. **Opinion:** An admission is admissible even though it contains an *opinion* or a *conclusion of law*, and even though it is not based on the maker's *first-hand knowledge.* Thus it can be admitted more easily even than the same statement when made at trial.

B. **Personal admissions:** One type of admission is a *party's own statement*, offered against him ("personal admission"). [152-55]

1. **Pleadings:** Statements a party makes in his *pleadings* are treated as personal admissions for most purposes, and are thus admissible.

2. **Conduct as admission:** A party's conduct, even if it is intended as an assertion (and thus is hearsay under the modern rule) will be admissible under the exception for admissions. (*Example:* Proof of D's attempt to conceal V's body would be admissible as an admission by D of his guilt, even if the court decided that this was assertive conduct.)

C. **Adoptive:** Under common law and the Federal Rules, a party may be deemed to have *adopted* another person's statement, in which case the statement will be admissible as an admission by the former party. [155-58]

1. **"Real and knowing" test:** If a party is claimed to have adopted another's statement and the adoption is merely *implied*, the test is: whether, taking into account all circumstances, the party's conduct or silence justifies the conclusion that he *knowingly agreed* with the other person's statement.

2. **Silence:** Often, the party's *silence* in the face of the other person's statement will, under the circumstances, indicate that the party agrees with the statement. If so, he will be held to have made an adoptive admission, which will thus be admissible. (*Example:* While D flashes a large wad of bills, X, his girlfriend, says to W, "D got that money as his piece of the National Bank job last week." D's silence in the face of this statement will probably be found by the court to show D's knowing agreement with X's statement, since otherwise, D would have denied the statement. Therefore, the statement will be admissible against D as an adoptive admission.)

   a. **Criminal cases:** In criminal cases, D's failure to respond to accusations made by the police while D is in *custody* will not be admissible against him as adoptive admissions, because this would violate the spirit of *Miranda.* But silence in the face of accusations made outside of police custody, or silence to accusations made by non-police, may be admitted against the criminal defendant under the adoptive-admission theory.

   c. **Writing:** A party's silence in the face of a *writing* will similarly be an adoptive admission, if the party can reasonably be expected to have objected were the writing untrue. (*Example:* D receives a bill from a creditor, reciting certain sums owed for specified work. If D does not respond, his silence in the face of the bill will be treated as an adoptive admission by him of the truth of the bill's contents.)

D. **Representative admission:** Even if a party did not make (or even learn of) another person's admission, that admission may be admissible against the party because he *authorized it* in some way. This is a "representative" or "vicarious" admission. [158-61]

1. **Explicit authorization:** This may occur because the party *explicitly* authorized another person to speak for him. (*Example:* Transport Co. authorizes any employee who is involved in an accident to make a statement to the police. A statement made by Employee arising out of such an accident will be admissible against Transport, because it was explicitly authorized.)

   a. **Statements to principal:** Even if the principal authorizes the agent only to make the report *to the principal,* the modern and federal approach is to treat this as an adoptive admission. Thus, an employee's accident investigation report, given only to the employee's boss, would nonetheless be admissible against the boss.)

2. **Vicarious:** Even if an agent is not explicitly authorized to make statements, statements he makes arising from a *transaction within his authority* will, under the modern view, be deemed to be authorized admissions by the principal. These are called *"vicarious"* admissions.

   a. **Common law:** At common law, this was not so: only "authorized" admissions, not "vicarious" ones, would be admissible against the principal.

   b. **Modern and Federal Rule:** But the modern and Federal Rule recognizes vicarious admissions. See, e.g., FRE 801(d)(2)(D), admitting a statement offered against a party if made "by the party's agent or servant concerning a matter within the scope of the agency or employment, made during the existence of the relationship." (*Example:* Truck Driver makes an accident statement to the police. Even if Employer, the company for which Driver works, never authorized him to make accident reports, under the modern/federal rule Driver's statement will be admissible against Employer because it relates to matters — driving and accidents — that were within Driver's employment. But the proponent of this admission will have to show by *other evidence*, not the statement itself, that Driver was acting Employer's agent at the time he made the statement.)

E. Co-conspirators: [161-67]

1. **General rule:** There is an important hearsay exception for statements by *co-conspirators*: a statement by one co-conspirator is admissible against other members of the *same conspiracy*, so long as the statement is made: (1) *during the course* of the conspiracy; and (2) in *furtherance* of the conspiracy. (*Example:* A says to X, "Don't you want to join B and me in robbing the First National Bank next Thursday?" This statement may be used against B in a prosecution for the robbery of that bank that took place on that date, since the statement was made by a member of the same conspiracy, made while the conspiracy was taking place, and made for the purpose of furthering its aims by recruitment.) See FRE 801(d)(2)(E).

2. **"During course of":** The requirement that the statement take place "during the course of" the conspiracy means:

   a. **After end:** Statements made *after the conspiracy has ended* are admissible only against the declarant, not against the other members. Thus, if the conspiracy is broken up by the *arrest* of A and B (the only members of the conspiracy), anything B says to the police will not be admissible against A, since the arrest has terminated the conspiracy.

   b. **Conspirator leaves:** If A leaves the conspiracy, but B and C continue the conspiracy without him, statements made by B and C after A leaves may not be admitted against A. (But the converse is not true: statements made by A to the authorities after he has left the conspiracy might be admissible against B and C, since their conspiratorial activities are still continuing at the time of A's statement).

   c. **Statements before:** Statements made by early conspirators **before** a later entry joins are admissible against the latter — when a conspirator enters an ongoing conspiracy, he is held to have adopted the earlier statements of fellow co-conspirators, so these are admissible against him.

3. **In furtherance:** The "in furtherance" requirement means that a statement should be admitted against a co-conspirator only if it was made for the purpose of advancing the conspiracy's objectives.

   a. **Weakly applied:** But this requirement is often not taken seriously. Thus, confessions by a co-conspirator, narratives of past events, or statements by the declarant blaming a crime on his co-conspirators rather than himself, are all frequently admitted under the exception even though, strictly speaking, they don't seem to meet the "in furtherance" requirement since they don't advance the conspiracy's objectives.

4. **No need to charge conspiracy:** Statements by one co-conspirator against another may be admitted under the exception *even if no conspiracy crime is formally charged*.

5. **Procedure:** It is the judge who decides whether a conspiracy has been shown, so that the exception applies. He reaches this decision as follows:

   a. **Preponderance:** He need only find that a conspiracy exists by a *preponderance of the evidence*, not "beyond a reasonable doubt."

   b. **Statements:** In determining whether a conspiracy exists by a preponderance, he may *consider the alleged statement itself*. (It is unclear whether there must be other, independent, evidence of a conspiracy's existence as well.)

II. AVAILABILITY IMMATERIAL — GENERALLY

A. **List of exceptions:** Four major hearsay exceptions apply even where the declarant is *available* to give courtroom testimony: [168]

   1. *Spontaneous, excited,* or *contemporaneous utterances* (including statements about *physical or mental condition*);

   2. *Past recollection recorded*;

   3. *Business records*; and

   4. *Public records* and *reports*.

III. SPONTANEOUS, EXCITED, OR CONTEMPORANEOUS UTTERANCES (INCLUDING STATEMENTS ABOUT PHYSICAL OR MENTAL CONDITION)

A. **Statements of physical condition:** There is a hearsay exception for statements by a person about his *physical condition*. [168-72]

   1. **Statement to lay person:** If the statement is made to a lay person, it is covered by the exception only if it relates to the declarant's **present** bodily condition or symptoms. Usually, it will relate to pain. (*Example:* X says to W, "I'm feeling terrible chest pains." W can testify about this statement even if it is offered for the purpose of showing that X did indeed suffer chest pains.)

   2. **To treating doctor:** For statements made by a person about his bodily condition, when made to a *physician* who is *treating* him, the exception is broader:

      a. **Past symptoms:** The statement may be about *past* pain or past symptoms.

    b. **Cause:** The statement may include references to the *cause* of the bodily condition (though statements about whose *fault* the condition is will generally not be allowed; thus W's statement that he was hit by a car will qualify, but his statement that the car was driven through a red light would not).

    c. **Non-M.D.:** Under FRE 803(4), statements made for purposes of getting medical treatment that are made to a *nurse*, ambulance driver, or other third person involved in the health-care process are covered by the exception.

    d. **Non-treating physician:** If the statement is made to a doctor who is not furnishing *treatment*, but who is consulted so that he can testify about the patient's condition at trial, the statement is covered by the federal exception (but not by the common-law exception).

B. Declaration of mental condition: There is a hearsay exception for statements by a person concerning his *present mental or emotional state*. [172-84]

  1. **State of mind directly in issue:** The exception is often used where a declarant's state of mind is directly in issue. (*Example:* P sues D for alienating the affections of W, who is P's wife. W's statement to P, "I don't like you anymore," if offered to show that W does not like P anymore — an element of P's *prima facie* case — comes within the exception.)

    a. **Presently existing:** The statement must relate to the declarant's *presently existing* state of mind. (*Example:* "I hate my husband," is acceptable to show the declarant now hates her husband. But, "Yesterday I was really furious at my husband," is not admissible, because it relates to a prior mental or emotional state, rather than the declarant's present one.)

    b. **Surrounding circumstances:** If statement of present mental state includes a reference to surrounding circumstances, the entire statement will normally be admitted, but with a limiting instruction. (*Example:* "I hate my husband because he's an adulterer." The whole statement will be admitted under the exception, if offered to prove that the declarant hated her husband at the time of the statement; the jury will be instructed that it may not use the statement as proof that the husband was an adulterer.)

  2. **Proof of subsequent event:** The exception also applies where a declaration of present mental state (especially present *intent*) is offered not because the mental state itself is in issue, but because that mental state is circumstantial evidence that a *subsequent event* actually took place. (*Example:* O says, "I plan to go to Crooked Creek." This statement of present intent is admissible to show that O probably subsequently went to Crooked Creek. *Mutual Life Ins. v. Hillmon.*)

    a. **Cooperation of other:** If the statement of present intent concerns an act which requires the *cooperation* of a third person, most courts will allow the statement to be used as circumstantial evidence that the declarant did the contemplated act with the third person's cooperation. However, in this situation, courts usually require that there be *independent evidence* either that declarant really did the intended act, or that the third person actually participated. (*Example:* V says, "I'm going to buy drugs from D in the parking lot." This statement of present intent will be admissible to show that V probably did meet D in the parking lot, but only if there is some independent evidence — other than the statement — either that D really went to the parking lot or that V did. *U.S. v. Pheaster.*)

  3. **Statements of memory or belief:** The "state of mind" exception does *not* to statements of *memory* or belief about *past actions or events*, when offered to prove that the past action or event took place. Thus FRE 803(3) excludes "a statement of memory or belief to prove the fact remembered or believed. . . ." (*Example:* O says, "I believe that my husband has poisoned me." Even though this is a statement of present belief, it is not admissible under the "state of mind" exception to prove that the husband really did poison O, since it is

offered to prove the fact believed. *Shepard v. U.S.*)

    a. Intent coupled with recital of past acts: If the statement is mainly an expression of intent to do a future act, the fact that it contains a brief recital about some past, relevant, fact will not cause the statement to be excluded. This is especially true where the declarant explains a ***past motive*** for his contemplated action. (*Example:* O says to W, "D has asked for some bribe money. I'm going to send it to him in Bridgeport." Most courts would probably allow in the entire statement, since it is mainly a statement of intent offered to show that the intended act — delivering the money — eventually took place, and the reference to the past act is merely by way of explaining the intended act.)

    b. Execution of will: A declarant's statement relating to his ***will*** is covered by the "state of mind" exception, even though the statement may be one of memory or belief offered to prove the fact remembered or believed. See FRE 803(3), making the hearsay exception applicable to a statement of memory or belief that "relates to the execution, revocation, identification, or terms of declarant's will." (*Example:* O says, "I changed my will yesterday to disinherit my no-good husband." If offered in a will contest to show that O intended to disinherit her husband, this statement will be admissible even though it is a statement of memory offered to prove the truth of the fact remembered.)

C. Excited utterance: There is a hearsay exception for certain statements made under the influence of a ***startling event***; this is called the ***"excited utterance"*** exception. [184-87]

    1. Requirements: Under the Federal Rules and most courts, there are two requirements for the exception: (1) the statement must relate to a ***startling event*** or condition; and (2) the statement must have been made while the declarant was still ***under the stress*** of excitement caused by the event or condition. See FRE 803(2).

    2. Time factor: In determining whether the declarant was still under the influence of the startling event, the ***time*** that has passed between the event and the statement is of paramount importance. Usually, statements made during the exciting event or within half an hour afterward are admitted, statements made more than an hour later are not, and statements between a half hour and an hour are decided based on the surrounding circumstances.

    3. Reflection: Since the rationale behind the exception is that statements made by a declarant who does not have the ***opportunity to reflect*** should be admitted as unusually reliable, facts showing that the declarant really did reflect will cause the exception not to apply. Thus if the statement is very self-serving, or is in response to a detailed question, the court is likely to find that the declarant reflected (rather than speaking spontaneously), so that the exception should not apply.

    4. Reference to startling event: Some courts insist that the excited utterance explain or refer to the startling event. But this is not required by the Federal Rules or other courts. (*Example:* Truck Driver, after getting in an accident, says, "Hurry up, I've got to get to my next customer." If offered to prove that Driver was on business on behalf of his employer, some courts would reject the statement because it does not refer to the startling event — the accident — but the Federal Rules and other state courts would admit the statement anyway.)

D. Present sense impression: Many courts, and the Federal Rules, today recognize an exception for "present sense impressions," even where the declarant is not excited. Thus FRE 803(1) gives an exception for a statement "describing or explaining an event or condition made while the declarant was perceiving the event or condition, or immediately thereafter." (*Example:* O sees a car speed by in the opposite direction, and says, "If the driver keeps up that rate of speed, he'll surely crash." In courts recognizing the exception for present sense impressions, this statement would be admissible to show that the car was traveling fast. *Houston Oxygen Co. v. Davis.*)

[187-88]

1. **Immediacy:** In contrast to the excited-utterance exception, the present-sense-impression exception applies only if *virtually no time passes* between the event being perceived and the declarant's statement about it.

2. **Must describe or explain:** The present sense impression must *describe or explain* the event that the declarant has perceived (in contrast to the usual rule for excited utterances).

IV. PAST RECOLLECTION RECORDED

A. **Four requirements:** A *written* record of an event, made shortly after the event has occurred, will be admissible under the hearsay exception for *"past recollection recorded,"* if four requirements are met: [189-91]

1. **First-hand knowledge:** The memorandum must relate to matters of which the sponsoring witness once had *first-hand knowledge*. (*Example:* W writes down an inventory. If he says at trial that some of the information in the inventory was known only to his assistant who supplied the information, not to W, the memorandum will not be admissible under the past recollection recorded requirement unless the assistant is also available to testify.)

2. **Made when fresh in memory:** The record must have been made when the matter was *fresh in the witness' memory*. Under the Federal Rules, even a record made several days after the events in question might be held to satisfy this requirement if there was evidence that the person doing the recording would still have had a clear memory of it.

3. **Impaired recollection:** A sponsoring witness' memory of the event recorded must now be *impaired* — if he can clearly remember the events, he must testify from memory rather than have the document admitted. Under the Federal Rules, he must merely have *some* impairment of his memory (in contrast to the common law requirement that he lack any present memory of the event).

4. **Accurate when written:** The sponsoring witness at the trial must testify that the record was *accurate* when it was made. (But the sponsoring witness does not have to be the person who made the record; thus if X made the record, it may be sponsored by W, X's assistant, who can testify that after the record was made, W checked it and determined it to be accurate.)

   a. **Multi-party problem:** If A knows the facts and B records them, both A and B will probably have to testify at the trial for the record to be admissible: A will testify that the facts he told B were ones that he, A, knew to be accurate; then B will testify that he accurately recorded what A told him.

B. **Status as exhibit:** Under the Federal Rules, the record cannot be taken into the jury room as an exhibit, unlike other forms of real or demonstrative evidence — the theory is that the record is in lieu of testimony, so it should not be given greater weight than testimony by being taken to the jury room. But the record is *evidence.* (This makes the past recollection recorded different from a document used to jog the witness' memory under the present recollection refreshed exception — the latter is not evidence, but is merely an aid to stimulate testimony.) [192]

V. BUSINESS RECORDS

A. **General/Federal Rule:** Nearly all states recognize a hearsay exception for certain types of business records. The Federal provision (FRE 803(6)) is typical; the business record is admissible if: [194]

1. **Routine of business:** The record was made in the *routine of the business*;

2. **Knowledge:** The record was made by, or from information supplied by, a person with *personal knowledge* of the matter recorded and who is *working in the business*; and

3. **Timeliness:** The entry was made *"at or near the time"* of the matter recorded.

> **Example:** The shipping department of Store records every shipment sent out to a customer. Store's ledger showing a shipment made to D will be admissible under FRE 803(6) if Store establishes that: (1) it regularly kept a written record of every shipment that went out; (2) the person who wrote the ledger entries did so either from his personal knowledge that a given shipment had gone out, or by being told that this had happened by a person with such direct knowledge and a business duty to disclose that knowledge; and (3) the ledger entries were made shortly after each shipment actually went out.

B. **"Business" defined:** "Business" is defined broadly under modern statutes. Thus, FRE 803(6) applies to schools, churches, and hospitals, even though these are not necessarily profit-making entities. [194]

C. **Person supplying info:** The person who originally supplies the information that goes in to the record must satisfy two requirements: (1) he must have first-hand knowledge of the fact he reports; and (2) he must do his reporting *while working in the business*. The latter requirement means that if the source of the information is not an employee of the business that keeps the record, the exception may not apply — thus statements by *witnesses to an accident*, even if made to a police officer or other person with a business duty to compile a report, will *not* be admissible. *Johnson v. Lutz.* [194-96]

D. **"Regular course of business":** Although the proponent must show that the report was made in the "regular course of business," even reports of a sort that are rarely made may qualify. For instance, if a business makes a practice of making a record of any *accident* that occurs during the transaction of business, the "regular course of business" requirement will be satisfied even though accidents happen rarely. (But the rareness with which a certain type of record is kept may suggest that the particular record is untrustworthy, violating a different requirement, discussed below.) [196-97]

E. **Opinion:** The modern trend is to accept even *opinions* contained in the report, if these would be admissible when given as part of live testimony. Thus, if the person supplying the report or making the record is an expert, his statement (e.g., "Patient seems to be suffering from schizophrenia") will be admitted if he would be permitted to make the same statement at trial. FRE 803(6) even allows lay opinions to be admitted, assuming there is no grounds for doubting their trustworthiness. [197-98]

F. **Untrustworthy:** If the surrounding circumstances make the record seem *untrustworthy*, the court has discretion to exclude it. For instance, if the facts indicate that the business that made record had a strong motive to create a *self-serving* record, the court may exclude it. (*Example:* After a train crash, Railroad conducts an internal investigation, and makes a report absolving the engineer. Railroad's strong incentive to cover-up so as to avoid liability may cause the court to exclude the report for untrustworthiness.) [198]

G. **Absence of entry:** If a regularly kept business record would otherwise qualify, it may usually be admitted to show that a particular entry is *absent*, if such an entry would normally have been made had a particular event occurred. (*Example:* Merchant keeps regular records of every payment by a customer. If the issue is whether Customer has paid a particular bill, Merchant may admit its records to show that no indication that Customer paid this particular bill was ever placed on its records.) [198-99]

H. **Oral reports:** Most courts hold that the record must be *in writing*. (*Example:* Foreman reports to Boss that Employee has hurt his hand on a machine. Even if making such an oral report is part of Foreman's job, Boss will not be permitted to testify that Foreman made the report, because the report was not in writing.) [199-200]

I. **Proving the record:** The business record is not "self admitting." Instead, a *sponsoring witness* must be called who can testify that the requirements of the business-records statute were satisfied. Typically, this will be someone who knows enough about the record-keeping routine of the business to testify that the records were appropriately kept in the particular instance (even if this witness did not make or observe the particular entry in question). [200]

J. **Special situations:** Here are two recurring situations where the business records exception is often applied: [200-04]

    1. **Hospital records:** *Hospital records* are often introduced to prove the truth of statements contained in them. Even statements contained in the record that are not declarations of symptoms (e.g., "Patient said he was hit by a truck") will be admitted if part of the record. But totally extraneous matter (e.g., "Patient says that the car that hit him ran a red light") will not be admitted.

        a. **Patient under no duty:** If the information comes from the patient, it will not normally satisfy the requirement that the person supplying the information must have been working for the business (in this case, for the hospital). However, the hospital record can usually be admitted for the limited purpose of showing that the patient made a particular statement; then, some other exception may apply to allow the patient's statement to be offered for the truth of the matter asserted. For instance, if the patient is the plaintiff, the defendant will be able to introduce the statement against him because it is an admission; similarly, if the patient is reporting his current symptoms or other bodily condition, the "statement of present physical condition" exception will apply.

    2. **Computer print-out:** Computer print-outs will often be admissible to prove the truth of matters stated in the print-out. However, the proponent must show that: (1) the print-out comes from data that was entered into the system relatively promptly; and (2) the procedures by which the data was entered, the program written, the report prepared, etc., are all reasonably reliable.

VII. PUBLIC RECORDS AND REPORTS

A. **Common-law rule:** At common law, there is an exception for admission of a *written report or record* of a *public official* if: (1) the official has *first-hand knowledge* of the facts reported; and (2) the official had a *duty* to make the record or report. [204-05]

B. **Federal Rule:** The federal public records and reports exception is even broader. FRE 803(8) admits three different types of public records and reports: [205]

    1. **Agency's own activities:** Subsection (A) allows admission of a government agency's records of its *own activities*, if offered to show that those activities occurred. (*Example:* P sues the FBI for invading his privacy; he could introduce the agency's own surveillance records to prove that the agency tapped his phone.)

    2. **Matters observed under duty:** Subsection (B) makes the written records of *observations* made by public officials admissible if: (1) the observation was made *in the line of duty*; and (2) the official had a *duty to report* those observations. (*Example:* An IRS agent does a field audit of Smith's tax return at Smith's house. If Smith claims a deduction for "home office," and the agent finds no evidence of one, his written report to his superior can be introduced in a later civil suit on the issue of whether Smith had a home office. But the agent's observation that Smith possessed cocaine would not be admissible, since the agent had no duty to report non-tax related matters.)

    3. **Investigative reports:** Subsection (C) allows the admission of *"factual findings"* resulting from *investigations*, except when used against a criminal defendant. (*Example:* Following an accident, the police send an accident investigator, who writes a report that concludes

that the crash was caused when the vehicle traveling east-west went through a stop light. This report would be admissible in a civil suit arising out of the crash.)

C. Criminal cases: Use of FRE 803(8) in criminal cases raises special issues: [207-10]

    1. No use of (B) and (C): Subsections (B) and (C) may *not* be used against the *defendant in a criminal case.* Thus a police officer's written report stating that he has seen D commit a robbery, or a detective's report concluding that a previously unsolved crime has probably been committed by D, could not be admitted against D in his trial. (Probably each of these reports, however, could be used *by* D against the government in the criminal trial.)

    2. "Other law enforcement personnel": Subsection (B) does not apply in criminal cases to matters "observed by police officers and *other law enforcement personnel.*" Observations by *laboratory technicians* working in government laboratories (e.g., the results of substance analysis performed by a police department chemist) have sometimes been excluded under this provision.

    3. Use of other exceptions: It is not clear whether a report that would otherwise come within subsection (B) or (C), and that is excluded under those provisions because it is used against a criminal defendant, may nonetheless be admitted under *some other* exception, e.g., the business records exception.

        a. Minority view: Some courts have flatly rejected all such evidence. (*Example:* The prosecution offers a substance analysis report prepared by a chemist working for the government, to prove that substance taken from D was heroin. Even though this was a "regularly kept record" by an organization, and thus would otherwise have qualified under the business records exception, it was disallowed because it fell within the explicit exclusion of 803(8)(B). *U.S. v. Oates.*)

        b. Majority view: But probably the majority would allow a report of direct observations or investigations to be admitted against D at least where the maker of the report is produced in court and is subject to cross-examination. (*Example:* If the government chemist above were produced as a witness, most courts would admit his report concluding that the substance taken from D was heroin.)

D. Other issues: Other issues arise in both a civil and criminal context: [210-14]

    1. Evaluations: Subsection (C) refers to the "factual findings" in investigative reports. But so long as an investigative report includes factual findings, other *"evaluative"* parts of the report — *opinions, evaluations* and *conclusions* — may *also* be admitted. [*Beech Aircraft Corp. v. Rainey*] (*Example:* The government, after investigating the crash of a Navy plane, produces a report containing numerous factual findings. The report then says that "the most probable cause of the accident was pilot error." This statement may be admitted, even though it is an "opinion" or "conclusion". *Beech Aircraft.*)

    2. Multiple hearsay: A government report must be carefully scrutinized for *multiple hearsay* problems.

        a. Report by one government agent to another: If government employee A tells facts to employee B, who writes them up into a government report, A's statements will be admissible if A had a duty to give the report to B. (*Example:* Officer Jones witnesses a car accident, and later says to Officer Smith, "I saw the green Plymouth run a red light and cause the accident." Smith includes this statement in a report on the accident. The entire report, including Jones' quoted statement, will be admissible under 803(8)(B), because Jones had a duty to furnish the information to Smith, and Smith's report was otherwise covered as a "report of matters observed.")

        b. Statement by one without duty to talk: But if information is supplied by one who does *not* work for the government and does not have a duty to give the report, the resulting written report may not include the quoted statement, unless the quoted statement independently falls within some exception. (*Example:* Bystander tells Officer Jones, "I saw the blue car jump the light and cause the accident." Jones' report will be generally admissible as an investigative report under subsection (C), but Bystander's statement will have to be removed, because he did not observe the accident pursuant to any duty, or have any duty to make a report.)

3. **Trustworthiness:** If the "sources of information or other circumstances indicate lack of *trustworthiness*," the judge can keep the report out of evidence. This is probably the case with respect to reports falling under any of the three subsections. (*Example:* Evidence that the public official who prepared a report had been bribed, or was motivated by ulterior motives, would cause it to be excluded for lack of trustworthiness.)

VIII. MISCELLANEOUS "AVAILABILITY IMMATERIAL" EXCEPTIONS

A. **Learned writings and commercial publications:** A learned writing (e.g., a *scientific treatise* or article) may be admitted for the truth of the matter asserted, under FRE 803(18). (The common law allowed such learned works to be used only for impeachment of the other side's expert witness.) [214-16]

1. **Use on direct:** The application may come in as part of a party's *direct* case, if a favorable expert testifies that the treatise is authoritative.

2. **Cross-examination:** The publication can be used as part of the *cross-examination* of the other side's expert, even if the expert refuses to admit that the publication is authoritative. (But the cross-examiner must establish the authoritativeness of the publication by some other means, such as another witness.)

3. **Expert must be on the stand:** Whether it is introduced as part of the direct or cross-examination, the publication may only be introduced if there is an *expert on the stand* who can help the jury interpret its meaning.

4. **Commercial publications:** The Federal Rules recognize a similar exception for *commercial publications* that are commonly relied upon by business people. See FRE 803(17), allowing admission of "market quotations, tabulations, lists, directories, or other published compilations, generally used and relied upon by the public or by persons in particular occupations."

B. **Ancient documents:** [216-18]

1. **Common law:** The common law makes it easy to admit *"ancient documents."* A document will be presumed to be authentic if it is: (1) at least 30 years old; (2) unsuspicious in appearance; and (3) shown to have come from a place of custody natural for such a writing. However, in most courts this is merely a rule of authentication, not an exception to the hearsay rule, so the statements contained in it may not be shown for their truth. But some courts do treat it as a hearsay exception.

   a. **Ancient deeds:** *All* courts allow statements contained in an ancient *deed* to be shown for their truth. Thus a statement in a will, "O purchased this property from X in 1872," could everywhere be used to show that O really did purchase the property in 1872, if the above three requirements are satisfied.

2. **Federal Rules:** The Federal Rules explicitly make the ancient documents rule a hearsay exception. The document need merely have been in existence *20* years (not the 30 required at common law). The proponent must prove that the document is "authentic" (i.e., that it is at least 20 years old and meets the "no suspicion" and "likely place of custody" requirements). See FRE 901(b)(8).

b. Newer title documents: A separate federal hearsay exception exists for less-than-20-year-old documents that relate to ***title to property***. See FRE 803(15). (*Example:* A 10-year-old deed recites, "O sold this property to X in 1973." This will be admissible to prove that O did indeed sell the property to X in 1972.)

C. Reputation: There is a hearsay exception for several types of ***reputation*** evidence: [218-19]

1. **Birth, marriage, etc.:** There is an exception for a person's reputation within his family regarding some aspect of ***birth***, ***marriage***, or ***relationship***. (*Example:* Reputation within the family that A is B's son, offered to prove that A really is B's son.) FRE 803(19) extends this to cover a reputation among one's ***business*** colleagues or one's reputation in a ***community***, concerning some fact of the person's personal or family history.

2. **General historical facts:** There is an exception for proof of ***facts of general history*** and for proof of land boundaries. See FRE 803(20). (*Example:* To prove that there was an earthquake in San Francisco in 1906, a party could call a historian who would testify that in Northern California, it is commonly believed or remembered that there was an earthquake in that year.)

3. **Reputation for character:** There is an exception for proof that a person had a particular ***reputation*** for character. (*Example:* W may testify that P has a reputation in his hometown for being a liar, if offered by D to prove that P really is a liar and that therefore D did not commit libel by calling him one.)

D. Miscellaneous: [219-22]

1. **Vital statistics, marriage certificates:** Statements of fact contained in public records have an exception. (*Examples:* A report that X died on a certain day, offered to prove that fact. A statement in a marriage certificate that X married Y on a certain day, offered to prove that fact.)

2. **Absence of public record:** There is an exception for the fact that a certain record is ***absent*** from the public records, offered to prove that fact. (*Example:* Testimony that a search of the IRS's records does not disclose D's 1985 tax return, offered to prove that D did not file a return that year.)

3. **Previous felony conviction:** Proof that X is guilty of a particular ***crime*** may be made by showing that X was convicted of that crime. (But the fact that X was convicted of a misdemeanor may not be used in a subsequent case to prove that he did the act charged.)

IX. UNAVAILABILITY REQUIRED — GENERALLY

A. Four exceptions: There are four main hearsay exceptions that do ***not*** require that the declarant be unavailable to testify at trial:

1. ***Testimony*** given in a ***prior proceeding***;

2. Statements made while the declarant believed his death was impending (so-called ***"dying declarations"***);

3. Statements which were ***against the declarant's interest*** when made; and

4. Statements concerning either the declarant's or his relatives' ***personal or family history*** (so-called statements of "pedigree").

B. Meaning of "unavailable": [223-25]

1. **Federal:** FRE 804(a) defines five situations in which the declarant will be deemed to be unavailable:

    a. He is *privileged* against testifying about the subject matter of his out-of-court statement;

    b. He *refuses* to testify despite a court order;

    c. He testifies that he *cannot remember* the statement's subject matter;

    d. He cannot be present to testify because of *death*, or physical or mental *illness*; or

    e. He is absent, and the proponent of his statement has been unable to procure his attendance (or his deposition) by *process* or other reasonable means (e.g., persuasion).

    f. Proponent's fault: But none of the above reasons will make the declarant "unavailable" if his unavailability is due to "procurement or *wrongdoing*" by the *proponent*.

2. States follow: Most states recognize the first four exceptions. But with respect to the fifth, absence from the jurisdiction, most courts automatically treat the declarant as being "unavailable" if he is outside the jurisdiction — they don't require the proponent to make non-subpoena efforts (e.g., persuasion or the taking of a deposition) to procure his attendance or testimony.

3. Constitutional problems: If the hearsay exception is one traditionally requiring unavailability, a criminal defendant's Sixth Amendment *Confrontation Clause* rights may be violated if the court admits the out-of-court statement without a showing that the declarant really was unavailable. For this purpose, a witness will be deemed sufficiently "unavailable" (and the use of his out-of-court declaration will not violate his Sixth Amendment right) if the state shows:

    a. that the witness is *beyond that state's own process*; and

    b. that either the government made a *good faith effort* to get the witness to attend by means other than process, or such efforts would have been *very unlikely to succeed*.

X. FORMER TESTIMONY

A. General rule: There is a hearsay exception for *former testimony* — that is, testimony given in an *earlier proceeding* — if the witness is unavailable for trial. FRE 804(b)(1), which basically follows the common law, imposes these requirements: [225]

1. Hearing or deposition: The testimony was given either at a *hearing* in the same or earlier action, or in a *deposition* in the same or different proceeding;

2. Party present: The party against whom the testimony is now offered was *present* at the earlier testimony (or, in a civil case, that party's "predecessor in interest" was present); and

3. Opportunity to cross-examine: The party against whom the testimony is offered had the *opportunity* and *similar motive* to develop the testimony. Usually, this opportunity will have been the chance to *cross-examine*, but it may have been a chance to expand the testimony by *direct* or redirect examination.

    Example 1: P sues D for negligence. At a deposition in which D is present, P asks questions to X, a witness to the accident. Because D has had the chance to cross-examine X during the deposition, X's deposition answers may be introduced against D in the eventual suit, if X is unavailable to testify at trial (even if D did not use his right to cross-examine X at the deposition).

    Example 2: W gives testimony unfavorable to D before a grand jury while D is not present. At D's eventual criminal trial, this testimony cannot be introduced against D even if W is now unavailable, because D had no opportunity to cross-examine (but some courts might apply the residual or "catch all" exception, discussed below).

B. Identity of issues: There must be enough overlap between the issues existing at the time of the prior hearing or deposition, and the issues existing at the present trial, that the above opportunity for cross-examination was a meaningful substitute for cross-examination in the present case. At common law, there must be "substantial identity" between issues; under the Federal Rules, the opponent must have had a *"similar motive"* in the earlier situation. [227-28]

    1. Different contexts: This requirement can be satisfied even though the earlier and present proceedings are quite different contexts. (*Examples:* Testimony given at a **preliminary hearing** can be used at a later criminal trial, even though the issues are not absolutely "identical" in the two situations. Similarly, testimony given at a criminal trial can be admitted at a later civil proceeding, even though the issues and burdens of proof are not identical.)

C. Identity of parties: The **proponent** of the former testimony need **not** have been a party to the taking of the former testimony. Only the **opponent** must have been present. [228-31]

    1. Similar party in interest: Furthermore, even if the opponent was not present, under the Federal Rule the testimony can be used so long as the present opponent's "predecessor in interest" was present, if the case is a civil case. This probably means merely that a person with a very similar motive must have been present. (But in criminal cases, there is no "predecessor in interest" provision. Thus a statement may not be offered against a criminal defendant who was not present, even if another person — e.g., a co-defendant — was present at the prior proceeding and had a highly similar motive to cross-examine.)

XI. DYING DECLARATIONS

A. General rule: There is an exception for *"dying declarations."* The common law version is narrow: a declarant's statement, while believing that his death is imminent, concerning the cause or circumstances of his impending death, is admissible in a subsequent homicide prosecution concerning that death. FRE 804(b)(2) loosens several of these restrictions. [231]

B. Requirements in detail: [231-33]

    1. Awareness of imminent death: The declarant must, at the time he made his statement, have been aware of his impending death. It is not enough that he knows he is seriously ill or wounded, or that he will probably die — at common law he must have **lost all hope** of recovery. (Under the Federal Rule, he must "believe . . . that his death [is] imminent.")

    2. Actual death: At common law, the declarant **must in fact be dead** by the time the evidence is offered. But this is not required under the Federal Rule (though the declarant must of course be unavailable, since this is one of the "unavailability required" exceptions).

    3. Homicide: At common law, the declaration may be used **only in a homicide case.** Thus it may not be used in civil cases, or in criminal cases not charging homicide (e.g., a case in which D is charged with rape alone, even though V died after the rape). Under the Federal Rules, dying declarations are usable in civil suits and homicide cases, but not in non-homicide criminal cases.

    4. Declarant is victim: At common law, declaration may be offered only in a trial for the killing of the **declarant**, not the killing of someone else. (*Example:* D has probably murdered both H and W. He is prosecuted for the murder of H only. At common law, the prosecution cannot introduce W's dying declaration, "D did this to H and me.") The Federal Rules drop this requirement.

    5. Relating to circumstances of killing: Both at common law and under the Federal Rules, the declaration must relate to the **causes or circumstances of the killing**. (*Example:* Declarant, while dying, says, "X and I have been enemies for years." The exception probably does not apply, since it does not relate directly to the causes or circumstances of declarant's death. But, "X has been stalking me for two days," would satisfy this test.)

6. **For accused:** The statement may be admitted *on behalf of* the accused (though usually, it is admitted *against* him.)

XII. DECLARATIONS AGAINST INTEREST

A. **Generally:** There is a hearsay exception for declarations which, at the time they are made, are *so against the declarant's interest that it is unlikely that they would have been made if they were not true*. [234]

   1. **Common law:** At common law, there are three main requirements for the exception:

      a. The declaration must have been against the declarant's *pecuniary or proprietary interest* (not his penal interest) when made;

      b. The declarant must now be *unavailable*; and

      c. The declarant must have had first-hand knowledge of the facts asserted in the declaration.

   2. **Federal Rule:** FRE 804(b)(3) follows this approach, except that declarations against *penal interest* are also admissible (except uncorroborated statements exculpating the accused).

B. **Meaning of "against interest":** [236-42]

   1. **When made:** The declaration must have been made against the declarant's interest *at the time it was made*. The fact that later developments have turned what was an innocent-seeming statement into one that now harms some interest of the declarant is *not* enough to satisfy this requirement.

   2. **Pecuniary interest:** At common law, only statements against the declarant's pecuniary or proprietary interest qualify.

      a. **Property:** Thus, a statement limiting the declarant's *property* rights, or a creditor's statement that a debt has been paid, will qualify. Modern cases also allow a statement subjecting the declarant to possible *tort liability* to qualify.

   3. **Penal interest:**

      a. **Common law:** At common law, statements against the declarant's *penal* interest — that is, statements tending to subject him to *criminal* liability — do *not* qualify. (This is due mainly to fears that people will falsely confess, or falsely claim to have heard others confess, in order to exculpate the defendant.)

      b. **Federal approach:** The Federal Rules treat statements against penal interest as *qualifying*. However, a statement against penal interest that is offered to exculpate the accused is not admissible unless "*corroborating circumstances* clearly indicate the trustworthiness of the statement." (*Example:* D is charged with burglary. W offers to testify that while in jail, he heard X, another inmate, confess to having done this burglary alone. Because both W and X are felons whose word is somewhat doubtful, this testimony will be allowed only if there is independent evidence that X may well have done the burglary — e.g., he was out of prison at the time, and is known to have performed other, similar burglaries.)

   4. **Collateral statements:** If statement includes a disserving part but also a self-serving part, the court will try to excise the self-serving part. If the statement has both a disserving and a neutral part, the court will probably let in the whole statement. (*Example:* "It was Joe and I that pulled off that bank job," will be admissible against Joe, even though the part of the statement referring to Joe was not directly against the declarant's interest.)

C. **Constitutional issues:** [242-43]

1. **Use by prosecution:** When the prosecution tries to introduce a third party's declaration to inculpate the accused, the Sixth Amendment Confrontation Clause rights of the accused may help him keep the statement out. For instance, a statement exposing the declarant to criminal liability, given while the declarant is in ***police custody***, will almost always be excluded, because of the declarant's motive to try to gain favor by inculpating the accused and minimizing his own guilt. *Lee v. Illinois.*

2. **Use by accused:** Where it is the accused who seeks to ***exculpate*** himself by use of third person's declaration against interest, the accused may be able to rely on the Due Process Clause and the Sixth Amendment right to compulsory process to get the statement into evidence. (*Example:* D tries to show that X has confessed to the crime that D is charged with. If there are some solid facts corroborating X's confession, and X is unavailable to testify, D probably has a due process or compulsory process right to have X's out-of-court confession introduced.)

XIII. STATEMENTS OF PEDIGREE

A. General rule: There is a hearsay exception for statements of ***"pedigree,"*** i.e., statements about a person's birth, death, marriage, genealogy, or other fact of personal or family history. Here are the requirements at common law and under the Federal Rules: [243-45]

1. **Declarant unavailable:** The declarant must be unavailable to testify;

2. **Person or relative:** At common law, the declarant must be either the person whose history the statement concerns, or a ***relative*** of the person whom the statement concerns. Under FRE 804(b)(4), it will also suffice if the declarant is so "intimately associated" with the family of the person the statement concerns that it is "likely [that the declarant would] have accurate information concerning the matter declared." (*Example:* O is the servant for X's family during X's entire lifetime. If O tells W, "X is the illegitimate son of Y," under the federal but not the common-law approach, W will be permitted to repeat the statement in court, even though O was not a member of the family.)

3. **Before controversy:** The statement must have been made before the ***present controversy arose***, under the common-law approach. (But this requirement is completely dropped by the Federal Rules.)

4. **Not motive to falsify:** The declarant must not have had any ***apparent motive*** to falsify.

XIV. PRIOR STATEMENTS OF AVAILABLE WITNESS

A. Common-law rules: At common law, it is very difficult to make use of ***prior statements*** by a person who is a ***witness*** at the current trial: [245-47]

1. **Prior inconsistent statement:** The trial witness' prior ***inconsistent*** statement is inadmissible hearsay at common law. (However, the prior inconsistent statement may used to ***impeach*** the witness at the present trial.)

2. **Prior consistent statement:** Similarly, the trial witness' prior ***consistent*** statement is not substantively admissible at common law. (But if the witness is accused of having recently fabricated his trial testimony, or of having been improperly influenced or motivated, the prior consistent statement may be used for the non-substantive purpose of rehabilitating his credibility.)

3. **Prior identification:** Proof that the trial witness has previously made an ***eyewitness identification*** is technically hearsay, but many common-law courts allow it as substantive evidence if it seems to have probative value. (*Example:* D is charged with robbing V. Many common-law courts would allow trial testimony by W, a police officer, that shortly after the episode, V pointed to D in a police lineup and said, "That's the one who robbed me.")

B. Federal Rule on prior inconsistent statements: [247-48]

    1. General rule: FRE 801(d)(1) makes certain prior ***inconsistent*** statements of the trial witness substantively admissible (i.e., not hearsay). If the defendant testifies at trial and is ***subject to cross-examination*** concerning his prior statement, that statement is admissible if it is "inconsistent with the declarant's [trial] testimony, and was given ***under oath*** subject to the penalty of perjury at a ***trial, hearing,*** or other ***proceeding***, or in a ***deposition***."

        a. Proceeding: In other words, only statements given under oath as part of a formal proceeding (generally a trial, preliminary hearing, or deposition) may be substantively introduced if the witness' trial testimony differs. An ***informal oral*** statement previously made by the witness will ***not*** be substantively admissible. (*Example:* In an accident case, W testifies at trial on behalf of P, "D went through the red light." D cannot introduce for substantive purposes a previous statement by W to her husband H, "The light was green when D went through it." But if W had made that same statement during the course of a deposition under oath, or during testimony at a prior trial, it could be substantively admitted in the present trial.)

    2. Cross-examination not required: This Federal Rule allows the prior inconsistent statement into evidence even when there was ***no cross-examination***, or even any ***opportunity*** for cross-examination. (*Example:* W testifies in favor of D at a criminal trial. The prosecution may substantively introduce W's prior inconsistent grand jury testimony, even though D and his lawyer were not present and had no opportunity to cross-examine W at that grand jury session — the theory is that D has the opportunity to cross-examine W *now*.)

C. Federal Rule on prior consistent statements: If the prior statement is ***consistent*** with the witness' trial testimony, it is substantively admissible, but only if it is "offered to rebut an express or implied charge against [the witness] of recent fabrication or improper influence or motive." FRE 801(d)(1)(B). (*Example:* W, a witness to a robbery, testifies at trial that the robber was not D. The prosecutor asserts in cross-examination that D has recently intimidated W and gotten him to change his story. D's lawyer may substantively introduce a statement made long ago by W at a grand jury, in which W told the same story.) [255]

D. Federal Rule on prior identifications: A statement of "***identification***" of a person made after perceiving him" is substantively admissible, if the declarant testifies at the trial and is available for cross-examination. FRE 801(d)(1)(C). [255-57]

    1. No oath or proceeding: Unlike a prior inconsistent statement, a statement of identification is substantively admissible under this provision even though it was ***not made under oath*** or at a formal ***proceeding***. (*Example:* V, a robbery victim, is walking down the street the day after the robbery when she spots D. She says to H, who is with her, "That's the robber." H will be permitted to repeat this statement at D's trial, even though W's statement was not made under oath or at a proceeding.)

XV. RESIDUAL ("CATCH ALL") EXCEPTION

A. Federal Rule generally: Modern courts now tend to admit hearsay evidence that does not fall within any well-defined exclusion, if it is highly reliable and badly needed in the particular case. The Federal Rules codify this ***residual*** or ***"catch all"*** exception in FRE 803(24) and 804(b)(5) (depending on whether the witness is available). These sections impose five requirements: [257-61]

    1. Circumstantial guarantees of trustworthiness: The statement must have ***"circumstantial guarantees of trustworthiness"*** that are equivalent to those inherent in the other, more specific, federal hearsay exceptions. (Factors the courts consider are summarized below.)

2. **Material fact:** The statement must be offered as evidence of a ***material fact***.

3. **More probative:** The statement must be ***"more probative"*** on the point for which it is offered than any other evidence which is available through reasonable efforts. (*Example:* If the declarant can give equally probative live testimony, or if there is some other witness who can give the same evidence as that contained in the out-of-court declaration, the catch all exception does not apply.)

4. **Interests of justice:** Use of the evidence must be consistent with "the general purposes of [the Federal] Rules and the interests of justice."

5. **Notice:** The proponent of the evidence must give ***notice*** of his intention to offer the statement "sufficiently in advance of the trial or hearing to provide . . . a fair opportunity to prepare to meet it." The notice must include the particulars of the statement, including the declarant's name and address. (But federal courts often disregard the precise language of this requirement, and allow use of evidence without a pre-trial notice if the need for the evidence does not become apparent until the trial starts; the court will usually give a continuance to the opponent in order to let him prepare to meet the evidence.)

> **Example 1:** W has given detailed, credible, and important ***grand jury testimony***, and is not available to testify at trial. The residual exception will probably apply. (The "former testimony" exception of 804(b)(1) does not apply to this testimony, because the opponent did not have the opportunity to cross-examine.)

> **Example 2:** X took contemporaneous ***hand-written notes*** of an event he witnessed, but is not available to testify at trial. If the notes seem to be reliable, and there is no equally probative or better testimony available, the notes will be admitted under the residual exception. (The document cannot constitute Past Recollection Recorded, under FRE 803(5), because the author is by hypothesis not available as a witness to authenticate it.)

> **Example 3:** W, D's building superintendent, orally tells P not to use a particular safety measure because it will inconvenience W's pets. P is injured. W is not available as a trial witness, and P has no other way to rebut D's claim that P was contributorily negligent. Assuming that there is some corroboration of W's alleged statement (e.g., some independent proof that the safety measure would indeed have inconvenienced W's pets), the court will probably apply the residual exception.

B. **Circumstantial guarantees of trustworthiness:** In determining whether the statement has "equivalent circumstantial guarantees of trustworthiness" (requirement 1 above), the court is likely to consider these factors, among others: [261-64]

    a. **Oath:** Whether the declaration was ***under oath***. (If so, it is more reliable.)

    b. **Time lapse:** How much ***time elapsed*** between the event and the statement. (The longer the time lapse, the less reliable the statement.)

    c. **Motive:** The declarant's ***motive*** for telling the truth. (The stronger the motive to tell the truth, the more reliable.) (*Example:* D1, who is been arrested on a criminal charge, tells a grand jury that the crime was committed by D2, and that D1 was just a bystander. Because D1 had a strong motive to exculpate himself by incriminating another, his statement will probably be viewed as unreliable.)

    d. **First-hand knowledge:** Whether the declarant had ***first-hand knowledge*** of what he said. (If he merely repeated what someone else said, this makes the statement less reliable.)

    e. **Written vs. oral:** Whether the statement is ***written*** or oral. (Written statements, whether written by the declarant or transcribed stenographically as in a confession to police, are presumed to be more reliable than oral statements.)

f. Corroboration by other evidence: In some but not all courts, the extent to which the declaration is corroborated by other evidence in the case. (*Example:* Grand jury testimony by D1 implicating D2 matches detailed physical evidence inculpating D2. Some but not all courts would treat this corroboration by other evidence as making D1's statements more reliable.)

g. Whether the declarant has subsequently **recanted** his statement. (A statement that has subsequently been recanted is less reliable.)

C. "Near miss": When a particular fact pattern comes very close to matching the requirements for a recognized hearsay exception, but just misses, a few courts refuse to apply the residual exception. But most courts are willing to apply the residual exception in this situation, if the other requirements are met. [264-66]

CONFRONTATION AND COMPULSORY PROCESS

I. INTRODUCTION

A. Confrontation Clause: The Confrontation Clause of the Sixth Amendment guarantees a criminal defendant the right "to be confronted with the witnesses against him." This Clause may give a criminal defendant the right to keep out of evidence out-of-court declarations that are unreliable, where the declarant is not available to be cross-examined in court. [269]

B. Compulsory process: The Sixth Amendment's Compulsory Process Clause gives the criminal defendant the right "to have compulsory process for obtaining Witnesses in his favor." This Clause may allow the defendant to **gain admission** of otherwise-inadmissible evidence. For instance, this Clause may give the defendant the right to introduce an out-of-court declaration (e.g., a confession to the crime by someone else) that would otherwise be excluded under traditional hearsay principles. [269]

II. CONFRONTATION CLAUSE

A. General principles: [270-79]

1. **Preference for live testimony:** The Confrontation Clause reflects a **preference for live testimony** in lieu of out-of-court declarations wherever possible. Therefore, if the declarant is available to testify, but the prosecution instead offers his out-of-court declaration, the trial judge is more likely to find a confrontation violation than where the declarant is not available. For instance, the declarant's **former testimony** may normally not be admitted if the declarant is available. (But other types of out-of-court declarations, such as statements by co-conspirators made during the course of the conspiracy, are admissible even though the declarant is available, on the theory that the defendant has the right to subpoena a declarant to cross-examine him about the statement.)

2. **Indicia of reliability:** Whether or not the declarant is unavailable, his out-of-court declaration will not be allowed into evidence unless it contains **"indicia of reliability."**

   a. "Firmly rooted exception": However, if the out-of-court declaration is sought to be introduced under a **"firmly rooted hearsay exception,"** this will **by itself** be enough to establish the required reliability. Therefore, the court will **not** look at the facts surrounding the particular declaration in question, and will allow the declaration even if there is reason to believe that it may be unreliable in this particular case. (*Example:* While A and B are planning a burglary, A tries to recruit C by saying, "B's in this with me." At B's subsequent trial on burglary charges, this statement may be admitted against him because it falls within the well-established hearsay exception for co-conspirators' statements; this is true even though there may be evidence in this particular case that A was falsely seeking to use the name of B, a well known local mobster, as a recruitment device.)

b. Particularized facts: If the out-of-court statement does **not** fall within a "firmly rooted hearsay exception," the prosecution must show that the **particularized facts** surrounding it demonstrate that it is probably reliable. One important factor in this determination is whether the defendant has at some stage gotten the right to **cross-examine** the declarant about the statement. (*Example:* D1 is arrested for robbery. While in custody, he gives the police a statement implicating D2. At D2's trial, D1 refuses to testify on self-incrimination grounds. D1's statement will not be allowed against D2, because it is not within a firmly rooted, narrow, hearsay exception — the "declaration against interest" exception is too broad — and the particular facts of this case do not establish its reliability, since D1 had a strong motive to curry favor with the police by helping them catch and convict D2. *Lee v. Illinois.*)

i. Can't use corroborating evidence: In deciding whether there are "particular guarantees of trustworthiness" for the out-of-court statement, only the facts surrounding the particular statement, **not** other evidence that **corroborates** the statement's **truth**, may be considered. (*Example:* W, a child, says she was sexually abused. Evidence that W had no motive to lie may be considered. But physical evidence showing that abuse took place, thus corroborating the truth of W's statement, may not be considered in determining whether the statement had "particular guarantees of trustworthiness." *Idaho v. Wright.*)

3. Right to confront testifying witnesses: In addition to hearsay situations, the Confrontation Clause may also give the defendant a right to **cross-examine** a testifying witness, even where the usual rules of evidence would prohibit or limit such examination. (*Example:* A state rape shield statute prohibits the defendant from asking the victim any questions whatsoever about any prior sexual act. If this were interpreted to prevent D from demonstrating consent by showing through the cross-examination of V that V and D had had sex together on numerous prior occasions, D's Confrontation Clause rights would be violated.)

a. Right to be face-to-face with W: Also, D's Confrontation Clause right generally gives him a right to be **face-to-face** with the witness against him. (*Example:* In child-abuse cases, normally the state may not put a screen between the witness stand and D, or otherwise prevent the witness from seeing D, unless there is evidence that this particular witness needs special protection. *Coy v. Iowa.*)

B. Specific contexts: [279-84]

1. W present and testifying: If W is present at trial, testifies, and is available for cross-examination, the only time D's Confrontation Clause rights are likely to be violated is if W denies any recollection of the underlying event, and the court believes that W is lying.

2. Co-conspirator's statement: Where the out-of-court declaration is a statement made by a **co-conspirator** during the course of the conspiracy and in furtherance of it, D is very **unlikely** to succeed with a confrontation claim. This is true regardless of whether the co-conspirator is available to testify. (Nor will the court look at the reliability of the particular statement, since it falls within the general firmly rooted hearsay exception for co-conspirator's statements.) *U.S. v. Inadi.*

3. "Declarant's unavailability immaterial" exceptions: Where hearsay is allowed under one of the traditional "declarant's availability immaterial" exceptions (excited utterances, statements of existing mental or physical condition, recorded recollections, business records, etc.), D's Confrontation Clause argument is unlikely to succeed. Even if W is available at trial to testify, the prosecution need not produce him, so long as it cooperates with D's ability to subpoena W. Nor will the court look into the particularized facts surrounding the declaration, since by hypothesis it falls within a firmly rooted hearsay exception.

4. **Declarant unavailable:** As to those hearsay exceptions requiring the unavailability of the declarant, D will also generally find it hard to keep the testimony out on confrontation grounds:

    a. **Former testimony:** *Former testimony* given at a prior proceeding or deposition under oath, where D had an opportunity to cross-examine W, can be admitted at D's trial without confrontation problems, if W is now unavailable. (But if W is available, the Confrontation Clause requires that he be produced, even if the local evidence rule deviates from the traditional approach by not requiring that the declarant be unavailable.)

    b. **Dying declaration:** Statements meeting the traditional dying declaration requirements are almost certainly admissible without any Confrontation Clause problems.

    c. **Statement against interest:** A *statement against interest* is the defendant's best opportunity to invoke the Confrontation Clause successfully. If his co-defendant has given a confession implicating D, the confession will be allowed against D only if the particular facts surrounding it give a special assurance of reliability (something that will rarely be the case, because of the co-defendant's motive to curry favor with the authorities). *Lee v. Illinois*. Furthermore, even if the co-defendant's statement has indicia of reliability, the prosecution must probably produce him at trial if he is available.

III. COMPULSORY PROCESS

A. **Generally:** The Compulsory Process Clause gives the defendant the right to obtain and present all evidence helpful to his defense. [284-85]

B. **State rules restricting evidence:** This means that a state evidence rule that restricts the defendant's ability to present exculpatory evidence may run afoul of his Compulsory Process rights. [285-86]

    1. **Ban on accomplice's testimony:** For instance, a statute providing that if A and B are charged as co-participants, A may not testify in B's defense, violates B's compulsory process rights.

    2. **Restrictive hearsay rule:** Similarly, a state hearsay rule that prevents D from showing that someone else has made an out-of-court declaration confessing to the crime, may violate D's compulsory process rights. However, this will only happen if D convinces the court that the third person's alleged out-of-court confession is somewhat *corroborated* by surrounding circumstances. Thus if D offers X's out-of-court confession, but the prosecution shows that X was in jail at the time of the crime, D has no compulsory process right to present that confession.

C. **Equality principle:** State rules that consistently *favor the prosecution* are especially likely to violate the Compulsory Process Clause. (*Example:* A state rule banning one accomplice from testifying on behalf of another, but not banning one accomplice from testifying against the other, favors the prosecution consistently, and therefore, violates the Compulsory Process Clause.) [286-87]

PRIVILEGES

I. PRIVILEGES GENERALLY

A. **Not constitutionally based:** Most privileges are not constitutionally based. (The privilege against self-incrimination is the only exception.) Therefore, each state is free to establish whatever privileges it wishes and to define the contours of those privileges as it wishes. [288-90]

   1. **Federal:** There were a number of specific proposed federal rules of privilege. But these were never enacted. Instead, FRE 501 is the only Federal Rule dealing with privileges. It provides that privileges "shall be governed by the principles of the common law as they may be interpreted by the [federal] courts in the light of reason and experience." That is, normally federal judges will decide what privileges to recognize based on *prior federal case law* and the court's *own judgment.*

      a. **Diversity:** But in *diversity* cases, the existence and scope of a privilege will be decided by the law of the *state* whose substantive law is being followed.

   2. **States:** The states vary greatly on what privileges they recognize. All recognize the husband-wife and attorney-client privileges, most by statute. All recognize a privilege for certain government information. Nearly all recognize some kind of physician-patient and clergyman-penitent privileges. Three other privileges are recognized only in a minority of states: journalist-source, parent-child, and accountant-client.

B. **Proceedings where applicable:** If a privilege not to disclose certain information exists, that privilege applies *regardless of the proceeding.* That is, it will apply to protect the holder against disclosure in a trial, administrative hearing, deposition, or any other proceeding. [290]

C. **Who may assert:** The privilege *belongs* to the *person whose interest or relationship is intended to be fostered* by that privilege. Therefore, he is the *only one* who may assert it. (*Examples:* The client is the one protected by the lawyer-client privilege, so it may be asserted only by him, or on his behalf, not by the lawyer on the lawyer's behalf. Similarly, the physician-patient privilege is meant to protect only the patient, so only he, not the doctor, may assert it.) [290]

D. **Third person learns:** Most privileges protect communications between two parties to a specified relationship. If a *third party* somehow learns of the conversation, the privilege may be found to have been *waived.* [290-91]

   1. **Older, strict view:** The traditional view is very strict: if a third party somehow learns of the conversation, even if the original parties to it had no reason to anticipate this, the privilege will be held to be lost. (*Example:* Telephone operator eavesdrops on a phone conversation between lawyer and client; the privilege is held to lost, and the operator may testify as to what she heard.)

   2. **Modern view:** But modern courts usually hold that the communication is protected even if intercepted, as long as the interception was not reasonably to be anticipated. (So the prior example would be decided differently today.) But if the party protected should reasonably have anticipated the interception, he will not be protected. (*Example:* Patient or client discloses a confidence to his doctor or lawyer in a crowded elevator; the risk of it being overheard is so great that if it is overheard, the privilege will be held waived.)

II. THE ATTORNEY-CLIENT PRIVILEGE

A. **Generally:** The privilege is basically that a client has *right not to disclose* (and the right to prevent his lawyer from disclosing) *any confidential communication between the two of them relating to the professional relationship.* The key elements are: [292-94]

1. **Client:** The "client" can be a *corporation* as well as an individual.

2. **Belongs to client:** The privilege *belongs to the client*, not to the lawyer or any third persons. The lawyer may assert it, but only if he is acting on behalf of the client in doing so.

3. **Professional relationship:** The privilege applies only to communications made for the purpose of facilitating the rendition of *professional legal services*.

4. **Confidential:** The privilege applies only to communications which are intended to be *"confidential."*

5. **Fact of employment or client's identity:** The fact that the lawyer-client relationship *exists*, and the *identity* of the client, are normally *not* privileged. Only the substance of the confidences exchanged between them is generally privileged (though there are a couple of exceptions).

6. **Physical evidence:** Normally, the privilege does not permit the lawyer to conceal *physical evidence* or documents given to him by the client; the lawyer may not only have to turn over the physical evidence but describe how and where he got it.

7. **Crime or fraud exception:** The privilege does not apply where the confidence relates to the commission of a *future crime or fraud*.

B. **Professional relationship:** The privilege applies only in the context of a professional lawyer-client relationship. [296]

   1. **No retainer:** The required relationship can exist even though the client does *not pay a fee.* (*Example:* Client receives a free initial consultation; the privilege applies even though, at the end of the consultation, either lawyer or client decides that the lawyer will not handle the case.)

   2. **Non-legal advice:** But the mere fact that the person giving the advice is a lawyer is not enough — the relationship must involve the giving of legal advice. Thus, if the lawyer gives *business* advice, *friendly* advice, political advice, etc., the privilege does not apply.

   3. **Reasonable belief:** So long as the client *reasonably believes* that the person he is talking to is a lawyer, the privilege applies even though the other person is in fact not a lawyer. Similarly, the privilege applies if the person is a lawyer who is not, and is known to the client not to be, admitted to practice in the state where the advice is given.

C. **Confidential communications:** Only *"confidential"* communications are protected. [296-300]

   1. **Client-to-lawyer:** Disclosures by the *client to the lawyer* are protected if they are intended to be confidential.

      a. **Lawyer's observation:** However, if the lawyer makes an *observation* that third parties could also have made, this will not be a confidential communication. (*Example:* Lawyer observes scratch marks on Client's face, in a meeting that takes place right after Client's wife has been found stabbed to death. Since anyone could have made this observation, it is not privileged, and Lawyer can be forced to testify at Client's trial about the scratches.)

   2. **Lawyer-to-client statements:** The privilege also applies to statements made *by the lawyer* to the client.

   3. **Information involving third parties:**

      a. **Representative of lawyer:** If a *third party* is assisting the lawyer, he is treated as being a representative of the lawyer and communications involving him are treated the same way as if he were himself a lawyer. (*Example:* Lawyer retains Private Detective to help investigate the case; statements made by Client to Detective, Lawyer to

Detective, Detective to Client, Detective to Lawyer, are all privileged.)

    b. Not assisting lawyer: But if a third person is *not* assisting the lawyer, there is *no* privilege for communications between that third person and the lawyer, even if these communications relate to the lawyer's providing of legal services. (*Example:* Lawyer interviews Witness; statements made by Witness that incriminate Client are not privileged, because Witness is not working on behalf of Lawyer. However, if the only reason Lawyer knew to interview Witness is because Client told him to do so, the privilege might apply to Witness' statements.)

4. Presence of third person: The *presence* of a *third person* when the communication takes place, or its later disclosure to such a person, may indicate that the communication was never intended to be "confidential." If so, it will be deemed waived. But if the third party's presence is reasonably helpful to the conference, that presence will not destroy the confidentiality. (*Example:* Client's friend or relative attends the meeting in order to help supply facts or to cope with language difficulties; this will not cause the privilege to be waived.)

5. Underlying facts: It is only the *communication* that is privileged, not the underlying fact communicated.

D. Fact of employment; client's identity: Generally, the *fact* that the attorney has been hired, and the *identity* of the client, are *not* privileged. (*Example:* At a grand jury investigating local cocaine trafficking, L, a well known specialist in defending high-level cocaine importers, may be required to say whether he is representing X, one such importer.) [300-01]

2. Exceptions: Some courts have recognized one or both of the following exceptions to this general rule of non-privilege:

    a. Anonymous restitution: Some courts allow Lawyer to make anonymous restitution on behalf of Client. (*Example:* Lawyer sends tax money to the IRS, without disclosing that it comes from Client — the purpose is to give Client a restitution defense if his taxes are ever audited. Some courts will allow Lawyer to refuse the IRS' demand to identify the Client.)

    b. "Missing link": Most courts will allow the lawyer to keep the client's identity secret where so much other information is already public that disclosure of the client's identity would have the effect of disclosing a privileged communication, or violating the client's self-incrimination privilege. (*Example:* X and Y are both suspected of murdering V. L represents X before a grand jury. A court might allow L to refuse to say whether Y is paying L's fee for representing X, on the theory that an affirmative answer might tend to incriminate Y.)

E. Physical evidence: If the client turns over to the lawyer *physical evidence*, the lawyer may generally not conceal this evidence or refuse to answer questions about whether he has it, on attorney-client privilege grounds. [301-07]

1. No ongoing fraud: The most important rule concerning this problem is that the attorney-client privilege does not apply where the lawyer's assistance is sought to enable the client to *commit a future crime or fraud.* Since all states prohibit the concealment or destruction of evidence in a pending proceeding, a lawyer who helps his client conceal or destroy evidence is a co-conspirator to a new crime, and the lawyer's assistance is thus not privileged. This is especially true where the evidence is contraband, stolen money, or a weapon or other instrument used to commit the crime.

3. Destruction advice: Similarly, the lawyer may not advise his client to destroy the evidence, and if he does so, the giving of that advice is not privileged.

4. **Lawyer's choices:** The lawyer may, however, simply return the evidence to the client with the advice not to conceal it; if the lawyer does this, he is probably privileged not to disclose the evidence's existence to the other side (usually the prosecution). Alternatively, he may take the evidence for a reasonable time for inspection or testing, and then return it to the client, without disclosing this fact to the other side. (But if the property is stolen, the lawyer must take steps to return it to his rightful owner. Similarly, if the lawyer believes that the client will destroy the evidence, he probably must turn it over to the other side, and is not privileged to keep silent about the evidence's existence.)

5. **Evidence of source:** If the other side (e.g., the prosecution) learns of particular physical evidence in the lawyer's possession, some courts hold that the lawyer is not privileged to refuse to say how he came into possession of it. (*Example:* D is charged with murdering and robbing V. From prison, D tells L to inspect D's garbage can; L does so, and finds V's wallet, which he takes with him and puts in his safe. At trial, many courts would require L to testify about how he came into possession of the wallet, since otherwise the prosecution is unfairly impeded in its efforts to tie the wallet to D.)

   a. **No custody:** But if the lawyer merely learns of an item's existence for his client, or inspects it and then gives it back to the client, the lawyer may not be required to say at trial how he learned about the item.

F. **Corporations as clients:** [307-09]

   1. **Corporations have privilege:** A *corporation* may possess the attorney-client privilege just as an individual may.

   2. **Who may communicate:** Only communications made "on behalf" of the corporation's business are covered. But probably no matter how low level an employee is, if he is really acting in what he reasonably perceives to be the corporation's interests, communications made between him and the corportion's lawyer will be privileged as to the corporation.

   3. **Must concern employment:** The mere fact that one party to the communication is an employee is not sufficient — the communication must *relate to the employee's performance of corporate duties.* (*Example:* Driver, who works for Bus Co., happens to see an accident involving one of the company's buses while he is off duty. Statements about the accident by Driver to Bus Co.'s lawyer are not privileged, because they do not relate to anything that happened while Driver was performing his corporate duties.)

   4. **Reports and routine communications:** The communication must be primarily for the purpose of obtaining legal services. Therefore, if the communication is a *routine report* generated in the ordinary course of the corporation's business, the privilege will not apply merely because the report happened to be received by one of the corporation's attorneys. (*Examples:* Accident reports, personnel records, and financial documents probably won't be privileged even if circulated to the company's attorneys, because none of these is typically created for the primary purpose of obtaining legal services.)

   5. **Confidentiality:** The requirement of confidentiality means that only those communications that the corporation handles on a *"need to know"* basis will be privileged.

H. **Exceptions:** There are several situations where the privilege will be held not to apply even though the usual requirements are met: [310-12]

   1. **Crime or fraud:** As noted above, a communication relating to the carrying out of a future *crime or wrong* is not privileged. (*Example:* Client says to Lawyer, "If X and I were to rob the First National Bank, and X were then to get caught and give a confession implicating me, could the police use this confession against me?" If the robbery is later committed, the statement may be used against Client, since even though he was seeking legal services, he was doing so with reference to a future crime.)

2. **Death of client:** In general, the privilege **survives** the **death** of the client. But there is a key exception: if the suit is a will contest or other case in which the issue is who receives the deceased client's property, the privilege does not apply. (*Example:* In will contest, Son may call Lawyer to testify about Lawyer's conversations with Testator, in which Testator said that he wanted to provide for Son in his will.)

3. **Attorney-client dispute:** The privilege does not apply to a **dispute between lawyer and client** concerning the services provided by lawyer. (*Examples:* The privilege does not apply if Lawyer sues Client for a fee, or if Client sues Lawyer for malpractice.)

4. **Joint clients:** The privilege may be inapplicable to a dispute between multiple clients who were originally on the same side of a transaction.

   a. **Same lawyer:** If two clients **retain a single lawyer**, and a dispute later breaks out between the two, the privilege does not apply. This is true regardless of whether the other client was privy to the communication in question. (*Example:* Driver is sued by Passenger for injuries from a car crash. Insurer, who insures Driver, hires Lawyer for the case. Driver makes confidential communications to Lawyer. Later, Driver and Insurer have a dispute about policy limits. In that dispute, Insurer may probably compel Lawyer to disclose otherwise-privileged statements between Driver and Lawyer.)

   b. **Different lawyers:** But if two clients retain **separate** lawyers, and both lawyers and both clients meet together and discuss common legal issues, the privilege applies even in the event of a later dispute between clients.

I. **Work product immunity:** Separately from the attorney-client privilege, the doctrine of **work product immunity** prevents an attorney from being required to disclose certain information that he obtains **while preparing for a lawsuit**. [313-14]

   1. **Qualified protection:** Generally, documents prepared in anticipation of litigation may be discovered by the other side only if the party seeking discovery shows that he has a **substantial need** for the materials, and that he cannot get the substantial equivalent by other means. This is a **"qualified"** immunity. Fed. R. Civ. Proc. 26(b)(3). (*Example:* Client fills out a questionaire about the facts of his injuries, to help Lawyer prepare the case for trial. Even if the questionaire is not covered by the attorney-client privilege — perhaps because Client has disclosed it to a journalist — Lawyer can refuse to release it in response to a discovery request by the other side.)

      a. **Absolute immunity:** Documents that show a lawyer's "mental impressions, conclusions, opinions, or legal theories" concerning litigation are probably **absolutely** privileged, in the sense that no showing of need by the other side will be sufficient to overcome the work product immunity.

III. PHYSICIAN-PATIENT PRIVILEGE

A. **Generally:** All but 10 states have a statutory physician-patient privilege. These statutes usually apply to: [315]

   1. a **confidential communication**;

   2. made to a **physician** (including psychiatrist);

   3. if made for the purpose of obtaining **treatment**, or diagnosis looking toward treatment.

B. **Constitutional underpinning:** Some aspects of the privilege may be constitutionally compelled. At least one state court (California) has held that the "confidentiality of the psychotherapeutic session" falls within one of the "zones of privacy" created by the U.S. Constitution (though California has held that its statute, with exceptions for the patient-litigant situation, see below, is constitutional). [316-17]

C. **Relationships covered:** All statutes that cover general physician-patient confidences also cover *psychiatrist*-patient confidences. A few states even give greater protection to the psychiatrist-patient relationship than to the general physician-patient one. [316-17]

    1. **Psychologist:** A general physician-patient statute does not protect disclosures made to non-M.D.s, such as *psychologists*. However, some states have specially covered psychologists. Disclosures to other health professionals (dentists, druggists, or social workers) are rarely covered.

    2. **Consulted for litigation:** Consultations that take place concerning *litigation* rather than for purposes of treatment or diagnosis are *not* covered. For instance, examination by or disclosures to a court-appointed physician, or an expert witness consulted so that he can testify at trial, are not covered.

D. **Patient-litigant exception:** Nearly all statutes have some kind of exception for the *"patient-litigant"* situation, under which a patient-litigant who puts his *medical condition in issue* is deemed to have in effect waived the privilege. (*Example:* Car collision case; P sues D for a broken leg. P's doctor and hospital records, including notations of disclosures made by P to the doctor, will be admissible, because P has placed the nature and extent of his injuries in issue by seeking damages for them.) [317-19]

IV. THE PRIVILEGE AGAINST SELF-INCRIMINATION

A. **Generally:** [320-22]

    1. **Constitutional basis:** The privilege derives from the U.S. Constitution. The Fifth Amendment provides that "no person . . . shall be compelled in any criminal case to be a witness against himself. . . ."

        a. **Applicable to states:** This provision is binding not only on the federal judicial system but also on the *states*, by operation of the Fourteenth Amendment's Due Process Clause.

        b. **Two types:** The privilege applies not only to criminal defendants, but also to any other person who is asked to give testimony that may incriminate him (e.g., witnesses in grand jury proceedings, congressional investigations, other people's criminal trials, etc.)

B. **Requirements:** The privilege applies only when four requirements are met: (1) it is asserted by an *individual*; (2) the communication sought is *testimonial*; (3) the communication is *compulsory*; and (4) the communication might *incriminate* the witness. [323-26]

    1. **Individuals:** The requirement that the privilege be individual and "personal" means that:

        a. **Another's privilege:** A person may not assert *another's* privilege. (*Example:* D is on trial for robbery. The prosecution puts on testimony by X, an unindicted co-conspirator, in which X says that he and D did the robbery together. D may not exclude this testimony by claiming that it violates X's privilege — since it is X who is testifying, only he may assert or waive the privilege.)

        b. **Business organization:** *Business organizations* do *not* have the privilege. Thus, neither *corporations*, partnerships, nor labor unions may claim the privilege. (But a person doing business as a sole proprietorship may assert it — it is not the fact of doing business that removes the privilege, but rather the use of an "artificial organization.")

        c. **Agent:** An employee or other *agent* of a business organization will usually have to produce and identify the organization's books and records on request, even though those books and records (or the fact that the agent has them) might incriminate him. But he will usually not have to do anything more if this would incriminate him (e.g., he usually will not have to state the whereabouts of corporate records that he does not possess).

  2. Testimonial: Only *"testimonial"* activity is covered. Thus, the suspect may be required to furnish a blood sample, fingerprints, handwriting samples, or even to speak so that his voice may be compared with a previously recorded conversation. Also, a suspect may be required to appear in a lineup for identification.

  3. "Compulsory": A communication must be *"compulsory."* The main importance of this requirement is that if a person *voluntarily* puts the information in *written form*, the document is not privileged. (But the writer may have a privilege against *producing* the document for the government, as discussed below.)

  4. Incriminatory: The response must have a *tendency to incriminate* the person. Thus if there are procedural reasons why no prosecution can take place (e.g., the statute of limitations has run, or the witness has been given immunity), the privilege does not apply. The fact that answering the question might subject the witness to ridicule or civil liability is not enough.

C. Proceedings where applicable: The privilege applies not only where asserted by a defendant in a criminal trial, but also by any witness in *any kind of proceeding.* Thus it may be asserted by witnesses to a grand jury investigation, to another person's criminal trial, to a civil proceeding, to pre-trial discovery proceedings (e.g., W's deposition is being taken), or to questioning by the police. [324-25]

D. Procedure for invoking: [326-27]

  1. Criminal defendant: When the assertion is made by the defendant in a criminal trial, he may invoke the privilege merely by *declining to testify*. In that event, he does not have to take the stand at all, and cannot even be questioned.

  2. Non-defendant witness: But if the privilege is being claimed by a *witness* (i.e., someone other than the defendant in a criminal trial), the procedure is different: the witness must *take the stand*, be sworn, listen to the question, and then assert the privilege. In this event, it is the judge who decides whether the response might be incriminatory; but the person seeking the testimony bears an extremely heavy burden of proving that the response *could not possibly* incriminate W, a showing that can only rarely be made.

E. Waiver: A person who takes the stand and gives some testimony may be held to have *waived* the privilege with respect to further questions: [327-30]

  1. Criminal defendant: If a criminal defendant does take the stand, and testifies in his own defense, he has waived his privilege at least with respect to those questions that are *necessary for an effective cross-examination*. (*Example:* In a murder trial, D testifies that he was not anywhere near the scene of the crime. The prosecution would certainly be entitled to ask D where he was, and D could not assert the privilege in refusing to answer.)

  2. Witness: Since an ordinary witness must take the stand and listen to each question, a witness who answers non-incriminating questions will not be held to have waived the privilege with respect to later, incriminating, questions. However, if W makes a general and incriminatory statement about a matter, he must then answer *follow-up questions eliciting the details*, at least where these details would not add significantly to the incrimination.

  3. Later proceedings: If the defendant or witness does waive the privilege, this waiver is effective *throughout the current proceedings*, but not for subsequent proceedings. (*Example:* W's waiver during grand jury proceedings would not prevent him from asserting the privilege when called as a witness at a subsequent trial of X on an indictment returned by that same grand jury.)

F. Documentary evidence: When a document is subpoenaed by the government, the person receiving the subpoena may have a fifth amendment right not to comply: [330-33]

1. **Contents:** The *contents* of the subpoenaed document will practically never be protected by the Fifth Amendment: so long as the taxpayer was not originally compelled to create the document, its contents are not protected by the privilege.

2. **Act of producing:** But a person's act of *producing* the documents in response to a subpoena may implicitly incriminate him, in which case he probably has a Fifth Amendment privilege not to produce it. For instance, if there were no way that the government could obtain or authenticate a certain personal diary kept by D except through production of this diary by him, D might be allowed to plead the Fifth by arguing that his production would implicitly mean that he is stating: (1) that the diary exists; (2) that the diary was in his possession or control; and (3) that he believes that this is indeed the genuine diary the government is seeking. (But if the government can show that it has other ways of authenticating this diary, then the privilege will not apply.)

3. **"Required records" exception:** Even if a person is *compelled* to keep a certain type of record, he may not have a Fifth Amendment right to refuse to do so: the record keeper must turn the record over even though it might incriminate him, if: (1) the record is one that a party has customarily kept, (2) the law requiring the keeping of it is "essentially regulatory," and (3) the records are analogous to a "public document." This is the *"required records"* exception to the privilege against self-incrimination. (*Example:* Records of prices charged to customers, kept under a mandatory price control law, still have to be turned over because they are essentially regulatory.)

G. **Inference and comment:** When a criminal defendant pleads the Fifth, he gets two other procedural safeguards to extend the privilege's usefulness. [333-36]

1. **"No comment" rule:** First, neither the judge nor the prosecution may *comment adversely* on D's failure to testify (e.g., by saying, "If D is really innocent, why hasn't he taken the stand to tell you that?")

2. **Instruction:** Second, D has an affirmative right to have the judge *instruct the jury* that they are not to draw any adverse inference from his failure to testify.

3. **Prior silence:** If the criminal defendant has remained silent at *prior proceedings*, the judge and prosecutor may not comment if the silence was the result of clear exercise of a constitutional privilege:

   a. **Arrest:** Thus, if D was previously silent during *custodial police interrogation*, the prosecutor and judge may not comment on this fact at D's later criminal trial.

   b. **Pre-arrest silence:** But if D remained silent *before being arrested*, this fact may be comment on, since D was not exercising any formal Fifth Amendment privilege. (*Example:* D pleads self-defense to a murder charge. The prosecution may comment upon the fact that for the two weeks between the killing and D's arrest, he did not go to the police to tell them his story.)

4. **Civil suit:** If the suit is a *civil* one, either side may freely comment adversely on the other party's (or a witness') failure to testify. (*Example:* P sues D for causing a car accident; D fails to take the stand because he is afraid that if he does so, the fact that he was drunk will come out, and he may be prosecuted. P may nonetheless say to the jury, "If D wasn't driving drunk, why doesn't he take the stand and tell you that?")

H. **Immunity:** If W is given *immunity* from prosecution, he may not assert the privilege (since he has received the same benefit — freedom from having his testimony used against him — that the privilege is designed to provide). [336-38]

1. **"Transactional" vs. "use" immunity:** There are two types of immunity: *"transactional"* and *"use."* Transactional protects the witness against any prosecution for the *transaction* about which he testifies. Use immunity is much narrower — it merely protects against the

direct or indirect use of the ***testimony*** in a subsequent prosecution.

   2. **Use immunity sufficient:** Use immunity is ***sufficient*** to nullify the witness' Fifth Amendment privilege. (But the prosecutor then bears a heavy burden of showing that he could not have used the testimony, even indirectly, in preparing for the subsequent case.)

   3. **Defense witness immunity:** If a person could give testimony that a criminal defendant thinks would help exonerate him, but the witness refuses to testify without immunity, the defendant may attempt to have ***"defense witness immunity"*** conferred upon this witness. But the vast majority of courts have refused to grant such defense witness immunity.

I. **Prosecutorial discovery:** A criminal defendant is sometimes required to ***disclose to the prosecution***, as part of discovery proceedings, certain facts about his defense. Such "prosecutorial discovery" might conceivably violate D's Fifth Amendment right, but only if D can show that: (1) the information will not be disclosed by D at trial (so that D may be forced to disclose such anticipated trial claims as an alibi defense); and (2) the information derives from him and not from some third party (so that D may be required to disclose statements obtained from X, a witness). But D might be able to refuse to turn over a report by a private investigator hired by D, containing statements made in confidence by D to the investigator. [338-39]

V. THE MARITAL PRIVILEGES

A. **Generally:** [339-42]

   1. **Two privileges:** In most states, two distinct privileges protect the marital relationship:

      a. **Adverse testimony:** The ***adverse testimony*** privilege (sometimes called "spousal immunity") gives a spouse ***complete*** protection from adverse testimony by the other spouse. (*Example:* H is on trial for murder; the adverse testimony privilege protects H from having W take the witness stand to testify against him, regardless of whether her testimony concerns anything he said.)

      b. **Confidential communication:** The ***confidential communications*** privilege is narrower: it protects only against the disclosure of confidential communications made by one spouse to the other during the marriage. (*Example:* H is on trial for murder. The confidential communications privilege protects H against having W disclose that H confessed to her, "I shot V," but does not protect him against having W describe to the jury how she witnessed H kill V.)

   2. **Distinctions:** Here are some of the practical differences between the two privileges:

      a. **Before marriage, or after marriage ends:** The adverse testimony privilege applies only if the parties are still married at the time of the trial, but applies to statements made before the marriage took place. Conversely, the confidential communications privilege covers only statements made during the marriage, but applies even if the parties are no longer married by the time of the trial.

      b. **Civil vs. criminal:** The adverse testimony privilege is usually allowed only in criminal cases, but the confidential communications privilege is usually available in civil as well as criminal cases.

      c. **Acts:** The adverse testimony privilege prevents the non-party spouse from testifying even as to ***acts*** committed by the spouse, but the confidential communications privilege does not (since it covers only "communications").

   3. **State coverage:** Only a slight majority of states recognize the adverse testimony privilege, but virtually all recognize the confidential communications privilege. In ***federal*** courts, ***both*** privileges are recognized.

B. Adverse testimony privilege: [342-43]

    1. Who holds: Courts disagree about who holds the adverse testimony privilege:

        a. Federal: In federal cases, the privilege belongs only to the ***testifying spouse***, not the party spouse. Thus, D in a federal criminal trial may not block his spouse's testimony; only the witness-spouse may assert or waive the right.

        b. States: Of those states recognizing the adverse testimony privilege, a slight majority give the privilege to the party (i.e., the criminal defendant); the rest follow the federal approach of giving the privilege only to the witness-spouse.

    2. Criminal vs. civil: Most jurisdictions (including the federal courts) grant the adverse testimony privilege only in ***criminal*** cases.

    3. Special marriage: If D is worried about his girlfriend's being required to disclose something she has heard or seen, he may marry her the night before the trial, and thereby keep her off the stand using the adverse testimony privilege.

C. Confidential communications: Virtually every state recognizes the confidential communications privilege. [343-45]

    1. Federal: Federal courts apply this privilege on the basis of ***general federal common law***, since there is no federal rule granting it.

    2. Who holds: In most states, ***either spouse*** may assert the privilege. (But a few states grant it only to the spouse who made the communication.)

    3. "Communication" required: Only "communications" are privileged. Strictly speaking, an "act" that is not intended to convey information is not covered. (But some states have held that if an act is done in front of the spouse only because the actor trusts the spouse, the privilege should apply. Thus if H allows W to see his recently-fired shotgun before putting it away, the court might hold that this was the equivalent of a "communication" since it would not have happened had H not trusted W.)

    4. Marital status: The parties to the communication must be married at the time of the communication. If so, the privilege applies even though they have gotten divorced by the time of the trial.

    5. Exceptions: Here are some common exceptions to the confidential communications privilege:

        a. Crime against other spouse: Prosecution for crimes ***committed by one spouse against the other***, or against the ***children*** of either;

        b. Suit between spouses: Suits by ***one spouse against the other*** (e.g., a divorce suit);

        c. Facilitating crime: Communications made for the purpose of ***planning or committing a crime***. (*Example:* H brings home loot from a robbery, and asks W to help him hide it. Since H is seeking W's help in committing an additional crime — possession of stolen goods — most courts would find the privilege inapplicable to H's request for assistance.)

VI. MISCELLANEOUS PRIVILEGES

A. Priest-penitent: Virtually all states recognize a privilege for ***confidential communications*** made to a ***clergyman*** in his profession capacity as ***spiritual advisor***. [345-46]

B. Journalist's source: Most states now recognize a privilege for a journalist's sources: [346-48]

    1. Statutes: A slight majority of states have enacted ***"shield laws"*** preventing a journalist from being compelled to testify about his confidential sources. All of these statutes at least protect the journalist from having to disclose the ***identity*** of his sources; some protect him against forced disclosure of his ***notes and records*** of information learned from the source.

2. **Constitutional argument:** Some state and lower-federal courts have recognized a ***First Amendment*** basis for the privilege in some situations. (*Example:* If the information being sought is not very central to the case of the litigant who is seeking it, or can be gotten from other sources, the court may find that the journalist has a constitutional right not to supply it.) But the Supreme Court has never found such a First Amendment privilege to exist, and in one major case, a four-justice plurality concluded that no such privilege exists. *Branzburg v. Hayes.*

3. **Conflict with defendant's rights:** If the journalist's statutory or constitutional privilege ***conflicts*** with a criminal defendant's Sixth Amendment right to ***compulsory process*** or ***confrontation***, the journalist's privilege will probably have to give way. (*Example:* Reporter conducts a murder investigation, leading to charges against D; D's constitutional right to compulsory process outweighs Reporter's rights under the state shield provision, so Reporter is required to supply his notes on his investigation. *In re Farber.*)

C. **Government information:** The government may have a privilege not to disclose ***information in its possession***: [348-54]

1. **Military or diplomatic secrets:** The government has an ***absolute*** privilege not to disclose ***military*** or ***diplomatic*** secrets. No matter how badly a litigant needs such information, the government is privileged not to disclose it.

2. **Other government information:** Other types of government information receive merely a ***qualified*** privilege. That is, the privilege applies only where the harm to the public welfare from disclosure outweighs the litigant's need for the information.

   a. **Internal deliberations and policy making:** Thus internal government opinions, deliberations, and recommendations about policies are qualifiedly privileged. (But factual reports are not.)

   b. **Law enforcement investigatory files:** Similarly, ***investigatory files*** compiled by a law enforcement agency are qualifiedly privileged. (*Example:* A criminal defendant has no general evidence-law right to force the government to turn over to him the files it has compiled in investigating and preparing the case against him, though criminal discovery rules may give him the right to certain items, such as witnesses' statements.)

3. **Informers:** The government has a special privilege to decline to disclose the ***identity of informants*** who have given information about crimes.

   a. **I.D. only:** Usually, the government informant privilege protects only the ***identity*** of the informant, not the substance of the ***information*** that he gives to the government (unless that information would effectively reveal the informant's identity).

   b. **Qualified:** The privilege is only a ***qualified*** one. Thus if disclosure of the informant's I.D. is likely to materially help the criminal defendant in his defense, the government must disclose it or drop the case. Participants and eyewitnesses are usually held to be so central that their I.D.'s must be disclosed; but a mere "tipster" is not, so his identity may usually be concealed. Anyone called as a ***witness*** by the prosecution must be identified.

4. **Consequences of upholding claim:** If the court upholds the government's claim of privilege, and the government is the plaintiff (as in a criminal prosecution or a civil suit brought by the government), the government must normally ***choose*** between releasing the information or ***dropping the case***.

D. **Trade secrets:** Some courts recognize a qualified privilege for ***trade secrets***; that is, special secrets which a business possesses that aid it in competing. (*Examples:* Information about a company's relative market position; secret information about a device or process; design information about a product.) If the judge does partly override the privilege because of a litigant's great need for the material, he may issue a ***protective order*** limiting the use to which the information may be put (e.g., by ordering that the litigant not disclose it to anyone else). [354]

E. Newly emerging privileges: [354-55]

    1. Parent-child communications: Three states have recognized a privilege for communications ***from minor child to parent*** (but not from parent to child).

    2. Other professional relationships: One third of the states have granted a privilege for communications made to ***accountants***. A few have granted a privilege for communications made to professional counselors (e.g., social workers, marriage counselors, etc.)

REAL AND DEMONSTRATIVE EVIDENCE, INCLUDING WRITINGS

I. INTRODUCTION

A. "Real" vs. "demonstrative" evidence: [356-58]

    1. "Real": "Real" evidence is a tangible object that ***played some actual role*** in the matter that gave rise to the litigation. (*Example:* A knife used in a fatal stabbing.)

    2. "Demonstrative": Demonstrative evidence is tangible evidence that merely ***illustrates*** a matter of importance in the litigation. (*Examples:* Maps, diagrams, models, summaries, and other materials created especially for the litigation. For instance, if the prosecution cannot find actual knife used in stabbing, a newly-acquired knife believed to be similar to the one actually used may be presented as a model to help the jury understand.)

    3. Significance of distinction: The foundation requirements needed to authenticate the two types of evidence are different. See below.

II. AUTHENTICATION

A. Generally: All real and demonstrative evidence must be **"authenticated"** before it is admitted. That is, it must be shown to be **"genuine."** This means that the object must be established to be ***what its proponent claims it to be***. See FRE 901(a). [359-60]

    1. Real evidence: If the object is real evidence, authentication usually means showing that the object is ***the*** object that was involved in the underlying event (e.g., the actual knife used in the stabbing).

    2. Demonstrative: If the evidence is demonstrative, authentication usually means showing that the object ***fairly represents or illustrates*** what it is claimed to represent or illustrate (e.g., proof that a diagram offered in evidence really shows the position of the parties and witnesses at the time of the murder).

B. Methods of authentication: [360-64]

    1. Real evidence: For real evidence, authentication generally is done in one of two ways:

        a. Readily or uniquely identifiable: If the item is ***readily*** or ***uniquely*** identifiable, it can be authenticated by showing that this is the case, and that the object is therefore the one that played the actual role. (*Example:* "I found the knife at the stabbing, and marked it with my initials; the knife you have just shown me has my carved initials, so it must be the knife found at the murder scene.")

b. Chain of custody: Otherwise, the item's ***"chain of custody"*** must be demonstrated. That is, every person who handled or possessed the object since it was first recognized as being relevant must explain what he did with it. (*Example:* Each person who handled the white powder taken from D must testify about how he got it, how he handled it during his custody, and whom he turned it over to.)

2. Demonstrative evidence: If the evidence is demonstrative, authentication is done merely by showing that the object ***fairly represents*** some aspect of the case.

3. Federal Rules: The Federal Rules have a simple, basic principle of authentication that applies to all evidence (real, demonstrative, writings, and intangibles): the proponent must come up with evidence ***"sufficient to support a finding*** that the matter in question is ***what its proponent claims."*** FRE 901(a). (901(b) gives illustrations of proper authentication.)

4. Judge's role: The judge does not have to decide whether the proffered item *is* what its proponent claims it to be (the jury does this). But the judge does have to decide whether there is ***some evidence*** from which a jury could reasonably find that the item is what it is claimed to be.

C. Authentication of writings and recordings: Special rules exist for authenticating ***writings*** and other recorded communications: [364-71]

1. Authorship: Usually, authentication of a writing consists of showing ***who its author is.***

2. No presumption of authenticity: A writing or other communication (just like any non-assertive evidence like a knife) carries ***no presumption of authenticity.*** Instead, the proponent bears the ***burden*** of making an affirmative showing that the writing or communication is what it appears to be and what the proponent claims it to be.

a. Signature: Thus, a ***writing's own statement*** concerning its authorship (e.g., its ***signature***) is ***not*** enough — the proponent must make some independent showing that the signature was made by the person who the proponent claims made it.

3. Direct testimony: One way to authenticate a writing or communication is by ***direct testimony*** that the document is what its proponent claims. (*Example:* If proponent wants to show that X really signed the document, he may produce W to testify that W saw X sign it.)

4. Distinctive characteristics: A writing's ***distinctive characteristics***, or the ***circumstances*** surrounding it, may suffice for authentication. See FRE 901(b)(4). (*Example:* The fact that a diary contains the logo of D Corp.; its entries match testimony previously given by X (D Corp.'s employee); it was produced by D Corp. during discovery; and it is similar to other diaries previously authenticated, all suffices to authenticate the diary as having been kept by X.)

5. Signature or handwriting: A document's author can be established by showing that it was signed or written in the hand of a particular person. Even if no witness is available who saw the person do the signing or writing, the document may be authenticated by a witness who can identify the ***signature or handwriting*** as belonging to a particular person.

a. Expert: If W, the person identifying the signature or handwriting, is a handwriting ***expert***, he may base his testimony based solely on handwriting specimens from X that he examined in preparation for his trial testimony.

b. Non-expert: But if W, the authenticating witness, is ***not*** a handwriting expert, his testimony may not be based on comparisons and studies made directly for the litigation; instead, he must testify that he saw X's handwriting at some time before the litigation began, and that he recognizes the signature or handwriting in question to be that of X.

    c. Exemplars: Exemplars (specimens prepared by the person claimed to have written the document in question) may be shown to the jury, which is then invited to make its own conclusion about whether the exemplar and the questioned document were by the same person.

6. Reply letters and telegrams: A *letter or telegram* can sometimes be authenticated by the circumstantial fact that it appears to be a *reply* to a prior communication, and the prior communication is proved. (*Example:* P proves that he wrote a letter to D on Jan. 1; a letter purporting to have been written by D to P on Jan. 15, that alludes to the contents of the earlier P-D letter, is authenticated by these circumstantial facts as indeed being a D-P letter.)

7. Phone conversation: When the contents of *telephone conversation* are sought to be proved, the proponent must authenticate the conversation by *establishing the parties to it*.

    a. Recognition of voice: One way to do this is by presenting testimony from one party to the conversation, who says that he was able to *recognize the voice* of the person at the other end of the line.

    b. Surrounding circumstances: Where this is not possible, the surrounding circumstances may furnish enough evidence. (*Example:* W testifies that the person on the other end of the phone knew certain facts. The proponent of W's testimony then shows that those facts could only be known to X. This will be enough to identify X as the person on the other end of the line, even if W never met X face to face and thus could not recognize his voice.)

8. Attesting witnesses: If a document is *attested to* or subscribed to by witnesses (e.g., a will), special rules sometimes apply:

    a. Common law: At common law, at least one attesting witness must be called to testify (even if he does not authenticate the document) before non-attesting witnesses may authenticate it.

    b. Federal Rule: But FRE 903 drops this requirement (except where the relevant state law imposes it).

10. Ancient documents:

    a. Common law: At common law, a writing is automatically deemed authenticated as an *"ancient document"* if it: (1) is at least *30 years old*; (2) is *unsuspicious* in appearance; and (3) has been found in a place of custody *natural* for such a document.

    b. Federal Rules: FRE 901(b)(8) applies the same requirements as the common law (above) for ancient documents, except that: (1) the document needs to be only *20* years old; and (2) the rule covers not only "documents" but "data compilations" (e.g., a computer tape, and probably photos, X-rays, movies, and sound tapes as well).

    c. No guarantee of admissibility: But keep in mind that a document that satisfies these requirements for the "ancient document" rule of authentication merely overcomes the authentication hurdle. The document still has to survive other obstacles (e.g., it must be not hearsay or fall within some exception; but there is also an ancient document exception to the hearsay rule; see *supra*, p. 27).

D. Self-authentication: A few types of documents are *"self-authenticating,"* because they are so likely to be what they seem, that no testimony or other evidence of their genuineness need be produced. [371-72]

1. **State provisions:** Under most state statutes, the following are self-authenticating: (1) deeds and other instruments that are *notarized*; (2) *certified* copies of *public records* (e.g., a certified copy of a death certificate); and (3) books of statutes which appear to be printed by a government body (e.g., a statute book appearing to be from a sister state or foreign country).

2. **Federal Rules:** FRE 902 recognizes the above three classes, and also adds: (1) all *"official publications"* (not just statutes); (2) *newspapers* or periodicals; and (3) *labels, signs,* or other inscriptions indicating "ownership, control, or origin" (e.g., a can of peas bearing the label "Green Giant Co." is self-authenticating as having been produced by Green Giant Co.).

E. **Ways to avoid:** Authentication is not necessary if: [372]

1. **Admission:** The proponent has served on the opponent a written *request for admission*, and the opponent has granted this.

2. **Stipulation:** The parties have jointly *stipulated* to the *genuineness* of a particular document or object.

IV. THE "BEST EVIDENCE RULE" FOR RECORDED COMMUNICATIONS

A. **Generally:** [375-77]

1. **Text of rule:** The Best Evidence Rule (B.E.R.) provides that *"in proving the terms of a writing, where the terms are material, the original writing must be produced unless it is shown to be unavailable for some reason other than the serious fault of the proponent."*

2. **Components:** The B.E.R. has three main components:

   a. **Original document:** The *original document* must be produced, rather than using a copy or oral testimony about the document;

   b. **Prove terms:** The Rule applies only where what is to be proved is the *terms* of a *writing* (or, under the modern approach, an equivalent recorded communication such as an audio tape of a conversation); and

   c. **Excuse:** The Rule does not apply if the original is *unavailable* because it has been destroyed, is in the possession of a third party, or cannot be conveniently obtained, and the unavailability is not due to the serious fault of the proponent.

3. **Not applicable to evidence generally:** The B.E.R. does *not apply to evidence generally*, only to writings (or equivalent recorded communications).

4. **Federal Rule:** FRE 1002 gives the federal version of the B.E.R.: "To prove the content of a writing, recording, or photograph, the original writing, recording, or photograph is required. . . ." The federal approach changes the common-law rule in two major ways:

   a. **Broadened coverage:** Not just writings, but also *recordings* and *photographs* are covered by the Federal Rule in contrast to the common-law rule. (*Examples:* An audio tape of a conversation, or a computer tape of data, would be covered under the federal approach, so that if these items are available, they must be introduced instead of using oral testimony to describe their contents.)

   b. **Duplicate:** But unlike the common law, the federal rules allow a *duplicate* (e.g., a photocopy) in lieu of the original unless the opponent raises a genuine question about authenticity or it would be unfair in the circumstances to allow the duplicate. FRE 1003.

B. **What is a "writing" or other recorded communication:** [377-78]

1. **Short inscription:** An object that contains a short *inscription* (e.g., a pocket watch with words of affection engraved on it) might be held to be a "writing" covered by the B.E.R., depending on the surrounding circumstances (e.g., how important its precise, rather than approximate, content is to the litigation).

2. **Photographic evidence:** Under the modern and federal approach, a *photograph* or X-ray will be covered by the rule, if offered to prove the contents of the item. (*Example:* P, to prove that she has been injured, wants to prove that her X-rays show a spinal injury; the X-rays themselves must be used if available, rather than a radiologist's testimony about what the X-rays show.)

3. **Sound recordings:** Similarly, if a party tries to prove the contents of a *sound recording*, he must do so by presenting the actual recording rather than an oral or written account of what it provides.

C. **Proving the contents:** The B.E.R. only applies where what is sought to be proved are the "terms" or "contents" of the writing. [378-81]

1. **Existence, execution, etc.:** Thus if all that is proved is that a writing *exists*, was *executed*, or was *delivered*, the B.E.R. does not apply. (*Example:* Prosecution of D for kidnapping; a prosecution witness, W, mentions that a ransom note was received but does not testify about the note's contents. Since this proof that the ransom note was delivered does not constitute proof of its terms, the note need not be produced in evidence. But if W goes on to give the details of what the note said, the note would have to be produced if available.)

2. **Incidental record:** The fact that there happens to be a writing memorializing a transaction does not mean that the transaction can only be proved by the introduction of a writing. Here, the writing is treated as an *incidental by-product* of the transaction. (*Example:* The earnings of a business can be proved by oral testimony, rather than by submitting the books and records, because those books and records are merely an incidental memorializing of the earnings.)

   a. **Transcript:** A person's prior *testimony* can generally be proved by an oral account of a witness who heard the testimony, even if a *transcript* exists. The transcript is merely an incidental by-product of the testimony. (But a *confession* by a defendant to the crime charged must generally be proved by the transcript or recording.)

   b. **Photo:** If a photograph, X-ray, audio recording, video tape, etc., has been made of an object or event, live testimony about the object or event will generally be *allowed* in lieu of introducing the photograph, etc. (*Example:* W may testify to seeing D shoot V, even though there happens to be a home movie showing the shooting. The movie is an incidental memorial of the event, so the event can be proved without the movie.)

   c. **Contract:** But if a document truly *embodies* a transaction, the document comes within the B.E.R. and must be produced if available. (*Example:* If two parties to an agreement have signed a formal written *contract*, that contract must be produced at the litigation, even though the parties could have bound themselves orally to the same terms; the contract embodies their arrangement, rather than merely being an incidental by-product of it.)

D. **Collateral writings:** The *"collateral writings"* exception means that a document which has only a *tangential connection* to the litigation need not be produced, even though its contents are being proved. See FRE 1004(4) (original need not be produced if the writing, recording, etc., is "not closely related to a controlling issue"). [381]

E. **Which is original:** If one writing is derived from another, the earlier one is not necessarily the "writing itself" that must be produced. The proposition being proved may be such that the derivative writing is the one whose contents are being proved, in which case it is the original of that derivative writing that must be produced. (*Example:* D writes a handwritten letter to X possibly defaming P; D then hands the letter to his secretary, who retypes it and sends the typed version. At P's libel suit against D, it is the derivative typed version, not the handwritten version, which is the "original" that must be produced if available.) [381-83]

F. Reproductions: [383-84]

   1. Common law: At common law, no subsequently-created copy was the equivalent of the original. Therefore, if the B.E.R. applied, no copy (e.g., a handwritten version) could suffice.

   2. Modern statutes: But today, most states have a statute by which regularly-kept *photocopies* of business and public records are admissible even if the original is available. Such statutes override the B.E.R.

   3. Federal: The Federal Rules have a broad copying provision: copies produced by *any reliable modern method* (including photocopying) are "duplicates" that are *presumptively admissible*. Such a duplicate is admissible even if the original is available, unless the opponent raises a "genuine question . . . as to the authenticity of the original" or it would be unfair in the circumstances to admit the duplicate instead. FRE 1003; 1001(4). (*Examples:* Photocopies, mimeograph copies, carbon copies, images scanned into a computer and then printed out, copies of an original video or audio tape made by re-recording, etc., would all qualify as "duplicates" under the federal approach. But any copies produced *manually*, whether by typing or handwriting, are *not* "duplicates" and therefore may not be used if the original is available.)

G. Excuses for non-production: There are several types of *"excuses"* for non-production, which will allow the proponent to use derivative evidence (e.g., a manual copy or oral testimony) instead of the original: [384-86]

   1. Loss or destruction: If the proponent can show that the original has been *destroyed* or *lost* he may use a copy (unless the loss or destruction is due to the proponent's *bad faith* or serious fault).

   2. Inconvenience: In some courts, *extreme inconvenience* of producing the original will suffice.

   3. Possession by third person: If the original is in the *possession of a third person*, and cannot be obtained by judicial efforts (e.g., a subpoena duces tecum), this will excuse non-production.

   4. Original in opponent's possession: If the original is in the hands of the *opponent*, or under the latter's control, and the proponent has *notified him* to produce it at the trial but the adversary has failed to do so, the proponent may use a copy instead. See FRE 1004(3).

H. Summaries: If original writings are so *voluminous* that they cannot conveniently be introduced into evidence and examined in court, most courts permit a *summary* to be introduced instead. FRE 1006. [386-87]

   1. Sponsoring witness: The summary must be sponsored by a witness (usually an expert) who testifies that he has reviewed the underlying writings and the summary, and that the summary accurately reflects the underlying documents.

   2. Originals: Usually, the court requires that the underlying documents be made available for examination by the opponent, and that the underlying documents be at least generally admissible. (But the underlying documents need not be individually admitted, since the purpose of the summary is to avoid this.)

I. Admission by adversary: An adversary's *admission* about the terms of a writing is sometimes usable in lieu of the writing itself, to prove the terms of the writing. [387-88]

   1. Written: A *written* admission or an admission under *sworn testimony* is always usable to prove the terms of the writing. (*Example:* D writes to P, "Remember that I wrote you in

December offering to buy your farm." This later letter is evidence that D made this statement in his December letter. Similarly, D's oral deposition testimony — "I wrote to P in December asking to buy his farm" — would suffice to prove that the December letter contained such an offer.)

    2. Oral: But courts are more reluctant to allow an ***unsworn oral*** admission by a party to be used by the other party to prove the terms of a writing. Thus FRE 1007 does ***not*** allow such proof of an unsworn oral admission.

J. Preferences among secondary evidence: If the original does not exist, courts are split as to whether the ***next best available*** evidence must be used. [388]

    1. Majority rule: Most American state courts ***do*** recognize "degrees of substantive evidence," and hold that where there is a choice between a written copy and oral testimony, the ***written copy must be used.***

    2. Minority/Federal Rule: A minority of states (but also the ***Federal Rules***) hold that "there are no degrees of substantive evidence." Thus under FRE 1004, even if handwritten notes or a typed copy of a writing exist, a party may instead prove the terms of the writing by oral testimony.

K. Judge-jury allocation: The judge, not the jury, decides most questions relating to application of the B.E.R. Thus under FRE 1008, it is the judge who decides such questions as: (1) whether a particular item of evidence is an "original"; (2) whether the original has been lost or destroyed; and (3) whether the evidence relates to a "collateral matter." [389-90]

V. SPECIAL TYPES OF REAL AND DEMONSTRATIVE EVIDENCE

A. Pictorial evidence: [389-91]

    1. Authentication: There are now usually two ways to authenticate ***pictorial*** evidence (e.g., photographs, X-rays, movies, and video tapes):

        a. Illustration of what W saw: First, the proponent puts on a sponsoring witness, W, who says that the picture illustrates what W saw. (*Example:* W testifies, "I observed the scene of the crime just as the police photographer was arriving, and this photograph accurately depicts the scene as it was at that moment.")

        b. "Silent witness" method: Alternatively, most courts allow a photograph to be verified not by the testimony of any witness who actually witnessed the scene or event portrayed, but rather from testimony about the ***reliability of the process*** by which the photo was produced. This is often used for X-rays and automatic picture-taking devices. (*Example:* W, an engineer for a company that makes bank surveillance photographic equipment, testifies, "Our machine reliably creates a photo with an image of a person doing a transaction at the teller's window on one side, and the document presented by that person to the teller on the other side. Therefore, this piece of film accurately shows that the person pictured presented the check pictured.")

B. Computer print-outs: [391-92]

    1. Authentication: If a computer print-out is offered as evidence of the facts contained in the print-out (e.g., financial or numerical facts), the print-out must be authenticated. This is usually done by a witness who testifies that the methods used to put data into the computer, to program it, and to produce a print-out of the data, were all reliable.

    2. Best Evidence Rule: Generally, a computer print-out can be used to prove the facts represented in the print-out without B.E.R. problems (the opponent can claim that the print-out is merely a "duplicate" of the original pre-computer paper documents, but he would then have the burden of showing that the print-out is not an accurate reproduction of the original paper record).

C. **Maps, models, diagrams, etc.:** [392]

   1. **Evidentiary status:** Courts will treat maps, models, diagrams, etc., as being *incorporated into the witness' testimony*, so that they become evidence for purposes of trial and appeal.

D. **Views:** The judge may permit the jury to journey outside the courtroom to visit and observe a particular place, if this would help them understand an event. The excursion is called a *"view."* [393-94]

   1. **Discretion:** The judge has *broad discretion* about whether to allow the jury to take a view.

   2. **Presence of judge:** In civil cases, the judge need normally *not be present.* In criminal cases, most states have statutes requiring the judge to be present at the view.

   3. **Defendant's right to be present:** A criminal defendant usually has a statutory right to be *present* at the view (and may have a constitutional Confrontation Clause right to be present).

   4. **Evidentiary status:** Courts are split as to whether the view is *evidence*, or merely an aid to the understanding of the evidence.

E. **Experiments:** An *experiment* conducted by a party may sometimes be admitted. If the experiment takes place out of court, its admissibility will depend mostly on whether the conditions are sufficiently *similar* between the experiment and the event that it is attempting to explain. (*Example:* Where P complains that his crash was caused by a defective transmission in a car produced by D, an experiment to see if the transmission breaks in a different car will be allowed only if both the test car and the conditions are shown to be highly similar to the original conditions.) [394-95]

OPINIONS, EXPERTS, AND SCIENTIFIC EVIDENCE

I. FIRST-HAND KNOWLEDGE AND LAY OPINIONS

A. **First-hand knowledge required:** An ordinary (non-expert) witness must limit his testimony to facts of which he has first-hand knowledge. [397-98]

   1. **Distinguished from hearsay:** You must distinguish the "first-hand knowledge" requirement from the hearsay rule. If W's statement on its face makes it clear that W is merely repeating what someone else said, the objection is to hearsay; if W purports to be stating matters which he personally observed, but he is actually repeating statements by others, the objection is to lack of first-hand knowledge.

   2. **Experts:** The rule requiring first-hand knowledge does not apply to experts. (See below.)

B. **Lay opinions:** [398-400]

   1. **Traditional view:** The traditional view is that a non-expert witness must state only facts, not "opinions." (*Example:* If W observes D's driving behavior leading to a crash, W may not testify that D "drove very carelessly," but must instead give more specific testimony, e.g., D's estimated rate of speed, degree of attention, etc.)

      a. **Exception for short-hand renditions:** Even under the traditional view, W may give an "opinion" that is really a *"short-hand rendition."* That is, if W has perceived a number of small facts that cannot each be easily stated, he may summarize the collective facts with a "shorthand" formulation. (*Example:* W may testify that D was "mentally disturbed," even though this has a conclusory aspect.)

   2. Modern/federal approach: But the modern/federal view is that lay opinions will be *allowed* if they have *value* to the fact-finder. See FRE 701, allowing opinions or inferences that are "(a) rationally based on the perception of the witness and (b) helpful to a clear understanding of his testimony or the determination of a fact in issue."

C. Opinion on "ultimate issue": Of those courts that allow lay opinions, a few bar opinions on "*ultimate* issues." But most today allow even opinions on ultimate issues. Thus FRE 704(a) allows opinions on ultimate issues except where the mental state of a criminal defendant is concerned. [400-02]

   1. Exceptions: But even the liberal federal approach excludes a few types of opinions on ultimate issues. For instance, a witness will not be permitted to express his opinion on a *question of law* (except foreign law), or an opinion on how the case should be decided.

II. EXPERT WITNESSES

A. Requirements for allowing: Expert testimony must meet two requirements to be admissible: [403-05]

   1. Qualifications: First, the expert must be *"qualified."* That is, he must have knowledge or skill in a particular area that distinguishes him from an ordinary person.

   a. Source of expertise: This expertise may come from either *education* or *experience*.

   b. Need for sub-specialist: Generally, a specialist in a particular field will be treated as an expert even though he is not specialist in the particular *sub-field* or branch of that field. (*Example:* If a medical condition involves kidney failure, a general practitioner would probably be found a qualified expert, even though he is not a sub-specialist in nephrology.)

   2. Suitable subject matter: Second, the expert's testimony must concern a topic that is *so specialized* that without the testimony, the jury would be less able to reach an accurate conclusion.

   a. Traditional rule: Traditionally, the subject matter of the expert testimony had to be so specialized that it was "beyond the ken" of laymen.

   b. Modern and federal rule: But the Federal Rules illustrate the modern trend: the expert's testimony must merely be *"helpful"* to the jury's understanding of the case. (FRE 702). This requirement will generally be found to be satisfied if the issue is a technical one. But where the matter is one that juries and ordinary people are often called upon to evaluate, the requirement may be found not to be satisfied. (*Example:* Since juries and ordinary people are often called upon to evaluate the reliability of an eyewitness identification, expert testimony purporting to tell the jury why such I.D.s are often unreliable will often be rejected as not satisfying this requirement of "helpfulness.")

B. Basis for expert's opinion: The expert's opinion may be based upon any of several sources of information, including: (1) the expert's *first-hand knowledge*; (2) the expert's observation of prior witnesses and other evidence at the trial itself; and (3) a hypothetical question asked by counsel to the expert. [405-08]

   1. Inadmissible evidence: Today, the expert's opinion may be based on evidence that would otherwise be *inadmissible*. Under FRE 703, even inadmissible evidence may form the basis for the expert's opinion if that evidence is "of a type *reasonably relied upon by experts* in a particular field in forming opinions or inferences upon the subject. . . ." (*Example:* Driver tells an accident investigator that the accident occurred when his brakes

C
A
P
S
U
L
E

S
U
M
M
A
R
Y

failed. The investigator writes a report, which is read by Expert, an accident analysis specialist. Even though Driver's statements are probably otherwise-inadmissible hearsay, if experts in the field of accident analysis would rely on such hearsay statements, Expert's opinion may be based upon this statement.)

    2. Disclosure of basis to jury: Some courts require the expert to *state the facts or assumptions* that he has based his opinion on, as part of his direct testimony. But most courts, and the Federal Rules, do not require this. Thus FRE 705 provides that the expert need not make prior disclosure of the underlying facts or data, except that the court may in a particular case require him to do so, and in any event the cross-examiner may require the expert to state these underlying facts or data.

C. The hypothetical question; basis for: If the expert's underlying facts and assumptions come from a *hypothetical question*, courts today are liberal about the source of these underlying facts and assumptions. Thus: (1) the underlying assumptions need not be supported by evidence in the record at the time of the question, or even by admissible evidence at all; (2) the assumptions may be based upon opinions by others, if an expert in that situation would rely on such an opinion. But there must be *some basis* for the assumptions in the hypothetical — if the assumptions are so far-fetched that no jury could possibly find them to be true, the hypothetical question will be stricken. [408-11]

D. Some procedural aspects: [411-14]

    1. Cross-examination by use of learned treatise: All courts allow an expert to be cross-examined by use of a learned treatise that contains a differing view. (*Example:* "Isn't it true, Doctor, that according to Smith's Handbook of Pathology, lung cancer is sometimes caused by asbestos exposure or other factors, not always smoking as you have asserted?") Most courts today allow the use of the treatise as impeaching evidence even if the expert did not rely upon it in forming his opinion, so long as the expert concedes that the treatise is authoritative; the Federal Rules even allow the treatise to be used substantively, not just for impeachment.

    2. Court-appointed expert: The Federal Rules allow the appointment of an expert *by the court*, in which case each party may cross-examine the expert.

III. SCIENTIFIC EVIDENCE — THE *FRYE* STANDARD

A. The *Frye* ("general acceptance") standard: Some courts hold that when the results of a *scientific test* or principle are sought to be introduced, the proponent must show that the test or principle has been *generally accepted* in the scientific community. This is the so-called *"Frye"* standard. [414-16]

    1. Lie detector tests: The *Frye* standard is most likely to be applied to exclude the results of *lie detector tests*, and is also sometimes used to keep out the results of hypnosis, truth serum, psychological stress evaluators, and voice prints. In all these situations, courts generally distrust the reliability of the test, and use the lack of general scientific acceptance as a rationale for exclusion.

    2. Federal Rules unclear: The Federal Rules do not explicitly adopt or reject the *Frye* "general acceptance" standard. Commentators and federal courts are split about whether the standard should be applied in federal cases.

IV. PARTICULAR TYPES OF SCIENTIFIC EVIDENCE AND EXPERTISE

A. Probabilities: Courts increasingly accept *probability* evidence where it supplies a scientifically reliable way of estimating the probability that a disputed event occurred. (*Example:* In a paternity case, most courts will now accept the results of analysis of genetic markers, whereby an expert testifies that not only are D's genetic markers consistent with those of the child, but only, say, one adult American male out of 3,000 would have markers consistent with those of the child. Similarly, some courts would allow evidence in a rape case that only one in 10,000 males would have semen containing genetic markers consistent with the markers found in the semen in the victim, and that D's semen has such markers.) [416-19]

B. Speed detection: The results of *radar* and VASCAR are commonly admissible to prove the speed at which D's vehicle was traveling. But most courts require the prosecution to prove that the particular speed detection equipment in question was properly calibrated and properly used. [419-20]

C. Voice prints: Courts are almost evenly split as to the admissibility of *"voice print"* analysis, whereby the voice of an unidentified suspect on a taped telephone call is compared with a sample given by D after his arrest. [420-21]

D. Neutron activation analysis: Neutron activation analysis (NAA) is generally admitted as a method of identifying a small sample of material (e.g., whether a hair found near a crime scene belongs to D). [421-22]

E. Psychiatry and psychology: [422-26]

    1. Mental condition of criminal defendant: Courts generally allow a psychiatrist or psychologist to testify as an expert on the *mental condition* of a criminal defendant. However, courts try hard to keep the expert from crossing over into areas that are properly the province of law rather than medicine (e.g., whether the defendant knew right from wrong). Thus, FRE 704(b) provides that "no expert witness testifying with respect to the mental state or condition of a defendant in a criminal case may state an opinion or inference as to whether the defendant did or did not have the mental state or condition constituting an element of the crime charged or of a defense thereto." (*Example:* In a federal case in which D claims insanity, the defense psychiatrist would be permitted to say that D is a schizophrenic, but will probably not be permitted to say that this condition prevented D from appreciating the wrongfulness of his conduct, now the substantive federal insanity standard.)

    2. Reliability of evidence: Courts hesitate to allow expert psychiatric or psychological testimony concerning the reliability of other witnesses' testimony. Thus evidence that a particular eyewitness identification is likely to be unreliable for psychological reasons, or that a particular alleged victim is probably telling the truth because she shows the signs of Rape Trauma Syndrome, will be rejected by many courts.

BURDENS OF PROOF, PRESUMPTIONS, AND OTHER PROCEDURAL ISSUES

I. BURDENS OF PROOF

A. Two burdens: There are two distinct burdens of proof, the burden of *production* and the burden of *persuasion*. [427-31]

    1. Burden of production: If P bears the burden of *production* with respect to issue A, P has the obligation to come forward with some evidence that A exists. This burden is sometimes also called the burden of "going forward."

       a. Consequence of failure to carry: If a party does not satisfy this burden of production, the court will decide the issue against him as a matter of law, and will not permit the jury to decide it.

2. **Burden of persuasion:** If P has the burden of *persuasion* on issue A, this means that if at the close of the evidence the jury cannot decide whether A has been established with the relevant level of certainty (usually "preponderance of the evidence" in a civil case), the jury must find against P on issue A. This burden is also often called the ***"risk of non-persuasion"*** — if neither P nor D have persuaded the jury about whether A exists, to say that P bears the burden of persuasion or the risk of non-persuasion means that he is the one who will lose when the jury decides this issue.

3. **One shifts, other does not:** The burden of production as to issue A can, and often does, shift throughout the trial. (*Example:* Suppose P has the burden of showing that D received notice of a fact. If P comes up with evidence that D received notice — e.g., P's own testimony that he told the fact to D — the burden will shift to D to come up with evidence that he did not receive notice.) The burden of persuasion, by contrast, always remains on the party on whom it first rests.

B. **Allocating the burdens in civil cases:** [431-33]

1. **Factors:** In most issues in civil cases, both the burden of production and the burden of persuasion are on the ***plaintiff***. (*Example:* In a negligence case, the plaintiff bears the burdens of production and persuasion with respect to showing D's negligence, P's harm, and the causal link between the two. But D bears both burdens with respect to contributory negligence, in most jurisdictions.) Courts consider a number of factors in determining where to place the burdens, including: (1) which party is trying to change the *status quo* (he is more likely to bear the burdens); (2) who is contending that the more unusual event has occurred (he is more likely to bear the burdens); and (3) which way do policy considerations cut (the court may allocate the burdens in a way that promotes some extra-judicial social policy).

2. **"Prima facie" case:** The collection of issues on which a civil plaintiff has the burden of ***production*** is sometimes called his ***"prima facie case."*** (*Example:* P has established a *prima facie* case for negligence if he has produced enough evidence of D's negligence, P's own harm, and a causal link between the two, to permit the case to go to the jury.)

C. **Allocation in criminal cases:** In criminal cases, the Due Process Clause of the U.S. Constitution places limits on the extent to which the burdens of proof may be placed on the defendant: [433-36]

1. **Element distinguished from affirmative defense:** The state is more limited in allocating the burdens as to an ***"element"*** of the offense than it is on allocating the burdens as to an ***"affirmative defense."*** An element of the crime is an aspect that is part of the basic definition of the crime; an affirmative defense is an aspect that is not part of the basic definition, but which the defendant is allowed to show as a mitigating or exculpating factor. (*Examples:* "Intent to kill" is an element of the crime of murder, but "self defense" is generally an affirmative defense.)

2. **General rules of allocation:**

   a. **Elements:** The ***state*** is constitutionally required to bear ***both*** the burdens of production and persuasion with respect to ***all elements*** of the crime.

   b. **Affirmative defense:** The ***defendant*** may constitutionally be required to bear both burdens with respect to affirmative defenses.

   c. **Overlap:** If the state defines an affirmative defense in a way that causes that defense to overlap almost completely with some element of the crime, the state must bear both burdens. (*Example:* Suppose the state makes "malice aforethought" an element of murder, and defines malice aforethought to include "any deliberate act committed by one person against another." If the state makes "heat of passion" an affirmative defense, the state, not D might have to bear the burden of proof and persuasion, because a court might hold that proof that D acted in the heat of passion is tantamount to proof that he did not act with malice aforethought.)

    d. Allowable affirmative defenses: At least the following may be established as affirmative defenses on which D bears both burdens: *insanity, self-defense,* and *extreme emotional disturbance.*

D. Satisfying the burden of production: [436-39]

    1. Civil case: In civil cases, on most issues (those as to which the persuasion burden follows the "preponderance of the evidence" standard), the party bearing the production burden must come forward with enough evidence *so that a reasonable jury could conclude, by a preponderance of the evidence, that the fact exists.*

        a. Judge decides: It is the judge, not the jury, who decides whether the party bearing the production burden has satisfied that burden. (*Example:* At the close of P's case, the judge decides whether P has come up with evidence of negligence that a reasonable jury could find that D was negligent by a preponderance of the evidence. The judge may find that P has done this even though the judge himself believes that it is less likely than not that D was negligent.)

        b. Cross-examination of adversary: If the burden of proof on issue A in a civil case is borne by P (as is usually the case), P will have to come up with a witness or real evidence tending to prove that A exists. It will not be enough that P conducts a withering cross-examination of a defense witness' denial of A. (But if it is D who bears the burden of proving A, his cross-examination of P and P's witnesses may be enough for him to avoid a directed verdict against him.)

    2. Criminal case: In a criminal case, the prosecution, to satisfy its burden of production on all elements of the case, must come forward with enough evidence on each element that a reasonable jury could find that the element was *proved beyond a reasonable doubt.* (In other words, the persuasion burden affects the production burden.)

E. Satisfying the burden of persuasion: [439-41]

    1. Civil cases: On most civil issues, the burden of persuasion must be satisfied by a showing that A exists *"by a preponderance of the evidence."* That is, the party bearing the burden must show that the existence of A is "more probable than not."

        a. Sheer statistics: Most courts refuse to find that this burden has been met by evidence that is *purely statistical.* (*Example:* If P testifies that he was hit by a blue bus, and shows that 60% of all the blue buses in the town are owned by D, this will not be enough to meet P's persuasion burden.) Instead, the party bearing the persuasion burden must come up with some evidence that will lead the jury to have an *"actual belief"* (rather than a mere statistical estimate) in the truth of the fact in question.

    2. Criminal cases: In criminal cases, the prosecution's burden of persuasion on all elements of the crime means that these elements must be proved *"beyond a reasonable doubt."* This is required by the Due Process Clause. *In Re Winship.* (But issues other than elements of the crime may be decided according to a lesser standard. For instance, a confession usually only has to be shown to be voluntary by a preponderance of the evidence.)

II. PRESUMPTIONS

A. Generally: The term "presumption" refers to a relationship between a "basic" fact (B) and a "presumed" fact (P). When we say that fact P can be presumed from fact B, we mean that once B is established, P is established or at least rendered more likely. [441-43]

B. Effect of presumptions in civil cases: In civil cases, most courts hold that a presumption has one of two types of effects: (1) a *"bursting bubble"* effect; or (2) a so-called *"Morgan"* effect. [443-49]

1. **"Bursting bubble":** Most courts believe that a presumption should be given the following effect: if B is shown to exist, the burden of production (but not the burden of persuasion) should be shifted to the opponent of the presumption. This is called the ***"bursting bubble"*** approach, because once the opponent discharges his production burden by coming up with some evidence that the presumed fact does not exist, the presumption ***disappears from the case***, and the jury decides the issue as if the presumption had never existed. (*Example:* A presumption is established that where a letter has been properly addressed and mailed — the basic fact — the letter will be presumed to have been received by the addressee — the presumed fact. Suppose that P is the beneficiary of this presumption, and that P starts out bearing the burden of proving that D received the letter. If P shows that the letter was properly addressed and mailed, under the bursting bubble view D will have to come up with some evidence that he never received the letter, but once he does so, the presumption will not be mentioned to the jury, which will be told that P has the burden of persuading the jury that D received the letter.)

2. **Morgan (minority) view:** A ***minority*** of courts follow the so-called ***"Morgan"*** view, that the presumption should not only shift the burden of production, but ***also the burden of persuasion***, to the presumption's opponent. (*Example:* On the above letter scenario, once P showed that he properly addressed and mailed the letter, it would become up to D to not only come forward with evidence that he never received the letter, but also to persuade the jury by a preponderance of the evidence that he never received it.)

3. **Federal Rules:** The Federal Rules adopt the ***majority, "bursting bubble"*** view. Under FRE 301, "a presumption imposes on the party against whom it is directed the burden of going forward with evidence to rebut or meet the presumption, but does not shift to such party the burden of proof in the sense of the risk of nonpersuasion, which remains throughout the trial upon the party on whom it was originally cast."

   a. **Instructions to jury:** Under the majority/federal "bursting bubble" approach, the judge normally will ***not mention*** that the presumption exists (e.g., he will not say, "The law presumes that a properly addressed and mailed envelope was received by the addressee unless there is evidence to the contrary"). But the judge has discretion to tell the jury that it ***may*** presume P if B is shown.

4. **Conflicting presumptions:** If a case presents two ***conflicting presumptions***, and neither is rebutted by the opponent, the court will generally apply the presumption that reflects the weightier social policy. If neither presumption reflects a social policy (both merely reflect an estimate of probabilities, or concerns for trial convenience), both presumptions will generally be held to have ***dropped*** from the case.

5. **Constitutional questions:** A civil presumption that is given either the "bursting bubble" or "Morgan" effect presents no significant constitutional issues. But a so-called ***"irrebuttable presumption"*** (which is really a substantive rule) must meet the same constitutional standard as any other substantive rule of law — the legislature must have had a ***rational reason*** for linking the basic fact to the presumed fact.

C. **Effect in criminal cases:** The constitutionality of a presumption in a ***criminal case*** depends on precisely the effect given to the presumption: [449-52]

   1. **Permissive presumptions:** A so-called ***"permissive"*** presumption (one in which the judge merely instructs the jury that it "may" infer the presumed fact if it finds the basic fact) will almost always be constitutional, so long as the fact finder could "rationally" have inferred the presumed fact from the basic fact, the presumption will be upheld. (*Example:* The jury is told that where a weapon is found in a car, the jury may infer that each person in the car possessed that weapon. Since the presumption was rational on these circumstances, it was constitutional even though it relieved the prosecution from showing that each D actually knew of or possessed a gun.)

2. **Mandatory:** But a *"mandatory"* presumption is subjected to much more stringent constitutional scrutiny:

   a. **Shift of persuasion burden:** If the presumption *shifts the burden of persuasion* to D, and the presumed fact is an *element of the crime*, the presumption will normally be **unconstitutional.** Such a presumption runs afoul of the rule that the prosecution must prove each element of the crime beyond a reasonable doubt. (*Example:* D, a dealer in second-hand goods, is charged with knowingly receiving stolen goods. The judge tells the jury that a dealer who buys goods that are in fact stolen, and who does not make reasonable inquiries about the seller's title to the goods, shall be presumed to have known they were stolen unless he shows that he didn't know this. Since this presumption has the effect of shifting to D the burden of showing that he did not know the goods were stolen — an element of the crime — it is unconstitutional.)

   b. **Possibly constitutional:** But even a presumption that shifts the burden of persuasion on an element of the crime will be constitutional if the presumed fact flows from the basic fact beyond a reasonable doubt, and the basic fact is shown beyond a reasonable doubt. However, few if any presumptions can satisfy this stringent pair of requirements.

D. **Choice of law:** In federal diversity cases, the court must apply the presumptions law of the state whose substantive law applies. (FRE 302). (*Example:* P sues D for negligence in a diversity suit in New Jersey federal court. If New Jersey law controls on the issue of negligence, then New Jersey law on the effect to be given to a presumption that one whose blood alcohol is more than .1% is legally drunk, must be applied by the federal court. Therefore, if New Jersey would apply a "Morgan" rather than "bursting bubble" approach to presumptions, the federal court must do the same.) [452-53]

III. JUDGE-JURY ALLOCATION

A. **Issues of law:** Issues of *law* are always to be decided by the judge, not the jury. Therefore, when the admission of a particular piece of evidence turns on an issue of law, it is up to the judge to decide whether the item should be admitted. (*Example:* W refuses to disclose a statement she made to L, asserting the attorney-client privilege; L is a law school graduate but is not admitted to practice. It is the judge, not the jury, who will decide the legal issue of whether the privilege applies on these facts.) [454]

B. **Issues of fact:** If admissibility of evidence turns on an issue of *fact,* the division of labor between judge and jury depends on the nature of the objection: [454-57]

   1. **Technical exclusionary rule:** If an objection to admissibility is based on a *technical exclusionary rule* (e.g., hearsay), any factual question needed to decide that objection belongs solely to the judge. Thus for factual issues in connection with a hearsay objection, an objection based on privilege, or most issues regarding the Best Evidence Rule, the judge decides.

      a. **Rules of evidence not binding:** Under FRE 104(a), when the judge makes such a finding he is *not bound by the rules of evidence* except those regarding privileges. (*Example:* In deciding whether V's out-of-court statement, "X shot me," qualifies as a "dying declaration" exception to the hearsay rule, the judge may consider other, inadmissible, hearsay declarations by V at about the same time that shed light on whether V knew he was dying.) The judge will normally decide such a factual issue by a *preponderance of the evidence* standard.

   2. **Relevance:** If the objection is that the evidence is *irrelevant*, the judge's role may be more limited:

a. **Ordinary relevance problem:** Ordinarily, a relevance objection may be decided without any finding of fact — the judge merely has to decide whether, **assuming** the proffered fact is true, it makes some material fact more or less likely; this is purely a legal conclusion, so the judge handles it himself.

b. **Conditional relevance:** In some cases, the proffered evidence is logically relevant only if some other fact exists. If fact B is relevant only if fact A exists, B is **"conditionally relevant."** It is the jury that will decide whether fact A exists, but the judge decides **whether a reasonable jury could find that fact A (the preliminary fact) exists**. (Example: P is injured when his tire blows out; D claims that he warned P of the problem. The preliminary fact is whether P heard the warning; the conditionally relevant fact is the warning's contents. The judge will decide whether a reasonable jury could find that P heard the warning; if he decides that the answer to this question is "yes," he will let the jury hear the warning's alleged contents, and it will be up to the jury to decide whether P really heard that warning and its contents.) The judge may allow the conditionally relevant fact into evidence prior to his showing of the preliminary fact; the conditionally relevant evidence is said to be admitted **"subject to connecting up."** (Example: In the tire blow-out example, D might be allowed to say what the warning's contents were, subject to subsequent proof by some other witness that P really heard the warning. If D does not come up with that later evidence, his testimony about the contents of the warning will be stricken.)

C. **Limiting instructions:** If evidence is admitted that should properly be considered only on some issues, the judge will on request give a **limiting instruction**, which tells the jury for what issues the evidence can and cannot be considered. [457-58]

D. **Non-jury trials:** [458-59]

1. **Same rules:** In general, **all rules of evidence applicable to jury trials also apply to bench trials**. Thus if an item of evidence would be inadmissible in a jury trial, it is inadmissible in a bench trial.

2. **Practical relaxation:** On the other hand, appellate courts are generally less strict in reviewing evidentiary rulings made in a bench trial than in a jury trial.

a. **"Sufficient competent evidence" rule:** Thus even if the trial judge in a bench trial admits inadmissible evidence over objection, the appellate court will not reverse if there was also admissible evidence in the case **supporting** the findings. The trial judge is presumed to have disregarded the inadmissible and relied on the admissible evidence. (But if the trial judge in the bench trial erroneously **excludes** evidence, the appellate court will be strict, and will reverse if that exclusion is likely to have damaged the losing party. Therefore, judges in bench trials err on the side of admitting too much rather than too little.)

IV. APPEALS AND "HARMLESS ERROR"

A. **"Harmless error":** Appellate courts will only reverse if the error may have made a **difference to the outcome**. An error that is unlikely to have made a difference to the outcome is called **"harmless,"** and will not be grounds for reversal. See FRE 103 (error must affect a "substantial right" of a party). [459-60]

1. **Standards for determining:** The test for determining whether an error is "harmless" varies depending on the context:

a. **Constitutional criminal issue:** In a criminal case in which evidence is admitted in violation of the defendant's **constitutional** rights, the appellate court will find the error non-harmless unless it is convinced "beyond a reasonable doubt" that the error was harmless. (Example: A co-defendant's confession implicating D, given to the police while in custody, and admitted against D in violation of his Confrontation Clause rights, will almost never be found to be harmless beyond a reasonable doubt, and will thus generally be grounds for reversal.)

    b. Other errors: But in civil cases, and in criminal cases involving non-constitutional errors, the error will be ignored as harmless unless the appellate court believes it *"more probable than not"* that the error affected the outcome.

B. Sufficiency of evidence: If the appellate court needs to decide whether the evidence was *sufficient* to support the findings of fact, the standard will depend on whether the case is civil or criminal: [461-62]

    1. Civil: In civil cases, the sufficiency test mirrors the "preponderance of the evidence" standard used at the trial. (*Example:* If P wins, the appellate court will ask, "Could a reasonable jury have concluded that P proved all elements of his case by a preponderance of the evidence?")

    2. Criminal: In a criminal case where D is appealing, the appellate court will ask, "Could a reasonable jury have found, beyond a reasonable doubt, that D committed all elements of the crime?"

JUDICIAL NOTICE

I. JUDICIAL NOTICE GENERALLY

A. Function: Under the doctrine of judicial notice, the *judge* can accept a fact as true even though no evidence to prove it has been offered. In a civil jury case, if the judge takes judicial notice of a fact he will instruct the jury that it must find that fact. [463]

B. Three types: The doctrine of judicial notice has evolved to recognize three distinct types of judicial notice: (1) *"adjudicative"* facts; (2) *"legislative"* facts; and (3) *law*. [463-65]

    1. Adjudicative facts: Adjudicative facts are those facts which relate to the *particular event* under litigation.

    2. Legislative facts: Legislative facts are more general facts that do not concern the immediate parties. (*Example:* A judge considering whether to impose an implied warranty of habitability for urban apartment buildings would take notice of legislative facts concerning the low bargaining power of urban tenants.)

    3. Law: Judicial notice of *"law"* relieves a party from having to formally plead and prove what the law is, in certain situations.

    4. Federal Rules: The only Federal Rule dealing with judicial notice, FRE 201, deals only with notice of adjudicative facts, not legislative facts or law.

II. ADJUDICATIVE FACTS

A. General rule: At common law, there are two different types of adjudicative facts which may be judicially noticed: (1) those that are "generally known"; and (2) those that are "capable of immediate and accurate verification." A fact will not be found to fall into either of these categories unless the court is convinced that it is virtually *indisputable*. [465-66]

    1. "General knowledge": An instance of *"general knowledge"* in the community might be that a particular portion of Mission Street in San Francisco is a business district, or that traffic going towards Long Island beaches on Friday afternoon during the summertime is frequently very heavy.

   a. Judge's own knowledge: The fact that the *judge himself* knows a fact to be so does *not* entitle him to take judicial notice of it if it is not truly common knowledge.

2. **Immediate verification:** Some of the kinds of facts that are capable of *"immediate verification*" by consulting sources of *indisputable accuracy*" include: (1) facts of *history and geography*; (2) *scientific principles*, and the validity of certain types of scientific *tests* (e.g., the general reliability of radar for speed detection); and (3) a court's own record of things that have happened in the same or other suits in that court.

3. **Federal Rule:** FRE 201 treats as being an adjudicative fact any fact that is "beyond reasonable dispute" because it is either: (1) "generally known" within the community; or (2) "capable of accurate and ready determination" by the use of "sources whose accuracy cannot reasonably be questioned." (This basically matches the common-law approach.)

B. **Jury's right to disregard:** [466-68]

1. **Civil case:** In civil cases, courts usually treat judicial notice as being *conclusive* on the issue. Therefore, the judge instructs the jury that it *must* treat the fact as being so. (FRE 201(g)).

2. **Criminal:** But in criminal cases, courts usually hold that the notice fact is *not conclusive* on the jury — if it were, D's constitutional right to a jury trial might be impaired. (FRE 201(g)).

   a. On appeal: This means that if the prosecution has failed at trial to ask for judicial notice of a fact, the appeals court may not take notice of that fact.

C. **When taken:** Most courts hold that judicial notice of an appropriate adjudicative fact may be taken *at any time* during the proceeding. Thus notice may be taken before trial, or even on appeal (except in criminal cases). (See FRE 201(f).) [469]

III. LEGISLATIVE FACTS

A. **General rule:** A court may generally take notice of a *"legislative* fact" (i.e., a fact that does not pertain to the particular parties, but is more general) even though the fact is *not "indisputable."* [469-70]

1. **Standard:** Most jurisdictions allow the judge to take notice of a legislative fact so long as the judge *believes it to be true*, even though it is not indisputable.

2. **Examples:** (1) A fetus does not generally become viable until 28 weeks after conception (relevant to the constitutionality of state abortion rules); (2) Urban tenants have very little bargaining power (relevant to whether there should be an implied warranty of habitability of city apartments).

3. **Federal Rules silent:** The Federal Rules, and most state evidence statutes, are *silent* about whether and when judicial notice of legislative facts may be taken. This is simply an implicit part of the process of deciding cases.

B. **Binding on jury:** A judicially-noticed legislative fact will be *binding on the jury* even in a *criminal* case. (*Example:* The judge's decision that cocaine falls within the statutory ban on importing "cocoa leaves and any derivative thereof" is binding on the jury.) [471]

IV. NOTICE OF LAW

A. **Generally:** Judges may take judicial notice of some types of *law*. When they do so, the consequence is that a party need not plead the provisions of the law, and need not make a formal evidentiary showing that the law is such-and-such; also, the judge may do his own research into the law. [471]

B. **Domestic law:** A judge may always take judicial notice of ***domestic*** law. [472]

    1. **State courts:** For a state court, "domestic" law is the ***law of that state***, plus federal law. A state's own law is generally held to include ***administrative regulations*** (but usually not municipal ordinances, which must therefore be proved).

    2. **Federal:** In federal courts, "domestic" law is usually held to include not only federal law, but also the law of ***all states*** if relevant.

C. **Laws of sister states:** At common law, one state may ***not*** take judicial notice of a ***sister state's laws***; instead, the sister state's laws must be "proved" by submitting evidence as to what that sister state's law really is. (But most states have now adopted a uniform act that allows judicial notice of a sister state's laws.) [472]

D. **Law of other countries:** The law of ***other countries*** may not be judicially noticed, according to most states. Therefore, a party must generally plead and prove such law. [472]

    1. **Federal Rules:** But this is not true in the federal courts: FRCP 44.1 allows the judge to conduct his own research on an issue of foreign law (though a party who intends to raise an issue concerning foreign law must nonetheless give notice of this fact in his pleadings).

C
A
P
S
U
L
E

S
U
M
M
A
R
Y

BASIC CONCEPTS

I. FIRST PRINCIPLES

A. Only admissible evidence usable: Probably the most basic rule of evidence law is that whether the case is tried to a judge or jury, the trier of fact must *decide the case based solely on what is presented in court*. L&S, p. 4. This rule does not mean that the trier cannot use common sense, or general knowledge gained from experience (e.g., that it is usually hotter in the summer than in the winter). But it does mean that "no information pertaining to the parties or to the specific incident giving rise to the litigation may be considered by the decision maker unless the law permits the information to be received by a court." *Id.* The rules governing what may be received by the court constitute, of course, the law of evidence.

B. Roles of judge and jury: In cases tried to a jury, the judge and the jury divide the responsibility of dealing with the evidence:

1. **Judge's role:** The role of the *judge* is to determine *whether the evidence is admissible*.

2. **Role of the jury:** Once the judge has decided to admit the evidence, the jury's role is to determine what *weight* the evidence should be given. The mere fact that the evidence has been admitted does not mean that the jury must attach any significant weight to it at all — for instance, it is up to the jury to judge the *credibility* of a witness, and the jury may choose to completely disregard quite admissible testimony because it believes the witness who is giving that testimony is mistaken or lying.

   a. **Jury assumed:** Throughout this book, we assume (unless otherwise noted) that the case is being decided by a jury. However, the rules of evidence are with very few exceptions exactly the same whether the case is tried to a jury or to a judge. For a discussion of the few differences, see *infra*, p. 458.

3. **Questions of fact:** Another way of looking at the roles of judge and jury is to say that the judge decides the *law* applicable to the case, and the jury decides the *facts*. The admissibility of a given piece of evidence is simply one type of issue of law; the believability of that piece of evidence is one type of factual question.

   a. **Preliminary question of fact:** Occasionally, however, the admissibility of a given piece of evidence cannot be determined without first making a *preliminary* determination of fact. Depending on the situation, it may be the *judge*, not the jury, who decides that preliminary factual issue. For a more complete discussion of preliminary questions of fact, see *infra*, p. 456.

C. The Federal Rules: In 1975, the *Federal Rules of Evidence* became effective, after having been enacted by Congress. These Rules apply to *all trials in federal courts,* whether civil or criminal, and whether to a judge or a jury. See FRE 101.

1. **Importance:** The Federal Rules are of increasingly great importance in the classroom, on bar examinations (e.g., the Multistate Bar Exam's Evidence questions test only the Federal Rules) and in practice. Therefore, we pay great attention to the Federal Rules in this book. However, we also in most instances talk about the common-law approach that preceded adoption of the Federal Rules, and we sometimes talk about the statutory approach of particular states.

2. **Adoption by states:** The Federal Rules of Evidence are so influential, and generally regarded as so-well drafted, that ***more than half the states*** have adopted them in one form or another. As of late 1986, 31 states had adopted the Federal Rules (Alaska, Arizona, Arkansas, Colorado, Delaware, Florida, Hawaii, Idaho, Iowa, Maine, Michigan, Minnesota, Mississippi, Montana, Nebraska, Nevada, New Hampshire, New Mexico, North Carolina, North Dakota, Ohio, Oklahoma, Oregon, South Dakota, Texas (civil only), Utah, Vermont, Washington, West Virginia, Wisconsin, and Wyoming). Puerto Rico and the military have also adopted them, and other states are considering adoption (including New York, New Jersey, and Rhode Island). See W&B, pp. T-1 through T-4.

II. ORGANIZATION OF THE TRIAL

A. **Flow of the case:** In the usual case, the plaintiff's case is presented first, followed by the defendant's. This is because the plaintiff generally has the burdens of proof (see *infra*, p. 431), and is given the compensating advantage of presenting his case first to the jury (as well as having the last word in closing argument). M, p. 6, n. 1. Thus, the typical case flows as follows:

1. **Opening statement:** The plaintiff (or, in a criminal case, the prosecutor) makes his ***opening statement*** first. Then, the defendant may make his opening statement (though many courts allow him to reserve his opening statement until the end of the plaintiff/prosecutor's case).

2. **Plaintiff's case:** Then, the plaintiff (or prosecutor) puts on his ***case in chief.*** That is, he presents the witnesses, as well as documents and other tangible evidence, to establish the facts needed for him to prevail.

3. **Defendant's case:** After the plaintiff or prosecutor "rests" his case, it is the defendant's turn. The defendant presents witnesses and documents to disprove the elements of the plaintiff's case and/or to establish ***affirmative defenses***.

4. **Plaintiff's rebuttal:** After the defendant rests, the plaintiff or prosecutor gets another turn at bat. This is called the plaintiff's ***rebuttal*** — the plaintiff may present additional witnesses, recall former witnesses, or present new exhibits, but ***only to rebut the defendant's evidence***, not to buttress his own case in chief.

5. **Defendant's rejoinder:** Likewise, after the plaintiff's rebuttal, the defendant has a ***rejoinder*** — here, he may only rebut evidence brought out in the plaintiff's rebuttal. M, p. 7.

6. **Closing arguments:** After both parties have presented all of their evidence, the two sides make ***closing arguments***. Usually, the plaintiff (or prosecutor) goes first,

the defendant goes second, and the plaintiff/prosecutor gets a last chance to rebut the defendant's closing remarks. L&S, p. 83, n. 45.

7. **Instructions:** Finally, the judge gives *instructions* to the jury, in which he explains to them the applicable law. In some jurisdictions, he may also comment upon, or summarize, the evidence. See *infra*, p. 458.

B. **Examination of witnesses:** Let us focus now on the steps by which witnesses are examined.

1. **Four stages:** The examination of a given witness proceeds through up to four stages:

   a. **Direct:** First, the party who has called a witness engages in the *direct examination*. Generally, the direct examiner may *not* use *leading questions*, i.e., questions that suggest the desired answer. Instead, the direct examiner must let the witness give his own testimony, though the examiner may gently guide the path of the testimony. See *infra*, p. 68.

   b. **Cross-examination:** After the side that called the witness has finished the direct examination, the other side has the chance to *cross-examine* the witness. Here, because the witness may be expected to be hostile to the examiner, leading questions are permitted. See *infra*, p. 70.

   c. **Re-direct:** The calling side then has an opportunity to conduct *re-direct* examination of the witness. Re-direct is generally limited to rebutting points made on cross-examination. See *infra*, p. 73.

   d. **Re-cross:** Finally, the cross-examining side gets a brief opportunity to conduct *re-cross*. This is limited to rebutting the effect of re-direct.

2. **Sequestration of witnesses:** If a witness were permitted to observe the testimony of other witnesses for the same side, he would be able to tailor his testimony (perhaps by perjury) so that it matched this other testimony. To prevent this, nearly all courts have, and often use, the power to *exclude all other witnesses* from the courtroom while one witness is testifying.

   a. **Federal Rule:** The trial judge's right to sequester witnesses is codified in FRE 615, which begins: "At the request of a party the court shall order witnesses excluded so that they cannot hear the testimony of other witnesses and it may make the order of its own motion."

      i. **Exceptions:** The Federal Rules, like most state courts, recognize several exceptions to this principle of sequestration. Under FRE 615, the court may not order the sequestration of: "(1) a party who is a natural person, or (2) an officer or employee of a party which is not a natural person designated as its representative by its attorney, or (3) a person whose presence is shown by a party to be essential to the presentation of the party's cause."

      ii. **Investigating officer:** The most controversial issue is whether the *prosecution* may have the *law enforcement officer* who investigated the case present at the prosecutor's table, even though that officer will later be a witness. Most courts that have faced the issue have held that the investigating officer may remain present under exception (2) above, partly on the theory that this counter-balances an advantage held by the defense (since the defendant, as a natural person, may always be present to assist his attorney). L&S, p. 39, n. 19.

III. MAKING AND RESPONDING TO OBJECTIONS

A. Making objections: When inadmissible evidence is offered, it is not the judge's responsibility to notice this and to exclude the evidence. Instead, our adversary system places *upon the other party* the responsibility of *objecting* to the evidence; only after a timely objection will the trial judge determine whether the evidence is admissible.

   1. Waiver: A corollary of this rule is that where the non-offering party does not make a timely objection, he will normally be held to have *waived* any claim on appeal that the evidence was wrongfully admitted. (There is an exception, however, for "plain error," usually applicable in criminal cases. See *infra*, p. 460.)

B. Time for objection: The objection must be *timely*. If the question alone makes it clear that the answer would be inadmissible, the objection should come *before the witness answers*. "Counsel is not free to sit back, gambling that the witness will give a harmless or even a favorable answer, and then object when the answer proves to be damaging." K&W, p. 39.

   1. Answer shows inadmissibility: Sometimes, however, it is not feasible to object before the answer. The inadmissibility may not become apparent until the answer is given (e.g., the witness gives an unresponsive and inadmissible answer that could not have been anticipated from the question). Or, the witness may simply answer so quickly that counsel does not have a reasonable opportunity to frame an objection beforehand. In these situations, an "after-objection" may be made following the witness' answer. The lawyer moves to have the witness' answer *stricken*, and to have the jury instructed that it should disregard this evidence. M, p. 127.

C. General vs. specific objections: How *specific* must the objection be? Generally, the objection should be "sufficiently specific for the judge and opposing counsel to know which of the many rules of evidence is being invoked." Lilly, p. 473. Thus the general statement, "I object," will not be specific enough to tell the judge whether the objection is based on the theory that the answer would be irrelevant to the case, that it would be inadmissible hearsay, that it would violate a privilege, etc.

   1. Federal Rules: The Federal Rules codify this requirement of specificity. FRE 103(a)(1) allows the appeals court to consider an evidentiary ruling only if the opponent made a timely objection "stating the *specific ground of objection*, if the specific ground was not apparent from the context. . . ."

   2. Effect of specificity on appeal: The handling of the ruling on appeal varies depending on whether the objection is specific or general:

      a. General objection: If the objection is *general*, here are the rules on appeal:

     i. Objection overruled: If the general objection was ***overruled***, the objector will rarely win on appeal — "only if there is no purpose or theory of admissibility to support the trial judge's ruling will it be overturned." Lilly, p. 474.

     ii. Objection sustained: Conversely, if the general objection was ***sustained***, the appellate court will ***uphold*** the ruling unless there is "no basis for it whatsoever." *Id*.

     iii. Summary: In other words, a trial judge's ruling on a general objection, whichever way the judge decides, will ***rarely be reversed on appeal.***

  b. Specific objection: If the objection is ***specific***, here is how it will be handled on appeal:

     i. Correct ground cited: If the objector has ***correctly*** pointed out a specific rule of exclusion to the judge, and the trial judge overrules the objection, the appellate court will reverse (unless it finds the error to have been "harmless"; see *infra*, p. 459).

     ii. Wrong ground; objection overruled: Suppose that the objector picks a specific ground that is ***erroneous***, and the objection is overruled. Here, the objector will generally ***lose*** on appeal ***even if there was a different specific ground which merited exclusion.*** For instance, if a document is objected to on hearsay grounds and the objection is overruled, the objector will lose on appeal even if he convinces the appellate court that the document violated the Best Evidence rule. The rationale is that it is the party's duty to select the correct ground for objection, and all the trial judge can be expected to do is to rule correctly on that specific ground. Lilly, p. 475.

     iii. Wrong ground; objection sustained: The most difficult question arises when the specific ground cited in the objection is ***erroneous***, but the trial judge erroneously ***sustains*** the objection even though there is a different, unnamed, valid ground for objection. Here, the courts are split — some sustain the trial judge's ruling on the grounds that the result was correct even though the reason was wrong; others reverse on the theory that the proponent, had he known of the valid ground, could have offered different evidence to support the point or otherwise cure the defect. The latter seems the better rule; see Lilly, p. 475. (Again, keep in mind that there will never be a reversal if the appellate court finds the error to have been "harmless.")

D. Taking of "exceptions": At common law, a party did not by the mere act of objecting preserve an objection for appeal — after the objection was overruled, the objecting counsel had to say, "I take ***exception***," or similar words. Today, however, most states (as well as the federal courts) have dispensed with the need for taking an exception, so that a timely and specific objection is all that is needed to preserve the evidentiary issue for appeal. See, e.g., Fed. R. Civ. P. 46, dispensing with the need for exceptions. See also M, pp. 132-33.

E. Offer of proof: If the trial judge sustains an objection, the proponent of the evidence must normally make an *"offer of proof"* if he wishes to be able to contend on appeal that the exclusion was reversible error. This "offer of proof" must normally consist of two parts: (1) a description of the evidence being proposed; and (2) an explanation of how that evidence relates to the case, if its relevance is not clear from context. L&S, p. 54, n. 30.

> **Example:** P is suing D for battery. P's counsel calls W to the stand to ask about an altercation between D and X. During the testimony, the lawyer asks, "What did X say to you when you asked him why he was grimacing in pain?" D's counsel objects on hearsay grounds. P's counsel argues that a hearsay exception (for statement of present physical condition; see *infra*, p. 168) applies. The judge sustains the objection. To preserve his position on appeal, P's counsel should now make the following offer of proof: "Your Honor, if W were permitted to testify, he would state that X told him that he was grimacing in pain because he had just been struck in the face by D, for no apparent reason. This evidence is relevant because it shows that D has in the past made unprovoked attacks, and thus impeaches the testimony D has previously given in this trial in which he said that his attack upon my client was self-defense."

1. **Rationale:** The main rationale for the rule requiring an offer of proof is that only by such an offer can the *appellate court* be *completely informed* of what the offered evidence would have been and how it would have been significant to the trial; this in turn helps the appellate court decide not only the issue of admissibility but also the issue of whether the error, if there was one, was harmless. (The offer also gives the trial judge the chance to reassess his ruling sustaining the objection, and gives the opponent a chance to refine or withdraw his objection. Lilly, p. 470.)

2. **Not needed on cross:** Generally, an offer of proof is required only on direct examination, *not cross-examination*. K&W, p. 50. There are two common reasons for this limitation: (1) the cross-examiner will often not know what the witness would have testified to had the objection not been sustained; and (2) the likely answer of the witness will often be obvious to everyone, because the question was probably a "leading" one (permitted on cross-examination but not generally on direct; see *infra*, p. 67). L&S, p. 54, n. 30.

3. **Question-and-answer form:** Generally, the court will allow the offer of proof to be in the form of a statement by the proponent as to what the witness would say if permitted to testify, as in the above Example. (In this situation, the trial court is relying on the good faith of the proponent's counsel, since counsel could theoretically lie, and claim that the testimony would be more favorable than it would in fact be.) Alternatively, counsel may engage the witness in *question-and-answer* form, just as if the testimony were being admitted.

4. **Presence of jury:** Regardless of the form of the offer of proof, it will normally be made *outside the presence of the jury*, since if the jury hears the evidence, the whole point of a sustained objection will be lost.

5. **Federal Rules:** The Federal Rules codify the requirement of an offer of proof. Under FRE 103(a)(2), an appellate court will be permitted to consider a ruling excluding evidence only if "the substance of the evidence was *made known to the court by offer* or was apparent from the context within which questions were asked." FRE 103(b) allows the court to require that the proponent make the offer in question-and-answer form. FRE 103(c) requires, where practicable, that the offer of proof be made outside of the jury's hearing.

F. **The "plain error" and "harmless error" doctrines:** Not every error in the admission or exclusion of evidence will be grounds for reversal. Conversely, not every error to which no objection (or an incorrect objection) is made, will lead to affirmance. An error will not lead to reversal if it is *"harmless"*; conversely, an unobjected-to error may nonetheless lead to reversal if it is *"plain."* See *infra*, pp. 459-60, for a discussion of these two concepts.

IV. COMPETENCY

A. **Meaning:** A witness is said to be *"competent"* if she possesses the qualifications necessary to give testimony. At common law, the competency of witnesses was an important topic, because there were a substantial number of ways in which a person could lose her competency. Today, nearly all of these have been eliminated.

B. **General common-law approach:** At common law, a witness would be found incompetent, and thus not permitted to give any testimony at all, if he occupied one of a number of statuses. Some of the types of persons automatically ruled incompetent were: (1) those who did not believe in a *supreme being* (i.e., agnostics and atheists); (2) convicted *felons*; (3) persons with an *interest* in the outcome of the litigation (e.g., *parties*); (4) *young children*; and (5) *insane* persons. Lilly, p. 85. The common law believed that all such people were either incapable of telling the truth or unwilling to do so.

C. **Modern approach:** Today, nearly all the automatic rules of incompetency have been *abolished* by statute. *Id.* For instance, no state now treats lack of belief in a supreme being as a disqualification. K&W, p. 714.

   1. **Presumption of competence:** Instead, witnesses are presumed competent, and the common-law grounds for disqualification are today at most factors that go to the witness' *credibility*, not to whether he may give testimony at all. For instance, the fact that a witness has an interest in the outcome of the case can be used to *impeach* his credibility, even though it cannot be used to prevent him from testifying entirely; see *infra*, p. 99.

   2. **Federal Rules:** The approach to competency of the Federal Rules is similar to that of most states.

      a. **Two reasons:** Under the Federal Rules, witnesses (other than the judge and the jury in the particular case) will be incompetent to testify *only for two reasons*:

         i. **Lack of personal knowledge:** First, a witness "may not testify to a matter unless evidence is introduced sufficient to support a finding that the witness has ***personal knowledge*** of the matter." FRE 602. Thus if a witness describes a particular event, his testimony will be stricken if it turns out that he did not personally observe that event, and instead heard about it from someone else. This requirement of personal knowledge is discussed more extensively *infra*, p. 397.

    ii. Oath: Second, if the witness will not solemnly ***promise to tell the truth***, the court will not hear his testimony. FRE 603 requires that "before testifying, every witness shall be required to declare that the witness will testify truthfully, by ***oath*** or ***affirmation*** administered in a form calculated to awaken the witness' conscience and impress the witness' mind with the duty to do so."

  b. Mental incapacity or immaturity: Thus under the federal approach, even a witness who is quite insane, or very young, will not be prevented from testifying if the trial judge is convinced that he has relevant first-hand knowledge and understands the obligation to tell the truth. (Of course, the witness' mental impairment or extreme youth could be used to impeach his credibility, if there was evidence that the defect impaired the accuracy of his observation, recall or narration. See *infra*, p. 101.) Similarly, even if the witness was ***intoxicated*** or under the ***influence of drugs*** when he witnessed an event, he will be permitted, under the federal approach, to testify about it.

  c. Diversity cases: However, occasionally federal courts may be required to follow the ***state*** rule on competency. The second sentence of FRE 601 provides, "[I]n civil actions and proceedings, with respect to an element of a claim or defense as to which ***State law supplies the rule of decision***, the competency of a witness shall be determined in accordance with State law." This provision applies most frequently in ***diversity*** cases, as to which the federal court is required to follow state substantive principles; Congress decided to treat state rules of competency as if they were substantive provisions.

    Example: In a diversity action, P sues D's estate for breach of an oral contract. If the state whose substantive contract law applies to this case has a strict Dead Man's Statute (*infra*) preventing P from testifying about any transaction with the decedent, the federal court is required by FRE 601 to similarly disqualify P from testifying to that transaction.

3. Dead Man's Statutes: The one important rule of competency that survives from the common-law days relates to civil suits in which one of the parties is ***deceased***. When the states all abolished the rule that no one with an interest in the outcome of the suit could testify, most states enacted a small compromise, colloquially referred to as a ***Dead Man's Statute***. These statutes vary in their precise effect, but they all attempt to "***equalize the opportunities of proof*** in litigation involving a decedent and survivor where the subject matter of the suit is a transaction or event that occurred when both were living." Lilly, p. 88.

  a. Extreme form: In their most extreme form, Dead Man's Statutes prevent the survivor from testifying *at all* about the transaction between him and the decedent. Under such a statute, if P claimed that D made an oral agreement with him, and D is dead, P will have to come up with some evidence other than his own testimony, or be thrown out of court; he will not be permitted to testify at the trial as to the alleged oral agreement.

b. **More liberal:** But an increasing number of states have enacted less Draconian Dead Man's Statutes. These typically permit the survivor to testify, but equalize his advantage by allowing the decedent's estate to introduce ***hearsay statements made by the decedent*** or other evidence that would otherwise be inadmissible. Lilly, p. 89.

c. **Federal Rules:** There is no federal Dead Man's Statute. That is, the Federal Rules do not directly limit a survivor's ability to testify against a decedent. However, as noted above, if the federal suit is brought in diversity, and the state whose substantive law applies has a Dead Man's Statute, the federal court is required by FRE 601 to honor the state Dead Man's Statute.

RELEVANCE

I. RELEVANCE GENERALLY

A. All relevant evidence admitted: The concept of "relevance" is the cornerstone of the law of admissibility of evidence. For instance, FRE 402 provides that, except as otherwise provided by the Rules or by other specific enactment, ***"all relevant evidence is admissible. . . ."*** The Rule goes on to say that "evidence which is not relevant is not admissible."

B. Two aspects of relevance: When we say that a piece of evidence is "relevant" to the case, we mean that there exist two distinct links between that piece of evidence and the case:

    1. Link One (probative relationship): First, there must be a ***"probative"*** relationship between the piece of evidence and the factual proposition to which the evidence is addressed. Lilly, p. 24. That is, the evidence must make the factual proposition more (or less) likely than it would be without the evidence.

        Example: P is injured when he is hit by D's car. In a negligence suit against D, he offers testimony by W that she saw D driving at what she believed to be around 55 miles per hour. There is a link between W's testimony and a factual proposition asserted by P (that D was travelling at 55 miles per hour) — W's testimony makes it more likely that D was actually travelling at 55 mph than if W didn't so testify.

    2. Link Two (materiality): Second, the evidence must be ***material***. That is, there must be a link between the factual proposition which the evidence tends to establish, and the ***substantive law***. Lilly, p. 24.

        Example: On the facts of the above example, assume that the speed limit at the site of the accident was 35 mph. W's testimony satisfies this second link, because evidence that D was exceeding the speed limit by 20 mph affects a fundamental substantive law issue in the case, namely, whether D was negligent. If, on the other hand, the local speed limit was 55 mph, this link would not be present (though D's speed might relate to some other substantive law issue in the case).

      a. Significance of substantive law: This second type of link, that between the factual proposition sought to be established and the underlying substantive law, illustrates that there is ***no such thing as relevance "in the abstract."*** For any given proposition of fact which the evidence tends to establish, the evidence may be relevant to some claims or defenses, and not to others.

    3. Rule 401: These two aspects of relevance are combined in FRE 401's definition of relevant evidence: " 'Relevant evidence' means evidence having any tendency to make the existence of any fact that is of consequence to the determination of the action more probable or less probable than it would be without the evidence." The first link — a probative relationship between the evidence and the factual proposition — is indicated by the requirement that the existence of the fact be made "more probable." The second link — the requirement that the factual proposition be relevant to the substantive law — is indicated by the requirement that the fact be "of consequence to the determination of the action. . . ."

C. **"Direct" vs. "circumstantial" evidence:** Evidence is either ***"direct"*** or ***"circumstantial."***

    1. **"Direct" evidence:** Direct evidence is "evidence which, if believed, *resolves* a matter in issue." M, p. 543.

        Example: W testifies that she saw D strangle V with a stocking. W's testimony is direct evidence on the issue of whether D did in fact strangle V with a stocking, since if that testimony is believed, the issue is resolved.

    2. **"Circumstantial" evidence:** Circumstantial evidence is evidence which, even if believed, does not resolve the matter at issue unless **additional reasoning** is used to reach the proposition to which the evidence is directed. *Id.*

        Example: Prosecution of D for strangling V. W, a policeman, testifies that shortly after hearing V's screams, he saw D running from the scene of the crime, and, after stopping D, found a stocking in D's pocket. While this testimony (if believed) is direct evidence on the issues of whether D was at the scene of the crime, was fleeing, and had a stocking in his pocket, it is merely circumstantial evidence as to whether D did the strangling. This is so because only by the application of additional reasoning ("A man seen fleeing from the scene of a strangling, who is found with a stocking in his pocket, is at least somewhat more likely to be guilty of the strangling than most other people are") does the evidence lead to the proposition to which it is addressed.

    3. **Consequences of distinction:** The relevance of proffered evidence differs dramatically depending on whether the evidence is direct or circumstantial.

        a. **Direct evidence never irrelevant:** When the evidence is ***direct***, so long as it is offered to help establish a material issue (i.e., so long as Link 2, *supra*, p. 10, exists), ***it can never be irrelevant***. *Id.*

        b. **Circumstantial evidence:** By contrast, ***circumstantial*** evidence, even if offered to prove a material fact, will nonetheless be found to be irrelevant if the evidence has no ***probative value***, i.e., it does not affect the probability of the proposition to which it was directed. (That is, Link 1, *supra*, p. 10, must exist as well as Link 2.)

II. PROBATIVE VALUE

A. **The problem generally:** As noted, evidence is relevant only if it has "probative value," that is, only if it affects the probability of the existence of a fact consequential to the action. Assessing the probative value of particular evidence is, therefore, a major part of what a judge must do in assessing relevance. (Also as noted, this is an issue that arises ***only*** in the case of circumstantial evidence, not direct evidence.)

B. Experience and logic, not law: The judge normally does not make this assessment of probative value by applying cut-and-dried legal principles. Rather, he applies his "own experience, his general knowledge, and his understanding of human conduct and motivation." M, p. 544.

> **Example:** Suppose that D, after being charged with a crime, is caught attempting to flee the jurisdiction. If the prosecution offers evidence of the flight on the grounds that it tends to establish D's consciousness of his guilt, "the answer will not be found in a statistical table of the attempts at escape by those conscious of guilt as opposed to those not conscious of their guilt." *Id.* Instead, the judge will ask himself whether a reasonable juror could believe that the fact that D tried to escape makes it more probable than it would otherwise be that he was conscious of his guilt of the crime charged. *Id.* This inquiry is a matter of common sense, experience and logic, not the application of any legal principle.

1. **Common patterns:** Certain types of circumstantial evidence, however, are so frequently offered that a body of legal precedent has been built up concerning them. Indeed, the probative value of an escape attempt, offered to show consciousness of guilt, is probably one such type, so a judge might look to cases on this issue in making his decision. But the precise circumstances of the present case are always of ultimate significance in assessing probative value. For instance, if D in the above example had been charged with two unrelated crimes at the time he fled, and was only being tried for one of them, the probative value of his escape on the issue of his consciousness of guilt for the one crime at trial would be weaker than where only the one charge had been pending at the time of escape.

C. Chain of inference: In assessing probative value, the judge must determine what proposition the evidence is being offered to establish, and he must then follow the *"chain of inference"* between the evidence and that proposition. Sometimes this chain may be a complex and subtle one.

> **Example:** Suppose the contested issue is whether D is the person who killed H, and the evidence is a love letter from D to W, H's wife. The "chain of inference" would be something like this: (1) A man who writes a love letter to a woman probably loves her ("probably" in the sense that he is more likely to love her than is a man who does not write a love letter); (2) A man who loves a woman probably wants her for himself alone; (3) A man who wants a woman for himself alone probably would like to get rid of her husband; (4) A man who wants to get rid of the husband of the woman he loves probably plans to do so; (5) A man who plans to get rid of someone probably does so, by killing him. W,M,A&B, p. 3.

1. **Evaluation:** Obviously, the more steps there are in the chain of inference, the less probative value the evidence has. Similarly, the less convincing any of the individual steps is, the less the probative value. K&W, p. 70.

   a. **"A brick is not a wall":** On the other hand, for an item of circumstantial evidence to have probative value as to a particular fact, *it is not necessary that* *the evidence render the fact more probable than not*. Rather, all that is required is that the evidence make the existence of the fact *more probable than it would be without the evidence*. As the idea has been most famously put, *"a brick is not a wall."* That is, if the particular fact in dispute is the wall, an item of evidence need merely be a valid brick in that wall. M, p. 543. Or as the idea is sometimes put, "it is not to be supposed that every witness can make a home run." Adv. Comm. Note to FRE 401.

> **Example:** D is charged with murdering V. D claims self defense, and tries to prove that he had reason to fear V by testifying that he had been told that V had seriously injured or killed an old man. The prosecution offers the testimony of the doctor who treated the old man, that the old man died of natural causes and that there were no marks of violence. The defense argues that the doctor's testimony is irrelevant, since the issue is not whether the story of D's attacking the old man is true, but whether D had in fact heard the story.
>
> *Held*, the evidence was relevant to the truth of D's self-defense claim. The evidence showed that "somewhere between the fact and [D's] testimony there was a person who was not a true speaker." Since D could not or would not identify his informant, the doctor's testimony had a tendency to make D's claim of what he heard less likely to be true than it would be without the doctor's testimony. *Knapp v. State*, 79 N.E. 1076 (Ind. 1907).

b. Proposition can remain improbable: Because all that is required is that the evidence make the disputed fact more probable than it would be without the evidence, it follows that evidence can have probative value even though, following receipt of the evidence, the proposition for which it is offered still seems quite improbable. M, p. 543. Thus the common objection that the proposition sought to be proved "does not follow" from the evidence offered by the other side, makes no sense. *Id.*

> **Example:** Suppose that D is charged with murdering V. The state's first piece of evidence is that D was the beneficiary of an insurance policy on V's life. If this were the only piece of evidence in the case, it would be quite unlikely that D was the murderer: after all, an empirical study of murderers would undoubtedly show that less than half of all insured murder victims are murdered by their beneficiaries. But the evidence is nonetheless of probative value, because a reasonable juror could conclude that someone who stands to gain financially from another person's death is at least somewhat more likely to murder that other person than is one who does not stand to gain.

i. Almost always some probative value: In fact, very few pieces of circumstantial evidence are proffered that do not have at least *some* probative value. That is, almost every piece of evidence that is offered at least slightly increases the probability of the existence of the fact to which it is directed. Therefore, in point of fact, evidence should rarely be excluded for lack of probative value. On the other hand, evidence is very frequently excluded because its probative value is *outweighed* by prejudice, tendency to confuse, or other discretionary considerations. (These countervailing considerations are discussed extensively *infra*.) Even when a court states that it is excluding evidence for lack of probative value, it is probably doing so because the modest probative value is outweighed by one of these "counterweights." M, p. 544, n. 23. See, e.g., FRE 403, allowing such weighing and exclusion.

   ii. Credibility not a factor: When the court measures probative value to determine whether it is outweighed by prejudicial effect, the court should **not** factor in doubts it may have about the **credibility** of the evidence. Rather, the test is what probative value the evidence would have **if believed**. See, e.g., *Ballou v. Henri Studios, Inc.*, 656 F.2d 1147 (5th Cir. 1981), in which the trial court's exclusion of the results of a blood alcohol test in a car crash case, on the grounds that the trial court believed the results to lack "credibility," was overturned on appeal; the Court of Appeals reasoned that "weighing probative value against unfair prejudice under FRE 403 means probative value with respect to a material fact if the evidence is believed, not the degree the court finds it believable." The choice of whether to believe an item of evidence should be left to the jury.

III. PREJUDICE, CONFUSION, AND WASTE OF TIME

   A. "Counterweights" to relevance: Even if evidence is relevant, the trial judge may exclude it on the basis of several largely discretionary countervailing considerations. FRE 403, for instance, allows the judge to exclude relevant evidence "if its probative value is **substantially outweighed** by the danger of **unfair prejudice**, **confusion** of the issues, or misleading the jury, or by considerations of undue **delay**, **waste of time**, or needless presentation of cumulative evidence." These countervailing considerations can be thought of as falling into three main classes: (1) prejudice; (2) confusion; and (3) waste of time.

   B. Prejudice: Relevant evidence may be excluded because its probative value is outweighed by the likelihood that it will cause **"unfair prejudice."** The word "unfair" is an important aspect: any highly material evidence is likely to be prejudicial (in the sense of damaging) to the party not introducing it. "Unfair" prejudice means "an undue tendency to suggest decision on an **improper basis**, commonly, though not necessarily, an **emotional** one." Adv. Comm. Note to FRE 403.

   > **Example:** D is charged with first degree murder in a state permitting the death penalty for that crime. After black and white photographs of the victim have been introduced (showing him lying in his bed with two bullet holes in the head), the prosecution projects colored slides onto a screen. The slides show the victim's head during the course of an autopsy; several show the empty brain cavity.
   >
   > *Held* (on appeal), these slides should have been excluded on the grounds that their probative value was outweighed by their prejudicial impact. Any fact the slides could have suggested had already been demonstrated by the black and white photos, so the slides' only purpose was to "inflame and arouse

the jury," and to induce them to recommend the death penalty instead of life imprisonment. *State v. Poe*, 441 P.2d 512 (Utah 1968).

1. **Evidence of other crimes:** One common situation in which evidence is excluded because of unfair prejudice is a showing that the defendant in a criminal case has in the *past* been convicted of crimes similar to the one with which he is now charged. The principal reason why such evidence is considered unfairly prejudicial is that it "may lead a juror to think that since the defendant already has a criminal record, an erroneous conviction would not be quite as serious as would otherwise be the case. A juror influenced in this fashion may be satisfied with a slightly less compelling demonstration of guilt than he should be." M, p. 545.

   a. **Special rule:** Indeed, the problem of prior convictions is so serious, and recurs so often, that the Federal Rules have a special provision barring such evidence in most instances (including most instances where the evidence is used against a criminal defendant). The special rules governing this situation are discussed *infra*, p. 22.

   b. **Other evidence of guilt:** Even where a prior conviction is not shown, evidence suggesting that the defendant is in fact guilty of past crimes may similarly be excluded on the grounds of unfair prejudice. See, e.g., *State v. Ball*, 339 S.W.2d 783 (Mo. 1960), in which the government in a robbery prosecution introduced evidence that several hundred dollars was found on D's person more than two weeks after the robbery, at a time when he was unlikely to have come by it honestly (since he was unemployed and only a few months out of jail). The evidence was ordered excluded as unfairly prejudicial on the theory that the jury may have inferred that D was guilty of a different robbery.

C. **Confusion:** Relevant evidence may be excluded if its probative value is outweighed by its tendency to **confuse** or **mislead** the jury, or unduly distract it from the main issues. M, p. 546. For instance, evidence that the accused has committed past crimes may not only be prejudicial (as discussed above), but it may also distract the jury from the fact that there is only weak evidence that the accused was the person who did the act charged.

D. **Waste of time:** Evidence may also be excluded if it would be a **waste of time.** This is especially likely to be the case where the evidence is cumulative. For instance, in a case in which the accused is charged with having poisoned the decedent, presentation by either side of more than two or three witnesses all testifying as to the cause of death might be deemed to be needlessly cumulative and therefore excluded.

E. **No "unfair surprise":** FRE 403 does *not* recognize "unfair *surprise*" as a ground for excluding otherwise relevant evidence. If the proposed evidence takes the other side by surprise, the appropriate remedy is a continuance. See Adv. Comm. Note to FRE 403.

F. **Standard for appellate review:** The exclusion of relevant evidence because its probative value is outweighed by the chance of prejudice, confusion, waste of time, etc., necessarily requires the trial court to perform a difficult balancing task. Appellate courts have generally given trial courts **wide discretion** in conducting this balancing — only where there is a **clear abuse of discretion** will the trial court's decision be overturned on appeal. The Federal Rules tip the scale in favor of the inclusion rather than exclusion of doubtful evidence, by allowing exclusion only where the probative value is "***substantially*** outweighed" by the prejudice, confusion, etc.

CIRCUMSTANTIAL PROOF: SPECIAL PROBLEMS

Introductory Note: This chapter considers special problems that exist only with respect to circumstantial, as opposed to direct, evidence. Most of the chapter deals with evidence of *"character,"* especially with the use of evidence of *other crimes* committed by the defendant. Other topics include: (1) *habit* and *custom*; (2) *similar happenings*; (3) *compromise* (settlements); (4) *subsequent precautions*; and (5) *liability insurance.* What these areas have in common is that they all involve evidence which most people would regard as relevant (in the sense of affecting the probability of a material fact's existence — see p. 10 *supra*), but which poses such a high risk of unfair prejudice that it is generally not admissible.

I. CHARACTER EVIDENCE IN GENERAL

A. Nature of the problem: The fundamental problem of *"character evidence"* is this: To what extent may evidence of a person's character be used to show that in the particular instance in dispute, he acted in *conformity* with that character? The issue arises in many different contexts. Here are some illustrations:

> **Example 1:** D, a mailman, is charged with stealing from the mails. The prosecution wants to introduce evidence that D has been convicted in the past for stealing from the mail, as well as for embezzlement and robbery.

> **Example 2:** P and D are in a car collision, and P sues D for negligent driving. P offers to prove that D has been involved in numerous car accidents in the past, some of which involved D's being intoxicated or otherwise driving improperly.

> **Example 3:** D is charged with killing P in a fight. As part of D's claim of self-defense, D offers evidence to show that P had a reputation for violence, as well as evidence that he himself has always been a peaceful person.

1. The problem: In all of these instances, the offered evidence of "character" is probably at least loosely relevant. For instance, in Example 1, the fact that D has been convicted (or even merely charged with) larcenous offenses in the past probably makes it more likely that he is guilty of the present charged offense than if he had not been the subject of prior charges. Similarly, on the facts of Example 3, a jury could reasonably conclude that a person with a reputation for violence is more likely to have started a fight than a person without such a reputation.

2. Countervailing considerations: There are two major problems with this type of evidence, however:

a. Change: First, we do not always act in conformity with our "character" — our moods change, and contexts change, and the notion of "character" is an imprecise one anyway. Therefore, a strong case can be made that the fact-finder should concentrate on evidence bearing directly on what happened in an episode in question, and less on evidence of the form "X is a ___-type of person; therefore, he probably acted in conformity with this character trait."

b. **Prejudice:** Second, the risk of **unfair prejudice** is unusually great when character evidence is involved — the jury is especially likely to punish (or reward) X for being the "kind of person he is" rather than for what he did on the particular occasion in question.

   i. **Criminal cases:** This is particularly true in *criminal* cases where evidence of the defendant's bad character (e.g., evidence that he has committed other, similar crimes in the past) may induce the jury to convict him not because of evidence that he actually committed the deed in question, but because he is a "bad person."

3. **General rules:** In theory, the admissibility of character evidence could be left to trial judges to handle on a case-by-case balancing basis, whereby the evidence would only be admitted if its probative value was greater than its unfairly prejudicial effect. But this scheme would be the farthest thing from a "bright line" rule, and would be hard to administer. Instead, the courts have formulated specific rules, and exceptions, to deal with the major contexts in which character evidence is sought to be introduced.

   a. **General rule and exceptions:** As is discussed more extensively below, the general rule in most jurisdictions is that character evidence may not be admitted to show that a person acted in conformity with his character. However, there are a number of vital exceptions to this rule.

4. **Distinctions:** Two sets of distinctions should be kept in mind during the discussion which follows:

   a. **Character in issue:** First, situations in which character evidence is used as circumstantial evidence of conduct must be distinguished from those in which character is itself *in issue* in the case. In the character-as-circumstantial-evidence situation, the presumption is against the admissibility of the character evidence, because there is generally more direct evidence of the conduct in question. But where character is itself in issue (e.g., an action for defamation, in which the plaintiff complains that the defendant has said the plaintiff's character is bad, and the defendant raises the defense of truth), character evidence will be permitted since it is the **only** evidence available on a material issue. The "character in issue" problem is discussed *infra* at p. 19.

   b. **Types of circumstantial evidence:** The second distinction is that among the various types of circumstantial character evidence. There are three types, ranging from least to most specific: (1) evidence of a person's **reputation** for possessing a certain character trait; (2) the witness's own **opinion** as to whether a person has a particular character trait; and (3) evidence of particular **acts** showing that the person has a particular character trait.

i. Significance: As we progress from the most general to the most specific of these kinds of evidence, the "pungency and persuasiveness" of the evidence increases. But so does its tendency to inspire undue prejudice, and to confuse and distract the jury from other issues. M, p. 550.

ii. Traditional rule: Therefore, the traditional rule has been that in those few instances where circumstantial evidence of character may be admitted, only the neutral and unexciting *reputation* evidence could be used. *Id.*

iii. Federal Rules: The Federal Rules have made a major change in this traditional approach. Under FRE 405(a), *opinion*, as well as reputation, evidence may be admitted. (Evidence of specific acts may not be brought out in direct examination of the witness; but on cross-examination of a witness who has already given opinion or reputation testimony, "inquiry is allowable into relevant specific instances of conduct.")

iv. Character in issue: Where a person's character is directly in issue (the situation discussed directly below), specific instances have almost always been permitted; FRE 405(b) continues this permissive rule.

II. CHARACTER IN ISSUE

A. General rule: A person's general character, or a particular character trait that he has, may be an *essential element* of the case, in the sense that, under the substantive law, that character or trait determines the rights and liabilities of the parties. In such a situation, character evidence is *not only allowable, it is essential.*

> **Example 1:** P is injured when a train owned by D Railroad fails to be given a "stop" signal at a crossing. The signal should have been given by a flagman who is employed by D. P offers evidence that the flagman was drunk at the time. He also offers evidence that the flagman had been drunk several times before, and that these prior episodes were known to D's employees who had the right to hire or fire the flagman.
>
> *Held,* the evidence of the flagman's prior drunkenness was admissible. P was attempting to recover punitive damages, so D's knowing and continuing employment of an alcoholic flagman was directly relevant to P's claim. *Cleghorn v. New York Central & H. River Ry. Co.,* 56 N.Y. 44 (1874).

> **Example 2:** D, a newspaper, prints an article calling P "the sort of man who would steal his mother's bones from the grave and sell them to buy flowers for a harlot." P sues D for libel. D may introduce evidence of P's despicable character, both to support the defense of truth and to minimize the damages (on the theory that P's reputation was already low and could not have been much damaged by the article). Since P's character is "in issue," the evidence about it is admissible. K&W, pp. 349-50.

B. Type of evidence: Most courts, and the Federal Rules, allow all three types of evidence of character when character is in issue. That is, the evidence may consist of: (1) *specific acts* to demonstrate character; (2) a witness' *opinion* of that character; or (3) evidence as to the subject's *reputation* for the character trait in issue.

1. **Specific instances:** Since FRE 405(a) *always* allows reputation and opinion evidence wherever character evidence is admissible at all, it is only proof of "specific instances" that needs a special provision to deal with the character-in-issue situation. 405(b) provides that "in cases in which character or a trait of character of a person is an essential element of a charge, claim, or defense, proof may also be made of specific instances of his conduct."

2. **Minority rule:** A few courts allow *only* evidence of specific acts, not reputation or opinion evidence, where character is in issue. M, pp. 552-53.

III. CHARACTER AS CIRCUMSTANTIAL EVIDENCE — GENERALLY

A. **General rule:** We now turn to the use of character as *circumstantial evidence* of what a person did (or thought) on a particular occasion. The theory behind such evidence runs something like this: "Because X has the character trait of [honesty, trickery, intoxication, or whatever], during the episode in question he probably acted [honestly, trickily, drunkenly, or whatever]."

   1. **General rule of exclusion:** As a general rule, *such use of character evidence for circumstantial purposes is not admissible*.

      a. **Federal rule:** The Federal Rules follow this approach. FRE 404(a) provides that "evidence of a person's character or a trait of character is not admissible for the purpose of proving action in conformity therewith on a particular occasion," except under a few special circumstances.

         Example: P brings a civil suit against D, alleging that D negligently drove his vehicle thereby injuring P. P offers evidence that D has been found to have driven negligently several times in the past, in suits by other accident victims. He also offers evidence that D has a reputation for being a careless driver, and offers the testimony of a witness who would express the opinion that D is a careless driver. All three of these types of evidence will be ruled inadmissible, because they are offered for the purpose of demonstrating that D is a careless driver who probably acted in conformity with this trait for carelessness during the accident involving P.

IV. USE OF CIRCUMSTANTIAL CHARACTER EVIDENCE IN CIVIL CASES

A. **General rule:** The general rule that circumstantial evidence of character is inadmissible, is applied in *civil* cases. The prior example is an illustration of this principle.

B. **Character for care:** The issue arises most frequently where a party in a case involving claims of negligence tries to prove that the other party had a character trait of *carelessness*, or that he himself had a trait of *carefulness*. Regardless of whether it is carelessness or carefulness that is sought to be proved, the virtually universal rule is that the evidence is *inadmissible*.

1. **Rationale:** This rule of exclusion is based upon the theory that the probative value of such "character for care" evidence is nearly always outweighed by its tendency to arouse unfair prejudice and to distract or confuse the jury. The probative value of such evidence is questionable, principally because even generally careful or generally careless people act, in some instances, quite out of conformity with their usual character.

C. **Quasi-criminal acts alleged:** Suppose that one party to a civil suit charges the other with conduct that, in addition to being actionable, is *criminal*. As will be seen *infra*, p. 36, a criminal defendant receives the benefit of an exception to the no-character-evidence rule that permits him to introduce evidence of his own good character. Should a party to a civil suit who is charged with acts constituting crimes be given the benefit of a similar exception? The issue arises most frequently in tort cases for assault and/or battery, where the defendant wishes to show that the other party was the aggressor.

1. **Minority view:** A *minority* of courts have **allowed** such good-character evidence, usually on the theory that the same general notion of fairness that dictates admissibility of the evidence in the criminal context also requires its admission where the defendant's reputation for being law-abiding is at stake.

    Example: P brings a tort suit against D, claiming D assaulted him with a meat cleaver and wounded him. D denies cutting P with the cleaver, and claims that P's injuries occurred as part of a general brawl. D offers evidence that he is a quiet and peaceable man.

    Held, the evidence is admissible. While the general rule is that "evidence of the good character of the defendant is not admissible in a civil case," there is an exception: "[W]here it is necessary to the recovery which the plaintiff seeks that he prove against the defendant facts which constitute a crime, and [in order for there to be a] recovery the defendant must have had criminal intent when he did the acts complained of, it is proper for the defendant to introduce character evidence . . . for the purpose of overcoming the proof offered to show criminal intent." (Also, P seeks punitive damages, and D's character is highly relevant on this issue, since "surely the jury would not conclude that a man of good character for peace and quietude in the community should be punished by a fine as large as one who is a notorious bully.") *Hess v. Marinari*, 94 S.E. 968 (W.Va. 1918).

    a. **Evidence of other party's aggression:** Courts that follow the minority rule allowing character evidence in assault and battery cases usually allow the defendant to show not only that he has a good peaceable character but also that the plaintiff/victim has a *propensity for violence or aggression.* Lilly, p. 130. The defendant, of course, offers the evidence to show that the victim, not he, was the aggressor.

2. **Majority view:** The majority view, exemplified by the Federal Rules, is that even in this "conduct constituting a crime" situation, evidence of good character is *inadmissible*.

Example: P, the beneficiary of an insurance policy on X's life, sues D, the insurance company, when D refuses to pay on the policy. The policy excludes coverage in cases where the decedent dies from his own criminal action. At trial, D shows that X was killed when he trespassed upon a cottage and was shot by a spring gun. P offers evidence that X was a peaceable and law abiding citizen.

Held, the evidence of X's character is inadmissible. "It is the generally accepted rule that in civil actions, even where fraud is imputed or dishonesty is charged, evidence of a party's good or bad character is incompetent in evidence unless it be made an issue by the pleadings or the proof. . . . 'The business of the court is to try the case and not the man; and a very bad man may have a very righteous cause.' " *Mutual Life Ins. Co. v. Kelly*, 197 N.E. 235 (Ohio 1934).

a. **Actual claim of self-defense:** The majority rule disallowing proof by the defendant of his good character even where he is charged with acts constituting a crime, must be distinguished from the rule in one special situation: where the defendant in an assault and battery action claims *self-defense*, nearly **all courts** allow him to introduce evidence of the victim's reputation for violence or aggression. However, this nearly universal rule allowing admission applies only where the defendant shows that he was *aware* of the victim's reputation for violence at the time of the episode. This situation is not really an exception to the general rule disallowing circumstantial evidence of character, since the evidence is directly relevant to a claim or defense — "The theory is that the victim's reputation bears upon defendant's apprehension and, of course, the defendant's state of mind is a significant factor in determining whether he acted reasonably." Lilly, p. 130, n. 9. A similar rule is universally applied in criminal cases where the claim of self-defense is raised. (A more complete discussion of reputation evidence in the self-defense context is given *infra*, p. 41, as part of the general discussion of evidence of a victim's character in criminal cases.)

V. OTHER CRIMES AS EVIDENCE IN CRIMINAL CASES

A. **General principle:** A prosecutor would always love to be able to introduce evidence that the defendant has committed *other, similar crimes* in the past. The theory behind such evidence is that it shows that the defendant has a bad or criminal disposition, making it more likely that he committed the crime in question. But the universally-applied principle is that *such evidence of other crimes is not admissible when offered for the purpose of suggesting that because the defendant is a person of criminal character, it is more probable that he committed the crime with which he is charged.* M, pp. 557-58.

Example: D is charged with the murder of V. The prosecution shows that V and some others insulted D's wife, leading D to threaten to "bump them all off" if they didn't leave within five minutes. D then returned to his apartment, selected a gun from his weapons collection, went back out to the scene of the insult, and as part of an argument, shot V to death. At trial, the prosecution seeks to introduce into evidence the fact that, at the time of the encounter and of the subsequent arrest of D, D kept three pistols and a tear-gas gun in his apartment. (There is no claim that D had all of these weapons with him at the time of the shooting.)

Held (on appeal), the weapons at the apartment should not have been admitted. They were introduced to persuade the jury that "here was a man of vicious and dangerous propensities, who because of those propensities was more likely to kill with deliberate and premeditated design than a man of irreproachable life and amiable manners." It is a fundamental principle that "character is never an issue in a criminal prosecution unless the defendant chooses to make it one. . . . In a very real sense a defendant starts his life afresh when he stands before a jury, a prisoner at the bar. . . . 'The natural and inevitable tendency of the tribunal — whether judge or jury — is to give excessive weight to the vicious record of crime thus exhibited, and either to allow it to bear too strongly on the present charge, or to take the proof of it as justifying a condemnation irrespective of guilt of the present charge.' " It would be a different story if the weapons had been brought to the encounter, since they would then show preparation and design; similarly, the result would be different if they identified the possessor in a case where identity was in dispute. *People v. Zackowitz*, 172 N.E. 466 (N.Y. 1930).

A dissent argued that the evidence was properly admitted because it stood not for the proposition that the defendant had a propensity towards crime or violence, but rather for the proposition that the murder was premeditated — the evidence furthered the prosecution's portrayal of D "as a man having dangerous weapons in his possession, making a selection therefrom and going forth to put into execution his threats to kill; not as a man of a dangerous disposition in general, but as one who, having an opportunity to select a weapon to carry out his threats, proceeded to do so. . . ."

B. Proof of element of crime: Now suppose, however, that the prosecution offers evidence of the defendant's prior crimes not to show that he has a criminal disposition, but to ***establish circumstantially an element of the crime charged***. In this situation, the fact finder is asked to infer from the fact of the prior crime something about the defendant's conduct or state of mind in connection with the crime charged.

   1. Admissible: In this situation, the other crimes are thus being used to establish a material fact, and the general rule of exclusion does ***not*** apply. So long as the probative value of the evidence outweighs its tendency to cause undue prejudice, confusion, etc., the evidence will be ***admitted.***

   Example: On the facts of *Zackowitz, supra,* suppose that the several weapons not used in the shooting had been brought by D to the scene of the crime and had been left there. If D had denied that he was the person who shot X, the weapons would have been admissible on the issue of identity. This would be the case even though proof that D had possessed the weapons would establish his guilt of another crime (illegal possession of weapons), and even though the fact-finder might infer from those weapons D's propensity for crime and violence. That is, so long as evidence of other crimes is relevant to some element of the crime charged (here, identity) it is admissible even though it may also show criminal disposition (again, assuming that its probative value is not outweighed by undue prejudice, confusion, etc.)

2. **No catalogue:** Some courts and statutes impose a list of particular elements (e.g., intent, motive, knowledge, identity, etc.) as to which other-crimes evidence is admissible; if the evidence is not relevant to one of those enumerated elements, it is not admissible. But the majority rule, and that followed by the Federal Rules, is more inclusive.

   a. **Federal Rule's formulation:** Thus, FRE 404(b) enumerates some specific elements which may be proven by other-crimes evidence, but does not foreclose the possibility of others: "Evidence of other crimes, wrongs, or acts is not admissible to prove the character of a person in order to show action in conformity therewith. It may, however, be admissible for other purposes, such as proof of motive, opportunity, intent, preparation, plan, knowledge, identity, or absence of mistake or accident. . . ." The Advisory Committee's Note on this subdivision observes that "no mechanical solution is offered." Instead, the probative value of the evidence is to be weighed against the danger of undue prejudice "in view of the availability of other means of proof and other factors appropriate for making decisions of this kind under Rule 403."

      i. **Advance notice required:** Because other-crimes evidence may unfairly catch the defendant by surprise, FRE 404(b) now requires the prosecution in a criminal case to give the defendant ***advance notice***, normally before the start of trial, of its intention to use the other-crimes evidence. (FRE 404(b), second sentence, last clause, as amended in 1991.)

C. **Specific situations:** Here are some of the special purposes for which other-crimes evidence has been admitted:

D. **Context:** Other-crimes evidence may be used to place the crime in ***context***, by describing other events or conduct that were part of the ***same transaction***.

   Example: Suppose that D is charged with murdering V, a policeman. The evidence shows that the murder occurred when V was trying to arrest D on a robbery charge. V's partner on the police force, W, testifies that while V and W were trying to arrest D, D not only shot V to death but also shot and wounded W. The "telling of the story" of the murder inevitably involves evidence of an additional crime by D — the attempted murder of W. Because this information is part of the overall context in which the murder took place, the other-crimes evidence is admissible. (Probably the evidence that D may have been guilty of robbery, the charge for which V and W were trying to arrest him, would also fall within the "same transaction" exception.)

E. **Larger plan:** Other-crimes evidence may be used to prove the existence "of a larger ***plan, scheme,*** or ***conspiracy,*** of which the crime on trial is a ***part***." M, p. 559.

   Example: D is charged with stealing money from the person of V. The state shows that D came to V's place of business, put her hands all over him and propositioned him for sex, while picking his pocket. X and Y testify that in separate incidents, D came to their offices and picked their pockets in a similar way.

Held, the evidence of the crimes upon X and Y was admissible because it showed that D's acts concerning V were part of a "common plan or scheme." *Jones v. State*, 376 S.W.2d 842 (Texas 1964).

1. **Why "common plan or scheme" is relevant:** The existence of a "common plan or scheme" is not itself generally an element of a crime (though it would be if the crime charged were that of conspiracy). However, the existence of a common plan or scheme in turn tends to show the defendant's intent, motive, identity, or other actual element of the crime charged. This illustrates the principle that for other crimes evidence to be admissible, it need not directly establish an element of the crime; all that is required is that it be reasonably strong circumstantial evidence of some element of the crime charged. Lilly, p. 149.

F. **Preparation:** Other-crimes evidence may be used to show *preparation* for the crime charged. Like "common plan or scheme," a showing of preparation is likely to reveal the defendant's state of mind — for instance, to show purposefulness and to negate the possibility of accident. It also increases the likelihood that the act prepared for in fact took place. Lilly, p. 157.

> **Example:** Recall *People v. Zackowitz* (*supra*, pp. 22-23), in which D, after hearing his wife be insulted by V, went back to his apartment and selected a gun before returning to the scene and shooting V. If D argued self defense, or involuntary manslaughter of the "heat of passion" variety, evidence of D's deliberativeness in selecting an appropriate weapon would be admissible because it would negate these defenses.

G. **"Signature" or *modus operandi*:** Such evidence may be used to prove other crimes by the accused that are so similar in method to the crime charged that all bear his ***"signature."***

1. **Requirements:** This kind of evidence of "signature" crimes is only admissible where two requirements are satisfied:

   a. **Denial by accused:** First, the accused must ***deny his participation*** in the crime charged. Thus if, in a murder case, D admits that he killed V by breaking his neck with a karate kick, and the only issue is D's state of mind, the prosecution may not use the "signature" rationale to show that D committed other killings with a neck-snapping karate kick (though these other killings may be admissible to negate, say, D's claim of self-defense).

   b. **Proof of identity:** Second, the methods involved in the other crimes must be ***so very similar*** to those used in the crime charged that the similarity is "substantially probative of identity." Lilly, p. 159. "A mere showing that D has committed other crimes in the same class as the offense charged is insufficiently probative of identity to justify admission." *Id*.

Example: Recall the facts of *Jones v. State*, *supra*, pp. 24-25, in which D was charged with entering V's place of business, sexually propositioning him while putting her hands on his body, and then pickpocketing him. Other business people who had different places of business were permitted to testify that D had picked their pockets by use of exactly the same ruse. The "signature" rationale could have been used to admit this evidence of other crimes, since the overall *modus operandi* used was so idiosyncratic that it strongly suggested that all of the crimes must have been by the same person (and the victims of the other crimes identified D as the perpetrator). But the "signature" rationale would not have been usable had D conceded that she visited V, and the only dispute was whether she picked his pocket. (But the other crimes evidence would still have been admissible under the "common plan or scheme" exception, since it suggested that pickpocketing was the whole object of D's repeated office visits.)

2. *Modus operandi*: A crude way to determine whether the precise method used in all of the crimes is so similar and so idiosyncratic that it is probative of identity, is to ask whether the method can plausibly be described as what readers of detective fiction would call a *"modus operandi"* or "m.o." (Latin for "method of operation.")

H. Intent: Other-crimes evidence may be used to show that the defendant acted *maliciously*, *deliberately*, or with the *specific intent* required for the crime.

1. **Rebutting an innocent explanation:** Generally, the way other-crimes evidence becomes relevant to the defendant's mental state is that the defendant admits the act charged, but asserts an *innocent explanation* for that act; evidence of similar acts is admitted on the theory that "the oftener a like act has been done, the less probable it is that it could have been done innocently." 2 Wigmore §312.

2. **Requirement of similarity:** For the defendant's guilty state of mind relative to the crime charged to be proved by the other crimes, there must be a substantial degree of *similarity* between the crime charged and the other crimes. For instance, the fact that D has committed many burglaries would not indicate the untruthfulness of his claim of self-defense in a murder case; but it might indicate the untruthfulness of his claim that, when he was arrested on a window ledge outside of V's apartment, he was there because he was fleeing from muggers in the street.

3. **Degree of similarity:** Some courts have required a very high degree of similarity between the other crime and the act charged, in the sense that the "essential physical elements" of the two crimes must be alike. But the *majority* view now seems to be that the two must be alike *only in the sense that a guilty state of mind as to the other crime suggests a guilty state of mind as to the act charged.* The leading case representing this majority view is *U.S. v. Beechum*, 582 F.2d 898 (5th Cir. 1978). Because this case contains probably the most important and detailed discussion of the entire FRE 404(b) "other crimes" provision, it is worth discussing in some detail. (The court used the phrase "extrinsic evidence" instead of "other-crimes evidence.")

a. **Facts:** D, a substitute mail carrier, was charged with unlawfully possessing a silver dollar that he knew to be stolen from the mail. Because D had been suspected of rifling the mails, postal inspectors placed the silver dollar in a letter that was part of D's route; inspectors watched D receive the letter in the mailbox, saw him stop in a record store, noticed that the silver dollar had been removed when D turned in the mail at the post office, and found the dollar in D's pocket when he was arrested and frisked. During the frisk, D was also found to be carrying two unsigned Sears credit cards which had not been issued to him, and which had been mailed some ten months previously to two different addresses on routes that he had served.

b. **Issue:** D claimed at trial that the silver dollar had accidentally fallen out of the envelope, and that he had intended to turn it in as lost property but was arrested before being able to do so. The government sought to introduce the credit cards and evidence about where and when they had been mailed. This evidence was intended to suggest that because D had unlawfully kept the credit cards for ten months knowing that they were probably stolen from the mails, D's assertion that he planned to turn in the silver dollar was unlikely to be true. (The government did not attempt to prove that D himself had stolen the cards.) Thus, the extrinsic evidence (unlawful possession of the cards) was, the government asserted, directly relevant to D's unlawful intent concerning the silver dollar. The trial judge admitted the evidence.

c. **Trial court upheld:** The Fifth Circuit, *en banc*, agreed with the trial judge that the evidence was correctly admitted. This decision reversed a prior 3-judge panel's decision that had held that extrinsic evidence could only be admitted where: (1) the main **physical elements** of the other crime and the main physical elements of the act charged were the **same**; and (2) each physical element of the other crime was established by "plain, clear, and convincing evidence." Instead, the court *en banc* instituted a new two-step test, which will usually be easier for the proponent of the extrinsic evidence to satisfy: (1) the extrinsic evidence must be "relevant to an issue other than the defendant's character"; and (2) the evidence must "possess probative value that is not substantially outweighed by its undue prejudice or the other countervailing considerations of Rule 403." The physical elements of the other crime and the crime charged need not be identical, or even similar, under this new test.

d. **Evidence admissible:** In concluding that the evidence here satisfied this new two-step test, the court reasoned as follows:

   i. **Step One:** Step One was satisfied because the credit card evidence was relevant to D's intent with respect to the silver dollar — if D possessed the cards with illicit intent, this would diminish the likelihood that at the same moment he intended to turn in the silver dollar.

   ii. **Step Two:** As for Step Two, the balancing of the card evidence's probative value against its prejudicial or other countervailing impact came out in favor of admission: (1) On the "probative" side of the balance, D's state of mind in holding the cards was not only a major, but virtually the only contested fact in the case. Without the credit card evidence, the government's case on intent was weak, since the resolution of that issue would have turned solely upon the jury's belief in the credibility of opposing witnesses. The other crime (possession of the cards) and the charged crime were sufficiently similar that D's intent in possessing the cards was strongly probative of his intent with respect to the coin, since both crimes involved possession of items which the defendant knew to belong to others (even if the jury did not believe that the cards, like the coin, were stolen from the mail). Also, the probative value of the cards was enhanced because the two wrongful possessions overlapped in time: D's continued wrongful possession of the cards meant that his "state of mind with respect to the . . . cards continued through his arrest. He maintained contemporaneously the wrongful intent with respect to the cards and the intent as regards the coin." (2) On the "prejudice" side of the balance, the other-crimes evidence here was "not of a heinous nature; it would hardly incite the jury to irrational decision by its force on human emotion."

e. **Dissent:** A dissent in *Beechum* forcefully argued that the majority was replacing a good test with a much worse one. The dissenters especially objected to the fact that the majority's test requires the trier of fact to evaluate the relevancy of the extrinsic offense by determining whether the defendant "indulg[ed] himself in the ***same state of mind*** in the perpetration of both the extrinsic and charged offenses." The dissenters did not know how one could answer this question; for instance, if a person "snatches a purse, cheats on his income taxes, and then steals a coin from the mail," the dissenters asked, is he "indulging himself in the same state of mind" in perpetrating these three offenses? Arguably, the answer is "yes," since he intends to possess property rightfully belonging to another. Yet the crimes seem very different from each other, and a wrongful intent as to one could indicate relatively little about the nature of the intent as to the others. In preference to this "Freudian and ill-defined type of psycho-analysis," the dissenters preferred the earlier test (rejected by the majority), which relied upon comparison of the physical elements of the two crimes.

I. **Abnormal sex:** Other-crimes evidence may be used to show a "passion or propensity for unusual and abnormal ***sexual relations***." M, p. 560.

1. **Same victim:** Where the other sex crimes are with the ***same victim*** as the crime charged, most courts have been willing to admit the other crimes.

2. **Different victim:** But where the other crimes are with a ***different victim*** than the crime charged, courts are generally stricter. Some courts that allow same-victim evidence completely exclude different-victim crimes. Others allow it, but only where the surrounding circumstances give reassurance that the other-crimes evidence is not fabricated. For instance, in *State v. Spreigl*, 139 N.W.2d 167 (Minn. 1965), an incest case in which D was charged with taking liberties with his eleven-year-old stepdaughter, the trial court permitted a younger stepdaughter and a younger stepson to testify that D had forced each of them to take part in similar acts. While the

appellate court's decision to remand for a new trial was motivated mostly by the unfairness to D of the prosecutor's failure to warn D of the other children's testimony, the court was clearly influenced by the lack of probative value of the other children's testimony: all three children lived in the same house with their mother, so "the opportunity for suggestion and for influencing their testimony was great"; also, neither of the other victims complained either to their mother or anyone else until after the act charged.

3. **Rationale for exception:** It is not clear why there should be a special exception to the rule against other-crimes evidence, that applies only to abnormal sexual relations. In theory, the exception is based on a theory that sex offenders are more likely than other types of criminals to be recidivists. But the whole idea behind the ban on the use of other crimes as evidence of character is that the prosecution is not permitted to make the argument that "because the defendant has committed other crimes in the past, he's more likely to be guilty of the present charge than had he not committed the other crimes." The other-sex-crimes exception seems to invite the prosecution to make exactly this forbidden argument.

J. **Knowledge:** Other-crimes evidence may be used to show, by similar acts, that the act in question "was *not performed inadvertently,* accidentally, involuntarily, or without guilty knowledge." M, p. 561.

1. **Similar to intent:** The line between other-crimes evidence used to prove intent (*supra*, p. 26) and other-crimes evidence used to prove knowledge is often a very blurry one. Where the other crimes are used to rebut the defendant's claim that he was unaware that a criminal act was taking place, the distinction is usually meaningless. But the exception is quite distinct in those situations where knowledge is *statutorily* made an *essential element* of the offense.

   Example: D is prosecuted for knowingly receiving stolen goods (blank video cassette tapes). D, who bought the tapes from one Wesby, claims that he did not know they were stolen. The prosecution offers evidence showing that on prior and subsequent occasions, D bought other stolen goods from Wesby, thus suggesting that D must have known that the tapes were stolen. This evidence of other possessions will be admitted, since it tends to prove knowledge, an element of the offense. See *Huddleston v. U.S.*, 485 U.S. 681 (1988), in which the Supreme Court affirmed D's conviction based in part on this evidence.

K. **Motive:** Other-crimes evidence may be used to establish *motive*. Since motive itself is never an essential element of a crime, the use of other-crimes evidence to establish motive is always part of a chain of reasoning. Thus the proof of motive may be probative either of conduct (did D commit the act charged? — if D had a motive to do so, it is more likely that he did the act than if he had no motive) or of intent (given that D did the act, did he do so intentionally, purposefully, maliciously, etc.?)

   Example: D is charged with car theft. The prosecution offers evidence that, two weeks before the theft, D had escaped from a jail 80 miles away. *Held*, the evidence of D's jail escape was relevant to show that he had a motive for stealing the car (and thus that he was more likely to have stolen the car than if he had had no motive to do so). *U.S. v. Stover*, 565 F.2d 1010 (8th Cir. 1977).

L. Opportunity: Other-crimes evidence may be used to establish ***opportunity*** to commit the crime. Usually, this exception will be used to show that the defendant had access to the scene of the crime, or was present at the scene at the time of the crime. It may also apply where the other-crimes evidence shows that the defendant had special skills or abilities used in committing the crime charged.

> **Example:** On the facts of *Stover*, *supra*, if D claimed that he could not have committed the car theft because he was in prison at the time, the prosecution would have been allowed to show evidence of the prison escape (a prior crime) in order to show that D had access to the place where the car was stolen. Furthermore, if D's prison sentence had been for car theft, and at the prior car theft trial the prosecution had shown that D knew how to pick an automobile lock, this could be used as evidence that D had special technical car-thieving ability which he could have used in the theft charged.

M. Identity: Other-crimes evidence may be used to prove ***identity***.

1. **Must be issue:** This exception can only apply, of course, where the identity of the person who committed a particular act is truly ***in issue***. Thus if the defendant admits that it was he who performed certain conduct (e.g., a shooting), and the only issue is the defendant's state of mind, other-crimes evidence suggesting that the act charged must have been the work of the defendant will not be admissible because it would be irrelevant.

2. **Relation to other exceptions:** Generally, the other-crimes evidence will be relevant to identity only indirectly, through one of the other exceptions. For instance, the other crime and the crime charged may both bear the same clear "signature," i.e., reflect the same unusual *modus operandi* (*supra*, p. 25). If there is evidence establishing that the person who committed the other crime was D, the other crime will suggest that the perpetrator of the crime charged was also D. Similarly, other-crimes evidence that shows a common plan or scheme (*supra*, p. 24) will tend to establish that the crime charged was done by the same person who carried out other parts of the common plan.

> **Example:** D is charged with forgery. The state attempts to prove that D received one of a number of blank checks stolen from the General Roofing Company, that he made it payable to one Harold Camden, and that he used it to purchase groceries. This check is introduced as exhibit A. The prosecution then offers exhibits B, D, and F, each of them a check drawn on the account of and signed by one Arthur Martin; for each of the checks, the state produces a different witness who testifies that D was the person who passed the check at the witness' store. D then offers, as exhibits 1 and 2, two additional forged checks, each drawn on the General Roofing Company account, together with testimony from two witnesses that D was *not* the person who passed exhibits 1 and 2. The trial court refuses to allow introduction of exhibits 1 and 2, and D is convicted.

Held (on appeal), D is entitled to a new trial, because exhibits 1 and 2 should have been admitted. Exhibits B, D, and F were properly admitted, on the theory that they appeared to be part of a common scheme or plan carried out by D, and thus indicated that D was also the person who passed exhibit A. But given this, "[T]here appears to us no good reason why an opposite inference that [D] was not the person who offered exhibit A is not permissible from a showing that checks identical to exhibit A [i.e., exhibits 1 and 2] were offered or passed on the same day and in a like manner by someone other than [D]. . . . [Where] the state has introduced evidence of other crimes to establish identity, the defendant is entitled to rebut the inference that might be drawn therefrom by showing that the crimes have been committed by someone else." *State v. Bock*, 39 N.W.2d 887 (Minn. 1949).

Note: *Bock* is a striking example of how decisions on the admissibility of evidence can alter the outcome of a trial. While it cannot be ascertained whether D was ever retried, a person reading the appellate decision is left with the moral certainty that D was the victim of a false identification. After the trial, but before the appeal, one Roland Miller pled guilty to a different forgery charge; D submitted an affidavit of Miller in which Miller said that it was he who had passed exhibits B, D, and F. Since the eyewitnesses who said that D was the one who passed B, D, and F were almost certainly wrong, and since exhibits 1 and 2 (as to which D would have presented exculpatory eyewitness testimony) were far more like the all-important exhibit A than were exhibits B, D, and F, it is hard to believe that the prosecutor would have stood a chance had exhibits 1 and 2, the eyewitness testimony absolving D of passing them, and the Miller affidavit, all been allowed into evidence.

N. Impeachment: Other-crimes evidence may be used to ***impeach*** an accused who takes the stand, by showing a prior conviction. In this situation, the evidence is being used not to prove directly that the defendant is guilty of the crime charged, but rather, to suggest that because he is a convicted criminal, his credibility as a witness is suspect. The use of criminal convictions to impeach an accused on the witness stand is discussed extensively *infra*, p. 81.

O. Other exceptions: Under the Federal Rules approach, as noted, a piece of other-crimes evidence does not have to fit into an enumerated "slot" to be admissible; the categories enumerated in FRE 404(b) ("proof of motive, opportunity, intent, preparation . . . ") are intended to be illustrative rather than exhaustive. The point is that the evidence must relate to some ***particular element*** of the crime charged, and must not be offered solely to suggest that because the accused had certain criminal traits, he probably acted in conformity with those traits on the occasion at issue. Two examples will hint at the virtually infinite variety of fact patterns, and underlying issues, for which other-crimes evidence may be admissible, even where none of the defined categories above is applicable:

Example 1: D is charged with a narcotics violation. The prosecution offers evidence that D has been convicted in state court of murdering one Ellis, who was to have been the government's principal witness in the narcotics case; the government also offers evidence that prior to the murder, D learned that Ellis was an informer against him. *Held*, these pieces of evidence are admissible, since "an inference may arise therefrom of an admission of guilt or an act inconsistent with the innocence of the defendant [on the narcotics charges]." *U.S. v. Howard*, 228 F.Supp. 939 (D.Neb. 1964).

Example 2: D is charged with the first degree murder of her 8-month-old foster child, Paul, who died after a number of cyanotic attacks. The prosecution offers expert testimony, based on autopsy and hospital records, that Paul was smothered to death. The prosecution then offers evidence that over a 23-year period, nine other children had experienced cyanotic attacks while under D's care, five of whom died.

Held, the evidence concerning the other children's attacks is admissible. None of the well-defined exceptions is precisely applicable — the "signature" exception is most nearly applicable, but D's argument that cyanosis among infants is "too common to constitute an unusual and distinctive device unerringly pointing to guilt on [D's] part" has some merit. However, the evidence is admissible under a broader, less mechanistic, approach than the mere fitting of evidence into a previously recognized exception. "[E]vidence of other offenses may be received, if relevant, for any purpose other than to show a mere propensity or disposition on the part of the defendant to commit the crime, provided that the trial judge may exclude the evidence if its probative value is outweighed by the risk that its admission will create a substantial danger of undue prejudice to the accused." Here, the possibility that so many infants would suffer cyanotic episodes without D's being at fault is so remote, and the unmistakable pattern so clear, that the evidence must be admitted. *U.S. v. Woods*, 484 F.2d 127 (4th Cir. 1973).

P. Other aspects: Even where the other-crimes evidence fits within one of the categories discussed above, other issues may arise. Here are a few:

1. Degree of certainty: Must the other crime have led to a *conviction*, and thus have been proved beyond a reasonable doubt? The answer is ***"no."***

    a. "Substantial" evidence: Virtually no courts require that the defendant have been convicted of the other crime. However, it may not be enough that the prosecution in the present case merely presents some evidence that the defendant committed the other crime — some courts require that evidence of the defendant's guilt in the other crime be ***"substantial"*** or ***"clear and convincing."*** See *Tucker v. State*, 412 P.2d 970 (Nev. 1966). (Before evidence of a collateral offense is admissible for any purpose, the prosecution must first establish by "plain, clear and convincing evidence" that the defendant committed that offense; here, there was no proof of this, only "conjecture and suspicion.")

        i. Federal standard: But under the Federal Rules, the evidence of the defendant's guilt in the other crime can be given to the jury even though that other crime has ***not*** been proved by a preponderance of the evidence (let alone by "clear and convincing" evidence). In *Huddleston v. U.S.*, 485 U.S. 681 (1988), the Supreme Court held that all that FRE 404(b) requires is that the evidence of the other crime be strong enough that the jury could *"reasonably find"* that the other crime was committed by D. Thus in *Huddleston*, the evidence of the other crime (D's knowing purchase of stolen T.V. sets from X) was properly admitted on the issue of whether D knew that blank tapes he bought from X were stolen — the low price of the televisions, the large quantity D had for sale, and D's inability to produce a bill of sale, coupled with D's involvement in still other purchases of stolen goods from X, were enough to allow a reasonable jury to conclude that D knew the T.V. sets were stolen, and therefore, enough to let the jury consider this other-crimes evidence.

b. Acquittal: Suppose the accused was tried and *acquitted* of the other crime. Should this acquittal by itself make the evidence of that crime inadmissible?

   i. Pros and cons: There are strong arguments on either side of this question. Against admission, it can be argued that admission causes the defendant, as a practical matter, to "defend against the same charge a second time . . . raising policy concerns that are related to those underlying collateral estoppel and the prohibition against double jeopardy. . . ." Lilly, p. 151. In favor of admission, it can be pointed out that acquittal in a criminal case means only that the finder of fact concluded that there was a reasonable doubt as to the existence of one or more essential elements of the offense; thus an acquittal is not inconsistent with the existence of "substantial" or even "clear and convincing" evidence of guilt.

   ii. Split decisions: Paralleling these opposing arguments, courts are split on whether to allow other-crimes evidence where there was an acquittal. Probably a majority will *not automatically bar* the evidence in such cases. Lilly, p. 151. Contrast *People v. Massey*, 16 Cal. Rptr. 402 (Cal. Dist. Ct. App. 1961) (allowing the evidence) with *State v. Little*, 350 P.2d 756 (Ariz. 1960) (barring it on the grounds that "a verdict of acquittal should relieve the defendant from having to answer again, at the price of conviction for that crime or another, evidence which amounts to a charge of a crime of which he has been acquitted.")

   iii. No constitutional problem: There is *no constitutional problem* with receiving other-crimes evidence where there was an acquittal. The Supreme Court has held that neither the Double Jeopardy Clause nor the Due Process Clause prevents the prosecution from putting on such evidence. *Dowling v. U.S.*, 493 U.S. 342 (1990).

   iv. Pattern: The case for allowing other-crimes evidence despite an earlier acquittal is strongest where the proof of guilt is *cumulative*. Recall, for instance, *U.S. v. Woods, supra*, p. 32, in which it was shown that the victim was the ninth child entrusted to D's care to have suffered a cyanotic attack. Suppose that when the first of these children died, D had been prosecuted and acquitted. A reasonable doubt may have existed at the time of this first death; but when the death is viewed in the light of eight subsequent similar deaths, the doubt is far less — therefore, it does not seem unfair to allow introduction of the first death.

2. **Genuine controversy:** The other-crimes evidence will be admissible only if it bears upon some issue that is the subject of a ***genuine controversy***. M, p. 564.

> **Example:** D is charged with possession of heroin with intent to distribute it. The government's main witness, a DEA agent, testifies that D had the heroin in a bag in his pocket, and threw the bag into a crowd (from which it was never recovered) as the agent arrested D. The government seeks to introduce evidence that D was previously convicted of selling heroin.
>
> *Held*, the prior conviction should not have been introduced, because there was no disputed issue to which it was relevant. It is true that the conviction would have been relevant to the issue of whether the substance in the bag was heroin or was, rather, coffee grinds (as D's co-defendants urged). But D's lawyer made it clear that D's defense was that the episode recounted by the DEA agent never happened, not that the bag contained something other than heroin. The prior conviction was totally irrelevant to this contention. *U.S. v. Figueroa*, 618 F.2d 934 (2d Cir. 1980).

3. **Subsequent acts:** Thus far, we have assumed that the "other crimes" sought to be introduced are ones which occurred before the crime currently charged. While most of the time this will indeed be the case, it is not necessarily so: the same principles apply to determine the admissibility of criminal acts that took place ***after*** the acts charged.

> **Example:** D (Patty Hearst) is charged with participating in a bank robbery committed by a terrorist group. The prosecution anticipates that, since D was originally held for ransom by the group, she will assert the defense of duress. The prosecution, therefore, introduces evidence of other criminal acts committed by D *after the bank robbery,* to counteract the duress defense. *Held*, these subsequent crimes were properly admitted. *U.S. v. Hearst*, 563 F.2d 1331 (9th Cir. 1977).

4. **Balancing:** Even where the other-crimes evidence bears directly on some element of the crime charged, it is not automatically admissible. The judge is still required to ***balance*** the probative value of that evidence against the disadvantages of allowing it. Under the Federal Rules, this is the same kind of balancing that is required for *any* relevant evidence pursuant to FRE 403. But there are some special factors that courts normally consider in the other-crimes context. These include: (1) the ***strength*** of the other-crimes evidence; (2) the degree of ***similarity*** between the other crime and the crime charged; (3) the ***interval of time*** between the two crimes; (4) the strength of the prosecution's ***need*** for the evidence coupled with the availability of ***alternative*** evidence on the same issue; and (5) the extent to which the evidence will rouse the jury to ***unfair prejudice***. See M, p. 565.

> **Example:** D is charged with selling heroin to an undercover agent. D asserts the defense of entrapment, and the prosecution counters by trying to show that D was predisposed to commit the offense. It does this by putting on the stand a narcotics officer who testifies that nine months prior to D's arrest, the agent saw D sell heroin to other addicts, but that no arrest was made.

Held (on appeal), the evidence of the prior sale should not have been admitted. While it was relevant to the issue of predisposition and hence entrapment, its probative value was outweighed by countervailing considerations. Because there was only one alleged incident, with no arrest, no official report of the incident by the agent, and no corroborating witnesses, the evidence was extremely weak. Furthermore, D had no opportunity to combat it except by his own unsupported testimony placed against the agent's word. Thus the possibility for unfair prejudice to D outweighed the evidence's value. *Hansford v. U.S.*, 303 F.2d 219 (D.C.Cir. 1962).

5. **Procedure:** Two ***procedural*** issues are specific to the problem of other-crimes evidence:

   a. **Notice:** To what extent must the prosecutor give the defendant ***advance notice*** of its intent to use other-crimes evidence at the trial? In general, most courts have answered that ***no*** advance notice at all is needed. In this view, other-crimes evidence is like any other evidence, and is simply introduced at a convenient time, either as part of the prosecution's case in chief (e.g., by entering into evidence an official document proving a prior conviction — see *infra*, p. 221 — or by using witnesses who have knowledge of the prior crime) or on cross-examination of the defendant during the defense case (e.g., "Have you ever been convicted of . . . ?")

      i. **Unfairness:** However, absence of any advance notice can ***unfairly surprise*** the defendant. This is especially true where the other-crimes evidence relates not to prior convictions, or even prior prosecutions, but rather to episodes in which the defendant was never prosecuted. A defendant in a narcotics sale case, for instance, is quite unfairly surprised if the prosecution suddenly introduces evidence by an undercover agent that the agent saw the defendant on a prior occasion make a sale of narcotics but that no charges were ever filed. Therefore, some courts have required advance notice before other-crimes evidence may be used, at least in those instances where there was no prior prosecution. See, e.g., *State v. Spreigl*, 139 N.W.2d 167 (Minn. 1965), requiring such notice to be given "within a reasonable time before trial. . . ." Failing such an advance notice rule, the court should at least grant a ***continuance*** to give the defendant time to combat unexpected other-crimes evidence.

   b. **Limiting instruction:** Whenever other-crimes evidence is admitted, it is never for the purpose of showing that the defendant has a propensity for criminal conduct and probably acted in conformity with that propensity. (See *supra*, p. 22.) Yet if the evidence is admitted for some other reason (i.e., it bears directly on some element of the crime), the jury may nonetheless ***use it*** for precisely the prohibited reason. How can such use be discouraged? Trial judges will often give a ***"limiting instruction"*** to the jury guiding them in the purpose for which the evidence may be used.

      Example: Recall the facts of *U.S. v. Beechum*, *supra*, pp. 26-28, involving the postal worker charged with rifling the mails. Either before allowing the evidence that the postal worker had possessed credit cards not issued to him or as part of the judge's charge to the jury, the judge might issue a limiting instruction along the following lines: "You are to consider the evidence regarding D's possession of the credit cards only for the purpose for determining D's state of mind regarding the coin; you are not to assume that because a person has acted unlawfully on one occasion, he is a 'bad person' or is more likely to have behaved criminally on another occasion."

    i. Request by defendant: If the defendant's counsel requests such a limiting instruction, the judge's refusal to give it may well be held to be ***reversible error***. W&B, Par. 404[19].

    ii. Probably useless: However, there is reason to doubt the efficacy of limiting instructions both generally and as to other-crimes evidence. One study has concluded that "[J]urors have an almost universal inability and/or unwillingness either to understand or follow the court's instruction on the use of a defendant's prior criminal record for impeachment purposes. The jurors almost universally used defendant's record to conclude that he was a bad man and hence was more likely than not guilty of the crime for which he was then standing trial." L&S, p. 220, n. 54.

VI.   EVIDENCE OF CRIMINAL DEFENDANT'S GOOD CHARACTER

A. General rule: Recall that as a general rule, evidence of a person's character is not admissible for the purpose of proving that he acted in conformance with that character. The rule against other-crimes evidence, discussed above, is one application of this general rule. It might, therefore, be supposed that a ***defendant*** in a criminal trial would not be permitted to give evidence of his ***good character*** for the purpose of showing that it is unlikely he committed the crime for which he is charged. However, in fact such evidence ***is allowed by all courts***.

> **Example:** D is charged with murdering a business rival. He calls a witness to testify that D has a well-established reputation in the community for being a peaceful and kind soul. Assuming that a proper foundation for the testimony is laid (i.e., that the witness discloses a basis for knowing about D's reputation in the community), all courts will accept the testimony. See, e.g., *People v. Van Gaasbeck*, 82 N.E. 718 (N.Y. 1907).

    1. Rationale: The principal rationale for allowing the defendant to offer favorable evidence about his character, in the face of the general exclusion of other types of "conformity with character" evidence, is that in the former situation there is (of course) ***no prejudice to the defendant***. Therefore, whereas evidence that the defendant has committed similar crimes in the past is excluded in large part because of such evidence's unfairness to the defendant, this factor is not present in the character-evidence-favorable-to-the-defendant situation. Once this prejudice is removed, in theory the probative value of the evidence outweighs the disadvantages of allowing its admission.

a. **Prejudice in favor of defendant:** Indeed, such evidence may unfairly prejudice the jury *in favor of* the defendant, since the jury's "regret at mistakenly convicting an innocent defendant of good character is likely to be quite high, while their regret at mistakenly acquitting a guilty defendant is likely to be less than it would otherwise be." L&S, p. 237 (suggesting that allowing such evidence may be unwise, since "the ability to get strong character witnesses does not necessarily guarantee that one's previous life has been exemplary." *Id.*)

2. **Relevance:** The admissibility of such character evidence is not restricted to "general character" (e.g., the trait of being law-abiding). It also applies to particular, possibly *narrow*, character traits. However, the trait on which evidence is offered must be *relevant to the crime charged*.

> **Example:** D is charged with murder. He will be permitted to show that he has a reputation for being peaceable. But he will not be permitted to show that he has a reputation for being *truthful*, since the trait of truthfulness is irrelevant to the issue of guilt or innocence of murder. Conversely, if D were charged with embezzlement, he would be permitted to show that he has a reputation for truthfulness, but not that he has one for peaceableness. M, p. 567.

B. **Method of proof:** The fact that the defendant may put on evidence of a favorable and relevant character trait does not mean that all types of evidence bearing on that trait are admissible. The common-law rule, probably still in force in most states, is that *only "reputation" evidence may be admitted*. That is, witnesses may testify that the defendant has a reputation for a certain favorable trait, but they may not state *their own opinion* that he has the trait, nor may they cite *specific incidents* demonstrating that he has that trait. See, e.g., *People v. Van Gaasbeck*, 82 N.E. 718 (N.Y. 1907); Lilly, p. 132.

1. **Rationale:** The rationale for barring witnesses from reciting specific acts or incidents showing the defendant's favorable character trait is clear: such testimony would be voluminous, and it would be nearly impossible for the prosecution to disprove. The rationale for barring witnesses from expressing their own opinion that the defendant possesses a certain trait is less clear. It has been argued that such testimony must be barred precisely because once it is allowed, the witness "cannot logically be prohibited from stating the particular incidents . . . which have led him to his favorable conclusion," which presents the evils just mentioned. *People v. Van Gaasbeck, supra.*

a. **Contrasting view:** Virtually no one quarrels with the bar to specific-acts evidence. But there is much dispute about the wisdom of barring opinion testimony. Wigmore, for instance, asks whether the jury is helped "more by the witnesses whose personal intimacy gives to their belief a first and highest value, or by those who merely repeat a form of words in which the term 'reputation' occurs?" 7 Wigmore §1986, at 166.

2. **Federal Rules:** The Federal Rules ***allow*** the witness to state his **opinion** that the defendant possesses the favorable character trait. FRE 405(a) provides that "in all cases in which evidence of character or a trait of character of a person is admissible, proof may be made by testimony as to reputation or by testimony **in the form of an opinion.**" But even this liberalized rule does ***not*** allow the witness to give evidence of **specific incidents.** M, p. 568.

3. **Other communities:** When reputation (as opposed to opinion) evidence is allowed, the reputation being referred to has traditionally been that of the defendant in the **community in which he lives.** If the defendant lives in a small town, where everybody knows pretty much everybody else, the concept of a "community reputation" still has some validity. But with the increasing urbanization of our society, most defendants will be unknown to the community at large. Therefore, most courts now allow proof of the defendant's reputation in any substantial group where he is well known. In particular, a defendant's reputation at his **place of employment** is generally admissible. M, p. 568.

C. **Rebuttal by prosecution:** The defendant's right to offer favorable character evidence sounds like a key advantage which would be frequently exercised. However, in order to keep this advantage from being unduly great, the prosecution is given two means of **counteracting** it: (1) if defense witnesses testify that the defendant's reputation is good, the prosecution may then put on witnesses who say it is **bad**; and (2) the defense character witnesses may not only be cross-examined, but they may be asked about **specific instances** of bad conduct. L&S, p. 241. The second of these is by far the more important.

1. **Character "in issue":** Judges and lawyers sometimes say that the reason that the prosecution is permitted to introduce evidence of bad conduct in this situation is that the defendant, by putting on his character evidence, has "put his character in issue." However, this is a misleading expression — the defendant's character is not "in issue" in the sense that it now becomes an essential element of the crime. Instead, all the phrase "places his character in issue" means is that the prosecution is free to counter the defendant's good-character evidence with bad-character evidence.

2. **Cross-examination of defendant's witness:** In states following the common-law rule that only reputation evidence, not opinion evidence, may be given by the defendant's character witnesses, the prosecution's cross-examination is similarly limited. That is, if the cross-examiner wishes to impeach the witness by calling attention to some specific bad conduct by the defendant, he may not ask, "Do you know that D was convicted of . . . ?" Instead, he must ask, "**Have you heard** that D was convicted of . . . ?"

   a. **Rationale:** The rationale for this rule is that only things which go to reputation may be inquired into — the witness might know of the act even though the community as a whole does not (in which case the act would be irrelevant to reputation). Questions of the form, "Have you heard . . . ?" are appropriate because either: (1) the witness has heard reports about the defendant's bad act, in which case his truthfulness or accuracy as a witness are suspect in light of his statement that D's reputation is good; or (2) the witness has not heard the reports, in which case his claim to be knowledgeable about D's reputation is suspect, if the bad act is of a sort that would normally be known and would lead to a bad reputation. *Id.*

    i. Unfounded rumors: Under this theory, even an ***untruthful rumor*** should logically be relevant and therefore a valid subject of cross-examination — after all, an untruthful rumor may influence the defendant's reputation just as much as a truthful one. However, because the use of an unfounded rumor in cross-examination is so clearly and hugely prejudicial to the defendant, "most courts require that the prosecutor have a ***good faith belief*** that the defendant has ***committed the act alleged*** before propounding such questions." L&S, p. 242.

    ii. Outside of jury: Procedurally, the way this good-faith requirement is carried out is that, before the prosecutor asks the question regarding the specific act, he should, outside the presence of the jury, ***disclose to the judge*** his reason for believing in good faith that the defendant committed the act in question. The judge will then make a ruling about whether the question may be asked. If the prosecutor does not make this side-bar showing, he runs the risk that either there will be a mistrial, or a resulting guilty verdict will be reversed on appeal.

b. Opinion testimony: Similarly, a witness who gives favorable ***opinion*** testimony about the defendant's character may be cross-examined by the prosecution. Here, the questions are usually of the "Did you know?" rather than "Have you heard?" variety. Lilly, p. 138. FRE 405(a), recognizing that either reputation or opinion evidence is allowed, does not specify the format to be taken by questions on cross-examination. Instead, the rule simply provides that "on cross-examination, inquiry is allowed into relevant specific instances of conduct."

c. Scope of questioning: Not all bad acts believed to have been committed by the defendant may the subject of cross-examination of the character witness. Rather, only bad acts that relate to the ***specific character traits*** testified to by the witness may be mentioned.

    Example: W testifies, on behalf of D, that D has a reputation for peaceableness. On cross-examination, the prosecution may not ask whether W has heard that D was once convicted of embezzlement, since embezzlement does not bear on the trait of peaceableness. L&S, p. 242.

d. Arrest without conviction: Suppose the "bad act" referred to on cross-examination is a criminal act that led to the defendant's arrest, but ***not*** to a conviction. May the act be referred to on cross-examination? The answer of most courts appears to be ***"yes,"*** assuming that there is evidence that the arrest really took place, and assuming that the crime alleged bears upon the character trait as to which the character witness has testified.

i. *Michelson* case: The leading case on this issue is *Michelson v. U.S.*, 335 U.S. 469 (1948), in which the Supreme Court allowed the arrest to be mentioned on cross-examination. In 1947, D was tried for, and convicted of, bribing a federal revenue agent. D claimed that he was entrapped by the agent. D put on five character witnesses, all of whom testified either that D had a good reputation for honesty and law-abidance or that he did not have a bad reputation. Each of these witnesses was asked by the prosecution "Did you ever hear that [in 1920, D] was arrested for receiving stolen goods?" The question was proper, the Supreme Court held, because "reports of [D's] arrest for receiving stolen goods, if admitted, would tend to weaken the assertion that he was known as an honest and law-abiding citizen." It was irrelevant that the alleged receipt of stolen goods was a different crime from the bribery crime being tried — what was relevant was the character trait(s) for which the witness was giving reputation testimony, not the character traits involved in the crime being tried.

ii. Age of arrest: The Supreme Court was clearly troubled by the fact that the arrest referred to took place twenty-seven years before the trial. But while such an old arrest might shed "little light on the present reputation and hence propensities of the defendant," the Court could not conclude that its admission was an abuse of discretion.

e. No extrinsic evidence: Suppose the prosecutor, in cross examining the defendant's character witness, asks a question of the "Have you heard . . . ?" sort. If the witness denies that he has heard of the act in question, *the issue is at an end.* The prosecutor may not put on a witness to show that the act took place. Conversely, "neither the questioned witness nor the accused may attempt to erase the damaging inference of the question by proving the nonexistence of the arrest or any such rumors. Additional inquiry into this collateral subject is considered not worth the impairment of judicial expedition and efficiency." Lilly, p. 137. For this reason, the prosecutor's good faith is doubly important in this situation. (See the discussion of the "collateral issue" rule *infra*, p. 102.)

VII. CHARACTER OF VICTIM, ESPECIALLY IN CASES OF ASSAULT, MURDER, AND RAPE

A. Problem generally: The general rule forbidding character evidence to show that a person behaved in conformity with his character would prevent a criminal defendant from showing quite relevant evidence about the character of his *victim*. Therefore, special rules have evolved to allow the defendant to introduce evidence about the character of his victim in two recurring situations: (1) where a defendant charged with murder or assault claims *self-defense*, and wants to show that the victim's propensity for violence makes it more likely that the victim, not the defendant, was the first aggressor; and (2) where a defendant charged with rape wants to show the victim's *previous sexual history*, usually for the purpose of showing that her previous unchastity supports the defendant's defense of consent. We consider each of these special situations in turn.

B. Murder and assault victims: In homicide and assault cases in which the defendant claims that the victim was the first aggressor, virtually all jurisdictions **allow** the defendant to introduce evidence that the victim had a **violent character**. M, pp. 571-72.

    1. Knowledge unnecessary: This exception applies even where the defendant cannot show that he was **aware** of the victim's violent character.

> **Example:** D is charged with manslaughter in the shooting of V. D admits that he shot V, and testifies that he acted in self-defense when V attacked him with a knife. D attempts to show that V has been convicted of breaching the peace, carrying a dangerous weapon, and assault at various times in the past. D concedes that at the time of the shooting, he was unaware of V's history of violence.
>
> *Held*, it was error to exclude the proof of V's history of violence. If character evidence is offered to show that the deceased was the aggressor, the defendant's knowledge of that character is irrelevant: "[F]or the question is what the deceased probably did, not what the defendant probably thought the deceased was going to do. The inquiry is one of objective occurrence, not of subjective belief." (quoting Wigmore.) *State v. Miranda*, 405 A.2d 622 (Conn. 1978).

> **Note:** There may, however, be cases in which evidence of the victim's character is offered for the purpose of showing that the defendant's belief that he needed to defend himself was a reasonable one. For instance, D's knowledge that V had a reputation for being "quick on the draw" would be admissible for the purpose of showing that D was reasonable in thinking that the situation was "kill or be killed." If the reasonableness of D's belief in the need for self defense is at issue, only a reputation of which D was **aware** will be admissible. But in a *Miranda* situation, the defendant need not be aware of the character for violence, because the issue is, "Who was the aggressor?" not "Was D's belief in the need for self-defense a reasonable one?" Sometimes, of course, evidence of the victim's violent character will be admissible for *both* the "Who was the aggressor?" and "Was the self-defense reasonable?" issues.

    2. Type of evidence: Generally, the evidence offered by the defendant on his victim's character for violence must be **reputation** (or, in some states, opinion) evidence. Evidence of **specific past acts** of violence by the victim is **not** admissible in most jurisdictions. See, e.g., *Government of the Virgin Islands v. Carino*, 631 F.2d 226 (3d Cir. 1980) (past convictions for violent acts by the defendant are not admissible, because evidence of character is limited by FRE 405(a) to opinion and reputation testimony). Observe that the *Miranda* case, *supra*, is apparently an exception to this rule prohibiting proof of specific past violent acts.

    3. Rationale: Allowing evidence of the victim's bad character does not suffer from one problem that evidence of the defendant's bad character suffers: unfair prejudice against the defendant. This helps explain why the former is admissible while the latter is, generally, not. However, victim character evidence does suffer a shortcoming from the standpoint of justice: the jury may conclude that, because the victim was a "bad person," he merely "got what he deserved," and the defendant should therefore be acquitted. M, p. 572. Nonetheless, courts have universally concluded that when the identity of the first aggressor is in doubt, the advantages of evidence of the victim's bad character outweigh its disadvantages. *Id.*

4. **Federal Rules:** The Federal Rules embody this approach. In fact, they extend it to cover *all* pertinent traits of the victim. FRE 404(a)(2) removes from the general character-evidence exclusionary rule "evidence of a ***pertinent trait of character of the victim*** of the crime offered by an accused. . . ."

    a. **Other contexts:** The overwhelming majority of uses of this sentence are in the contexts of murder and assault, where the defendant claims that the victim was the first aggressor. But uses of the rule in other contexts can be imagined. For instance, one writer has speculated that "a defendant accused of bribing a public official might show that the official in question had exhibited the trait of greed or abuse of power in order to advance a defense of extortion. Perhaps a person accused of 'joy riding' might be able to prove the owner's characteristic trait of generosity to support his claim that he was operating the car with the permission of the owner." 130 U. Pa. L. Rev. 845, 856 (quoted in M, pp. 571-72, n. 1).

    b. **Rape and exception:** But there is a critical exception to the broad coverage of FRE 404(a)(2). Evidence of the sexual character of a ***rape victim*** is severely circumscribed by a special rule on that subject, FRE 412, discussed *infra*, p. 44.

5. **Rebuttal by prosecution:** Once the defense has introduced evidence of the victim's character for violence to support the assertion that the victim was the first aggressor, the prosecution then has the right to ***rebut*** this evidence by showing the victim's ***peaceable character***. The prosecution may do this by cross-examining the defendant's reputation (or, where allowed, opinion) witness. Alternatively, it may present its own witnesses who give reputation (or, where allowed, opinion) evidence that the victim was peaceable. Lilly, p. 139.

    a. **Defendant's indirect slur on victim:** Suppose the defendant does not expressly present evidence of the victim's aggressive character, but through the pleadings or the evidence, he attempts to prove that, at least on the occasion in question, the victim was the first aggressor. In this situation, the courts are split about whether the prosecutor may present rebuttal evidence. Traditionally, most courts have allowed defendants to plead self-defense and produce non-character evidence that the victim was the first aggressor, ***without opening the door*** to the prosecution evidence that the victim had a peaceable character. L&S, p. 238, n. 88.

        i. **Federal Rules approach:** The Federal Rules take an approach that, at least traditionally, has been the ***minority*** view. Under FRE 404(a)(2), the general rule of exclusion does not apply to "evidence of a character trait of peacefulness of the victim offered by the prosecution in a homicide case to rebut evidence that the victim was the first aggressor." In support of this rule, it can be argued that in a homicide case, the victim is obviously not around to testify that the defendant was the aggressor; therefore, in the absence of other eyewitnesses, the only way that the prosecution can rebut the defendant's claim about who was the first aggressor is to show the victim's character for peaceableness.

   b. **Prosecution evidence on defendant's character:** Suppose that the defendant has argued the victim's violent character, either explicitly or implicitly (by claiming that the victim was the first aggressor). Has the defendant thereby opened the door to prosecution evidence showing that the ***defendant*** has a violent character? On this issue, too, the courts are split. Those courts that give the prosecution the right to introduce such evidence argue that "in order to make a rational judgment based upon character, the trier needs to know the propensities of both defendant and victim: a direct attack by the accused upon the victim's character should permit counterbalancing evidence of the accused's character." Lilly, p. 141. Courts following the opposite view (that unless the defendant first offers evidence of his own character, the prosecution may not do so) argue that evidence of the defendant's bad character is prejudicial to him, and that it is unfair to require him to submit to such evidence as a condition for his exercise of the right to reveal the victim's violent character. *Id.*

      i. **Federal Rules' approach:** The Federal Rules follow the latter, pro-defendant, approach. Under 404(a)(1), no special relief is given from the general exclusion of character evidence in the case of the accused's character except for "evidence of a pertinent trait of character offered by an accused, or by the prosecution to ***rebut the same***." That is, no special provision entitles the prosecution to rebut evidence of the victim's bad character with evidence of the defendant's bad character.

      ii. **Narrow evidence:** Even in those jurisdictions allowing the prosecution to rebut evidence of the victim's violent character by evidence of the defendant's bad character, the relief is narrowly fitted to the ***particular relevant trait***. Thus the prosecution may show that the defendant has a violent or turbulent character, but not that he is generally a criminal or that he is, say, dishonest. *Id.*

C. **Rape:** In cases of ***rape*** and ***sexual assault***, courts have, until recently, been quick to admit evidence of a victim's "character for ***chastity***." In particular, they have traditionally given the defendant wide latitude to introduce evidence of the victim's ***prior sexual activities*** in cases where the defendant asserts that the woman ***consented.***

   1. **Rationale:** Allowing such evidence was usually justified on one or both of the following theories: (1) that a woman who has been "unchaste" is more likely to have in fact consented than one who is not; and (2) that where a woman had a ***reputation*** for unchastity (whether or not deserved) and that reputation was known to the defendant, this fact bears upon the credibility of his assertion that he believed (even if wrongly) that the woman was consenting.

   2. **Disadvantages:** However, this traditional approach has the terrible effect of allowing the defendant to subject the victim to a great invasion of privacy and

embarrassment — some victims have likened their role in the prosecution of their assailant to being raped a second time.

> **Example:** D is charged with the rape of V. The prosecution shows that D accosted V in the parking lot of a singles bar, spoke to her briefly, and forced her to have sex. At trial, D contends that V "led me on" during their initial conversation, and that he reasonably believed she was consenting to his advances. Under the traditional approach, D would be permitted to cross-examine V at trial, forcing her to disclose the names of any past lovers and the circumstances under which she met them; he could justify the relevance of this questioning on the grounds that if V had sex in the past with men who "picked her up" in places like singles bars, this makes it more likely that she consented, or seemed to consent, to D's advances. D might also be allowed to present the former lovers as witnesses, and to question them on the details of their affairs with V.

3. **"Rape shield" laws:** In recent years, nearly all jurisdictions have enacted some form of *"rape shield"* law. These laws attempt, in sharply differing ways, to channel or limit evidence about the victim's past sexual history. Some of the statutes merely set up special procedures, including notice and a preliminary screening by the judge, before such evidence can be used. Other statutes include substantive limits on the extent to which victims' past sexual behavior may be presented or explored at trial. The laws have withstood constitutional attack. M, pp. 573-74.

   a. **Cases:** A few *cases* have similarly had the effect of furnishing a "rape shield." See, e.g., *State ex rel. Pope v. Superior Court*, 545 P.2d 946 (Ariz. 1976), holding as a matter of common law that the victim's past sexual history will normally no longer be admissible merely because consent is in issue (but not barring such evidence in a number of special circumstances, such as evidence of prior consensual sex with the defendant, evidence that directly refutes physical or scientific evidence such as origin of the semen or disease, and evidence concerning the victim's reputation or profession as a prostitute when offered in support of a defense based on prostitution.)

4. **The federal rape shield provision:** The Federal Rules of Evidence, as initially enacted, did not contain any special rape shield provision. Therefore, evidence of the victim's sexual history and reputation was governed by FRE 404(a)(2)'s allowance of "evidence of a pertinent trait of character of the victim of the crime offered by an accused. . . ." However, in 1978 a special provision, FRE 412, was added governing specifically the "Relevance of Victim's Past Behavior" in rape cases.

   a. **Protective:** FRE 412 "is, from the victim's standpoint, one of the more protective of the rape shield laws that have been enacted." L&S, p. 637.

   b. **Particular provisions:** FRE 412 is long and complex, and its full provisions are beyond the scope of this book. However, its key provisions can be summarized as follows:

   c. **Reputation or opinion evidence:** Evidence relating to the victim's *reputation* for past sexual behavior, and *opinion* testimony about that past behavior, is *absolutely excluded* in federal trials. FRE 412(a). That is, in those comparatively rare instances where, under other provisions of FRE 412, evidence concerning the victim's past sexual behavior is admissible, that evidence must always take the form of proof of *specific acts*. Thus FRE 412 carries out an exact reversal of the usual pattern of general character evidence under the Federal Rules, whereby *only* reputation and opinion testimony, not a showing of specific instances of conduct, may be used. (See FRE 405(a).)

d. **Specific acts evidence:** *Specific acts* evidence concerning the victim's past sexual behavior is also *inadmissible* in federal rape trials, unless it falls into one of three categories:

　i. **Constitutional requirement:** The evidence is *constitutionally required* to be admitted (FRE 412(b)(1));

　ii. **Source of semen or injury:** The evidence concerns the victim's past sexual behavior with persons other than the accused, offered by the accused on the issue of whether the accused was *"the source of semen or injury"* (FRE 412(b)(2)(A)); and

　iii. **Consent:** The evidence relates to the victim's past sexual behavior *with the accused*, and is offered on the issue of whether the victim *consented*. (FRE 412(b)(2)(B))

e. **Exclusions:** Most significantly, FRE 412 *prevents the defendant from introducing evidence of the victim's past sexual behavior with persons other than himself, when offered on the issue of whether there was consent.* Thus on the facts of the example on p. 44 *supra*, D would not, in a federal trial, be permitted to ask questions about V's past relationships with others, or to put those others on the stand.

f. **Procedural rules:** FRE 412, like most rape shield statutes, imposes strict rules governing the *procedures* that must be followed before a victim's past sexual behavior may be admitted in those circumstances where admission is substantively permitted. Highlights of the procedures include:

　i. **Notice:** The accused give *prior notice* of his intent to use such evidence. He must make a written motion saying that he wants to introduce such evidence, and the motion must be filed at least fifteen days before the trial date (unless the evidence is newly discovered or the issue has newly arisen in the case). FRE 412(c)(1). At the same time, the defendant must submit a written "offer of proof" (see *supra*, p. 6). FRE 412(c)(2).

　ii. **Hearing:** The court then conducts a hearing in chambers to determine the admissibility of the evidence. This hearing may include inquiry into whether any "condition of fact" needs to be fulfilled (see *infra*, p. 456) before the evidence becomes admissible. For instance, if the defendant denies that he was the source of semen found in the victim, and contends that the semen found belonged to the victim's boyfriend, X, the judge would probably have to make some preliminary determination about whether the semen found in the victim and X's semen matched up. FRE 412(c)(2).

   iii. Balancing: Even if the judge concludes that the evidence falls within one of the exceptions in 412(b), he may not admit it unless he concludes that it is relevant and that "the probative value of such evidence outweighs the danger of unfair prejudice. . . ." The judge must then issue an order specifying what evidence may be offered and which areas may be the subject of a physical examination or cross-examination of the victim. FRE 412(c)(3).

g. Possible constitutional problems: No one has so far successfully challenged any part of FRE 412 on constitutional grounds. However, a number of *constitutional questions* about the Rule arise. Here are two of the more interesting:

   i. Reputation: Recall that under FRE 412(a), the victim's reputation for sexual behavior will *never* be admissible. In cases where the victim's reputation is relevant to the issue of whether the victim consented, exclusion of that evidence might be unconstitutional.

   Example: D and V, two college students, are engaged in heavy petting when, just before intercourse, V (she later claims) refuses. V's version is that she pushed D away and said, "That's it. I want to get dressed — quickly." D's version is that V may have said that, but he thought her pushing was teasing, and that what he thought she meant was, "Do it quickly, I want to get dressed." D offers to show that V had a reputation within D's fraternity for promiscuity and also a reputation for not liking afterplay. Exclusion of this reputation evidence would probably be a violation of D's constitutional rights (e.g., his right to due process). See L&S, p. 638.

   ii. Best available evidence: *Reputation* or *opinion* evidence may, even if not known to the defendant at the time of the incident, be the best available evidence of *how the victim behaved* during the episode.

   Example: D claims that V is a prostitute who threatened to accuse him of rape if he didn't pay her an extra $50 beyond the agreed price. D puts on the stand the man he believes to be V's pimp, as well as one of her "clients," but each declines to testify, citing the Fifth Amendment. D then calls a vice squad officer who will testify that although he has never seen V engage in sex for pay, he has seen her behavior on the streets and has witnessed a steady stream of men coming to her apartment, and that he is of the opinion that she is a prostitute. Exclusion of this opinion evidence would probably be an unconstitutional violation of D's rights. *Id.* (FRE 412(a) would not bar the officer from testifying about V's behavior on the street and the men entering her apartment, but without the officer's opinion that this is strong circumstantial evidence of prostitution, the jury is less likely to believe D's story. *Id.*, n. 7.)

h. Specific acts evidence: Assuming that the procedural aspects of FRE 412(c) do not have an unconstitutional effect, specific acts evidence can never be barred in an unconstitutional way under FRE 412, for the simple reason that

412(b)(1) automatically allows any evidence that is "constitutionally required to be admitted." Here is an illustration of how this "constitutionally required" provision might come into play:

Example: V is engaged to be married, and has sexual relations with her fiance, X. One evening, X believes that V is acting suspiciously, and he questions her about where she has been earlier that evening. She tells X that she has been out with another man, D, with whom she had sex; V claims that she did not consent and was raped by D.

At trial, D's lawyer wants to show the relationship between V and X, to show that V falsely accused D in order to protect her relationship with X. The relationship between V and X, especially the fact of their having had sex, will be highly relevant to this defense. Yet the prosecutor will be able to argue that neither branch of FRE 412(b)(2) applies, and that the proffered evidence falls into the category of "past sex life of the victim with persons other than the accused, offered on the issue of consent," the very class whose exclusion is the principal purpose of FRE 412. In this situation, the trial court should probably conclude that the evidence of the V-X relationship is so central to D's defense that to exclude it would unconstitutionally violate D's right of due process and confrontation, and should therefore admit the evidence under 412(b)(1). See S&R, p. 329.

i. **Limits to clause:** However, the "constitutionally required" clause of 412(b)(1) is likely to be read fairly tightly by courts. For instance, "where the circumstances of a rape suggest that there was a very low probability of consent, the Constitution should not be read so as to require the admission of sexual history evidence for whatever bearing it might have on that issue. Thus, if a woman is raped and beaten by a stranger in a parking lot and afterwards complains immediately to the police, evidence that the woman was promiscuous or, indeed, was a prostitute should not be admissible simply because the defendant has the gall to claim that the woman consented." L&S, p. 639.

VIII. HABIT AND CUSTOM

A. **General rule allows:** Evidence of a person's character, of course, is generally not admissible to show that he acted in conformity with that character on a particular occasion. Yet evidence of a person's *habit*, in most jurisdictions, *is* admissible to show that he followed his habit on a particular occasion.

Example: P, an auto mechanic, is injured while trying to warm up a can of refrigerant manufactured by D. At the trial of his products liability case, P asserts that he heated the refrigerant by surrounding it with warm tap water. D offers the testimony of W, who would testify that on prior occasions, he saw D use an immersion heating coil to heat the same kind of refrigerant, in violation of warnings on the label.

Held, W's testimony should have been allowed. Evidence that P regularly serviced auto air-conditioning units by use of refrigerant, and that he routinely used a coil to heat the refrigerant, was sufficient to establish a habit on P's part. Such evidence of habit is admissible to prove conformity on a specific occasion, because "one who has demonstrated a consistent response under given circumstances is more likely to repeat that response when the circumstances arise again. . . ." *Halloran v. Virginia Chemicals, Inc.,* 361 N.E.2d 991 (N.Y. 1977).

B. Distinction between habit and character: The distinction between "habit" and "character" is, in theory, not hard to draw: "Character" is a "generalized description of a person's disposition, or of the disposition in respect to a general trait, such as honesty, temperance, or peacefulness." M, p. 574. "Habit," by contrast, is "more specific. It denotes one's *regular response* to a *repeated situation*." M, p. 575.

> **Example:** Evidence that X generally drives carefully goes to his "character," since it relates to a relatively general trait. Therefore, such evidence will normally be inadmissible. But evidence that every work day, X crosses a particular railroad, and that he always stops, looks both ways, and then proceeds, would be evidence of his "habit." Such evidence will, therefore, generally be admissible to prove that on the particular day in question (e.g., the day that X is hit by an oncoming train), X stopped and looked before crossing the tracks. Lilly, p. 146.

1. Blurry line: Of course, like any dividing line, the line between character and habit may be blurry in particular instances. For instance, suppose that on the facts of the above example, X offered evidence that he always stops and looks before crossing *any* railroad tracks. It is not clear whether this evidence should be deemed "character" or "habit" evidence; whichever way the trial judge decides, he is unlikely to be reversed on appeal, since the decision would be held to be within his discretion. *Id.*

C. Minority rule: A very few states reject habit evidence entirely. M, p. 576. An additional minority allow it, but only as to those events for which there are *no available eyewitnesses*. *Id.*

1. Rationale: The "no available eyewitnesses" minority view is premised on the general undesirability of habit evidence. Because such evidence is undesirable, the theory goes, it should be allowed only where there is no other choice, and the availability of an eyewitness provides an alternative.

a. Criticism: The eyewitness rule is of dubious soundness, however. "Perception and memory are subject to many kinds of distortion. Evidence of an established habit may be more reliable as an indicator of behavior than the testimony of an eyewitness." L&S, p. 248. This is especially true when the eyewitness is *associated with the party* who is opposing the habit evidence. (For instance, in our railroad example, *supra*, the eyewitness rule would mean that if the driver of the locomotive was available to testify that X did not look or stop before driving onto the tracks, even well-documented evidence of X's habit of stopping and looking before that particular crossing every morning would be inadmissible — yet the engineer has every reason, conscious and unconscious, to misdescribe X's behavior. *Id.*)

2. Difficulties with habit evidence: On the other hand, it's not hard to see why some courts have been hesitant to welcome habit evidence. Here are a few reasons for distrusting such evidence:

    a. Taking advantage: A person can consciously *take advantage* of the fact that he is known to have a certain habit. "A murderer, in the habit of taking the six-o'clock bus home from work, may kill someone at six-fifteen, counting on evidence of habit to establish an alibi." L&S, p. 249.

    b. Sometimes disregarded: Second, "even well-established habits do not always govern behavior." For instance, again considering our example of the railroad crossing, no matter how well-established X's habit was of stopping at that particular crossing and looking carefully, it is unlikely that he did so on the day he was run over there (if he had, he wouldn't have been on the tracks!) *Id.*

    c. Fabrication and refutation: Finally, habit evidence is especially *easy to fabricate*, and *hard to refute*. On our railroad crossing example, suppose that X's wife were to testify that she sometimes drove to work with him, and that every single time she did so, he stopped and looked at that particular crossing. This is the kind of evidence that the wife could easily falsify, and yet evidence that the railroad would find it almost impossible to refute.

    d. Conclusion: Nonetheless, these problems do not seem insurmountable. For one thing, a jury will ordinarily be astute enough to identify those instances where the habit is either intentionally taken advantage of or falsified — it's unlikely that a jury would be so dumb as to miss the possibility that the murderer might have intentionally capitalized on his habit of taking the six-o'clock bus in deciding to commit the crime at six-fifteen.

D. Federal Rule: FRE 406, in keeping with the rule of most states, allows *very liberal use of habit evidence.* The Rule provides that "evidence of the habit of a person or of the routine practice of an organization, whether corroborated or not and regardless of the presence of eyewitnesses, is relevant to prove that the conduct of the person or organization on a particular occasion was in conformity with the habit or routine practice."

    1. No eyewitness requirement: Observe that this Rule expressly rejects the eyewitness requirement.

    2. How proved: The Rule does not say anything about *how* the existence of a habit is to be proved. As in most state proceedings, proof will normally be made by the testimony of a witness who has observed the habit over a long enough time for him to be able to say that it is a routine, repeated practice. Lilly, p. 147. Sometimes, however, the opponent will have to prove a number of *separate instances* (perhaps by a number of different witnesses) which, when taken together, demonstrate the required regularity. *Id.* This method of proof by individual instances is generally acceptable, so long as there are a sufficient number of instances and they have enough in common with each other.

E. Business practice: All courts, even those that disallow or restrict habit evidence, freely allow evidence of the ***routine practice*** of an ***organization***. This greater acceptance probably stems from the fact that "the need for regularity in business and organizational sanctions which may exist when custom is violated provide extra guarantees that the questioned activity followed the usual custom." L&S, p. 250.

> **Example:** A party wishes to prove that a certain letter was mailed by X Corp., a business. The party need not produce testimony by the person who actually mailed the letter. It is sufficient that the party show that the letter was placed in an "out box" at X Corp., if X Corp.'s mail clerk testifies that it was part of his job to collect all letters in the out box and mail them every day. This would be sufficient proof that that particular letter was mailed, even if the mail clerk testified that he could not remember whether he mailed the letter in question. L&S, p. 250, n. 8.

1. **Need for testimony:** In many states, however, the routine business practice must be proven via the testimony of the individual whose behavior is in question (e.g., the mail clerk in the above example). In other jurisdictions, ***anyone*** who has knowledge of the custom may testify as to its existence. This liberal approach is implicitly followed in FRE 406.

IX. SIMILAR HAPPENINGS

A. General problem: A party will sometimes want to introduce evidence of an event that is ***similar*** to the event under litigation. Generally, the similar event will be one which took place prior to the event under litigation, but it may have taken place subsequently.

> **Example 1:** P trips on a stairway in D's movie theater. She wishes to show that in the six months prior to her accident, two other people slipped and fell on the same stairway. She offers this evidence to prove that the carpet on the stairway was maintained in an unsafe condition, which D knew of or ought to have known of.

> **Example 2:** P loses money on a stock touted to him by his broker, D. P claims that D knowingly made several specific misrepresentations about the stock. If D denies having made the statements to P, P would like to be able to show that D made the same statements to several others about the same stock at about the same time.

1. **Objections:** Yet there are several potential problems with such "similar happenings" evidence. In the stair-fall example, for instance, the earlier fall may have taken place under such different circumstances that it has no probative value on the fall under litigation; this would be the case, for instance, if the earlier fall were while the lights were dim and the later one while the lights were bright, or the earlier one was by a woman in high heels and the later by a child running in sneakers. Furthermore, the jury might overestimate the importance to be attached to the similar happening, or overestimate the similarity between the two events.

2. **General rule:** For these and other reasons, courts are generally ***reluctant*** to allow evidence of similar happenings. In most jurisdictions, there are no black letter

rules governing when such evidence may be admitted. In general, such evidence is not flatly excluded, but the proponent must demonstrate that there is a **substantial similarity** between the collateral event offered as evidence and the event at issue in the case. L&S, p. 208.

> **Example:** P falls while going down the stairs at D's theater. She produces evidence that the carpet on the stairs was loose because the tacks holding it to the floor had pulled out, and that the carpet slipped under her feet. D produces evidence that the carpet was securely fastened. P offers evidence that two or three weeks before her injury, two girls fell at the same spot, and that after they fell, the carpet was found to be loose because the tacks fastening it had been pulled out.
>
> *Held* (on appeal), the evidence of the other falls should not have been admitted, because P did not show that on the earlier occasion, the tacks had been pulled out to the same distance, or that the carpet had the same degree of looseness, as during the time of P's accident. *Robitaille v. Netoco Comm. Theaters*, 25 N.E.2d 749 (Mass. 1940).

B. Similar accidents and injuries: Probably the most common use of "similar happenings" evidence is in suits for personal injuries from accidents or defective products. As with "similar happenings" evidence generally, courts will not exclude the similar accident evidence automatically, but will closely scrutinize it. The plaintiff will have to show substantial similarity between the two accidents.

1. **Narrow element:** Furthermore, in negligence actions, the evidence will rarely be admitted for the broad purpose of showing that the defendant was negligent. Lilly, p. 169. Instead, the plaintiff will have to show **what particular element** of the case the other accident is being offered to prove. Possible elements that the accident may demonstrate include the following:

   a. **Defect:** that a particular defect **existed**;

   b. **Causation:** that a defect, whether or not disputed by the defendant, **caused** plaintiff's accident;

   > **Example:** P, a housepainter, is working with a ladder at the side of a church, when he suddenly dies. An autopsy reveals an electrical exit wound, but also shows that P had cirrhosis of the liver and was drunk at the time of death. P's estate sues D, the local power company, contending that the power lines were in an unsafe condition and that they caused P's death by electrocution. D contends that the cause of P's death is a mystery. P offers evidence that another housepainter received an electrical injury at the same spot, six weeks after P's death.
   >
   > *Held*, since the cause of P's death was in dispute, and since the two situations were highly similar, the subsequent electrocution was admissible on the issue of causation. *Arkansas Power & Light Co. v. Johnson*, 538 S.W.2d 541 (Ark. 1976).

   c. **Risk:** that the defendant's conduct created a substantial **risk**; or

    d. Knowledge: that the defendant ***knew***, or should have known, of the danger.

        i. Subsequent happenings: If the other event is ***subsequent*** to the event under litigation, it will not for that reason alone be made inadmissible on the first three of these elements. But it will be inadmissible on the last, knowledge — the fact that someone was injured after the plaintiff was, obviously cannot prove that the defendant knew or should have known of the danger at the time of plaintiff's injury. M, p. 590.

2. Evidence of past safety: A defendant will sometimes want to show that there have been ***no accidents*** of the kind suffered by the plaintiff. Logically, this kind of evidence should be admissible in courts allowing the plaintiff to introduce evidence of similar accidents. Most courts indeed ***allow*** such evidence of a safe history if conditions were the same during the historical period as during the moment of plaintiff's injury.

    Example: Let's return to the example of P falling on the carpeted stairway of D's theater. Assume that P does not have any evidence of other accidents. Most courts would allow D to introduce the fact that of the thousands or tens of thousands of customers who have gone up and down those stairs in the last year, none fell. However, this evidence would be admissible only if conditions had remained the same over the last year — if D had recarpeted the stairs just prior to P's injury, or relighted the premises, the situation might be deemed to be so different that the history of safety would be of too little probative value to be admitted.

    a. Difficulty: Some courts, probably a minority, refuse to allow such safe-history evidence. These courts reason that the mere fact that no suits or complaints had been reported to the defendant does not mean that accidents have not occurred — other customers might have fallen on the same loosely carpeted stair in defendant's theater, but did not complain because they were in a hurry and not badly injured. These courts also point out the difficulty of assuring that the same conditions really prevailed during the safe history as during the plaintiff's accident — that is, "the plaintiff may in fact be among the first to encounter a newly dangerous situation." L&S, p. 210.

C. Other kinds of events: There are a number of other common settings in which similar-happenings evidence is sought to be admitted. Some of the common contexts are as follows:

1. Contracts: In a dispute about a contract or a transaction, a party will sometimes try to introduce evidence of ***similar contracts*** or ***transactions***. The court's response is likely to depend in part upon whether the parties to the different contracts or transactions are the same.

    a. Both parties the same: When the collateral contract or transaction and the one in issue both involve ***the same parties***, the courts will generally accept evidence of the collateral one, assuming that the situations are similar. Thus if the suit concerns the meaning to be given to a term in a contract between A and B, the meaning given to the same term in other contracts between A and B will be admitted. M, p. 583. The same would be true of an unwritten "course of dealing" followed by the parties in their various transactions.

b. Contract between opponent and third party: Where the suit concerns a contract between A and B, and A seeks to introduce the terms of a contract or transaction between B and *C*, courts are markedly more reluctant to admit the evidence. The theory seems to be that any deal B made with C simply has little or no probative value as to what kind of deal he made with A.

> **Example:** P sues to regain title to Blackacre from D. He claims that although he deeded Blackacre over to D, the deed was merely security for a loan, not an outright sale. D claims that there was an outright sale. P offers evidence that P's brother, W, deeded the adjacent Whiteacre to D as security for a loan, and when the loan was repaid D reconveyed to W.
>
> *Held*, the evidence of W's transaction with D should not have been admitted. "Persons capable of contracting have the right to make such contracts as they deem proper, and the fact that a defendant has made a particular contract with a third person does not tend to show that he has made a similar contract with the plaintiff." *Linthicum v. Richardson*, 245 S.W. 713 (Tex. Civ. App. 1922).

> **i. Some courts allow:** Nonetheless, some courts allow such evidence of a contract or transaction to which only one of the present litigants was a party. This is particularly likely to be the case where the issue is the meaning to be given to a standardized "boilerplate" item like a warranty.

c. Neither party the same: When the collateral contract or transaction does not involve *either* of the parties to the present litigation, courts almost universally refuse to allow it (except in one special context discussed *infra*). L&S, p. 210. Thus on the facts of the above example, if P had tried to show that a deed from X to Y for Whiteacre (located in the same town as Blackacre) was really just a form of mortgage, and that the property was redeemed from Y to X after full payment, probably no court would allow the evidence — no matter how similar the situations, X's dealings with Y would be held to be insufficiently probative of P's dealings with D.

> **i. Fair market value:** The one exception is where the issue is the *fair market value* of an item. Here, evidence of the price paid for a similar item in a competitive market is viewed as being a good indicator of market value. (But if the item is not a *standardized commodity*, the other-sale evidence generally will *not* be admitted — no two valuable gems, or thoroughbred race horses, are likely to be sufficiently similar to be admitted directly into evidence, though they may enter into the opinion of an appraiser who gives expert testimony. *Id.*)

> **ii. Land:** *Land* presents special problems. Traditionally, the law has regarded each piece of land as being "unique." Today, however, most courts allow evidence of sales of comparable parcels to be admitted, provided that the sales are reasonably recent, and the parcels are sufficiently similar in terms

of location, condition, etc. M, p. 585.

2. **Criminal allegations:** When the plaintiff in a civil suit alleges that the defendant has committed conduct which amounts to a crime, evidence of *other acts by the defendant* are admissible on the same basis as they would be in a criminal trial of that defendant.

    a. **Fraud:** The most common illustration is a civil suit for *fraud*. Similar past acts by the defendant will be admissible to show the defendant's guilty knowledge, deceitful intent, or a broad plan or scheme, assuming that such element is a disputed issue in the civil case.

        Example: P, an investor, sues D, a new-issues stock broker, for fraud. P claims that D sold him stock in X Corp. by means of untrue statements, including that "the prospectus is out of date and should be disregarded" and that "the initial offering of the stock will be closed this weekend." D denies having made the representations. P offers the testimony of two witnesses that at about the same time D made essentially the same representations to them on the same stock.

        Held, all the claimed representations are so strikingly similar that they should be admitted to show a general plan or scheme by D. *Karsun v. Kelley,* 482 P.2d 533 (Or. 1971).

3. **Prior claims by same plaintiff:** A party (usually the defendant) will sometimes want to show that his adversary has previously raised *fraudulent claims* similar to the claim in the present action. If the proponent can show that these other claims were indeed fraudulent, and were similar to the present claim, most courts will accept the evidence.

    a. **Repeated claims:** The more difficult case is where the defendant shows that the plaintiff has made a number of very similar claims in the past (far more than would be actuarially expected) against the same defendant or others, but the proponent has no hard evidence that any of the claims were fraudulent. Without evidence of fraud, most courts are reluctant to accept the evidence — whatever the laws of probability, some people are indeed unlucky and more frequently injured or victimized than others, and it would be unfairly prejudicial to allow other-claims evidence where only the sheer frequency suggests wrongdoing. See, e.g., *San Antonio Traction Co. v. Cox,* 184 S.W. 722 (Tex. Civ. App. 1916) (P and his relatives had made 17 claims against D, a streetcar company, within a one-year period, 15 of them for injuries claimed to have been suffered in stepping down from streetcars; although this state of affairs was "remarkable," there was no direct evidence of conspiracy or other wrongdoing, so the evidence was excluded).

4. **Accident proneness:** The defendant in a negligence action may try to show that the plaintiff is *"accident prone,"* either to suggest that the defendant was not negligent, or to show that there was contributory negligence by the plaintiff. Courts have generally *refused* to allow evidence of accident proneness on the issue of negligence.

a. Rationale: One reason for this reluctance is that, as a purely statistical matter, *some* people will simply will end up in markedly more accidents than others, even though they may be every bit as careful as their more fortunate peers. If 100 people in a village had 100 accidents, and the accidents "found their victim" in a totally random way, it would nonetheless probably turn out that some few unfortunates had two, three, even four accidents — that's simply the way the bell-shaped probability distribution works. These unfortunates would be called "accident prone," yet only the laws of chance, not their own carelessness, would have been the cause. L&S, pp. 211-12, n. 41.

X. SUBSEQUENT REMEDIAL MEASURES

A. Problem generally: After an accident, the owner of premises or property involved in it will often take *remedial measures*. For instance, when a pedestrian trips on a pothole in the sidewalk in front of a building, the building owner may have the pothole paved over. When suit is brought by the injured party, he will often want to introduce evidence of the subsequent repair, on the theory that that repair shows the defendant's consciousness of negligence or other fault. For instance, in the pothole situation, the plaintiff would be saying something like, "By paving over the pothole, Mr. Landowner, you acknowledge that prior to the repair the pothole made the sidewalk unsafe." Should such evidence of subsequent repairs be admissible?

1. General rule: Courts generally *do not allow* such evidence of subsequent repairs, when offered to the show the repairer's culpability.

2. Rationale: At first glance, this rule seems hard to understand. After all, the defendant's prompt repair does suggest that the defendant realized that prior to the accident, he had not been as careful as he might have been. Two reasons are usually given for the rule:

a. Little probative value: First, such evidence is of relatively little probative value on the issue of negligence. "Certainly a conscientious individual, newly alerted to a dangerous condition, will do everything reasonable to remedy that condition regardless of his or her earlier care." L&S, p. 192. Subsequent repair is at best indicative only of the defendant's *belief* that he may have been negligent, a belief which does not necessarily correspond to the fact of negligence, since a non-lawyer party does not necessarily have an accurate knowledge of the law. *Id.*

b. Discouragement of repairs: The second, and probably more important, reason for the general rule of exclusion is that if such evidence were allowed, it might have the effect of *discouraging repairs*. That is, a defendant might reason, "If I make this repair while suit is threatened or pending, the plaintiff will be able to use it against me. I'm better off not doing anything until the suit is resolved." This second rationale thus amounts to a rule of policy: For reasons having nothing to do with accuracy in the fact-finding process, the courts impose a rule of exclusion in the hopes that defendants will be encouraged to make things safer for the public in the future, or at least not discouraged from doing so.

      i. Criticism: This second rationale is highly questionable. First, "if a defendant knows enough law to realize that evidence of subsequent remedial measures will not be admissible on the issue of negligence he is also likely to realize that such evidence may be admissible for other purposes. . . ." *Id.* (See, *infra.*) Second, a rational defendant would probably conclude that not making repairs after being put on notice of a dangerous condition may lead to additional accidents, additional lawsuits, and the possibility of punitive damages for gross negligence. *Id.*

  3. Remedial actions generally: In any event, the law of exclusion is almost universally established (except in Maine, where it is abolished by statute).

    a. Extension: In fact, the rule has been extended beyond "repairs," and has been applied in the following situations:

      i. Installation of a new *safety device*;

      ii. Lowering of a speed limit or beefing up some other *safety rule*;

      iii. *Firing the employee* responsible for the accident.

    b. "Subsequent remedial measures": None of these actions is, strictly speaking, a "repair." For this reason, the rule is now stated as covering not just repairs, but *"subsequent remedial measures."*

  4. Federal Rule: The Federal Rule on the subject, FRE 407, follows the common-law approach in general. However, it is broadly written to cover all remedial measures: "When, after an event, measures are taken which, if taken previously, would have made the event less likely to occur, evidence of the subsequent measures is not admissible to prove negligence or culpable conduct in connection with the event." (The Rule then makes it clear that it does not apply to evidence offered for purposes other than negligence or culpability — see *infra*, p. 57.)

B. Permissible purposes: The rule against subsequent repairs evidence applies *only* where the evidence is offered on the issue of negligence or culpability. If the evidence is relevant to *some other contested element* in the case, the exclusionary rule does not apply.

  1. Typical issues: Some of the more common issues as to which subsequent repairs evidence may be relevant and thus admissible, are:

    a. Feasibility: The issue of *feasibility*. If the defendant claims that he was not negligent or culpable because there was no safer way to handle the situation, evidence that the defendant implemented a safer way following the accident is strongly probative on this issue.

    b. Ownership or control: *Ownership* or *control* of the property that caused the accident.

      Example: P, a pedestrian, is hit by a car driven by D. P brings a negligence action against D. D defends by showing that the car was not registered to him, and by claiming that the collision occurred because, unbeknownst to D, the brakes were faulty. P wants to introduce evidence that D had the brakes repaired after the collision. If he offers this evidence to prove directly that D was negligent in not inspecting the brakes beforehand, the evidence would be barred under the general rule of exclusion. But if P offers the subsequent repair to show that D had enough control over the vehicle to have it repaired (and thus had enough control to have had a duty to inspect the brakes before the accident), the evidence will be admitted. S&R, pp. 265-66.

c. **Impeachment:** To *impeach* an opposing witness.

Example: P is killed when her car is run over at a railway crossing. The train was traveling just within the then-prevailing 90 mph speed limit at the time of the collision. In the suit between the railroad and P's estate, the railroad calls W, the motorman on the train that hit P. W testifies on direct that in the "fourth district" (a many-mile stretch of track that includes the crossing), the speed limit "is 90 mph now. . . ." On cross-examination, P's lawyer gets W to concede that in the crossing area, the speed limit is now 50 mph.

Held, W's admission about the current reduced speed limit at the crossing is admissible, because it occurred in response to a question properly designed to impeach W's earlier testimony that the limit was 90 mph. *Daggett v. Atchison, Topeka & Santa Fe Railway Co.*, 313 P.2d 557 (Cal. 1957).

Note: Observe that the impeachment exception is a broad one, probably broad enough so that a skilled plaintiff's lawyer will usually be able to get his evidence in under it. In *Daggett*, for instance, a dissent argued that "any confusion as to speeds, times, and districts or areas appears from the record to have been invited and brought about by counsel for plaintiffs, who then seized upon such alleged confusion as an excuse to get before the jury otherwise inadmissible evidence of a change in the speed limit after the accident."

2. **Federal Rule:** FRE 407 expressly recognizes that the general rule of exclusion should not bar use for purposes other than the showing of negligence or culpable conduct. The second sentence of 407 states that the rule does not apply when evidence is offered for "another purpose, such as proving ownership, control, or feasibility of precautionary measures, if controverted, or impeachment." This list is illustrative, not exhaustive.

3. **Must be controverted:** For repair evidence to be admitted because it is relevant to a specific element other than negligence/culpability, that element must be *disputed*. Thus evidence of a post-accident design improvement cannot be introduced to prove that that improved design is feasible, if the defendant concedes that such an improvement is feasible, and instead merely disputes the issue of negligence. For instance, in a drug product liability case presenting the issue of whether the manufacturer's warning was adequate, evidence that the manufacturer had later made the warning stronger was not allowed under the "feasibility" exception, since the manufacturer conceded that a stronger warning was feasible, and merely disputed whether it was required. *Werner v. Upjohn Co. Inc.*, 628 F.2d 848 (4th Cir. 1980).

      a. Strategy: If the defendant asserts that a particular issue (e.g., feasibility) is not in dispute, the trial judge may force the defendant to "put its money where its mouth is" by agreeing to a ***stipulation*** conceding that issue.

C. Third persons: Another exception to the exclusionary rule is that a remedial action carried out by a ***third person*** rather than by the defendant is admissible. M, p. 816. For instance, suppose that P, a worker, is injured on the job by a machine owned by X and manufactured by D. If, after the accident, X puts a new safety feature on the machine, this fact will be admissible in a suit brought by P against D. *Id.*

      1. Rationale: The reason for this exception is that the usual safety rationale does not apply. For instance, in the above example, employers will not be dissuaded from installing safety features merely because the features would be admissible in suits against manufacturers.

D. Product liability: The most controversial issue concerning the repairs exclusion involves suits brought in ***strict product liability***.

      1. The problem: In a strict product liability case, the negligence or culpability of the defendant is not, legally speaking, at issue — if a product is "dangerously defective," there is liability even though the manufacturer, at the time of manufacture, neither knew nor had reason to know of the defect. Since the rule barring admission of repair evidence applies only when the evidence is offered on the issue of negligence or culpability, arguably the rule should not apply in the product liability case. Especially where the rule is embodied in a statute that limits the rule to evidence used to prove "negligence or culpable conduct" (FRE 407's language), this argument has apparent merit.

      2. Trend: Indeed, the trend seems to be to ***allow*** remedial-measure evidence in the strict product liability context. Some courts have reached this result simply as a matter of statutory interpretation; see, e.g., *Ault v. International Harvester Co.*, 528 P.2d 1148 (Cal. 1975), holding that evidence of a remedial measure in a product liability case does not fall within Cal. Evid. Code §1151, since that section applies only to negligent or culpable conduct. Other cases reaching the same result have done so on the theory that the risk of deterring repairs is not present to the same extent in strict product liability cases as in negligence cases; as the court in *Ault* phrased it, "it is manifestly unrealistic to suggest that [a mass-market] producer will forego making improvements in its product and risk innumerable additional lawsuits and the attendant adverse effect upon its public image, simply because evidence of adoption of such improvement may be admitted in an action founded on strict liability. . . ."

      3. Contrary view: But a number of recent cases have reached the opposite conclusion. Some have concluded that allowing such evidence does indeed dissuade defendants from making repairs even in the product liability context. Others have focused on the low probative value of such evidence in a products case; see, e.g., *Grenada-Steel Industries v. Alabama Oxygen Co.*, 695 F.2d 883 (5th Cir. 1983), in which the court said that "changes in design or in manufacturing process might be made after an accident for a number of different reasons: simply to avoid another injury, as a sort of admission of error, because a better way has been discovered, or to implement an idea or plan conceived before the accident."

4. **Summary:** At this juncture, neither the pro- nor anti-exclusion forces have won a clear majority in the product liability situation. As noted, however, "the trend is to admit such evidence." L&S, p. 193.

XI. LIABILITY INSURANCE

A. **General rule:** Both the common law and the Federal Rules provide that evidence that a person carried or did not carry *liability insurance* is *not admissible* on the issue of whether he acted negligently. This rule bars such evidence when it is offered by a plaintiff to suggest that because the defendant was insured, the defendant was probably careless. Conversely, such evidence is barred when offered by the defendant to show that because he did not have adequate insurance, he had an incentive to be careful. S&R, p. 316.

1. **Federal Rule:** The Rule on the subject, FRE 411, codifies the common-law approach. The Rule provides that "evidence that a person was or was not insured against liability is not admissible upon the issue whether the person acted negligently or otherwise wrongfully. This rule does not require the exclusion of evidence of insurance against liability when offered for another purpose, such as proof of agency, ownership, or control, or bias or prejudice of a witness."

2. **Rationale:** As with several of the other rules of exclusion which we have considered above (e.g., the rule dealing with evidence of subsequent repairs), the rule barring liability insurance evidence has both a relevance and a prejudice rationale behind it: (1) The evidence is of relatively little probative value, because most people agree that "whether one has insurance coverage reveals little about the likelihood that he will act carelessly." M, p. 593. (2) A jury may well be prejudiced by information about insurance; it can be argued that "the mention of insurance invites higher awards than are justified, and conversely, the sympathy that the jury might feel for a defendant who must pay out of his own pocket could interfere with its evaluation of the evidence. . . ." M, pp. 593-94.

3. **Other purpose:** Again as with other rules of exclusion, the rule does not apply where the evidence is offered for some *other purpose*. The possible purposes listed by FRE 411 are in fact the most commonly applicable ones, but the list is merely illustrative.

   a. **Insurance investigator:** A common way for the existence of insurance to come out in trial is if the defendant decides to put an insurance company *investigator* on the witness stand; in this situation, the plaintiff may inquire into the witness' relationship to the defendant both to show possible prejudice and as part of the general right to put a witness' testimony in context. (Of course, for this reason the defendant will often choose not to put an insurance company employee on the stand.) For instance, if the plaintiff gave his statement to a representative of the defendant's insurance company, the statement typically cannot be admitted into evidence without the testimony of the person who took it, and plaintiff's counsel will then be permitted to test the reliability of that person by inquiring on cross-examination into sources of possible bias.

b. Voir dire: Also, most states allow questions during the *voir dire* of prospective jurors concerning a juror's employment by or interest in insurance companies. A juror who hears such questions being asked is likely to assume (not necessarily correctly) that the defendant has insurance. Such questions are proper even when the defendant is not insured, because if a juror has a bias in favor of or against insurance companies, this may influence his deliberation because of his mistaken belief that the defendant is covered by insurance.

XII. COMPROMISES, OFFERS TO PLEAD GUILTY AND OFFERS TO PAY MEDICAL EXPENSES

A. Compromises: Most lawsuits are settled before trial. Where a trial does take place, it has usually been preceded by attempts at settlement. The things that parties say during the course of settlement negotiations are often at least arguably relevant. Nonetheless, it has long been established that the fact that a party has *offered to settle a claim* may *not be admitted* on the issue of the claim's validity. M, p. 811.

> **Example:** P, a pedestrian, is injured by a car driven by D. P sues for $10,000. D offers to settle the case for $5,000. P declines. At trial, P may not introduce D's settlement offer into evidence on the theory that it constitutes an admission by D of liability. Conversely, had P offered to take $5,000 in settlement and D had refused, D could not introduce P's offer to show that P had serious doubts about the merits of his claim.

1. Rationale: There are two reasons for this rule, which are similar to those we have seen for several of the other rules discussed in this chapter: (1) Settlement offers are of low probative value, since a litigant may be attempting to "buy peace" by settling, rather than expressing his real belief about the merits of his case; and (2) Admission of such information would give the parties a strong disincentive to pursue settlement negotiations.

2. Actual dispute required: The rule of exclusion applies only where there is an *actual dispute* between the parties concerning either the validity of the claim or the amount at issue. Thus if D agrees that P's claim has merit and both parties agree on the sum owed, their discussions will not be classified as "settlement discussions" merely because D admits liability or says he can't pay the full amount but will pay less.

> **Example:** P's decedent is a passenger in a car driven by D; she is killed when the car hits another car. P (the decedent's mother) testifies at trial that after the accident, D talked to her about the accident and "he said he would settle with us if it wasn't taken care of." P offers this statement as an admission of liability.
>
> *Held,* the testimony is admissible, because it related to an admission of liability by D, and was not an offer of compromise. There was no controversy between P and D at the time, and no demand was being made upon D at the

time. *Nehring v. Smith*, 49 N.W.2d 831 (Iowa 1951).

3. **What is excluded:** Exactly what is excluded under the rule? Clearly the offer itself. But what about collateral ***admissions of fact*** that are made during the course of settlement negotiations? The common-law rule is that such factual admissions are ***generally admissible.***

> **Example:** P, a pedestrian, is run over by D and badly injured. P sues D; shortly thereafter, D says to P, "I'm so sorry about this — it's all my fault, because I was drunk that night. I'll pay you $5,000 to drop your action." P may not introduce the fact that D offered $5,000 to show that D believed he is liable. But she may, under the common-law rule, introduce D's admission to having been drunk, since that is an admission of fact.

a. **Exceptions:** There are two exceptions to the common-law rule on factual admissions. The factual admissions will be ***inadmissible*** if they are either:

   i. ***Inextricably bound up*** with the settlement offer so that one cannot be introduced without the other; or

   ii. ***Phrased in a hypothetical form*** (e.g., "Assuming for the moment that you may be able to prove that I was drunk that night, I'll offer you $5,000) or are preceded by the statement that the discussion is ***"without prejudice."***

b. **Federal Rule:** The Federal Rules take a ***broader*** approach to exclusion. FRE 408 provides in full as follows:

"Evidence of (1) furnishing or offering or promising to furnish, or (2) accepting or offering or promising to accept, a valuable consideration in compromising or attempting to compromise a claim which was disputed as to either validity or amount, is not admissible to prove liability for or invalidity of the claim or its amount. Evidence of conduct or statements made in compromise negotiations is likewise not admissible. This rule does not require the exclusion of any evidence otherwise discoverable merely because it is presented in the course of compromise negotiations. This rule also does not require exclusion when the evidence is offered for another purpose, such as proving bias or prejudice of a witness, negativing a contention of undue delay, or proving an effort to obstruct a criminal investigation or prosecution."

   i. **Collateral statements also barred:** Observe closely the second sentence: "Evidence of conduct or statements made in compromise negotiations is likewise not admissible." This sentence means that an admission of ***fact*** ("I was drunk that night"), if it occurs during the course of settlement negotiations, is ***not admissible*** even if it is quite separable from the settlement offer. This sentence reflects the desire of the rule's draftsmen to encourage free-wheeling settlement negotiations in which the parties simply do not have to worry that some of what they say may come back to hurt them.

   ii. **No ability to "immunize":** Suppose a party admits a certain fact during settlement negotiations. Under the Federal Rule, does this mean that the other party may not prove that fact by means independent of the settlement admission? The answer is "no" — the third sentence of FRE 408 makes it clear that the rule does not require exclusion of "any evidence otherwise discoverable merely because it is presented in the course of compromise negotiations." This sentence also means that when a party gives a ***document*** to his adversary during settlement negotiations, the document is ***not*** automatically ***"immunized"*** from admission — if the same document is or could be found through discovery or other techniques independent of the settlement negotiations, it may be admitted.

4. **Other purposes:** Like most of the other rules of exclusion discussed in this chapter, the rule excluding settlement offers applies only where the evidence is offered in order to prove a core fact (here, the weakness of the opposing party's claim or defense) — it may be admitted for ***other purposes***. FRE 408 mentions some of the possible "other purposes": "proving bias or prejudice of a witness, negativing a contention of undue delay, or proving an effort to obstruct a criminal investigation or prosecution."

   a. **Settlement with third person:** The most common situation in which the "other purpose" exception applies occurs when what is at issue is a settlement between a party (usually the defendant) and a ***third person*** who is not a party to the present action.

      Example: P and W are both employees of D, a railroad. At the trial of P's suit against D, D calls W as a witness, and W gives testimony that is largely favorable to D. P's lawyer elicits from W in cross-examination that W was injured in the same collision as P. P then asks W, "Didn't you make a claim against D that D settled with you?" D objects on the ground that the answer would be inadmissible as evidence of settlement negotiations.

      Held, the question was proper. Proof of D's settlement with W was not offered for the purpose of showing the validity of W's (and by inference P's) claim. Rather, it was asked for the purpose of testing W's credibility as a witness (e.g., W may feel beholden to D, or he may have explicitly agreed to give favorable testimony in return for the settlement payment by D). *Joice v. Missouri-Kansas-Texas Ry.*, 189 S.W.2d 568 (Mo. 1945).

      i. **Courts split:** Not all courts would agree with the result in *Joice*. The somewhat confused state of the law in this three-party situation may be summarized as follows:

      ii. **Basic privilege:** The basic rule of exclusion applies to the third-party situation just as in the two-party case. In other words, if in the above example P had sought to introduce D's settlement with W to prove that D thought it was liable for the collision, all courts would have excluded the evidence for the same reasons that they would have excluded similar evidence of an attempted P-D settlement.

      iii. **Bias:** Where, as in our example, the offering lawyer is careful to explain that the evidence is sought only to indicate the witness' ***bias***, the courts are not in complete agreement. The need to show bias roughly counterbalances the need to promote settlements. If the witness has actually received or been promised money in settlement of his claim, most courts would probably allow this fact to be brought out as suggestive of bias. M, p. 813. (The more generous a settlement is to the witness, the more likely the court is to allow the evidence, since the more the settlement suggests bias. L&S, p. 198.)

iv. **Inconsistency:** Even if the witness has not received or been promised money, things he said during his settlement negotiations with D may be used to impeach his own testimony, if these things are *inconsistent* with what he says on the witness stand. M, p. 813. Thus in the factual setting of *Joice*, *supra*, if W had said on the witness stand, "The engineer had no way of knowing that there was anybody on the track," most courts would allow P to show that W had insisted during his settlement negotiations with D that the engineer did have time to spot P and himself.

v. **Balancing:** Remember that even in a court which takes a sympathetic view of the need to show bias or inconsistency on the part of a witness, evidence is always subject to a *balancing* between probative value and countervailing disadvantages. For instance, in the *Joice* situation, a federal court (following FRE 403's mandate to balance probative value against countervailing values) might conclude that it would be more unfair to the railroad to let the jury hear about the settlement with W than it would be unfair to P to disallow him this opportunity to show W's bias. The court's decision might turn on how important W's testimony seemed to be (and thus how important it was to P to be able to show bias). If the court did allow the testimony, it would probably issue a limiting instruction to the jury, to the effect that the evidence is relevant only to show possible bias by W, not to show anything about D's belief in the merits of its case.

5. **Completed compromises:** Suppose a settlement is not only attempted but *completed*, in the sense that the parties have signed a formal agreement. That agreement can be sued upon as a contract, and in the suit the agreement itself is always admissible. But suppose that defendant never pays the agreed-upon amount, and plaintiff instead reinstates his original claim (for more money than the amount called for in the settlement agreement). May either party introduce the settlement agreement to show that the other lacked confidence in its case?

> **Example:** D signs a settlement agreement in which he promises to pay $10,000 to P next June 15th. If June 15th comes and goes and D does not pay, P may well prefer to sue for $50,000 and use the agreement as an admission by D of liability, rather than having to go through all the trouble of suing just to collect the $10,000 called for in the agreement.

a. **States split:** The states are split on this issue. Some apply the general rule of exclusion. But others reason that since the purpose of settlement (to cut down on litigation) has not been achieved, the policy encouraging settlements should not apply. L&S, p. 198.

i. **Federal Rule:** The Federal Rule *excludes* the completed settlement in this situation. See Advisory Committee's Note to FRE 408.

B. Guilty pleas: On the criminal side, the equivalent of the settlement is the ***guilty plea***. The process of plea bargaining raises two major evidentiary questions: (1) If D offers to plead guilty, but the prosecution does not accept, may D's offer (or factual admissions accompanying it) be introduced against D at trial? and (2) If D actually enters a guilty plea as part of a plea bargain, but later withdraws the plea, may the fact of the initial plea be introduced against him at the trial? In general, the Federal Rules and most states are in accord that the answer to each of these questions is ***"no."***

1. **Offer of plea:** With respect to the defendant's offer to plead guilty, and any statements he makes in connection with that offer, FRE 410(4) is in accord with the rule of most states. FRE 410(4) excludes from use against the defendant (either in the criminal trial on the very charge in question, or in ***any other*** similar criminal proceeding) "any statement made in the course of plea discussions with an attorney for the prosecuting authority which do not result in a plea of guilty or which result in a plea of guilty later withdrawn."

   a. **Rationale:** Once again, there is a two-fold rationale for the rule of exclusion: (1) an offer to plead guilty has relatively little probative value on the issue of guilt, since a defendant who fears conviction may find the lesser charge or lighter sentence offered to him to be attractive even though he is in fact innocent; and (2) because of the overcrowded criminal justice system, there is a strong public policy in favor of encouraging plea bargains.

   b. **Factual admissions:** Observe that the Federal Rule, like the rule in most states, protects the defendant from having the prosecution use against him either the fact of the guilty plea or any ***factual admissions*** made by him during the course of plea-bargaining negotiations. Thus if D's lawyer says to the prosecutor, "My guy admits that he pulled the gun against the storekeeper that night, but will plead guilty to the lesser crime of burglary instead of robbery," the admission of facts constituting robbery would not be admissible, nor would the offer to plead guilty to the burglary.

   c. **Must be with prosecutor:** Under the version of FRE 410 that existed prior to 1980, statements made to ***any law enforcement officer*** in the hopes of obtaining leniency were inadmissible. This required the courts to engage in a lot of case-by-case determinations about whether a particular factual admission made to a police officer, IRS agent, etc., was made in the hopes of gaining leniency. Under the rule as amended in 1980, only statements made to "an ***attorney for the prosecuting authority***" are covered. Therefore, if an IRS agent, police officer, or corrections official tells the defendant or his lawyer that he may be able to arrange leniency or a plea bargain, any resulting statement may be ***used against the defendant***. (However, such statements may be inadmissible because of the *Miranda* rule's ban on uninformed statements made during custody.)

   d. ***Nolo contendere***: FRE 410(2), like the rule in most states, also excludes pleas of ***nolo contendere***. In fact, the very purpose of entering a plea of *nolo contendere* is that it may not be admitted in any subsequent proceedings (e.g., civil ones alleging the same facts that gave rise to the criminal plea).

2. **Withdrawn pleas:** FRE 410(4) makes it quite clear that the rule of exclusion applies to a plea of guilty that is entered and later ***withdrawn***. Most states agree with this approach. L&S, p. 200.

3. **Impeachment:** If the defendant introduces into evidence a statement made during plea bargaining that he believes is exculpatory, the prosecution is then free to use other statements made during the same discussions to ***impeach*** him, if the statement the prosecution seeks to introduce "ought in fairness to be considered contemporaneously with" the one introduced by the defendant. FRE 410(i). "The obvious purpose is to prevent a defendant from taking advantage of FRE 410 by introducing a statement that is exculpatory only when taken out of context." L&S, p. 201.

C. **Payment of medical expenses:** The fact that a party has paid the ***medical expenses*** of an injured person is likewise excluded in nearly all states, when offered on the issue of the party's liability for the accident that caused the injury. FRE 409 follows this common-law approach: "Evidence of furnishing or offering or promising to pay medical, hospital, or similar expenses occasioned by an injury is not admissible to prove liability for the injury."

1. **Communications:** But unlike the compromise and guilty plea contexts, in the medical-payment context only the ***fact of the payment*** is excluded. Other admissions of fact (e.g., "I'm paying your medical expenses because if I hadn't have been drunk that night, I wouldn't have been driving on the shoulder and hit you") are not excluded under the rule.

EXAMINATION AND IMPEACHMENT
OF WITNESSES

Introductory Note: We examine two broad topics in this chapter: (1) the general methods by which testimony is developed, including an overview of *direct* and *cross-examination*; and (2) methods of *impeaching* the *credibility* of a witness.

I. DIRECT EXAMINATION

A. Definition of direct examination: When a lawyer calls a witness, the lawyer's questioning of that witness is called the *direct examination*. The direct examination is generally used to establish those facts that are *essential* to the claim or defense of the party calling that witness. For instance, in a negligence action, the plaintiff will need to show, by direct examination of his witnesses, that the defendant was negligent and caused injury to the plaintiff.

   1. Hope that witness is believed: Normally, the direct examiner hopes that the factfinder will *believe* the witness. (But there are exceptions; for instance, one party may call the other party as a witness, in which case the calling party hopes that the direct testimony by the witness-party will be disbelieved).

B. Free narrative vs. specific questions: The direct examiner, in eliciting testimony from the witness, has two broad choices about how to question the witness: (1) to ask *specific questions* about the facts; or (2) to ask general questions eliciting a *narrative* from the witness. Each has its dangers and advantages.

   1. Specific questions: *Specific questions* about the facts have the advantage that they give the questioner tight control over how the witness testifies, so that the facts can be presented in the desired, and most comprehensible, order, and with the greatest clarity. The disadvantage is that very specific questions may, by their nature, suggest to the witness what answer is desired by the questioner, and thus be held to be *leading* (and therefore disallowed; see *infra*, p. 67).

   2. Narrative: Questions calling for a *narrative* (e.g., "Tell us, Mr. Plaintiff, what happened to you on the afternoon of June 13, 1987?") have the advantage that the witness is testifying completely in his own words, so that there is no danger that he is being "led." The main disadvantage is that the witness may blurt out inadmissible evidence (e.g., hearsay statements; see *infra*, p. 117), and the opposing lawyer will not have the ability to object to the question before the answer is given, as he could in the case of a more specific question. (If this does happen, the court's only remedy is to order the inadmissible portion of the testimony stricken, and to attempt to explain to the witness what kinds of statements he should not make.)

   3. Neither required nor preferred: Neither form of questioning is required or preferred as a matter of law. M, p. 10. So long as the questions are not leading, and the statements are not inadmissible, the choice of whether to ask specific questions or merely request a narrative is entirely up to the direct examiner.

C. Leading questions: The most important rule concerning direct testimony is that, generally, the examiner *may not ask leading questions*.

1. **Definition of "leading":** A leading question is one that *suggests to the witness the answer desired by the questioner*. M, p. 11.

    Example: D is charged with armed bank robbery. W, a teller, has just testified that D walked up to her and demanded money. The prosecutor then asks, "Did D point a gun at you?" This is a leading question, since it would suggest to a reasonable person in the witness' position the answer desired by the questioner (namely, "yes").

    a. **Re-phrasing:** A leading question can always be *rephrased* to make it non-leading. Thus, in the facts of the above example, the prosecutor could rephrase the question as follows: "What else, if anything, did the defendant say or do?" The court might also allow the prosecutor to ask a slightly more specific question: "What, if any, gestures did the defendant make?" On the other hand, probably any question calling the witness' attention to the fact that the defendant had or used a gun would be impermissibly leading.

2. **No mechanical formula:** There is no mechanical formula for determining whether a question is leading. The issue is always: Would a reasonable person in the witness' position understand what answer the questioner desired?

    a. **"Didn't" questions:** Questions beginning with "Didn't" will almost always be leading, since they almost always suggest that the questioner desires a "yes" answer. For instance, in a contract suit, where the plaintiff claims that the defendant refused to deliver, a question to the plaintiff, "Didn't the defendant then say that he wouldn't deliver the goods?" will certainly be leading. *Id.*

    b. **"Yes or no" questions:** Often, a question that lends itself to a simple "yes" or "no" answer will be leading. But this is not always the case. For instance, "Was the water hot?" will probably not be leading. *Id.*

    c. **Specific:** In general, the more *specific* the question, the more likely it is to be leading. Thus, "Did the defendant then punch you in the nose and stomp on you?" will almost certainly be leading, since the very specific facts contained in the question suggest to the witness that the questioner thinks that these things happened. Conversely, a question with almost no factual predicate (e.g., "What happened next?") will hardly ever be leading.

3. **Rationale for ban:** Why are leading questions prohibited on direct examination? A party who calls a witness will normally expect that that witness will give testimony favorable to the calling party. Courts reasonably fear that such a "friendly" witness will tend to "adopt whatever words the lawyer puts in his mouth." L&S, p. 255. Our judicial system's ability to ascertain the truth depends on the factfinder's ability to judge the knowledge and credibility of each witness; therefore, it is important that the factfinder hear the story in the *words of the witness*, not the words

of the calling lawyer.

4. **Exceptions:** There are several situations in which leading questions are **allowed** even on direct examination:

   a. **Unfriendly witness:** If the usual assumption that the witness is "friendly" to the party calling him is **incorrect**, leading questions may be asked. In this situation, there is little danger that the unfriendly witness will let the questioner put words in her mouth.

      i. **Party:** Thus, the **opposing party** will almost always be deemed to be unfriendly and therefore open to leading questions. See, e.g., FRE 611(c), allowing leading questions to an "adverse party" in all situations.

      ii. **Witness identified with party:** Similarly, a witness who is biased in favor of an opposing party, or otherwise identified with that party, may be examined by leading questions. For instance, a **relative** of the opposing party (e.g., the son of the defendant, when being questioned on direct by the plaintiff) will normally be found to be a hostile witness.

      iii. **Other indications:** The witness' **demeanor** on the witness stand may similarly make it clear that he is "hostile" to the examiner, in which case leading questions may be used. For instance, the witness may claim that he cannot remember the transaction in question, under circumstances which lead the court to believe that the witness is being deliberately uncooperative rather than honestly forgetful. If so, leading questions may be used.

   b. **Other situations:** Apart from the "hostile witness" situation, leading questions may be used in a few other situations:

      i. **Preliminary matters:** They may be used to develop **preliminary matters**, or matters that are not really in dispute. For instance, in our bank robbery example above, if neither side disputes that W, the teller, was on duty when a bank robbery took place (and the only question is whether D was the robber), the question, "Were you on duty at the Bank on the afternoon of August 12, 1987?" would be acceptable even though it is leading (it suggests that the questioner desires a "yes" answer).

      ii. **Suggestion of topic:** Similarly, a quite specific question will be allowed, if it merely suggests a **subject** rather than the desired answer. Thus in our bank robbery example above, the question, "Did you or anyone else make any attempt to summon the authorities while the robbery was in progress?" might well be allowed, despite its specificity, since it merely introduces a new topic (summoning of the authorities).

      iii. **Forgetful witness:** If the witness is **forgetful**, leading questions may sometimes be used to refresh his memory, by drawing his attention to the specific transaction. Lilly, p. 95. Such "memory jogging" questions, however, will usually be allowed only briefly, and only if the judge is convinced that their effect is not to put the questioner's words into the witness' mouth. *Id.*

        iv. Less competent witness: The witness may have some kind of **handicap** that makes it difficult for him to respond to non-leading questions. This may be the case, for instance, if the witness is very **young**, has trouble **speaking English**, is unusually **unintelligent**, or very **timid**. M, p. 13. In all of these situations, leading questions may be permitted. This is true even though the very disability may make it more, rather than less, likely that the witness will be very suggestible and thus will adopt the answer suggested by the leading question — in this situation, courts will usually hold that it is better to have possibly flawed testimony, subject to testing by cross-examination, than to have no testimony at all. *Id.*

    c. Reversals rare: In any event, the trial judge has **wide discretion** to determine what is or is not a leading question. No matter which way he decides, it will be **very rare** for him to be **reversed** on appeal. M, p. 12.

        i. Unfair trial: Occasionally, however, the judge's rulings on the issue of leading questions will be so one-sided that they amount to the **denial of a fair trial** for one party. This is more likely to happen when the judge repeatedly **allows** what are obvious and intentional leading questions objected to by the other side. For instance, in *Straub v. Reading Co.*, 220 F.2d 177 (3d Cir. 1955), the plaintiff was repeatedly asked obviously leading questions by his lawyer; for instance, in order to show that the defendant was involved in interstate commerce (a necessary element of plaintiff's case), P's lawyer was allowed to ask him, "And do you personally have to go to these different states and go in interstate commerce yourself personally?" The appellate court held that although the trial court has broad discretion as to what questions are leading and whether to allow them, "Where [the judge's control] is lost or at least palpably ignored and the conduct is a set piece running the length of the trial which produces a warped version of the issues as received by the jury," the other side has not received a fair trial and the verdict must be set aside.

D. Impeachment of own witness: Apart from the rule against leading questions, there is a second technique that is traditionally not permitted on direct examination: the direct examiner **may not "impeach his own witness."** That is, under the traditional rule, the direct examiner may not attempt to cast doubt on the accuracy or truthfulness of the witness he has called. This rule against impeaching one's own witness has been modified or abandoned in many jurisdictions, including the federal system; the rule is discussed more extensively *infra*, p. 78.

II. CROSS-EXAMINATION

A. Nature of cross-examination: After the party calling a witness has finished the direct examination, that party's adversary has the opportunity to **cross-examine** the witness. Cross-examination is usually thought to be indispensable to the truth-finding process. For instance, in some situations a criminal defendant's lack of opportunity to cross-examine a witness against him may be found to be a violation of the defendant's constitutional Confrontation Clause rights; see *infra*, p. 276. Similarly, lack of the opportunity to cross-examine is the main reason for the rule against hearsay (*infra*, p. 117), which prevents the use of out-of-court declarations to prove the truth of matters asserted therein.

B. Leading questions allowed: In contrast to direct examination, ***leading questions*** are usually ***permitted*** during cross-examination. M, p. 50.

   1. **Rationale:** Recall that the reason for not allowing leading questions on direct is that the witness is presumed to be friendly, and a friendly witness will all too readily acquiesce to the direct examiner's suggested answers. In cross-examination, by contrast, the witness will generally **not** be friendly, so there is little danger that the witness will adopt the questioner's suggested answers as his own.

   2. **Federal Rules:** The Federal Rules follow the usual practice of allowing leading questions on cross-examination. FRE 611(c) provides that "ordinarily leading questions should be permitted on cross-examination."

   3. **Exceptions:** But as in the direct examination context, the usual rule will be suspended if the typical relationship between questioner and witness is not present. Thus, if the witness is ***biased in favor of the cross-examiner***, the trial judge has discretion to prevent leading questions. This will be true, for instance, if the witness is a ***party*** adverse to the side who called him. Thus if P calls D to the stand, not only will P's lawyer be allowed to use leading questions in the direct examination, but D's lawyer will **not** be allowed to use leading questions on the "cross" (since it is not really a "cross"-examination at all).

C. Scope of cross: Most jurisdictions impose ***limits*** on the ***scope*** of cross-examination. There are three views, the most restrictive of which is followed by most jurisdictions:

   1. **"Restrictive" majority rule:** Most states, and the Federal Rules, ***limit the cross-examination to the matters testified to on the direct examination***. M, p. 52. This is sometimes known as the ***"scope of direct"*** rule.

> **Example:** P, a passenger in a car, is injured in a collision with a truck owned by D and operated by D's employee, W. P calls W as a witness, and covers only two items on his direct examination (whether W was on company business at the time of the accident, and whether W can identify an accident report made by him to the authorities). On cross, D's lawyer elicits from W W's entire version of the accident, none of which was touched on the direct exam by P.
>
> *Held*, the trial court erred in allowing this so-called "cross"-examination. In this jurisdiction, "cross-examination shall be limited to the subject-matter of the direct examination." Here, the trial judge's failure to follow this rule gave D "the distinct advantage of placing before the jury, at the outset of the trial, a version of the circumstances favorable to his contentions, proceeding from a witness called and in a sense vouched for by [P]. . . ." Normally, the trial judge has substantial discretion as to the scope of cross-examination and the order of proof; but here, the so-called cross-examination of W was so unfair to P that the court's discretion was abused and constituted reversible error. *Finch v. Weiner*, 145 A. 31 (Conn. 1929).

a. **Credibility:** Even in states following the restrictive majority rule, questions that are relevant to the witness' *credibility* are always regarded as within the proper scope of cross-examination. Thus FRE 611(b), which follows the majority rule, provides that "cross-examination should be limited to the subject matter of the direct examination and matters *affecting the credibility* of the witness."

b. **Trial court's discretion:** The trial court generally has *discretion* to permit cross-examination on matters that are not literally within the scope of direct, so long as the discretion is not abused. Thus FRE 611(b) concludes by stating that "the court, may in the exercise of discretion, permit inquiry into additional matters as if on direct examination."

c. **Same transaction or statement:** Even in states following the majority "scope of direct" rule, the cross-examiner may bring out facts that relate to the *same transaction*, *conversation*, or statement that was the subject of direct examination. M, p. 53. For instance, suppose that on direct, P's lawyer asks W, "What did D say to you after the collision?" D's lawyer will be permitted to ask W on cross, "What did you say in return?" since W's response was part of the same conversation that was testified to on direct. As some courts put it, P, by his question on direct, has *"opened the door"* to the rest of the conversation. See, e.g., *U.S. v. Segal*, 534 F.2d 578 (3d Cir. 1976) (where prosecution asked W on direct about a conversation with D, D's lawyer should have been allowed on cross-examination to play parts of a tape of that same conversation or to read a transcript of it; the fact that D was given the right to re-call W to the stand during D's own case was not sufficient to undo the unfairness to D of being denied the right to perform a full cross-examination about the conversation).

d. **Tactics:** The majority "scope of direct" rule gives the direct examiner a substantial ability to *control the facts* and testimony brought out in his case.

> **Example:** In a negligence suit arising out of a car crash, P's lawyer wishes to withhold from the jury the fact that P was intoxicated while driving at the time of the accident. P does not testify, but his lawyer calls W, who was a passenger in the car, to testify that D went through a red light.
>
> So long as W confines his testimony solely to D's conduct, P's lawyer will probably be able to ensure that during P's case, the jury does not learn about P's intoxication. (Questions by D's lawyer on cross-examination of W concerning P's intoxication cannot be justified on credibility grounds so long as P never takes the witness stand.) P's lawyer cannot keep this information from the jury indefinitely — during D's case, D will be able to call W as a witness and ask whatever he wishes; furthermore, D will be able to call P and ask him about drunkenness. But the majority "scope of direct" rule does allow P's lawyer to see to it that this information does not come in until D's case, and that it does not come in from witnesses who have been called (and in a sense "vouched for") by P.

> i. **Leading questions:** The "scope of direct" rule may also permit a direct examiner to deprive his adversary of the benefit of leading questions. Even

if the trial judge permits the cross-examiner to go beyond the scope of direct, the trial judge has discretion to order the cross-examiner not to use *leading questions* to cover matters that go beyond the scope of direct. (Similarly, in "wide open" jurisdictions, discussed below, that permit cross-examination about matters not covered in direct, leading questions may be barred on cross as to the new material. See L&S, p. 257.)

2. **Traditional "wide open" rule:** A minority of states follow the English rule, sometimes known as the *"wide open"* rule. In these states, the cross-examiner may inquire about *any subject* relevant to the issues in the entire case. Most significantly, the cross-examiner may bring up subjects relating solely to the examiner's own claim or affirmative defense. M, p. 51. Thus in our above example concerning plaintiff's intoxication, in a wide-open jurisdiction D could ask W about P's intoxication, even though that intoxication relates solely to D's affirmative defense of contributory negligence.

3. **Middle ground:** A few states take a *middle ground* between the majority restrictive "scope of direct" rule and the minority "wide open" rule. Under this view, the cross-examiner may ask about any subject so long as it is not part of the examiner's *own claims or affirmative defenses.* M, p. 53.

D. **Art of cross-examination:** A real treatment of the "art of cross-examination" is beyond the scope of this outline, and is usually covered in trial advocacy courses. Here, however, briefly stated, are four cardinal rules of cross-examination:

1. **Preparation:** Even great "talent" at cross-examination is no substitute for *preparation*. Most successful cross-examinations are less the product of talent than they are the fruits of extensive review of documents, depositions of hostile witnesses, interviews with favorable witnesses, and other forms of pre-trial preparation.

   Example: See the description of the cross-examination of the defendant in *U.S. v. Owens, infra,* p. 90. Had the prosecutor not gone to police and court records to discover D's prior arrests and convictions, and then compared these with D's job application, the most brilliant cross-examination technique would not have produced the impeachment that in fact occurred.

2. **Know the answer:** "Never ask a question to which you do not know the answer." While this is probably an overstatement, it reflects the well-established principle that the examiner must be at least reasonably confident that the question will produce a *favorable response*.

   Example: D is arrested and charged with pick-pocketing. She tells her lawyer (W.S. Gilbert, shortly before he teamed up with Sullivan) that she was on her way to church, with her hymn-book in her pocket, when she was arrested, and that the purse found on her must have been planted by some unknown evil person. Gilbert performs the first cross-examination of his career, of the arresting policeman; he is determined to call attention to the hymn-book in D's pocket. The examination goes like this:

Gilbert: You say you found the purse in her pocket, my man?

Constable: Yes, sir.

Gilbert: Did you find anything else?

Constable: Yes, sir.

Gilbert: What?

Constable: Two other purses, a watch with the bow broken, three handkerchiefs, two silver pencil-cases, and a hymn-book.

See K&W, p. 442.

3. **No broad questions or ones calling for explanation:** Control the witness with tightly-phrased, **narrow** questions. Don't give the witness a chance to expand or buttress his testimony by asking broad questions or questions that request an explanation.

> **Example:** D is charged with theft. D does not take the stand, but his lawyer shakes the testimony of the only eyewitness. D's lawyer then cross-examines the arresting policeman, bringing out the fact that D is a veteran and that D's wife is pregnant. He then asks one last question: "Having regard to this man's splendid record, how did you come to arrest him?"
>
> The policeman "drew a bundle of blue documents from the recesses of his uniform, and, moistening his tongue, read therefrom. [D's lawyer] learned in silent horror that the prisoner's record included nine previous convictions." Mathew, Forensic Fables by O (quoted in K&W, pp. 442-43).

4. **Make one or two big points:** End on high note: try to make one or two big points, and don't dull them by also making a lot of insignificant points. When you make a big point, pass immediately on to another issue, so that the witness does not have a chance to recant or wriggle out of the trap. "When you have struck oil, stop boring." M, p. 67.

See generally M, pp. 66-67.

III. REDIRECT AND RECROSS

A. Redirect: After cross-examination, the party who called the witness has the opportunity to question him again, in what is called **redirect** examination.

1. **Scope:** The party who calls a witness is normally required to elicit on the original direct examination every part of the witness' story that is of interest to the calling party. Thus the redirect examination must normally be limited to aspects of the witness' testimony that were **first brought out during cross-examination.**

   a. **Drawing the sting:** As to these matters first revealed on cross, the redirect examiner's job is normally to **"draw the sting"** of the cross-examination by giving the witness an opportunity to explain or avoid the troublesome facts or

74 EXAMINATION AND IMPEACHMENT

statements that came out on cross. M, p. 70.

> **Example:** Let's return to our automobile collision example from p. 71. W (the passenger in a car driven by P) testifies on direct that D drove carelessly, but does not say anything about P's conduct. Assume that the jurisdiction follows the "wide open" rule, and that D's lawyer is permitted on cross to draw out the fact that W saw P have three beers just before the accident. On redirect, P's lawyer would not be permitted to have W testify to any additional facts concerning D's carelessness, since that carelessness was the subject of the original direct exam. But he could ask W, "Did you notice any change in P's behavior after the three beers?" or "Did P's ability to drive seem to be impaired?" since the entire issue of P's intoxication did not come out until the cross-examination of W.

    2. Discretion of judge: As with most issues regarding the order and scope of examination, the trial judge has **broad discretion** in what to allow on redirect. While he usually does not have discretion to refuse to allow entirely new matters to be brought out, he does generally have discretion to allow matters to be amplified that were first presented on direct. For instance, if the direct examiner can show that he honestly overlooked one aspect of an issue that was developed on direct, and that the aspect is very important, the trial judge may well allow redirect on this point (though the judge's refusal to allow it would not be grounds for reversal).

B. Recross: After redirect, the cross-examiner will have a limited opportunity to conduct **recross** examination. As with redirect, the recross may not cover subjects that were covered by the examiner in his previous questioning (in this case, the cross-examination) — only matters **newly brought up in the redirect** may be touched upon.

> **Example:** On direct, W, a prosecution witness, testifies that he previously picked D out of a police lineup. On cross, W admits that his identification of D was only because D was wearing a blue shirt. On redirect, W changes his story to add that D's face and hair were also factors in his identification. On re-cross, D's lawyer tries to return to the identification issue, but the trial judge refuses.
>
> *Held*, D's lawyer had no right to cover the identification in recross: "There comes a time when examination on a given subject must close. Here the state on redirect examination did not bring out something new and on which defendant had not already fully examined the witness . . . [so] recross-examination was properly denied." (But observe that it was not until redirect that W testified that he had recognized D's face or hair, so the court's ruling did deprive D of the right to challenge these aspects of the identification.) *State v. McSloy*, 261 P.2d 663 (Mont. 1953).

IV. REFRESHING RECOLLECTION AND OTHER TECHNIQUES

A. Refreshing the witness' recollection: Suppose that a witness' recollection of an event is hazy. It may be possible to **refresh** his recollection by showing him a statement, picture, or other item; the item triggers an association in the witness' mind, enabling him to recall the event more clearly.

1. **Traditional rule:** Nearly all courts permit *any item* to be shown to the witness while he is on the stand, to refresh his recollection. The examiner need not establish the authorship, time of making, or even correctness of the object. M, p. 19. This technique is usually called that of *"present recollection refreshed."*

   a. **Rationale:** The rationale for this liberal rule is that the item shown to the witness is *not evidence* at all. It is merely a stimulus to the witness' memory. After the witness' memory is refreshed, the evidence comes *from the witness*, not the document or other item shown to him.

   b. **Distinguished from "past recollection recorded":** This "present recollection refreshed" technique must be distinguished from the technique of "past recollection recorded," by which a witness is shown a writing that he has prepared or authenticated, and that was made shortly after an event. If the tests for past recollection recorded (see *infra*, p. 189) are satisfied, the writing *becomes evidence*, and can be used to prove the truth of the matters asserted in the writing, even if the witness testifies that he has no independent recollection of the events described.

2. **Danger:** Assume that the witness' memory of an event is hazy, that he is shown a document to refresh his recollection, and that he then proceeds to give refreshed testimony about the event. There is a danger that the witness' memory has not really been refreshed, and that he is instead simply reciting what the document says. This danger is increased by the rule, followed in most courts, that the witness may *repeatedly consult* the writing while testifying. M, p. 21. To guard against this danger, there are two main safeguards:

   a. **Judge's discretion:** First, the trial judge has discretion to determine whether the witness really *is* testifying from refreshed memory rather than simply reciting the contents of the document. M, p. 20. The judge may examine the memorandum in reaching this decision. If he concludes that the witness is merely parroting what the document says, he may strike the testimony. See, e.g., *U.S. v. Riccardi*, 174 F.2d 883 (3d Cir. 1949) (trial judge "should in the first instance satisfy himself as to whether the witness testifies upon a record or from his own recollection.")

   b. **Given to adversary:** Second, the cross-examiner may *examine the document*, and test whether the witness really has an independent recollection of the event. In most jurisdictions, the cross-examiner can introduce into evidence those portions of the document that relate to the witness' testimony. See, e.g., FRE 612(2).

   Note: Other aspects of the "present recollection refreshed" technique are discussed in the treatment of hearsay, *infra*, p. 192.

3. **Document consulted before trial:** The careful trial lawyer always *prepares* each of his witnesses beforehand, by reviewing with him the testimony that the witness will give. As part of this preparation, the lawyer will often show the witness a statement or other item to refresh his recollection. If the witness then gives trial testimony without consulting the item on the stand, and the opposing lawyer learns

that the item was consulted prior to the testimony, does he have the right to demand the item so that he can use it for cross-examination?

    a. Rarely required: Courts *rarely* require the document to be shown to the cross-examiner. L&S, p. 439, n. 24. (A party has a better chance of getting the evidence as part of pretrial *discovery* proceedings.)

    b. Federal Rule: But the Federal Rules explicitly give the trial judge discretion to order production of a document consulted by the witness before testifying "if the court in its discretion determines it is *necessary* in the interests of justice." (FRE 612)

B. Argumentative and misleading questions: We now treat briefly two other techniques for shaping a witness' testimony, both of which are *improper:* (1) argumentative questions; and (2) misleading questions.

    1. Argumentative: An *argumentative* question is one which is "designed to induce the witness to affirm counsel's interpretation of the evidence." Lilly, p. 97. Argumentative questions are disallowed because the interpretation of the evidence is to be done by the jury, not by the lawyer or the witness. *Id.*

        Example: In a prosecution against D for mayhem, D's lawyer asks W, "Isn't it a fact that [D's] mouth is so small that he could not reach up and get it wide enough open to get [Complainant's] ear in there?" *Held*, question is argumentative, since both mouth and ear were visible to jury. *White v. State*, 210 P. 313 (Ok.Cr. 1922).

        a. Cross-examination: Argumentative questions are heard more often on cross than on direct. On cross, trial judges have discretion, which they sometimes exercise, to allow a question that is, strictly speaking, argumentative. Lilly, p. 97.

    2. Misleading questions: A *misleading* question is one that assumes as true a fact that is either *not in evidence* or is *in dispute*. Most misleading questions have a "trick" aspect about them, since by answering the witness implicitly affirms the correctness of the assumption.

        Example: Lawyer to witness: "When did you stop beating your wife?" If there is no evidence that the witness ever beat his wife, or the evidence is in dispute, the question will be stricken as misleading, since any answer by the witness will be an implicit admission that he has beaten her.

V. EXAMINATION BY COURT

    A. General rule: Virtually all states, and the Federal Rules, allow the trial judge to *call her own witnesses*, and to *question any witness* (whether called by the judge or by a party). L&S, p. 275. See FRE 614(a) and (b).

    1. Witness called by judge: If the judge calls a witness, either side may question the witness as if in *cross-examination*. Thus, each side may use leading questions.

2. **Judge's discretion:** The decision whether to call a witness is generally left to the judge's *discretion.* One common situation for the discretion to be exercised arises in criminal cases in which the prosecution needs testimony from a particular witness, but does not want to call the witness itself, because either: (1) the witness will be uncooperative but not hostile (so that the prosecutor will not be allowed to use leading questions unless the court calls the witness); or (2) the prosecution does not wish to be seen to be vouching for or "sponsoring" the witness' testimony (perhaps because the witness is of clearly bad character, or has told inconsistent stories in the past), yet the prosecution needs the testimony. L&S, p. 275; M, pp. 16-17.

3. **Questioning by judge:** Most states do not permit the judge to **comment on the evidence** in jury trials. Therefore, although the trial judge has discretion to question the witnesses, he must be careful that his questioning does not seem so one-sided that it will seem to the jury to be an implied comment on the evidence. L&S, pp. 275-76. In the minority of states allowing the judge to comment on the evidence, and in bench trials, the judge can be much freer in his questioning of witnesses. *Id.*

VI. IMPEACHMENT — GENERALLY

A. **Meaning of "impeachment":** In ordinary cross-examination, the questioner tries to show flaws in the witness' *testimony.* For instance, he may try to get the witness to change his story, or expose gaps in the account, or otherwise render the testimony less damaging. *Impeachment*, by contrast, is a technique to show *flaws in the witness*, rather than in the testimony. That is, the tool of impeachment is designed to destroy the witness' *credibility.* Thus whereas in the usual cross-examination the witness' honesty and ability are usually not questioned, in a successful impeachment these personal characteristics of the witness will be not only questioned but perhaps destroyed. L&S, p. 282.

B. **Five types:** There are five common techniques for impeaching a witness, one of which has three sub-techniques:

1. **Character:** The witness' general *character*, especially his character for *truthtelling*, may be attacked. This is usually done in one of three ways:

   a. **Convictions:** By showing that he has previously been *convicted* of one or more *crimes*;

   b. **Bad acts:** By showing that he has previously committed *bad acts* that have not led to a criminal conviction; or

   c. **Reputation:** By showing that he has a *bad reputation* (usually a reputation for not telling the truth).

2. **Prior inconsistent statement:** The witness' credibility may be attacked by showing that on a prior occasion, he has made a *statement* that is *inconsistent* with his present testimony.

3. **Bias:** Credibility may be attacked by showing that the witness is *biased* in favor of or against one side, because of family relationship, financial interest, or other

ulterior motive.

4. **Sensory or mental defect:** Credibility may be weakened by a showing that the witness suffers from a *sensory* or *mental* defect (e.g., the witness is hard of hearing so he could not have heard what he claims to have heard, or the witness is psychotic so his description of an event cannot be trusted).

5. **Contradiction:** Lastly, the witness may be impeached by the production of other evidence (e.g., testimony by a second witness) that statements made by the first witness are not correct. This is so-called "impeachment by contradiction."

We will be examining each of these types of impeachment in detail below.

C. **Impeaching one's own witness:** At common law, the rule has long existed that *"a party may not impeach his own witness."* To put it another way, impeachment is generally *not allowed on direct examination.* L&S, p. 282.

1. **Rationale:** Several rationales have been asserted in support of this traditional rule. None is very convincing. Here are the two most persuasive:

   a. **"Vouching" for one's witness:** First, by calling a witness, a party in a sense *"vouches for the credibility"* of that witness, and should therefore have no need to attack that credibility.

      i. **Criticism:** However, the assumption that a party vouches for the credibility of his witnesses is badly flawed. Usually, "the party has little or no choice of witnesses. The party calls only those who happened to have observed the particular facts in controversy." M, p. 82. See, e.g., *Johnson v. Baltimore & Ohio R.R. Co.,* 208 F.2d 633 (3d Cir. 1954) (wrongful death suit against railroad; only living witness to episode was employee of defendant railroad, whose conduct was at issue. *Held,* P could impeach W even though it called him, despite "vouching" rationale, because "when witnesses are called, in some stranger's lawsuit, to tell about things they saw, heard, or did, there is no reason in logic or common sense or fairness why the party who calls them should have to vouch for everything they say.")

   b. **Subterfuge:** Second, there is a danger that juries will incorrectly view material introduced to impeach a witness as being substantive evidence. This is especially true where the impeaching material is the witness' own prior inconsistent statement. If we allow a party to call a witness, elicit testimony from him, then put in a prior inconsistent statement that the jury may regard as substantive evidence, the party is given the chance to intentionally evade the hearsay rule. (See *infra,* p. 117.) L&S, p. 282.

      i. **Criticism:** One answer to this rationale is that the modern trend (following the Federal Rules approach) is to treat a witness' prior inconsistent statement as being *non-hearsay* and thus substantively admissible evidence. See *infra,* p. 252. When this approach is taken, allowing the direct examiner to introduce the witness' prior inconsistent statement does not give the jury access to otherwise-inadmissible evidence. L&S, p. 282.

2. Exceptions to common-law rule: Because of the weakness of these rationales for the common-law prohibition on impeachment during direct, most courts following the common law rule recognize several *exceptions* to it:

a. Surprise: If the witness' damaging testimony comes as a *surprise* to the direct examiner, the examiner will be allowed to impeach him by showing that he has made *prior inconsistent statements* on the subject. Lilly, p. 340.

i. Surprise must be genuine: But courts that recognize the "surprise" exception generally take pains to make sure that the examiner's surprise is genuine, and not just a subterfuge for getting a prior inconsistent statement before the jury. For instance, in *U.S. v. Miles*, 413 F.2d 34 (3d Cir. 1969), W gave a pre-trial statement implicating the Ds in an armed robbery, but repudiated her statement to the prosecutors both before the trial began and during *voir dire* of the witness; by the time W took the stand in front of the jury (the appellate court later held), the prosecutor could not have been surprised that W gave damaging testimony, so the prosecution should not have been allowed to rely on the "surprise" doctrine to introduce the prior statement as impeachment.

ii. Must be actually injurious: A second requirement for the "surprise" doctrine is usually that the witness' testimony "must affirmatively be damaging: he must make a positive assertion adverse to a material part of the proponent's case." Lilly, pp. 340-41. For instance, a statement by a witness that he *cannot remember* will usually *not* be found to be affirmatively damaging, and will therefore not justify use of the prior (helpful) statement. *Id.*

b. Adverse parties and hostile witnesses: Most jurisdictions allow impeachment on direct of an *adverse party*, on the theory that the "direct" examination of one party by the other is really in the nature of cross, rather than direct, examination. Lilly, p. 340. A witness whom the court finds to be *"hostile"*, even though not a party, may also usually be impeached on direct. L&S, p. 283.

c. Necessary witness: A witness may be impeached on direct if the calling party is *required* to call that witness as a matter of law. For instance, the proponent of a will is often required to call anyone who attested the will, in order to establish that the will was properly executed; such a witness could then be impeached. Lilly, p. 340.

d. Judge calls: If the witness is called by the *judge* (*supra*, pp. 76-77), each side may impeach.

e. "Refreshing" recollection: Finally, a skillful direct examiner may, under the guise of "refreshing" the witness' recollection, ask the witness whether he has previously told a different story. Even if the witness sticks to his present version, the possible existence of the prior version has at least been called to the jury's attention. L&S, p. 283.

3. **Modern and Federal rule:** In recent years, a number of jurisdictions have wholly or partly ***abandoned*** the common law rule against impeachment on direct. See, e.g., Cal. Evid. Code §785 (complete abandonment of rule). Most dramatically, the Federal Rules ***completely abandon the common-law rule.*** FRE 607 provides that "the credibility of a witness may be ***attacked by any party***, including the ***party calling the witness.***"

   a. **Constitutional requirement:** In some instances, it may even be ***constitutionally required*** that a party be permitted to impeach a witness that it has called. In a criminal case, if the defendant calls a witness and is then prevented from impeaching that witness, this may be a denial of the defendant's rights under the Constitution's ***Confrontation Clause.***

      i. ***Chambers:*** For instance, in *Chambers v. Mississippi*, 410 U.S. 284 (1973) (discussed more extensively *infra*, pp. 285-86), D, charged with murder, was prevented at trial by the state's "no impeachment of one's own witness" rule from showing that one McDonald had previously confessed in writing to the crime; this, together with other errors, was enough to violate D's constitutional right to a fair trial, the Court held.

      ii. **Limited right:** Courts have so far not accepted arguments by criminal defendants that the defendant is *always* constitutionally entitled to impeach his own witnesses. L&S, p. 283. But clearly there will be many situations, such as that in *Chambers*, where adherence to the strict common-law "no impeachment upon direct" rule will violate the Confrontation Clause. *Id.*

4. **Leading questions:** One way to impeach a witness is to ask him ***leading questions*** designed to test his credibility (e.g., "Isn't it true that you told a different story previously?") As we've just seen, some states, and the Federal Rules, now allow a party to impeach his own witness. Yet leading questions are not normally allowed on direct. How can these two rules be reconciled?

   a. **Hostility:** First, remember that where the witness is ***hostile***, leading questions are normally allowed even on direct (see *supra*, p. 68).

   b. **Non-hostile:** Where, however, the witness is not truly hostile, but gives testimony that is less favorable than expected, it is not clear whether impeachment by leading questions should be allowed. Recall that FRE 611(c) provides that "leading questions should not be used on the direct examination of a witness except as may be necessary to develop the witness' testimony." S&R (p. 565) suggest that in federal trials, any time a witness on direct gives unfavorable testimony (even if he is not truly "hostile"), FRE 611(c) should be interpreted to allow leading questions for purposes of impeachment.

VII. IMPEACHMENT BY PRIOR CRIMINAL CONVICTIONS

A. **Problem generally:** Of all the techniques of impeachment, probably the most controversial is that of showing that the witness has previously been ***convicted of a crime***. The controversy is especially great when the issue is whether prior convictions can be used to impeach the credibility of the ***accused*** in a criminal case who takes the stand in his own defense. On the one hand, the fact that the witness has been convicted of a crime (especially a crime involving dishonesty) may be legitimately relevant to whether his present testimony is believable. But on the other hand, there is a danger that the factfinder will use the prior convictions not only for evaluating credibility, but also for impermissible substantive purposes. (Recall that use of prior crimes for the substantive purpose of showing that the defendant has a propensity to commit crimes, and therefore probably committed the presently-charged crime, is not allowed; see *supra*, p. 22.)

B. Common law approach: The common-law approach to this problem is, in general, that two types of prior convictions may be used to impeach the witness: (1) *any felony conviction*; or (2) a misdemeanor conviction, but only if the crime involved dishonesty or a *false statement*. L&S, p. 284. However, states following the general common-law approach vary widely in defining exactly what kinds of convictions can be used. M, p. 93.

1. **Criminal defendant:** The common-law rule places a *criminal defendant* who has prior convictions in a terrible dilemma: if he takes the witness stand in his own defense, all of his prior felony convictions, and even misdemeanors that bear on veracity, can be disclosed to the jury. The jury may react not only by disbelieving the accused's testimony, but by further reasoning either that: (1) "If he did it before, he did it this time"; or (2) "If he did it before, we'll all be better off if we get him off the streets whether or not he did it this time." Yet if the accused does *not* take the stand, the jury is likely to hold this silence against him (even if it is instructed not to do so by the trial judge); this is especially likely to be so where the facts are such that the defendant is the only one who can give a convincing explanation of why the defendant is innocent.

   a. **Relevance to veracity:** Furthermore, the common-law rule will often allow introduction of prior convictions that have practically nothing to do with the witness' veracity. Since all felony convictions are usable under the common-law approach — regardless of whether they have anything to do with truthfulness — even a prior murder or child molestation conviction is usable. Yet the prejudicial effect of such a conviction is far greater than any relevance that that conviction may have to the issue of whether the witness is now telling the truth.

C. Federal Rules: The Federal Rules follow a *middle approach* between the widespread right to use prior convictions at common law, and the narrow admissibility urged by the common law rule's critics. FRE 609(a) provides as follows:

"For the purpose of attacking the credibility of a witness, (1) evidence that the witness other than an accused had been convicted of a crime shall be admitted, subject to Rule 403, if the crime was punishable by death or imprisonment in excess of one year under the law under which the witness was convicted, and evidence that an accused has been convicted of such a crime shall be admitted if the court determines that the probative value of admitting this evidence outweighs its prejudicial effect to the accused; and (2) evidence that any witness has been convicted of a crime shall be admitted if it involved dishonesty or false statement, regardless of the punishment."

1. **Criminal defendant as witness:** Thus where the witness is the accused in a criminal trial, the Federal Rules' approach works like this:

a. **Felony without dishonesty:** If the prior conviction is a felony that does not involve "dishonesty or false statement," the trial judge must conduct a balancing: only if the judge finds that the probative value (presumably its value in determining whether the accused is telling the truth now) is greater than the prejudice to the defendant, may the prior conviction be admitted.

b. ***Crimen falsi***: But if the prior conviction involved ***"dishonest or false statement,"*** it will ***automatically*** be admissible against the defendant, ***whether it was a felony or misdemeanor***, and ***no matter how prejudicial*** to him its introduction will be. (A crime involving "dishonesty or false statement" is often referred to as a ***"crimen falsi."***)

2. **Definition of *crimen falsi*:** It is not clear exactly what crimes will constitute *crimen falsi*, and thus be admissible regardless of punishment and regardless of the degree of prejudice to the defendant. The Conference Report on FRE 609 said that Congress intended to cover crimes such as "perjury or subornation of perjury, false statement, criminal fraud, embezzlement, or false pretense, or any other offense in the nature of *crimen falsi*, the commission of which involves some element of **deceit**, **untruthfulness**, or **falsification** bearing upon the accused's **propensity to testify truthfully**."

   a. **Larceny:** It is not clear whether crimes of ***larceny*** that do not directly involve deceit are *crimen falsi*. Thus while embezzlement clearly is a *crimen falsi*, simple car theft may not be. See, e.g., *U.S. v. Dorsey*, 591 F.2d 922 (D.C.Cir. 1978), holding that shoplifting and other ***petit larceny*** crimes are not *crimen false*, because although they involve stealth, they do not involve deceit or fraud.

3. **No discretion:** If the court does hold that the prior conviction is for a *crimen falsi*, the court apparently has ***no discretion*** to exclude it, ***no matter how prejudicial*** to the defendant it may be.

   a. **Argument by defendant:** Some criminal defendants have argued that even where the prior crime is a *crimen falsi*, the judge has discretion to exclude it under FRE 403, by which relevant evidence "may be excluded if its probative value is substantially outweighed by the danger of unfair prejudice. . . ."

   b. **Rejected:** But every court to have considered this argument has **rejected** it, on the theory that Congress was quite specific in not allowing the weighing of prejudice against probative value in the case of *crimen falsi*. See, e.g., *U.S. v. Toney*, 615 F.2d 277 (5th Cir. 1980) ("Congress meant what it said in Rule 609(a)(2) — that the fact of a prior conviction for an offense such as mail fraud is always admissible for impeachment purposes.") Similarly, *U.S. v. Wong*, 703 F.2d 65 (3d Cir. 1983) (trial judge had no discretion to weigh probative value of prior mail fraud and Medicare fraud convictions against their prejudicial effect on the defendant, because the legislative history of FRE 609 makes it clear that the general balancing test of FRE 403 was not to apply in this *crimen falsi* situation).

4. **Similar prior felonies:** Where a crime that is not a *crimen falsi* is involved, one situation presents an especially high risk of prejudice to the defendant: if the prior

offense is *very similar* or *identical* to the presently-charged offense, the jury is even more likely than usual to reason that "if he did it before, he'll do it again."

a. **Sanitizing:** Some courts have tried to deal with this problem by allowing evidence of the prior similar events, but in a *"sanitized"* version that does not identify the crime. Thus in an auto theft prosecution, a prior conviction for auto theft might be allowed for impeachment, but the prosecution might be permitted only to introduce the fact that the witness-defendant was previously convicted of "a felony involving theft."

   i. **Sanitizing rejected:** But not all courts have found the "sanitizing" technique helpful. See, e.g., *People v. Barrick*, 654 P.2d 1243 (Cal. 1982), holding that the technique "in fact tends to focus the speculation towards the conclusion that the prior crime was identical, which inevitably leads to the improper presumption that 'if he did it once, he will do it again.' " (Incidentally, a line of California Supreme Court cases restricting use of prior convictions, of which *Barrick* is a part, was abruptly reversed by the California voters. In 1982, voters approved by initiative an amendment to the California Constitution called the Victims' Bill of Rights, which included a provision that "any prior felony conviction of any person in any criminal proceeding, whether adult or juvenile, shall subsequently be used without limitation for purposes of impeachment or enhancement of sentence in any criminal proceeding." Cal. Const. Art. I, §28.)

5. **Balancing:** When a trial judge balances prejudice against probative value in deciding whether to allow impeachment use of a non-*crimen falsi* prior conviction, here are some of the factors that the judge is likely to consider:

   a. **Impeachment value:** The *"impeachment value"* of the prior crime. The more probative the prior crime is on the issue of whether the defendant-witness is now telling the truth, the more likely it is to be admitted (so that heat-of-passion manslaughter would be less likely to be admitted than, say, shoplifting, since the former has no bearing whatsoever on veracity, whereas the latter's factor of stealth has a least a slight connection to truthtelling);

   b. **Recency:** The *recency* of the prior conviction. The older the conviction, the less relevant it is and thus the less likely to be admitted;

   c. **Similarity:** The *similarity* between the prior crime and the charged one. As noted, the more similar, the more prejudicial and thus, the less likely to be admitted;

   d. **Importance of defendant's testimony:** The *importance* of the defendant's *testimony*. Thus if the defendant is the only witness who does or could testify for the defendant's case, the prior conviction is less likely to be admitted than if the defendant's case is also buttressed by numerous other eyewitnesses; and

   e. **Centrality of credibility issue:** The *centrality* of the *credibility issue*. Thus if the case is likely to come down to a "swearing contest" between the defendant-witness and, say, a police officer, the prior conviction is less likely to be admitted than if the case turns mostly on non-credibility issues such as the results of scientific tests or the interpretation of documents.

See *U.S. v. Mahone*, 537 F.2d 922 (7th Cir. 1976), listing these factors.

6. **Witnesses other than an accused (prosecution witnesses, defense witnesses, witnesses in civil cases):** As the prior discussion of FRE 609(a) shows, a witness who is a criminal defendant gets special protection before he can be impeached with prior felony convictions not involving dishonesty: the prosecution must show that the conviction's probative value is greater than the prejudice to the defendant, for the prior conviction to be admitted. But *witnesses other than the accused* do *not* get the same special protection against past-conviction impeachment: 609(a) now reads that "evidence that the witness other than an accused had been convicted of a crime shall be admitted, subject to Rule 403, if the crime was punishable [as a felony]." This language was added in 1990, to make it clear that witnesses other than criminal defendants don't get the benefit of the special burden of proof — instead, FRE 403 applies, allowing the prior conviction to be excluded only if the person opposing its introduction shows that the conviction's probative value "is substantially outweighed by the danger of unfair prejudice. . . ." So the following types of witnesses don't get special protection against having their past felony convictions used to impeach them:

   a. **Prosecution witnesses:** Witnesses *for the prosecution* in a criminal case;

   b. **Defense witnesses:** Witnesses for a *criminal defendant* (other than the accused himself); and

   c. **Civil witnesses:** Witnesses for either the plaintiff or the defense in a *civil* case.

   Example: D is prosecuted for bank robbery. The prosecution offers testimony by W, an accomplice of D's in the crime, who has turned state's evidence. D's lawyer wishes to impeach W by showing that W was previously convicted of bank robbery, and is therefore not worthy of belief. The prosecution will be able to keep out this past felony conviction only if the prosecution can carry its burden under FRE 403 of showing that the probative value of the conviction is "substantially outweighed" by the danger of unfair prejudice to the prosecution, confusion of the issues, or one of the other items listed in FRE 403. The prosecution will probably not be able to bear this burden, and the prior conviction will be used for impeachment of W.

7. **Time limit:** As noted, the *older* the conviction, the less probative value it has. FRE 609 contains a special provision making very old convictions hard to get into evidence: 609(b) provides that if more than *10 years* has elapsed from both the conviction and the prison term for that conviction, the conviction is not admissible "unless the court determines, in the interests of justice, that the probative value of the conviction supported by *specific facts and circumstances substantially outweighs* its prejudicial effect." The requirement of specific facts and circumstances, and the requirement that value "substantially" outweigh prejudice, make it much harder to get a 10-year-old conviction into evidence than a more

recent one. Furthermore, the last sentence of 609(b) requires that the party seeking admission of the more-than-10-year-old conviction must give **advance written notice** of its intent to use the conviction, so that the other party may have "a fair opportunity to contest the use of such evidence."

8. **In limine motions:** Before a defendant who has prior convictions decides whether to testify, he will often want to know whether these convictions can be introduced against him. Therefore, he will often before taking the stand ask the trial judge for an **in limine** ruling, in which the judge specifies which, if any, of the prior convictions can be used against the defendant.

   a. **Clever technique no longer allowed:** Before 1984, such *in limine* rulings provided a clever defendant a riskless way of possibly developing an appealable error. A defendant who had no intention of testifying could ask for an *in limine* ruling; if the judge ruled that the convictions could be used against the defendant, the defendant could then claim reversible error on appeal. For this reason, trial judges often refused to rule on the admissibility of prior convictions until the defendant actually took the stand, or required the defendant to state in writing that he would take the stand if the convictions were held inadmissible.

   b. ***Luce* case removes technique:** But this defense technique no longer works, as the result of the Supreme Court's ruling in *Luce v. U.S.*, 469 U.S. 38 (1984). There, the Court held that if the trial judge in its *in limine* ruling allows use of a prior conviction, and the defendant then does **not in fact testify**, the trial judge's decision to allow use of the conviction will **not be reviewed on appeal** (at least in federal courts).

      i. **Rationale:** The Court reasoned that if the defendant does not take the stand, any harm from the district court's *in limine* ruling permitting use of the prior convictions for impeachment is "wholly speculative," since there is no way to know that the defendant would have testified absent the ruling, or even any way to know whether the prosecution would in fact have used the prior conviction for impeachment.

      ii. **Consequence:** As a result of *Luce*, in federal cases the use of prior convictions is a battle that will largely be fought out at the trial level. If the trial judge, prior to the defendant's taking the stand, rules that the prior convictions will be admissible, the defendant who then elects not to take the stand because he is afraid of this impeachment has no possibility of appellate review of the judge's decision, no matter how wrong it may have been. If the defendant decides to go ahead and testify anyway, he at least has a theoretical possibility of appellate review of the decision to allow the convictions into evidence (but even here, because FRE 609(a)(1) requires the trial judge to balance probative value against prejudice, the matter is likely to be left to the trial judge's discretion unless that judge's decision is very clearly wrong).

9. **Procedure:** If use of the prior convictions is allowed, there are two main ways in which this evidence can be introduced. First, the opposing lawyer (usually the prosecutor) can ask the witness during cross-examination to admit the fact of the conviction. Alternatively, the cross-examiner may introduce a ***certified copy*** of the prior judgment. Lilly, p. 345.

10. **Details:** Courts disagree on what ***details*** about the previous conviction may be disclosed to the jury. The name of the crime and the date and place of the conviction are almost always allowed into evidence. Some, but not all, courts also allow the jury to learn the ***sentence***. Most courts ***disallow a detailed description*** of the underlying acts; for instance, the court might allow disclosure that there was a conviction for assault, but not disclosure of the fact that the victim was the witness' wife. *Id.* Regardless of whether the details of the prior conviction are disclosed, the court will usually allow the impeached witness to give a short statement explaining the circumstances of the prior conviction (though this may be dangerous for the witness to do, since it may open the door to a rebuttal by the other side). L&S, p. 291.

11. **State or federal:** The conviction need not be in the same jurisdiction as the present case. Thus a conviction from any state may be used in a federal trial, and vice versa. M, p. 95.

12. **Pardon:** Most state courts allow use of a conviction even if the witness was ***pardoned***. M, p. 96. Under the Federal Rules, the effect of a pardon depends on the reason for it: (1) If the pardon was granted because the person convicted was found to have been ***rehabilitated***, the conviction cannot be used for impeachment as long as the witness has not been convicted of a ***subsequent felony***; (2) If the pardon is based upon a finding of ***innocence***, the conviction may never be used for impeachment, even if the witness is convicted of subsequent crimes. FRE 609(c).

13. **Juvenile adjudications:** At common law, evidence that the witness has been the subject of a ***"juvenile adjudication"*** (i.e., found to have committed an act which would have been a crime had the defendant been an adult), is generally ***not admissible***. S&R, p. 525. But the federal rules change this slightly: FRE 609(d) states the general rule that juvenile adjudications are not admissible, but adds that "the court may, however, in a criminal case allow evidence of a juvenile adjudication of a ***witness other than the accused*** if conviction of the offense would be admissible to attack the credibility of an adult and the court is satisfied that admission in evidence is necessary for a fair determination of the issue of guilt or innocence."

   a. **Consequence:** This means that juvenile adjudications are never admissible in civil cases, and that an accused who takes the stand can never be impeached by his own juvenile adjudication.

14. **Appeals:** The fact that the prior conviction is being ***appealed*** does not make the conviction inadmissible, either at common law or under the Federal Rules. See FRE 609(e). But the pendency of the appeal is, under FRE 609(e), a fact that can be disclosed to the jury. Some commentators have argued that if a criminal defendant is impeached by the use of a conviction that is later overturned on appeal, a new trial should be required in the second suit. S&R, p. 526.

15. *Nolo contendere* **pleas:** It is not clear whether a conviction based upon a plea of *nolo contendere* is admissible. In federal cases, FRE 410(2) makes pleas of *nolo contendere* inadmissible in later proceedings. However, since FRE 609 does not exclude convictions based on *nolo* pleas, it is probably the case that a conviction based on a *nolo* plea is admissible, even though the fact that the conviction came about by a *nolo* plea rather than by trial is not admissible. See M, p. 97, n. 24, urging this interpretation.

VIII. IMPEACHMENT BY PRIOR BAD ACTS

A. Use of bad acts generally: Just as a witness' prior criminal convictions may impeach his credibility, so may his past ***misconduct*** that has not led to a conviction. If it can be shown that the witness has lied on a job application, embezzled from an employer, evaded taxes, or done some other act that reflects poorly on his veracity, but that has not led to a criminal conviction, the witness will be shown to be less worthy of belief. Yet such prior misconduct by hypothesis has not been the subject of independent judicial proof "beyond a reasonable doubt," so in a sense it is more troubling to allow the witness to be impeached by such conduct than by a past conviction.

   1. Common-law view: Most common law jurisdictions have adopted a compromise between freely allowing evidence of prior bad acts and completely excluding it. The majority rule at common law ***allows*** prior bad acts, but subject to the following limitations:

   a. No extrinsic evidence: Most importantly, the questioner must introduce the prior bad act ***solely through cross-examination*** of the witness. For instance, he may ask the witness, "Isn't it true that you lied on your job application by falsely stating that you had never used drugs?" But if the witness denies the allegation, the examiner may ***not*** introduce ***extrinsic evidence*** to show that the witness is lying; thus, the questioner could not put on a second witness to testify that the first witness had indeed used drugs and lied on his job application. As the concept is often expressed, the examiner ***must "take the witness' answer."*** (But this restriction does not prevent the cross-examiner from hammering away at the witness, trying to overcome his denial of the allegation; it merely means that he may not introduce extrinsic evidence.)

   b. Veracity: Second, in some but not all jurisdictions that allow prior bad act impeachment, only those prior bad acts that relate to ***veracity*** may be introduced. Under this view, prior bad acts that do not have an element of dishonesty or deceit (e.g., an assault with a deadly weapon that never led to a conviction) could not be introduced, since they are not probative of whether the witness is telling the truth in the present testimony.

   i. Minority view: But a minority of jurisdictions allow even evidence of prior bad acts that do not reflect on truthfulness, so long as they are relevant to the witness' "credibility" in the broad sense. See, e.g., *People v. Sorge*, 93 N.E.2d 637 (N.Y. 1950), a prosecution for abortion, where the prosecutor was allowed to ask D about numerous past abortions she had performed, on the theory that "a defendant, like any other witness, may be 'interrogated

upon cross-examination in regard to any vicious or criminal act of his life'
that has a bearing on his credibility as a witness."

   c. **Discretion of court:** Most courts allowing prior bad act impeachment give the
       trial court wide ***discretion*** about whether to allow or exclude such evidence.
       M, p. 91. For instance, the trial judge may consider the degree of prejudice to
       the witness, the nearness or remoteness in time of the misconduct, and the
       relevance of the misconduct to the witness' truthfulness. *Id.*

   d. **Good faith basis:** The cross-examiner must have a ***good faith basis*** for ask-
       ing about a particular prior bad act. Otherwise, an unscrupulous cross-
       examiner could convince the jury that the witness had committed a particular
       act even though there was no evidence that that act ever occurred at all. For
       instance, in *People v. Sorge, supra,* the prosecutor asked D highly specific, and
       incriminating, questions about past abortions, e.g., "During the month of Janu-
       ary 1947 did you perform an abortion in your home at 64 Eleanor Street on
       Mrs. John Peeler of Willow Springs, North Carolina, also known as 'Sandy'?"
       Although D denied each allegation, the allegations were so precise that the jury
       was almost certainly left with the sense that the past deeds occurred as
       alleged. Extensive and specific probing about an alleged prior misdeed would
       be a breach of professional ethics if the questioner did not have a good faith
       basis for believing that the witness in fact committed the bad act in question.
       L&S, p. 299.

2. **Federal Rules:** The Federal Rules follows the common-law approach in general.
   FRE 608(b) provides as follows:

"Specific instances of the conduct of a witness, for the purpose of attacking or supporting the
witness' credibility, other than conviction of crime as provided in Rule 609, may not be
proved by extrinsic evidence. They may, however, in the discretion of the court, if probative
of truthfulness or untruthfulness, be inquired into on cross-examination of the witness (1)
concerning the witness' character for truthfulness or untruthfulness, or (2) concerning the
character for truthfulness or untruthfulness of another witness as to which character the
witness being cross-examined has testified.

The giving of testimony, whether by an accused or by any other witness, does not operate as
a waiver of the accused's or the witness' privilege against self-incrimination when examined
with respect to matters which relate only to credibility."

   a. **Summary:** Thus FRE 608(b) incorporates several restrictions on the use of
       prior bad acts for impeachment:

       i. **No extrinsic evidence:** As at common law, the prior bad act may be
           proved ***only through cross-examination,*** not through the presentation of
           testimony by other witnesses or other ***extrinsic evidence.*** In other words,
           in federal courts (as at common law), the cross-examiner must "take the
           witness' answer."

       ii. **Probative of truthfulness:** Only those prior bad acts that are ***"probative
           of truthfulness or untruthfulness"*** may be brought up. So a prior act of,

say, manslaughter or armed robbery not leading to conviction would not be admissible, because the fact that the witness had committed that deed does not make it more likely than it would otherwise be that he is now lying.

 iii. Discretion of the judge: The cross-examiner has no absolute right to bring up even those prior bad acts that clearly bear on truthfulness. All inquiry into "specific instances of the conduct of a witness" are explicitly left to *"the discretion of the court."* The court will weigh the probative value of the evidence against the prejudice that will result to the opposing party. The exercise of this discretion will rarely be reversed on appeal.

b. Self-incrimination: The examiner's right to inquire about prior bad acts may run afoul of the witness' *privilege against self-incrimination* (see *infra,* p. 320).

 i. The problem: The problem is most likely to arise where the witness is the accused, who has taken the stand in his own defense. Normally, the accused or any other witness who voluntarily takes the stand and discloses part of a transaction is deemed to have waived the privilege against self-incrimination as to the rest of the transaction. See, e.g., *U.S. v. Hearst, infra,* p. 328.

 ii. No waiver: But where the accused takes the stand in his own defense and speaks on direct only about the present crime, as a constitutional matter the accused does *not waive* his right to claim the privilege when asked about prior bad acts that have nothing directly to do with the present charged offense and are relevant only to credibility.

 iii. Federal Rule: Therefore, the last sentence of FRE 608(b) provides that testimony by an accused (or by any other witness) "does not operate as a waiver of [his] privilege against self-incrimination when examined with respect to matters which relate only to credibility."

 iv. Note on *Sorge*: Observe that had FRE 608 been in force in *People v. Sorge, supra,* p. 87, the defendant would presumably been able to claim self-incrimination in refusing to answer whether she had previously performed abortions. Indeed, the Advisory Committee's Note to FRE 608(b) says that the final sentence of that rule "constitutes a rejection of the doctrine of . . . *People v. Sorge* . . . that any past criminal act relevant to credibility may be inquired into on cross-examination, in apparent disregard of the privilege against self-incrimination." (But the prosecutor might confer immunity on the witness, in which case presumably the privilege would no longer apply, and the witness could be forced to answer. See *infra,* p. 336. See also L&S, p. 298, n. 39.)

c. Relation to prior convictions: The fact that the witness has been convicted of a crime must normally come into evidence, if at all, via FRE 609's special rules dealing with convictions. But a clever questioner will often be able to get the fact of a prior conviction before the jury under Rule 608 even though the conviction could not have come in under 609, if the witness has *lied* in the past about his criminal record. In this situation, it is the lie, not the fact of conviction, that is the prior bad act admissible under Rule 608; but the conviction, arrest, or other misdeed being lied about can be alluded to as well.

> **Example:** D, a soldier, is subjected to military prosecution for murdering his wife. After D takes the stand in his own defense, the prosecutor asks D, "Isn't it a fact that as to your application for appointment as a Warrant Officer in the United States Army . . . that you knowingly omitted the fact . . . that you had been convicted . . . for the possession of marijuana and marijuana paraphernalia in 1976?" Also, "Is it not a fact that you intentionally omitted from [the application] the fact that you had been arrested in 1976 . . . for assault and battery on your second wife . . . [and] convicted . . . for carrying a .22 caliber pistol in your automobile without a permit in 1976?" D claims that he disclosed these offenses to the personnel specialist who was processing his application, and that the omission of these prior misdeeds from his signed application was thus inadvertent. On appeal, D claims that these questions improperly prejudiced him.
>
> *Held,* for the prosecution. It is true that the prior convictions could not have been admitted under the military equivalent of FRE 609 to show D's poor character for veracity. Nor could the drug, assault, and weapons misdeeds have been directly admitted under FRE 608(b) to show D's poor character for truthfulness, since those misdeeds were not probative of a person's truthfulness. However, lying on a job application *is* probative of truthfulness, and the prior convictions and arrests were "necessary and inseparable parts" of D's deceit on the application, and were thus relevant to establish the lie on the job application. (The prosecutor's identification of the victim of the assault and battery arrest as being D's second wife was, however, not probative of truthfulness, and was prejudicial to D; but this was harmless error.) *U.S. v. Owens,* 21 M.J. 117 (Ct. Mil. App. 1985).

d. Prior arrest: The prior bad act may be admissible for impeachment even though, if it occurred, it **constitutes a crime** for which there was no conviction. That is, in both state courts that allow prior bad act impeachment and under the Federal Rules, there is no rule that says that a crime must come in as a prior conviction or not at all. However, whereas a prior felony conviction can come in even if it is not especially probative of truthfulness under FRE 609(a), a crime not leading to conviction (or a misdemeanor conviction not involving a *crimen falsi*) may come in under 608(b) only if it is "probative of truthfulness," and only in the discretion of the court.

e. Direct examination: FRE 608(b) on its face allows inquiry into prior bad acts only "on cross-examination." However, FRE 607 (allowing impeachment of a witness even on direct examination) probably means that 608(b) should be read to allow inquiry about prior bad acts on **direct examination** as well. See S&R, pp. 494-95, urging such an interpretation. This would mean that: (1) the direct examiner who is interrogating a hostile witness may impeach the witness' credibility by inquiring into prior bad acts; and (2) possibly, the direct examiner who is interrogating a friendly or neutral witness and who fears that his adversary will impeach by bringing up prior bad acts on cross, may "draw the sting" by bringing up these acts on direct.

IX. IMPEACHMENT BY OPINION AND REPUTATION REGARDING CHARACTER

A. **Issue generally:** We turn now to the third and final way in which the witness' general character for veracity may be impeached. The two prior methods rely upon specific past acts by the witness to infer that he has a general character for lying, and is thus likely to be lying now. The final method of character impeachment is more direct: the opponent offers testimony from a second witness that the first witness has a *bad character for truthfulness*.

1. **Distinguished from substantive evidence:** Recall that a party may not usually use character evidence to prove substantive elements of his case. For instance, the prosecution may not show that because the defendant has a character for drunken driving, he was probably driving while drunk in the present case. (See *supra*, p. 20.) Allowing the prosecution to show that because D has a general character for lying, he is probably lying in his present testimony, should logically be equally forbidden. L&S, p. 304. Such evidence is likely to be just as prejudicial to the witness as use of character as substantive evidence would be to the party against whom it is directed. Nonetheless, nearly all courts allow at least limited use of "character for truthfulness" evidence on impeachment.

B. **Common-law rule:** The general common-law approach allows some but not all types of proof that the witness has a bad character for truthfulness.

1. **Reputation:** Most importantly, most common-law jurisdictions allow a witness to impugn the truthfulness of the principal witness only by stating that the principal witness has a *bad reputation* for truthfulness. The second witness may *not*, in most jurisdictions, recite his own *opinion* of the principal witness' veracity, nor may he recite *specific instances* of conduct by the principal witness leading to that witness' bad reputation for truthfulness. Lilly, p. 356. The rationale for this limitation is that it *prevents delay*, and also minimizes prejudice.

   Example: D, a criminal defendant, takes the stand in his own behalf. The prosecutor then calls W, a former associate of D, for the purpose of establishing D's poor character for truthfulness. In most jurisdictions, the prosecutor may not ask, "In your opinion, what is D's character for truthfulness or untruthfulness?" Nor may he ask W to describe any particular instances in which D has acted untruthfully. The prosecutor may, however, ask, "Do you have knowledge of D's *reputation* for truthfulness?" W may then respond that he does have such knowledge, and that D's reputation for truthfulness is bad. (The prosecutor must first establish a foundation for this reputation testimony, by showing that W lives in the same community as D, or otherwise has reason to know D's reputation.)

2. **General character not allowed:** The vast majority of jurisdictions do *not* allow evidence of the witness' reputation for *general* good or bad "character," only

evidence of his reputation for the particular trait of ***truthfulness***. M, p. 101.

3. **Opinion:** As noted, most courts do not allow the second witness to state his personal ***opinion*** as to the principal witness' truthfulness. However, a growing ***minority*** of courts does allow such evidence. Furthermore, even more courts water down the no-opinion rule by allowing the questioner to ask the following question of the second witness: "If [the principal witness] were to say something under oath, would you believe him?" Even though a negative answer by the witness clearly reflects his personal opinion, the question is usually allowed. L&S, p. 305. (When this happens, the other side is usually allowed to call witnesses who say that they *would* believe the witness under oath. *Id.*, n. 47.)

4. **Opening the door:** The need to impeach the witness' character for truthfulness arises most often when the witness is the accused in a criminal case, who takes the stand in his own behalf. If the accused affirmatively states that he is a truthful person, it is easy to see why the prosecution should be able to impeach with witnesses who testify that the accused is a liar. But where the accused merely tells his side of the facts, and makes no assertion that he is a generally honest person, the defense has not really put the defendant's "character for truthfulness" in issue. Nonetheless, nearly all courts hold that ***merely by taking the stand***, the defendant has ***opened the door*** to evidence of his general character for untruthfulness. See, e.g., *State v. Ternan*, 203 P.2d 342 (Wash. 1949) ("The character of a defendant in a criminal case is not open to inquiry unless he himself puts it in issue, but when a defendant in a criminal case takes the witness stand he subjects himself to cross-examination the same as any other witness, and the state has the right to impeach him as a witness to the extent of proving by witnesses that his general reputation for truth and veracity in the community where he resides is bad.")

5. **Proof that others have disbelieved witness:** Normally, proof of a witness' bad character for truthfulness must be made by putting a second witness on the stand. Occasionally, however, the main witness' character for truthfulness can be proved out of the witness' own mouth. However, most courts have held that the questioner may not do this by eliciting the fact that ***previous judges or juries*** have ***disbelieved*** the witness' testimony.

> **Example:** The prosecutor asks W (a co-defendant who has been tried and convicted in a different trial), "When you gave similar testimony in your own trial, the judges convicted you, didn't they?" *Held*, on appeal, for D. This question — whose "obvious purpose was to induce the jury to believe that, as the testimony of the witness . . . had already been discredited by three judges sitting in the same court in another case . . . they should discredit it in this case" — was unfairly prejudicial. *Newton v. State*, 127 A. 123 (Md. 1924)

C. **Federal Rule:** The Federal Rules follow the general common-law approach of allowing some types of evidence of the witness' character for truthfulness. FRE 608(a) provides as follows:

"The credibility of a witness may be attacked or supported by evidence in the form of opinion or reputation, but subject to these limitations: (1) the evidence may refer only to character for truthfulness or untruthfulness, and (2) evidence of truthful character is admissible only after the character of the witness for truthfulness has been attacked by opinion or reputation evidence or otherwise."

1. **Summary:** Only subsection (1) of 608(a) is relevant to us now (since subsection (2) relates to rehabilitation, and is discussed *infra*, p. 106). That subsection directly or indirectly includes the following provisions:

    a. **Reputation:** As at common law, the second witness may recite that the first witness has a ***bad reputation*** for truthfulness.

    b. **Opinion:** Unlike most common-law jurisdictions, FRE 608(a)(1) also allows the second witness to state his own ***opinion*** about the first witness' character for truthfulness.

    c. **Specific instances:** The second witness may ***not***, on direct, refer to any ***specific instances*** of untruthful conduct by the first witness. This limitation comes from 608(b)'s ban on the use of "extrinsic evidence" to show "specific instances of the conduct of a witness." Thus if D takes the stand to deny the crime, and the prosecution calls W to testify that W has a bad opinion of D's truthfulness, W may not recite the particular past lies by D that have led W to this unfavorable opinion of D's veracity. The rationale is that were the details of past lies allowed, these details would be unduly prejudicial to D, and a lot of trial time would be used up while D's counsel tried to show that D did not really lie on the prior occasions.

        i. **Cross-examination:** However, the ban on specific instances of past conduct does not apply to ***cross-examination***. Thus, if W has testified on direct that he has a bad opinion of D's veracity, the defense counsel could, for instance, ask W, "Don't you remember when D was undercharged at the Bonanza Steakhouse restaurant, and he insisted on paying the proper amount?" See FRE 608(b)(2). However, past striking instances of truthfulness (unlike past instances of lying) are rare, so the right to use past instances of truthfulness on cross-examination is of little utility. L&S, p. 305.

    d. **General character:** As at common law, the second witness may testify only to the principal witness' character for ***truthfulness***, not his character for other traits (e.g., physical aggressiveness), nor his "general" character.

X. IMPEACHMENT BY PRIOR INCONSISTENT STATEMENTS

A. **General principle:** Perhaps the most important technique for impeaching a witness is by showing that he has made a ***prior inconsistent statement***. Evidence of prior inconsistent statements is impeaching in two ways: (1) it directly casts doubt on the truthfulness of the current statement; and (2) insofar as it suggests that the witness has told two stories, at least one of which must be incorrect, it suggests that the witness has a general tendency to lie, so that other aspects of his present testimony should be disbelieved.

1. **Relation to hearsay rule:** Our present discussion concerns the use of prior inconsistent statements for impeachment only. Traditionally, impeachment use was the *only* use to which a prior inconsistent statement could usually be put, since the hearsay rule prevented use of the prior statement for substantive purposes. But the modern trend is to treat at least some types of prior inconsistent statements as not being barred by the hearsay rule, and thus as substantive proof of the matters contained therein. (For instance, FRE 801(d)(1) treats prior statements made in an earlier trial or proceeding, where the declarant spoke under oath and subject to perjury penalties, as not being hearsay. See *infra*, p. 252.) Our discussion of prior inconsistent statements here assumes that the statement is not admissible for substantive purposes, and is therefore admissible only for impeachment if at all.

B. General rule: The general rule, both at common law and under the Federal Rules, is that when a witness testifies at trial, evidence of his prior inconsistent statement is *admissible* to impeach his credibility. L&S, p. 306.

1. **Limits:** But there are two important rules that limit the use of prior inconsistent statements for impeachment:

   a. **Foundation:** First, at common law (and to a lesser extent under the Federal Rules), a rigid *foundation* must be laid before the prior inconsistent statement may be introduced for impeachment. In brief, before the statement may be introduced, the witness must be given a chance to deny having made it or to explain away the inconsistency. See *infra*, p. 95, for a fuller discussion.

   b. **No extrinsic evidence on collateral matters:** Second, if the prior statement involves only a "*collateral* matter," the statement may not be proven by "*extrinsic*" evidence (e.g., another witness' testimony that the first witness made the statement).

      Example: D is charged with robbing W by taking W's wallet. W testifies that the mugging occurred just after W left the Roxy theater where "Sound of Music" was being played. Defense counsel learns that shortly after the mugging, W told his friend X that the crime took place just after W had left the Sleazeball Cinema, where "I Was a Teenage Nymphomaniac" was playing. This prior inconsistent statement may be introduced to impeach W's testimony. However, defense counsel must first satisfy two common-law requirements: (1) He must ask W whether he made the earlier statement to X, and give W a chance to deny having made it or to explain away the inconsistency as to the movie seen; and (2) He may bring out the fact of the earlier statement in cross-examination, but since the inconsistency relates to a collateral matter (the movie W saw), he may not use extrinsic evidence (e.g., testimony by X that W really made the earlier statement to X) to prove the earlier statement — he must "take W's answer."

2. **Parties not covered:** The rules governing prior inconsistent statements (i.e., the foundation requirement and the "no extrinsic evidence of collateral matters" rule) apply only where the *witness is not a party*. If the witness *is* a party, his prior inconsistent statement is substantively admissible as an *admission*, since

admissions do not fall within the hearsay rule (see *infra*, p. 149). Therefore, the remainder of our discussion of prior inconsistent statements involves only prior statements by non-party witnesses. See, e.g., the last sentence of FRE 613(b), making that Rule's foundation requirement inapplicable to admissions of a party-opponent.

C. Foundation requirement: Let us examine more closely now the requirement that before the prior inconsistent statement can be proved, preliminary questions must be asked to lay a *foundation* for it.

1. **Common law:** As noted, the common law imposed a very rigid foundation requirement. The witness must be told the substance of the alleged statement, the time, the place, and the person to whom it was made. M, p. 79. This foundation gives the witness a chance to deny ever having made the statement, or to explain away the inconsistency. L&S, p. 306.

   a. **Rationale:** There seem to be two rationales for the common-law foundation requirement. First, there is the sense of *fairness* to the witness: the cross-examiner should not be allowed to plant a trap and "spring" the prior statement on the witness without any advance warning. Second, if the witness is not given a chance to explain or deny the prior statement, and extrinsic evidence of the prior statement is then presented (e.g., testimony by a person who heard the prior statement), time will be wasted, since the primary witness might have, if asked, been able to explain away the inconsistency.

   Example: P sues D for having alienated the affections of P's wife. One of the acts complained of is that D wrestled with P's wife on several occasions, including a picnic held on the banks of the Pudding River. W, the main witness for D, testifies that D's conduct towards P's wife was the same as his conduct toward other women friends, and was proper and harmless. On cross, the only question relating to the Pudding River picnic is whether W recalls talking to P about that trip, which W says he does not. P then testifies that W told him, while they were in W's garage, that D's conduct with P's wife at the Pudding River picnic was disgraceful. P objects to this testimony.

   Held, P's testimony about his conversation in the garage with W should have been held inadmissible. While W was on the stand, he was asked only in the most general terms about his conversation with P concerning P's conduct at the picnic, and this was an insufficient foundation. Therefore, P should not have been permitted to impeach W's credibility by giving the particulars of the prior inconsistent statement in the garage. Before a prior inconsistent statement may be used to impeach a witness, "the statements must be related to [the witness], with the circumstances of times, places, and persons present; and he shall be asked whether he has made such statements, and if so, allowed to explain them." This rule is intended to "afford all witnesses ample opportunity to recall a fact before they may be assailed as dishonest." It also reduces confusion of issues by "eliminating unnecessary impeachments." *Coles v. Harsch*, 276 P. 248 (Or. 1929).

2. **Federal Rule:** The common-law foundation requirement has been criticized as being unduly rigid; criticism has focussed on the requirement that the foundation be laid *before* the impeachment. For instance, suppose the cross-examiner does not learn of the prior inconsistent statement until the witness has not only left the stand but is now unavailable; the common-law rule prevents the prior statement from being shown. M, p. 80. Furthermore, the foundation rule is a trap for the unwary, since in the heat of cross-examination it is easy to neglect to lay a sufficiently specific foundation (as happened in *Coles*, where the prior statement was referred to on cross, but not specifically enough to please the appellate court). Therefore, the Federal Rules have **liberalized** the foundation requirement by requiring the foundation, but allowing it to be made either before *or after* the impeachment. FRE 613(b) provides:

"Extrinsic evidence of a prior inconsistent statement by a witness is not admissible unless the witness is afforded an opportunity to explain or deny the same and the opposite party is afforded an opportunity to interrogate the witness thereon, or the interests of justice otherwise require. This provision does not apply to admissions of a party-opponent as defined in Rule 801(d)(2)."

   a. **Illustration:** Thus FRE 613(b) might have made P's life easier in *Coles*. After P testified that W told a different story to him about his view of the picnic than W had told on the stand, P's lawyer could have recalled W, and given him a chance to deny having made the statement to P in the garage, or to explain away the apparent inconsistency between that statement and W's trial testimony. But if P's lawyer had not recalled W, P's testimony about the prior inconsistent statement would probably have had to be stricken even under the liberalized Federal Rules approach, since P's lawyer's casual reference to the garage conversation during the original cross-examination of W was probably not specific enough to constitute "an opportunity to explain or deny" the prior inconsistent statement as required by FRE 613(b). (But note that the trial judge has discretion to dispense with the requirement of a foundation if "the interests of justice otherwise require." For instance, if W had become unavailable after leaving the stand, and P's lawyer's failure to lay a precise foundation during the original cross was apparently inadvertent, a trial judge applying FRE 613(b) might have concluded that justice required dispensing with the full foundation requirement and allowing P to testify about the prior inconsistent statement.)

3. **Writing:** The common-law foundation requirement is especially strict where the prior inconsistent statement is **written**. Under the rule of *The Queen's [Caroline's] Case*, 129 Eng. Rep. 976 (1820), the beginning of the foundation for impeachment by a contradictory writing is that the writing must be **presented to the witness** for his examination. Lilly, p. 362.

   a. **Criticism:** This rule makes effective cross-examination of the witness much more difficult. First, the examiner loses the ability to trap a deceitful witness who would otherwise deny having made the prior inconsistent written statement. Second, the early disclosure to the witness gives him time to gather his thoughts, and perhaps make up an explanation of the inconsistency. *Id.*

   b. Modern and Federal Rule: Many modern courts, and the Federal Rules, abrogate the rule of *Queen's Case* for these reasons. *Id.* Thus FRE 613(a) provides that the prior written statement need not be shown to the witness before or during examination (though "on request the same shall be shown . . . to opposing counsel.")

D. Extrinsic evidence: Often, the prior inconsistent statement can be proved "out of the mouth" of the witness who made it. That is, after the witness testifies at trial to assertion A, the examiner can ask him, "Don't you remember saying not-A in a conversation with X on June 24, 1986?" If the witness admits having made the prior inconsistent statement, that is all that the cross-examiner needs. If the witness denies having made the earlier statement, however, the examiner will wish to prove the prior statement by *"extrinsic" evidence*, i.e., evidence other than the testimony of the witness who made the statement. If the prior statement was in writing, the writing itself would be extrinsic evidence. If the prior statement was oral, testimony by another witness who heard the statement would be extrinsic.

   1. Limits: There are two important common-law rules limiting the use of extrinsic evidence to prove a prior inconsistent statement:

   a. Must be material: First, the inconsistency between the trial testimony and the prior statement must be *"material."* In other words, if the prior statement varies only slightly from the present testimony (so that it would *not cast doubt* on the truthfulness of the witness' present testimony), the prior statement cannot be proved by extrinsic evidence.

   b. No proof of collateral facts: Second, extrinsic proof of the prior inconsistent statement is not allowed if that statement involves only *"collateral"* matters. M, p. 77. This means that the statement must deal with either: (1) facts relevant to the issues in the case; or (2) facts which are themselves provable by extrinsic evidence to discredit the witness.

   i. Explanation: Category (2) above refers to facts which could be proved by extrinsic evidence *even if there were no claim that the witness had contradicted himself.* Facts showing that the witness is *biased*, and probably facts showing that the witness had no opportunity to know the facts that he testified to, fall within this category. L&S, p. 308.

   Example: D is charged with rape. W testifies that D was with W during the entire evening on which the rape allegedly took place, and that the rape did not take place. W testifies that she has no romantic involvement with D or any motive to lie on his behalf. On cross, the prosecutor asks W, "Isn't it true that before trial, you told X that you loved D and would lie to get him acquitted?" W denies having made this statement, and repeats that she has no reason to help D. The prosecutor will now be permitted to call X to testify that W did indeed tell him that she was in love with D and would lie for him. This is extrinsic proof of a prior inconsistent statement, and the subject of the statement is not directly relevant to the issues in the case. However, the prior statement shows bias, and a witness' bias may be shown even where the cross-examiner does not claim that the bias contradicts the witness' present testimony. Therefore, this statement falls into category (2) above. Similarly, the prosecutor would be permitted to introduce extrinsic evidence that W told X, "I was out of town on the night of the rape, so I don't know whether D did it or not."

2. **Federal Rule:** The Federal Rules do not expressly state whether the prohibition on extrinsic proof of prior inconsistent statements dealing with collateral matters is maintained or not. The trial judge can achieve the result of keeping out such extrinsic evidence by exercising his discretion, under FRE 403, to exclude evidence whose probative value is "substantially outweighed by the danger of . . . confusion of the issues . . . or by considerations of undue delay, [or] waste of time. . . ."

3. **Use for substantive purposes:** Observe that allowing prior inconsistent statements for their impeachment value may often result in the jury using the prior statement as **substantive** evidence as well. For instance, suppose that in a negligence action, W testifies at trial, "I didn't see whether D ran the red light or not," and P's lawyer is allowed to introduce W's prior out-of-court statement to a policeman, "I saw D run a red light." The jury is likely to look to the prior statement by W not just for what it implies about W's credibility as a witness, but also for substantive proof that D really ran the red light. Yet the prior inconsistent statement would not be admissible as substantive evidence at common law, because of the rule against hearsay (*infra*, p. 245). The rule allowing impeachment by prior inconsistent statements thus presents a danger of subterfuge, especially where it is a **direct** examiner who elicits the present testimony, and then introduces the prior inconsistent statement. Prevention of this kind of subterfuge is one of the reasons why the common law prevented a direct examiner from impeaching his own witness. (See *supra*, p. 78.)

   a. **Federal courts:** The danger is especially great in federal courts, since the common-law rule preventing impeachment of one's own witness has been abrogated. (See FRE 607.) However, the trial judge can probably prevent subterfuge by use of his discretion to balance probative value against prejudice and relevance under FRE 403. Thus, in the case of our "running the light" hypothetical above, the federal trial judge could reason as follows: Since W's trial testimony does not show whether she saw D run the red light or not, that evidence is not especially relevant on this issue; therefore, it is of little importance whether W has previously testified differently on the issue, so I will not allow time to be wasted by extrinsic proof of W's prior statement. See L&S, p. 310.

XI. IMPEACHMENT FOR BIAS

A. **Proof of bias generally:** All courts allow proof that the witness is **biased**.

B. **Types of bias:** A witness is biased whenever his emotions or feelings towards the parties or towards some aspect of the case make the witness **desire one outcome rather than another.** Here are some of the types of bias:

1. **Friendly feeling:** The witness may feel *friendly* to one of the parties. This may be due to a *personal relationship* between the two (e.g., a romantic or familial tie). Or, it may be because one employs or does business with the other. It may even be because the party has paid the witness money in *settlement* of a claim related to the transaction involved in the suit.

     Example: P and W are in a car driven by P, which collides with a car driven by D. In the P-D suit, W testifies that D was negligent and that P was careful. D may show that W is biased by showing that P paid W money to settle W's claims for injuries arising out of the accident. M, p. 86.

2. **Hostility:** Conversely, the witness may be *hostile* to a party. Hostility may be evidenced by the fact that the witness and the party have argued in the past, or one has sued the other, or the witness has said nasty things about the party to others.

3. **Self-interest:** The witness may have an *interest in the outcome*, apart from any feeling of favor or hostility to the parties.

     Example 1: If W is an expert witness, the fact that he is being paid for his testimony is usually allowed as evidence that he has an interest in having the case come out in favor of the party for whom he is testifying (even if the expert's receipt of payment for his time and testimony is completely proper). M, p. 87.

     Example 2: In a criminal case, W's own legal status may be affected by the outcome. For instance, if W has pled guilty to some related event, has agreed to cooperate with the prosecution, and is awaiting sentencing, these facts may be shown to establish bias — it is plausible that W will get less jail time if his testimony aids in convicting the defendant. (In the recent prosecution of insider-trader Ivan Boesky, the prosecution made sure to have Boesky sentenced before he gave testimony in other cases, to defuse the anticipated defense arguments that Boesky was lying in order to help the prosecution gain convictions and thereby reduce his own sentence.)

4. **Membership in group:** Bias may even be shown by the fact that the witness belongs to a particular organization and subscribes to its beliefs. Thus, in *U.S. v. Abel*, 469 U.S. 45 (1984), the Supreme Court held that the prosecution was entitled to show that a defense witness, W, and D were both members of a secret prison organization which had a creed requiring members to lie to protect each other. "A witness' and a party's common membership in an organization, even without proof that the witness or party has personally adopted its tenets, is certainly probative of bias."

C. **Foundation:** The examiner may cross-examine the witness to show bias *without laying any foundation.*

  1. **Extrinsic evidence:** However, most jurisdictions do not allow a party to use *extrinsic evidence* to show a witness' bias (e.g., testimony by another witness as to the first witness' bias) unless a foundation has been laid. The questioner must first *ask* the principal witness about the alleged bias; only if he denies it may the

extrinsic evidence be used, in courts following this majority approach. M, p. 87.

> **Example:** Consider the facts of *U.S. v. Abel*, *supra*: in a criminal prosecution of D, W gives evidence favorable to D. The prosecutor has evidence that W and D belong to the same secret prison organization whose central tenet is that members must lie to protect each other. Under the majority rule, the cross-examiner must first ask W whether he and D are members of such an organization, and whether it has that belief. If W concedes this to be so, the prosecutor may not use extrinsic evidence. But if W denies this, the prosecutor may then call X to testify that X knows that W and D belong to the secret society and that lying for mutual protection is its creed.

2. **Federal Rules:** The Federal Rules do not explicitly require a foundation before extrinsic evidence of bias may be introduced. (In fact, the Federal Rules do not explicitly mention bias as a form of impeachment at all.) However, FRE 611(a), by giving the federal judge control over the "mode and order of interrogating witnesses and presenting evidence so as to . . . avoid needless consumption of time," probably gives the federal judge discretion to require that a foundation be laid before the extrinsic evidence is introduced. W&B, Par. 607[03]. Thus, in *Abel*, *supra*, such a foundation was laid — it was not until W denied being a member of the secret society that the prosecution called X to testify that W was a member.

3. **Bias never collateral:** Recall that extrinsic evidence of prior inconsistent statements may not be introduced if the statements relate to "collateral" matters. (See *supra*, p. 97.) A similar rule does ***not*** apply to extrinsic proof of bias. That is, ***facts showing bias are not "collateral,"*** and if the main witness denies being biased, the cross-examiner is not required to "take his answer" — he may instead call other witnesses to prove the facts suggesting bias. M, p. 89.

D. **Confrontation Clause rights in criminal cases:** In criminal cases, the defendant's right to show that a prosecution witness is biased will often be ***constitutionally protected.*** Thus in *Davis v. Alaska*, 415 U.S. 308 (1974), the Supreme Court held that the trial court's denial of cross-examination to show the witness' bias violated D's Confrontation Clause rights under the Sixth Amendment, as applied to the states through the Fourteenth Amendment. (See *infra*, p. 270.) In *Davis*, the defendant's Confrontation Clause rights were so important that he should have been allowed to bring out the fact that W had a prior juvenile adjudication against him and thus had a motive to cooperate with the authorities — these Confrontation Clause rights even outweighed the conflicting state policy making such juvenile adjudications secret.

1. **Sexual history of rape victim:** Similarly, the trial judge's refusal to allow a ***rape defendant*** to cross-examine his victim to show bias arising from her sexual history, may represent a denial of the defendant's Confrontation Clause rights. Thus in *Olden v. Kentucky*, 488 U.S. 227 (1988), D, the rape defendant, tried to show that W, the victim, was living with her boyfriend at the time of the alleged rape, and that W falsely claimed to have been raped by D in order to convince the boyfriend that W had been faithful to him. The Supreme Court held that the trial judge's refusal to allow D to bring out these points during cross-examination of W violated D's Confrontation Clause rights.

XII. IMPEACHMENT BY SENSORY OR MENTAL DEFECTS

A. General rule: A witness can always be impeached by showing that his capacity to *observe, remember,* or *narrate events correctly* has been impaired. W&B, Par. 607[04].

1. Sensory defect: Thus, a witness can be impeached by showing that he has a *sensory deficiency* that impaired his ability to observe the events in question.

> **Example:** If W claims to have overheard, from 10 feet away, a whispered conversation in which D and X plotted a murder, D's lawyer can show that W was hard of hearing and could thus not have heard the conversation. Similarly, W's credibility could be attacked by showing that his vision was too poor to have seen an event that he claims to have seen.

2. Mental defect: As a general rule, a *mental defect* that the witness has, that can be shown to have impaired his ability to *remember* events or to *narrate them* correctly, may also be shown for impeachment.

3. Drugs and alcohol: The most controversial issue concerning proof of sensory and mental incapacity involves evidence of *alcohol* or *drug addiction*.

    a. Proof of intoxication: All courts agree that the witness may be impeached by showing that he was *drunk* or *high on drugs* at the time of the events he purported to witness.

    b. Addiction: But there is no unanimity about whether the witness may be shown to be a *habitual*, i.e., addicted, user of alcohol and drugs. Probably most courts would not allow proof of alcoholism or drug addiction in the absence of proof that the witness was drunk or high on drugs at the time of the events in question. M, pp. 105-06.

       i. Criticism: The blanket exclusion of addiction evidence has been criticized as illogical: "We fail to see a 'bright line' between the person with hearing difficulties who swears he overheard a particular conversation [whose hearing difficulties could be shown as impeachment] and the alcoholic who swears he was 100% sober on a particular occasion" (whose disease cannot be shown, according to the majority rule.) L&S, p. 325 (arguing that addiction evidence should be handled on a case-by-case basis, and admitted if relevant, unless some other interest — perhaps extreme prejudice — demands exclusion).

4. Psychiatric testimony: A party will sometimes wish to impeach a witness' credibility by presenting expert *psychiatric* testimony that the witness is incapable of accurately observing, remembering or narrating the events in question. This happens most often in rape cases, where the defendant wants to introduce psychiatric testimony to prove that the prosecutrix is fantasizing or distorting what happened. In general, use of such testimony to impeach the witness is frowned upon. The matter is discussed more extensively *infra*, p. 110.

XIII. IMPEACHMENT BY CONTRADICTION; THE "COLLATERAL ISSUE" RULE

A. General theory of contradiction: The final method of impeachment is simply to present a second witness who will **contradict the first witness** on some point. As we will see below, impeachment by contradiction is quite restricted in most courts — impeachment is not allowed as to "collateral" matters, so only if the point on which the first witness' testimony is being contradicted is material to the issues in the case, or is relevant to the witness' credibility apart from the contradiction, may the contradiction be shown by use of a second witness.

> **Example:** In an armed robbery prosecution of D, W1 testifies for the defense that she saw the robbery take place, and that the robber was not D. She also testifies that she remembers the episode vividly because she had just stopped to tie the laces on her running shoes when she saw the robbery. The prosecutor seeks to impeach W1 by putting on the testimony of W2 (a policeman), who says that when he arrived at the scene of the crime and questioned W1, he noticed that she was wearing high heels. This is impeachment by contradiction; most courts would probably hold that the contradiction deals solely with a "collateral issue" (shoes worn by W1), and is thus not allowed.
>
> Suppose, however, that W2 instead testifies that W1 picked D out of a police lineup shortly after the crime. This impeachment by contradiction would be allowed by all courts, because it is directly relevant to one of the issues in the case (whether D was the robber).

B. "Collateral issue" rule: The *"collateral issue"* rule may be summarized as follows:

 1. Summary: If Witness 1 makes an assertion of fact (let's call the assertion "A"), then testimony by Witness 2, whose sole purpose is to contradict Witness 1 by asserting not-A, will be allowed only if the A/not-A issue is either: (1) a **material issue** in the case; or (2) an issue as to which Witness 2 could assert not-A **even if Witness 1 had never asserted A.**

  a. Explanation: Category (2) above means that if the extrinsic evidence could be used for impeachment **even in the absence of contradiction,** it may be used to show the contradiction. By this sub-rule, extrinsic evidence that the witness is biased, has been convicted of a crime, or had a relevant sensory or mental defect, may be used to contradict the witness' statement to the contrary, since such facts could be proved even if the witness did not otherwise assert. Application of the collateral issue rule to each of these categories is discussed further *infra*, p. 103.

 2. The *Oswalt* case as illustration: To illustrate operation of the collateral issue rule, let us consider *State v. Oswalt*, 381 P.2d 617 (Wash. 1963).

  a. Facts: D was charged with a robbery that took place in Seattle on July 14, 1961. On behalf of D, W1 testified that he operated a restaurant in Portland, Oregon, that D was in the restaurant at such a time on July 14 that he could not have been in Seattle at the time of the robbery; and that D was in the restaurant every day for the two months prior to the robbery. To impeach W1 by contradiction, the prosecutor offered testimony by W2 (a police detective) who testified that D admitted to having been in Seattle on June 12. D never denied at trial having been in Seattle on June 12, so the only importance of whether he was in Seattle on that date was that if he was, W1's testimony on this point was incorrect and W1's credibility would be impeached.

b. **Holding:** The Washington Supreme Court held that W2's testimony should not have been allowed — the prosecutor was entitled to cross-examine W1 to try to show that he was wrong about D's June 12th location; but the prosecutor was not permitted to impeach W1 by the use of "extrinsic" evidence (i.e., testimony by another witness), since the issue was "collateral" to the main issues in the case.

c. **Application of test:** Analyzing *Oswalt* in terms of our test above, W2's testimony was properly rejected because: (1) it was offered solely to contradict the testimony of another witness; and (2) the issue to which it related (D's location more than a month before the robbery): (a) was not a material issue in the case (since his presence in either Seattle or Portland had no real probative value on whether he committed the robbery 32 days later); and (b) could not have been proved by W2's testimony in the absence of W1's testimony on that issue (e.g., it would not have impeached any other aspect of W1's testimony).

3. **Solely for contradiction:** The "collateral issue" rule does not mean that Witness 2 can never contradict Witness 1 on a collateral issue. It merely means that if *all* that Witness 2 does is to contradict Witness 1 on the collateral issue, Witness 2's testimony should not be allowed. Thus in *Oswalt*, had Witness 2 (the police detective) gotten on the stand to cover a number of points that were directly relevant to the facts in the case, he would have been allowed to state in passing that D had admitted to being in Seattle on June 12. L&S, p. 330.

4. **Rationale:** The rationale for the collateral issue rule is that it *saves time* and eliminates confusion. In *Oswalt*, for instance, had Witness 2's testimony been properly allowed, D would then have been entitled to produce two or three additional witnesses to prove that he had been in the Portland restaurant, not in Seattle, on June 12; the prosecution could have rebutted these witnesses, and so on. This would have led to a "trial within a trial," all for no purpose except to determine the credibility of Witness 1's testimony on other unrelated points.

5. **Various contexts for rule:** In prior sections of this chapter, we have already seen two instances of the collateral issue rule: (1) the ban on showing that the witness has made a *prior inconsistent statement* as to a collateral issue (*supra*, p. 97); and (2) the ban on using extrinsic evidence to show *prior bad acts* by the witness. Yet, the collateral issue rule is *not* applied to some types of impeachment evidence (e.g., proof of *bias*). Therefore, it's worth looking briefly at each of the major techniques for impeachment to see whether the collateral issue rule applies:

a. **Prior convictions:** Witness 1's *prior criminal convictions* are *never* deemed "collateral," so that they may always be proved by extrinsic evidence if they otherwise meet the tests described above (*supra*, p. 81).

b. Prior bad acts: In sharp contrast, Witness 1's **prior bad acts** that did not lead to a criminal conviction **are** deemed "collateral," and thus are not provable by testimony from Witness 2 or other extrinsic evidence (*supra*, p. 88.) This is true even if Witness 1 has flatly denied the prior bad acts on the stand — since the prior bad acts could not be proved had Witness 1 been silent on the issue, the fact that Witness 2 would contradict him is deemed not to add enough impeachment value to justify Witness 2's testimony. This result is summed up in the phrase, noted above, that the cross-examiner "must take the witness' answer" as to prior bad acts.

c. Bad character for truthfulness: Witness 1's **bad character for truthfulness** is **not** collateral, so it can be proved by testimony from Witness 2. Again, this is so regardless of whether Witness 1 has affirmatively asserted his good character for truthfulness. See *supra*, p. 93.

d. Prior inconsistent statements: The fact that Witness 1 has made a **prior statement** inconsistent with his trial testimony **is** collateral, if the contradiction does not relate to a main issue in the case. In other words, if Witness 1 testifies to fact A on the stand, Witness 2 will not be allowed to testify that Witness 1 previously said not-A if A/not-A is not directly relevant to the case, any more than Witness 2 would be allowed to testify directly to not-A. To put it another way, what matters is the materiality of the A/not-A issue, and the fact that Witness 1 has made a prior inconsistent statement is irrelevant in this determination.

e. Bias: The fact that Witness 1 is **biased** is **never collateral**. Therefore, regardless of whether Witness 1 has testified to his own lack of bias, Witness 2 may testify that Witness 1 is biased.

f. Sensory or mental defect: Witness 1's **sensory or mental defects** are **not** collateral. Therefore, if a particular sensory or mental defect could be brought out on cross-examination of Witness 1, that defect could also be brought out by later testimony from Witness 2.

g. Contradiction of direct testimony about case: Finally, if Witness 1's testimony relates directly to the facts of the case (not to Witness 1's own qualifications or credibility), the collateral issue rule applies to contradictory testimony from Witness 2 — only if Witness 1's testimony relates to a fact that is important to the outcome of the case will Witness 2 be permitted to contradict the underlying fact. This category is where the *Oswalt* case fits.

h. No explanation: In summary, the collateral issue applies to three categories of impeachment (prior bad acts, prior inconsistent statements, and direct contradiction of testimony about case) and does not apply in four other categories (prior convictions, bad character for truthfulness, bias, and sensory/mental defect). There is no convincing explanation for this split. Probably, however, it is fair to think of the latter four categories as usually involving types of impeachment evidence that are either more reliable and convincing, less prejudicial, or less time-wasting, than the former three categories. See Lilly, p. 373.

6. **Fact about which no honest mistake possible:** Let us return now to one aspect of the use of contradiction relating to Witness 1's testimony about the case. Suppose Witness 1's testimony does not relate to a fact that is material to the outcome, but does relate to a fact about which *an honest witness would be very unlikely to be mistaken*. In this situation, the trial judge probably has discretion to allow contradictory evidence by Witness 2, even though the issue is, strictly speaking, "collateral." M, pp. 111-12.

> **Example:** Return to our example of the witness to armed robbery (*supra*, p. 102), who claims that she tied her sneakers just before viewing the robbery. Whether Witness 1 tied her sneakers, or indeed whether she was wearing sneakers at all, is not strictly material to whether D did the robbery. However, a reasonable jury could conclude that if Witness 1 really saw the robbery, and had really stopped to tend to her shoes just before witnessing it, she could not have been innocently mistaken about whether she was wearing sneakers or high heels. Therefore, the judge should have discretion to allow Witness 2's testimony that Witness 1 was really wearing high heels.

7. **Federal approach:** The Federal Rules do *not* contain any explicit "collateral issue" rule. However, the trial judge has general discretion under FRE 403 to exclude evidence whose probative value is substantially outweighed by, *inter alia*, "confusion of the issues . . . or by considerations of undue delay [or] waste of time. . . ." This discretion allows the judge to keep out evidence that would, under the common-law approach, be banned as extrinsic evidence of a collateral issue. See W&B, Par. 607[05], urging that federal judges should "substitut[e] the discretion approach of Rule 403 for the collateral test advocated by case law."

XIV. RELIGIOUS BELIEFS

A. **Issue:** May the credibility of the witness be impeached by proof that he does not believe in a *God* who punishes untruths?

  1. **Minority view:** At common law, persons who did not believe in a God who would punish untruths were not even deemed competent to be witnesses. M, p. 157. Such a rule today would almost certainly be found to be a violation of the U.S. Constitution, and virtually all states have abandoned it. However, a few states have converted this rule of competency into a rule allowing *impeachment* of a witness who does not believe in a lie-punishing God, on the theory that this fact makes it less likely than it would otherwise be that the witness is telling the truth. M, p. 114.

  2. **Majority view:** However, the vast majority of courts do *not* allow impeachment of the witness' credibility for any reason relating to his religious beliefs. *Id.* There are several reasons. First, it is highly doubtful whether the witness' religious beliefs have any probative value at all on his truthfulness. Second, use of such evidence is likely to have a prejudicial effect on the jury. L&S, p. 332. Finally, use of such evidence would violate at least the spirit, and possibly the letter, of the U.S

Constitution's various provisions regarding freedom of worship (e.g., the First Amendment's Free Exercise and Establishment Clauses). *Id.*

3. **Federal Rules:** The Federal Rules explicitly adopt this majority view. FRE 610 provides that "evidence of the beliefs or opinions of a witness on matters of religion is not admissible for the purpose of showing that by reason of their nature the witness' credibility is impaired or enhanced."

4. **Political beliefs:** The rationale for prohibiting impeachment on grounds of religious beliefs would seem to apply also to impeachment by proof of the witness' *political* beliefs. For instance, if a prosecutor were to attempt to prove that the defendant is unworthy of belief because he is a member of the Socialist Party, the prejudice to the defendant would seem to substantially outweigh the evidence's probative value; use would also undermine First Amendment free speech and free association values. See S&R, p. 561, urging that FRE 610 be expanded to cover political beliefs. A judge could also achieve this result by using his discretion to balance probative value against prejudice pursuant to FRE 403 (*supra*, p. 14).

XV. REHABILITATING THE IMPEACHED WITNESS

A. **General rules:** So far, we have talked about the ways in which a lawyer may impeach, or attack, the credibility of opposing witnesses. Now, we turn to how he may *support*, or *rehabilitate*, the credibility of his own witnesses.

1. **No bolstering:** A basic rule on which all courts agree is that a lawyer may *not* offer evidence *supporting his witness' credibility*, unless that credibility has first been *attacked* by the other side. This is sometimes known as the *rule against "bolstering" one's witness.* See FRE 608(a)(2).

   Example: In a civil suit, W testifies on behalf of P that D behaved negligently. On direct examination, P's lawyer will not be permitted to bolster W's credibility by showing that in a report to the police right after the accident, W told the same story as she is now telling in court. (But if D attacks W's credibility by asserting that she has recently concocted her trial testimony, P will be allowed to "rehabilitate" W by showing that right after the accident, she told the police the same story as she is now telling. Rehabilitation is discussed immediately below.)

2. **Exceptions:** There are two frequently-recognized *exceptions* to the rule against bolstering one's witness' credibility:

   a. **Prior identification:** First, if the witness has made a *prior out-of-court identification*, many courts will let that fact into evidence if the identifying witness is in court and available for cross-examination. Lilly, p. 374. (See *supra*, p. 255.) Sometimes this prior identification is substantive evidence (as under the Federal Rules), not merely bolstering of the witness' in-court testimony. In other courts, however, its function seems to be mainly to bolster the in-court identification.

b. Prompt complaint: Second, where the witness is a crime victim, many courts will allow evidence that he made a *"fresh complaint"* promptly following the crime, where the crime is one that is likely to be **known only to the criminal and the victim.** Lilly, p. 374. This rule is often applied to complaints by **rape** victims, and also sometimes to attempted bribery. *Id.*

B. Rehabilitation: Except in the two situations just described, a party may support the credibility of its witness only if that credibility has **previously been attacked by the other side.** This process of repairing the credibility of one's witness is usually called *"rehabilitation."*

> **Example:** W testifies on behalf of D. P asserts, either on cross-examination of W or by separate direct evidence, that W has a romantic attachment to D and is therefore biased. D may now rehabilitate W's credibility by showing that W is not in fact romantically interested in D. This may be done either by W's own testimony or by extrinsic evidence (e.g., testimony by W's best friend that W has never indicated any interest in D).

C. Must meet the attack: The basic rule of rehabilitation is that the rehabilitative evidence "must respond **as directly as possible** to the theory of the impeaching evidence." L&S, p. 333. Or, as McCormick puts it, "The wall, attacked at one point, may not be fortified at another and distinct point." M, p. 116.

> **Example:** P attempts to show that W, a defense witness, is biased because he is D's son. D may rehabilitate W's credibility by showing that W is not D's son, or that although they are related, they do not especially like each other — the charge of bias is met with evidence of non-bias. But D may *not* rehabilitate W by showing that W has a good reputation for truthfulness, or that W has made prior out-of-court statements that are consistent with his trial testimony — these attempts to boost W's credibility do not respond directly to the charge of bias, and are thus excluded on grounds of relevance.

1. Two categories: Whether the rehabilitating evidence is sufficiently directly related to the impeaching evidence to justify admission, varies from court to court and depending on the particular facts. The most troublesome issues involve the use of two types of rehabilitative evidence: (1) evidence that the witness has a **good character** for truthfulness; and (2) evidence that the witness has made **prior statements** that are **consistent** with his trial testimony. Each of these techniques can be used to meet some, but not other, types of attacks.

2. Good character: Evidence that the witness has a **good character for truthfulness** is more likely to be accepted when the impeachment relates to the witness' general bad character for truthfulness, than when it merely casts doubt on the accuracy of his testimony in the present case.

a. Attacks on general veracity: Thus if the witness is attacked by evidence that he has a **bad reputation** for truthfulness, that a second witness has a **bad opinion** of the first witness' truthfulness, that the witness has been **convicted of a crime**, or that he has committed a prior **bad act**, evidence of good reputation will be allowed. M, p. 116. In all of these situations, the attack implies not only that the witness has given incorrect testimony in this case, but also that he is a generally unreliable person — therefore, evidence of good reputation is quite relevant to the attack. Similarly, the judge may allow good-reputation evidence if the witness has been attacked by a slashing cross-examination that implies or states that the witness is a liar. M, p. 117.

b. **Attack on present testimony:** Where, by contrast, the attack is merely on the witness' testimony *in the present case*, and does not assert that the witness is generally unreliable, evidence of good reputation will probably *not* be allowed. Evidence that W is biased because he is related to the other party, or evidence by X that W has given erroneous testimony, are attacks on W's present testimony alone, not his character — therefore, these attacks will have to be met not by evidence of W's good character, but rather by evidence that the particular testimony attacked is worthy of belief. M, p. 117.

c. **Inconsistent statement:** If the attack is by showing that W has made a *prior inconsistent statement*, the courts are split. Most treat this as an implicit attack on the witness' general credibility, and therefore allow it to be rebutted by a showing that the witness has a good character for truth. *Id.*

3. **Prior consistent statement:** The greatest confusion comes where a party tries to meet attacks on the credibility of its witness by showing that the witness has made *prior statements* that are *consistent* with the witness' trial testimony.

a. **Attack on general character:** If the attack is based upon the witness' *general character*, evidence of prior consistent statements is usually *not permitted*, again on the theory that it does not meet the attack. Thus, if W is attacked by showing his prior *criminal convictions*, *prior bad acts*, or his *bad reputation* for veracity, the fact that he has made prior consistent statements will be treated as irrelevant.

b. **Charge of recent fabrication or improper influence:** In fact, most courts allow prior consistent statements to be used *only* where there has been an *express or implied* charge that the witness' trial testimony is a *recent fabrication* or the product of *improper influence* or *motive*. L&S, p. 334. Unless one of these elements is present, no type of impeachment may be rebutted by prior consistent statements, according to most courts.

c. **Prior inconsistent statement:** Most cases concerning prior consistent statements arise where the proponent of the witness is attempting to repair the damage done by a showing that the witness has made a *prior inconsistent statement*. Unless the proponent can demonstrate that his adversary's use of the prior inconsistent statement amounts to an express or implied claim that the witness has recently made up his trial testimony, or is lying because of improper influence or ulterior motives, the prior consistent statement will *not* be allowed.

    i. **Before motive:** Furthermore, the proponent who wants to use a prior consistent statement must, according to most courts, show that the prior statement was made *before* the alleged motive to fabricate or improper influence arose. Only in this situation does the fact of the prior consistent statement rebut the implication of deceit.

Example: P, while on business for D, is involved in an accident. In the suit, he claims to have been injured during this accident. D shows that P made no complaint of injury to passers-by or to his boss; D's lawyer points out on cross-examination that P didn't say anything about an injury "till you decided to make a case and when you decided to make a case, you started hunting those kinds of doctors . . . that would swear there was something wrong with you." P now offers testimony by his wife that the night following the accident, he complained of being hurt.

Held, P's wife's testimony is admissible. A mere allegation by D that P made up the story could not have been rebutted by P's wife's testimony, since P had a motive to lie immediately after the accident. However, because D's claim of recent fabrication was even more specific — that P remained silent after the accident — P was entitled to rebut those specifics by showing that he did not remain silent. *Barmore v. Safety Casualty Co.*, 363 S.W.2d 355 (Tex. Civ. App. 1962).

d. **Federal Rule:** The Federal Rules agree that if the use of a prior inconsistent statement amounts to a charge of recent fabrication or other wrongdoing by the witness, a prior consistent statement may be used to rehabilitate the witness. FRE 801(d)(1)(B) provides that where a witness testifies at trial and is available for cross-examination, his prior statement is admissible if it is "consistent with [his] testimony and is offered to rebut an express or implied charge against [him] of *recent fabrication* or *improper influence* or *motive*. . . ." In fact, if these conditions are met, the prior consistent statement may be used not only to rehabilitate the witness' credibility, but also as *substantive* evidence to prove the truth of the matters contained in the statement. In other words, in these circumstances, the prior consistent statement is *not hearsay* (see *infra*, p. 255.)

   i. **Existence of motive to falsify:** Observe that FRE 801(d)(1)(B) does not explicitly repeat the common-law rule that the prior consistent statement must have been made before the witness had a motive to falsify. However, the fact that the prior consistent statement was made after a motive to falsify arose makes it less likely that the trial judge will conclude that that prior statement does indeed tend to demonstrate the truthfulness of the witness' present story, than if the prior statement was made before there was such a motive. L&S, p. 334. Furthermore, even if a court holds that the prior consistent statement must have been made before the witness had a motive to falsify in order for it to qualify as substantive evidence under 801(d)(1)(B), it could be argued that the requirements of that rule do *not* have to be satisfied in order for the prior consistent statement to be used solely for purposes of *rehabilitation*. See, e.g., Judge Friendly's concurrence in *U.S. v. Rubin*, 609 F.2d 51 (2d Cir. 1979), so arguing.

    e. Other contexts: The use of prior consistent statements is not limited to rebutting a prior inconsistent statement. If the adversary charges by **any means** that the witness has recently fabricated his story or has been improperly motivated, a prior consistent statement that rebuts this implication may be admitted. For instance, if the adversary states or implies in cross-examination that the witness has recently changed his story or is lying for ulterior motives (even though the cross-examiner does not put in evidence of a prior inconsistent statement), the direct examiner may rehabilitate the witness by showing that he made a prior consistent statement.

        i. Before motive to lie: But here too, the prior consistent statement is much more likely to be admitted if it was made before the witness had a motive to lie — a prior consistent statement made after a motive to lie arose will usually not be a sufficiently convincing rebuttal of a charge of recent fabrication or improper motivation to justify admission. L&S, p. 334.

    f. Rationale for limits on use of prior consistent statement: There is a simple reason why courts resist the use of the prior consistent statements except to rebut charges of recent fabrication or improper influence: general admissibility of such statements would offer parties a large incentive to **manufacture evidence**. If the witness were a party, he could through careful planning buttress his anticipated trial testimony by making numerous pre-trial statements consistent with what he expected to say at trial. If the witness was a non-party, each party would have an incentive to pester him to make repeated prior statements consistent with the way that party hoped the witness would testify at trial. The rule restricting prior consistent statements to situations where they rebut a charge of recent fabrication or improper influence removes this incentive, since not until the adversary "opens the door" by making such charges can the prior consistent statement be used.

XVI. SOME SPECIAL TECHNIQUES FOR DEVELOPING OR EVALUATING TESTIMONY

  A. Scope: We conclude our treatment of the general rules on testimony by examining several scientific techniques that are arguably useful for developing or evaluating testimony: (1) the use of expert **psychiatric** testimony to help the jury evaluate the truthfulness of the witness; (2) the use of **hypnosis** and **truth serum** to help the witness remember facts; and (3) the use of the **lie detector** (polygraph) to evaluate the witness' truthfulness.

    1. General view of courts: In general, courts take a dim view of these types of "scientific" assistance. Most courts regard them as interfering with the jury's right and duty to observe and judge the witness directly. However, a growing minority of courts do allow some of these kinds of evidence.

  B. Psychiatric testimony: A party may wish to discredit an opposing witness by the use of **psychiatric expert testimony** to show that the witness' accuracy is doubtful because of some **mental illness** or **defect.** For instance, the defense in a criminal case might offer evidence by a psychiatrist that the prosecution's key witness is a paranoid schizophrenic who cannot distinguish fact from fantasy, and whose testimony therefore cannot be believed even if the witness himself believes it.

1. **Sex cases:** The issue of psychiatric expert testimony on credibility arises most frequently in *rape* and other sex cases. Typically, the defendant argues that the prosecutrix is making up or distorting the facts. The defendant asks the court to order the prosecutrix to submit to examination by a court-appointed psychiatrist who will then give an opinion as to whether the victim has any mental abnormality that should lead her testimony to be doubted.

   a. **Discretion:** Generally, the trial court is given broad *discretion* to decide whether to appoint a psychiatrist in this situation, and whether to allow the jury to hear his resulting opinion. Usually, that discretion will be exercised only for *compelling reasons*. M, p. 107.

      i. **Lack of corroboration:** A court-ordered exam is more likely if there is no evidence *corroborating* the victim's story, or if there is hard evidence of prior relevant mental illness or defect.

      ii. **Privacy right of victim:** Courts typically give heavy weight to the *privacy interests* of the victim. See, e.g., *U.S. v. Benn*, 476 F.2d 1127 (D.C. Cir. 1973), upholding the trial court's refusal to order a psychiatric examination of a mentally defective rape victim — the court relied on the strong evidence corroborating the victim's account, as well as on the fact that a compulsory psychiatric examination "may seriously impinge on a witness' right to privacy; the trauma that attends the role of complainant to sex offense charges is sharply increased by the indignity of a psychiatric examination; the examination itself could serve as a tool of harassment; and the impact of all these considerations may well deter the victim of such a crime from lodging any complaint at all."

      iii. **Treating psychiatrist:** Where the victim has previously been *hospitalized for mental illness,* the court may allow the *treating* psychiatrist to testify, perhaps on a theory that at least there is no court-ordered psychiatric examination to add to the victim's burdens. See, e.g., *Mosley v. Commonwealth*, 420 S.W.2d 679 (Ky. 1967), allowing the treating psychiatrist to testify that the victim was a schizophrenic who had fantasies that extended to the area of sex. But observe that such testimony runs afoul of the victim's physician-patient privilege (*infra*, p. 315), so it should be allowed only under compelling circumstances.

2. **Other cases:** Courts take a similar approach in non-sex cases. That is, the trial judge has broad discretion about whether to order the witness to undergo psychiatric examination, and about whether to admit the resulting evidence. Again, only where the need for the evidence is highly compelling will most courts force the witness to undergo such an exam.

   a. **Testimony without examination:** If the court refuses to order the witness to undergo a psychiatric exam, the opposing party may then attempt to introduce psychiatric testimony in response to a *hypothetical* question about the witness, or testimony based upon the psychiatrist's observation of the witness *in court*. Very occasionally, courts have allowed such testimony. The most famous instance is *U.S. v. Hiss*, 88 F.Supp. 559 (D.C.N.Y. 1950), in which the judge let a defense expert testify that, on the basis of his in-court observation of the star prosecution witness, that witness was a psychopathic personality with "a tendency towards making false accusations. . . ."

     i. Criticism: Evidence based on such casual observation seems of very questionable value, and should usually be excluded. M, p. 109. (It is also fairly easy to rebut. For instance, in the *Hiss* case, the expert's opinion was based in part upon the fact that the prosecution witness looked up frequently at the ceiling; the prosecution impeached the psychiatrist by pointing out that he looked at the ceiling more frequently than did the supposedly psychopathic prosecution witness!)

C. Hypnosis and truth serum: Two techniques, *hypnosis* and *truth serum*, are sometimes used to help the witness remember the details of an event (especially a crime of which the witness was a victim). Such techniques raise two different types of admissibility questions: (1) whether the statement given under the influence of the hypnosis or truth serum may itself be admitted; and (2) whether a witness whose recollection has been sharpened by one of these techniques may then give live testimony at trial about the event in question. (During our discussion, we will refer to hypnosis only, but the same rules generally apply to truth serum.)

  1. Statement made under influence: Where admission is sought of the statement made under hypnosis, courts have almost always *rejected* the statement. M, pp. 632-33. This is true whether the statement is offered as substantive evidence or for its bearing on the credibility of the witness' live testimony at trial. This rule stems both from fears of the technique's unreliability and also from hearsay problems (*infra*, p. 117).

  2. Testimony at trial: Where what is to be introduced is the witness' *live testimony* about an event, his recall of which has been refreshed through hypnosis, courts are split.

    a. Majority view: Most courts in this situation, too, *exclude* the live testimony. See, e.g., *People v. Shirley*, 641 P.2d 775 (Cal. 1982) (California will flatly refuse to allow a witness to testify about events that have been the subject of hypnotic refreshment; the dangers of inaccurate recollection and testimony — including the likelihood that the witness will develop an "unwarranted confidence in the validity of his ensuing recollection" — make it impossible to develop workable "safeguards"). See also *State v. Mack*, 292 N.W.2d 764 (Minn. 1980) ("A witness whose memory has been 'revived' under hypnosis ordinarily must not be permitted to testify in a criminal proceeding to matters which he or she 'remembered' under hypnosis.")

     i. Rationale: This majority view stems mainly from judges' fear of the *unreliability* of testimony that derives from hypnosis or truth serum. The key danger is that of "confabulation," i.e., "pseudomemories where plausible fantasy has replaced gaps in recall." *State ex rel. Collins v. Superior Court,* 644 P.2d 1266 (Ariz. 1982). As the *Mack* court explained, "the problem is that hypnosis can create a memory of perceptions which neither were nor could have been made, and, therefore, can bring forth a 'memory' from someone who cannot establish that she perceived the event she asserts to remember." Furthermore, "because the person hypnotized is subjectively convinced of the veracity of the 'memory', this recall is not susceptible to attack by cross-examination."

b. Minority view: A small (but probably increasing) minority of courts *allow* testimony influenced by prior hypnosis. These courts have generally imposed stringent safeguards to increase reliability and reduce the danger of suggestion. See, e.g., *State v. Hurd*, 432 A.2d 86 (N.J. 1981), requiring, *inter alia*, a written record of all information about the event given to the hypnotist before the session, a recording (preferably videotape) of all contacts between hypnotist and subject, and a limitation of attendance at the session to just hypnotist and subject.

c. Pre-session recollections: If the jurisdiction does not allow hypnotically-influenced testimony, or if it does allow it but the conditions have not been satisfied, it is not clear whether the witness will be found to be totally incompetent (*supra*, p. 7) to testify about the event. The issue is whether the witness may repeat those recollections he had prior to the session. Some courts hold that the witness' testimony must be completely excluded, because the session will inevitably increase the witness' confidence in his prior recollections, and therefore make it unfairly hard to cross-examine him. Other courts allow testimony limited to the pre-hypnotic recall. See, e.g., *State ex rel. Collins v. Superior Court, supra*, allowing testimony as to the pre-hypnotic recall, but only if there is a complete record made before the session showing the extent of the witness' pre-hypnotic recall.

d. Leads: Even if the state completely forbids testimony of witnesses who have been hypnotized about the event, hypnosis may be worthwhile. The hypnosis may generate *leads* which an investigator can then follow up on. These leads may in turn produce admissible evidence (e.g., other witnesses, forensic evidence, etc.) This hypnotically-derived evidence will presumably be admissible no matter how dim a view the jurisdiction takes of the reliability of hypnosis, since the derivative evidence will have to have its own foundation.

e. Criminal defendant's right to testify: Most hypnotized-witness cases have involved witnesses other than criminal defendants. Where the ***criminal defendant*** himself has been hypnotized, the trial court's ability to restrict hypnosis-influenced testimony may impair the defendant's ***constitutional*** right to ***testify in his own defense***.

Example: D, while fighting with her husband, V, picks up a handgun. The gun goes off, shooting V in the chest. D is charged with manslaughter. D cannot remember all the details of the incident, and so undergoes hypnosis by a licensed neuropsychologist/hypnotist. The hypnosis sessions are recorded on tape. During the sessions, D remembers that her finger was not on the trigger at any time during the fight, and that the gun went off when V grabbed D's arm. At trial, D offers testimony by a gun expert that the gun was defective and prone to fire if hit or dropped without the trigger's being pulled. D then offers her own hypnotically-refreshed testimony. The judge limits D's testimony to "matters remembered and stated to the examiner prior to being placed under hypnosis"; this ruling prevents D from testifying on the finger-on-the-trigger issue. D is convicted.

Held (by the Supreme Court), for D. D's constitutional right to testify in her own defense was violated by the trial judge's ruling. States have the broad right to restrict hypnotically-refreshed testimony by a non-criminal-defendant witness. Even where the testimony is by a criminal defendant, the states have some right to guard against unreliable hypnotic evidence. But the judge's ruling in this case — that all of D's testimony that D could not prove to be the product of pre-hypnosis memory must be excluded — went too far. For instance, testimony by D that was corroborated by other evidence should have been allowed. Since D's testimony that she did not pull the trigger was corroborated by the gun expert's testimony that the gun was defective and prone to fire if hit or dropped, D's testimony should have been allowed even though it was not remembered until hypnosis. *Rock v. Arkansas*, 483 U.S. 44 (1987).

D. Lie detector tests: The *lie detector* (polygraph) purports to determine whether the subject is lying by detecting changes in his physiological functions, such as pulse rate, blood pressure, and perspiration, on the theory that a person is more anxious when he is lying than when he is not, and these physiological reactions accompany anxiety. The polygraph is widely used in private industry to check employee honesty, and also widely used in the investigative stages of law enforcement (though generally only with the consent of the subject). Therefore, its proponents urge that it be accepted as *evidence* of the *credibility* of the subject. Its evidentiary use would be most applicable in criminal cases, where test results could be offered either by the defendant (to show that he is not lying when he denies involvement in the crime) or by the prosecution (to show that the story the defendant has been telling the police is a lie).

1. General rule: Except where both parties stipulate to allow the lie detector results in evidence, virtually all courts still *reject* polygraph evidence on the issue of whether the statements made by the subject during the test are true. M, p. 628. See, e.g., *People v. Leone*, 255 N.E.2d 696 (N.Y. 1969), completely excluding polygraph results on the grounds that the polygraph is not yet "sufficiently established to have gained general acceptance in the particular field to which it belongs" (the general standard for scientific evidence; see *infra*, p. 414).

2. Rationale: The traditional rule barring polygraph evidence on the issue of truth is supported by a number of rationales:

a. Unreliable: The technique is of *questionable reliability*. Even its strongest advocates concede that it is wrong about 5% of the time and inconclusive another 10% of the time. L&S, p. 328. Opponents say the error rate is much higher. Also, accuracy depends upon a highly trained expert to administer and interpret the test, and many testers lack the necessary training.

    i. Anxiety rather than guilt: In particular, the test really measures only *anxiety*, not lying. As one critic put it, "there is no reason to believe that lying produces distinctive physiological changes that characterize it and only it. . . . No doubt when we tell a lie many of us experience an inner turmoil, but we experience a similar turmoil when we are falsely accused of a crime, when we are anxious about having to defend ourselves against accusations, when we are questioned about sensitive topics — and, for that matter, when we are elated or otherwise emotionally stirred." 17 Law & Soc. Rev. 85, 87 (1981) (quoted at M, p. 627, n. 32).

  b. Seemingly scientific: Conversely, the jury is likely to regard the results as *more scientific* than they are, and consequently to give them *too much weight*. M, p. 630.

  c. Waiver of self-incrimination: Finally, if polygraph evidence were generally available, and juries learned of this fact, they might presume that a particular criminal defendant who did not introduce such evidence had flunked or refused to take the test. Especially given the fact that the polygraph is certainly not always accurate, this reasoning by juries would amount to an unfair burden on a criminal defendant's Fifth Amendment right to remain silent (*infra*, p. 320). See L&S, p. 328.

3. Stipulation: A substantial and growing minority of courts allow use of polygraph results where both parties have *stipulated* that the results may be admitted. M, pp. 628-29. See, e.g., *State v. Valdez*, 371 P.2d 894 (Ariz. 1962) (polygraphs and expert testimony relating thereto are admissible upon stipulation in Arizona criminal cases, if trial judge is convinced that the examiner is qualified and that the test was conducted under proper conditions).

  a. Before test: Generally, the stipulation will be entered into before the test is administered, so that neither party knows for sure whether the results will be beneficial to him.

4. Credibility: Finally, a very few courts allow polygraph evidence even in the absence of stipulation, but only in the discretion of the trial judge, and in most instances only on the issue of the *credibility* of the subject, not as substantive evidence of the truth or falsity of the statements he makes on the test. See, e.g., *Commonwealth v. Vitello*, 381 N.E.2d 582 (Mass. 1978), allowing either side to use polygraph evidence to impeach or corroborate the testimony of a criminal defendant. The court pointed to several benefits, including that a defendant who has a criminal record, instead of being afraid to take the stand because of fear that the past record will destroy his credibility, can take the stand and rely on a favorable polygraph to shore up that credibility.

5. Constitutional argument: A criminal defendant could make a plausible (though probably not successful) *constitutional* argument in favor of his right to introduce favorable polygraph evidence. Such a defendant could argue that where respectable scientific evidence and an expert opinion indicate that the defendant is telling the truth, basic fairness (as guaranteed to the defendant by the Fourteenth Amendment's Due Process Clause) requires that the evidence be received. *Chambers v. Mississippi, infra*, pp. 285-86, gives some support to this argument, since it stresses the defendant's fundamental right to present testimony that bears "persuasive assurances of trustworthiness." See L&S, p. 328.

6. **Expert testimony:** When polygraph evidence is admitted, it is usually presented in the form of expert testimony by the examiner, who describes to the jury the questions and answers, interprets the technical test results, and gives his opinion as to the veracity of the subject.

7. **Psychological Stress Evaluation:** Nearly all courts have declined to admit the results of *Psychological Stress Evaluation (PSE)* tests. The PSE is a type of "voice stress analysis," which purportedly shows whether a person is lying by measuring stress in his voice. Most scientific literature has concluded that the PSE has no validity. M, p. 628. Presumably any court that excludes lie detector evidence would exclude PSE results, and probably even some courts that allow lie detector evidence under certain conditions would exclude PSE results on the grounds that the latter are less reliable. See, e.g., *Barrel of Fun, Inc. v. State Farm & Casualty Co.*, 739 F.2d 1028, (5th Cir. 1984) (PSE results are inadmissible for same reasons as polygraph; therefore, testimony by arson investigator who stated that he believed, based on PSE, that D knew the fire was going to be set, should have been excluded).

HEARSAY

I. INTRODUCTION

A. Nature of hearsay: The prohibition on the use of hearsay evidence is probably the single most important rule of evidence. It is not possible to give a statement of the rule that is both succinct and totally accurate. However, for the early part of our discussion of the topic, the following definition will be adequate:

1. **Basic definition:** Hearsay is "a statement or assertive conduct which was made or occurred out of court and is offered in court to prove the truth of the facts asserted." L&S, p. 356. Evidence that falls into this hearsay category is simply **inadmissible**.

   a. **More simplified version:** The gist of the rule against hearsay can be stated even more simply: "The trier of fact may only be asked to believe those statements made by witnesses testifying at the trial." *Id.*, p. 347. In other words, the fact-finder may not be presented with out-of-court statements and asked to believe that the statements are true.

      Example: P sues D for negligence, claiming that D drove her car into the back of P's tractor. D argues that the cause of the accident was not her negligence, but P's contributory negligence in driving a tractor without a rear light. D calls as a witness the insurance adjuster who investigated the accident. The adjuster testifies that P's son told him that the rear light on the tractor had been out for some time before the accident occurred.

      Held, the adjuster's testimony was inadmissible hearsay, since it repeated an out-of-court statement (by P's son) that was offered to prove the truth of the matter asserted in the statement (that the light was indeed out). *Leake v. Hagert*, 175 N.W.2d 675 (N.D. 1970).

2. **Written hearsay:** The non-lawyer generally thinks of hearsay as including only oral declarations made out of court. However, the rule in fact covers any kind of statement, whether oral or **written**, so long as the statement is offered to show the truth of the matter asserted.

   Example: Same facts as above example, but the adjuster tells the jury that P's son wrote a written statement that the rear light was out; D then offers the statement into evidence. The statement would be inadmissible hearsay evidence if offered to prove that the light was out.

B. Truth of matter asserted: The key to the concept of hearsay is to remember that an out-of-court declaration is not, by itself, either hearsay or non-hearsay. The **purpose for which the declaration is offered** is dispositive: an out-of-court declaration may be offered into evidence for many purposes other than to prove the truth of the matter asserted in the declaration; in that event, there is no hearsay problem.

   Example: P, while shopping in a grocery store operated by D, slips on a puddle of ketchup. In defense of P's negligence suit against D, D claims that P failed to keep a proper lookout and failed to heed a warning from D's store manager. D offers the testimony of the store manager's wife (who happened to be in the store at the time) that just before the accident, her husband shouted to P, "Lady, please don't step in that ketchup."

Held, the testimony is not hearsay. The manager's declaration is relevant to whether P was on notice of the dangerous condition, and is not being offered for the purpose of proving the truth of assertion (i.e., that there was ketchup on the floor). *Safeway Stores, Inc. v. Combs*, 273 F.2d 295 (5th Cir. 1960).

C. Dangers of hearsay: The use of hearsay testimony presents four main dangers: (1) *ambiguity*; (2) *insincerity*; (3) *incorrect memory*; and (4) *inaccurate perception*. All of these relate to the fact that the person making the out-of-court statement (the *declarant*, as he is usually called) is *not available for cross-examination*.

1. The four dangers: To understand the four dangers, it is worthwhile to use a triangle diagram first proposed by Professor Tribe. (See *Triangulating Hearsay*, 87 Harv. L. Rev. 957.) To make our use of the triangle technique concrete, assume that the facts are those of *Leake*, summarized in the Example on p. 117, *supra*, (out-of-court statement by O, "The tail light was broken before the accident"). We can represent the process by which the fact-finder can go from this out-of-court statement ("The tail light was broken") to the ultimate issue (Was the tail light broken?) by the following diagram:

Figure 3-1

Adapted from L&S, p. 351

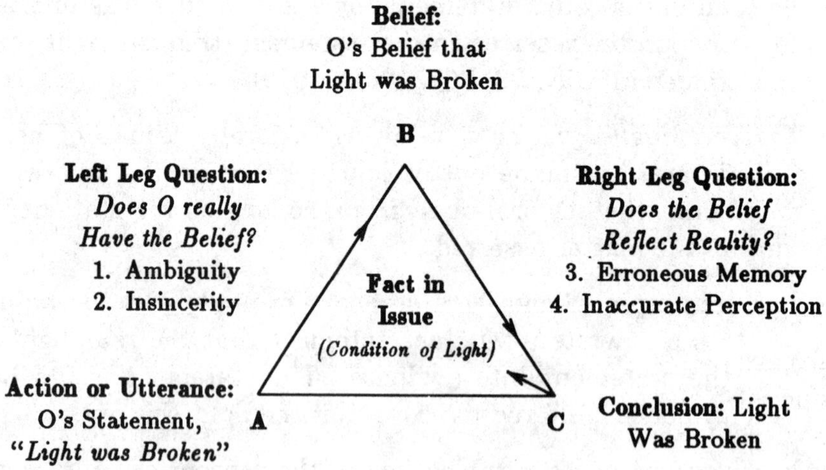

Belief:
O's Belief that
Light was Broken

B

Left Leg Question:
*Does O really
Have the Belief?*
1. Ambiguity
2. Insincerity

Right Leg Question:
*Does the Belief
Reflect Reality?*
3. Erroneous Memory
4. Inaccurate Perception

**Fact in
Issue**
(Condition of Light)

Action or Utterance:
O's Statement,   **A**
"Light was Broken"

C   **Conclusion: Light
Was Broken**

2. Trip around the triangle: In terms of the diagram, the fact-finder's process of inference goes as follows:

a. **Step 1:** We start at point A (O's out-of-court statement).

b. **Step 2:** We first want to get to point B (the conclusion that O really believed that the light was working). To do so, we must avoid two dangers:

   i. **Ambiguity:** The danger of *ambiguity*. O may not really have meant to say that the light was broken. For instance, English might be a foreign language for him, and he really meant to say, "The tail light was on."

   ii. **Insincerity:** The danger of *insincerity*. For instance, O may have known full well that the tail light was working, but because he hated his father, he lied to the insurance adjuster to get his father in trouble.

c. **Step 3:** Once we pass these dangers, we are at point B — that is, we're satisfied that O really believed that the light was broken. Now, we want to get to point C (the conclusion that the light was indeed broken). Here too, there are two principal dangers, problems which might prevent O's truly held belief from accurately representing reality:

   i. **Erroneous memory:** The risk of *incorrect memory*. For instance, O might have honestly believed that the light was broken, but he might be forgetting that it was the family's other car that had a broken light.

   ii. **Inaccurate perception:** The danger of *inaccurate perception*. For instance, O may have seen the car right before the accident, but because of weak eyesight or a blinding sun did not notice that it was really lit and working.

3. **Significance of diagram:** The triangle diagram is of value in two respects. First, it helps illustrate the four principal hearsay dangers. Second, it is a good tool for determining whether evidence is indeed hearsay. Techniques for using the diagram for this purpose will be developed more subsequently; for now, it is enough to note that evidence will be hearsay *only if the trier of fact is asked to travel from point A to point B to point C* in order to get to the fact to which the declaration is relevant. If the evidence is relevant before the trier of fact gets to point B (i.e., the point at which it is satisfied that the declarant truly held the belief which his declaration suggests he held), or if it is relevant before the fact-finder gets from point B to point C (i.e., before he concludes that that belief accurately reflects reality), there is no hearsay problem. See pp. 122-24 for examples of the diagram's use.

D. **Dangers of out-of-court declaration:** The four dangers summarized above (ambiguity, insincerity, erroneous memory, and inaccurate perception) would all exist even if O took the witness stand at the trial and made the same declaration, "The tail light was broken before the accident." However, the dangers are collectively (and probably individually) *greater* when the declaration is made out of court rather than from the witness stand.

1. **Explanation:** To understand the dangers of hearsay testimony, we must first consider the safeguards that are present when a witness testifies at trial about facts of which he has personal knowledge. Consider, for instance, the safeguards that surround O's testimony *directly from the witness stand*, "The tail light was broken."

a. **Oath:** First, O would be testifying **under oath.** The oath "emphasizes the solemnity of the occasion and raises in potential liars the fear of perjury." L&S, p. 352.

b. **Demeanor:** Second, the jurors would be able to **observe O's demeanor** as he testifies. At least in theory, liars may appear shifty-eyed or nervous, or may squirm uncomfortably while telling their story.

   i. Criticism: However, there is little if any empirical evidence to support the view that observation of a witness' demeanor aids materially in determining whether she is telling the truth. *Id.*

c. **Context:** O will be making his statement in the **context of a larger story** (e.g., how he happened to notice that the tail light was broken; how he knows that it was still broken at the time of the accident, etc.) This context may help the jury evaluate the sincerity and accuracy of O's testimony.

d. **Cross-examination:** Most of all, O's testimony will be subject to **cross-examination** by the opposing lawyer. No technique known to jurisprudence is a better instrument for uncovering the truth.

2. **Hearsay contrasted:** Contrast this set of safeguards with the situation in which an out-of-court declaration is offered for the purpose of establishing the truth of the assertions made in that declaration. Where W testifies, "O said that the tail light was broken at the time of the accident," here's what the situation looks like:

a. **No oath:** O's statement is **not** made under **oath**, so at least to the extent that O was tempted to lie (and perhaps to the extent that he was merely being sloppy), his statement may be less accurate than had he been under oath.

b. **Demeanor:** The jury has **not** gotten a chance to **observe O's demeanor** while he made the remark.

c. **Context:** O is **not** telling his story as part of a **larger context** which the jury gets to hear. Probably the jury will get to hear only the one sentence that is most closely relevant ("The tail light was broken at the time of the accident"), and supporting clues to the accuracy or inaccuracy of O's statement will be lost.

d. **Cross-examination:** Most significantly, the adversary will have **no opportunity to cross-examine O, the absent declarant**. If O was telling an outright lie, there will be no opportunity for this lie to be exposed. Perhaps more importantly, if O was honestly mistaken, or his statement was slightly misleading or taken out of context, there will be no opportunity for the adversary to bring these facts to the jury's attention.

3. **Four dangers:** One way to assess the importance of cross-examination is to observe that where such examination is possible, all four of the potential dangers to the jury's correct evaluation of the factual assertion discussed above — ambiguity, **insincerity**, erroneous memory, and faulty perception — could be **exposed** by cross-examination, which by definition is not available in the hearsay situation. (Context, similarly, might help avoid each of these four dangers, but probably in a

less direct way.)

    a. Oath and demeanor: By contrast, oath and demeanor, even if present, would only help avoid the declarant's **_insincerity_**, not the other three potential dangers.

4. Mistakes in transmittal: Absence of oath, demeanor, context, and cross-examination all relate to the testimony of the out-of-court declarant. A **_fifth difficulty_** with hearsay testimony relates to the testimony of the in-court witness who is repeating the out-of-court declaration. This is the danger of a **_mistake in transmittal_**. While the usual safeguards (e.g., cross-examination) are available to make sure that the in-court witness is speaking accurately, these traditional safeguards are probably less effective where the in-court witness is repeating someone else's out-of-court statement than where more complex events are being described in court. L&S, p. 353.

    Example: Return to our example of the broken tail light (*supra*, p. 117). If W had actually witnessed the condition of the tail light, he would be telling a story that is somewhat complicated, with lots of surrounding detail and context. A small error in perception by W is unlikely to be conclusive. If, on the other hand, W is testifying about what O said, and W failed to hear the word "not" in O's statement, "The light was not broken at the time of the accident," the entire significance of O's statement will be distorted when W repeats it. Thus the risk of an inadvertent mistake in transmission by the in-court witness is probably greater when what is being described is someone else's statement rather than an actual event.

5. Cross-examination: Another reason why the in-court witness' testimony is less likely to be accurate when what is being recounted is someone else's statement rather than an actual event, is that **_cross-examination is less valuable_**. L&S, pp. 353-54.

    Example: Once again in our broken tail light example, consider the position of an adversary who wants to cross-examine W (the in-court witness). If W is describing the event itself as he witnessed it (e.g., his seeing the broken tail light), W will have to fit his story into a complicated fact pattern composed of evidence proved by other means (e.g., where W was on that day; what model the car was; what time the accident took place, etc.) If W's story doesn't fit, cross-examination can bring this fact out. If, by contrast, W is merely repeating O's statement, "The tail light was broken," W doesn't have to make the story fit with anything else; so cross-examination of W is largely useless as it relates to the underlying story — W can simply stubbornly repeat, "That's what O said." The lack of cross-examination is especially damaging where W is intentionally lying. *Id.*

II. THE DEFINITION OF HEARSAY

    A. The problem generally: There is no single universally-accepted definition of hearsay. However, it is possible to state a common-law definition that squares with most decisions; after that, we will discuss the Federal Rule, which makes some modifications to the common-law one.

1. **Common-law definition:** The best common-law definition of hearsay is probably the one with which we began this chapter: Hearsay is "a statement or assertive conduct which was made or occurred out of court and is offered in court to prove the truth of the facts asserted." M. Ladd, Cases on Evidence 384 (quoted in L&S, p. 356).

> **Note:** From here on, as a shorthand we'll generally use the word "statement" to include not only the term's conventional meaning of "declaration or remark," but also to include nonverbal behavior that is intended as an assertion. (Such behavior is discussed *infra*, p. 135.)

   a. **Issues:** There are three types of issues raised by this common-law definition, each of which will be considered in turn below:

   i. **"Out of court":** What types of statements will be deemed to have occurred *"out of court"*? See *infra*, p. 126.

   ii. **Truth:** When is a statement offered to prove "the **truth** of the facts asserted"? or, more precisely, what kinds of statements are **not** deemed to be offered for the truth of the facts asserted? See *infra*, p. 127.

   iii. **"Statement or assertive conduct":** What is included within the phrase "statement or assertive conduct"? More precisely, what is the difference between conduct that is *"assertive"* and that which is not? See *infra*, p. 135.

2. **Use of triangle:** The common-law definition can be tied into the testimonial triangle first presented on p. 118, *supra*, and reprinted in slightly different form here:

Figure 3-2

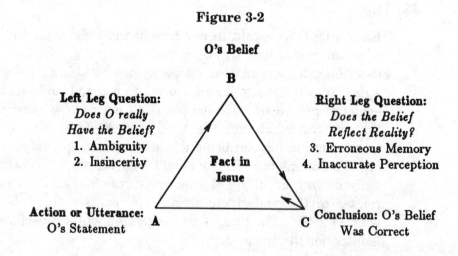

a. **Must raise questions on both legs:** In the terms of this diagram, the statement of the out-of-court declarant (O) constitutes hearsay **only if the**

inference that the proponent seeks to establish requires a "yes" answer to the questions raised by both legs. L&S, p. 359.

Example 1: The issue is whether O is conscious after an accident. W testifies, "After the accident, I heard O say, 'I've been shot.' " The proponent of this testimony (the party who put W on the stand) is trying merely to establish that O was conscious. The inference which the proponent desires the trier of fact to make (that one who speaks must necessarily be conscious) can be reached by the factfinder without ever even getting to point B (that O believed his statement that he had been shot), let alone getting to point C (that O's belief that he had been shot was correct).

In diagrammatic terms, the trier of fact can go directly from point A to the center of the triangle, so neither the Left Leg questions nor the Right Leg questions require an affirmative answer:

Figure 3-3

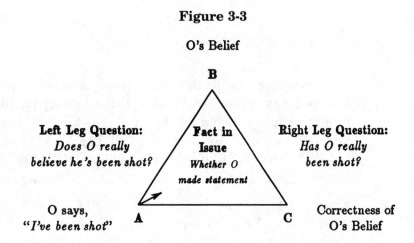

To put it another way, even if the trier of fact believes that O was lying or mistaken about having been shot, the inference is the same. Since neither the Left Leg nor Right Leg dangers exist, O's statement is not hearsay.

Example 2: O is prosecuted for robbery. He defends on the grounds that he was a hostage, and that he was threatened with death if he did not participate in the robbery. W, O's wife, testifies at the trial that during O's captivity, he smuggled out a hand-written message to her that said, "If I don't take part in a robbery they're going to pull, they'll kill me." This situation can be diagrammed as follows:

Figure 3-4

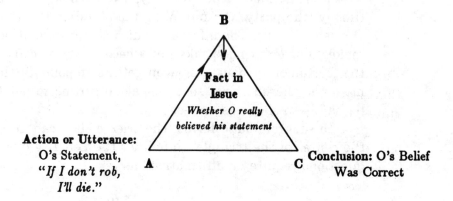

O's Belief that if
he doesn't rob, he'll die

B

**Fact in
Issue**
*Whether O really
believed his statement*

Action or Utterance:
O's Statement,
*"If I don't rob,
I'll die."*
A

C
Conclusion: O's Belief
Was Correct

O, the proponent of this testimony, is merely trying to establish that O **believed** that he would be shot if he did not participate in the robbery, not that the captors would really have shot him. Therefore, to get to the desired inference, we have to travel the Left Leg ("Did O really believe that he would be shot?"), but not the Right Leg ("Was O's belief correct?"). Since the Right Leg question never arises, the statement is not hearsay.

Example 3: D is on trial for shooting O. In order to establish D's guilt, the prosecution offers the testimony of W, that when he found O lying in pool of blood, O said to him, "D shot me." Here is the appropriate diagram:

Figure 3-5

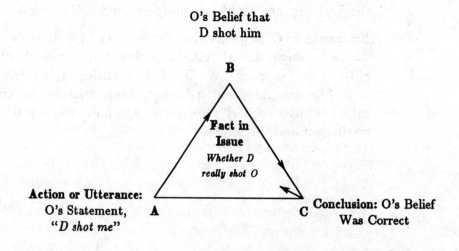

O's Belief that
D shot him

B

**Fact in
Issue**
*Whether D
really shot O*

Action or Utterance:
O's Statement,
"D shot me"
A

C
Conclusion: O's Belief
Was Correct

Because the prosecution is trying to use this testimony to directly establish D's guilt, it is asking the factfinder to make the following chain of inferences: because O said that D had shot him, O in fact believed that D shot him; a person who believes that another has shot him is probably correct in that belief. Thus to reach the inference that the prosecution desires it to reach, the trier of fact must travel to point B and then to point C, giving affirmative answers to both the Left Leg question and the Right Leg question. Therefore, the use of O's statement constitutes hearsay.

3. **Federal Rule:** The Federal Rule's definition of hearsay occurs in FRE 801. Since this provision is also in effect, in substantially identical form, in about half the states, it is especially worthy of close scrutiny:

"The following definitions apply under this article:

(a) *Statement.* A "statement" is (1) an oral or written assertion or (2) nonverbal conduct of a person, if it is intended by the person as an assertion.

(b) *Declarant.* A "declarant" is a person who makes a statement.

(c) *Hearsay.* "Hearsay" is a statement, other than one made by the declarant while testifying at the trial or hearing, offered in evidence to prove the truth of the matter asserted.

(d) *Statements which are not hearsay.* A statement is not hearsay if —

(1) *Prior statement by witness.* The declarant testifies at the trial or hearing and is subject to cross-examination concerning the statement, and the statement is (A) inconsistent with the declarant's testimony, and was given under oath subject to the penalty of perjury at a trial, hearing, or other proceeding, or in a deposition, or (B) consistent with the declarant's testimony and is offered to rebut an express or implied charge against the declarant of recent fabrication or improper influence or motive, or (C) one of identification of a person made after perceiving him; or

(2) *Admission by party-opponent.* The statement is offered against a party and is (A) the party's own statement, in either an individual or a representative capacity or (B) a statement of which the party has manifested an adoption or belief in its truth, or (C) a statement by a person authorized by the party to make a statement concerning the subject, or (D) a statement by the party's agent or servant concerning a matter within the scope of the agency or employment, made during the existence of the relationship, or (E) a statement by a coconspirator of a party during the course and in furtherance of the conspiracy."

a. **Difference from common-law rule:** The basic definition given in 801(c) is essentially identical to the common-law approach. To the extent that FRE 801 changes common-law principles, it does so through 801(a) and (d). These deviations will be considered in greater detail when the relevant common-law aspect is discussed. For now, here are the important departures:

i. **Non-assertive conduct:** Where non-verbal **conduct** that is **not intended as an assertion** is introduced to show a belief on the part of the actor, the traditional common-law approach was that this was hearsay. See the classic case of *Wright v. Doe d. Tatham*, discussed extensively *infra*, p. 138. FRE 801(a)(2) by negative implication provides that non-verbal conduct that is not intended as an assertion will **not be hearsay.**

    ii. Prior inconsistent statements: At common law, a witness' ***prior inconsistent statement*** is hearsay, and is therefore not admissible to prove the truth of the matter stated in the prior inconsistent statement (though it is admissible to impeach the witness' credibility). FRE 801(d)(1)(A) changes this by providing that the witness' prior inconsistent statement will not be hearsay, and is thus admissible for its truth, if the witness made it while testifying **under oath** in a previous **proceeding or deposition.** See the more detailed discussion *infra*, p. 252.

    iii. Prior consistent statement: At common law, a prior ***consistent*** statement by the witness is not admissible for its truth, although it is admissible for the limited purpose of rebutting the opposing party's claim that the witness was improperly influenced. FRE 801(d)(1)(B) makes such a statement non-hearsay (i.e., admissible for truth) where such a charge of recent fabrication or improper influence is made. (Observe that a consistent statement, unlike an inconsistent one, does not have to be made under an oath or in a proceeding.) See *infra*, p. 255.

    iv. Identification: Under the common-law definition, the fact that A has previously given an ***eyewitness identification*** of B is hearsay. FRE 801(d)(1)(C) makes such an identification non-hearsay, provided that the person who makes the identification is a witness at the trial. See *infra*, p. 256.

    v. Admissions: *Admissions* by a party-opponent are, at common law, treated as exceptions to the hearsay rule (which means that such admissions may be admitted for their truth). FRE 801(d)(2) makes such admissions non-hearsay rather than an exception to the hearsay rule. The distinction has little practical significance. S&R, p. 726. See *infra*, p. 152.

B. Statement made "out of court": What does it mean for a statement to be made *"out of court"*?

    1. Meaning: An "out-of-court" statement is any statement except one that is "made by witnesses during the trial while testifying before the trier of fact." L&S, p. 357. This means that the following statements will be deemed "out of court":

        a. Statement by non-witness: *any* oral or written statement by someone other than the at-trial witness; and

        b. Prior statements by witness: *prior statements* by the *at-trial witness*, where the prior statement was not made in the present trial before the trier of fact. Thus a witness' prior statement made in a *deposition* or in an *earlier trial*, or even when spoken in the judge's chambers during the present trial, are all "out of court," and so will constitute hearsay if the other aspects of the hearsay definition are met.

Note: But don't forget that under FRE 801(d)(1), some prior statements by a witness that would be deemed "out of court" and thus hearsay under common-law rules, are treated as not being hearsay. See *infra*, p. 247.

C. **"Truth of matter asserted":** Most of the close questions involved in analyzing whether a statement is hearsay involve the requirement that the statement be "offered to prove the *truth of the matter asserted*" in the statement. Our discussion of this aspect of the definition will consist mainly of detailing the important uses of statements that are not for the truth of the matter asserted.

   1. **Significance of assertions for truth:** First, let's examine *why* only those statements offered to prove the truth of the matter asserted should fall within the hearsay rule. Recall the basic hearsay diagram (Figure 3-2, *supra*, p. 122). Only if the statement is offered to prove the truth of the matter asserted therein does the Right Leg question ("Does the declarant's belief reflect reality?") arise. Only then does the danger that the declarant misremembered the event, or inaccurately perceived it, matter.

      a. **Left Leg dangers:** Of course, an out-of-court statement that is offered to prove that the declarant *believed* something, but not offered to prove that the belief was correct, would not satisfy the "truth of the matter asserted" requirement and would thus not be hearsay. Yet the use of such evidence at trial raises Left Leg dangers. (Remember that the Left Leg question is, "Did the declarant really have the belief that his statement suggests he did?") Thus the danger that the declarant's statement ambiguously reflected his belief, or that the declarant is lying, is present even though Right Leg questions are absent. Why, then, should the mere fact that the statement is not being introduced for its truth be enough to remove the statement from hearsay classification?

      Example: D is charged with extorting money from O. A substantive element of the crime of extortion is that the victim must have believed that he would be harmed if he did not comply with the demand. The prosecution offers a statement made by O to his wife shortly after O paid money to D: "If I hadn't paid D, he would have shot off my kneecaps." Since the prosecution is not offering this statement for the truth of the matter asserted (that D would in fact have shot off O's kneecaps if he hadn't made the payment), the statement is not hearsay. Yet for the jury to reach the inference desired by the prosecutor (that O in fact believed that harm would befall him if he didn't pay up), the jury must answer the Left Leg question, "Did O really have the belief?" This inference in turn requires the jury to make a correct assessment that O was sincere in his statement. Yet O is not available for cross-examination, so his sincerity cannot be tested by this means. The situation thus seems to share the principal weakness of hearsay: the inability to test the out-of-court declaration by cross-examination.

         i. **Explanation:** There is no totally convincing explanation of why a statement like the one in the above example should be treated as not hearsay. Two commentators give the following explanation: "Since the Right Leg problems are probably the most significant hearsay dangers, and since many hearsay exceptions are justified by only some support to one of the legs, it makes sense to classify statements used so as to eliminate the Right Leg dangers entirely as not hearsay." L&S, p. 358.

2. **Approach:** We now proceed to examine the various uses to which a statement may be put that do not constitute offering the statement for the truth of the matter asserted.

3. **Verbal acts:** A statement may be, by itself, an ***operative fact*** which gives rise to ***legal consequences***. Such a statement, which is usually called a ***"verbal act,"*** is not offered for the truth of the matter asserted.

> **Example 1:** D is prosecuted for running a brothel. W, a vice officer, testifies that while at the bar in D's establishment, he was propositioned by Pattie and Jean, who offered to have sex with him in return for money.
>
> *Held,* the girls' out-of-court statements (the offers to have sex for money) were not hearsay. These statements were "operative facts," since the mere fact that they were made is relevant to the charge, ***even if the statements were untrue*** (e.g., even if the girls would not have performed sex for money). *Los Robles Motor Lodge, Inc. v. Dept. of Alcoholic Beverage Control,* 246 Cal.App.2d 198 (Cal. Dist. Ct. App. 1966).

> **Example 2:** D says to P, "You're a no-good thief who'd sell his mother for a dollar." P sues for slander, and testifies that D spoke these words. The speaking of the words was a "verbal act" which has legal effect (since it constitutes slander), ***regardless of the truth of the words spoken***. In fact, not only is P not offering the words to prove the truth of the matter asserted, he would be barred from recovery if the words *were* true.

> **Example 3:** D says, "I'll sell you my house for $24,000." P says, "O.K., I accept." D refuses to perform, and P sues for breach of the oral contract. If P testifies that D spoke the words of the offer, this will not be hearsay — the words of the offer had an independent legal effect (they gave give rise to a power of acceptance in P) regardless of their "truth."

4. **Verbal parts of acts:** Closely related to "verbal acts" are situations in which a physical act is ambiguous, but words that accompany it resolve the ambiguity. In such situations, the accompanying words are called the ***"verbal part of the act,"*** and are not hearsay.

> **Example:** O hands money to X, a friend who happens to be mayor of the town in which they live. If the jury can't learn of the words that accompanied the transfer, it will not be clear whether the transfer was a loan, gift, or bribe. Therefore, O's statement to X at the time of the transfer, "This is to repay you for the money you lent me last year," will be non-hearsay, since it is the verbal part of the act of transferring the money.

   a. **Diagram:** Now let's analyze the "verbal part of the act" exception in terms of the triangles, Figures 3-3 and 3-4, *supra*, pp. 123-24. In some situations, ***the mere utterance*** of the words (without regard to the declarant's intent) will be, under the applicable substantive law, enough to determine the nature of the act. In this situation, Figure 3-3 supplies the correct analysis. For instance, if, in the above example, X had been a bank teller rather than the mayor, applicable banking law would probably provide that O's payment should be treated as a loan repayment regardless of whether O secretly intended to be making a deposit to his own account — the mere speaking of the words gives rise to the legal effect.

b. **Declarant's belief:** But in other situations, the applicable substantive law may make the declarant's *belief* the relevant question. For instance, if X is O's friend, and X claims that the money is a gift, O's accompanying statement will be looked at as evidence of O's underlying donative intent or lack of it. In this situation, the relevant diagram is Figure 3-4.

c. **Significance:** It probably doesn't matter whether, in a particular case, the verbal part of an act is best analyzed under Figure 3-3 or Figure 3-4 — in either event, the verbal act should not be hearsay, since no complete trip around the triangle is required; that is, the truthfulness of the declarant's belief is irrelevant no matter which diagram is used. L&S, p. 360. But some authorities assert that the "verbal part of an act" exception only applies where the declarant's belief is irrelevant. See, e.g., M, p. 733 (exception applies only where "under the substantive law the inquiry is directed only to objective manifestations rather than to the actual intent or other state of mind of the actor.") This limitation seems wrong, for the reason just stated.

5. **Effect on hearer or reader:** If a statement is offered to show its *effect on the listener*, it will generally *not* be hearsay. This is so because the statement is not being offered to prove its truth, merely to prove the effect that that statement (whether true or false) had or should have had on the listener. This principle applies where the out-of-court declaration is offered to show that the listener (or reader) was *put on notice*, *had certain knowledge*, had a certain *emotion*, behaved reasonably or unreasonably, etc.

a. **Murder defense:** For instance, suppose that D, who is on trial for the murder of V, raises a self-defense claim. If D presents W's testimony, "Just before the killing, I heard V say to D, 'I'm going to cut off your [expletive deleted] and shove it up your [expletive deleted],' " this will not be hearsay. The reason is that the evidence is not being offered for the truth of the assertion (that V would really have done this to D), but rather to show that D probably had an actual, and reasonable, fear for his own safety. L&S, pp. 360-61. See also *Subramaniam v. Public Prosecutor*, 100 Sol. J. 566 (Jud. Comm. Privy Coun. 1956) (where D was charged with illegal possession of ammunition, his testimony that he had been captured by terrorists, and that they threatened him with death if he would not comply with their demand that he carry the ammunition, was not hearsay; the terrorists' statements were relevant to D's defense of duress regardless of whether the threats were "true," i.e., regardless of whether they would have been carried out).

b. Notice: Statements admitted to show the effect on the hearer are often admitted in negligence cases, where the issue is whether the hearer or reader was on *notice* of a dangerous condition.

> **Example:** P sues D, a hospital, for its negligence in hiring X as a doctor and allowing him to operate on P's hip. P introduces the records from two other hospitals, showing these hospitals' refusals to allow X on their staffs.
>
> *Held*, the records were not hearsay, because they were not offered to show the truth of those hospitals' conclusions regarding X's competence, merely to show that D knew or should have known that X was of questionable competence. The state of D's actual or constructive knowledge of X's competence was, in turn, highly relevant to whether D was negligent. *Johnson v. Misericordia Community Hospital*, 294 N.W.2d 501 (Wis. 1980).

> **Note 1:** Of course, particular evidence may have both a hearsay and a non-hearsay purpose. The *Johnson* case illustrates this. In this situation, all the objecting party can do is to ask for a *limiting instruction*, by which the jury is told to consider the evidence only for the non-hearsay purpose. Thus in *Johnson*, the trial judge should have, at the hospital's request, told the jury, "You are to consider the other hospitals' actions only on the issue of whether D knew or should have known that there were questions about X's competence, not on the issue of whether X was really competent." Also, if P produced no other evidence of X's actual incompetence, D would have been entitled to a directed verdict — "the tendency of [a] statement to prove . . . hearsay inferences may not be considered on a motion for a directed verdict." L&S, p. 362.

> **Note 2:** Observe that the *Johnson* case also illustrates that hearsay analysis must be applied even where the out-of-court statement is *written*, rather than oral. In that case, it turned out that the other hospitals' written records were not hearsay, but this had nothing to do with the fact that they were written.

c. Emotion: Out-of-court statements may be introduced to show that they produced a certain *emotion* in the hearer or reader.

> **Example:** P is injured when she slips in the lobby of D's hotel. She suffers a repeatedly collapsed lung, and sues for pain and suffering, including suffering from the fact that she is afraid to pursue many activities that she has formerly enjoyed. She testifies that X, her doctor, has "told me that I would have to live with myself and to be careful never to strain myself."
>
> *Held*, the doctor's statement was not hearsay, because "it is well-settled that evidence of an out-of-court statement to show its effect upon the mental attitude of the person who hears it is properly admissible." The statement was not offered to show the accuracy of the doctor's diagnosis, but only to show the state of fear it introduced in P's mind. *194th St. Hotel Corp. v. Hopf*, 383 So.2d 739 (Fla.App. 1980).

> **Note:** But other courts have found the hearsay rule applicable in this situation of a plaintiff testifying about the mental effects upon him of his doctor's

statements regarding the condition. See, e.g., *Central of Georgia Railway Co. v. Reeves*, 257 So.2d 839 (Ala. 1972), holding that "the proposition that a patient may testify in court as to statements made to him out-of-court by his doctor in order to show that he, the patient, was caused mental anguish as a result of such statements . . . [would] 'open wide the door to hearsay evidence' without the opportunity afforded to cross-examine the declarant." As a matter of analysis, the *Central of Georgia* case seems flatly wrong; any abuses can be handled by a limiting instruction and/or by cross-examination of the patient about the details of his alleged mental anguish.

    d. Diagram: In all of the above situations involving a statement's effect on the listener or reader, the relevant diagram is Figure 3-3, *supra*, p. 123. That is, we never even reach the issue of the declarant's belief in the truth of his statement — all that matters is that the statement was made (and that the other party to it responded in a certain way). The situation is thus especially clearly non-hearsay, since neither Left Leg nor Right Leg problems arise.

    e. Account of arresting officer: A more troubling situation arises when, in a criminal prosecution, the ***arresting officer describes how he came to make the arrest.*** The officer may recite all kinds of out-of-court declarations that he heard or read, and that led him to suspect D of the crime. Strictly speaking, this is not hearsay, because the prosecution is merely putting the arrest in context, a use to which the actual truth of the out-of-court declarations are irrelevant. But use of the statements may be very unfair to the defense, since the statements are likely to be used by the jury for purposes that are clearly hearsay (i.e., the jury is likely to assume that the statements implicating D in the crime and leading to his arrest are evidence of his guilt). Therefore, some courts have labelled it hearsay.

        Example: D is on trial on narcotics charges. The prosecution puts on the stand W, a narcotics officer, who testifies that he began surveillance of D after he ran D's name through a computer and obtained a print-out that D was a "known narcotics smuggler."

        Held (on appeal), this was hearsay testimony and was reversible error. *U.S. v. Escobar*, 674 F.2d 469 (5th Cir. 1982). (McCormick (p. 734) suggests that in this situation, the officer should merely be permitted to testify that he acted "upon information received" regarding the defendant, and that he not be entitled to give in detail the information upon which he acted.)

6. Declarant's state of mind: Statements introduced to show the ***state of mind*** of the ***declarant*** are, similarly, not barred by the hearsay rule. As with the statements discussed immediately above concerning the hearer's or reader's state of mind, a statement offered to show the declarant's state of mind is not offered to prove "the truth of the matter asserted," i.e., the truth of the declarant's statement.

    a. Knowledge: Most frequently, such statements are introduced to show the declarant's ***knowledge*** of some matter, as manifested by his statement.

Example: P, a pedestrian, is hurt when D runs him over. P claims that D was negligent in not having his brakes checked after he knew that there was a problem. P introduces a statement made by D to X just before the accident: "I need to get my brakes checked; they don't seem to have been working too well recently." Because the state of D's knowledge is in issue in the suit, D's statement to X will not be hearsay — it is offered to show the state of D's knowledge, not to show that the brakes were in fact defective at the time of the statement. (On the other hand, P will have to come up with some independent evidence that the brakes were in fact defective at the time of the accident in order to withstand a directed verdict motion by D. All of this ignores the exception to the hearsay rule for admissions by a party; see *infra*, p. 149.)

i. Knowledge relevant to other issue: In the above example, the issue of the declarant's knowledge was itself an issue in the case. In other situations, knowledge may not be an actual issue, but it may be a fact tending to resolve some other issue in the case. Here, too, the statement is not hearsay, because it merely shows something about the declarant's state of mind (the possession of knowledge), and is not offered for the purpose of proving the statement's truth.

Example: D is accused of having enticed O, a young girl, to come to his room and of then having sexually assaulted her. The prosecution seeks to introduce O's out-of-court statement describing the room and its contents, in order to show that O was in the room. Other evidence independently establishes that the room and its furnishings exactly match O's description of them.

Held, O's out-of-court description is not hearsay, because it is not offered for the truth of the matter asserted (what the room really looked like), but rather to show that O knew what the room looked like, and therefore, by inference, that she must have been in it. *Bridges v. State*, 19 N.W.2d 529 (Wisc. 1945).

Note: But observe that in the *Bridges* case, the desired inference (that because O knew what the room looked like, she had been in it) only applies if one assumes that no one else could have described the room to O. O's out-of-court statement apparently included the assertion that she was able to give the description because she had been there, and had not heard the description from anyone else. This aspect of her statement seems to be hearsay, since it is only relevant if looked at for its truth. L&S, p. 362, n. 29. Therefore, the case is probably wrongly decided.

b. Other states of mind: Like knowledge, other states of mind of the declarant can be shown by her statement, without violating the hearsay rule.

i. Sanity: For instance, the declarant's *sanity* may be shown by his statements.

Example: D, charged with murder, raises an insanity defense. He offers in evidence letters written by him while a psychiatric patient. The letters are addressed to the Pope, the FBI, the Secret Service, and others, and expert witnesses for D testify that they are "classic paranoid letters." The prosecution objects on the grounds of hearsay.

Held, the letters are not hearsay, because they are "offered not to establish the truth of the statements they contained but as evidence of the mental state of the writer at the time they were written." *Sollars v. State*, 316 P.2d 917 (Nev. 1957).

ii. **Fear:** Similarly, a declarant's statement may be used to show that he felt a certain **emotion**, such as **fear**.

Example: In a custody fight between W and H for their daughter, Tracey, H tries to show that he should be given custody because W's paramour, Ray, is a violent criminal who has probably murdered H and W's other child, James. During the trial of Ray for this murder (which ended in a hung jury), Tracey was placed in a foster home. H now offers the testimony of the foster mother that when she told Tracey that her mother and Ray had gotten married, Tracey started crying and said, "He killed my brother and he'll kill my Mommie too." W objects to this statement as hearsay.

Held, not hearsay. Tracey's out-of-court declaration was not admitted to prove the truth of the assertion she made (that Ray killed her brother), but "merely to indirectly and inferentially show [her] mental state . . . at the time. . . ." (Nor is it relevant that Tracey would not be competent to testify as a witness in court; putting aside the question of whether statements made by persons not competent as witnesses can be admitted as *exceptions* to the hearsay rule, statements that are simply not hearsay at all will be admissible even though the speaker would not have been competent as a witness.) *Betts v. Betts*, 473 P.2d 403 (Wash. 1970).

c. **Statements of mental state:** Now consider an intriguing problem: How should we treat a statement **asserting that the speaker has a particular state of mind**, where the speaker's state of mind is the very fact in issue?

Example: D, on trial for the murder of X, asserts the defense that he was provoked by X's affair with D's wife, and that he is guilty of at most voluntary manslaughter. Applicable substantive law requires D to show that he was under extreme emotional distress at the time of the killing. D introduces a statement he made to X just before the killing: "I'm so furious at you for what you've done to me that I'll never be able to look at you again." Is D's statement, offered for the purpose of showing extreme mental disturbance, hearsay?

i. **Alternative views:** On the one hand, the statement looks like hearsay, because it is offered for the truth of the matter asserted therein (that D was uncontrollably furious at X). Yet the Right Leg hearsay dangers (see Figure 3-2 on p. 122, *supra*) are absent, since we don't have to worry about whether the declarant's belief corresponds with any external reality — the issue is precisely what the declarant's mental state *is*. The issue does not matter as much as might appear, since there is an **exception** to the hearsay rule for "statements evincing states of mind" (*infra*, p. 172), so the statement would be admissible under this exception theory anyway. Probably most courts would treat it as being hearsay, but would then apply the exception. See L&S, pp. 363-64.

7. Reputation: When a witness testifies that a certain community *reputation* exists as to a matter, this may be a form of hearsay. After all, a reputation is what people in the community are saying about the matter; the witness is thus summarizing the out-of-court declarations of others. Therefore, if reputation testimony is given for the ***truth of the matter reputed***, it is hearsay.

    a. Other uses: As with other types of statements discussed above, however, reputation evidence may be used for purposes other than proving the truth of the matter reputed. For instance, in a defamation action, proof by the plaintiff that his reputation used to be good and is now bad would not be hearsay, because the reputation is proved not for truth of the matter asserted (that the reputation is correct) but, on the contrary, to prove that the matter asserted in the reputation statements is false. Similarly, reputation evidence when offered as tending to prove that a particular person had knowledge of a particular fact (e.g., a neighborhood's reputation for dangerousness as bearing on whether a landlord knew of the need for security measures) is not hearsay, since what is being proved is not the correctness of the reputation, but rather, the fact that a given member of the community probably knew of the reputation. M, p. 735.

8. Opinion surveys: *Opinion surveys* pose a problem similar to that posed by reputation. There are a number of situations in which public opinion, or the opinion of some segment of the public, is relevant. These include motions for change of venue in criminal cases because of the alleged unavailability of a fair trial; trademark cases involving the issue of consumer confusion; and the ascertaining of community standards in obscenity prosecutions. M, p. 642. If the person who did the survey testifies in court as to its results, a hearsay argument could plausibly be made, on the theory that the witness is asserting the out-of-court survey responses in order to prove the truth of what those responses assert.

    a. Most courts allow: Most courts, however, ***allow*** opinion surveys that are conducted with reliable methodology. Some stretch to conclude that there is no hearsay, usually on the ground that the survey responses are being offered for some purpose other than proving the truth of the matters asserted in the responses. Others hold that the survey results, even if hearsay, are admissible under the exception for present statements of mental state (*infra*, p. 172).

        Example: P (Zippo Manufacturing Co.) brings a trademark infringement and unfair competition suit against D. P claims that D's pocket lighters so closely resemble P's that consumers are confused. P relies on a consumer study, in which interviewees were shown each company's lighters, and asked which brand of lighter they thought they were seeing. The results of the survey are described to the jury by the executives of the survey firm (who did not personally conduct the interviews). D objects on grounds of hearsay.

Held, the surveys are admissible. The surveys probably should not be treated as hearsay since three of the four basic hearsay dangers (faulty memory, faulty perception, and faulty narration) are either absent or only minimally present, and the fourth (insincerity) is minimal where unbiased respondents are used. (In any event, the "state of mind" exception to the hearsay rule would apply. See *infra*, p. 172.) A possible argument could be made that even though the actual interviewer would be entitled to testify about the responses made to him, the executives should not be permitted to testify as to the contents of the interviewers' reports; this is arguably a second level of hearsay. But the court does not accept this objection either, in part because there is a great necessity for this type of evidence in this type of case — the alternative would be to present testimony by all of the nation's 115 million smokers. *Zippo Mfg. Co. v. Rogers Imports, Inc.*, 216 F.Supp. 670 (S.D.N.Y. 1963).

   b. **Reliability:** But the court will carefully scrutinize survey evidence to make sure that those who conducted it used appropriate methodology, so that the results are reliable.

9. **Impeachment:** When a witness tells a story at trial, the opposing lawyer will often confront him with a previous out-of-court statement, in which the witness told a different story. Such an *impeachment* use of an out-of-court statement is not hearsay, because the out-of-court statement is introduced not for the purpose of showing that it (rather than the in-court testimony) contains the truth, but rather, to suggest that a witness who changes his story is not credible. Impeachment of a witness by use of his prior inconsistent statements is discussed further, both *infra*, p. 248 and more generally *supra*, p. 93, as part of the treatment of cross-examination.

D. **Statements and conduct:** Recall that a hearsay problem exists only where there has been an out-of-court *"statement."* (See *supra*, p. 117.) What is a "statement" for hearsay purposes?

1. **Open question:** The most common type of "statement" for hearsay purposes is, in the words of FRE 801(a), *"an oral or written assertion."* But more difficult problems are hinted at by the second part of FRE 801(a)'s definition: A statement can also consist of "nonverbal conduct of a person, if it is intended by the person as an assertion." We will treat in some detail several significant issues relating to the meaning of "statement": (1) What kind of conduct is likely to be "intended . . . as an assertion"?; (2) When can silence constitute hearsay?; (3) What is the proper treatment of non-assertive conduct?; and (4) What about intended assertions that imply additional facts or assertions?

2. **Assertive conduct:** The most easily understood of these categories is *assertive conduct*. There are many illustrations of conduct that, although nonverbal, is nonetheless intended as an assertion. Such conduct is universally recognized as capable of being hearsay, since its use presents the same dangers as do the use of verbal assertions.

Example: O, a robbery victim, is hospitalized with her injuries. When she is shown a series of "mug shots" and asked whether she recognizes any of them as being the perpetrator, she pulls D's photo out of the stack and hands it to the detective. If the detective testifies in court that O picked out the photo of D, this will clearly be hearsay even though O made no verbal statement. O's picking out of the photo and handing it to the detective was intended by her to be the equivalent of an assertion, "This is the photo of the man who robbed me." The same hearsay dangers (e.g., that O's memory or perception are flawed, or that she is insincere) are present whether O picks out the photo silently, or points to it saying, "That's the one."

3. **Silence:** A person's *silence* may in some situations lead to the reasonable inference that a particular fact, X, is true. Usually the inference goes like this: If X were not the case, the person would have said something; therefore, by the person's silence we may deduce that X is so. In this situation, is evidence of the person's silence, when offered to prove X, barred by the hearsay rule? The issue arises most frequently in two contexts: (1) the *absence of complaints* by others to prove that a danger or defect did not exist; and (2) silence by a person *accused* of something, to prove that the person was guilty. In each context, the courts are split.

   a. **Absence of complaints:** Suppose that P claims to have been injured by some defect or danger caused by D. This might be allegedly poisonous food served by D to P; a slippery floor in D's store fallen on by P; or any other situation in which D's negligence or sale of a defective product is claimed to have caused injury to P. D will frequently try to make at trial the argument familiar to every disgruntled consumer: "We've never had any complaints about this from anybody else." Most courts will *allow* the absence of complaints into evidence.

      Example: P is a passenger on a train operated by D railroad. The car she is riding in is detached and stands for four hours in a railroad yard awaiting a connection. P, who suffers from a circulatory ailment, claims that during this wait the car became too cold for her, and that she suffered injury. D offers the testimony of the porter in P's car that none of the eleven other passengers in that car at the time complained about the cold.

      Held, the porter's testimony should have been admitted. If these other passengers had been cold, at least one of them would probably have complained to the porter; since all faced the same temperature conditions as P, it was reasonable to assume that neither they nor she actually suffered from cold. *Silver v. New York Central R.R.*, 105 N.E.2d 923 (Mass. 1952).

      i. **Hearsay argument:** Notwithstanding the result in *Silver*, the plaintiff who wants to keep out evidence of others' silence can make a plausible-sounding hearsay argument. He can point out that the others' silence is the functional equivalent of their statement, "Everything is O.K." Since the defendant is offering the evidence of silence precisely to prove that everything was indeed O.K., this use of silence is for proof of the truth of the matter asserted, and is thus arguably hearsay.

ii. **No assertion intended:** However, most modern courts (as well as the Federal Rules — see FRE 801(a)(2)) treat a person's non-verbal conduct as being a "statement" only if it was *intended* by the person as an *assertion*. It is doubtful whether a person who remains silent because he does not suffer a particular ill consequence is intending to assert, "Everything's O.K." The other passengers in *Silver*, for instance, were almost certainly not reciting to themselves, or intending to say to the porter, "I'm not feeling cold" — it's unlikely that they focused on the issue of whether they were cold at all. Therefore, they don't seem to have intended to make any assertion, and under the modern (and Federal Rule) approach *their silence should not be treated as hearsay.* Thus the result in *Silver* would be followed by most courts today. M, p. 743.

b. **Silence in face of accusation:** A more troublesome situation is posed by a person's silence in the face of an *accusation against him*, where that silence is later offered to prove that the accusation was true.

Example: W, a police officer, sees D smoking a cigarette that, in W's judgement, looks and smells like marijuana. As W approaches, D throws the cigarette in the street. W picks up the cigarette, determines that it seems to be marijuana, and says, "This is pot that you were just smoking, isn't it?" D remains silent. At trial, W testifies to these facts, including the fact of D's silence at the accusation. Putting aside any issue as to whether this testimony violates D's *Miranda* rights, can D keep the fact of his silence out of evidence on the grounds of hearsay? The correct result is not clear.

i. **Countervailing arguments:** On these facts, D can argue that the prosecution's very theory for wanting to introduce the evidence is the following syllogism: An innocent person in D's situation would have protested his innocence; therefore, D's silence proves that he believed he was guilty, and that belief means that he was indeed guilty. Thus, D can argue, the prosecution is claiming that D's silence amounts to an assertion of his guilt, used to prove the truth of the matter asserted (the guilt). Furthermore, D can argue, the basic hearsay dangers are present; most spectacularly, there is an extreme risk of *ambiguity*, since D's silence may have nothing to do with consciousness of guilt — for instance, he may just have been applying a reasonable or unreasonable personal policy that it is never wise to speak to the cops.

ii. **Favoring admission:** But the prosecution here can argue that D, by his silence, has not intended to assert anything at all. His silence is being offered not as a statement, but merely as non-assertive conduct that is circumstantial evidence of guilt.

iii. **Probable result:** Most courts in this situation have held that the person objecting to the evidence has the better of the arguments, and have therefore treated the evidence as *hearsay*. L&S, p. 365. But this is usually an empty victory — even if the silence is hearsay, one of the exceptions to the hearsay rule will usually be available; most commonly, the exception for *admissions* by a party (*infra*, p. 149) will apply. This would be the result, for instance, on the facts of our marijuana example.

4. **Non-assertive conduct:** We've already suggested that the modern view is that nonverbal conduct will not be treated as a "statement" unless it was intended by the actor as an assertion. However, this was not the traditional rule; in fact, the contrary rule — that nonverbal conduct implying a fact is hearsay if offered to prove that fact, even if no assertion was intended — was established in perhaps the most famous evidence case of all time, ***Wright v. Doe d. Tatham***, 112 Eng. Rep. 488 (House of Lords 1837).

   a. ***Wright v. Doe:*** Because of *Wright v. Doe*'s historical importance (and the fascinating intellectual issue it presents), we consider it in detail:

      i. **Facts of *Wright*:** A testator, John Marsden, left his estate to his steward, one Wright. Tatham, Marsden's legal heir, contested the will, claiming that Marsden was mentally incompetent when he wrote it. In support of the will, Wright offered in evidence several letters that had been written to the testator by persons no longer living. The theory behind this offer was that the tone of the letters suggested that the authors thought they were corresponding with a man of ordinary intelligence and sanity; from their belief in Marsden's mental competence, it could be inferred that he was in fact competent when he wrote the will.

      ii. **Holding:** In an initial trial, the letters were admitted and the will sustained; in a retrial after appeal, the letters were excluded and the will was voided. The litigation was finally ended by the House of Lords, which ruled the letters ***inadmissible***, on the theory that they amounted to a ***hearsay declaration of Marsden's sanity***, offered to prove that sanity.

      iii. **Parke's summary:** The rationale for this result was explained by Baron Parke: "[P]roof of a particular fact, which is not of itself a matter in issue, but which is relevant only as implying a statement or opinion of a third person on the matter in issue, is inadmissible in all cases where such a statement or opinion not on oath would be of itself inadmissible. . . . The letters, which are offered only to prove the competence of the testator . . . were properly rejected, as the mere statement or opinion of the writer would certainly have been inadmissible."

      iv. **Analogue:** Baron Parke provided a number of hypothetical examples illustrating the Lords' view that a statement implied by conduct should be treated the same as an actual statement for hearsay purposes. For instance, he suggested, consider the conduct of a sea captain who examines every part of his vessel, and then loads it with his family for a trip. If this conduct is offered to prove that the vessel was seaworthy at the start of the voyage, it should be excluded on hearsay grounds. The proponent of the evidence is asking the fact-finder to reason as follows: (a) The fact that the captain boarded the ship with his family indicates that he believed the vessel was seaworthy; and (b) When a captain, after inspection, believes that a vessel is seaworthy, it probably is. In the view of Parke (and the House of Lords), this evidence is functionally no different from the captain's out-of-court statement, made immediately after his inspection, "This vessel seems to be seaworthy" — clearly inadmissible hearsay.

b. **State of the law:** In the years after *Wright*, most American courts faced with the issue of "statements implied from conduct" failed even to notice that there was a potential hearsay problem. Of those that did notice the problem, probably most agreed with the conclusion in *Wright* that such evidence is hearsay. L&S, p. 367.

c. **Modern view:** But there has clearly been a shift, begun even before the enactment of the Federal Rules. Modern courts have tended to attach great importance to the fact that in the "statement implied from conduct" situation, there is a key difference from the explicit verbal assertion of a fact: In the implied statement situation, there is *no intent* to make an assertion.

　　i. **Federal Rules:** Thus the Federal Rules, in FRE 801(a), limit the meaning of "statement" to "(1) an oral or written *assertion* or (2) nonverbal conduct of a person, if it is *intended* by him as an *assertion*."

　　ii. **How *Wright* would come out under Federal Rules:** The facts of *Wright* do not seem to fall within either (1) or (2) of FRE 801(a). The Federal Rules do not define "assertion," but one court has held that the term means "a forceful or positive declaration." *U.S. v. Zenni*, 492 F.Supp. 464 (E.D.Ky. 1980), discussed *infra*, pp. 140-41. The letters in *Wright* were clearly verbal, but they were not "assertions" under this definition, at least not assertions of the matter whose truth was to be proven, i.e., the testator's sanity. (One of the letters urges the testator to have his attorney meet with the writer's attorney to discuss some business matters; others invite him to come to certain meetings to discuss public business; a letter from a cousin who had emigrated to America discusses conditions there. M, p. 737, n. 5.) In none of these letters did the writer make a "forceful or positive declaration" of the testator's sanity. Nor was the "nonverbal conduct" of any of them (e.g., the mere act of writing the letter, without reference to its contents) intended by them as an assertion of Marsden's sanity. So it seems pretty clear that under the Federal Rules, the letters would have been *admitted*, and Wright would have probably won his case.

d. **Pros and cons:** Like most great legal debates, there are plausible arguments to be made on either side. The best arguments speak in terms of the underlying hearsay dangers.

e. **In favor of *Wright* approach:** Here is how one could defend the approach taken by the House of Lords in *Wright*, treating the non-assertive conduct as hearsay: To some extent, both non-assertive verbal communications (like those in the letters in *Wright*) and nonverbal conduct not intended as an assertion, share some of the traditional hearsay dangers. Consider the letters in *Wright*. There are possible problems of *perception* and *memory*, since the authors may not have had the occasion to witness the testator's behavior in recent years; the letter from the cousin in America, for instance, had both of these possible weaknesses. Furthermore, the correspondents may not have been *"sincere"*; they may have believed that Marsden was incompetent, but wrote as if he were sane in order to spare his feelings. Finally, there was a large risk of ***ambiguity***; even if the correspondents believed Marsden was incompetent, they may have written in the tone they did because of their knowledge that the trusted steward, Wright, would read the letters and act upon them. L&S, p. 367.

f. **In favor of Federal Rules' approach:** But the contrary arguments are probably stronger. The four hearsay dangers are almost certainly less extreme in the case of non-assertive writings or conduct not intended as assertions, than in the case of intended assertions. For instance, problems of memory and perception are likely to be less grave, because the conduct will usually take place during or shortly after the event that is perceived.

   i. **Insincerity:** Most dramatically, the risk of ***insincerity*** is almost always less in the conduct situation, since a person who does not intend to make an assertion is (*Wright* to the contrary notwithstanding) unlikely to attempt to deceive. Consider the case of a man who puts up his umbrella, where this fact is offered as proof that it was raining. The man almost certainly did not intend to assert to himself or anyone else, "It's raining." Therefore, it's very unlikely that he was trying to mislead anyone. Furthermore, conduct has an additional guarantee against insincerity: it generally includes ***reliance*** by an actor. For instance, when a sea captain inspects the vessel and boards it with his family, his actions speak much more loudly about the sincerity of his belief in the vessel's trustworthiness than would any mere verbal statement about the vessel's condition.

   ii. **Ambiguity:** But one of the hearsay dangers, ***ambiguity***, is probably ***more severe*** in the case of conduct. A person who makes a verbal statement normally tries to make himself clear. But one who takes a certain action that is not intended to communicate anything to others is by definition not interested in clarity of communication. For instance, the sea captain may have been merely looking for his wallet, not inspecting the vessel for seaworthiness. L&S, p. 368. However, the danger of ambiguity is likely to be very apparent to factfinders who are asked to make an inference from conduct, so the danger of ambiguity is probably not that great. *Id.* On balance, the inclusive approach of the Federal Rules is probably better, in part because it spares trial judges from having to make difficult analyses of the admissibility of particular non-assertive conduct.

g. **Illustration of modern approach:** The operation of the Federal Rules' modern approach to non-assertive conduct is illustrated by the following example.

   Example: Government agents search D's premises, under a search warrant which allows them to search for evidence of bookmaking activity. While there, the agents answer D's telephone several times. The unknown callers attempt to place bets on various sports events. At D's trial, the prosecution attempts to introduce evidence of these calls to show that the callers believed that the premises were used in betting operations, and thereby prove that the premises were in fact so used. D contends that the calls are hearsay when used for this purpose.

Held, the evidence is admissible. Under FRE 801(a), verbal or nonverbal conduct is a "statement" only if it is intended as an "assertion." "Assertion" is not defined in the Rules, but "has the connotation of a forceful or positive declaration." Consequently, "the effect of the definition of 'statement' is to exclude from the operation of the hearsay rule all evidence of conduct, verbal or nonverbal, not intended as an assertion. The key to the definition is that nothing is an assertion unless intended to be one." (Quoting the Advisory Committee Note to FRE 801.) The utterances of the bettors telephoning in their bets were "nonassertive verbal conduct," offered as relevant for any proposition that could be inferred from them, i.e., that bets could be placed at the premises. "The language is not an assertion on its face, and it is obvious these persons did not intend to make an assertion about the fact sought to be proved or anything else." Since FRE 801(a)(2) "removes implied assertions from the definition of 'statement' and consequently from the operation of the hearsay rule," the offered evidence, as an implied assertion, is excluded from operation of the hearsay rule and is admissible. *U.S. v. Zenni*, 492 F.Supp. 464 (E.D.Ky. 1980).

  i. **Clarification:** When FRE 801(a) applies to nonverbal conduct, its application is quite clear — evidence of such conduct can never be barred by the hearsay rule, except in those relatively rare instances (e.g., pointing a suspect out from a lineup) where the conduct is intended as an assertion. But where what is involved is an oral or written **utterance**, 801(a) is trickier. The utterance can fall within the hearsay rule only if it is an "assertion." The Federal Rules don't define "assertion," but the *Zenni* court seems correct in defining this to mean "a forceful or positive declaration." Putting it another way, an utterance must, in order to be an assertion, be offered with the **intent to state that some factual proposition is true.** The bettors who were placing their bets were not intending to make a factual statement about whether the premises were to be used for betting, so their words were not an "assertion."

5. **Assertions not offered to prove truth of matter asserted:** Our discussion of the "implied assertion" problem and *Wright v. Tatham* has focused on nonassertive conduct. A similar problem is faced by *assertive* conduct that is offered to prove not the truth of what is asserted, but the truth of some factual proposition that is *inferred* from the matter asserted.

  a. *Wright v. Tatham*: Indeed, *Wright v. Tatham* itself falls into this category of "assertions inferred from other assertions." The letters to the testator were, at least to some extent, clearly assertive — the letter from the cousin in America, for instance, clearly contained positive declarations about the status of life in America. Yet, the letter from the cousin was not offered to prove conditions in

America; it was offered to prove a proposition that could be inferred from the assertion, namely, that the writer thought the recipient was sane.

b. Treatment: The modern view is to treat "assertions inferred from other assertions" the same way as "assertions inferred from nonassertive conduct." That is, **assertions inferred from other assertions are not barred by the hearsay rule.** FRE 801 carries this out by its definition of "hearsay" in subsection (c) — hearsay is a statement "offered in evidence to prove the truth of the matter asserted." The Advisory Committee's Note to 801(a), after describing the reasons for not including nonassertive conduct within the definition of hearsay, goes on to say that "similar considerations govern nonassertive verbal conduct and verbal conduct which is assertive but offered as a basis for inferring something other than the matter asserted, also excluded from the definition of hearsay by the language of subdivision (c)."

c. Difficulty: However, where an utterance that is intended to be an assertion is used to imply some other assertion, a significant hearsay danger is present that is not present in the case of nonassertive conduct that is used to imply an assertion: the danger of **insincerity** by the speaker.

> **Example:** When a person raises his umbrella and carries it over his head (nonassertive nonverbal conduct), the use of this fact to show that it was probably raining does not involve any danger of that person's insincerity — he is not trying to communicate anything, so there is no danger of lies. Compare this with the cousin writing from America in *Wright v. Tatham*; if he says, "You would love it in America, cousin, because the weather is drier and warmer than in England," he is making an assertion. Use of this statement to prove that he thought the recipient was sane runs the traditional hearsay risk of declarant's insincerity — the letter writer may be lying for some reason we don't know anything about (e.g., to induce his cousin to come to America).

d. Balancing: However, on balance, the risk of insincerity in this context is usually thought to be relatively small. The most important reason is that a court will (or rightly should) treat the statement as being offered for a purpose other than its truth only where the proposition being proven (the proposition inferred from the statement) **would be equally true whether the assertion is sincere or insincere**.

> **Example:** Consider the cousin writing the letter from America. This letter has about the same tendency to prove that the writer thought the recipient was sane whether the writer honestly believed that the weather was nice in America or was lying about how he felt about the weather in America. Now, however, assume that the letter from the cousin said, "The last letter I received from you, dear cousin, showed you to be alert and not suffering any mental consequences of old age." If the letter is offered to show that at the time the testator wrote his will (a year after the American cousin wrote this letter), the testator was sane, the letter is not literally offered to prove the truth of the matter asserted (which is that the testator appeared to be sane and alert at some prior time). Yet whether the letter has value as evidence

certainly very much depends on: (a) whether the American cousin really believed in his cousin's sanity; and (b) the accuracy of that belief. Therefore, this use should be treated as hearsay.

e. **L&S summary:** L&S, p. 369, put the test as follows: "An out-of-court statement, offered not for its literal truth but for the truth of some proposition therein implied, should be considered hearsay so long as the validity of the desired implication depends on the existence and accuracy of a belief arguably implied by the intended statement." This test seems to be the equivalent of asking, "At the time he made his declaration, was the declarant thinking about the proposition that his statement is now being used to prove?" If the answer is "yes," the statement can be hearsay; if "no," the statement cannot be.

E. **Other hearsay problems:** We turn now to several miscellaneous problems that arise in attempting to define hearsay.

1. **Lack of first-hand knowledge:** The rule against hearsay is sometimes confused with the rule disallowing testimony of facts not based upon the witness' *first-hand knowledge* (discussed *infra*, p. 397). The policy behind the two rules is similar, but they apply in differing circumstances.

   Example: Suppose that the witness, W, says, "The car which hit P was a red Volvo." If from other testimony by W it is clear that W was not present during the accident, the proper objection is, "The witness is not testifying from personal knowledge," not an objection based on hearsay. This is true even if the factfinder can reasonably infer that W has received his information from something that P told him.

   Now, assume that W testifies, "P told me that the car that hit him was a red Volvo." Here, the correct objection is hearsay — W is certainly testifying to something within his own first-hand experience (since he personally experienced P's declaration), but his testimony is the recitation of someone else's out-of-court declaration, offered to prove the truth of that declaration.

   a. **Resemblance:** Observe that the two rules are supported by comparable rationales. Each stems from the belief that the search for truth requires cross-examination of the person with the most direct knowledge of the fact offered as proof.

   b. **Confusion:** Courts, however, have not always carefully distinguished between the two types of objections. When the witness' statement literally sounds as if it comes from the witness' own knowledge, but it is clear from context that the statement is really based upon a declaration made to the witness by an out-of-court declarant, a hearsay objection is not unreasonable — it is an objection against hearsay from an anonymous informant, and the courts have sometimes so treated it.

   Example: D, a tax return preparer, is prosecuted for making false statements on the returns of his taxpayer clients. W, an IRS agent, testifies that over 90% of the 160 returns prepared by D contained overstated itemized deductions. From other evidence, it is clear that W's "proof" of the overstatements must have come from her conversations with the taxpayers, in which they either confessed their overstatements or said that they did not have records to sustain those deductions.

Held, W's testimony is hearsay. "The information obtained by [W] from the out-of-court statements made by the 160 taxpayers whose returns she audited, was absolutely vital to her ultimate in-court conclusion that [over] 90% . . . of the 160 returns she audited contained substantially overstated itemized deductions. [Therefore, D] had no opportunity to test her ultimate assumptions through cross-examination. . . . Given the rationale of the hearsay rule, a clearer case of hearsay testimony would be difficult to imagine." *U.S. v. Brown*, 548 F.2d 1194 (5th Cir. 1977).

(But a vigorous dissent argued that W was testifying "from her own personal knowledge about the results of tax audits she conducted," and that there was thus no hearsay. The dissent pointed out that the majority could cite no "statement" made by any taxpayer out-of-court and repeated in-court by W.)

    i. Criticism: Probably a better way for the court to have handled the issue in *U.S. v. Brown* would have been to allow the testimony on a theory similar to that used in cases of **opinion surveys** (see *supra*, p. 134). Recall that a pollster will be permitted to testify as to what a scientifically constructed sample of respondents said about a certain matter. In *Brown*, the taxpayers who were interviewed by the agent could be regarded as survey respondents. Without some sort of accommodation, it is hard to see how the government could ever successfully prosecute an offense like the one in *Brown* if what is charged is the consistent and repeated overstating of deductions on a large number of returns — the only alternative would be to subpoena each taxpayer to testify, a very unwieldy and time-wasting prospect.

c. Consequences of difference: Often, it will not make any practical difference whether an objection is based upon hearsay or a lack of first-hand knowledge — in either event, the evidence will be excluded. However, there can be instances where the theory used *does* make a difference:

    i. No exceptions to first-hand knowledge rule: Whereas the hearsay rule has many exceptions (discussed *infra*, beginning p. 149), the rule requiring first-hand knowledge has no formal exceptions. Therefore, in those situations where a hearsay objection would be defeated by the existence of an exception, the first-hand knowledge rule might nonetheless apply. L&S, p. 370. (However, in some instances, an informal exception to the requirement of first-hand knowledge is made where the witness is an **expert**, and he is asked to testify based upon a factual situation that he does not know first-hand. See *infra*, p. 406. Also, a "party's own statements may be admitted against him although they are not based on first-hand knowledge." *Id.* at n. 46.)

    ii. Hearsay declarant's first-hand knowledge: Suppose that in a case where an out-of-court declaration's admissibility is at issue, the out-of-court declarant is shown not to have had first-hand knowledge of the subject of his declaration. In this situation, even if the hearsay rule for some technical reason does not apply, or the facts fall within some exception to it, the lack of first-hand knowledge will still keep the declaration from being admitted. *Id.*

2. **"Not offered in presence of party":** A lawyer will sometimes object to an out-of-court statement on the grounds that it was ***"not made in the presence of the party against whom it is offered."*** This is, as a general rule, not a valid objection; rather, it is a "remarkably persistent bit of courthouse folklore." M, p. 730.

   a. **Significance:** There are only a few situations in which the presence of the party against whom the statement is offered makes a difference. One is where a statement spoken in a party's presence is relied on to charge him with ***notice*** of some fact mentioned in the statement. (See *supra*, p. 130.) Another is where the party's silent failure to deny a statement (usually an accusation against him) is introduced to show that the party ***acquiesced*** in the statement. (*Supra*, p. 137.) *Id.*

3. **Multiple hearsay:** An out-of-court declaration may quote or paraphrase another out-of-court declaration. If each of the declarations is offered to prove the truth of the matter asserted, the situation will amount to ***"double hearsay"*** or "hearsay on hearsay." (Indeed, three or more declarations, each referring to one of the others, may be involved. This is usually called ***"multiple hearsay."***)

   a. **Rule:** In this double or multiple hearsay situation, the rule is the obvious one: The evidence will be inadmissible if ***any*** of the declarations are hearsay that does not fall within an exception. If both or all are covered by an exception, the package is admissible.

   b. **Written report of oral statement:** The problem most frequently arises where a party wants to admit a ***written report*** of someone's ***oral out-of-court statement.***

   Example: In a negligence suit arising out of a car accident, P seeks to introduce a report written by W, an employee of D's insurance company. In the report, W states, "D told me that at the time of the collision, he was traveling at 65 miles per hour." P offers the report to show that D was speeding and therefore negligent.

   The proper analysis is as follows: First, we look at the report to see if it is hearsay. It is hearsay because it is an out-of-court declaration by W, offered for its truth (namely, what D told W). If there is no applicable exception, we need look no further — the report is not admissible. Here, however, the report would probably be admissible under the business records exception. (See *infra*, p. 193.) We now look at the incorporated statement, i.e., D's statement to W. This is hearsay since it, too, is being offered for its truth, namely, that D was speeding. Again, if there is no applicable exception, the whole report must be excluded. But the exception for admissions by a party would probably apply. Assuming that each statement falls within some exception to the hearsay rule, the report will be admitted. See L&S, p. 370.

c. **Federal Rule:** FRE 805 follows the approach outlined above: "Hearsay included within hearsay is not excluded under the hearsay rule if each part of the combined statements conforms with an exception to the hearsay rule provided in these rules."

4. **"Statements" by machines or animals:** The hearsay rule applies only to out-of-court declarations that are *made by human beings.* This proposition sounds self-evident, but it is not as obvious as it seems. A number of cases have involved out-of-court "statements" made by *machines* or *animals*, in which serious hearsay objections were raised; however, the courts have all but universally rejected such arguments.

a. **Machines:** The "hearsay by machine" objection can be raised whenever a party seeks to introduce in court a *measurement* or other reading given by a machine. In such a situation, it can be plausibly argued that the machine has "spoken," and that that "statement" constitutes an out-of-court "declaration," offered for the truth of the matter asserted. But, as noted, such efforts have almost always failed.

Example: D is charged with speeding (40 mph in a 30 mph zone). W, the arresting police officer, testifies that he knew D was speeding because he used an electric timer. The timer is a specialized device that includes two tubes placed on the street, one at the start of a 132-foot zone and the other at its end; the device measures the time that a car takes to get from one tube to the other, and then indicates on a clock face how many miles per hour the car must have been going. D objects on the grounds of hearsay, claiming that in effect the readings of the timer were an out-of-court declaration.

Held, there is no hearsay. "Evidence is called hearsay when its probative force depends . . . on the competency and credibility of some person other than the witness by whom it is sought to be produced. . . . [Here,] the evidence as to the results obtained by the witness is not dependent on the perception, memory, and sincerity of an absent declarant." If D's objection had merit, evidence of measurements made by the use of scientific instruments would never be admissible; for instance, a doctor would not be permitted to testify as to the results heard through a stethoscope. *City of Webster Groves v. Quick*, 323 S.W.2d 386 (St. Louis Ct. App., Mo. 1959).

i. **Rationale:** As the *Webster Groves* case indicates, "declarations" that emanate from a machine are not regarded as the kind of "statement" to which the hearsay rule applies. This is an entirely sensible result — the principal hearsay dangers relate to problems of memory, perception, and sincerity on the part of the absent declarant, and it is not reasonable to ascribe these peculiarly human frailties to a machine. In any event, the purpose of the hearsay rule is to bring the out-of-court declarant into court where he can repeat the same factual assertion and be cross-examined about it. One cannot bring the machine into court and cross-examine it (although one can demonstrate it; see *infra*, p. 394).

ii. Foundation for evidence: On the other hand, a machine may emit *incorrect information*, either because it is fed incorrect data (analogous to problems of perception) or because it processes the data in a flawed manner (analogous to faulty memory or insincerity). Therefore, evidence about data produced from a machine will only be accepted if a proper foundation (see *infra*, p. 359) is laid for it; this foundation must include information by which the court can conclude that the machine was accurate. Thus in the *Webster Groves* electric timer situation (or its more modern equivalent, radar detection), the prosecution will bear the burden of demonstrating that the device was of a sort that is scientifically accepted as accurate; that the device was properly calibrated and maintained; that the person using it was properly trained, etc.

b. Retrieval by machine: A different problem is presented where a machine is used not to "create" a factual proposition (as in *Webster Groves*) but rather to *retrieve* or compile *human statements*. In this situation, any proponent of the evidence must overcome two obstacles: (1) he must show that the machine functioned properly in its retrieval or compilation; and (2) he must show that the original statements that were compiled or retrieved fall within some hearsay exception, if they are offered to prove the truth of what they assert. See L&S, p. 371.

Example: D is charged with spying for the Russians. The prosecution introduces computer printouts, which are claimed to be the decoded form of coded messages sent by and to D and his alleged spy masters. (E.g., from KGB headquarters to head of KGB Chicago station: "We have recruited D and he will be giving you reports of U.S. missile silos via dead drop.") First, the prosecution will have to show that the computers were functioning accurately when they intercepted and decoded these messages. Second, the prosecution will have to show that the statements themselves fall within some exception to the hearsay rule, since they are being offered for the truth of the matter asserted (e.g., that D has indeed been recruited).

c. Animals: Occasionally, a party will attempt to introduce evidence that an *animal* has behaved in a certain way, in an attempt to prove some factual proposition that may be deduced from the animal's behavior. Courts have taken the position that an animal's behavior is never the sort of "statement" that the hearsay rule applies to, and that there is thus no hearsay problem.

Example: V is found dead in her isolated rural cottage. A scrap of clothing is found at the scene which is shown by forensic evidence to have probably been left by the murderer. Soon after the body is discovered, a trained bloodhound sniffs the clothing, and then heads off on a long trail culminating at the cottage of D, miles away. When D comes to the door, the dog barks furiously while sniffing at him. At D's murder trial, the prosecution, after producing evidence to demonstrate the dog's great training and expertise in pursuing criminals by scent, offers evidence of the dog's conduct to prove that D must have been present at V's cottage at around the time of the murder. A hearsay objection by D will almost certainly be unsuccessful, since the dog's conduct will not be treated as the sort of "statement" to which the hearsay rule applies. See, e.g., *Buck v. State*, 138 P.2d 115 (Okla. Crim. Ct. App. 1943) (allowing conviction to stand where based almost solely on evidence of the trailing of the defendant by bloodhounds, although not discussing the hearsay problem *per se*).

i. Criticism: Recent zoological evidence, however, suggests that certain animals can make "statements" about past events, can fail to remember those events accurately, and perhaps more amazingly, can intentionally deceive. See, e.g., "Conversations with a Gorilla," 154 Natl. Geographic 438 (1978) (partially reproduced in K&W, pp. 121-23), recounting sign-language lies by the "talking" gorilla Koko. Evidence of a sign-language "statement" by a chimpanzee or gorilla, offered for the truth of the proposition stated, may thus reflect classical hearsay dangers and should be treated as presenting a hearsay problem.

EXCEPTIONS TO THE HEARSAY RULE

I. INTRODUCTION

A. Significance: The rules about hearsay might be better thought of not as a rule of exclusion coupled with exceptions, but rather as a general rule allowing hearsay, coupled with a narrow exception excluding it. As one commentator has put it, "In the sea of admitted hearsay, the rule excluding hearsay is a small and lonely island." Weinstein, 46 Iowa L. Rev. 331, 346 (quoted in L&S, p. 381). In this chapter, we examine the large number of exceptions to the rule against hearsay, exceptions which cumulatively apply more often than not in real-life situations.

B. Availability of declarant: In considering the various exceptions to the rule against hearsay, one distinction should be constantly kept in mind: Some exceptions apply only where the *declarant is unavailable* to give testimony at the trial; others apply regardless of whether the declarant is available.

   1. Rationale: In the case of the exceptions for which unavailability is required, the theory is that live testimony by the declarant is preferable, so that he can be cross-examined under oath; however, if his live testimony is not available, the judgment is made that the factfinding process will be more accurate with the less-than-perfect out-of-court evidence than without it. In the case of the exceptions for which the declarant's availability is irrelevant, the theory is that the out-of-court declaration is, because of the circumstances, at least as accurate as in-court testimony would be.

C. Confrontation Clause of Constitution: A second distinction to keep in mind is that between the common-law rule against hearsay and the *Confrontation Clause* of the Sixth Amendment to the U.S. Constitution. That Clause provides that "in all criminal prosecutions, the accused shall enjoy the right . . . to be confronted with the witnesses against him." To the extent that a particular hearsay exception permits an out-of-court declaration to be used against a defendant in a criminal prosecution, there is a risk that the Clause is violated. In general, however, the use of declarations falling within well-established common-law hearsay exceptions has been held not to violate the Confrontation Clause, or the related Due Process Clause. The entire issue of these constitutional guarantees and their relation to the hearsay rule is discussed extensively in a separate chapter beginning *infra*, p. 269.

II. ADMISSIONS

A. Neither category: Our discussion of hearsay exceptions will first consider those in which the declarant's availability is immaterial, then those where it is a requirement. First, however, we consider a subject that does not fall neatly into either category: *admissions made by a party-opponent*.

   1. Reasons for separate treatment: There are two reasons for treating admissions separately.

a. Not more reliable: First, all other exceptions to the hearsay rule are based on the theory that they involve special circumstances which furnish *special guarantees of trustworthiness* not present in the usual hearsay situation. (For instance, a "dying declaration," see *infra*, p. 231, is thought to be more reliable because a person who knows he is dying has no motive to lie.) An admission by a party, by contrast, has *no* special circumstantial guarantees of reliability. M, p. 775.

b. Arguably not hearsay: Second, it's not really clear that admissions should be viewed as an "exception" to the hearsay rule. Things a party says could be more properly viewed as part of the context of the litigation rather than as an out-of-court declaration, just the way statements made in pleadings would not be thought of as hearsay. In fact, FRE 801(d)(2) treats admissions by party-opponents as not being hearsay at all, rather than as falling within an exception to the hearsay rule.

B. General rule: The general rule regarding admissions is this: *A party's words or acts may be offered as evidence against him*. Thus the rule allowing admissions of a "party-opponent" is a rule of evidence echoing the police interrogator's warning, "Anything you say may be used against you." M, p. 774.

  1. Exception or outside of scope: Authorities differ on whether the rule allowing admissions should be arrived at by treating admissions as being non-hearsay, or rather by treating them as an exception to the rule barring hearsay. FRE 801(d)(2) treats admissions as being *non-hearsay*.

  2. Rationale: The rationale for the rule allowing admissions is not obvious. As noted above, admissions do not by their surrounding circumstances carry any special guarantees of trustworthiness, as all other traditional hearsay exceptions do. It has been suggested that the rule stems from "the adversary theory of litigation. A party can hardly object that he had no opportunity to cross-examine himself or that he is unworthy of credence save when speaking under sanction of an oath." Morgan, quoted in M, p. 775. This theory — tied to the notion that people should take responsibility for their own words and acts — probably supplies the best rationale. L&S, p. 384.

  3. Distinguish from declaration against interest: An admission by a party-opponent must be distinguished from a *declaration against interest* (discussed *infra*, p. 234). An admission will usually be against the declarant's interest at the time it is made, but this is *not a requirement* — even statements that seem neutral or self-serving at the time they are made may be introduced against the party who made them. Thus to speak of the admissibility of "admissions against interest," as many courts do, is inaccurate.

    a. Other distinctions: Apart from the fact that admissions need not have been against interest when made, there are two other important distinctions between admissions and declarations against interest: (1) The declaration-against-interest exception applies only when the declarant is *unavailable* as a trial witness, whereas the admission by a party or a party's representative is admissible even where he is available to be a witness at trial; and (2) admissions must be made by a party (or his representative), and must be admitted **against**, not for him, whereas the declaration-against-interest exception applies to statements offered in evidence by the party who made them as well as statements made by third persons. M, p. 777.

4. **Not binding:** Once an out-of-court admission by a party is entered in evidence against him, may he offer evidence which **contradicts** his own out-of-court statement? The answer is universally **"yes."** That is, out-of-court admissions are different from "judicial" admissions (e.g., admissions made in the pleadings of a case), which may not be contradicted by the party who made them. L&S, p. 385.

   a. **Party's testimony against himself:** A more difficult issue arises when a party makes an **in-court statement** which is unfavorable to him. This does not raise any hearsay questions, since the hearsay rule only applies to out-of-court declarations. But such statements do raise a policy question on which courts are split: May the party who made the unfavorable statement then contradict his own statement with other, more favorable, evidence? Some courts do not allow this, on the theory that a party's own in-court statements are the equivalent of judicial admissions. But the better approach seems to be to allow the contradictory evidence, and to leave for the factfinder the job of weighing the conflicting evidence. M, p. 786.

5. **Can be opinion or conclusion:** All other hearsay exceptions merely remove the hearsay obstacle; they do not overcome any non-hearsay related deficiency in the evidence. But the rule allowing admissions is different: The rules barring admissibility of **opinions** and of **conclusions of law** do **not** apply to an admission used against the party who made it. M, pp. 779-80.

   Example: After an auto accident, D tells a police officer, "The accident was my fault." Even though a witness' in-court expression of an opinion is normally not admissible (see *infra*, p. 398), this out-of-court expression of an opinion will be admissible against D. Of course, D is always free to take the stand to explain why his opinion is mistaken, taken out of context, etc. The same rule of admissibility would apply where D expressed a conclusion of law (e.g., "P will probably be able to sue my rear end off.")

   a. **First-hand knowledge not required:** Similarly, the usual rule that a witness may speak only of facts of which he has **first-hand knowledge** (*infra*, p. 397) does **not** apply to out-of-court admissions used against the party who made them.

   Example: Sophie is a wolf owned and raised by D (a wildlife research center). While she is in a fenced-in yard of the Center's Education Director, Mr. Poos, she is found licking the face of P, a 3-year-old boy who had climbed over the fence, and who is lying on his back screaming. P has lacerations of the face, chest, stomach, and legs. P's parents bring suit against D on the theory that Sophie attacked P. At trial, P introduces a note written right after the incident by Mr. Poos to the President of the Center, which says, "Sophie bit a child that came in our backyard," and also offers to prove that Mr. Poos later orally told the President, "Sophie bit a child." The trial judge refuses to admit the evidence, on the grounds that Mr. Poos did not have any personal knowledge of the facts. The jury finds for the defense.

Held (on appeal), Mr. Poos' written and oral statements should have been admitted. FRE 801(d)(2)(D) prevents from being hearsay a statement offered against a party (here, the Center) that is "a statement by [the party's] agent or servant concerning a matter within the scope of [the] agency or employment, made during the existence of the relationship." Nothing in this Rule requires that the statement be based upon facts personally known to the agent. Nor does anything else in the Federal Rules require an implied condition of personal knowledge. New trial ordered. *Mahlandt v. Wild Canid Survival & Research Center, Inc.*, 588 F.2d 626 (8th Cir. 1978).

6. **Federal Rule:** As noted, the Federal Rules treat admissions as non-hearsay rather than as exceptions to the rule barring hearsay. FRE 801(d)(2) treats five different kinds of admissions by a party as non-hearsay; our detailed discussion below will be similarly organized into these five categories. The full text of 801(d)(2) is as follows:

"(d) *Statements which are not hearsay.* A statement is not hearsay if — . . .

(2) *Admission by party-opponent.* The statement is offered against a party and is (A) the party's own statement, in either an individual or a representative capacity or (B) a statement of which the party has manifested [his] adoption or belief in its truth, or (C) a statement by a person authorized by the party to make a statement concerning the subject, or (D) a statement by the party's agent or servant concerning a matter within the scope of the agency or employment, made during the existence of the relationship, or (E) a statement by a coconspirator of a party during the course and in furtherance of the conspiracy."

a. **Significance:** The Federal Rule essentially codifies the common law. While most common-law courts have treated admissions as being exceptions to the hearsay rule rather than non-hearsay, the Federal Rules' treatment of admissions as non-hearsay makes very little practical difference.

C. **Personal admissions:** The clearest kind of admission is that defined by FRE 801(d)(2)(A): a ***party's own statement***, offered against him.

Example: D is charged with murdering his wife by stabbing her. At the beginning of their investigation, police believe that the stabbing took place at 7:00 p.m. D tells them, "I left the house at 6:45 p.m." It later turns out that the murder probably took place at 6:30. The prosecution may introduce D's statement against him (assuming that there are no *Miranda* problems), since it is an admission. This is so even though the statement is not a "declaration against interest," since at the time he made it, D believed the statement was exculpatory.

1. **Representative capacity:** Observe that under the federal approach, the statement is admissible against its maker, regardless of whether the statement was made in an ***individual*** or ***representative*** capacity, and regardless of in which capacity suit is brought. For instance, if a trustee gossips to a friend about some property in the

trust (a statement made in the trustee's individual rather than representative capacity), it may be used by the other side in a suit involving the trust, where the trustee is sued in his representative rather than individual capacity. L&S, p. 386.

2. **Pleadings:** The statements a party makes in his **pleadings** are treated as admissions for most purposes, and thus may be admitted as evidence against him. A number of situations can arise:

    a. **Civil pleadings, same case:** First, a party may make statements in his pleadings in a civil case. These statement are "judicial admissions," and their maker cannot controvert them except by amending his pleadings. If he does amend them, his adversary may use the original pleadings as evidence. L&S, p. 387.

    b. **Subsequent case:** Statements made by a litigant in one case may be introduced against him in **subsequent cases**, under the admissions rationale.

    c. **Inconsistent pleadings:** Statements that are part of "inconsistent" or "alternative" pleadings, allowed in most jurisdictions, will **not** be admissible as admissions, since a contrary rule would defeat the utility of the alternative pleading technique. Thus if D says in his answer, "Even if I was negligent, the statute of limitations has already run," this is not admissible against D, whether in the present or a later suit, as evidence that he was negligent. M, p. 781.

    d. **Multiple defendants:** A more interesting question occurs where an injured plaintiff is not sure which of two defendants, D1 and D2, is responsible for his injury. For instance, suppose that P is injured by a truck, and is not sure whether the accident was caused by the negligence of the driver (D1) or by faulty brakes installed by the manufacturer (D2). If P sues D1 and loses, and then sues D2, may D2 introduce the pleading in the suit against D1 in which P asserted that "my injury was caused by D1's negligence in driving the truck"? Cases are split, but the modern (and better) trend seems to be to **exclude** the pleadings on the grounds that they are similar to alternative counts in a single pleading. M, p. 782.

    e. **Guilty pleas:** A **guilty plea** that is not withdrawn is generally **admissible** as an admission. In the case for which the plea was entered, the plea is of course a judicial admission. But the plea is also generally admissible in later civil or criminal cases. However, a guilty plea to a minor offense will usually not be admissible; for instance, a guilty plea to a traffic offense will generally not be admissible in a later civil suit arising out of the same incident, on the theory that the plea may have been entered simply because the cost of litigating the traffic offense was greater than the cost of paying the ticket. L&S, p.387.

        i. **Withdrawn guilty plea:** Suppose that the defendant in a criminal case enters a guilty plea, and then is allowed to **withdraw** that plea. May the fact that he initially made the plea be introduced against him as an admission, either in the same criminal case or in a later civil or criminal one? As a matter of evidentiary logic, the plea is an admission, and should be admissible under the rule allowing admissions. But as a matter of policy,

FRE 410 flatly excludes, from any civil or criminal proceeding, "a plea of guilty which was later withdrawn." This rule has the advantage of making withdrawal of a plea an effective rather than a futile device, and also safeguards the accused's privilege against self-incrimination (since otherwise, he would be virtually forced to take the stand to explain why he pleaded guilty). However, not all states follow the federal approach. M, p. 783, n. 21.

3. **Conduct as admission:** Recall our extensive discussion (*supra*, p. 138) about whether ***nonassertive conduct*** can constitute hearsay. In those jurisdictions that treat such conduct as raising hearsay problems, the rule allowing admissions into evidence means that such conduct is admissible even though it is hearsay. The issue is most likely to arise in two situations:

   a. **Manifestation of guilt:** First, conduct by a party outside the courtroom may justify the inference that he has a ***guilty conscience*** or believes he has a weak case. Thus a criminal defendant's ***flight*** after a crime, or his attempt to ***obstruct justice***, are admissible against him in the criminal prosecution as admissions. See, e.g., *Matthew v. State*, 337 N.E.2d 821 (Ind. 1975) (D charged with reckless homicide while driving under the influence of alcohol; W, D's employee, permitted to testify that D persuaded her to falsely tell the grand jury that D had dinner at her home on the evening in question, and that he coerced her false testimony by reminding her that she was divorced and had children to support).

   b. **Failure to testify or produce:** Second, a defendant's ***failure to testify*** (in a civil case, but not in a criminal case) or his failure to ***produce a witness*** close to him or to produce some item of real evidence within his control, or his refusal to undergo a physical examination on a relevant issue, all justify the factfinder in inferring that the unproffered evidence would not have been favorable to that party. This is in a sense an application of the admissions exception.

      i. **Not substantive evidence:** However, this inference from failure to testify or to produce evidence is merely permissible, not mandatory. Furthermore, if the other party has the burden of producing evidence on a particular issue, he will rarely be held to have met that burden merely by virtue of such a negative inference from the first party's silence. L&S, p. 387.

4. **Admissions in criminal cases:** Admissions by a ***criminal defendant*** are admissible against him, so long as no specific constitutional guarantee (e.g., the *Miranda* rule) is infringed. That is, an admission by a criminal defendant falls within the general rule that admissions are admissible against the party who made them.

   a. **Possible unfairness:** Observe that this application of the general rule may be unfair, and may even threaten constitutional freedoms. For instance, suppose that a police officer in a drug prosecution testifies that he spotted a vial of crack near D's feet, and that, before he arrested D, D admitted that the vial was his. Suppose further that the police officer's testimony is false, and that D never said anything. Because this alleged admission is admissible against D, D is under great pressure to take the stand to deny having made the admission. Once he takes the stand, he will open himself up to cross-examination on all manner of things that he might prefer to avoid (e.g., what he was doing in the presence of other known drug users at the time of his arrest). D's practical ability to assert his privilege against self-incrimination is thus impaired. L&S, p. 387. Nonetheless, courts unanimously agree that the "admission" is admissible against D.

D. Adoptive admissions: Subsection (B) of FRE 801(d)(2) codifies the common-law notion of an "*adoptive* admission." Under subsection (B), a statement is not hearsay if it is offered against a party and is "a statement of which he has manifested his **adoption or belief** in its truth."

1. **Test for adoption:** Occasionally, A will adopt B's statement explicitly: "What B has just said is correct." This kind of express adoption clearly is sufficient to have B's statement entered in evidence, and presents no special problems. However, most issues in the area of adoptive admissions involve *implied* adoptions: A is present while B makes a statement, and A either then takes an action which arguably amounts to an adoption of B's statement, or remains silent in circumstances in which, arguably, the silence means acquiescence. In all "implied adoption" situations, the test is *whether, taking into account all circumstances, A's conduct or silence justifies the conclusion that he knowingly agreed with B's statement.*

   Example: D is charged with bank robbery. W testifies that: prior to the robbery, D told him he was going to rob a bank; three weeks after the robbery, he saw D with money and diamond rings; and in the presence of D, D's girlfriend said, regarding D's sudden affluence, "That ain't nothin', you should have seen the money we had in the hotel room." The prosecution offers the girlfriend's out-of-court statement as an admission by D, on the theory that D, by remaining silent when the statement was made, adopted it.

   Held, admissible. "Under the total circumstances, we believe that probable human behavior would have been for [D] promptly to deny his girlfriend's statement if it had not been true — particularly when it was said to a person to whom he had previously related a plan to rob a bank." In some circumstances, a person's silence in the face of an inculpatory statement might not amount to an adoption (e.g., if D was in custody and knew that anything he said might be held against him); but here, no such reasoning was at all likely to have been in D's mind. *U.S. v. Hoosier*, 542 F.2d 687 (6th Cir. 1976).

2. **Real acquiescence:** The court will thus look to all the circumstances to determine whether the party's conduct or silence manifested a *real and knowing agreement* with the other person's statement.

   a. **Insurance claims:** The issue frequently arises where a claimant under a life insurance policy submits a *death certificate*, and that certificate lists a cause of death that turns out to be one not covered by the policy. Can the insurance company introduce the death certificate on the theory that its contents were "adopted" by the claimant, or must the insurer put the maker of the death certificate on the stand? Many courts permit the insurer to introduce the death certificate on an adoption theory.

    i. Criticism: But this will often be unfair and unrealistic, since the claimant was typically trying to show merely *that* the insurer died, not *how* he died. (Indeed, it probably never occurred to the claimant that by attaching the death certificate, he might be deemed to have "adopted" the statements in that certificate.)

    ii. Factors: A claimant's odds of keeping the certificate out of evidence improve if either (a) the insurance company required the death certificate as part of the claims process; or (b) a representative of the insurance company assisted the claimant in filing the claim papers. L&S, p. 388.

3. Silence: The most difficult problems in connection with adoptive admissions are those in which the party remains **silent** in the face of the statement. All courts agree that the mere fact that the party remained silent does **not** by itself amount to an adoption. But there is no agreement about what else must be shown, and in any event the entire factual setting must be considered. As with adoption by conduct, the issue is always "whether a reasonable person would have denied under the circumstances. . . ." M, p. 801.

> **Example:** The issue in the case is whether a tire on D's car, which later blew out, was known by D to be defective. P shows that before the blowout, D was filling the tire at a garage, when X said, "Your tire is in poor shape, and with 38 pounds of pressure it might go to pieces in a few miles." D responded that he would "take a chance" on the tire. P argues that X's statement should be admitted as one adopted by D.
>
> *Held*, inadmissible. "Silence is not evidence of an admission, unless there are circumstances which render it more reasonably probable that a man would answer the charge made against him than that he would not." Here, D's statement that he would "take a chance" is "as reasonably to be construed as a dissent to [X's] opinion of the condition of the tire as an assent to it. . . ." *Pawlowski v. Eskofski*, 244 N.W. 611 (Wis. 1932).

    a. Special factors: Here are some of the particular factors which courts have required before silence will be taken to be acquiescence to another's statement: (1) The statement must have been **heard** by the party claimed to have acquiesced; (2) It must have been **understood** by him; (3) The subject matter must have been **within his knowledge**; (4) Impediments to a response must not have been present (e.g., confusion or injury after an accident); and (most generally and most importantly) (5) "The statement itself must be *such as would, if untrue, call for a denial under the circumstances.*" M, p. 801.

    b. Incentive to manufacture evidence: Observe that the adoption-by-silence doctrine may furnish the other party with a strong incentive to *"manufacture" evidence*. For instance, suppose cars driven by P and D collide, and P, a lawyer knowledgeable in the rules of evidence, keeps his wits about him immediately after the accident. He has a strong incentive to say to D, "You ran the stop sign and this accident is your fault." P knows that if D remains silent, his (P's) statement can come into evidence as an adoption by D. And the statement is equally admissible whether it is true or totally fabricated by P.

c. **Criminal cases:** The problems with adoption by silence, especially the manufacture-of-evidence problem, are at their greatest in *criminal* cases. The adoption theory gives the police every incentive to make (possibly false) accusations against and to the accused, and then to argue that his silence constituted an adoption.

    i. *Miranda*: If the accusation comes at a time when the accused is *in custody*, the accused's silence *cannot be treated as an adoption* by him of the charges. The Supreme Court has so held in *Doyle v. Ohio*, 426 U.S. 610 (1976). In this situation, treating the silence as an adoptive admission would virtually nullify that part of the *Miranda* warnings informing the suspect that he has the right to remain silent.

    ii. **Other contexts:** But in non-custodial contexts, the accused's failure to respond to police accusations may be treated as an adoptive admission without violating the constitution. For instance, in *Jenkins v. Anderson*, 447 U.S. 231 (1980), D claimed self-defense at his murder trial, but the prosecution brought out the fact that he did not report the death to anyone for two weeks after it occurred, and suggested that if it had really been self-defense, D would have spoken out. The Supreme Court held that use of D's silence to impeach him in this way would not violate his privilege against self-incrimination. This suggests that at least where no governmental action induces the defendant to remain silent, his silence in the face of accusations may constitutionally be admitted under the adoption-by-silence rationale.

    iii. **Police not present:** Where the accused is silent in the face of an accusation and the police are *not present*, it is quite clear that the adoption-by-silence rationale will apply if the circumstances are such that a false accusation would have been rebutted. That is, as long as it is not the police who make the accusation, there is nothing special about the fact that the adoption-by-silence rationale is used in a criminal, rather than civil, case.

Example: D, the executor of an estate, is charged with evading estate taxes on the estate. At trial, the prosecution puts on testimony by W to show that more money was involved than was reported. W testifies that when D took the decedent's money out of his safe in the presence of others, D said that there was $500 in each bundle, and X corrected him by saying, "No. $5,000," and that D said nothing in response.

Held, X's statement and D's silence were admissible under the adoption theory. Since the very purpose of opening the safe in the presence of witnesses was to prevent any future dispute or suspicion about the property which D was taking into his hands, D's silence in the face of X's correction presented "a very clear and strong inference of [D's] assent" to X's correction.

U.S. v. Alker, 255 F.2d 851 (3d Cir. 1958).

d. Letter or other writing: Suppose that the statement as to which acquiescence is urged is not an oral declaration, but rather a *letter* or other *written* communication. Will the letter be admitted on the theory that the recipient's silence constituted an admission by adoption?

  i. General rule: In general, courts are less quick to recognize an admission by adoption where the statement is written than where it is oral. Nonetheless, the modern trend seems to be that the failure to reply to a letter (or the failure to contradict certain statements in the letter if there is a response) is *admissible* as evidence under the adoption-by-admission rationale. M, p. 802. Admissibility is made more likely by the fact that either (a) the recipient wrote back, but did not deny the statement; or (b) the parties were in some business or other relationship such that the recipient would be unlikely to remain silent in the face of an incorrect statement.

  ii. Bill or statement: The most common illustration of (b) above is where the writing is a *bill or statement* of indebtedness sent to a customer. The customer's *failure to question the bill* is always *admissible* as evidence of an admission of its correctness. *Id.*

E. Representative admissions: We now turn to three kinds of admissions that can be thought of as *"representative"* or *"vicarious"* ones. That is, the admission is made by a person other than the party against whom it is sought to be introduced, but it is usable against that party because it was in some way *authorized* by him. These three categories of authorized admissions correspond to subsections (C), (D), and (E) of FRE 801(d)(2); the first two have to do with express or implied agency; the third has to do with the specific problem of statements by a co-conspirator.

  1. Explicitly authorized admission: The easiest of the three categories is that represented by subsection (C) of FRE 801(d)(2): A statement may be offered against a party if it is "a statement by a person authorized by the party to make a statement concerning the subject." Thus subsection (C) applies in the situation where the party has *expressly agreed* that his agent may make a statement on the particular subject. Thus if A says, "On this subject, refer all questions to my associate, B," anything B says on the subject will be admissible against A as if it were said by A.

  a. Corporations: The most common application of this rule of express authority is where the party is a *corporation* that has designated one of its employees to speak for it on a certain matter. Thus if X Corp.'s plant explodes, and X appoints Employee to furnish the police with details about what caused the accident, anything Employee says will be admissible against X.

  b. Statements to principal: The rule allowing into evidence expressly authorized admissions clearly applies where the agent is authorized to speak to third persons and does so. The more interesting question is, what happens if the principal only authorizes the agent to speak *to the principal*? The issue arises in the case of internal reviews, inspections, and other investigations undertaken at the request of a corporation, where the corporation intends that outsiders not see or hear the results. The courts are split.

i. Inadmissible: The majority common-law approach is that such "for in house use only" statements are ***protected*** against disclosure at trial. L&S, p. 389. Courts following this approach have often relied on the substantive law of agency, under which the doctrine of *respondeat superior* (employer is responsible for acts of employee) does not apply to transactions between the agent and the principal.

Example: P is crushed by a truck owned by D (a trucking corporation), and driven by Employee, who works for D. After the accident, Employee gives a report about it to a vice president of D.

Held, this report is not admissible against D. Unless a principal intends his agent's report to be made to others, the fact that it is authorized to be made to the principal himself is not enough to make it admissible against the principal at trial. Here, there was nothing to indicate that D authorized Employee to release the report to the world. *Big Mack Trucking Co., Inc. v. Dickerson*, 497 S.W.2d 283 (Tex. 1973).

ii. Admissible: The modern trend, however, seems to be to treat such communications to the principal as being ***admissible*** against him. One of the reasons is that considerations of ***reliability*** favor admissibility. "Intra-organization reports are generally made as a basis for some action, and when this is so, they share the reliability of business records." M, p. 790. Furthermore, those who prepare such reports usually have an insider's access to information, so the reports are likely to be accurate. L&S, p. 390.

iii. Federal Rules: The Federal Rules follow the modern approach, and allow reports from agent to principal to be ***admitted*** against the principal. While FRE 801(d)(2)(C) does not make this clear, the Advisory Committee's Note states: "The question arises whether only statements to third persons should be so regarded [as admissions], to the exclusion of statements by the agent to the principal. The rule is phrased broadly so as to encompass both."

iv. Books and records: Under the modern and Federal approaches, a party's ordinary ***books and records***, prepared by employees for the company's internal use alone, will be admissible as admissions. Advisory Committee's Note to FRE 801.

2. Vicarious admissions by agents: Now suppose that the agent is ***not*** explicitly authorized to speak on a particular matter, but that the matter arises out of a ***transaction*** that is ***within the agent's authority***. The question is: Does the fact that the agent had authority to engage in the transaction also mean that he will be deemed to be authorized to speak about it, so that admissions he makes will be admissible against the principal? In general, the answer is: (a) under the traditional common law approach, ***"no"***; and (b) under the modern and Federal Rules approach, *"yes."*

a. **General common-law approach:** There is *no concept at common law of "vicarious" admissions*, only "authorized" admissions. The common law approach is based on the wooden theory that speaking is like any other act, and only *authorized* acts are binding against the principal.

   i. **Truck drivers:** Most frequently, the question arises where a truck driver (the agent) who works for a corporate employer (the principal) has an accident while on the job, and makes a statement about the accident (e.g., "Gee, I'm sorry I ran that red light"). Under the traditional common-law approach, the only way the truck driver's statement can be admitted against the employer is if the employer authorized the truck driver to *make statements* about accidents. Since in the normal situation the employer will not be found to have authorized speaking about accidents (even though it clearly authorized the truck driver to do the driving that led to the accident), the admission is not admissible against the company at common law.

b. **Modern and Federal Rules:** But the traditional rule seems to be giving way to a modern rule embodied by FRE 801(d)(2)(D). 801(d)(2)(D) admits a statement offered against a party if it was made "by the party's agent or servant concerning a *matter within the scope of the agency or employment, made during the existence of the relationship.*"

   Example: Consider our illustration of the truck driver who has an accident while on the employer's business, and then gives a damaging account of what happened, in the form of a report to the police (e.g., "I'm sorry I ran that red light"). Under the modern and federal rule, the driving of the truck was "a matter within the scope of his agency or employment." Therefore, a statement concerning that matter would be admissible, so the truck driver's admission would be admissible against the employer.

   i. **Rationale:** The modern rule (admitting statements relating to matters that the agent was authorized to handle) can be justified on the grounds of *reliability*. For instance, the agent is typically well-informed about the transactions he is commenting on, since they occur within his work for the employer. Also, while the employment continues the worker is not likely to make the statements unless they are true. M, p. 788.

c. **Showing fact of agency:** How can the proponent of an agent's admission *prove* that there was an agency relationship (a showing required under either the common law or modern approach), or that the agent had speaking authority (required under the common law but not the modern view)? Most importantly, these showings *may generally not be made by use of the very statement in question*.

   Example: Suppose that after Truck Driver has an accident while on business for Employer, he says to the policeman, "I was driving on business for Employer when I ran a red light and crashed." In deciding as a preliminary matter whether Truck Driver's statement was "concerning a matter within the scope of [Truck Driver's] agency or employment, made during the existence of the relationship . . ." (the federal test), the court will *not* consider evidence contained in the very statement by Truck Driver to the police. Thus the plaintiff who is seeking to get Truck Driver's statement into evidence will have to prove by *other means* (e.g., employment records, or the testimony of Truck Driver on the stand) that Truck Driver was really on business for Employer at the time of the crash. L&S, p. 391.

3. **Other exceptions:** Whether in a common-law or modern/federal jurisdiction, an admission by an employee may come in under some *other exception* to the hearsay rule even if the authorized or vicarious admissions rules fail to apply. Always consider, for instance, the *excited utterances* exception (*infra*, p. 184): thus P in the *Big Mack Trucking* case (*supra*, p. 159) argued that the truck driver's statement immediately after the accident to the police was such an utterance; P lost on this argument because there was no showing that the truck driver was in the requisite high emotional state, but on slightly different facts the argument might have succeeded.

F. **Co-conspirators:** We turn now to special problems that are posed by admissions involving *conspiracies*.

1. **Partners:** Before we consider conspiracies, let us briefly consider *partnerships*, because the rules covering admissions by co-conspirators are often justified on the theory that co-conspirators are "partners in crime." The courts have generally assumed that when a partner purports to speak for a partnership, he is in fact authorized to do so since he is a part owner of the partnership. L&S, pp. 391-92. Therefore, in a suit involving the partnership, a statement by a partner made while he purported to speak for the partnership will be admissible against the partnership. *Id.*

   a. **Liability of an individual partner:** As a matter of substantive law, each partner is fully liable for the debts of the entire partnership. Assume Partnership has two partners, A and B. P sues Partnership, and introduces a statement made by A on behalf of the partnership. This statement will be admissible (for the reason given in the prior paragraph). And assume Partnership loses the suit, and has a large judgment entered against it. If the assets of the partnership are not sufficient to pay the judgment, and A has no resources, B will end up paying the full amount of the shortfall. Thus in a sense, the statements of one partner (A) will end up having been used "against" the other (B). But this result does not derive from any rule of evidence providing that statements by one partner are admissible against the other; rather, it stems from a combination of a presumption about partnership affairs (that each partner, as part owner, is presumed to be authorized to speak for the firm) and a substantive rule of partnership law (that each partner is liable for the debts of the partnership). If A had made a statement confessing to a *crime* this evidence would not be admissible in a prosecution against B (assuming that the co-conspirators exception discussed below was not involved), because criminal activities are presumed to be beyond the authorized business of a partnership. L&S, p. 392.

2. **General rule on co-conspirators:** Now let us turn to conspiracies. Courts have long recognized a special *conspiracy exception* to the hearsay rule: *statements made by one co-conspirator are admissible against other co-conspirators, so long as the statement was made during the course of the conspiracy and in furtherance of it.*

> **Example:** A and B are charged with robbing, and conspiring to rob, the First National Bank. The prosecution charges that A aided in all the master planning and got a share of the proceeds, and that B actually pulled the robbery. The prosecution calls as a witness W, a friend of A, who testifies, "B tried to recruit me to join in the robbery by telling me 'A's in this with me, and we're gonna make a million bucks.' " If this testimony is introduced to prove the truth of B's statement (i.e., that A really was part of the conspiracy), it will be hearsay, but it will fall within the co-conspirator exception to the hearsay rule. This is so because the statement was: (1) made by a co-conspirator (B); (2) made during the course of the conspiracy; and (3) made in furtherance of the objectives of the conspiracy (since recruitment of W would have added to the conspiracy's chances of success).

3. **Rationale:** As noted, the rule allowing statements by one conspirator to be admitted against the other is often justified on the theory that the conspirators are "partners in crime." But as was discussed above, there is no real rule of evidence permitting statements by one partner to be admitted against another. Thus the true rationale for this exception to the hearsay rule is not so clear after all.

   a. **Substantive law:** Before we look at possible rationales in support of an exception to the hearsay rule for co-conspirator statements, first observe that in many instances there will not really be a hearsay problem at all. This is because, as a matter of *substantive law*, in a conspiracy prosecution all conspirators are liable for the acts of any of them. Thus if A and B are shown to have conspired to rob a bank, A is liable for the actual robbery even if only B walked into the bank lobby and carried away the money. This rule of mutual liability for actions applies to "verbal acts" just as much as it does to physical acts. Statements made by one conspirator in furtherance of the conspiracy are thus admissible against all conspirators if conspiracy is charged, since the statement is part of the illegal plan of action.

   > **Example:** Return to our example above, in which A and B are charged with conspiring to rob, and actually robbing, Bank. B's statement to W while trying to recruit him ("A's in this with me") is a verbal act taken in furtherance of the illegal aims of the conspiracy, and is thus part of the crime of conspiracy itself. Therefore, that statement is admissible against not only B, but also A (since he is jointly liable for all substantive acts taken in furtherance of the conspiracy). In this instance, the statement is not offered to prove the truth of the matter asserted (that A is really part of the conspiracy), but rather, to prove an act that is part of the substantive crime of conspiracy (a

statement made as part of the recruitment). Therefore, no hearsay question need even arise. L&S, p. 393.

Note: If this is the theory on which W's testimony is admitted, the judge should warn the jury, "Consider W's testimony only on the issue of whether statements were made in furtherance of the alleged conspiracy; do not consider it for the truth of what B said about A's participation." But it would be a rare jury that would be able to listen to that testimony without considering its most interesting aspect: as proof that A really *was* part of the conspiracy (i.e., a hearsay purpose rather than the "official" non-hearsay purpose). For this reason, the trial judge should be careful not to let in the evidence unless there is at least some independent proof that a conspiracy really existed, and that A was part of it. See *infra*, p. 167.

b. **Hearsay problem:** Sometimes, however, a statement by one co-conspirator will, if admitted against another conspirator, involve clear hearsay problems. This is most dramatically the case if the prosecution has ***not charged conspiracy***, but is only prosecuting for the substantive crimes committed (e.g., bank robbery). In this situation, the statement is not admissible as part of any substantive crime, so it is likely to be relevant only insofar as it proves the truth of the matter asserted; in this instance, it is hearsay, and must therefore fall within some exception.

Example: Again return to A, B, and their bank robbery. Assume that the prosecution has not charged conspiracy to rob, only the actual robbery. Now, B's recruitment statement to W ("A's in this with me") is not admissible as a substantive act in furtherance of any crime, since it is not part of the completed crime of bank robbery. It is only relevant for the truth of the matter asserted (that A was an accomplice to the robbery), so if it does not fall within some exception to the hearsay rule it will be excluded.

c. **Rationale:** The best rationales for admitting one conspirator's statement against another are probably those that take account of ***reliability*** and ***necessity***.

i. **Necessity:** The "necessity" argument runs this way: conspirators will rarely give testimony implicating each other at trial; each will have a Fifth Amendment right against self-incrimination on any matter having to do with the conspiracy. Therefore, live testimony will rarely be available, and the only way to get one conspirator to implicate the other is by introducing his out-of-court declarations against the other or against both of them. Without an exception allowing such out-of-court statements, convictions will be hard to get, and necessity for particular testimony is a legitimate consideration in deciding whether a particular hearsay exception should be recognized. L&S, p. 395.

ii. **Reliability:** The "reliability" argument goes like this: "Active conspirators are likely to know who the members of the conspiracy are and what they have done. When speaking to advance the conspiracy, they are unlikely to describe non-members as conspirators, and they usually will have no incentive to misdescribe the actions of their fellow members." *Id.* (Observe that this analysis would not apply in a number of situations. For instance, if B is arrested, and his declaration, "A's in this with me," is made to the police, he may have a strong motive to falsely accuse A in order to work out a plea bargain. Similarly, if B is trying to recruit X and A is known to X to be a powerful mobster, B's statement, "A's in this with me," may well be a lie stemming from B's desire to use A's reputation as a recruitment device. *Id.*)

4. **Requirements for exception:** In any event, the co-conspirators exception to the hearsay rule is well-established. FRE 801(d)(2)(E) codifies the common-law requirements for the exception: a statement falls within the exception (or, in the approach of FRE 801, is non-hearsay) if it is offered against a party and is "a statement by a co-conspirator of a party during the course and in furtherance of the conspiracy."

   a. **Three requirements:** There are thus ***three requirements*** that must be made for the statement to be admissible: (1) it must be by a member of the ***same conspiracy*** of which the party against whom it is admitted (typically the defendant in a criminal action) is a member; (2) it must have been made while the conspiracy was ***still in force***; and (3) it must have been made in order to ***further the aims*** of the conspiracy. The first of these requirements poses little problem (except for issues of proof and procedure, which are discussed below). We concentrate on the second and third.

5. **"During course of":** The requirement that the statement have taken place ***"during the course of"*** the conspiracy has several implications:

   a. **Termination:** Statements made ***after the conspiracy has ended*** are admissible only against the declarant, not against the other members of the conspiracy.

      i. **Arrest:** Thus if the conspiracy has been broken up by the ***arrest*** of one or more of its key members, anything the arrestees say to the police will not be admissible against the others. (But the prosecution may be able to argue successfully that the conspiracy continued after the arrest of some members. If so, statements by the arrestees would be admissible against the other members who continued with the conspiracy.)

      ii. **Achieving goal:** Similarly, the conspiracy will be treated as ending when it ***reaches its goal***, and statements made after that time will not be admissible.

      Example: A and B conspire to rob the First National Bank. They carry out the robbery successfully, and split the proceeds. One year later, B mentions to X, whom he thinks is his friend, "A and I were the ones who pulled off the First National Bank job last year." This statement will not fall within the conspirator-statement exception to the hearsay rule, and may thus be introduced only against B, not against A, because it took place after the conspiracy was over.

   iii. Concealment: Some prosecutors have tried to argue that after the first phase of the conspiracy (the carrying out of the crime and splitting of the loot), there comes into existence a second phase: a conspiracy to **conceal** the crime. Therefore, so the argument goes, any statements made before the crime is solved are made during the course of the conspiracy, and are thus admissible against the non-declarant conspirators. However, courts have generally rejected such arguments. L&S, p. 398. See, e.g., *Krulewitch v. U.S.*, 336 U.S. 440 (1949), rejecting this notion of an implied conspiracy to conceal for purposes of the conspirator-statement exception, at least in the case of federal trials, for which the Supreme Court has authority to set the evidentiary rules.

  b. Conspirator leaves: A conspirator may of course leave the conspiracy while it goes on. As noted, statements made by him to the authorities probably satisfy the "in the course of" requirement if the conspiracy goes on without him. But the converse is not true: if A leaves the conspiracy, statements made thereafter by the continuing conspirators, B and C, will not be admissible against A. L&S, p. 398.

  c. Statements before: Now consider the situation in which A and B begin a conspiracy, and make statements after the conspiracy has begun, but before C has joined. Are these statements admissible against C? The answer is **"yes."** "When a conspirator enters an ongoing conspiracy, he is held implicitly to have adopted the earlier statements of fellow co-conspirators, so these statements may be introduced as admissions against him." *Id.*

   i. Criticism: This may make sense where the statements concern matters that C reasonably should have anticipated at the time he joined (e.g., statements about the basic aim of the conspiracy). But the basic rule extends even to statements that C had no reason to expect to have been made, and in this context the rule seems wooden and unfair.

6. "In furtherance" requirement: The **"in furtherance"** requirement means that a statement should be admitted against a co-conspirator only if it was made for the purpose of **advancing the conspiracy's objectives.**

    Example: D is charged with importation of marijuana and conspiracy to import marijuana. W, a law enforcement officer, repeats in his testimony statements made by one Bobby Flores. W says that Flores told him that he had just finished the last of several marijuana imports with D, that he (Flores) didn't like the way D ran things, and that he would rather be in business with W. D objects to this testimony.

    Held, W's testimony is inadmissible. Flores's statements to W may have been an attempt to further the aims of a *new* conspiracy (one not involving D); they were certainly not in furtherance of the charged conspiracy involving Flores and D. This was true even though Flores was complaining about not having been paid for the prior haul and was still hoping to get payment for that haul: "[T]he interests of . . . Flores and [D] were in such direct conflict, and Flores's claim for remuneration was so tangentially related to the accomplishment of the underlying transaction, that the policies of Rule 801(d)(2)(E) would not be served by admitting Flores' statement. . . ." *U.S. v. Fielding*, 645 F.2d 719 (9th Cir. 1981).

    a. Implications: If the "in furtherance" requirement is taken seriously, it renders inadmissible against a co-conspirator the following kinds of statements: (1) *confessions*, whether to authorities or to one the declarant thinks is a friend; (2) *narratives* of *past events*; and (3) *finger-pointing* by the declarant against a co-conspirator (as in *Fielding*).

    b. Ignored: But *most courts have not taken the "in furtherance" requirement very seriously*. *Fielding*, for instance, would probably have come out differently in most courts. Confessions, narratives, and finger-pointing are all frequently allowed even though a strict construction of "in furtherance" would dictate their exclusion. L&S, p. 394.

7. No need to charge conspiracy: Statements by one co-conspirator against another may be admitted *even if no conspiracy crime is charged*.

    Example: The prosecution believes that A and B worked together to carry out the robbery of the First National Bank. But since only B went into the bank and carried away the money, the prosecution decides to charge only B, and to charge him only with robbery, not conspiracy to rob. If the judge makes a preliminary finding (discussed *infra*) that A and B conspired together to carry out the robbery, A's statements incriminating B will be admissible against B for the truth of what those statements assert, even though no conspiracy is charged and A is not even a defendant.

    a. Previously-acquitted co-conspirator: Even statements by a *previously acquitted* co-conspirator may be introduced if the requirements of the conspirator exception are otherwise satisfied. S&R, p. 736.

8. Procedure: As the previous paragraphs make clear, a proponent (typically the prosecution) who seeks to use one conspirator's statement against another, must establish that there was a conspiracy of which both the declarant and the other party were members, that the statement took place during the course of that conspiracy, and that the statement was in furtherance of the conspiracy. *Who is to decide* whether these factual requirements have been met? And *by what standard* should this issue be decided? These questions have over the years caused much disagreement among courts.

    a. Emerging federal rule: The federal courts have finally agreed on a standard, which most state courts will also probably follow. L&S, p. 396. This standard seems to include the following rules:

        i. Judge: Existence of the conspiracy, and satisfaction of the other factual requirements, is to be decided *by the judge*. He must find that these requirements are satisfied *by a preponderance of the evidence*. *Bourjaily v. U.S.*, 483 U.S. 171 (1987).

ii. **How he finds:** The judge can use any of three ways of ascertaining enough facts to make this judgment: (a) he can conduct a "mini trial" outside of the presence of the jury to decide whether it is more likely than not that the defendant and the declarant were co-conspirators; (b) by the time the statement is offered, there may already be enough proof in the record to justify the judge in finding that the conspiracy exists; or (c) the judge can admit the statement subject to "connecting up," i.e., subject to the later introduction of evidence sufficient to allow the judge to find it more likely than not that the conspiracy existed. The third approach is dangerous for the prosecution, since if the later evidence never develops, the statement may be so damaging that a mistrial will have to be declared. However, in complicated cases involving many alleged conspirators and many crimes, this "subject to connecting up" approach is the only practical way of trying the case. L&S, pp. 396-97.

iii. **Independent evidence:** The most troublesome issue regarding procedure is this: In deciding whether it is more likely than not that a conspiracy existed, may the judge *take into account the very statement whose admissibility is in issue*? The Supreme Court has recently answered *"yes"* to this question, at least for federal cases. In *Bourjaily v. U.S.*, 483 U.S. 171 (1987), the Court held that the trial judge may at least consider the alleged statement as one of the factors in determining whether the conspiracy existed; the Court declined to decide whether a conspiracy could be found to exist if the alleged statement was the *only* evidence of conspiracy. (Other aspects of *Bourjaily* are discussed *infra*, p. 273 and 455.)

G. Privity: Most common-law jurisdictions have recognized one additional situation in which statements made by one person will be admissible as admissions against another. This is the situation of *"parties in privity"* with each other. If A and B hold an interest *jointly*, or if A first owns it and then sells it to B, statements made by A will in most jurisdictions will be admissible against B. The doctrine applies not only to real estate, but to personal property and even intangibles.

1. **Joint tenancy of real estate:** Thus if A and B hold Blackacre, a piece of real estate, as *joint tenants* or *tenants in common*, any statements made by A relating to the property will be admissible against B. Similarly, suppose A owns Blackacre in fee simple and makes a statement, "I know X is living illegally on the property." If A sells his interest to B, the statement will be admissible against B if X sues to gain title on the theory that he has lived openly on the property for more than the statutory period and is thus owner by adverse possession.

2. **Intangibles:** Since the doctrine covers *intangibles*, statements made by an owner of a note, contract right, copyright, etc., can be admitted against any successor in interest. Thus if A invents and then patents a device, any statements he makes that bear on the validity of the patent can be admitted against B if B buys the patent rights and then sues third parties for infringement.

3. **Absent from Federal Rules:** The Federal Rules do *not* recognize an exception for statements by predecessors in interest or other privies. M, p. 797. However, in

most instances such a statement will qualify as a declaration against interest (*infra*, p. 234) or under some other non-admissions exception. *Id.*

III. AVAILABILITY IMMATERIAL — GENERALLY

A. Rationale: We turn now to a group of exceptions to the hearsay rule that are *not conditioned upon the declarant's unavailability at trial*. The rationale behind applying these exceptions even where the declarant is available at trial is that these exceptions arise in situations "where courts have felt that a witness' account of an out-of-court statement was likely to be as probative of the issue in question as the declarant's courtroom testimony, or where the difficulty of proving unavailability or subpoenaing available witnesses was likely to outweigh the incremental benefits of courtroom testimony." L&S, p. 407.

B. List of exceptions: Here, then, are the major exceptions which will apply even where the declarant is available to give courtroom testimony:

1. *Spontaneous, excited,* or *contemporaneous* utterances (including statements about *physical* or *mental condition*);

2. *Past recollection recorded*;

3. *Business records*; and

4. *Public records* and *reports*.

IV. SPONTANEOUS, EXCITED, OR CONTEMPORANEOUS UTTERANCES (INCLUDING STATEMENTS ABOUT PHYSICAL OR MENTAL CONDITION)

A. General principle: Our first "availability of declarant immaterial" exception to the hearsay rule is really a collection of related exceptions. What they have in common is the element of *"contemporaneity"* — they are statements, usually (but not necessarily) oral, that concern something that is happening *at that moment*. Thus statements about one's present physical condition, statements about one's present mental state, as well as statements made under great excitement, all share this element of contemporaneity; so also do statements concerning "present sense impressions" (recognized under a modern exception). The sole exception to the contemporaneity requirement is that a person's statement to a physician concerning his medical condition or symptoms, if made in order to obtain *diagnosis* or *treatment*, may relate to past symptoms or causes.

1. **"Res gestae":** Some courts have traditionally lumped these various situations together under the phrase *"res gestae."* M, p. 835. However, this term is vague and unhelpful, and will be avoided in our discussion.

B. Statements of physical condition: A well-recognized exception has evolved for statements by a person about his *physical condition*. Most commonly, the exception is used to admit a person's statement about *pain* he is feeling, as proof that he really did feel the pain. Because the precise scope of the exception depends on whether the statement is made to a layperson or to a doctor, we consider each of these situations in turn.

1. **Statements to laypersons:** If the statement is made to a *layperson*, it will come under the exception only if it relates to the declarant's *present* bodily condition or symptoms.

   > **Example:** X says to W, "I'm feeling terrible chest pains." Even though W is not a doctor, X's statement falls within the bodily-condition exception to the hearsay rule. Therefore, either party would be permitted to prove at trial that X actually had chest pains by putting on W's testimony that X made the statement.
   >
   > If, on the other hand, X said, "I had terrible chest pains yesterday," the exception would not apply if W were a layperson, and not a physician. See L&S, p. 420.

   a. **Spontaneity:** The statement must also be *spontaneous*. The requirement of spontaneity is mainly an attempt to prevent the *manufacture of evidence*. In most states (and under the Federal Rules), the mere fact that the statement refers to the declarant's present condition will generally be sufficient to meet the requirement of spontaneity, unless there are particular reasons to suspect that the evidence is manufactured.

      > **Example:** X is in a car accident, in which his car is hit by a Rolls Royce driven by a famous and wealthy woman, D. X does not consult a doctor, but within earshot of witnesses, says, shortly after the accident, "Oh, my neck. I think I have whiplash. Maybe I can sue." A trial judge might well hold that these surrounding circumstances indicate that this statement was a self-serving attempt to manufacture evidence; if so, the judge would exclude it on the grounds that it lacked "spontaneity."

   b. **Federal Rules:** The Federal Rules handle statements of bodily condition made to non-doctors as part of a more general provision dealing with the declarant's then existing mental, emotional, or physical condition. FRE 803(3) creates an exception for "a statement of the declarant's then existing state of . . . physical condition (such as . . . pain and bodily health). . . ." Observe that the requirement that the condition presently exist is explicit; however, the requirement of spontaneity is merely implied from the fact that the rule is "a specialized application of the broader rule recognizing a hearsay exception for statements describing a present sense impression, the cornerstone of which is spontaneity." M, p. 839.

   c. **Statements not about pain:** As noted, statements allowed under this rule will generally be ones about pain. A statement by the declarant to a non-doctor that reports identifying the precise medical condition will probably be excluded on grounds that it is an uninformed opinion (*infra*, p. 398) or made without firsthand knowledge (*infra*, p. 397).

      > **Example:** X says to W (a friend who is not a doctor), "My leg must be broken." The judge will probably exclude the evidence on opinion or lack-of-firsthand-knowledge grounds. L&S, p. 420.

2. Statements to a treating physician: When a person goes to a doctor for treatment, he knows that any statement he makes about his condition will be relied upon by the doctor. Therefore, courts have long believed, statements made about a bodily condition, **made to a physician** in connection with **treatment**, carry this special guarantee of reliability. Therefore, courts have been more willing to accept such statements into evidence than in the case of statements made to non-doctors. This greater receptivity has three tangible consequences:

   a. Past symptom: First, the statement need not be in connection with a **present** bodily condition. Statements about **past** pain, past symptoms, or even past events that have given rise to pain or symptoms, are all admissible, if made to a physician in connection with treatment.

   b. Self-serving statements: The presumption of reliability is so strong that even statements that, if made to non-doctors would be rejected as clearly self-serving, will be admitted, as long as made in connection with procuring treatment. L&S, p. 421.

   c. Causation: Lastly, even statements that relate to the **cause** of the pain, symptoms, or other condition will be admitted, if they seem reasonably related to treatment. Thus FRE 803(4) admits "statements made for purposes of medical diagnosis or treatment and describing . . . the inception or general character of the cause or external source thereof insofar as reasonably pertinent to diagnosis or treatment."

   Example: D is charged with assault with intent to rape. The victim is a 9-year old girl, Lucy. The prosecution offers statements made by Lucy to Dr. Hopkins, the physician who treated her after the incident. Under the doctor's questioning, Lucy told him that she had been dragged into the bushes, that her clothes, jeans, and underwear were removed, and that the man had tried to force something into her vagina, which hurt. Dr. Hopkins repeats these statements at trial, and D objects on hearsay grounds.

   Held, these statements are admissible under FRE 803(4)'s exception to the hearsay rule. The statements related to the "cause or external source thereof," and were "reasonably pertinent to diagnosis or treatment." For statements regarding causation to be "reasonably pertinent to diagnosis or treatment," two tests must be satisfied: (1) the declarant's motive must be consistent with the purpose of the rule, which is to allow statements motivated by the patient's desire to obtain treatment; and (2) the information must be reasonable for the physician to rely upon in diagnosis or treatment. Here, both tests are satisfied. Even Dr. Hopkins' question, "Did the man take your clothes off" was one to which Lucy responded only because she was seeking treatment. (Importantly, the doctor's questions all related to *what* happened, not *who* did it.) All information was reasonably relied upon by the doctor in his examination and treatment; for instance, the information permitted him to pinpoint certain areas of the body and eliminate others. *U.S. v. Iron Shell*, 633 F.2d 77 (8th Cir. 1980).

i. Statements of fault or identity: The Federal Rules go farther than the common law in allowing statements about causation to come in under the exception for statements made to a doctor relating to treatment or diagnosis. But the requirement that the causal statements be "reasonably pertinent" to diagnosis and treatment has some bite. For instance, the Advisory Committee's Note to FRE 803(4) states that statements about *fault* will ordinarily not qualify; for instance, a patient's statement that he was struck by an automobile would qualify but not his statement that the car was driven through a red light. *Id.* Similarly, a patient's statement that he was shot would be admissible, but a statement that he was shot by a white man would not be.

3. Statements to third persons: Suppose the statement is made "for purposes of" getting medical treatment, but is made not to a doctor, but rather to a **nurse**, ambulance driver, or other person involved in the health care process. FRE 803(4) would allow such statements to be admitted, since that rule applies wherever the statement is made "for purposes of medical diagnosis or treatment . . . ," not merely where the statement is made to a physician. Indeed, the Advisory Committee's Note to 803(4) provides that "statements to hospital attendants, ambulance drivers, or even members of the family might be included."

a. Common-law approach: It is not clear whether most common-law courts would similarly apply the exception where the statement is made to a non-physician. In those cases where the statement was obviously made with the intent that the hearer repeat it to a physician (e.g., a nurse taking the patient's history), common-law courts would probably apply the exception. L&S, p. 421. This approach makes sense, since the patient has the same motive for truthfulness as he does when he is speaking to a physician.

4. Physician who does not treat but testifies: So far, our discussion of statements to physicians has assumed that the physician is giving treatment to the declarant. Often, however, a physician is consulted not because he will be treating the patient, but rather because he will be asked to form an opinion about the patient's condition as to which he can **testify at trial**. Such an examination will often take place after litigation has commenced, or when it is contemplated.

a. Common-law approach: In this situation, the declarant's incentive to tell the truth is obviously less than in the consultation-for-treatment situation, since the physician will not be rendering care based upon the declarant's statements. For this reason, most common-law courts **refuse** to apply the exception in this situation. However, either of two rules may as a practical matter allow the statements made by the patient to be admitted anyway. First, the testifying physician will also often be one who furnished some treatment (even if only a second opinion regarding the best course of treatment), and courts apply the exception where both treatment and testimony are involved. Second, most courts allow a non-treating physician to recount statements by the patient concerning existing conditions or past symptoms, if these statements are introduced solely for the non-hearsay purpose of showing how the expert arrived at his opinion. L&S, p. 421.

b. Federal rule: FRE 803(4) eliminates the problem by making no distinction at all between physicians consulted for treatment and those consulted for testimony only. As the Advisory Committee's Note to 803(4) makes clear, the Rule's reference to "medical diagnosis or treatment" covers statements made to a physician whose examination is made *solely in order to enable him to testify at trial.*

   i. Rationale: The drafters' rationale for this broadening of the rule is that the traditional rule (see *supra*), by which the expert is permitted to state the basis for his opinion, generally causes the evidence to come before the jury anyway, and the limiting instruction preventing the jury from considering the statements for their substantive value is very unlikely to be obeyed by the jury. *Id.*

C. Statements about the declarant's mental state: A declarant will often make statements that explicitly concern his own *mental* or *emotional* state. For instance, she may say, "I hate my husband." We'll address two conceptually distinct situations involving declarations of mental state: (1) such statements when offered to prove the very mental state asserted, because that mental state is directly at issue in the litigation (e.g., "I hate my husband," where the declarant's emotions concerning her husband are directly at issue, as in a contest concerning the declarant's will); (2) such statements when the mental or emotional state referred to in the statement is not directly in issue, but is *circumstantial evidence* of some other fact in issue; typically, the other fact will be a past or future *act by the declarant*.

   1. State of mind directly in issue: The declarant's state of mind will often be *directly in issue* in the litigation.

   a. Illustrations: The declarant's state of mind will often be in issue in a criminal case where the declarant is the defendant (for instance, the intent to kill X, or the intent to rob a store.) The declarant's statement of emotional suffering may be at issue in the computation of damages in a suit by the declarant for intentional infliction of emotional distress. Or, the validity of a document asserted to establish a trust or a will may depend on the author's state of mind.

   b. Not necessarily hearsay: Before we examine the exception to the hearsay rule for statements of present mental state, it's important to realize that often, the declarant's statement will *not* be hearsay at all. This is because the statement will often merely be *circumstantial evidence* of the declarant's state of mind (in which case it will not be offered to prove the truth of the matter asserted), rather than a direct assertion of the declarant's state of mind offered to prove the matter asserted (that state of mind).

   Example 1: Declarant says, "My husband, Norman, is a two-timing adulterous S.O.B." Shortly after making this statement, she executes a new will, disinheriting Norman. After she dies, Norman contests the will. Declarant's feelings about him at the time of the will are directly in issue, since the validity of the will depends in part on whether it accurately reflected her emotions. But her statement is not, strictly speaking, hearsay, since it is not offered to prove the truth of the matter asserted (that Norman was an adulterer); rather, it is offered as circumstantial evidence that Declarant did not like Norman. Thus a careful court should not even reach the question of whether a hearsay exception applies. Indeed, at least one of the principal reasons for the hearsay rule — avoiding problems of misperception — does not exist here, since the validity of the will simply does not depend at all on whether Declarant correctly or incorrectly perceived Norman's fidelity.

Example 2: Contrast the above example with one in which Declarant says, "I really hate my husband, Norman, because he's a two-timing adulterer." Here, the statement directly asserts the mental state (hatred of Norman) that is at issue in the suit. Therefore, the hearsay rule applies unless there is an applicable exception. This is true even though this remark also includes a statement that would not be hearsay (an assertion of Norman's adultery). In any event, the distinction is unlikely to make a difference, since the exception for statements of present mental state or emotion would apply here. (But procedural rules governing the handling of hearsay exceptions might make the distinction significant in a few instances.)

c. **General rule:** In any event, there is a general exception to the hearsay rule, both at common law and under the Federal Rules, for statements of the declarant's *presently existing state of mind*. FRE 803(3)'s formulation gives the exception for "[a] statement of the declarant's then existing state of mind, emotion, sensation . . . (such as intent, plan, motive, design, mental feeling . . .), but not including a statement of memory or belief to prove the fact remembered or believed unless it relates to the execution, revocation, identification, or terms of declarant's will." The Federal Rule is essentially a restatement of common-law rules.

Example: P, the husband of W, sues D for D's alienation of W's affections. As part of P's case, P repeats in court W's earlier statements that D could give W a better time than P could, and that W now dislikes P.

Held, these statements are admissible. "[W]hen the intention, feelings, or other mental state of a certain person at a particular time . . . is material to the issues under trial, evidence of such person's declarations at the time indicative of his then mental state, even though hearsay, is competent as within an exception to the hearsay rule." Since the statements were admissible under this exception, they were not rendered inadmissible by the fact that they also contained other information that might otherwise have been inadmissible (such as W's statements that D took her for automobile rides and dinners, and gave her flowers.) *Adkins v. Brett*, 193 P. 251 (Cal. 1920).

d. **Present state:** The most important thing to remember about the exception for statements of mental state is that it applies *only* to statements about the declarant's *then existing* mental state.

Example: Declarant says, "I hate my husband, Norman." The exception to the hearsay rule would apply, since this is a statement of Declarant's mental state *existing at the time of the statement*. If, however, Declarant said, "Yesterday after I had a big fight with Norman, my hatred of him grew to new heights," the exception would not apply, because Declarant is speaking of a past mental state, not a present one.

   i. Rationale: Like statements of present physical condition, statements of present mental condition are considered more trustworthy because they are probably *spontaneous* and because the declarant usually has no motive for insincerity. As Justice Gray said in the famous case of *Mutual Life Insurance Co. v. Hillmon (infra,* p. 175), the exception makes sense because even if the declarant were to testify at trial, "his own memory of his state of mind at a former time is no more likely to be clear and true than a bystander's recollection of what he then said. . . ."

   e. Present state as bearing on past or future state: So long as the declarant's statement concerns a present mental state, the hearsay exception applies even though the ultimate mental state at issue in the case is one that *pre-dates* or *post-dates* the statement. In the following examples, admissibility of the statement turns on *relevance*, not hearsay.

   Example 1: On Monday, Declarant takes her will out of her safe deposit box and rips it up; the issue is whether this was done with an intent to revoke. On Tuesday, she says, "I don't want my husband Norman to get a cent." This statement is admissible under the exception for present declarations of present mental state, since the statement refers to her feelings at the very moment she made the declaration. In determining whether the exception to the hearsay rule applies, it would not matter that the ultimate mental state in issue (Declarant's feelings about Norman on Monday) relates to Monday and the declaration was made on Tuesday. The judge might conclude that Declarant's Tuesday feelings are not relevant to how she felt on Monday — this would depend on the particular facts of the case (e.g., if other evidence showed that Declarant discovered Norman's infidelity on Tuesday morning, the court might conclude that the Tuesday declaration was not logically probative of her Monday feelings). But the exclusion would be for lack of relevance, not hearsay.

   Example 2: Similarly, a relevance, not hearsay, problem is raised where a declaration about a present mental state is used as circumstantial proof of a *later* mental state. Thus, if Declarant said on Tuesday, "I hate Norman and don't want him to receive a cent," and ripped up the will on *Wednesday,* the hearsay exception would apply and again the question would be one of relevance — are Declarant's Tuesday feelings probative of how she felt on Wednesday? See L&S, p. 423.

   f. Surrounding circumstances: Declarations concerning state of mind often also include *other assertions.* Commonly, for instance, the declarant will go on to say that the defendant's actions caused the declarant's state of mind. If one of the issues in the case is whether the defendant's actions did indeed cause the declarant's state of mind, then the declaration is hearsay as to this issue. The court will normally deal with this problem by *allowing* in the entire statement, but then instructing the jury that it is to consider the statement only on the issue of the declarant's state of mind, not on the issue of whether this state of mind was caused by the defendant's acts. M, p. 845. If the risk of prejudice is too great because the jury will probably be unable to heed this instruction, and there is other evidence of the declarant's state of mind, the judge has discretion to exclude the statement. *Id.*

2. **Proof of subsequent act:** We now turn to a quite different aspect of statements regarding mental condition: a proponent of the out-of-court declaration may be introducing it not to prove the mental state because the mental state is an issue in the case, but rather, to prove that a subsequent *act* took place, where the act is at issue. Most commonly, this will happen because the proponent wants to show that the declarant had the *intent* (mental state) to take a certain action, in order to prove that the declarant did in fact eventually take that action, where whether that act took place is an issue in the case.

   a. **General rule:** It is now generally accepted that the exception *applies* in this situation. "[O]ut-of-court statements which tend to prove a plan, design, or intention of the declarant are admissible . . . to prove that the plan, design, or intention of the declarant was carried out by the declarant." M, p. 847.

   b. **Limitation:** Of course, considerations of *relevance* must always be satisfied, as with any other declaration of mental state. A's statement that he plans to kill B tomorrow might be held by the trial judge to be probative of whether A did in fact kill B the very next day; the same statement would probably be held to be irrelevant to whether B's unexplained death three years later was caused by A — the remoteness in time is simply too great.

   c. **Sufficient reliability:** Observe that the case for recognizing an exception in this situation is less strong than where the statement about mental condition is offered only to prove that the mental condition actually existed. There is a high likelihood that when a person says, with apparent sincerity, "I have the following mental condition," the person really has that condition. It is much less certain that when the person says, "I plan to take the following action," the act will actually occur — plans change, circumstances change, etc. Nonetheless, courts have concluded that such statements of intent are sufficiently reliable indicators of whether the intended act took place that the hearsay exception should be applied to them.

   d. **The *Hillmon* case:** The classic case illustrating this rule, indeed one of the classic cases in all of evidence law, is ***Mutual Life Ins. Co. v. Hillmon***, 145 U.S. 285 (1892).

      i. **Facts:** The plaintiff in *Hillmon*, Sallie Hillmon, sued two insurance companies to recover on policies on the life of her husband, John Hillmon. She claimed that a body found in Crooked Creek, Colorado, was that of her husband. The defendants claimed that the body was that of one Walters. To support their defense, the defendants tried to introduce letters written by

Walters to his sister and fiancee, in which he said that he planned to accompany Hillmon on a trip to Colorado.

ii. Holding: The U.S. Supreme Court held that the letters should have been admitted. There was an issue in the case as to whether Walters went with Hillmon to Colorado. The letters were not directly evidence of whether Walters went on the trip. But the letters were the best available proof of his intention to go, and to go with Hillmon; that intention in turn "made it more probable both that he did go and that he went with Hillmon, than if there had been no proof of such intention."

iii. Rationale: The Supreme Court's reasoning and the result in *Hillmon* make sense, in terms of our triangular technique for assessing hearsay dangers. (See *supra*, p. 122.) When Walters' statement of intent is allowed to give rise to the inference that he took the act he intended to take, there is no Right Leg danger — we're not worried that the declarant, Walters, misremembered his own intentions, or inaccurately perceived them. L&S, p. 428. It's true that the chain of inference between his having the intent and his taking the trip is not necessarily a strong one — circumstances may have changed, or he may simply have changed his mind. But these are issues of relevance, not hearsay. For instance, cross-examination of Walters at the time he wrote the letters would have revealed little about his intentions — it would almost certainly not have shown that he misremembered or misperceived them.

e. Unavailability: Statements evincing an intent to perform an act, even when offered to show that the act probably took place, do **not** require proof of the declarant's **unavailability**. However, some commentators have suggested that the exception should be changed to allow such evidence only where the declarant is not available to testify at trial. For instance, Professor Tribe (87 Harv. L. Rev. at 971, quoted in L&S, p. 429) concedes that cross-examination at the time of the declaration would not be useful where the declaration concerns intent; however, he argues that cross-examination at the time of trial would be very useful, since the declarant could be asked whether he in fact did the act.

i. Significance: However, the problem is more theoretical than real. Direct evidence (through cross-examination or otherwise) about whether an individual in fact did an act is so obviously preferable to inferential evidence based upon his expressed intent to do an act in the future, that virtually the only time a proponent relies on intent evidence is where the declarant is indeed unavailable. This was, for instance, clearly the case in *Hillmon*, since Walters was never found or heard from after the letters at issue in the case.

ii. Federal Rules: However, neither the Federal Rules nor state courts impose a requirement of unavailability. Thus FRE 803(3), which incorporates the *Hillmon* intent-to-show-act exception, is placed within 803's general grouping of exceptions which apply "even though the declarant is available as a witness."

3. Cooperation of other: The most difficult issue involving declarations of intent arises when the stated intent is to do an act that requires the ***cooperation of another person***. That is, the declarant says, "I plan to do such-and-such with X." Most of the time, the proponent of this evidence is trying to prove that X did something with the declarant, not that the declarant did something with X.

   a. *Hillmon* case: The Supreme Court's opinion in *Hillmon*, *supra*, p. 175, almost — but not quite — deals with this problem. Recall that the declarant was Walters, and his out-of-court declarations amounted to the statement, "I plan to go to Colorado with Hillmon." Clearly, he could not have carried out this intent without Hillmon's cooperation. The Supreme Court held that his statement could be introduced as circumstantial evidence not only that he went, but that he went with Hillmon.

   b. Modern view: Most modern courts have followed the Supreme Court's apparent lead in *Hillmon*, and "allow a statement of an intention to engage in some action with another to support the inference that that action was done with the other and, since the two are not separable, to support the inference that the other did the action with the declarant." L&S, p. 429.

      i. Criticism: However, *Hillmon* is not really authority for the proposition that a declarant's statement can be used to prove action by a third person. In *Hillmon*, it was undisputed that the third person (Hillmon) went to Crooked Creek. The only issue was whether the *declarant*, Walters, went there. The Supreme Court would not necessarily have allowed Walters' declaration to be evidence of whether *Hillmon* went to Crooked Creek — it might have rejected this evidence, on the ground that Walters' statement of his own intent to go to Crooked Creek (even though that intent involved going with Hillmon) was reasonably probative of what Walters did, but much weaker evidence of what Hillmon did. After all, Walters might have decided to go alone after Hillmon changed his own mind. Nonetheless, most modern courts have been willing, in at least some circumstances, to allow the declarant's statement of intent to do something with a third person to serve as evidence that the third person did the act.

   c. Declarant is murder victim: The most fascinating cases raising this problem are those in which a murder victim tells friends beforehand, "I'm going to do such-and-such with X," and is never seen again; when X is charged with the crime, can the victim's statement be introduced as evidence to show that the victim and X were together, giving X the opportunity to commit the murder? At least one court, in the famous case set out in the following example, has ***allowed*** the statement into evidence.

      Example: Larry Adell, a sixteen-year-old boy, leaves a group of his high school friends in a restaurant, telling them that he plans to meet a man named Angelo in the parking lot, and that Angelo is supposed to give him a pound of free marijuana. Larry never returns to his friends, and is never seen again. At D's trial for kidnapping, the prosecution introduces other evidence to show that D was the man Larry knew as Angelo; it then seeks to introduce

Larry's declaration to his friends about the rendezvous.

Held (on appeal to the Ninth Circuit), the statement is admissible. The Advisory Committee's Note to FRE 803(3) states that "the rule of [*Hillmon*] allowing evidence of intention as tending to prove the doing of the act intended, is, of course, left undisturbed." It is true that the Notes of the House Committee on the Judiciary concerning FRE 803(3) would exclude this evidence; those Notes say, "However, the Committee intends that the Rule be construed to limit the doctrine of [*Hillmon*] so as to render statements of intent by a declarant admissible only to prove his future conduct, not the future conduct of another person." However, the court chooses to follow the Advisory Committee's implicit allowance of the use of such testimony, rather than the House Committee's explicit rejection of it. *U.S. v. Pheaster*, 544 F.2d 353 (9th Cir. 1976).

d. **Other evidence that declarant did act:** Observe that this problem of using the declarant's statement of intent to prove a third party's action arises in two conceptually distinct situations: in one, there is no evidence that the declarant ever carried out the act he said he intended to commit; in the other, there is evidence that the declarant carried out, or attempted to carry out, the act, and the only question is whether he did it **with the third person**. In the former situation, the chain of inference is quite weak — the declarant may have been lying, he may have been mistaken about X's intent and learned later of his mistake before he acted, or other events may have occurred to prevent X from ever carrying out his part of their shared conduct. In the latter situation, by contrast, the fact that the declarant actually carried out his part of the shared action furnishes greater assurance of reliability.

   i. **Corroboration required:** Most courts will, therefore, allow the declarant's statement to serve as evidence that X cooperated in the activity only if there is **independent, corroborative evidence** either that the **declarant actually participated** in the activity, or that **X** actually participated. Thus in *Pheaster*, there was no question that Larry walked into the parking lot in pursuit of some kind of rendezvous; the only question was whether Angelo met him there. By contrast, if Larry had told his friends *the day before* that he planned to meet Angelo the next night in the restaurant parking lot, and there was no independent evidence that Larry or Angelo ever went to the parking lot, the court probably would not have allowed the statement to be introduced for the purpose of proving that Angelo met Larry in the parking lot.

e. **In favor of admissibility:** Assuming that there is, as is usually required, this independent evidence that either the declarant or X participated in the activity, there are still strong arguments to be made on both sides of the admissibility issue. First, let's consider the arguments in *favor* of admissibility. These arguments can be understood in the context of *Pheaster*:

   i. **Probative:** It is unlikely that Larry would have gone into the parking lot and remained there for any length of time, unless Angelo arrived for a meeting. That is, Larry's **conduct** is at least somewhat **probative** on the issue of who met Larry in the parking lot.

ii. **Risk of misperception:** The *Right Leg* dangers (*supra*, p. 122) are not entirely present here. Even if Larry misperceived or misremembered the arrangements with Angelo, Larry's statement made it more probable than it would otherwise be that Angelo ultimately did away with him — for instance, even if Larry had the time or place wrong, he might have contacted Angelo and they might ultimately have rendezvoused somewhere else or at a later time, with the same ultimate fatal result.

iii. **Circumstantial guarantee:** Furthermore, there is an additional indication of reliability in the fact that Larry **did not return to the restaurant** immediately — had Larry been mistaken about where or when the rendezvous was to take place, it's reasonably likely that he would have gone back to his friends at the restaurant. Thus his failure to do so furnishes some (albeit minor) **circumstantial guarantee** that his statement was correct.

f. **Reasons against admission:** But the following arguments, also very plausible ones, can be made **against** admission of the evidence:

i. **Lying:** Larry may simply have been **lying.** He may have wanted to impress his friends with what a wheeler-dealer he was, while he was really covering up for the fact that he had to be home early (and was waylaid by somebody else on the way).

ii. **Misidentification:** He might really have had the rendezvous, but not with Angelo, and was trying to **cover up** his sources.

iii. **Mistake:** He might have really made an arrangement with Angelo, but **mistook** the time or place, and someone else coincidentally waylaid him.

iv. **Generally:** More generally, the Right Leg dangers of misperception and erroneous memory, as well as the Left Leg danger of insincerity, are somewhat present in the situation. Furthermore, any instruction to the jury limiting them to use of the declaration only insofar as it concerns Larry's own actions (e.g., "You may consider the statement only as it bears on what Larry did, not as it bears on what, if anything, Angelo did") would be not only impossible for the jury to apply, but even hypocritical — there is no dispute that Larry went into the parking lot, and the only relevance of his declaration is on the issue of whether Angelo met him there.

g. **Summary:** Thus this kind of issue is a very close one, and reasonable courts could disagree. See, e.g., L&S, pp. 429-30, in which the two co-authors disagree with each other. See also *People v. Alcade*, 148 P.2d 627 (Cal. 1944), a very similar case to *Pheaster* (in which the victim said, "I'm going out with Frank tonight," and Frank was charged with her murder) — the majority allowed the declaration into evidence, over the vigorous dissent of Justice Traynor.

i. **Factors:** Two factors that a court will consider in a particular situation are: (1) the strength of the **independent evidence** that the declarant or X in fact participated in the activity; and (2) the extent to which it is likely that the declarant would have participated in the activity ***only with the cooperation*** of X. Thus the court in *Pheaster* probably found it significant that no other plausible reason was advanced as to why Larry would have gone into the parking lot and failed to return. If, however, there had been evidence that he often met his girlfriend in the parking lot and necked with her (and the girlfriend was unavailable to testify as to whether this had happened on that fateful night), the court would probably not have been so quick to admit the evidence. Similarly, had there been evidence that Larry was wont to smoke marijuana by himself in the restaurant parking lot, again admission would not have been so likely. See Lilly, p. 253.

4. Proof of prior acts: Now, let us consider the converse problem: To what extent may a person's statement about his mental condition, memory, or belief be used as circumstantial evidence of something that happened ***before*** the statement? Whereas courts have been quite willing, as we've seen, to allow statements of intent to prove that the intended act later occurred, they have been very ***unwilling*** to allow statements of mental condition (especially statements of ***memory*** or ***belief***) as circumstantial evidence that a ***prior event*** caused the mental state. The reason, in brief, is that allowing such evidence would ***virtually abolish the hearsay rule.***

a. The *Shepard* case: Here, too, there is a classic Supreme Court case on point: ***Shepard v. U.S.***, 290 U.S. 96 (1933).

  i. Facts: Dr. Shepard was charged with the murder by poison of his wife. In the absence of Dr. Shepard, Mrs. Shepard, then ill in bed, asked her nurse to bring the bottle of liquor from which she had drunk just before collapsing. She then asked the nurse whether there was enough left to test for poison, and said that the smell and taste were strange; she added, *"Dr. Shepard has poisoned me."* At the murder trial, the nurse repeated these statements to the jury.

  ii. Result: The Supreme Court (in an opinion by Justice Cardozo) held that the statement, "Dr. Shepard has poisoned me," was admitted in violation of the hearsay rule.

  iii. Not dying declaration: The trial court had admitted the testimony under the "dying declaration" exception (*infra*, p. 231). However, the Supreme Court rejected this rationale, on the grounds that there was no showing of the declarant's consciousness of impending death or her abandonment of hope, as required for that exception.

  iv. Not state of mind: On appeal, the government argued that the statement was admissible under the "state of mind" exception, on the theory that there was evidence that Mrs. Shepard had thought of suicide, and the statement was relevant to whether she was indeed of a suicidal mind. The Court first rejected this argument on the narrow grounds that this was not the purpose for which the prosecution had really offered the testimony, and that a trial judge's decision to admit testimony for an illegitimate purpose (the dying declaration purpose) should not be sustained because the appellate court finds some other purpose, not even articulated at trial, that might sustain it.

v. Not usable to prove past act by another: But the Court also rejected the government's attempt to apply the "state of mind" exception for a much more fundamental reason, the one for which the case is remembered. The government would indeed have had the right to introduce Mrs. Shepard's declarations "to prove her present thoughts and feelings, or even her thoughts and feelings in times past." Here, however, the declarations were used "as proof of an *act* committed by someone else, as evidence that [declarant] was dying of poison given by her husband."

vi. Might not be backwards-pointing: The Court contrasted this situation with that in *Hillmon* (*supra*, p. 175). *Hillmon* involved a statement of intention used to prove that the intended act was *subsequently* accomplished. But in the *Shepard* court's view, "The ruling in [*Hillmon*] marks the high water line beyond which the courts have been unwilling to go. . . . Declarations of intention, casting light upon the future, have been sharply distinguished from declarations of memory, pointing backwards to the past." The testimony here ***"faced backward and not forward,"*** at least in its "most obvious implications." Furthermore, it "spoke to a past act, and more than that, to an act by someone not the speaker." The small tendency it might have had to establish the declarant's own present state of mind was clearly drowned by "the reverberating clang of those accusatory words."

vii. Rationale: The Court explained why the distinction between future-pointing statements (allowed under *Hillmon*) and past-pointing statements (disallowed under *Shepard*) was so significant: "***There would be an end***, or nearly that, ***to the rule against hearsay*** if the distinction were ignored."

b. Modern rule: The view of the *Shepard* court has essentially prevailed in every jurisdiction. The rule may be capsulized as follows: The "state of mind" exception to the hearsay rule does not apply to statements of ***memory*** or ***belief*** about ***past actions or events***. This is true whether the past action was by the declarant ("I believe I went to the store yesterday") or by another ("I believe that Dr. Shepard has poisoned me.") Observe that not only would allowing such statements swallow up the hearsay rule, such statements also suffer from all of the standard hearsay dangers — both the Left Leg and Right Leg dangers (*supra*, p. 122).

i. Illustration from *Shepard*: Thus on the facts of *Shepard*, the Left Leg dangers are clear: Mrs. Shepard may have been insincere (she may have committed suicide, and knowingly tried to get her husband blamed); also, her statement may have been ambiguous and been misheard by the nurse (e.g., she may have said, "Is it possible that Dr. Shepard has poisoned me?") Furthermore, the Right Leg dangers are equally present: Mrs. Shepard may have suffered from an erroneous memory of what had happened (e.g., she really put the poison in the liquor herself, and forgot that she had done so, in a paranoid delusion) or from inaccurate perception (e.g., she didn't notice that it was really the nurse who put poison in the bottle).

ii. **Federal Rule:** The Federal Rules follow *Shepard* in not allowing statements of memory or belief to prove previous acts. FRE 803(3), after establishing the general hearsay exception for statements of the declarant's "then existing state of mind, emotion," etc., excludes "a statement of **memory or belief to prove the fact remembered or believed** . . . ." (There is a special exception for statements regarding the declarant's will; see *infra*, p. 184.)

c. **Fear of another:** In one situation, a minority of courts have allowed into evidence the declarant's statement of memory or belief where that statement's principal tendency is to show another's action: where the declarant expresses *fear* of another, and the statement expressly or implicitly blames the fear on the other's acts.

Example: V says (out of court), "I'm afraid that D will kill me." If V is later found dead, and D is charged with killing him, a few courts might allow the declaration. See, e.g., *People v. Merkouris*, 344 P.2d 1 (Cal. 1959), accepting such evidence on the theory that it was shown not for the purpose of proving that D committed the crime, but merely for the purpose of showing V's state of mind. However, in most such cases the victim's state of mind is not directly in issue, and therefore most courts will not allow declarations concerning a victim's fear of the defendant, since the jury will probably view the declarations as direct evidence of the defendant's guilt. M, p. 854.

i. **Other purposes:** However, the generally-accepted rule that the victim's declarations of fear of the defendant do not fall within the state of mind exception applies only where the victim's statement is used as evidence that the defendant committed an act which caused the fear. In several other situations, the victim's declaration of fear of the defendant will be admitted, because that state of mind is directly relevant to **some other issue** in the case. This would be true, for instance, if: (1) The defendant claims **self-defense** as the justification for killing the victim; the victim's declaration that he fears the defendant will be admitted to rebut the defense, since it makes it less likely that the victim was the initial aggressor. (2) The defendant defends on the grounds that the victim committed **suicide**; the victim's statements of fear of the defendant will be admitted to rebut a suicidal bent. (3) The defendant claims that the decedent died **accidentally** (e.g., he claims that the victim picked up the defendant's gun and was accidentally killed). Here, a statement by the victim that he was afraid of the defendant (or, for that matter, that he was afraid of guns) would be admitted to rebut defendant's defense. See *U.S. v. Brown*, 490 F.2d 758 (D.C. Cir. 1973), listing these situations.

d. **Intent coupled with recital of past acts:** Sometimes, a statement of intent to commit an act (admissible under the *Hillmon* rationale to prove that the act probably occurred) is **coupled** with a reference to the declarant's recollection of some **past act** by himself or by a third person. The latter reference, if standing alone, would of course not be admissible, under *Shepard*. But where the **main thrust** of the statement is the future-looking part, many courts will allow the **entire statement** to come in.

- **i. Statements explaining motive:** The whole statement is especially likely to be allowed in where the reference to the remembered fact or belief is an explanation of **why** the future act is intended.

Example: D, a union official, is charged with taking an illegal payoff from a corporation of which one Harry Terker is President and Richard Terker, his son, is Secretary and Treasurer. At the trial, Richard is permitted to recount a conversation he had with Harry, in which Harry told him, "I've just received a call from [D]" and "[D] has asked for some money on the Bridgeport Harbor Bridge Project, which I intend to send up to Connecticut for him."

Held, the conversation is admissible. The part of the statement relating to the father's statement to send the money was clearly admissible under *Hillmon*. Since the "most obvious implications" of the father's statement looked forward — to the sending of the money to Connecticut — inclusion of the reference to the past remembered fact (the telephone call from D) could be admitted without great danger. The past event "is recent, is within the personal knowledge of the declarant and is so integrally included in the declaration of design as to make it unlikely in the last degree that the latter would be true and the former false." *U.S. v. Annunziato*, 293 F.2d 373 (2d Cir. 1961).

Note: The reasoning and result in *Annunziato* have been criticized on the grounds that "the evidence was much more powerful and probative in looking backwards — to show that the defendant had requested the payment as a bribe — than in looking forward. The elephant of the past was pulled in by the tail of the future." W&B, Par. 803(3)[05].

- **ii. Not all courts agree:** Not all courts have agreed with Judge Friendly in *Annunziato*, that references to the past act should be admitted where they are an integral part of explaining why a future act is planned. Thus in *U.S. v. Mandel*, 437 F.Supp. 262 (D.Md. 1977), the case against the defendant (the governor of Maryland) turned in part on whether he was aware that two of his associates had an interest in a race track. D offered testimony by Dorothy Rogers, the wife of co-defendant William Rogers, to the effect that William had told Dorothy not to mention the past acquisition of the race track to anyone, not even the governor. The court refused to admit the testimony, mainly on the grounds that: (1) there was not much need for it, since William Rogers and the other co-defendants could testify about the alleged concealment of the plan from the governor (in contrast to the *Annunziato* situation, where the father, who was the only other source of the evidence, was dead by the time of trial); and (2) there was a strong risk of **fabrication**. As to point (2), the court found the present case similar to the many cases in which defendants charged with operating moonshine stills defended on the grounds that they had been rabbit hunting near the still, and offered statements by friends that the defendant said, just before the episode, that he was going rabbit hunting.

   e. Execution of will: There is one very well-recognized exception to the ban on "memory or belief" statements: A person's statements relating to his own ***will*** are generally allowed, even if they are statements of memory or belief offered to prove the fact remembered or believed. This special exception exists not because this kind of out-of-court declaration is believed inherently more trustworthy, but simply because there is often a ***great need*** for it — no one else can know the decedent's wishes as well as the decedent, and he is of course not available.

   i. Scope: Generally, this special exception applies to the testator's statements that he has or has not made a will, that his will is intended to reach a certain result, or that he has or has not revoked a will. M, pp. 852-53.

   ii. Federal formulation: This special exception is carried over into the Federal Rules. FRE 803(3), after excluding statements of "memory or belief to prove the fact remembered or believed," carves out a special exception where the statement of memory or belief "relates to the execution, revocation, identification, or terms of declarant's will."

D. Excited utterances: All courts recognize a hearsay exception for certain statements made under the influence of a ***startling event***. This is usually called the *"excited utterances"* exception.

   1. Federal codification: The common-law formulation of this exception has been codified in FRE 803(2): The exception applies to "a statement relating to a ***startling event*** or condition made while the declarant was under the ***stress of excitement*** caused by the event or condition."

   a. Two requirements: There are thus two independent requirements that must be satisfied in order for the excited utterances exception to apply:

   i. Startling event: The event giving rise to the statement must be ***sufficiently startling*** to eliminate the declarant's capacity to reflect before speaking; and

   ii. Still under effect: The statement must be made while the declarant is ***still under the influence*** of the startling event. See L&S, p. 418.

   2. Rationale: The main rationale for the exception is that where the event is so startling that the declarant's reflective capacity is eliminated, the declaration is unlikely to be motivated by self-interest or otherwise insincere. Therefore, the statement is likely to be accurate, or so the theory says.

   Example: V, immediately after being brutally assaulted and raped, calls out to a passerby, "Help. D did this to me." Given the stress on V at the moment, it's very unlikely that she has had the time or ability to cook up a false story about who her assailant is.

a. **Mistake of perception:** However, the increase in sincerity due to the startling occurrence is partially offset by a probable increase in *errors of perception* due to the startling event. "[E]xcitement tends to distort perception and may cloud memory. There is reason to believe that excited utterances are, on balance, less reliable than much of the hearsay we refuse to admit." L&S, p. 417. Nonetheless, the exception is firmly grounded and unlikely eliminated.

3. **Sufficiently startling:** The requirement that the event be *sufficiently startling* to still reflective capacity, rarely causes problems. Physical violence is not required — even seeing a photograph in a newspaper may suffice. M, p. 855. The basic issue is whether the event is sufficiently startling that the court believes that a normal person would probably have spoken before thinking.

a. **Independent proof:** Courts are split about whether the existence of the startling event can be proved by the statement alone, or whether *independent evidence* of the event must be presented. Most courts allow the statement to be used for this purpose. L&S, p. 418.

4. **Time factor:** Most litigation has involved the second requirement, that the statement be made while the declarant is *still under the influence* of the startling event. In making this determination, courts look to all of the surrounding circumstances, including evidence that this particular declarant was in fact still under the event's sway (e.g., she was suffering from clinical shock). However, in making this determination, the courts have attached exceptional importance to the *amount of time that passed* between the event and the declaration.

a. **Rule of thumb:** One authority asserts that most cases fall within the following rule of thumb: "Statements made during the exiting event or within *half an hour* afterward are usually admitted, statements made an hour or more after the event are usually excluded, while statements made within thirty minutes to an hour of the event are dealt with . . . by a close look at the surrounding circumstances." L&S, p. 418.

b. **Shock or memory loss:** Occasionally the event may produce shock, memory loss, or some other medical condition that *delays the time for reflection* far beyond what it would normally be. In this event, courts will generally apply the excited utterance exception despite the long time interval.

Example: P is injured in an automobile accident. She is taken to the emergency room with serious leg injuries. After an unknown period of time during which she suffers either from memory loss or shock, she opens her eyes and tells the doctor that the accident occurred when she "stopped for [a] red light, started up on [the] green light and got hit."

Held, P's statement to the doctor is admissible under the excited utterance exception. The exact elapsed time between the accident and her declaration is not important. "The fact that her utterance about the accident was made very shortly after her return to reality and while she was in severe pain is the important circumstance. . . ." *Cestero v. Ferrara*, 273 A.2d 761 (N.J. 1971).

    c. Presence of reflection: Even where the time interval is short, a court may find that the surrounding circumstances indicate that the declarant **did** have time to reflect, so that the exception should not apply.

        i. Self-serving nature: For instance, if the statement is clearly **self-serving** (e.g., "The accident wasn't my fault, because I carefully stopped at the stop sign . . ."), the court will probably find that the required interference with reflective capacity did not exist. M, p. 857.

        ii. Questions: If the statement is made ***in response to a detailed question***, this will be evidence that there was not the required absence of reflection. However, a statement that comes in response to a simple "What happened?" will probably not be disqualified. L&S, pp. 418-19.

5. Reference to exciting event: Must the declaration ***explain*** or ***refer to*** the startling event? Or is it enough that the declaration is made while still under the influence of the event, and relates to it in some way? The courts are split.

    a. Federal rule: Under FRE 803(2), whose approach is also followed by some state courts, the declaration need **not** explain or refer to the startling event — it is sufficient that the excited utterance is one "***relating to*** a startling event or condition."

    b. Contrary rule: But other state courts insist that the excited utterance explain or refer to the startling event. M, p. 857.

    c. Statements of agency: The issue is most likely to arise where the declarant, while still under the influence of the startling event, makes a statement regarding his ***employment*** or other agency. Courts following the federal approach will allow the statement under the excited utterances exception; those following the opposite rule will not.

    Example: Declarant, a truck driver, gets in an accident. Immediately following the accident, he shouts, "Hurry up, I've got to call on a customer, and I want to get home." The statement is offered to prove that Declarant was really going to call on a customer (and therefore, by inference, that he was on business at the time of the accident so that his employer is liable). The statement does not explain or directly refer to the accident. Therefore, some state courts would exclude it; but the Federal Rules would allow it, since it "relates to" the accident. On these facts, see *Murphy Auto Parts Co. v. Ball*, 249 F.2d 508 (D.C. Cir. 1957), allowing the statement to be used to prove the employer's responsibility for the driver's actions.

    d. Distinguished from present sense impression rule: Observe that the Federal Rule on this point is quite different from the Federal Rule in the case of a statement of "present sense impression" under FRE 803(1) (*infra*, p. 187) — the statement of present sense impression must be one "***describing*** or ***explaining*** an event or condition."

6. Rape cases: A separate common-law exception to the hearsay rule has developed in ***rape*** cases, under which the prosecution may prove that the victim made a ***prompt***

complaint. M, p. 859. Today, such a declaration of complaint is more likely to be admitted under the excited utterances exception — whereas the special rape complaint exception usually allows only the fact of complaint to be admitted, the excited utterances exception will allow the content of the declaration (especially any statement about the identity of the assailant) to be admitted. The Federal Rules make no special provision for declarations of complaint in sex cases, so the excited utterances exception is typically the only way to get into evidence the contents of the victim's complaint. *Id.*

E. Present sense impressions: Recall that the exception for excited utterances has been criticized on the grounds that the startling event makes errors more, rather than less, likely. Consequently, it can be argued that a spontaneous statement by one who has witnessed an event should be admitted more readily if the speaker was **unexcited** than if he was excited. This reasoning was generally rejected traditionally, but in the last few decades, more and more courts have subscribed to it. Today, many if not most courts (and the Federal Rules) recognize a separate hearsay exception for what might be termed "***present sense impressions***."

    1. Federal formulation: The formulation of FRE 803(1) is typical of this trend: an exception is recognized for a statement "***describing*** or ***explaining*** an event or condition made while the declarant was ***perceiving the event*** or condition, or immediately thereafter."

    2. *Houston Oxygen* case: The case with which the present sense impression exception is usually associated is *Houston Oxygen Co. v. Davis*, 161 S.W.2d 474 (Tex.App. 1942).

        a. Facts: In *Houston Oxygen*, Mrs. Cooper and Mr. Sanders were riding together on the highway when a car containing P passed them. The defendants offered Mr. Sanders' testimony that as P's car passed by, Mrs. Cooper said that the people in P's car "must have been drunk, that we would find them somewhere on the road wrecked if they keep that rate of speed up."

        b. Holding: The declaration could not come in under the excited utterance exception, because there was no evidence that Mrs. Cooper was so startled by the event that she was incapable of reflection. Nonetheless, the court admitted the statement.

            i. Rationale: It did so on the theory that the statement was "sufficiently spontaneous to save it from the suspicion of being manufactured evidence. There was no time for a calculated statement." Since the statement was a report of an event at the moment the event was witnessed, there was no danger of any defect from memory. Furthermore, the statement was made to another (Mr. Sanders) who had an equal opportunity to observe the event and thus to correct any misstatement. In summary, the circumstances gave the statement a high degree of reliability. This was true even though the statement was made considerably before the principal event being litigated; (P's car did not crash until 4 miles later up the road).

3. **Immediacy:** In contrast to the excited-utterances exception, for the present-sense-impression exception **no material time may pass** between the event being perceived and the declarant's statement about it. FRE 803(1)'s requirement — that the statement take place "while the declarant is perceiving the event . . . or immediately thereafter" — is typical.

4. **Description:** Whereas the excited utterance need not describe the exciting event (it must merely take place under the influence of that event), the present sense impression must **describe** or **explain** the event that the declarant has perceived.

5. **Perception**: The declarant must be a "percipient witness" to the event. That is, he must have **perceived the event**, rather than have learned about it from some other means (e.g., reading the newspaper).

6. **Opinions allowed:** A declaration may be admitted under the exception even if it expresses an **opinion**, so long as it is an attempt to explain something that the declarant is perceiving. See, e.g., *Commonwealth v. Coleman*, *infra*.

7. **No corroboration required:** Although the listener (who will repeat the statement in court) will generally be present at the event and be able to corroborate the declaration, there is **no requirement** that there be **corroboration** of the statement.

> **Example:** V lives with her boyfriend, D. Early one morning, V telephones her mother, saying, "[D] won't let me leave the apartment, he's going to hang up the phone and then he's going to kill me." V begs her mother to call the police. The connection is broken, her mother calls the police, and D, blood spattered and with cuts on face and hands, is apprehended outside the apartment. V is found shortly thereafter dead of multiple stab wounds. V's mother testifies at trial about V's statements made during the phone call.
>
> *Held*, the mother's recounting of V's statements is admissible. The present sense impression exception applies. The fact that the mother was not physically present and thus cannot directly corroborate V's statements is irrelevant. Nor is admissibility nullified by the fact that part of V's statement ("he's going to kill me") is, arguably, an "opinion." The rule against opinion testimony applies to opinions rendered by a witness at trial; the statement here was an "impression of contemporaneous events," and falls within the exception for present sense impressions. (A concurring judge believed that the evidence was better classified as an excited utterance.) *Commonwealth v. Coleman*, 326 A.2d 387 (Pa. 1974).

8. **"Res gestae" label:** Recall (*supra*, p. 168) that the label *"res gestae"* is often applied to a variety of spontaneous or excited statements. This is especially likely to be the case in the present sense impression context — many courts have simply used the *res gestae* label instead of making it clear that the present sense impression exception is being applied. The better practice is to avoid the *res gestae* terminology entirely.

V. PAST RECOLLECTION RECORDED

A. The rule generally: Sometimes a person makes a written record of an event, shortly after the event has occurred. Time passes, the writer's memory of the event dims, and then a trial occurs at which the event is in issue. The witness cannot testify satisfactorily about the event, because by hypothesis he has forgotten some of the details. The written account of the event cannot be offered as evidence for the truth of the facts recited in the document, unless there is an exception to the hearsay rule — for the writing is an out-of-court declaration offered for the truth of what it asserts. The rule permitting introduction of *"past recollection recorded"* provides such an exception, if certain requirements are satisfied whose effect is to increase the reliability of the document.

1. **Typical applications:** Here are some situations in which the writing might be admissible as a past recollection recorded:

   a. W takes an inventory for the business which employs him, and writes down the inventory on a slip of paper;

   b. W is an insurance company accident investigator, who investigates a car accident and writes down information about the damage, location of the vehicles, etc.;

   c. W is a police officer who interviews a witness after a crime, and makes notes about the witness' statement;

   d. W is the admitting nurse at a hospital, who makes notes about the patient's symptoms and the patient's comments regarding pain.

2. **Relation to business records exception:** Observe that some of these types of documents might be alternatively admissible under the "business records" (or more generally, "regularly kept records") exception, *infra*, p. 193. However, the business records exception applies whether or not the person who made the entry is available to testify; the past recollection recorded exception applies only where the person who made the entry (or at least some person who approved the entry at the time it was made) is available to testify about the making of the entry.

3. **FRE 803(5) recognizes a hearsay exception for:** The Federal Rules follow the general outlines of the common-law exception. FRE 803(5) provides a hearsay exception for: "a memorandum or record concerning a matter about which a witness once had knowledge but now has insufficient recollection to enable him to testify fully and accurately, shown to have been made or adopted by the witness when the matter was fresh in his memory and to reflect that knowledge correctly. If admitted, the memorandum or record may be read into evidence but may not itself be received as an exhibit unless offered by an adverse party."

B. Requirements for the rule: There are four essential requirements which must be satisfied before a memorandum or record may be admitted under the past recollection recorded exception. These requirements exist in more or less the same form in most common-law jurisdictions as well as under the Federal Rules:

1. **First-hand knowledge:** The memorandum must relate to something of which the witness once had *first-hand knowledge*.

   > **Example:** W writes down the details of an inventory. If he testifies at trial that he had first-hand knowledge of the inventory details at the time he made the record, this requirement will be satisfied. If, however, he says on the stand that some of the information was supplied by his assistant (and the assistant is not available to testify that he, too, wrote or approved the record), the inventory records will not be admissible. M, pp. 865-66.

2. **Made when fresh in memory:** The record must have been made when the matter was *fresh in the witness' memory*.

   a. **Common law:** The traditional common-law rule was that the record had to be made "at or near the time" of the events recorded.

   b. **Modern/federal:** But the modern trend is somewhat more liberal. Thus FRE 803(5) requires merely that the record have been made "when the matter was fresh in the witness' memory." Under the modern/federal approach, a record made several days after the events in question would still have a reasonable chance of being found to meet this requirement.

3. **Impaired recollection:** Both traditional and modern cases have nearly always required that the witness have suffered at least some *impairment* of his memory of the events recorded. That is, if the witness' memory at the time of trial is perfectly clear about the events, the earlier record may not be introduced — a key part of the rationale for the past recollection recorded exception is that it applies only where, in a sense, the witness' memory is partly "unavailable." However, courts have, over the years, differed as to how complete the impairment of the witness' memory must be.

   a. **Traditional approach:** The traditional common-law approach was that the witness who made the record must testify at trial that he *lacks all present memory* of the event, and thus cannot testify concerning it at all. M, p. 867.

   b. **Federal and modern rule:** The Federal Rules approach, shared by most modern courts, is that the witness must suffer *some impairment* of his memory of the events, but this impairment need not be total. FRE 803(5)'s formulation is that the witness must now have "insufficient recollection to enable the witness to testify fully and accurately. . . ."

      i. **Rationale:** The reason most courts require a substantial impairment of memory is that they are afraid that otherwise, there would be an increase in the use of statements that are prepared for the express purpose of being used in litigation; such statements might be drafted or influenced by interested parties or lawyers. Lilly, p. 262.

   c. **No impairment needed:** A very few courts have abandoned the requirement of memory impairment entirely, on the theory that the written record, since it was made so much closer to the time of the events, is inherently more reliable than the witness' testimony at the time of trial could possibly be. L&S, p. 437.

4. **Accuracy when written:** The witness at trial must testify as to the *accuracy* of the record when made. As FRE 803(5) puts it, the record must be shown "to reflect [the witness'] knowledge correctly." "What this means in practice is that the witness must testify either that he remembers making an accurate recording of the event in question although he no longer remembers the facts recorded, or, if the witness has entirely forgotten the situation in which the recording was made, that he is confident he would not have written or adopted some description of the facts unless that description truly described his observations at the time." L&S, p. 437.

   a. **Adopted by witness:** It is *not* required that the witness at trial be the person who *made* the record. All that is required is that the witness have *approved* or adopted the record, after it was made, as being an accurate reflection of his knowledge.

   Example: W, a forensic pathologist, performs an autopsy. He dictates the results of the autopsy to an assistant, who carefully makes notes of what W says. So long as W looks over the notes and approves them shortly after they are made, only W's testimony (and not that of the assistant) is needed at trial in order for the notes to come in under past recollection recorded.

   b. **Multi-party problem:** Now suppose that, as in the above example, W describes to X facts of which W has first-hand knowledge, X puts them into a record, but W does *not* check the record for accuracy. W's testimony will not, in most courts and under the Federal Rules, be sufficient by itself — W cannot testify that the document "reflect[s] [his] knowledge correctly." In this situation, both W and X must testify at trial: W would testify that his oral statements to X correctly reflected the facts as he, W, then knew them; X would then testify that he accurately recorded what W told him. Together, the two witnesses would be found to have met the requirements of FRE 803(5). M, p. 869; L&S, p. 438.

C. **Other considerations:** Here are some miscellaneous aspects of the past recollection recorded exception:

   1. **Non-writings:** Normally, the "record" will be a writing. However, this is not a formal requirement. Thus if W makes a *tape recording* of facts known to him (e.g., a tape dictated by a pathologist during an autopsy), the tape recording is probably admissible under the exception, assuming all the above requirements are met. M, p. 866.

   2. **Best Evidence rule:** The Best Evidence rule (see *infra*, p. 375), which applies to any written document, means that the record introduced must be the *original*, unless the proponent can show that the original is unavailable through no fault of his own. L&S, p. 438. Thus if the record is, say, a police officer's notes on an accident investigation, the original notes, rather than a typed transcript of them, must be introduced at trial.

   3. **Not always admissible as evidence:** All courts allow the record, if it meets the requirements for the exception, to be *read out loud* to the jury and into evidence. However, courts disagree about whether the memorandum or record itself should

become an ***exhibit*** in evidence.

a. Allow as exhibit: Some courts allow it to be entered as an exhibit, in which case the jury may ***take it into the jury room***.

b. Don't allow: Other courts, and the Federal Rules, take the view that the record is essentially testimony; since transcripts of live witness' testimony are not exhibits intended to be taken into the jury room, these courts feel that the past recollection recorded should not be given better status, and therefore possibly greater probative value in the jury's eyes. Thus FRE 803(5) provides that "if admitted, the memorandum or record may be read into evidence but may not itself be received as an exhibit unless offered by an adverse party."

4. **Distinguished from present recollection refreshed:** The exception for past recollection recorded must be distinguished from the doctrine called ***"present recollection refreshed,"*** whereby a witness on the stand who has trouble remembering an event may be given a writing, a picture, or some other document to aid his recollection. See *supra*, p. 74.

a. Not hearsay: Strictly speaking, the use of the present recollection refreshed technique is not an exception to the hearsay rule at all — since the only thing that goes into evidence is the witness' present testimony, and not the document, there is simply no out-of-court declaration. The witness can, of course, be cross-examined on what he said. (Of course, often the witness' testimony is very similar to the contents of the document he has been shown, so that one may wonder whether he is really testifying from "refreshed memory" rather than merely reading the document. This is especially true where, as in some states, the witness is permitted to continually refer to the document during his testimony. L&S, pp. 438-39. Nonetheless, the official view in all jurisdictions is that the present recollection refreshed doctrine is not an exception to the hearsay rule.)

b. Rules for use: Because the use of the document is not evidence but merely "an aid to evidence," courts are generally much more liberal about the circumstances under which documents can be used for this purpose, than in the case of past recollection recorded.

i. Few restrictions: Most courts follow the following "non-rules": (1) The document need not have any guarantee of reliability; (2) It need not have been prepared near the time of the events it describes; and (3) The witness need not have been involved in the document's preparation.

Example: D is charged with the robbery and murder of V. After the attack on V, and before he died, D was brought before V, and V told officers Bolton and Hucke that D was not his assailant. A police report was prepared by Hucke. At the trial, officer Bolton is a witness for the prosecution. To stimulate officer Bolton's memory of V's statement, D's lawyer attempts to show Bolton the police report prepared by Hucke.

Held (on appeal), D was entitled to try to refresh officer Bolton's memory, even though Bolton did not prepare, or even subsequently read and verify, the document. "All that is required is that [the document] ignite the flash of accurate recall — that it accomplish the revival which is sought." *Baker v. State*, 371 A.2d 699 (Md. Ct. Sp. App. 1977).

    ii. Safeguards: For a discussion of how courts prevent abuse of the present recollection refreshed exception, see *supra*, p. 74.

VI. BUSINESS RECORDS

  A. Problem generally: Business enterprises keep records in the ordinary course of their business. For instance, a business typically keeps accounts that show who owes it money. If such a routine business record is offered as evidence, and offered to show the truth of the matter asserted in the document, a hearsay problem is presented.

    1. Illustration: For instance, suppose that P, a merchant, is suing D, a customer, for an unpaid balance. If P presents its ledger book to show that goods were sold to D on a certain date for a certain amount, and never paid for, the use of the document is hearsay — it is used to show that the matter asserted in the document (that D received the goods and never paid for them) is true. Yet there may be no other evidence available to P — the clerk who actually handed the goods to D may no longer be available; the clerk who made the notation in the records was not necessarily the one who delivered the goods; still another person may have been in charge of processing payments, and could thus give only a partial picture of the transaction, etc.

    2. Need for rule: In short, the complexities of modern business transactions mean that an enterprise's records, kept in the ordinary course of business, are often the best evidence of events that happen during the course of business. For this reason, a special hearsay exception for *"business records"* (or, somewhat more generally, *"regularly kept records"*) has arisen.

  B. History: The business records exception developed gradually over a long period of time.

    1. Two historical exceptions: At common law, two distinct exceptions were available to allow some types of business records into evidence.

      a. Shopbook rule: First, the *"shopbook rule"* developed. Under this rule, a merchant could submit his books of account into evidence to show that the defendant owed him money. Because of the potentially self-serving nature of such books of account, most jurisdictions imposed one or more pre-requisites to admissibility; for instance, many courts required testimony that the merchant generally kept honest accounts, or proof apart from the books that at least some of the goods were actually delivered to the defendant. M, p. 871.

      b. Regularly kept records: The second common-law rule admitted the *regularly kept records* of a business. The utility of the common-law rule was curtailed by four requirements: (1) the entries had to be "original entries made in the routine of a business"; (2) the entries had to be made upon the "personal knowledge of the recorder or of someone reporting to him"; (3) they had to be made "at or near the time of the transaction recorded"; and (4) the recorder and his informant had to be shown to be *unavailable*. M, p. 872. The requirement of unavailability was especially cumbersome; often the recorder was available to testify, but the records were clearly better evidence than the recorder's memory, since the recorder may have recorded hundreds or thousands of similar transactions.

2. **Statutory reform:** Today, in virtually every jurisdiction, the admissibility of business records is governed by *statute* or court rule. In general, these statutes or rules follow the common-law approach, except that the requirement of unavailability of the recorder has almost always been *omitted*.

3. **Federal Rule:** FRE 803(6) is more or less representative of these statutes, except that on most controversial issues, it tends to be more liberal (i.e., to include more). 803(6) gives a hearsay exception, without regard to availability of the recorder, for:

"Records of regularly conducted activity. A memorandum, report, record, or data compilation, in any form, of acts, events, conditions, opinions, or diagnoses, made at or near the time by, or from information transmitted by, a person with knowledge, if kept in the course of a regularly conducted business activity, and if it was the regular practice of that business activity to make the memorandum, report, record, or data compilation, all as shown by the testimony of the custodian or other qualified witness, unless the source of information or the method or circumstances of preparation indicate lack of trustworthiness. The term 'business' as used in this paragraph includes business, institution, association, profession, occupation, and calling of every kind, whether or not conducted for profit."

   a. **Summary of requirements:** Observe that FRE 803(6), like most modern-day statutes or court rules, imposes three of the four requirements of the common-law "regularly-kept records" rule:

      i. **Regular entries:** The entries must be made in the *routine* of a *business* ("kept in the course of a regularly conducted business activity, and . . . it was the regular practice of that business activity to make the [record]");

      ii. **Knowledge:** The record must have been made by, or from information from, a person with *personal knowledge* of the matter recorded;

      iii. **Timeliness:** The entries must have been made *"at or near the time"* of the matter recorded.

C. **Definition of a "business":** Originally, the regularly-kept records exception only applied to a *"business,"* and the term "business" was construed quite literally. Today, most statutes are far broader. Thus FRE 803(6) applies to any record kept by a "business, institution, association, profession, occupation, and calling of any kind, whether or not conducted for profit." Thus *schools*, *churches*, and *hospitals* would be covered. S&R, p. 831.

D. **Person who originally supplies information:** The statutes and court rules pay special attention to the person who *originally supplies* the information that goes into the record. In most jurisdictions, this person must satisfy two requirements: (1) he must have *first-hand knowledge* of the fact he reports; and (2) he must do his reporting *while working in the business.*

1. **First-hand information:** Courts have generally insisted that the original source of the information be one with *first-hand knowledge* of the matter. Observe that this original source need not be the person who is actually making the entry. Thus FRE 803(6) merely requires that the record be "made . . . by, or from information transmitted by, a person with knowledge. . . ." For instance, if a delivery boy for a retail store reports to the clerk that he has dropped off a shipment at X Corp., the fact that the clerk who records that information lacks personal knowledge is irrelevant, since the source of the information is one who has first-hand information (the delivery boy).

2. **Requirement of business duty:** Suppose the person who supplies information from his own knowledge is *not acting on behalf of the business* that is making the record. Is the requirement of a "regularly kept business record" satisfied? Most courts that have considered the question have said, *"no."* The classic case on this issue is *Johnson v. Lutz*, 170 N.E. 517 (N.Y. 1930).

   a. **Facts:** *Johnson v. Lutz* involved an accident report prepared by a policeman based on information supplied to him by people present at the scene of the accident.

   b. **Holding:** The New York Court of Appeals refused to apply its recently-enacted business records statute to this situation. The court pointed out that the statute was enacted to avoid the need for having every member of a business who had participated in the preparation of a given record testify. "It was not intended to permit the receipt in evidence of entries based upon voluntary hearsay statements made by third parties not engaged in the business or under any duty in relation thereto."

   c. **Rationale:** This rationale and result have seemed reasonable to most courts and commentators who have considered the problem. A person who works for the business that is making the record, or has some other relation of duty to that business, may make mistakes, but his conduct is subject to safeguards: a person's employment in a business makes it likely that he is operating in a well-established routine shared by other employees, and that he will be subject to punishment by superiors if he makes a mistake. L&S, p. 442. There are no such safeguards, however, in the case of information supplied by a third person who does not work for the business that is keeping the record.

      Example: If X, a bystander at the accident, says, "Y caused the accident by going through a red light," there is no special reason to believe that X's statement is correct, merely because it ends up in a police officer's report. X's statement would not be admissible if another bystander heard it, and repeated it in court; why should X's out-of-court statement come into evidence merely because it happens to be transcribed by a policeman? *Id.*

   d. **Two-step admission:** Most courts would, however, allow a report to be introduced for the *limited purpose* of proving that the statement was made. If some *other exception* to the hearsay rule would apply directly to the statement, the record and the statement it includes can therefore come into evidence. For instance, in *Johnson v. Lutz*, if the policeman's report contained a statement made by the plaintiff, and the report was sought to be introduced by the defendant, this two-step analysis would lead to admission of the report: the report would come in under the business records exception (or the related public records exception; see *infra*, p. 204) for the limited purpose of proving that P made the statement; the statement itself would then come in under the exception for admissions (*supra*, p. 149). *Id.*

E. Made in "regular course of business": The business records exception was originally designed to cover records made during the everyday routine of a business, and integrally related to its operations. Where the record is of a sort that the business prepares only **rarely**, and does not relate to its day-to-day operations, does the exception nonetheless apply? The issue usually arises in the case of **accident reports** prepared by a business.

   1. *Palmer*: The leading case, the Supreme Court case of **Palmer v. Hoffman**, 318 U.S. 109 (1943), suggests that the exception does **not** apply to such non-routine records. But more recent cases have limited *Palmer* fairly narrowly to its facts.

      a. Facts: In *Palmer*, the plaintiffs were the spouse and estate of a person killed in a railroad grade crossing accident. The defendant railroad company tried to introduce a statement made after the accident by the train's engineer, in an interview conducted by a railroad supervisor and a member of the state Public Utilities Commission at the railroad's office. The then-applicable federal business records statute required that the record have been made "in the regular course of [the] business."

      b. Holding: The Supreme Court concluded that the accident report did not qualify under the statute, since it was not in the "regular course" of the railroad's business. Unlike, say, payroll or accounts receivable records, the accident reports "are calculated for use essentially in the court, not in the business. Their primary utility is in litigating, not in railroading."

      c. Criticism: The Court's reasoning in *Palmer* can be criticized. The railroad made a routine of investigating *every* accident in which it was involved; indeed, it probably could not have continued successfully in business without doing so.

         i. Self-serving nature: However, the Court was clearly correct that this kind of report is fundamentally different from, say, a payroll account. This report was made only once litigation had become likely, and the railroad (as well as the engineer who was making the statement) had a strong incentive to take a **self-serving** position, an incentive which is not present in the payroll records situation. Yet at the same time, the Court did not want to base the result directly on the self-serving nature of the record; otherwise, it might have had a problem admitting, say, accounts receivable records, where the business keeping the record has at least an arguable incentive to overstate the money owed to it.

   2. Modern view: In interpreting modern statutes, courts have followed the precise result in *Palmer*, but have limited that case somewhat narrowly to its facts.

a. **Rareness not dispositive:** Thus the mere fact that the type of record in question is kept rarely rather than in the business's everyday routine, is *not* in most courts sufficient to take the record out of the relevant statute or court rule. "Most courts feel that an activity may be in the regular course of business without being so frequent as to be routine." L&S, p. 443.

b. **Self-serving motive:** But most courts will *exclude* the record where they sense a strong motive on the part of the business or the employee-declarant to behave in a *self-serving* manner. This is especially likely in the case of accident reports or other documents prepared in anticipation of litigation. Thus most courts today would reach the same result on the facts of *Palmer* itself.

c. **Federal Rule:** The Federal Rules are in agreement with this general modern approach. FRE 803(6) requires merely that it have been the "regular practice of that business activity to make the memorandum. . . ." There is no requirement that the making of such records be frequent or routine. Yet the rule does not apply if "the source of information or the method or circumstances of preparation indicate *lack of trustworthiness*." Thus in a *Palmer*-like situation, where the record is an accident report prepared in anticipation of litigation, the trial judge has discretion under FRE 803(6) to exclude the record, and might well exercise that discretion.

3. **Police reports and records:** Where an accident or crime report is maintained by the *police*, the record may qualify under the business records exception — modern statutes may well include police operations (e.g., their activities are a "regularly conducted business activity" under FRE 803(6), and it would be the "regular practice of that business activity" to make accident or crime reports). However, a separate exception exists in most jurisdictions for *public* records and reports, and the rules for that exception may be different. Therefore, a question arises about the treatment of a police or other government report that would not be admissible for a particular use under the public records exception, but would be admissible under the business records exception. The most interesting version of this question is whether a police report or other government record that would not be admissible against a criminal defendant under FRE 803(8)(B) may nonetheless be admitted under the general business records exception of 803(6). Courts have split on this matter; the issue is discussed more extensively *infra*, p. 208.

F. **Opinions:** Sometimes the business record will contain an *opinion*. Courts and statutes vary substantially as to when a record containing an opinion may be introduced for the truth of that opinion.

1. **Speculative opinion:** In general, "the more speculative the opinion, the greater the probability of exclusion." L&S, p. 443.

2. **Lay opinions:** Where the opinion is a *"lay"* (as opposed to "expert") opinion, it will usually be *excluded*. If the lay opinion were given from the witness stand, it would probably be excluded under the general rule prohibiting such lay opinion testimony (see *infra*, p. 398.) Most courts will not permit such otherwise inadmissible testimony to come in in the form of a business record.

3. **Expert testimony:** Most cases involve *expert* opinions contained in the business record. The most common situation involves *hospital records*, where the physician or nurse has written an opinion about the nature of the patient's ailment, its cause, or its prognosis. Courts vary significantly in their treatment of such opinions; the issue is discussed in detail *infra*, p. 200.

4. **Federal Rules:** FRE 803(6) rejects the tendency of some courts to exclude opinions contained in business records. 803(6) expressly allows a record of "acts, events, conditions, opinions, or diagnoses. . . ." However, the court will usually be at least as strict as it would be were the opinion given in courtroom testimony; thus if the opinion is unduly speculative, the court has discretion to exclude it.

   a. **Basis for opinion not disclosed:** Furthermore, the court may decide to keep out opinion evidence that does not disclose the factual basis for the opinions — if the opinion were given in courtroom testimony, the expert could be examined about the basis for it; with a mere physical record restating the opinion, no such examination is possible, and the court may therefore conclude that the evidence is not sufficiently trustworthy. In reaching such a decision, the court can rely on 803(6)'s special exclusion where "the source of information or the method or circumstances of preparation indicate lack of trustworthiness."

G. **Trustworthiness:** As noted just above, even where the formal conditions for the business records exception are satisfied, the court may still exclude evidence that it finds to be unduly self-serving or otherwise *untrustworthy*. Most statutes and rules contain an implied or explicit exception similar to that of FRE 803(6), which allows the exclusion of evidence if "the source of information or the method or circumstances of preparation indicate lack of trustworthiness."

   Example: P, who has been injured in the course of his employment, makes a worker's compensation claim. For purposes of this claim, he is examined by several doctors, some retained by the insurance company and some retained by P. P then brings a civil action arising out of the same accident. He wishes to introduce the reports prepared by each of these doctors, instead of calling them to give trial testimony.

   Held, the reports of the physicians retained by D may be admitted, but those prepared by P's treating physicians may not be. Even though all reports were made in anticipation of litigation, the trustworthiness of the reports prepared by D's physicians is enhanced by the fact that they are being offered by a party adverse to the one on whose behalf the reports were made. The reports by P's physicians, on the other hand, are "self-serving with no added degree of trustworthiness." *Yates v. Bair Transport, Inc.*, 249 F.Supp. 681 (S.D.N.Y. 1965).

H. **Absence of entry:** Suppose that a regularly kept business record *fails* to contain a record of a particular event, and the circumstances are such that had that event taken place, the records would probably have reflected it. May the absence of an entry be introduced as evidence that the event did *not occur*?

1. **General rule:** Most courts ***allow*** the absence of the entry as evidence of the non-occurrence of the event. M, p. 875.

> **Example:** P, a merchant, routinely records receipt of payments from customers against outstanding invoices. P sues D for failure to pay an invoice. D defends on the grounds that it paid the invoice. Most courts would allow P to introduce its receivables records, which do not show any payment by D, as evidence that there was no payment by D.

2. **Federal Rule:** The Federal Rules agree with this principle. In fact, they contain a special provision governing it: FRE 803(7) provides a special hearsay exception for "evidence that a matter is not included in the memorandum, reports, record, or data compilations, in any form, kept in accordance with the provisions of paragraph (6), to prove the nonoccurrence or nonexistence of the matter, if the matter was of a kind of which a memorandum, report, or data compilation was regularly made and preserved, unless the sources of information or other circumstances indicate lack of trustworthiness."

    a. **May not be hearsay:** Most of the time, absence of an entry would not, under the Federal Rules, be hearsay at all. Recall (see *supra*, p. 139), that under the Federal Rules, conduct can only be hearsay if it is assertive. A business person's failure to record a transaction will generally not be assertive — that is, the record keeper is not intending to express to the world the fact that no transaction took place; the occasion to record the transaction simply never occurs. It is only in the rare instance where failure to make a notation is intended as a declaration that nothing has happened (and, furthermore, where that declaration is "trustworthy") that FRE 803(7) is ever really necessary. L&S, p. 446, n. 40. The Advisory Committee's Notes to FRE 803(7) explain that this generally-unnecessary exception exists only to set to rest any possible doubts about the admissibility of such evidence.

I. **Oral reports:** Suppose that a business person, in the regular course of the business, makes an ***oral*** report to a co-worker, rather than making a written record. Can this oral report be introduced into evidence (by being recounted by the co-worker who heard it) under the business records exception? Most courts hold that oral reports ***cannot*** fall within the exception; but a few courts have allowed them under an analogy to the business records exception.

> **Example:** Foreman reports to Boss that Employee has hurt his hand on a machine. It is Foreman's duty to report, orally, all on-the-job accidents to Boss. Most courts would not allow the business records exception to be used to allow Boss to testify at trial about the contents of the report given by Foreman; a few courts might allow it on this ground, however. The courts that excluded it might nonetheless allow it under the "residual" hearsay exception (see *infra*, p. 257). M, p. 874, and n. 8.

1. **Federal Rules:** The Federal Rules are silent about whether an oral report can ever come within the business records exception. The use of the term "report" within 803(6) suggests that an oral report might qualify, but the further requirement that

the report be "kept" probably means that oral reports cannot qualify. M, p. 874.

J. Proving the record: We turn now to the issue: How does a party "prove" a business record?

   1. **Not self-proving:** Business records are not "self-proving." That is, for a business record to fall within the exception, witnesses must testify that it meets the requirements of the exception.

   2. **Who must be called:** It is not necessary, under modern statutes, to call as a witness each person who participated in the making of the record. For instance, if A reported facts known to him to B, and B wrote them in the business' records, it is not necessary that both A and B testify about the making of the records. All that is required is that there be a witness who knows enough about a particular record-keeping process to be able to testify that: (1) it was the business' regular practice to make such a record; (2) the particular record in question was made in the regular course of business on the personal knowledge of the recorder or someone reporting to him; (3) the person with the first-hand knowledge was acting in the regular course of the business; and (4) the entries were made at or near the time of the transaction. M, p. 881. Typically, that witness will be "a person in authority in the ***record-keeping department*** of the business." *Id.*

K. Special situations: We conclude our discussion of the business record exception by examining two special contexts that have raised special problems: (1) hospital records; and (2) computer printouts.

   1. **Hospital records:** *Hospital records* are often introduced to prove the truth of statements contained in them.

      a. **General rule:** Generally speaking, a hospital record will almost always be found to be one regularly made during the course of an ongoing business activity. Therefore, the requirements of the business records exception will generally be found to be satisfied. M, p. 882. However, two special kinds of problems can be presented by such records, which may lead to certain statements contained in the record being excluded.

      b. **Factual statements unrelated to treatment or diagnosis:** First, when the patient gives the history of his ailment, and this history is recorded, it may contain a variety of statements. Those statements that are ***relevant*** to ***treatment*** or ***diagnosis*** (e.g., "I was a hit by a car" or "I was hit in the head with a baseball bat") will be treated as having been recorded within the "regular course" of the hospital's business, since the business of a hospital is the giving of treatment and diagnosis. If, on the other hand, statements are recorded that are totally unrelated to any conceivable treatment or diagnosis, the recording of these statements will not be treated as falling within the hospital's regular course of business, and that aspect of the record will not be admissible under the business records exception. M, p. 883.

         Example: P is injured by being hit by D's car. At trial, P offers part of his hospital record. D then attempts to introduce a different part of the hospital record, which recites that P told a doctor at the hospital that "[P] was crossing the street and an automobile ran into another automobile that was at a standstill, causing this car (standstill) to run into him."

Held, this part of the hospital record is inadmissible. Only acts or occurrences cited in a hospital record that are "germane to diagnosis or treatment" are admissible under the business records exception. It might have been useful to the doctor to know that P had been struck by *an* automobile. "However, whether the patient was hit by car A or car B, by car A under its own power or propelled forward by car B, or whether the injuries were caused by the negligence of the defendant or of another, cannot possibly bear on diagnosis or aid in determining treatment." *Williams v. Alexander*, 129 N.E.2d 417 (N.Y. 1955).

But a dissenting judge pointed out that P had already put the hospital record in evidence. Therefore, this dissenting judge argued, P had "vouched for" the authenticity of the record, and it should have been treated as satisfying the requirement of being made in the regular course of the hospital's business. The underlying statement by P, in turn, should have been admissible under the "admission" exception. (See *supra*, p. 149.)

i. **Second-level problem:** If the statements recorded do not relate to diagnosis and treatment (as the majority in *Williams* found that that statement did not), the record is not admissible even for the limited purpose of proving that the statement was made, let alone to prove the truth of the statement. M, p. 883. If the recorded statement does relate to treatment and diagnosis, the business records exception allows the record to be admitted for the limited purpose of proving that the statement was made. But normally, the business records exception does not by itself allow the record to be used as evidence of the *truth* of the statement, because of the generally-accepted rule of *Johnson v. Lutz, supra*, p. 195 — since the statement about symptoms, causation, etc., is usually made by the *patient*, and since the patient has *no duty to the hospital* to relate the information, the patient is not acting in the course of the hospital's business. Therefore, the situation is like that of the bystander/informant in *Johnson*, and the admission of the record is *not evidence of the truth of the patient's statement. Id.*

ii. **Other exception:** However, often some *other exception* will make the patient's statement admissible notwithstanding the hearsay rule. For instance, if the patient is the plaintiff and the statement is offered by the defendant, the exception for admissions (*supra*, p. 149) will be enough to make the statement evidence of the truth of the matter asserted. Thus in *Williams*, if the majority had accepted the notion that P's statements were germane to treatment or diagnosis, not only would the overall record have been able to come into evidence, but the particular statement would then have been admissible against P as an admission.

c. **Expert opinions:** The second problem presented by hospital records is that they will often contain *opinions* by physicians, concerning causation, prognosis, etc. The physician, if he were giving that same opinion in live testimony at trial, would normally be qualified to do so as an expert. (See *infra*, p. 402.) Yet courts are somewhat more reluctant to allow such opinions to come in via the hospital record, because the physician is not available to explain the basis for his opinion, or to be cross-examined about it.

    i. General rule: Therefore, courts tend to be somewhat stricter about receiving such opinions in records than they would be about receiving the opinion in live testimony. "The more speculative the opinion, the greater the probability of exclusion." L&S, p. 443.

    ii. Objective criteria: Thus where the patient's symptoms are reasonably *objective*, and the diagnosis or prognosis is reasonably cut-and-dried (e.g., a fractured elbow or appendicitis), nearly all courts would allow the attending physician's notation of diagnosis and prognosis into evidence. But where the appropriate diagnosis is, on the facts, much less certain, courts may exclude the record containing the opinion, even where they would accept that same opinion from that same physician at trial.

    Example: Suppose the hospital record contains the following notation written by the physician: "Diagnosis: substantial lung damage resulting from black lung disease due to working in a poorly ventilated coal mine." L&S, p. 444, suggests that "most courts would admit the entry to show lung damage, some would admit it to show black lung disease, but few, if any, would admit it to show that the disease was caused by poor working conditions."

    iii. Causation and prognosis: Courts are more willing to admit medical opinions that relate to precise diagnosis of a medical condition, than opinions regarding *etiology* (i.e., what caused the illness), or *prognosis* (i.e., prospects for recovery). L&S, p. 443.

2. Computer print-outs: Many if not most business records today are kept *on computer* rather than on paper. If a party wishes to prove that a fact is as recorded on a computer maintained by the party, this will generally have to be done by presenting a computer *print-out*. Since the print-out is not a primary record, but merely a collection or arrangement of "real" data stored in the computer, use of print-outs under the business records exception poses special problems.

    a. Generally applicable: In general, courts have held that the business records exception *applies* to computer print-outs, so long as a proper foundation is laid.

    b. Time of entry: Recall that the business records exception requires that the record have been prepared "at or near the time" of the event being recorded. When a computer print-out is presented as evidence, when should the record be deemed to have been "made"? If the relevant time is when the *print-out* was prepared, this will generally be after litigation has begun, and long after the event being recorded. Therefore, the print-out would only rarely satisfy the rule. However, courts that have considered the issue have generally concluded that the requirement of timeliness means only that the data must have been *entered* into the computer at or near the time of the event.

c. Trustworthiness: Recall (*supra*, p. 197) that the business records exception will not apply where the judge concludes that the record is ***untrustworthy***. The proponent's need to make an affirmative showing of trustworthiness is stronger in the case of computerized records than for hard-copy records — the degree of reliability of a written record will often be evident from an inspection of the record itself, whereas a computer print-out may appear to be quite meticulous and accurate, yet be based upon some hidden flaw in the procedures used to prepare it. Therefore, the witness who vouches for a computer print-out must generally testify as to the following:

    i. Equipment: At least a general description of the equipment;

    ii. Programming: How the computer has been programmed, and how errors in programming are detected and corrected;

    iii. Data entry: How the data is ***entered*** into the computer;

    iv. Controls: What controls are used to ***detect errors*** at any stage in the procedure, especially errors in data entry and errors in the preparation of the final print-out; and

    v. Security: Ways that unauthorized ***access*** to the programs and data files is prevented.

    See M, p. 886.

d. *Monarch* case: The above requirements are taken seriously by at least some courts. See, e.g., *Monarch Federal Savings & Loan Assoc. v. Genser*, 383 A.2d 475 (N.J. Sup. Ct. 1977), excluding a print-out purporting to show that the defendant was behind on his mortgage, on the grounds that the sponsoring witness did not testify, *inter alia*, about "the type of computer used and its acceptance in the field as standard, efficient and accurate equipment [nor] as to the competency of those who program the computer and process the daily input, [nor about] the input controls or the mechanics of the machines."

e. Risk of error: Observe that even with the above safeguards, the opponent of computerized evidence faces a difficult burden. Suppose, for instance, that in the *Monarch* case both the foreclosing mortgage company and the defending debtor agreed that the defendant had made a particular payment, and the sole issue was whether it was before or after expiration of a grace period. The defendant would be unlikely to have kept a paper record showing when he sent the payment in (and his cancelled check would merely reflect the date the check was drawn, a quite different issue). If the mortgage company's director of data processing testified, in appropriate detail, that his department "always" entered checks promptly and verified its work, how could the defendant rebut this testimony, except by placing his word against "the word of the computer"? Yet in this particular instance, the clerks in plaintiff's office may well have erred; the result is that the individual defendant, rather than the large-company plaintiff, ends up bearing the burden of record keeping.

    i. Solution: L&S, p. 445, assert that "this seems unfair when the errors to be avoided are the organization's." They suggest that "perhaps businesses should be required to keep the original records of any transactions until their dealings indicate that there is no dispute about the accuracy of their computer entries. Only then would the computer entry be admissible in lieu of the original." *Id.*

VII. PUBLIC RECORDS AND REPORTS

A. Exception generally: There is a common-law hearsay exception for *public records* and *reports* that is similar to the exception for business records. This exception, as codified in most states and in the Federal Rules, is an extremely important one because of the wide variety of material that it allows into evidence in both civil and criminal trials.

B. Common-law rule: The common-law form of the rule allows the admission of a *written report or record* of a *public official* if: (1) the official (or perhaps his subordinate) had *first-hand knowledge* of the facts reported; and (2) the official had a *duty* to make the record or report. M, p. 888.

    1. Rationale: The rationale for the exception is similar to that for the business records exception: An official who has knowledge of the facts, and a duty to report them, is likely to produce a reliable record.

    2. Self-authenticating: Many government records and reports could qualify under the business records exception (*supra*, p. 193) as well as under the public records exception. But there is a key difference between these two exceptions that usually leads the proponent to use the public records exception: Whereas the business records exception applies only where a person with relevant knowledge of the record keeping system testifies at trial, the public records exception can be used *without any testimony at all*, if a certification procedure is used.

        a. Certification: If each time a public record were offered in evidence, testimony from the official in charge of the records was required, many officials would do little but give testimony. Similarly, if the *original* record were required (as is the case for most other kinds of documents; see *infra*, p. 375) filing problems would be unmanageable. Therefore, all states have established, by statute or court rule, *certification* procedures to deal with these two problems. Typically, the official in charge of a particular department makes a copy of a given public record, and attaches his certificate that the copy is a true copy of the original. This copy can then be entered into evidence, *without any testimony*. See, e.g., FRE 902(4) and 1005; see also *infra*, p. 371.

    3. Not necessarily open to public: The common-law exception is generally held to apply even to those records and reports which are *not* otherwise *open to the public*. M, p. 889. For instance, a state or federal Freedom of Information Act provision could be used to obtain otherwise secret government records, which could then be introduced under the public records exception.

4. **Evaluative reports:** Most courts have limited the common law rule to reports that are essentially *factual* in nature. Thus *evaluative* reports have not usually been allowed under the exception; for instance, if a police report contained a notation by the reporting officer, "Accident seems to have been caused by Smith's careless driving," most courts would not allow it into evidence under the exception. (But cases under the Federal Rules have been more liberal on this issue; see *infra*, p. 210.)

C. **Federal Rule:** The principal Federal Rule governing public records and reports, FRE 803(8), has been extraordinarily influential. That rule provides a hearsay exception for:

"Public records and reports. Records, reports, statements, or data compilations, in any form, of public offices or agencies, setting forth (A) the activities of the office or agency, or (B) matters observed pursuant to duty imposed by law as to which matters there was a duty to report, excluding, however, in criminal cases matters observed by police officers and other law enforcement personnel, or (C) in civil actions and proceedings and against the Government in criminal cases, factual findings resulting from an investigation made pursuant to authority granted by law, unless the sources of information or other circumstances indicate lack of trustworthiness."

1. **Focus:** Because of the importance of 803(8), our remaining discussion of the public records exception focuses on the Federal Rules' treatment. Many states have a nearly identical provision; but other states may have statutes, especially ones adopted before the enactment of the Federal Rules, that are quite different on key issues (e.g., the admissibility of investigative reports).

2. **Uses of Rule:** Because government today is so active, and performs investigations in so many situations, in a high proportion of litigations there will be a relevant government report or record. Here are some ways government reports may be relevant:

   a. **Accident:** In a vehicular accident, there will usually be a *police report*;

   b. **Antitrust:** In a civil antitrust case, there may well be industry market-share studies prepared by the Justice Department's Antitrust Division;

   c. **Plane crash:** In a suit arising out of an airplane crash, an *FAA report* on the causes of the crash will be highly relevant;

   d. **Job discrimination:** In a suit by an employee against an employer for *job discrimination* based on sex or race, various federal or state agencies may have already investigated and made a report.

   See generally, L&S, p. 447.

D. **Three categories:** As is obvious from the text of FRE 803(8), it divides public records and reports into three categories:

1. **Activities of the office:** The first, subsection (A), covers reports that are also covered under the traditional common-law approach. An agency's records of its *own activities* can be used to show that those activities occurred.

   Example: Following an airplane crash, the FAA sends an inspector to the crash scene, who attempts to determine the cause of the crash. Under subsection (A), the FAA's records may be used to show that the investigation took place (but not to show what the results of it were — that would have to come in under subsection (C) if at all).

2. **Matters observed under duty:** Subsection (B) also goes no further than the common-law exception. The written records of **observations** made by public officials are admissible if: (1) the observations were made in the **line of duty**; and (2) the official had a **duty to report** those observations.

> **Example:** Suppose an IRS auditor goes to the Smith household to conduct a field audit of the Smith's tax return. Mr. Smith claims a business deduction for "an office at home." The auditor finds no evidence of such an office, and says so in his report. In a subsequent civil suit between Mr. Smith and his business partner, Mr. Jones, either side could, under FRE 803(8)(B), use the report as proof of the fact that Mr. Smith did not maintain an office at home.
>
> Now, however, assume that the auditor also noticed that Mr. Smith possessed cocaine, and put this fact into his report. Since the auditor had no duty to report non-tax-related matters, this aspect of the report could not be introduced in the later civil suit.

a. **Oral reports:** Suppose, in the above example, the IRS auditor made an **oral** report to his supervisor about Mr. Smith's lack of a home office. By the literal language of FRE 803(8)(B), the hearsay exception extends to "statements," and it could be argued that the supervisor may testify about what the auditor told her. However, everything in the legislative history of FRE 803 suggests that Congress had in mind only written records, and a court would probably reject this attempt to use the rule to get oral statements into evidence. L&S, p. 448. (But if the **supervisor** made notes of the auditor's statements, those notes would be admissible under FRE 803(8)(B). *Id.*)

b. **Criminal cases:** Subsection (B) by its terms does not apply in **criminal cases** to "matters observed by police officers and other law enforcement personnel. . . ." It is clear that such police reports cannot be used **against** the criminal defendant; it is not so clear whether they may be used **by** the criminal defendant. The matter is discussed more extensively *infra*, p. 207.

3. **Investigative reports:** The last category in FRE 803(8), covered by subsection (C), involves **investigative reports**.

a. **Evaluative:** Subsection (C) allows into evidence only **"factual findings"** that result from investigation. However, most courts have viewed this requirement that the findings be "factual" somewhat liberally, and have accepted reports that include a substantial **"evaluative"** component. How evaluative a report may be and still be accepted as "factual" for purposes of subsection (C) is discussed more extensively *infra*, p. 210.

b. **No use against criminal defendant:** By the express terms of subsection (C), investigative reports may **not** be used **against** a criminal defendant. The purpose of this restriction is to prevent the prosecution from basing its case upon police reports and other inculpatory documents; law enforcement officials must give **personal testimony** at trial, rather than hiding behind the written report.

Example: Police Officer, investigating the murder of V, writes a report in which she concludes, "For all these reasons, this killing was certainly committed by D." Regardless of whether Police Officer is available to testify at the murder trial of D, the report will not be usable by the prosecution. Rather, Police Officer must give live testimony regarding the reasons why she believes the murder was done by D.

E. Criminal cases: Many of the issues involving FRE 803(8) have arisen in the context of criminal prosecutions, especially situations in which the prosecution desires to use the exception to admit evidence against the accused. Our discussion below applies to all three subsections of 803(8), unless otherwise noted.

1. **Federal language:** Both subsection (B) and (C), by their literal language, prevent the prosecution from using materials against the accused in a criminal case. Thus if a police officer happened to see D commit a crime, and put his observations into a required daily activity report, this report would not be admissible against D in a criminal prosecution under subsection (B). Similarly, if a police officer did not witness the crime, but conducted an after-the-fact investigation of the crime, his investigative report would not be admissible against D under subsection (C).

2. **Accused's use of subsection (B):** Subsection (B), by its literal language, excludes from the coverage of that section "in criminal cases matters observed by police officers and other law enforcement personnel." Thus the section does not merely exclude *prosecution* use of such materials in a criminal case, but ostensibly also *defense* use of such matters.

    a. **Liberal interpretation:** Observe that this phrasing is quite different from that of subsection of (C), where investigative reports are usable "against the government in criminal cases." The only reason why subsection (B) is drafted differently (and probably more clumsily) is that the language was hastily added on the floor of the House of Representatives, which was afraid that otherwise criminal defendants might be tried on the basis of police reports. Therefore, at least some of the courts that have interpreted subsection (B) have concluded that the section ***bars only the government, not the accused,*** from using such evidence. See, e.g., *U.S. v. Smith*, 521 F.2d 957 (D.C.Cir. 1975).

3. **"Other law enforcement personnel":** Subsection (B) does not apply to matters observed by police officers "and other law enforcement personnel." It is not clear what other types of individuals, apart from police officers, are included in this phrase "other law enforcement personnel." For instance, are ***laboratory technicians*** who work for law enforcement agencies doing substance analysis, to be treated as "law enforcement personnel" whose accounts of tests they make are therefore excluded?

    a. *Oates* **case:** The most important decision so far on this issue concluded that a Customs Service chemist who had identified a substance as being heroin was "without question, [an] important participant . . . in the prosecutorial effort," so that his report could not be admitted under subsection (B). See *U.S. v. Oates*, 560 F.2d 45 (2d Cir. 1977), discussed further *infra*, p. 208.

4. Routine observations: Does subsection (B)'s exclusion of "in criminal cases [reports of] matters observed by police officers and other law enforcement personnel" apply to *routine* police records? Or does it apply only to reports of episodes that are by their very nature confrontational, as when a police officer witnesses what he realizes at the time is a crime? The courts that have considered the question have generally answered that *routine*, non-adversarial observations that happen to be incorporated in police records are *not excluded* from criminal trials. M, pp. 891-92.

> **Example:** The Ds, who are involved on the Catholic side of the conflict in Northern Ireland, are charged with federal weapons violations. The prosecution seeks to introduce routine Irish police records of serial numbers and weapons receipts, showing that certain weapons were found in Northern Ireland after a certain date.
>
> *Held*, these records were admissible under FRE 803(8)(B), because the exclusionary language in that subsection covers only "police officers' reports of their contemporaneous observations of crime," not routine bureaucratic observations of events that were not in themselves criminal acts. *U.S. v. Grady*, 544 F.2d 598 (2d Cir. 1976).

5. Use of "business records" or other rules: Reports by the police of matters they have observed, or investigations they have conducted, will often appear to qualify under *other* hearsay exceptions apart from FRE 803(8). For instance, a laboratory report might appear to qualify as a *business record* under 803(6), and a police officer's contemporaneous notes of a crime he has witnessed will often appear to meet the requirements for past recollection recorded under FRE 803(5). The issue arises, therefore: Does the fact that a police report offered against the defendant in a criminal case is excluded from 803(8)(B) or (C) also mean that these other exceptions may not be used? The issue is probably the most important one that has arisen in the public records area. Courts are split, but the trend seems to be in favor of *allowing the use of other exceptions,* at least if the person who made the report is available for cross-examination at trial. M, p. 892.

    a. General principle: In general, hearsay exceptions *stand alone* — the fact that one exception is unavailable (even expressly made inapplicable) in a given situation does not mean that some other exception cannot be used. Thus if this general principle were to control, a police report would be allowed to come in under the business record exception, the past recollection recorded exception, or perhaps even FRE 803(24)'s residual exception (see *infra*, p. 258).

    b. *Oates* case excludes: Nonetheless, the first major case to consider the issue concluded unequivocally, and broadly, that "police and evaluative reports not satisfying the standards of FRE 803(8)(B) and (C) may not qualify for admission under FRE 803(6) or any of the other exceptions to the hearsay rule." *U.S. v. Oates*, 560 F.2d 45 (2d Cir. 1977).

        i. Facts: D was charged with heroin distribution. The prosecution offered as evidence a laboratory report prepared by a chemist who was a full-time employee of the United States Customs Service, reporting that analysis showed that the substance seized was indeed heroin. The government claimed that the chemist who prepared the report was "unavailable" (though it did not explain why, or appear to make any major any attempt to produce him); instead it put on the stand another chemist from the Department who explained the steps that the Department customarily goes through in performing a heroin test.

ii. **Result:** The Second Circuit Court of Appeals held that the report should ***not*** have been admitted.

iii. **Covered by (B) and (C):** First, the court concluded that the report was covered by the general provisions of 803(8)(B) and (C). It then found that under these two subsections, the report would be inadmissible, because of the exclusion for use against criminal defendants. This exclusion was quite clear in the case of (C); it was probable in the case of (B), since, in the court's view, "other law enforcement personnel" included full-time Customs Service Chemists. (See *supra*, p. 207.) Therefore, the issue became: Is a report that is expressly excluded from admission by 803(8) nonetheless admissible under some other hearsay exception, in this case the business records exception of 803(6)?

iv. **Excluded:** The court then concluded that "it was the clear intention of Congress to make evaluative and law enforcement reports ***absolutely inadmissible*** against defendants in criminal cases." Therefore, even though the report might seem to be admissible under the literal language of 803(6)'s business records exception, "803(6) must be read in conjunction with FRE 803(8)(B) and (C). . . . The prosecution's utilization of any hearsay exception to achieve admission of evaluative and law enforcement reports would serve to deprive the accused of the opportunity to confront his accusers as effectively as would reliance on a 'public records' exception. Thus, there being no apparent reason why Congress would tolerate the admission of evaluative and law enforcement reports by use of some other exception to the hearsay rule . . . it simply makes no sense to surmise that Congress ever intended that these records could be admissible against a defendant in a criminal case under *any* of the Federal Rules of Evidence's exceptions to the hearsay rule. . . ."

v. **Narrower ground rejected:** The court also observed that there was reason to doubt the trustworthiness of the particular report at issue, because of crossed-out notations and other reasons. But the court explicitly declined to rely on 803(6)'s exclusion on account of factors indicating "lack of trustworthiness."

c. **Subsequent cases:** The *Oates* court seemed to be saying that so long as a document is an "evaluative [or] law enforcement report," it is ***automatically*** absolutely inadmissible against a criminal defendant no matter what other hearsay exceptions it seems to fall under. If this is what the court meant, most subsequent decisions from other courts have ***not agreed***. Many have adopted the following modification: "The limitations of [FRE 803(8)](B) and (C) will not be extended to other hearsay exceptions if the maker is ***produced in court as*** *a witness*, subject to cross-examination, since the essential purpose of the Congress was simply to avoid uncross-examined evidence." M, p. 892. Thus under the view of most courts other than the Second Circuit, if the chemist who prepared the report in *Oates* were placed on the stand, the report itself could be introduced in evidence against the accused.

  i. Additional suggestion: Even where the maker of the report is not available, commentators have suggested a further modification of the *Oates* approach. Thus L&S, p. 451, agree that where the report is a record of the police's observation of what they believe, at the time they are observing, is a criminal act (e.g., an officer sees a burglary take place and writes it up in his report), the *Oates* court was correct to prevent the business records exception or some other exception from applying — this is exactly the sort of situation Congress had in mind when it enacted the explicit prohibition on admission into subsections (B) and (C). But where the report does not involve contemporaneous observation of a crime, other exceptions, like the business records exception, should be available; for instance, the recording of a weapon's serial number or the license plates of all cars crossing a certain checkpoint should be admissible under the business records exception, even in a court which would hold that these are not admissible under 803(8)(B) or (C). (But notice that, in most courts, these would be considered "routine" observations admissible under 803(8)(B) anyway.)

  ii. Laboratory: Furthermore, it has been suggested that since a report by a *private laboratory* in the *Oates* drug-test situation would clearly have been admissible under the business records exception, it is hard to see why the report by a full-time chemist who follows the same scientific procedures and has the same level of expertise (and as to whom there is no particular reason to question the impartiality) should be treated differently. S&R, p. 837. This, too, seems to be the kind of situation that Congress did ***not*** have in mind when it excluded police reports from (B) and (C); thus S&R believe that *Oates* itself was decided by wrong reasoning, and that the result, though it may have been correct, should have been based on the probable untrustworthiness of the particular report at issue there. *Id.*

F. Other issues: Other issues under 803(8) arise in all contexts, not just in the context of a criminal case where the prosecution tries to use the evidence.

  1. "Factual" versus "evaluative": Subsection (C), which applies to investigative reports, by its terms applies only to *"factual findings"* resulting from the investigation. The interpretation of the phrase "factual findings" has been the subject of much dispute; are *"opinions,"* *"evaluations,"* and *"conclusions"* contained in an investigative report admissible?

  a. Admission allowed: The Supreme Court finally answered *"yes"* to this question in *Beech Aircraft Corp. v. Rainey*, 488 U.S. 153 (1988). So long as the investigative report is based on factual statements, ***the conclusions or opinions stated in it are admissible***, along with the other portions of the report.

Example: The Ps die when the Navy plane they are piloting suddenly loses altitude, crashes and burns. The Ps sue D, the plane's manufacturer. The defense offers into evidence an investigative report prepared by the Nacy, which includes sections called "findings of fact" and "opinions." In the "opinions" section, the report contains a statement that "the most probable cause of the accident was the pilots [sic] failure to maintain proper interval." Over the Ps' objections, this "opinion" is allowed into evidence. The jury returns a verdict for the Ds.

Held (by the U.S. Supreme Court), the trial judge properly allowed the "opinions" portion of the report into evidence. Nothing in the legislative history of FRE 803 suggests that the drafters meant to distinguish between "facts" and "opinions" contained in investigative reports. Also, there is great analytical difficulty in drawing a line between fact and opinion. Therefore, portions of investigatory reports otherwise admissible under Rule 803(8)(C) are not inadmissible merely because they state a conclusion or opinion. "As long as the conclusion is based on a factual investigation and satisfies the Rule's trustworthiness requirement, it should be admissible along with other portions of the report." *Beech Aircraft Corp. v. Rainey, supra.*

b. **Examples from lower courts:** Before *Beech Aircraft*, most lower federal courts considering the issue agreed with the Supreme Court's ultimate decision in *Beech*, that evaluations, opinions and conclusions contained in investigative reports could be admitted. Here are two examples of opinions and conclusions allowed into evidence:

   i. FCC decisions concluding that AT&T's tariffs are "unreasonable" and "discriminatory." *Litton Systems Inc. v. AT&T*, 700 F.2d 785 (2d Cir. 1983); and

   ii. An HEW Hearing Examiner's finding that a particular school was established as a black school (admitted in a segregation suit). *U.S. v. School District of Ferndale*, 577 F.2d 1339 (6th Cir. 1978).

c. **Legal conclusions not allowed:** However, courts will generally not allow that portion of a report to be admitted that includes a ***"legal"*** conclusion. For instance, in a tort case, a report concluding that the defendant was "negligent" should probably not be admitted (or at least, that conclusion should be excised), since this is clearly a conclusion of law. (But a portion of the report concluding that the defendant was driving faster than the speed limit would probably be admitted; this may be a "conclusion" based upon other facts such as skid marks, but it would not be a conclusion of law. W&B, Par. 803(8)[03].)

2. **Trustworthiness in (C) cases:** Recall that 803(8) allows the judge to exclude a report that would otherwise be admissible if "the sources of information or other circumstances indicate ***lack of trustworthiness.***" This exception is discussed more extensively *infra*, p. 214. However, it is quite clear that it not only applies, but is very important, in subsection (C) cases.

a. **Factors:** In fact, the Advisory Committee's Note to subsection (C) lists several factors which should be taken into account in determining whether an evaluative report is sufficiently trustworthy to be admissible:

   i. The *timeliness* of the investigation;

   ii. The "special *skill* or *experience* of the official";

   iii. Whether a *hearing was held* and the level at which it was conducted; and

   iv. Possible *"motivation problems"* (e.g., the incentive that the railroad and its engineer had in *Palmer v. Hoffman, supra,* p. 196, when they gave statements about the railroad accident that were then contained in the government report on the accident).

b. *Baker* **case:** These factors were applied, and found to establish trustworthiness, in *Baker v. Elcona Homes Corp.,* 588 F.2d 551 (6th Cir. 1978).

   i. **Facts:** *Baker* involved the investigative report prepared by an Ohio State Highway Patrolman after a car accident. The report contained two items whose admissibility was questioned: (1) a transcription of a statement made by D to the police officer; and (2) the officer's notation that "apparently [the Ps' car] entered the intersection against their red light."

   ii. **Factors considered:** The court began by concluding that the report should be admitted, if at all, under 803(8) (rather than as a recorded recollection under 803(5), because that rule does not allow the document to be admitted as an exhibit unless offered by an adverse party, and the report was in fact offered as an exhibit by its proponent, D). The court then concluded that the report's contents constituted "factual findings" even though they were in some sense evaluative. Finally, the court applied the Advisory Committee's factors for measuring trustworthiness, listed above.

   iii. **Conclusion:** The court concluded that the report should be admitted: first, it was timely because the officer arrived at the scene of the accident soon after it occurred; second, the officer was highly experienced in accident reconstruction; the third requirement (hearing) was irrelevant; and finally, there was no sign of any lack of objectivity by the officer, who had no apparent motive to favor one side over the other. Therefore, the report had sufficient indicia of trustworthiness to be admissible.

3. **Multiple hearsay:** As was the case with the business records exception, public records may raise problems of *multiple hearsay*. This problem will arise any time the report *quotes statements made by others.* This can be the case either in a subsection (B) "report of matters observed" situation or in a subsection (C) investigative report context. Three distinct situations must be analyzed:

a. **Report by one government agent to another:** First, there may be two government agents involved, one who has knowledge of the facts and a duty to report them, and the other who makes up the report. In this situation, by analogy to the business records exception (*supra,* p. 193), it is clear that if the report quotes the first agent's statements, the quoted statements may come in as evidence of the truth of the matters they assert. L&S, p. 450.

Example: Police Officer Jones witnesses a car accident. He goes back to the station house and says to Officer Smith, "I saw the green Plymouth go through a light and cause an accident." Smith records this statement in a report he compiles on the accident. Almost certainly, the entire report, including the quoted statement by Jones, will be admissible under 803(8)(B), in a civil case concerning the accident.

b. **Statements by those without duty to talk:** The quoted statements may, by contrast, be ones made by third persons who had *no duty* to talk to the government. Unless these statements themselves fall under some other hearsay exception (e.g., they are made by a party and are offered against that party), they will *not* be admissible even though the report as a whole may fall within 803(8). In that event, the report will be entered, but with the quoted statements excised. L&S, p. 450.

Example 1: On the facts of the above example, assume that Officer Jones also took down a statement by Brown, a passer-by. If the final report prepared by Smith says, "Brown said that the car driven by D ran a red light," this statement will be excluded, because it is hearsay that does not fall within any independent exception.

Example: In the *Baker* case, *supra*, p. 212, D's statement to the police officer was not automatically admissible even though the report itself was, since D had no duty to make the report of the accident. However, because the cross-examination of D at trial suggested that D had changed his story, D's statement to the police officer was admissible on behalf of D under 801(d)(1)(B), which allows a witness' prior statement to be admitted if it is "consistent with his testimony and is offered to rebut an express or implied charge against him of recent fabrication or improper influence or motive. . . ."

c. **Reports based on statements:** Finally, it may happen that the report makes findings based on hearsay statements made by others, but the report does not quote those statements. When this happens, the report is not automatically rendered inadmissible because of this hearsay basis. Thus in the above example, if Jones' report merely stated his conclusion that the accident had been caused by D's car going through a red light, it would not be rendered inadmissible because it was based on statements from third parties with no duty to speak to the police, which statements would have been inadmissible hearsay had they been quoted in the report.

i. **Untrustworthy:** However, the extent to which investigative findings in a report are based on inadmissible hearsay is a factor that the court should consider in determining whether the report should be excluded because "the sources of information or other circumstances indicate lack of *trustworthiness*" (the last sentence of 803(8)). Thus a report that is based entirely on such inadmissible hearsay is far more likely to be excluded on grounds of untrustworthiness than one which is based upon a small amount of hearsay but mostly upon, say, scientific testing, observation by law enforcement officials, or other sources that would themselves be admissible. L&S, p. 450.

4. **Trustworthiness in (A) and (B) cases:** The last clause of 803(8) (" . . . unless the sources of information or other circumstances indicate lack of trustworthiness") creates a grammatical ambiguity. It is not clear whether that proviso applies only to cases falling under subsection (C) (investigative reports), or whether it also applies to situations falling under (A) and (B). However, it seems almost certain that, on policy grounds, the proviso should be interpreted to **apply to all three subsections.** Thus if a building inspector writes a report stating that he has inspected premises at 1865 Palmer Avenue and found them to be in good repair (a report that would normally be admissible under 803(8)(B)), the judge could and should use the proviso to exclude the report if other evidence is presented that the building inspector was bribed by the property owner to prepare a favorable report.

VIII. MISCELLANEOUS EXCEPTIONS — AVAILABILITY IMMATERIAL

A. **In general:** We cover now the remaining "declarant's availability immaterial" exceptions to the hearsay rule.

B. **Learned writings and commercial publications:** Suppose that a party wants to prove a proposition of science, medicine, or other fact by showing that the authoritative professional **treatises** on the subject say that that fact is so. Such proof would clearly present a hearsay problem — the out-of-court treatise writer's assertion of fact would be used to show the truth of that fact. Yet, a treatise, professional journal, or other learned writing is free from at least some of the traditional hearsay problems — for instance, "the treatise is written primarily and impartially for professionals, subject to scrutiny and exposure for inaccuracy, with the reputation of the writer at stake." Advisory Committee Note to FRE 803(18). Yet, the most fundamental hearsay problem — that the writer/declarant is **not available for cross-examination** — remains in full force. Furthermore, there is an additional problem — a work prepared for a professional may well be misunderstood and misused by a lay juror.

1. **Common law:** For these reasons, the vast majority of common-law courts have **refused to allow** learned writings to be introduced as **substantive evidence**.

   a. **Cross-examination:** However, nearly all courts have permitted at least some use of learned treatises as part of the **cross-examination** of an **expert witness**.

      Example: P, a plaintiff in a medical malpractice action, has not been able to find an expert witness to testify that D's treatment of P's condition failed to meet the relevant local standards of care. However, he has found a medical treatise by a leading medical professor that unambiguously criticizes the method used by D. Under the common-law approach, P cannot get the treatise into evidence as part of his substantive case. However, if D puts on an expert witness, W, who testifies that D's conduct comported with professional standards, P may be able to use the treatise on cross-examination of W. In virtually all courts, if W says that his opinion of the propriety of P's treatment was formed in part by W's reliance on the treatise, P can show that the treatise contradicts W's opinion. In some courts, even if W has not relied on the treatise, P can ask W whether he considers the treatise to be a recognized authority in the field, and if so, P can then use the treatise for impeachment. Other courts are even more liberal — so long as P can show by *any means* (even judicial notice) that the treatise is a recognized authority, he can use it to cross-examine W. M, p. 900.

b. Limited use: Remember that under the common-law approach, even though the treatise may be used on cross-examination, it is used only to undermine the witness' competency or dispute the accuracy of his conclusions; it may not be used for substantive evidence.

2. Federal Rules: The Federal Rules go *markedly further* than the common law in allowing use of learned writings. Indeed, this is one of the most important changes made by the Federal Rules. FRE 803(18) provides a hearsay exception for:

"To the extent called to the attention of an expert witness upon cross-examination or relied upon by the expert witness in direct examination, statements contained in published treatises, periodicals, or pamphlets on a subject of history, medicine, or other science or art, established as a reliable authority by the testimony or admission of the witness or by other expert testimony or by judicial notice. If admitted, the statements may be read into evidence but may not be received as exhibits."

a. Aspects of the Federal Rule: Let's look at some of the key aspects of this broadened rule:

b. Use upon direct: The writing can come in on *direct examination*. That is, if the party can find a favorable expert who will testify that the treatise is authoritative, parts of the treatise can be read into the record as part of that party's direct case. S&R, p. 840.

c. Use on cross-examination: The treatise can be used on cross-examination even if the expert being cross-examined not only has not relied on the treatise, but *refuses to recognize its authoritativeness*. The cross-examiner must still establish the authoritative standing of the treatise in some way (e.g., by some other expert, or perhaps even by judicial notice).

d. Use for truth: In sharp contrast to the common-law approach, any statements read in from a treatise that has been "qualified" in this manner can come in *for their truth*, not merely for impeachment purposes.

e. Expert must be on the stand: At the time the treatise is read into evidence, an expert *must be on the stand*. Because a treatise written for professionals might be misunderstood or misused by a lay jury, the expert's presence is needed to "interpret" it before the lay jury relies on it. S&R, p. 840.

i. Use in cross-examination: This "interpretation" may (and often will) be by a *hostile* expert under cross-examination. Thus, suppose P brings a medical malpractice action, and is cross-examining D's expert witness, W, by use of a treatise favorable to P. The "interpretation" of the treatise may consist of W's saying why the treatise does not help P's case. W may point out that the treatise is out of date, that it doesn't say what P says it says, or that it is too general and fails to deal with the particularities of P's situation under litigation.

f.   **Not admitted as exhibit:** Even if all of the requirements are met, the treatise *may not* be admitted as an *exhibit*. The jury has to be content with hearing the appropriate portions read to it (and "interpreted" by the expert who is on the stand at the time). This safeguard, too, prevents the jury from misunderstanding and misusing a work written for professionals. (Observe that this no-exhibits policy is similar to that for past recollection recorded, *supra*, p. 192.)

g.   **Other types of materials:** The classic use of FRE 803(18) is for a scientific or medical book. But the rule is written more broadly. It includes periodicals or pamphlets, and it includes materials not only on the sciences and medicine, but also on "history . . . or other . . . art. . . ." This language is broad enough to include "standards and manuals published by government agencies and industry and professional organizations." M, p. 901.

   Example: P is injured by a power saw, and sues on a product liability claim based upon defective design. He should be able to use FRE 803(18) to put into evidence Underwriters Laboratory Standards, and to show that the saw in question did not satisfy those standards. (Remember that he would have to have an expert on the stand while doing so. He might, for instance, call the chief engineer of D, and ask him whether Underwriters Laboratory Standards are recognized in the power saw industry as being a measure of the safeness of a saw.) See, e.g., *McKinnon v. Skil Corp.*, 638 F.2d 270 (1st Cir. 1981).

3.   **Commercial publications:** Related to "learned writings" are certain *commercial publications* that are commonly relied upon by business people. The impartiality and, in general, reliability of such publications has led to a separate Federal Rule giving them, too, an exception from the hearsay rule.

   a.   **Text of Rule:** FRE 803(17) gives a hearsay exception for "*market quotations, tabulations, lists, directories*, or other *published compilations*, generally used and relied upon by the public or by persons in particular occupations."

   b.   **Reliability:** The proponent of the list or other compilation bears the burden of showing that it is indeed generally reliable. See, e.g., *State v. Lungsford*, 400 A.2d 843 (N.J. 1979), reversing D's conviction for possessing a stolen vehicle, where the "proof" that the vehicle was stolen stemmed directly from serial-number records of the National Automobile Theft Bureau, and where the prosecution did not supply detailed information about how the NATB record-keeping system works or why it should be treated as sufficiently reliable to support a criminal conviction.

C.   **Ancient documents and documents relating to property:** We now consider two closely-related exceptions, one for "ancient documents" and one for documents relating to property.

1. **Ancient documents:** A special rule has evolved to allow the admission of *"ancient"* documents.

   a. **Common-law approach:** At common law, there has existed for a long time a rule of *authentication* governing ancient documents, whereby a document could be deemed to be authentic, and thus admissible, if it satisfies these requirements: (1) it is *at least 30 years old*; (2) it is *unsuspicious* in appearance; and (3) its proponent proves that it was produced from a *place of custody natural* for such a writing. M, p. 903.

      i. **Rule of authentication only:** However, this common-law rule has generally been regarded as a rule of *authentication only*, not a hearsay exception. That is, the document can come into evidence, but it is not admissible to show the truth of the matters contained therein. See, e.g., *Town of Ninety-Six v. Southern Railway Co.*, 267 F.2d 579 (4th Cir. 1959), holding that where the width of a railroad right-of-way was at issue, a letter found in the office of the court clerk relating to that right-of-way, even if admissible under the ancient documents rule, could not be used to prove the assertion contained therein (that the railroad was claiming a lesser right-of-way than in the present litigation), because the ancient documents rule "is a rule of authentication and not a rule of admissibility."

      ii. **Minority rule:** But some American courts have, on a common-law basis, extended this rule of authentication into a full-fledged hearsay exception, so that a document that meets these three requirements can be admitted for the truth of the matters asserted in it. M, p. 903.

      iii. **Recitals in deed:** Where the ancient document is a *deed* that contains *recitals*, nearly all courts allow it not only to be admitted, but to be admitted for the truth of the recitals. M, p. 904. Thus, if a properly recorded deed recites, "O, the present owner, purchased this property from X in 1872," virtually all courts would allow the deed into evidence to prove the truth of the assertion that X sold the property to O in 1872.

   b. **Federal Rules allow:** The Federal Rules explicitly recognize a *hearsay exception* for ancient documents. FRE 803(16) gives a hearsay exception for: "Statements in a document in existence *twenty years* or more the authenticity of which is established." (Authenticity is proven by the same three requirements as at common law, except that 20 years of age will suffice. See FRE 901(b)(8).)

      i. **Rationale:** This broad exception can be justified on several grounds: (1) Since a document is required, there is at least the somewhat greater assurance of reliability that comes from a written, rather than oral, out-of-court declaration; and (2) The requirement of 20-years-of-age makes it very likely that the writing predates the present controversy, thus removing a motive for the writer to have lied.

ii. Limitation: FRE 803(16) does not explicitly require that the writer be shown to have had ***first-hand knowledge*** of the events described. However, this requirement is probably applicable to all of the FRE 803 exceptions. Therefore, if it appears that the writer could not have had first-hand knowledge of the facts recited in the document, it will probably be excluded. W&B, Par. 803(16)[01].

c. Newspaper reports: Reports in ***newspaper articles*** will sometimes be admissible under the ancient documents exception. For instance, a contemporaneous newspaper report might be used to show that a particular building was destroyed by fire in 1930.

i. First-hand knowledge: However, the requirement, discussed above, that the out-of-court declarant (here, the newspaper reporter) have had ***first-hand knowledge*** may disqualify some articles — the issue is probably whether the reporter himself observed the event (in which case the article is admissible) rather than merely interviewed others about it (in which case it is inadmissible). See M, p. 904, n. 11.

2. Newer title documents: The Federal Rules also contain a narrower exception for certain ***newer*** documents (i.e., those less than 20 years old). FRE 803(15) gives a hearsay exception for:

"A statement contained in a document purporting to establish or affect an ***interest in property*** if the matter stated was relevant to the purpose of the document, unless dealings with the property since the document was made have been inconsistent with the truth of the statement or the purport of the document."

a. Relation to common-law rule: This Rule does not break very much new ground, since, as noted above, nearly all courts allow a hearsay exception for recitals in deeds. The Rule does expand the common-law approach in two respects: (1) It applies to documents less than 20 years old; and (2) It applies to any document "purporting to establish or affect an interest in property," thus making it applicable not only to wills and deeds, but also probably to contracts to sell real estate, as well as to contracts and bills of sale affecting ***personal property*** (e.g., a bill of sale for a piece of jewelry). W&B, Par. 803(15)[01].

D. Reputation: There is a cluster of situations in which evidence of ***reputation*** may be admitted even though it is technically hearsay.

1. Personal or family history: For instance, a person's reputation within his ***family***, regarding some aspect of his ***birth***, ***marriage***, blood relationship, etc., has always been given a hearsay exception at common law.

Example: If the issue is whether X is the son of Y, X could put on the stand Z, an acknowledged son of Y, who would be permitted to testify, "It was commonly understood in the family that X was Y's son."

a. Liberalization: The Federal Rules expand this exception for reputation regarding personal or family history. FRE 803(19) goes beyond the common-law exception — which in most instances was limited to reputation within the family — and extends it to cover reputation "among a person's **associates**" (e.g., his business colleagues), and also his reputation **"in the community."** It covers reputation as to the person's "birth, adoption, marriage, divorce, death, legitimacy, relationship by blood, adoption, or marriage, ancestry, or other similar fact of his **personal or family history**."

b. **Family records exception:** A related common-law exception allows the use of **contemporaneous family records** (e.g., entries in a family Bible) to prove such facts of personal or family history. FRE 803(13) carries forward this exception as well.

Example: If the issue is whether X is Y's son, a family genealogy could be introduced to prove that fact under 803(13), provided that the entry in the chart was made soon after the alleged birth of X to Y.

2. **Boundaries and general historical facts:** Both at common law and under the Federal Rules, there is an exception for proof of **land boundaries** and for **facts of "general history."**

a. **Federal Rules:** Thus, FRE 803(20) gives a hearsay exception for "reputation in a community, arising before the controversy, as to **boundaries of** or customs affecting **lands** in the community, and reputation as to events of **general history** important to the community or State or nation in which located."

Example: Suppose P is trying to prove that a particular building was destroyed in the San Francisco Earthquake of 1906. He could call W, a historian, who could testify that within northern California, an earthquake has a reputation for having occurred in San Francisco in 1906, and for having destroyed all buildings within a certain area. (Observe that this fact could also be proved, perhaps more conveniently, by use of newspaper accounts through the "ancient documents" exception of FRE 803(16), or by the doctrine of judicial notice, covered *infra*, p. 463.)

3. **Reputation for character:** Similarly, there is a hearsay exception for reputation concerning a person's **character**. Thus FRE 803(21) gives an exception for "reputation of a person's character among associates or in the community."

a. **Caution:** But this exception merely removes the hearsay problem. There remain some important restrictions on the use of character evidence generally (e.g., that a person's character is generally not admissible "for the purpose of proving that he acted in conformity therewith on a particular occasion." FRE 404(a)). See the discussion of character evidence generally *supra*, p. 17.

E. **Miscellaneous public and quasi-public records:** A last category of hearsay exceptions relates to certain public and quasi-public records that don't quite fall within the conventional "public records" exception (see *supra*, p. 204).

1. **Vital statistics:** There is an exception for **vital statistics**, such as official records of **births**, **deaths**, or **marriages**.

a. **Regular public records rule not applicable:** At first glance, it might seem that the regular *public records* rule (*supra*, p. 204) would apply to cover such vital statistics, and that the special exception is not necessary. However, recall that the general public records exception only applies where the out-of-court declarant had an *official duty* to make the report in question. In many instances, the person who reports the event to the keeper of the public records (e.g., a person reporting the death of a spouse) is not really acting under any official duty to make the report. Therefore, the special exception for vital statistics has arisen. See FRE 803(9), providing a hearsay exception for "records or data compilations, in any form, of births, fetal deaths, deaths, or marriages, if the report thereof was made to a public office pursuant to requirements of law."

b. **Cause of death:** Most applications of this exception are cut and dried. But what if a *death certificate* (which is clearly admissible to show the fact of death under this exception) also recites the *cause* of death? In such situations, the person filling out the death certificate — usually the treating physician — may not have had personal knowledge of all the facts that went into the determination of cause of death. For instance, the physician's conclusion that the decedent died of suicide may have been influenced by the decedent's spouse's declaration, "He had been depressed lately," a fact of which the physician has no first-hand knowledge. Nonetheless, most courts would allow the physician's statement on the death certificate as to the cause of death — "suicide on account of depression" — to be admitted under the vital statistics exception. See generally W&B, Par. 803(9)[01].

2. **Marriage certificates:** Statements of fact contained in a *marriage certificate* are given an exception. See FRE 803(12). Where the marriage is performed by a public official (e.g., a judge), no special exception is needed for the official's certificate that the marriage was performed, since the general "public records" exception covers this situation. But when the marriage certificate is signed by a *clergyman* or other private citizen, the certificate would not be admissible without this special exception.

3. **Vital statistics kept by religious organizations:** Various facts of personal or family history, when contained in the records of a *religious organization*, are given an exception. See FRE 803(11), covering statements of "births, marriages, divorces, deaths, legitimacy, ancestry, relationship by blood or marriage, or other similar facts of personal or family history, contained in a regularly kept record of a religious organization."

a. **Rationale:** The business records exception might seem to cover such religious records. However, remember that that exception applies only where the person supplying the information was acting in the course of the business or other regular activity. Since the religious organization's records are often based on information supplied by an "amateur" (e.g., a parent reporting the birth of a child), the business records exception does not apply, and this special exception is needed.

4. **Absence of public record:** Sometimes a party may wish to prove that there is *no* entry in the public records about a certain event, or that a particular document or filing does not exist in the public records. Just as there is an exception allowing proof of the absence of a particular business record (see *supra*, p. 198), so there is an exception to prove *lack of a public record.* See FRE 803(10).

   a. **Certificate or testimony:** The absence of a particular public record can be proved in either of two ways, under FRE 803(10): (1) by a *certificate* by the keeper of the records in question, that diligent search has failed to find the record; or (2) by testimony of the record keeper to that effect.

      Example: In a prosecution of D for failure to file tax returns, the IRS could prove failure to file either by a certificate from a person who works in the relevant IRS records center that a search of the Service's records failed to disclose the relevant return, or by live testimony of that custodian that the return could not be found.

5. **Previous felony convictions:** Often a party will wish to show that another party has received a prior *conviction* for a crime. If the previous conviction is sought to be introduced as evidence that the convicted person committed the crime in question, this is technically hearsay. (That is, the out-of-court declarant — the judge or jury in the earlier action — is saying, "D committed the crime," and this statement is offered to prove that D did in fact commit the crime.)

   a. **Traditional view:** Traditionally, therefore, courts have been unwilling to allow prior convictions into evidence. M, p. 894.

   b. **Modern and federal view:** However, a criminal conviction is accompanied by such safeguards that it is an unusually reliable piece of hearsay. Therefore, a special modern exception has evolved: prior *felony convictions* are generally admissible to prove any fact essential to the conviction. See, e.g., FRE 803(22).

      i. **Use in subsequent civil case:** This exception is most often used where the plaintiff in a *civil suit* wants to use the prior criminal conviction of the defendant or of a third person to prove some fact that is relevant to the civil case.

      Example: Suppose that D, a psychiatrist, is sued in a negligence action by the Ps, whose daughter was murdered by X, a patient of D who D knew had murderous tendencies. To prove that X killed their daughter, the Ps need merely prove that X was convicted of the murder — they don't have to relitigate the issue of whether X really did it. See *Semler v. Psychiatric Institute of Washington*, 538 F.2d 121 (4th Cir. 1976).

      ii. **Conviction of third person not usable in criminal case:** Where the current proceeding is a *criminal* trial, it would probably be unconstitutional for the government to use a *third person's conviction* as part of its case in chief. Therefore, FRE 803(22) disallows such a use.

      Example: D is charged with possession of stolen stamps. The prosecution cannot prove that the stamps were stolen by introducing the fact that the thieves (persons other than D) were convicted of the theft. Such use would violate D's constitutional right to confront the witnesses against him, since an essential element of his guilt — that the stamps were stolen — would have been established in a prior proceeding in which he was not represented and did not have the ability to question the witnesses. See *Kirby v. U.S.*, 174 U.S. 47 (1899).

iii. **Minor crimes:** Most courts do ***not*** allow a ***misdemeanor*** conviction to be used in a subsequent proceeding. This restriction is based on the theory that, when faced with a minor conviction, the defendant may have found it more sensible to pay a fine rather than litigate the charges, even though he was in fact innocent. Thus a driver's conviction on a minor traffic charge (e.g., speeding) will usually not be admissible in a subsequent civil case to show that he did the act charged. FRE 803(22) follows this policy, by allowing proof of convictions only where the crime was "punishable by death or imprisonment in excess of one year" (the traditional felony standard).

iv. **Prior civil judgments:** The exception for prior judgments applies only to prior ***criminal*** convictions. A prior judgment in a ***civil*** case is not covered, either under modern state-law approaches or the Federal Rules. M, p. 896. (However, general civil procedure principles of *res judicata* or collateral estoppel may cause the prior civil judgment to be dispositive, even though not formally admissible into evidence.)

v. **Acquittal:** Only convictions are covered. Judgments of ***acquittal*** are not excepted from the hearsay rule. *Id.*

IX. UNAVAILABILITY REQUIRED — GENERALLY

A. **Introduction:** All of the hearsay exceptions discussed so far apply regardless of whether the declarant is available to testify at the current trial. We turn now to the second major grouping of hearsay exceptions, those which apply only where the declarant is ***unavailable*** to testify at the current proceeding.

   1. **Theoretically less reliable:** These "declarant's unavailability required" exceptions would seem to cover evidence that is, on the whole, ***less reliable*** than the previously-considered exceptions, which apply regardless of whether the declarant is available.

   2. **Not necessarily so:** However, this lesser reliability often reflects only theory, not reality. For instance, it seems probable that former testimony (admissible only if the declarant is available; see *infra*, p. 225) is generally much more reliable than excited utterances (admissible regardless of whether the declarant is available; see *supra*, p. 184). See L&S, pp. 469-70. The breakdown between these two broad categories probably reflects historical accident more than sound policy.

   3. **Four main exceptions:** There are four basic exceptions that fall into this unavailability-required category:

a. **Former testimony:** *Testimony given in a prior proceeding*;

b. **Dying declaration:** Statements made while the declarant believed his **death was impending** (so-called **dying declarations**);

c. **Statements against interest:** Statements which were **against the declarant's interest** when made; and

d. **Pedigree:** Statements concerning either the declarant's or his relative's **personal or family history** (so-called statements of **"pedigree"**).

B. **Meaning of "unavailable":** To determine whether one of these exceptions applies, it is first necessary to determine whether the declarant is "unavailable."

1. **The Federal Rule:** The Federal Rules reflect general state policies on when the declarant should be deemed to be "unavailable." FRE 804(a) defines "unavailability as a witness" to include situations in which the declarant:

"(1) is exempted by ruling of the court on the ground of **privilege** from testifying concerning the subject matter of the declarant's statement; or

(2) persists in **refusing to testify** concerning the subject matter of the declarant's statement despite an order of the court to do so; or

(3) testifies to a **lack of memory** of the subject matter of the declarant's statement; or

(4) is unable to be present or to testify at the hearing because of **death** or then existing **physical or mental illness** or infirmity; or

(5) is absent from the hearing and the proponent of a statement has been unable to procure the declarant's attendance (or in the case of a hearsay exception under subdivision (b)(2), (3), or (4), the declarant's attendance or testimony) by **process** or **other reasonable means**.

A declarant is not unavailable as a witness if exemption, refusal, claim of lack of memory, inability, or absence is due to the procurement or **wrongdoing** of the **proponent** of a statement for the purpose of preventing the witness from attending or testifying."

2. **States generally follow:** The first four of these are pretty cut-and-dried, and nearly all states recognize these same ways of being "unavailable."

a. **Absence:** But where the asserted unavailability of the declarant stems from his **absence** from the jurisdiction, the Federal Rule is more strict than that of most states. In most state courts, the declarant's mere absence from the state will be enough to render him "unavailable," since that absence will make him not reachable by **process**. L&S, p. 471. But under the Federal Rules, it is not enough to show that the declarant is beyond the reach of process; the person offering the out-of-court declaration must show that it was also not possible to procure the witness's attendance by **other means** (e.g., persuasion). In fact, for the exceptions given in FRE 804(b)(2), (3), and (4) (dying declarations, statements against interest, and statements of pedigree), the person offering the out-of-court declaration in a federal trial must **also** show that attempts to take the declarant's **deposition** were unsuccessful.

3. **Constitutional problems:** In civil cases, and in criminal cases where the declaration at issue is sought to be introduced by the defense, the issue of unavailability has no constitutional dimensions. But where, in a criminal case, the **prosecution** seeks to introduce an out-of-court declaration for which the declarant's unavailability is required, the Constitution's **Confrontation Clause** comes into play. That is, the defendant's right to cross-examine the witnesses against him may be violated by the use of an out-of-court declaration, unless the declarant is "unavailable" measured by a constitutional standard.

   a. **Absence from state not sufficient:** For example, the mere fact that the declarant is out of the state and cannot be compelled by process to testify, will generally **not** be sufficient to satisfy the Confrontation Clause — the state must show that attendance could not be procured by means other than process (e.g., persuasion). *Barber v. Page*, 390 U.S. 719 (1968).

      Example: Thus, in *Barber v. Page, supra,* Oklahoma, in a state robbery prosecution against D, tried to introduce against him W's testimony from a preliminary hearing. At the time of the trial, W was in a federal prison in Texas, 225 miles away. Oklahoma argued that W was "unavailable" because he was outside of Oklahoma and thus not reachable by state process; it contended therefore that the "former testimony" exception to the hearsay rule (see *infra*, p. 225) could be used without violating D's confrontation rights. (The state also claimed that D had had the opportunity to cross-examine W at the preliminary hearing, even though he did not exercise that right.)

      The Supreme Court noted that the federal prison system had a policy of permitting federal prisoners to testify in state court criminal proceedings even if the proceedings were in a different state. Here, Oklahoma authorities had made no effort to use this policy or other means to procure W's attendance. Therefore, Oklahoma had not shown that W was truly "unavailable," and D's Confrontation Clause rights were denied by use of the transcript. "[A] witness is not 'unavailable' for purposes of . . . the Confrontation requirement unless the prosecutorial authorities have made a **good-faith effort** to obtain his presence at trial."

      i. **Degree of effort:** But, two later Supreme Court cases seem to have weakened this constitutional requirement of *Barber v. Page* that good faith efforts to procure the declarant's attendance must be shown. Thus in *Mancusi v. Stubbs*, 408 U.S. 204 (1972), the Court found that the prior witness, Holm, was unavailable for Confrontation Clause purposes, where he was living in Sweden at the time of the trial. There was no policy of international process or international cooperation comparable to the federal prison policy of cooperation in *Barber*. (A dissent contended that the state should still have been required to show that it made good faith efforts to procure the witness's voluntary presence, and that it had not made such a showing.)

      ii. **"Good faith effort" found:** Similarly, the witness was held "unavailable" for Confrontation Clause purposes, in *Ohio v. Roberts*, 448 U.S. 56 (1980). The government had issued five separate subpoenas to the witness in care of her mother, and showed that the mother did not know of the witness' whereabouts. However, the government did not contact a social worker who the mother said might know the daughter's address. On the entire set of facts, the Court concluded that the prosecution "did not breach its duty of good-faith effort. . . . The great improbability that [contacting the social worker] would have resulted in locating the witness, and would have led to her production at trial, neutralizes any intimation that a concept of reasonableness required [this step]."

   b. **Summary:** In summary, the following are about all that can be said about when a witness will be deemed sufficiently "unavailable" that use of his out-of-court declaration will not violate a criminal defendant's Confrontation Clause rights: (1) the state must show that the witness is *beyond that state's own process*; and (2) the state must show either that it made a *good-faith effort* to procure the witness' presence by means other than process, or that such efforts would have been *very unlikely to succeed.*

X. FORMER TESTIMONY

   A. **In general:** There is a long-established exception for *former testimony* — that is, testimony given in an earlier proceeding — if the witness is unavailable for trial.

   1. **Federal Rule:** The Federal Rules follow the common law, by and large. FRE 804(b)(1) provides a hearsay exception, if the declarant is unavailable as a witness, for:

   "testimony given as a witness in *another hearing* of the *same or a different* proceeding, or in a *deposition* taken in compliance with law in the course of the same or another proceeding, if the party against whom the testimony is now offered, or, in a civil action or proceeding, a *predecessor in interest*, had an *opportunity* and *similar motive* to develop the testimony by direct, cross, or redirect *examination*."

   2. **Rationale:** There is a very strong rationale in favor of allowing a hearsay exception for former testimony. "Cross-examination, oath, the solemnity of the occasion, and in the case of transcribed testimony the accuracy of reproduction of the words spoken, all combine to give former testimony a high degree of credibility." M, p. 760.

   a. **Not just for transcripts:** However, observe that the exception is *not limited* to *transcripts* of the prior hearing. For instance, a *first-hand observer* may *orally recount* the testimony, either from unaided memory or by refreshing his recollection by use of the transcript. M, p. 771. In this situation, the accuracy of the evidence — in the sense of avoiding errors in transmission — is not especially high. In the overwhelming majority of former testimony situations, however, a transcript will be used.

   B. **Opportunity for cross-examination:** A key requirement for the former testimony exception is that the party against whom the evidence is now offered must have had a reasonable opportunity to *cross-examine* the declarant at the time of the former testimony.

Example: X is arrested in connection with a robbery. At a preliminary hearing on the charges, X gives testimony implicating D, who so far has not been suspected and who is not present at the hearing. At a subsequent prosecution of D for the crime, the state will not be permitted to introduce X's preliminary hearing testimony (even if X is now unavailable), because D had no opportunity to cross-examine X at that hearing. (In this prosecution-witness context, the requirement of cross-examination is imposed not only by general evidence principles, but also by the Constitution's Confrontation Clause.)

1. **Actual examination not required:** There is no requirement that the party against whom the evidence is now offered have *actually* cross-examined the declarant at the earlier proceeding. All that is required is that the opponent have had a reasonable *opportunity* to do so.

   Example: Suppose that, on the facts of the above example, D and X had been arrested together, and both were present (with D represented by counsel) at the same preliminary hearing. If D's counsel was given the opportunity to cross-examine X at the hearing, and chose not to do so, lack of cross-examination will not furnish a reason for D to keep X's hearing testimony out of D's eventual trial.

   a. **Possible unfairness:** Where the opportunity to cross-examine is declined at a *non-trial* proceeding, it may sometimes seem unfair to allow the testimony to come in at the later trial. The party declining cross-examination may have made a perfectly reasonable tactical decision that cross-examination was not worthwhile and should be saved for the trial stage. For instance, the defense lawyer at a preliminary hearing, or a party taking his adversary's deposition, may shorten or eliminate cross-examination entirely, on the theory that this will only tip the examiner's hand and deprive him of the advantage of surprise at trial. Nonetheless, courts generally hold that this makes no difference: as long as there was a reasonable opportunity to cross-examine, the fact that sound tactics may have dictated dispensing with that opportunity is irrelevant. M, p. 762.

   b. **Lack of counsel:** However, if counsel has not had sufficient time to prepare a cross-examination, or counsel has not been appointed at the time of the earlier proceeding, the defendant will not be found to have had a reasonable opportunity to cross-examine.

2. **Direct examination:** Suppose the party opposing the former testimony at trial had the opportunity to do *direct* (rather than cross) examination at the prior proceeding. Such an opportunity is virtually always held to be the equivalent of an opportunity to cross-examine, so the requirement of cross-examination is satisfied.

   Example: At Trial 1 of a negligence action between P and D, P calls X, a witness who ends up giving testimony unfavorable to P. After a mistrial, Trial 2 is held, and X is no longer available as a witness. If D offers X's former testimony, P cannot claim that he lacked the opportunity to cross-examine X at Trial 1 — P's opportunity to do a *direct* examination of X is the equivalent of cross-examination (even though local trial rules might have substantially impaired P's right to attack the credibility of his own witness, or even though, from a tactical perspective, P's decision not to attack his witness' credibility was reasonable). See L&S, p. 475.

C. Identity of issues: It has never been a requirement of the former testimony exception that the former testimony have occurred in the *same case*. But the common law did originally require that the earlier and later proceedings both involve the *same issues*. This was a way of making sure that the handling of the witness (especially the nature of the cross-examination) in the earlier proceeding was comparable to the handling that would occur if the witness were available for the second proceeding.

1. **"Substantial identity":** Modern cases have generally been less strict. All that they usually require is that there be *"substantial identity"* of issues between the two situations. M, p. 768. This requirement of substantial identity of issues really amounts merely to a "requirement that the issues in the first proceeding and hence the purpose for which the testimony was there offered, must have been such that the present opponent (or some person in like interest) had an *adequate motive* for testing on cross-examination the credibility of the testimony now offered." *Id.*

2. **Federal Rule:** The Federal Rules go one step further. Instead of referring to "substantial identity of issues," FRE 804(b)(1) explicitly substitutes a requirement that the party against whom the testimony is now offered (or, in a civil action, a predecessor in interest) "had an *opportunity* and *similar motive* to develop the testimony by direct, cross, or redirect examination."

3. **Different contexts:** This modern trend (whether a state common-law approach requiring "substantial identity of issues" or the federal "similar motive" requirement) means that the former testimony exception can apply even where the two proceedings are in quite *different contexts*.

   a. **Preliminary hearing:** Thus testimony given at a *preliminary hearing* can be used at a later criminal trial, even though the issues are not, strictly speaking, "identical" in the two situations. (In the preliminary hearing, the issue is whether there is enough evidence to justify a trial; in the trial, the issue is guilt or innocence.) The point is that the defendant in both situations has a motive to try to knock down the prosecution's case against him. See, e.g., *California v. Green*, 399 U.S. 149 (1970), holding that use of preliminary hearing testimony at the later criminal trial did not violate D's Confrontation Clause rights, because "the right of cross-examination then afforded [at the preliminary hearing] provides substantial compliance with the purposes behind the confrontation requirement."

   b. **Criminal followed by civil trial:** Similarly, the former testimony may be admissible at a civil proceeding even though it was given at an earlier *criminal* trial.

      Example: P1 and P2, business partners, bring a civil action against D, an insurance company, to recover on two fire insurance policies. At the trial, D seeks to introduce a transcript of testimony from an earlier criminal prosecution against P1, in which two witnesses, W1 and W2, testified that P1 had helped them burn down the premises. The Ps argue that there is no "identity of issues" between the earlier criminal case and the later civil one.

Held, for D. The main issue on which the Ws' testimony was relevant is the same in both actions: whether P1 was responsible for the burning of the building. This satisfies the requirement of "identity of issues," since P1 had the same motive and interest in cross-examining in the earlier criminal proceeding as P1 and P2 have in the subsequent civil one. (Also, there is sufficient "identity of parties," see *infra*, since P1 was a party to both proceedings and has a common interest with P2, sufficient to overcome the fact that P2 was not a party to the earlier criminal case.) *Travelers Fire Insurance Co. v. Wright*, 322 P.2d 417 (Okla. 1958).

D. Identity of parties: The last important requirement for the former testimony exception is that there must be an **"identity of parties"** as between the two proceedings.

1. **Applies only to opponent:** In modern cases, it is never required that **both** parties be the same in the two actions. All that is required is that the party **against** whom the former testimony is offered must have been a party to the prior proceeding. (Earlier common-law decisions required that both parties be the same; this requirement of "mutuality" has been abandoned in Evidence, just as it has been abandoned in the analogous Civil Procedure area of collateral estoppel. See Emanuel on *Civil Procedure*.)

    Example: Byars (driving a truck for Mattress Co.) collides with Martin (driving his own car); Gaines, who is working on the highway near the point of impact, is injured, and Martin is killed. In Trial 1, Martin's administrator sues Mattress, and Byars gives testimony. Byars then dies. In Trial 2, Gaines sues Martin's estate, and seeks to use Byars' testimony from Trial 1. Martin's estate claims that the requisite "identity of parties" is lacking, because Gaines was not a party to Trial 1.

    Held, for Gaines. Gaines' absence from Trial 1 is irrelevant. All that matters is that Martin (the party against whom the testimony is now offered) was a party to the first action, since his presence assured that he had the opportunity to cross-examine Byars in the first action. The requirement that there be "identity of issues" is but a means of assuring that there was an adequate opportunity for cross-examination by the party now opposing the evidence. *Gaines v. Thomas*, 128 S.E.2d 692 (S.C. 1962).

2. **Similar party in interest:** In fact, some states now no longer even require that the party opposing the evidence have been a party to the earlier action, at least in civil cases. In these courts, it is sufficient that there have been **some** party in the earlier action whose opportunity and motive to cross-examine are **similar** to those held by the opponent in the subsequent hearing. L&S, p. 477.

    Example: On the facts of *Gaines*, *supra*, suppose that Martin had had a passenger, Y, and that Trial 1 was a suit by Y against Mattress. Since Y would have had the same motive in cross-examining Byars (to break down his testimony that Martin, rather than Byars, caused the accident) as Martin would have in Trial 2, a few states would allow Byars testimony to be used in Trial 2 against Martin. These states would apply the "former testimony" exception even though Martin, by our hypothetical, was not a party to Trial 1.

a. **Federal Rules:** The Federal Rules, as originally submitted to Congress, followed this minority view under which the party against whom the former testimony is offered need not have been present in the earlier proceeding. But Congress ultimately rejected this approach, believing that it is unfair to charge a party with the way a different party handled the witness in the earlier proceeding.

b. **Result:** Consequently, FRE 804(b)(1) requires that the following be the case: (1) The party against whom the former testimony is now offered must have had an opportunity to cross-examine in the earlier proceeding; *or* (2) In civil cases only, the present opponent's *"predecessor in interest"* must have had such an opportunity.

c. **Significance:** On the face of it, this looks like a stricter standard than the modern minority state rule described previously: a requirement that there have been a "predecessor in interest" sounds harder to satisfy than a requirement that there merely have been someone in the earlier action who had a "similar motive" to cross-examine.

d. *Lloyd* **case:** However, the leading case on this issue has held, in effect, that all the "predecessor in interest" requirement in FRE 804(b)(1) *means* is a person with a "like motive to develop the same testimony about the same material facts. . . ." *Lloyd v. American Export Lines, Inc.*, 580 F.2d 1179 (3d. Cir. 1978).

   i. **Facts:** In *Lloyd*, two members of a ship's crew (Lloyd and Alvarez) got into a fight. In Proceeding 1, the Coast Guard held a hearing to determine whether Lloyd's merchant mariner's document should have been suspended. Lloyd and Alvarez testified at this hearing, and each was represented by counsel. Proceeding 2 was a suit by Alvarez against the shipowner. The Shipowner tried to introduce the testimony of Lloyd (now unavailable) from the Coast Guard hearing, but Alvarez argued that he had had no opportunity to examine Lloyd at the first hearing (which was true), and that the Coast Guard was not a "predecessor in interest" to Alvarez.

   ii. **Result:** The former testimony was held *admissible* on appeal. "There was a sufficient community of interest shared by the Coast Guard in its hearing and Alvarez in the subsequent civil trial to satisfy Rule 804(b)(1)." The "nucleus of operative facts" — the conduct of Lloyd and Alvarez on the ship — was the same in the two proceedings, and the Coast Guard officer had the same motive — to establish Lloyd's wrongdoing — as Alvarez had in the later trial. Therefore, the Coast Guard was Alvarez's predecessor in interest because it had a "like motive to develop the testimony about the same material facts. . . ." (A concurring opinion pointed out that Rule 804(b)(1) has a separate requirement that there have been a "similar motive" to cross-examine in the two situations; given this "similar motive" requirement, the majority's interpretation of "predecessor in interest" to require merely a similar motive "eliminates the predecessor in interest requirement entirely.")

e. **Present status of Rule:** Thus if the *Lloyd* approach is followed, the "predecessor in interest" requirement virtually disappears, and it is sufficient that there was a different party in the earlier proceeding who had the same motive to cross-examine as the party who now opposes the former testimony. That is, the *Lloyd* court's interpretation restores FRE 804(b)(1) to essentially the form in which it was originally proposed to Congress. Most courts have apparently followed the *Lloyd* court's approach of interpreting "predecessor in interest" very loosely. W&B, Par. 804(b)(1)[04].

3. **Criminal cases:** In criminal cases, by contrast, the "same parties" requirement is *strictly construed*. FRE 804(b)(1) has no exception for a "predecessor in interest" in this situation — if the defendant was not an actual party to the earlier proceeding, the presence of a person with even an extremely similar motive to cross-examine will not be sufficient to allow the testimony to be used against the defendant at trial.

> **Example:** D1 and D2 are suspected of armed robbery. At D1's trial, W gives testimony implicating both D1 and D2. D1 vociferously cross-examines W, in a way designed to show that W is lying (and in a way that, if successful, will exculpate both D1 and D2). At D2's later trial, W is unavailable. The prosecution will not be permitted to offer against D2 the transcript of W's prior testimony at D1's trial, because D2 was not a party to that trial. This is true even though D1 had every opportunity and motive to cross-examine in a manner similar to that which would be expected from D2 at the latter's trial. This rule safeguards D2's Confrontation Clause rights, since otherwise he would be deprived of the ability to confront W, a witness against him.

a. **Defense witness:** Observe that FRE 804(b)(1)'s treatment of criminal cases requires that the party against whom the testimony is offered have been an actual party to the proceeding, without respect to whether that party is the defendant or the prosecutor. The above example shows why this is constitutionally required where the prior testimony is offered against the defendant. However, the Rule seems also to mean that if the testimony is offered against the **prosecution**, the **same prosecuting body** must have been involved. Such a result would probably be so unfair as to violate the defendant's due process rights, and "quite likely it was not intended by the Congress." M, p. 766.

> **Example:** In Trial 1, D is prosecuted by the state for murdering X. He presents testimony of W, who is extensively cross-examined by the state prosecutor. In Trial 2, D is prosecuted by the federal government for violating X's civil rights, based upon the same alleged facts. W has since died, and D offers a transcript of his testimony from the prior state action. A literal reading of FRE 804(b)(1) would indicate that the federal prosecutor can keep this evidence out, since the party against whom it is offered (the U.S. government)

was not a party to the earlier action, and since there is no provision for a "predecessor in interest" in criminal cases. However, such a result would probably violate D's due process rights, so the former testimony would probably be allowed. *Id.*

XI. DYING DECLARATIONS

A. General rule: As long as there has been a hearsay rule, there has been an exception for *dying declarations*.

1. **Statement of rule:** The common-law form of this rule is fairly narrow: *a declarant's statement, while believing that his death is imminent, concerning the cause or circumstances of his impending death, is admissible in a subsequent homicide prosecution concerning that death.*

2. **Rationale:** The rationale for this exception is more religious and psychological than it is legal — it stems from the belief that "the dying declarant, knowing that he is about to die, would be unwilling to go to his Maker with a lie on his lips." 6 How. L.J. 109, 111.

   a. **Criticism:** In earlier times, this was probably a reasonable assumption, since most people feared Hell. Today, fear of God and fear of Hell are probably less prevalent, so there is less reason to believe that the exception produces reliable evidence. Furthermore, "the desire for revenge or self-exoneration or to protect one's loved ones may continue until the moment of death. [Also] the declarant's physical and mental condition at the time he is awaiting death may have impaired his faculties of perception, memory and communication and may contribute to the unreliability of the statements." W&B, Par. 804(b)(2)[01].

   b. **Limitations:** Because of these doubts about the real reliability of dying declaration evidence, both the common law and the Federal Rules have restricted such evidence to a fairly small set of circumstances, discussed below.

3. **Federal Rule:** The Federal Rules provide the dying declaration exception in FRE 804(b)(2):

   "The following are not excluded by the hearsay rule if the declarant is unavailable as a witness: . . . (2) *Statement under belief of impending death.* In a prosecution for homicide or in a civil action or proceeding, a statement made by a declarant while believing that the declarant's death was imminent, concerning the cause or circumstances of what he believed to be his impending death."

B. Requirements: We now consider in detail the requirements for application of the dying declaration exception. At common law, there are five such requirements. As we discuss each, we will also cover the handling of that requirement under the Federal Rules (which relax several of them).

1. **Awareness of imminent death:** The declarant must, at the time he made his statement, have been *aware of his impending death*. It is not enough that he believed that he would probably die — "he must have lost all hope of recovery." M, p. 829.

a. **How proven:** There are a number of ways of showing that the declarant had the requisite awareness of his impending death. His own statements may demonstrate this knowledge (e.g., "I'm a goner"). His *wounds may be so severe* that he must have known that he was about to die. (But if there is no showing that the victim knew how severe his wounds were, their severity will not be enough.) Finally, statements made *to* the victim by others, especially doctors, can be evidence of the declarant's awareness of impending death.

b. **Federal Rules:** The Federal Rules continue the "awareness of impending death" requirement: FRE 804(b)(2) requires that the statement have been made by the declarant "while believing that his death was imminent."

2. **Actual death required:** At common law, the declarant *must in fact be dead* at the time the evidence is offered. That is, no matter how certain the declarant was that he would die, if he makes a miraculous recovery and is alive at the time of trial (even if unable to testify), the common-law exception does not apply. M, p. 830.

   a. **Temporary recovery:** On the other hand, it is *not* required that the declarant have died immediately or even soon after the declaration. "Periods even extending into months have been held not too long." M, p. 830.

   b. **Federal Rule:** The Federal Rules *completely remove* the requirement that death have actually ensued. FRE 804(b)(2) is one of the "declarant unavailable" exceptions, but it will suffice if the declarant is unavailable for some reason other than death (e.g., disability or forgetfulness).

3. **Homicide:** At common law, dying declarations may be used *only in homicide cases*. That is, they may *not* be used in *civil* cases. Nor may they be used in other kinds of criminal actions, even where the victim has died from the episode (e.g., a prosecution for rape where the woman has in fact died).

   a. **Rationale:** The only rationale for this strange limitation is that dying declarations are really not such reliable evidence after all, so their use should be curtailed. But it is hard to see why such declarations are more reliable in a murder prosecution (where the defendant's life may well be at stake) than in, say, a robbery prosecution.

   b. **Federal Rules:** The Federal Rules relax the "homicide only" requirement somewhat. Such declarations are usable in *civil suits*. But they remain unusable in *non-homicide criminal cases*.

4. **Declarant must be victim:** The most bizarre of all the common-law requirements is that the declaration may be offered only in a trial for the homicide of the *declarant*, not the homicide of someone else.

   Example: There is evidence that D has murdered both H and W. He is prosecuted for the murder of H only, because the evidence is strongest as to this crime. At common law, the prosecution will not be permitted to introduce W's dying declaration, "It's D who has done this to H and me." M, p. 831.

a. **Federal Rules:** This silly requirement has been dropped from the Federal Rules.

5. **Must relate to circumstances of killing:** Finally, the declaration must relate to the *causes or circumstances* of the killing.

> **Example:** Suppose that Declarant, in anticipation of his death, says, "X and I have been deadly enemies for the last 10 years." This statement will probably not be admissible, because it does not relate directly to the causes or circumstances of Declarant's death. But if Declarant had said, "X has been stalking me for two days," this statement would probably be allowed into evidence.

a. **Federal Rules:** The Federal Rules continue this requirement: 804(b)(2) requires that the declaration be one "concerning the cause or circumstances of what [declarant] believed to be his impending death."

C. **Miscellaneous:** Here are some miscellaneous aspects of the dying declaration doctrine:

1. **Usable on accused's behalf:** Such declarations may be admitted *on behalf of the defendant*, even though most of the time they are admitted against him. M, p. 832.

2. **First-hand knowledge:** As with other out-of-court declarations, the dying declaration will be admissible only if it appears to come from the declarant's *first-hand knowledge*.

> **Example:** Declarant says, "X shot me." If the other evidence shows that Declarant was shot in the back, and that he could not have had the opportunity to see that it was indeed X who was shooting him, the declaration will not be admitted. W&B, Par. 804(b)(2)[01]. This is true even though Declarant may have had other reasons to suspect that X was out to get him — the whole point is to exclude statements of suspicion, and to limit admissibility to statements that are unusually reliable because they come from the declarant's direct observation.

3. **Opinions:** Suppose the declaration includes an element of the declarant's *opinion*. A witness on the stand (other than an expert) will not usually be permitted to give an opinion. (See *infra*, p. 398.) However, the rule against opinion testimony is not strictly applied in the case of dying declarations. Thus a court will probably admit the declaration, "He shot me without cause." But if the judge finds that the opinion or speculation portion of the statement outweighs its factual portion, he can exclude the evidence on the grounds that it is prejudicial or not helpful. (Federal Rule 701, relating generally to lay opinion testimony, seems to apply to the dying declaration situation. See Advisory Committee's Note to 804(b)(2).)

4. **Belief in God not required:** Recall that the original reason for the dying declaration exception was that a person facing death would not want to "go to his Maker with a lie on his lips." Does it follow that the exception does not apply where the declarant is an *atheist* or agnostic? It is very unlikely that a court would take the religiosity of the declarant into account in determining whether to let the jury hear

the declaration; see, e.g., *Wilson v. State*, 468 P.2d 346 (Nev. 1970), holding that even though the declarant was a pimp (and therefore perhaps unreligious), the prosecution was entitled to have his statement go to the jury, which could decide how much weight or credence to give it.

5. **Preliminary fact questions:** Observe that before a declaration can be found to be an admissible "dying declaration," some preliminary questions of fact must be answered. In particular, it must be determined whether the declarant was indeed aware of his impending death. Who should decide this question, the judge or the jury? This issue is part of the broader issue of who should decide factual issues in connection with "conditional relevance," and is discussed further *infra*, p. 456. In brief, the answer is that in most state courts (and under the Federal Rules), the *judge* makes a *preliminary factual determination*: if he decides that there is enough evidence that the requisite awareness of death existed that a jury could reasonably find that there was such awareness, he will let the jury hear the declaration (even though he may personally believe that it is less likely than not that there was such awareness). It will then be up to the jury to determine what weight is to be given to this evidence, and they may (but probably need not) consider whether, in their opinion, the declarant was really aware that he was dying. See, e.g., *Soles v. State*, 119 So. 791 (Fl. 1929); M, pp. 137-38. See also FRE 104(b): "When the relevancy of evidence depends upon the fulfillment of a condition of fact, the court shall admit it upon, or subject to, the introduction of evidence sufficient to support a finding of the fulfillment of the condition."

XI. DECLARATIONS AGAINST INTEREST

A. **Generally:** There is a hearsay exception for declarations which, at the time they are made, are *so against the declarant's interest that it is unlikely they would have been made if they were not true*. At common law, the exception applies solely to statements against the declarant's financial interest; some states, and the Federal Rules, have expanded the exception to cover statements against penal interest.

1. **Summary of requirements:** The exception has only three requirements, in most jurisdictions: (1) the declaration must be against the declarant's *pecuniary or proprietary interest* when made; (2) the declarant must be *unavailable*; and (3) as with virtually all other hearsay exceptions, the declarant must have had *first-hand knowledge* of the facts asserted in the declaration. (Some states add a fourth requirement, that the declarant have had no probable motive to falsify. When this requirement is imposed, it is generally of importance as to statements that are partly disserving and partly self-serving. See *infra*, p. 240.)

> **Example:** P, an employer, sues D, its insurer, on a policy of fidelity insurance protecting P from wrongdoing by its employees. P seeks to introduce written and signed confessions by several employees admitting that they have misappropriated P's funds.
>
> *Held*, the confessions are admissible as third-party declarations against interest. "The courts have reasoned that a person does not make statements against his own pecuniary interest unless they are true and have thus

considered such statements trustworthy, even though there is no opportunity to confront the witness or to cross-examine him." Here, all requirements are met: (1) the employees could not be found by the sheriff, so they are unavailable; (2) they had first-hand knowledge of their own wrongdoing; (3) the confessions were against their pecuniary interest (since the confessions could be used to support a civil suit against them, in addition to criminal liability); and (4) they had no probable motive to falsify the facts in their confessions. *McKelvey Co. v. General Casualty Co. of America*, 142 N.E.2d 854 (Ohio 1957).

2. **Distinguished from admissions:** It is important to distinguish a declaration against interest from an ***admission*** (see *supra*, p. 149). The exception for admissions applies only where the declarant is a party, and his opponent is offering the statement. An admission does not have to meet any of the requirements that are applied to declarations against interest: (1) the party need not be unavailable; (2) the declaration need not have been against the party's interest when made; and (3) the party need not have had first-hand knowledge.

    a. **Strategy:** Therefore, if you represent a party and want to get a declaration by the opposing party into evidence, you should treat it as an admission, not a declaration against interest.

    b. **Practical use:** Conversely, the practical use of the declaration-against-interest exception is where the declarant is ***not a party***. Lilly, p. 297.

3. **Rationale:** As noted, the theory behind the exception is that a person will usually not make a statement against his own interest unless the statement is true. However, this rationale is not convincing in all cases: "Persons will lie despite the consequences to themselves to exculpate those they love or fear, to inculpate those they hate or fear, or because they are congenital liars. Others will not realize that they are making an admission against themselves, or will make ambivalent statements susceptible of differing interpretations." W&B, Par. 804(b)(3)[01]. It is for these reasons that there is a requirement of declarant unavailability — the evidence is better than no evidence at all, but not as good as having the declarant himself on the stand. These doubts are also the reason why, until recent years, declarations against penal interest (discussed *infra*, p. 237) have not been covered by the rule.

4. **Federal Rule:** The Federal Rules apply the declaration-against-interest exception in more or less its common law form. FRE 804(b)(3) provides an exception, if the declarant is unavailable, for:

    "A statement which was at the time of its making so far contrary to the declarant's pecuniary or proprietary interest, or so far tended to subject the declarant to civil or criminal liability, or to render invalid a claim by the declarant against another, that a reasonable person in the declarant's position would not have made the statement unless believing it to be true. A statement tending to expose the declarant to criminal liability and offered to exculpate the accused is not admissible unless corroborating circumstances clearly indicate the trustworthiness of the statement."

    a. **Covers penal interest:** The principal difference between this Federal Rule and the common-law rule is that the Federal Rule covers ***statements against penal interest***.

B. Meaning of "against interest": Most of the tough questions regarding the declaration-against-interest exception relate to whether the declaration really is *against the declarant's interest.*

1. **When made:** The declaration must have been against the declarant's interest *at the time it was made*. The fact that later developments have turned what was an innocent-seeming statement into one that now harms some interest of the declarant, is *not* enough to satisfy the requirement.

    a. **Rationale:** The rationale behind the exception is that a person will not speak against his own interest unless he is telling the truth, so this rationale would not apply where the statement was not against interest at the time it was made.

2. **Pecuniary interest:** As noted, the common-law version of the exception requires that the statement have been against the declarant's *pecuniary* or *proprietary* interest. Statements that would subject the declarant to criminal liability, or to social scorn, but not affect his financial well-being, have traditionally not been covered by the rule. Thus declarations against interest have tended to have a business or financial flavor.

    a. **Property:** For instance, the declarant's statement may concern his *property*, and may have the effect of limiting his property rights in some way.

        Example: P, a school board, brings an action against the Ds to quiet title to real estate on which its school is located. The Ds had previously received the property from one Lamm. P claims the property by adverse possession; the Ds claim that P merely received from Lamm the right to use the property for a school, after which it would revert to Lamm or his heirs. The Ds offer testimony by W1 and W2, who testify that, before the school buildings were constructed, the Ws heard Lamm say that he was allowing P to use the property only so long as it was needed for school purposes, and then it was to revert to him or his estate.

        Held, the statements were admissible. At the time of the statement, Lamm had an undisputed fee simple interest in the land, but by making the statement he limited his title by conceding that P had the right to use the land for school purposes. Therefore, his declaration was against his interest when made. Since Lamm is now unavailable, the declaration-against-interest exception applies. *Wilson County Board of Education v. Lamm*, 173 S.E.2d 281 (N.C. 1970).

    b. **Debts:** Similarly, statements by *creditors* about debts owed to them will often be against interest. For instance, a creditor's declaration that a debt has been all or partly paid will be treated as being against his interest, since it extinguishes his right to sue on the debt.

        i. **Receipt:** Observe that the out-of-court "declaration" may be *written* as well as oral. Thus, a *receipt* signed by the creditor acknowledging payment will be admissible to show that the debt was paid.

c. Tort liability: Modern decisions also generally treat a statement that may give rise to, or extinguish, ***tort liability*** as being against interest.

> **Example:** P is a passenger in a car driven by X. The car collides with a car driven by D, and P is killed. In a wrongful death action brought by P's husband, D testifies that, after the accident, he said to P, "I'm sorry, lady, but you pulled right out in front of me," and that P replied, "Yes, I know. It wasn't your fault."
>
> *Held*, P's response is admissible as a declaration against interest, at least with respect to its factual portion ("Yes, I know"). It had the effect of limiting her right to recover in a negligence action. (But the balance of the statement, concerning fault, is not admissible because it is a mere opinion rather than a factual declaration.) *Carpenter v. Davis*, 435 S.W.2d 382 (Mo. 1968).

> **Note:** *Carpenter* illustrates the wisdom of trying to get evidence in as a party admission, rather than a declaration against interest, wherever possible. Had P's statement been admissible as a party admission, the whole statement would probably have come in, even the part expressing P's opinion about fault. (See *supra*, p. 151). But because the court ruled that P was not really a "party" — it held (in a hypertechnical manner) that the real party was P's husband suing for damages — her statement had to come in as a declaration against interest or not at all. This ruling, in turn, resulted in excluding the opinion portion.

3. Against penal interest: At common law, statements against the declarant's ***penal*** interest — that is, statements exposing him to criminal liability — do ***not*** fall within the declaration-against-interest exception.

a. Rationale: This limitation stems mostly from the ***fear of false evidence.*** There are several related dangers:

i. False confessions: Many crimes, especially well-publicized ones, attract a substantial number of ***false confessions***. Thus suppose that D is charged with a murder, and that he offers testimony by W, that W has heard X confess to the murder. Even though W's testimony may be absolutely accurate — in the sense that he did indeed hear X confess to the crime — the underlying assertion (that X, not D, is guilty) may well be incorrect. Furthermore, it will waste a lot of prosecution and juror time if every false confession has to be admitted into evidence and then demonstrated to be false. See L&S, p. 490.

ii. False testimony: Conversely, there is a great risk that the witness will ***falsely testify*** that he has heard another person confess. For instance, suppose again that D is charged with murder, and that D's good friend (and sometime partner in crime), W, wants to help D out. W could falsely testify that he heard X confess to the crime. Especially where X is no longer available (a requirement for the declaration-against-interest exception), it may be hard for the prosecution to prove that W is lying.

b. Countervailing view: However, there is also a strong countervailing argument. Judicial refusal to allow evidence of out-of-court confessions by now-unavailable witnesses may cause an innocent man to be convicted.

> **Example:** The classic illustration comes from *Donnelly v. U.S.*, 228 U.S. 243 (1913), in which Justice Holmes dissented. D was convicted and given a death sentence for a murder that he claimed had been committed by Joe Dick. There was some evidence linking Dick to the crime, and some evidence that Dick confessed before dying. A majority of the Supreme Court upheld the trial court's decision to keep Dick's alleged confession out of evidence, on the grounds that it was not a declaration against his pecuniary interest, and that declarations against penal interest should not receive a hearsay exception. Holmes argued that the exception should be broadened to include evidence of Dick's confession: "The confession of Joe Dick, since deceased, that he committed the murder for which [P] was tried, coupled with circumstances pointing to its truth, would have a strong tendency to make anyone outside of a court of justice believe that [D] did not commit the crime. . . . The exception to the hearsay rule in the case of declarations against interest is well known; no other statement is so much against interest as a confession of murder, it is far more calculated to convince than dying declarations, which would be let in to hang a man; and when we surround the accused with so many safeguards, some of which seem to be excessive, I think we ought to give him the benefit of a fact that, if proved, commonly would have such weight."

c. The federal and modern approach: Some states (though probably still a minority) have broadened the declaration-against-interest exception to cover declarations against penal interest. The Federal Rules have also done so — indeed, this is the most important change from common law to Federal Rules in the area of declarations against interest.

    i. Corroborating circumstances: However, the Federal Rules have steered a ***middle path*** between keeping such evidence out entirely and letting it in wholesale: the last sentence of FRE 804(b)(3) states that "a statement tending to expose the declarant to criminal liability and offered to exculpate the accused is not admissible unless ***corroborating circumstances*** clearly indicate the trustworthiness of the statement."

    ii. Exculpatory statements: Most uses of declarations against penal interest are uses by the accused of a statement by a third person (often a confession) ***exculpating*** the accused. In this common situation, FRE 804(b)(3)'s corroboration requirement comes into play, and has significant bite.

d. Meaning of "corroboration": There can be no hard-and-fast standard as to what constitutes adequate ***corroboration*** (required for statements exculpating the defendant under FRE 804(b)(3)). Here are some of the factors the courts look at:

    i. Motive: Whether the declarant had an apparent ***motive*** to lie. For instance, if Declarant is shown to have been a friend of D, and was conveniently out of the jurisdiction or on his deathbed at the time he confessed to the crime with which D is now charged, Declarant's clear motive to falsify will probably be a strong non-corroborating factor.

ii. **General character:** The general *character* of the declarant. Thus if Declarant is a convicted criminal (especially a perjurer), his confession will be much less likely to be admitted.

iii. **Persons hearing statements:** Whether *more than one person* heard the statements. The more people who testify to having heard the out-of-court declaration, the more likely it is that the declaration was at least made (though this does not increase at all the likelihood that the declaration, when made, was truthful).

iv. **Spontaneous:** Whether the declaration was made *spontaneously* (if so, it is more likely to be received).

v. **Other:** The *timing* of the declaration, and the *relationship* between the declarant and the witness.

vi. **External connections:** Whether there is *other evidence* linking the declarant to the crime.

See *State v. Parris*, 633 P.2d 914 (Wash. 1981), applying factors i-v and concluding that corroboration was present.

Example: Suppose that D is charged with a robbery, and presents W, who testifies that shortly after the robbery, X told him, "It wasn't D who did it, it was me." If there is independent evidence that X could not have committed the crime because he was in prison at the time, the confession will be excluded. If, however, there is evidence that X was near the scene of the crime and had some motive or background connecting him to it, this will probably be enough. W&B, Par. 804(b)(3)[03]. "The court should only ask for sufficient corroboration to 'clearly' permit a reasonable man to believe that the statement *might have been made in good faith* and that it *could be true*." *Id.*

e. **Statements inculpating the accused:** The modern (and federal) tendency to allow statements against penal interest is not, by its terms, limited to statements introduced by the accused. That is, the *prosecution* may theoretically introduce an out-of-court declaration, made against the declarant's penal interest, that has the effect of *inculpating* the accused.

Example: D is charged with selling heroin. The prosecution offers testimony by W, an undercover narcotics officer, that he gave Declarant $100, that he (W) saw Declarant go to D's car and exchange something with him, and that when Declarant came back, W asked him whether he would get the drugs and Declarant responded, "Yes, I think so. There won't be any problem." The prosecution argues that Declarant's statement, taken in light of the surrounding circumstances, was against his penal interest, so the declaration-against-interest exception should apply.

Held, the exception applies, and the statement may be used against D. Declarant's statements "clearly indicated his involvement in an illicit drug transaction and 'strengthen the impression that he had an insider's knowledge of the crimes.' " At the time, Declarant did not know he was dealing with an undercover agent, and a reasonable person in his position would not have made the statements unless he believed them to be true. (Also, there was sufficient corroboration of the statement's reliability.) *State v. Parris*, 633 P.2d 914 (Wash. 1981).

   i. Need for corroboration: Observe that FRE 804(b)(3) does *not* explicitly impose a requirement that there be corroboration where the statement is used to *inculpate* (rather than exculpate) the accused. The draftsmen seem to have been mostly worried about false exculpations used by the accused, and seem to have ignored the possibility that a prosecutor might use an uncorroborated statement against the accused. Nonetheless, a number of courts have imposed a requirement of corroboration in this inculpatory situation as well. W&B, Par. 804(b)(3)[03]. *Parris*, *supra*, is one such decision.

4. **Collateral statements:** Perhaps the toughest issue concerning declarations against interest arises where a statement includes a part that is clearly against the declarant's interest and another part that is either "neutral" (in the sense that it doesn't affect the declarant's interest one way or the other) or self-serving.

   a. **Three choices:** If part is self-serving, the court has basically three choices: (1) It can admit the entire statement, on the theory that at least part of it is against the declarant's interest; (2) It can admit the whole statement if the disserving part predominates, and exclude the whole statement if the self-serving part predominates; and (3) It can admit just the disserving part, excluding the self-serving part. L&S, p. 488.

   b. **No general rule:** American courts prefer the second and third of these choices. L&S, p. 489. The third is probably the best, when the pieces can be separated. If they can't be, the court will generally choose the second, i.e., admit the whole statement if the disserving part predominates, and exclude the whole statement if the self-serving part predominates.

   c. **Neutral part:** If the other part of the statement is *neutral*, rather than self-serving, usually the court will allow the *whole statement* into evidence, on the theory that the neutral part should not mean that the whole statement is unreliable. This is especially likely where the statement inculpates the declarant, but also coincidentally inculpates or exculpates the accused.

   Example 1: Declarant tells a friend, "It was Joe and I that pulled off the First National Bank job the other day." Since the thrust of Declarant's statement is inculpatory to him, and since the other part (inculpating Joe) does not serve any apparent interest of Declarant, the whole statement will probably be admitted against Joe.

Example 2: D, whose nickname is Bucky, is charged with the federal crime of stamp theft. He offers testimony by Melvin that, during a cardgame, Tilley (Declarant) told Melvin that "Buzzy and I are going to have some trouble . . . [about] the stamp theft," that Melvin asked did he mean Bucky or Buzzy, and that Tilley replied, "No, Bucky wasn't involved. It was Buzzy." The prosecution argues that, although the first statement — that Declarant would be having some trouble — may be admissible as a declaration against interest, the Buzzy-not-Bucky part is not against Declarant's interest and should be excluded.

Held, the Buzzy-not-Bucky portion of the statement may be admitted as part of the overall statement (assuming that the general requirement of corroboration for exculpatory remarks is satisfied). First, the Buzzy-Bucky remark probably strengthened the disserving nature of the remark, since it strengthened the impression that Tilley had "an insider's knowledge of the crimes." Second, the Buzzy-Bucky remark was "sufficiently integral to the entire statement, and the latter sufficiently against interest, as to come within the first part of Rule 804(b)(3)." (But, on retrial, D will have to show that there is adequate corroboration before the entire statement can come in.) *U.S. v. Barrett*, 539 F.2d 244 (1st Cir. 1976).

5. **Factual background:** In determining whether a statement was against the declarant's interest when made, the ***factual background***, and the proposition for which the declaration is now offered, will be relevant.

   a. **Inferences:** Thus, a statement may be against the declarant's interest when used to support one inference, but not against his interest when used to support a different inference.

      Example: Declarant writes on his tax return that he earned $10,000 in 1986. If this statement is used to show that Declarant earned at least $10,000, it is against interest (since Declarant had financial incentives to minimize the amount of income he reported). However, if it is used to show that he earned no more than $10,000, it should not be admitted (because of the same incentive). L&S, p. 488.

   b. **Ignorance:** If there is evidence that the declarant ***did not realize***, at the time he made his declaration, that it was against his interest, it should probably be excluded (since lack of awareness of the danger removes the guarantee of reliability that is the whole basis for the exception).

      Example: D, a partner in a tavern, is charged with failure to pay cabaret excise taxes. A cabaret is defined as a place where dancing takes place. The IRS seeks to introduce a statement made to an IRS agent by D's partner, Declarant, that "there was dancing practically every weekend." There is no evidence that Declarant, at the time of the statement, realized that the presence of dancing would make the tavern a cabaret, and trigger excise taxes.

      Held, the statement is not admissible, because of the lack of evidence that Declarant knew the statement was against his interest when made. *Filesi v. U.S.*, 352 F.2d 339 (4th Cir. 1965).

c. **Reasonable person:** Keep in mind that, under the Federal Rules, a *"reasonable person"* standard applies on the question of whether the statement was against interest: FRE 804(b)(3) requires that the statement have been so far contrary to the declarant's interest "that a reasonable person in the declarant's position would not have made the statement unless believing it to be true." However, the "reasonable" person is one having the degree of awareness that the declarant had, so that, on the facts of *Filesi, supra,* if there was evidence that Declarant was unsophisticated in tax matters, the "reasonable person" would presumably be one with the same lack of sophistication and awareness.

C. **Constitutional issues:** When declarations against interest are sought to be introduced in criminal cases, various *constitutional issues* can arise. These vary, depending on whether the evidence is sought to be introduced by the accused or the prosecution.

   1. **Use by prosecution:** Where the *prosecution* seeks to introduce a third-party declaration to inculpate the accused, the Confrontation Clause of the Sixth Amendment may help the accused keep the statement out.

      a. **Corroboration required:** If the court allows a third-party statement exculpating the accused, and the judge does not insist on fairly stringent corroboration, the accused's right to confront and cross-examine the witness against him would seem to be violated. "Because of the dangers involved, exclusion should *almost always result* when a statement against penal interest is offered against an accused." W&B, Par. 804(b)(3)[03]. (However, it is not clear that the present Supreme Court would entirely agree with the just-quoted statement.)

         i. **In custody:** A Confrontation Clause argument by the accused is especially powerful where the declarant was *in custody* at the time he made the statement, or was otherwise in a situation that gave him a motive to *curry favor* with the authorities. Thus, if D can show that Declarant was motivated by the desire to get a *lighter sentence* for himself if he inculpated others, D has an excellent chance of keeping Declarant's statement against him out of evidence on a Confrontation Clause theory. See *Lee v. Illinois, infra,* pp. 273-74, where the Supreme Court held that the admission of one co-defendant's in-custody confession implicating the other violated the latter's Confrontation Clause rights, despite the applicability of the declaration-against-interest exception.

   2. **Use by accused:** Where it is the *accused* who seeks to *exculpate* himself by use of a third person's declaration against interest, the accused may be able to make an argument based upon the *Due Process Clause* and the Sixth Amendment's right to *compulsory process*.

      Example: Consider the facts of *Donnelly v. U.S., supra,* p. 238. Today, D could make a strong argument that depriving him of the right to prove that Joe Dick confessed to the crime violates D's due process rights and his right to "have compulsory process for obtaining witnesses in his favor" (Sixth Amendment).

a. ***Chambers* case:** The due process and compulsory process arguments are supported by a Supreme Court case, *Chambers v. Mississippi*, 410 U.S. 284 (1973). In *Chambers*, D sought to cross-examine one McDonald, who had, on previous occasions, admitted the crime for which D was on trial. (McDonald had later repudiated these confessions.) The state denied D both the right to cross-examine McDonald (because of a "voucher" rule that would not apply in federal courts; see *infra*, pp. 285-86) and the right to prove that McDonald had made the out-of-court confessions (finding the confessions to be hearsay). The Supreme Court held that D's due process rights were violated by this combination of factors.

i. Significance: In *Chambers* itself, McDonald was "available," so the declaration-against-interest exception would not have applied. But if McDonald had been unavailable, it seems clear that either the Due Process or the Compulsory Process clauses, or both, would have required that D be given the ability to prove McDonald's prior confessions, at least if there was some evidence corroborating those confessions. W&B, Par. 804(b)(3)[03].

XIII. STATEMENTS OF PEDIGREE

A. In general: There has always been a hearsay exception for statements of "pedigree," i.e., statements about a person's ***birth***, ***death***, ***marriage***, ***genealogy***, or other facts of personal or family history.

1. Requirements: At common law, there are four requirements which must be met before such a statement of personal or family history may be admitted:

a. The declarant must be ***unavailable***;

b. The declarant must be either the person whose history the statement concerns, or a ***relative*** of the person whom the statement concerns;

c. The statement must have been made ***before the present controversy arose***; and

d. The declarant must not have had any apparent ***motive*** to falsify.

M, p. 902.

Example: P, claiming to be Declarant's son, contests Declarant's will. P offers into evidence his own testimony that before Declarant died, Declarant told him, "You are my illegitimate son." P's testimony will be admissible at common law, because: Declarant is unavailable; Declarant is a close relative of the person whom the declaration concerns (i.e., P); the statement was made before the controversy (the will contest) began; and Declarant had no apparent motive to make a false statement. (It is irrelevant that *P* may have a motive to falsely quote Declarant's statement.)

Note: It is ***not*** required that the declarant have had ***personal knowledge*** of the facts stated, because such knowledge is often too hard to come by (e.g., a person's statement about his own year of birth, something that he could not know first-hand).

2. **Federal Rule:** The Federal Rules generally follow the common-law approach, but with a couple of liberalizations. FRE 804(b)(4) provides a hearsay exception for "statements of personal or family history":

> "(A) A statement concerning the declarant's own birth, adoption, marriage, divorce, legitimacy, relationship by blood, adoption, or marriage, ancestry, or other similar fact of personal or family history, even though declarant had no means of acquiring personal knowledge of the matter stated; or (B) a statement concerning the foregoing matters, and death also, of another person, if the declarant was related to the other by blood, adoption, or marriage or was so intimately associated with the other's family as to be likely to have accurate information concerning the matter declared."

   a. **Changes:** The main changes from the common law made by FRE 804(b)(4) are that: (1) the declaration need not have been made prior to the arising of the controversy; and (2) the declaration need not have been made by a relative of the person whom it concerns. These changes are discussed in more detail below.

B. **Family relationship:** As noted, most common-law jurisdictions require that the declarant have been a *relative* of the person whom the declaration concerns.

   1. **Minority view:** But some states allow declarations by *intimate associates* of the person or family whom the statement concerns. For instance, in *In re Lewis' Estate*, 242 P.2d 565 (Utah 1952), the court allowed W to testify that his wife, Declarant, told him that a baby boy was born in D's house in 1904, and that the mother was a daughter of D's cleaning woman. Because Declarant was present at the birth, and made arrangements for it, the fact that she was not a relative of the child or mother was irrelevant. "The likelihood of her declarations being true [is] very great. . . ."

   2. **Federal Rule:** As noted, part (B) of FRE 804(b)(4) embodies this liberal rule, allowing the declaration if the declarant is a non-relative who is "so intimately associated with the other's family as to be likely to have accurate information concerning the matter declared."

C. **Before controversy:** The common law required that the declaration have been made not only before the present litigation, but even before the *"controversy" arose*. This requirement is summed up in the Latin words *ante litem motam*. This was a way of assuring the reliability of the declaration.

   1. **Federal Rule:** The Federal Rule totally *drops* this requirement — the declaration may *even have been made after the litigation itself began*. (However, remember that the trial judge always has discretion under FRE 403 to reject evidence that is unfairly prejudicial or misleading.)

      a. **Rationale:** The theory behind the federal approach is that the fact that the statement was made after the controversy or litigation arose is a factor that the jury will take into consideration when it decides what *weight* it will give to the declaration.

b. Criticism: L&S criticize this rule as going too far, insofar as it allows declarations even by one who is himself involved in the controversy. They advocate "a compromise admitting statements whenever made, so long as the declarant is not shown to be involved in the controversy. . . ." L&S, p. 496.

D. Relation to reputation evidence: Observe that there may be overlap between the pedigree exception and evidence relating to *reputation* concerning a matter of personal or family history. See *supra*, p. 218, including discussion of FRE 803(19) ("reputation concerning personal or family history"). However, the two are not identical: reputation evidence requires at least moderately widespread knowledge of the fact reputed (as opposed to statements of pedigree, as to which only the declarant needs to have had the knowledge). Conversely, however, reputation evidence of pedigree is admissible even if the declarant is available, whereas the statement-of-pedigree exception requires that the declarant be unavailable.

   1. Family documents: Also, when the need to prove a fact of pedigree arises, don't overlook the *"family records"* exception (see *supra*, p. 219, and FRE 803(13)), by which statements of pedigree contained in family Bibles, genealogies, and the like can be introduced.

XIV. PRIOR STATEMENTS OF AVAILABLE WITNESSES

A. In general: We turn now to a special problem: the admissibility of *prior statements* made outside of a courtroom by a person who is, or is available to be, a witness at the current trial.

   1. Not necessarily exception: Although some types of "extrajudicial statements by available witnesses" have always been admissible, and under the Federal Rules even more kinds are, such statements do not necessarily, strictly speaking, constitute an "exception" to the hearsay rule. For instance, the Federal Rules treat those prior statements by available witnesses that are admissible as being *simply not hearsay at all*, rather than as falling within an exception to the hearsay rule. Nonetheless, we treat this problem in the present chapter on exceptions to the hearsay rule.

   2. Three different problems: The problem of "prior statements by a witness" really breaks down into three distinct problems: (1) Can prior *inconsistent* statements by the witness be admitted as substantive evidence? (2) Can prior *consistent* statements by him be admitted substantively? and (3) Can a prior out-of-court *identification* by the witness be admitted substantively? Our discussion below will take each of these cases in turn.

   3. Common-law rules in brief: The common law rules on the subject, in brief, are as follows:

      a. Prior inconsistent statement: A prior *inconsistent* statement by the witness is *inadmissible hearsay*. The reason is that the hearsay rule covers any statement offered for its truth other than one made from the witness stand *in the present proceeding*.

i. Impeachment use: The prior inconsistent statement may be used to *impeach* the witness at the present trial. But it may not be offered *substantively*, i.e., to prove the truth of the matter asserted.

Example: P brings a negligence action against D, alleging that D drove his car through a red light and hit P, a pedestrian. P's back was turned at the time, and the only witness other than D was W. At trial, D offers W's live testimony, "The light was green when D went through it." P offers to testify, "Right after D hit me, W rushed up and said, 'I saw D go through the intersection while the light was red.' "

At common law, W's prior inconsistent out-of-court statement (that the light was red) may be offered *only for purposes of impeaching W's credibility*, not as substantive evidence. Allowing the prior inconsistent statement as substantive evidence would mean that an out-of-court declaration is being offered for the truth of the matter asserted (that the light was red), and that's hearsay at common law. Therefore, unless P has some other evidence of D's negligence, P will lose because the judge will have to take the case away from the jury by awarding a directed verdict for D.

b. Prior consistent statement: Similarly, a witness' prior *consistent* statement is, at common law, not substantively admissible.

i. Rebut charge of recent fabrication: Again, use for non-substantive purposes is sometimes allowed. Most importantly, if the opponent claims that the witness has *recently fabricated* his trial testimony, or that the witness has been *improperly influenced* or *motivated*, the party offering that witness may show prior consistent statements by the witness, to rebut these charges. Again, as in the case of use of a prior inconsistent statement for impeachment purposes, the prior consistent statement is being used not to show the truth of the matter asserted (which would be a violation of the hearsay rule), but merely to support the credibility of the witness.

Example: As in the prior example, P asserts that D went through a red light. D offers W's testimony at trial, "The light was green when D went through it." P produces evidence suggesting that D has bribed W to change his story so that it is favorable to D. To rebut this charge of improper influence, all common-law courts agree that D may now testify that, at the time of the accident, W said to him, "The light was red." M, p. 119. But D's testimony goes only to W's credibility, and is not substantive evidence.

ii. Fresh complaint: Also, in a few circumstances the fact that there has been a *"fresh complaint"* has special probative value. In criminal cases where the wrongdoing is likely to be known only to the criminal and the victim — *rape* and *bribery* for instance — the court will usually allow the fact that the victim made a prompt complaint as substantive evidence that the crime occurred, even though this complaint is an out-of-court declaration offered to prove the truth of the matter asserted, and is consistent with the victim's at-trial testimony. Lilly, p. 206.

c. **Prior identification:** Proof that a witness has previously made an *eyewitness identification* is technically hearsay, but many (perhaps most) common-law courts allow the prior I.D. as substantive evidence if the circumstances make it appear to have probative value. M, pp. 747-48.

> **Example:** D is charged with robbing V. The prosecution offers testimony by W, a police officer, that shortly after the episode, V pointed to D in a police lineup and said, "That's the one who robbed me." Although V's declaration is technically hearsay — it is an out-of-court, uncross-examined statement offered to prove the truth of the matter asserted (that it really was D who robbed V) — many, if not most, common-law courts will allow it into evidence.

4. **Federal Rules:** The Federal Rules make some important modifications to these common-law rules, usually in the direction of increased admissibility. FRE 801 provides:

"(d) *Statements which are not hearsay.* A statement is not hearsay if —

(1) *Prior statement by witness.* The declarant testifies at the trial or hearing and is subject to cross-examination concerning the statement, and the statement is (A) inconsistent with the declarant's testimony, and was given under oath subject to the penalty of perjury at a trial, hearing, or other proceeding, or in a deposition, or (B) consistent with the declarant's testimony and is offered to rebut an express or implied charge against the declarant of recent fabrication or improper influence or motive, or (C) one of identification of a person made after perceiving the person. . . ."

a. **Modifications:** The Federal Rule broadens the common law in several very important ways:

b. **Inconsistent statement:** In the case of prior *inconsistent* statements, the Federal Rule: (1) allows *substantive* use (not just impeachment use) of (2) a previous statement made *under oath* at a "*proceeding*" or in a *deposition*.

> **Example:** Same facts as the example on p. 246, *supra*. W's prior inconsistent statement, "The light was red," will be admissible for its truth under the Federal Rules if it was made under oath at a prior trial, hearing (e.g., a preliminary hearing in a criminal negligence case against D), or even in a deposition. It will not be substantively admissible — any more than it would have been at common law — if it was merely an unsworn statement, say, to a casual bystander or a police officer investigating the accident.

c. **Prior consistent statement:** With respect to prior *consistent* statements, the Federal Rule follows the common-law principle of allowing admission to rebut a charge that the witness has *recently fabricated* his story, or has been *improperly influenced* or *motivated*. But the Federal Rule makes one big change from the common law: if the "rebuttal of accusation" requirement is satisfied, the prior consistent statement is *substantively admissible*, i.e., admissible to show the truth of the prior consistent statement.

d. **Identification:** With respect to prior *identifications*, the Federal Rule mirrors the approach of many common-law courts, by allowing the identification.

Observe that, unlike a prior inconsistent statement offered under 801(d)(1)(A), an identification under 801(d)(1)(C) need not have been made under oath, and need not have been made in a proceeding.

> **Example:** Return to the example on p. 247, *supra*. V's statement in the lineup, "That's the man who robbed me," will be admissible as substantive evidence that it was indeed D who did the robbery, even though V did not make this statement under oath, and even though an informal police lineup would probably not be a "proceeding" as used in 801(d)(1)(A).

B. Prior inconsistent statements: We turn now to a detailed consideration of prior inconsistent statements, the category of prior-witness-statement law that is the most difficult. Much of our discussion will be devoted to the unusually fascinating policy issues.

  1. In favor of admitting: Courts that would change the common-law rule against the substantive admission of prior inconsistent statements make the following arguments:

   a. Hearsay dangers absent: Generally, the classic dangers of hearsay are *absent* in this situation.

   b. Cross-examination: In particular, the witness is *now present to be cross-examined*. There is thus full opportunity to test the accuracy of his prior statement.

   c. Oath: The fact that the prior statement was not given *under oath* is of limited significance, since the oath is no longer as significant a guarantee of trustworthiness as it used to be, and since most of the other hearsay exceptions (e.g., dying declarations) are not given under oath.

   d. Demeanor: The fact that the declarant's *demeanor* at the time he made the statement cannot be witnessed by the trier of fact is also largely irrelevant, since his present demeanor can be viewed. "If, from all that the jury see of the witness, they conclude that what he says now is not the truth, but what he said before, they are nonetheless deciding from what they see and hear of that person and in court." *DiCarlo v. U.S.*, 6 F.2d 364 (2d Cir. 1925) (Learned Hand, J.)

   e. Recency: The earlier statement is likely to be *more reliable,* because it was given *earlier*, before the declarant's memory had a chance to fade. This is especially true of statements made immediately after the events in question.

   f. Improper influence: Finally, a statement made shortly after the events in question is likely to be more reliable because it is less likely that the witness has been *"gotten to,"* i.e., bribed or intimidated into changing his story.

  2. In favor of exclusion: Yet, those who would maintain the common-law rule, and exclude prior inconsistent statements as substantive evidence, have their own quite strong set of arguments:

   a. Hearsay dangers: Nearly all of the protections of the hearsay rule are absent, since the prior statement is: (1) not under oath; (2) not in the presence of the trier of fact; and (3) not subject to cross-examination.

b. **Cross-examination:** In particular, the absence of cross-examination ***at the time of the statement*** is critically important, and later cross-examination is no substitute. "The chief merit of cross-examination is not that at some future time it gives the party opponent the right to dissect adverse testimony. Its principal virtue is the immediate application of the testing process. ***Its strokes fall while the iron is hot***. False testimony is apt to harden and become unyielding to the blows of truth in proportion as the witness has opportunity for reconsideration and influence by the suggestions of others. . . ." *State v. Saporen*, 285 N.W. 898 (Minn. 1939).

3. **Superficial view favors admission:** Looking just at these classical intellectual arguments, it may appear that those favoring admission of the prior statement get the better of it. Superficially, there is no special reason to believe that the mere passage of time between the statement and the cross-examination should be so damaging to the examiner's ability to ferret out the truth. After all, the examiner can certainly pound away at *why* the witness changed his story, and the mere fact that the witness has changed his story will make the prior story hard-to-believe. As the argument has been stated, "the most successful cross-examination at the time the prior statement was made could hardly hope to accomplish more than has already been accomplished by the fact that the witness is now telling a different, inconsistent story, and — in this case — one that is favorable to the defendant." *California v. Green*, 399 U.S. 149 (1970) (White, J.)

4. **Ignorance of trial realities:** However, the view just summarized, favoring substantive admission of the prior inconsistent statement on the grounds that the cross-examiner has not been disadvantaged, ignores the practical realities of cross-examination. To see why this is the case, we will consider three separate Scenarios: (1) one in which there is no prior inconsistent statement at all; (2) one in which the witness concedes making the prior statement but says that he was wrong in what he said then, and (3) one in which the witness denies making the prior statement at all and tells a story that is different from the one he allegedly told previously. In each Scenario, the trial is about whether D shot V, and W is a prosecution eyewitness.

Scenario A: *No prior statement by W.*

Prosecutor (on direct): Would you tell us what you saw on August 12, 1987?

W: I saw D shoot V in the head.

Defense (on cross-examination): W, you say that you saw D shoot V, is that correct?

W: Yes

Defense: Did you see the gun in D's hand?

W: Well, not exactly. I saw D point something at V, then I heard an explosion, then I saw V fall down.

Defense: Did you see anything in D's hand?

W: I was too far away to see whether D was holding anything.

Defense: Isn't it possible that someone else had just shot V, and that what you saw was D pointing to a man who had just been shot?

W: Well, yes I guess that's possible.

Defense: So do you withdraw the testimony you just gave that you saw D shoot V?

W: Well, I guess I have to say I'm not sure anymore what I saw.

Scenario B: *Witness' prior statement remembered but repudiated.*

Prosecution: Would you tell us what you saw on August 12, 1987?

W: I heard an explosion, I saw V fall to the ground, and then I saw D pointing his finger at V.

Prosecution: Your Honor, I am taken completely by surprise by this testimony. I would like to show that this witness made a prior statement which is inconsistent with the testimony he has just given.

Judge: Permission granted.

Prosecution: Didn't you tell the police right after the shooting that you had seen D shoot V?

W: Yes, but I now realize that D was just a bystander, and that my prior statement was wrong.

Defense (on cross-examination): Do you mean to tell me, W, that my client *didn't* shoot V?

W: That's right.

Defense: So you were lying when you told the police that he did it?

W: No, I wasn't lying. I was simply mistaken, and later realized that I had been mistaken.

Defense: So you're telling the truth now and you weren't telling the correct story then?

W: Yes.

Prosecution (on re-direct): When you "changed your mind" about what you had seen, that didn't have anything to do with your being contacted by D, did it?

W: Absolutely not.

Prosecution: D or his representatives didn't by chance offer you anything in return, or threaten you, in order to get you to change your story, did they?

W: No.

Scenario C: *Prior statement not remembered and underlying facts denied.*

Prosecution: Would you tell us what you saw on August 12, 1987?

W: I heard an explosion, I saw V fall down, and then I saw D point his finger at V.

Prosecution: Your Honor, we're very surprised by this testimony. I'd like to show that the witness made an inconsistent statement on a prior occasion.

Judge: Permission granted.

Prosecution: Didn't you tell the police officer right after the event that you had seen D shoot V?

W: Naw, I never said anything to the police. I told them I didn't see what happened.

Prosecution: But now, suddenly, you "remember" what you couldn't remember when you spoke to the police three seconds after the accident?

W: Well, I don't like talkin' to the police. But I know what I saw, and what I saw was that V was already on the ground when D pointed at him.

[Prosecution calls Police Officer who came to scene of crime.]

Prosecution: Would you tell us what, if anything, W said to you when you arrived?

Officer: He told me that D had shot V.

Defense (on cross): W has just told us that he didn't tell you anything. Why should we believe your story that he told you he saw D do the shooting?

Officer: I guess you gotta believe him or believe me. Anyway, I made notes in my notebook about what he told me. Here they are. *[Hands notes to Defense.]*

Defense: Can we recall W to the stand?

[W recalled]

Defense (on cross): W, Police Officer has just told us that you said you saw D shoot V. Yet you say you never said this?

W: What do you want me to say? I already told you that I didn't say nothin' to the police 'cause I don't trust cops.

Defense: But it's now your testimony that you didn't see D shoot V?

W: That's right. Like I said, all I saw was V fall to the ground and D point his finger at him afterwards.

5. **Analysis:** Even though, in each of the three scenarios above, W has given the same ultimate version of what he saw, the defendant comes out much worse in scenarios

B and C than under A.

   a. Scenario A: After Scenario A, D is in great shape. W has been discredited right in front of the jury's eyes. After that testimony, there is simply **no evidence** (at least coming from W) that D shot V.

   b. Scenario B: After Scenario B, by contrast, D is in much less good shape. True, W has conceded on the stand that he did not see D shoot V. But W has not been really discredited; he has merely told why his earlier statement was inaccurate. D's lawyer was stripped of his ability to reach the key goal of cross-examination, the ***dramatic discrediting of the witness on the stand.*** "Instead of a plunge to the jugular, the examiner will have to be satisfied with applying a bandage to the witness, i.e., to showing that the witness is now telling the truth." *Ruhala v. Roby,* 150 N.W.2d 146 (Mich. 1967). The jury is quite likely to conclude that W told the truth then and is lying now.

   c. Scenario C: In Scenario C, D probably makes out even worse. D wasn't able to examine W about why he changed his story, since W denied ever changing the story. Yet, the jury will almost certainly believe the testimony of Police Officer (backed by Police Officer's notes) that W really did make the declaration, rather than W's unsubstantiated testimony that he never made the statement. If this is what the jury believes, then W's earlier statement stands in full force, without D's ever really having had the opportunity to attack its underlying details. Thus one court has referred to the "windmill-fighting nature" of cross-examination in these circumstances. *Ruhala, supra.* "However cooperative the witness, there can be no explanation for a discrepancy which is not acknowledged." L&S, p. 512.

6. Federal Rules compromise: Because of these practical realities, the drafters of the Federal Rules refused to provide a blanket hearsay exception for prior inconsistent statements. Instead, they pursued a ***compromise*** approach, which allows the prior statement in as substantive evidence only in those situations where there is some ***extra guarantee of reliability.***

   a. Oath and proceeding: In particular, the prior statement must have been given ***under oath***, and must have occurred at a "***trial, hearing***, or other ***proceeding***, or in a ***deposition* . . . .**" Thus in Scenarios B and C above, since W's statement to the police officer was neither under oath nor at a "proceeding," it would not be admissible under FRE 801(d)(1)(A). The theory behind the compromise is that the solemnity of the oath, when coupled with the regularity inherent in a "proceeding" (especially the probable preparation of a transcript) reduces the danger that the declarant lied, or that the purported statement was never made.

   b. Cross-examination not required: Observe, however, that the Federal Rule allows the prior inconsistent statement into evidence even where there was ***no cross-examination***, or even any ***opportunity*** for cross-examination. For instance, a witness' prior ***grand jury testimony*** is admissible against the accused if the witness tells a different story at trial, even though the accused not only did not have the opportunity for cross-examination at the grand jury, but did not even have the right to be present (or the right to object to leading questions by the prosecutor).

7. Special contexts: Let us now review several special contexts, and see how the common law and Federal Rules would apply to them:

8. Statement remembered but repudiated: First, suppose the witness concedes having made the prior statement, but says it was wrong, and tells a different story now. (This is Scenario B above.)

    a. Common law: At common law, the statement is *inadmissible* as substantive evidence.

    b. Federal: Under the Federal Rules, as long as the prior statement was made under oath in a "proceeding," it is substantively admissible, because it is clearly "inconsistent" with the witness' present testimony.

9. Prior statement denied: Suppose that the witness denies ever having made the prior statement, but there is independent evidence that the statement was made, and the witness now tells a story which is inconsistent with the prior purported statement. (This is Scenario C above.)

    a. Common-law rule: Again, at common law, the statement will be excluded as substantive evidence.

    b. Federal Rule: Under the Federal Rules, the Scenario will generally arise only under circumstances making the prior statement *inadmissible*:

        i. Transcript: If the statement was made under oath and in a trial, hearing, "other proceeding," or deposition, it will be admissible under the Federal Rules. However, if it was made in such a proceeding, there will normally be a *transcript* available. If there is a transcript, it is very unlikely that the witness will continue to deny having made the statement. Therefore, the whole Scenario is unlikely to arise.

        ii. Unrecorded oral statement: If, on the other hand, the statement was merely an informal one made to, say, a bystander or a police officer, and was not made under oath or in a "proceeding" (so that there is no transcript available), the statement will not be admissible under the Federal Rules.

    c. Use in state court: Suppose that a state court, not bound by the Federal Rules, decides to admit the prior statement in this situation against a criminal defendant. Can the defendant argue that his constitutional rights under the Sixth Amendment's Confrontation Clause have been violated? Probably not, under *Nelson v. O'Neil*, 402 U.S. 622 (1971).

        i. Facts of *O'Neil*: In *O'Neil*, D and W were arrested together and jointly tried. A police officer testified at trial that, after the arrest, W had made a statement implicating both himself and D. W then took the stand and denied having made the statement to the officer, and also denied that he or D committed the crime. D argued that introduction of W's prior statement (even though the judge cautioned the jury that it was admissible only against W, not D) violated his Confrontation Clause rights.

> **ii. Rejected:** The Supreme Court disagreed. "Where a co-defendant takes the stand in his own defense, denies making an alleged out-of-court statement implicating the defendant, and proceeds to testify favorably to the defendant concerning the underlying facts, the defendant has been denied no rights protected by the Sixth and Fourteenth Amendments." Had W admitted making the statement, D would have been in much worse shape than the way in which he found himself when W disavowed the statement. Therefore, D cannot claim that W's disavowal put him in a worse position than W's adoption of the prior statement would have (in which situation it is clear, from prior decisions, that D's Confrontation Clause rights will be satisfied by the opportunity to cross-examine W at trial).

10. Prior statement adopted but underlying facts not remembered: Suppose now that W admits making the prior statement, but claims that he does not now remember the underlying facts. That is, W says at trial, "Yes, I told the Grand Jury that I saw D shoot V, but now I don't remember whether that's what I really saw."

> **a. Common law:** Again, at common law, the prior statement is simply not substantively admissible.

> **b. Federal Rules:** Under the Federal Rules, the result would depend on whether the judge believes that W is being ***truthful*** in his assertion that he cannot remember.

>> **i. Truthful:** If the judge believes W is telling the truth about not being able to remember, then his prior statement is ***not inconsistent*** with his present testimony. Accordingly, the prior statement should not be found to be within FRE 801(d)(1)(A). W&B, Par. 801(d)(1)(A)[04].

>> **ii. Not truthful:** If, however, the judge concludes that W is now lying about not being able to remember, then the prior statement should probably be viewed as inconsistent, and would be ***admissible.*** (But even then, the judge could keep it out under FRE 403, if he felt that the lack of a real opportunity to cross-examine the witness made the statement unfairly prejudicial or confusing.)

> **c. Constitutional issue:** The above situation — W admits making the statement but claims not to remember the underlying facts now — was the setting of a major Supreme Court Confrontation Clause case, in which the Court held that D's right to confront the witnesses against him was ***not violated***. See *California v. Green*, 399 U.S. 149 (1970), discussed extensively *infra*, pp. 270-71. Under *Green*, if the trial judge finds that the witness who asserts lack of memory of the underlying facts is lying, the prior statement is probably not only an admissible prior inconsistent statement under the Federal Rules, but also one whose admission does not violate D's confrontation rights, so long as the jury had the opportunity to observe the demeanor of W.

11. **Prior statement eventually adopted by witness:** Finally, suppose that the witness testifies in a manner that is inconsistent with the prior statement, is shown that statement, and then agrees that the prior statement is correct. (E.g., "Oh yes, I see that I was correct when I originally told the Grand Jury that I saw D shoot V.")

   a. **Common law:** Here, even at common law, the prior statement is *admissible*. This is because it has now been adopted as *present testimony* — it has been repeated by the witness in court under oath, is subject to cross-examination, and the witness' demeanor while repeating it can be observed. W&B, Par. 801(d)(1)(A)[02].

   b. **Abuse:** However, there is a possible abuse. The witness' trial testimony might have been almost completely consistent with the prior statement, yet the person presenting that witness could seize upon the small deviations to claim that the prior statement is inconsistent and may now be admitted. This would lead to a "bolstering" of the witness by use of what is really a prior *consistent* statement. Since prior consistent statements are not normally admissible, the trial judge should not allow small variations to turn a statement into an admissible "inconsistent" one. *Id.*

C. **Prior consistent statements:** We now turn to prior *consistent* statements, i.e., those statements which match what the witness is now saying at trial.

   1. **Common-law view:** In general, the common law treats such consistent statements as *inadmissible hearsay.* However, as noted, if the opponent has claimed that the witness has been "gotten to," i.e., persuaded to change his story because of improper influence, the common law allows the proponent to show that the witness told the same story earlier. However, this exception only goes to credibility, and the prior statement is not treated as substantive evidence. M, p. 747.

   2. **Federal Rule:** The Federal Rules allow substantive use of the prior consistent statement if "offered to rebut an express or implied charge against [the witness] of recent fabrication or improper influence or motive." FRE 801(d)(1)(B). However, it is hard to see why this exception is even needed — if the prior statement is really consistent with what the witness is saying at trial, there already *is* substantive evidence on the point in question, so the only effect of the prior statement would be as to the witness' credibility. L&S, p. 516.

D. **Prior identification:** A *statement of identification* made by the witness on a prior occasion is theoretically hearsay. That is, if W says in court, "I picked D out of the lineup and told the police that that was who robbed me," W's statement at the time of the lineup is being used for the truth of the matter asserted (that it was D who did the robbery).

   1. **Common-law exception:** Nonetheless, most states, either by statute or by case law, *allow* such prior statements of identification, if the identifier is *available for cross-examination at trial.* Similarly, W2 will be permitted in these states to testify that W1 previously made a statement of identification to him, if W1 testifies and is available to be cross-examined.

Example: The Ds are prosecuted for an attack on Anderson. At trial, Anderson is permitted to testify that after the attack, he accompanied a police officer to a pool hall, where he pointed out the Ds as his assailants. The police officer also testifies that Anderson made the pool hall identification of the Ds.

Held, Anderson's and the officer's testimony about the prior statement of identification were admissible. As to Anderson's testimony, the identification of the Ds in the pool hall, made so close in time to the attack (the day after), was more reliable than an in-court identification would have been, especially since there was no showing that it was unfair or biased. The officer's testimony about the ID was not offered to prove the truth of the out-of-court declaration, but merely to prove that the declaration (the picking out of the Ds) had taken place, so it was not hearsay. *People v. Gardner*, 265 N.W.2d 1 (Mich. 1978).

2. **Federal Rules:** The Federal Rules contain a similar exception for prior identifications. FRE 801(d)(1)(C) treats as non-hearsay a statement of "identification of a person made after perceiving him," if the declarant testifies at the trial and is available for cross-examination.

   a. **No oath or proceeding:** Under the Federal Rules, prior identifications are easier to get into evidence than are prior inconsistent or consistent statements.

      i. **Compare with inconsistent statement:** The prior ID need not have been made under oath, and need not have been part of a "proceeding," in contrast to a prior inconsistent statement. Thus the pool hall ID in *Gardner* would be admissible under the Federal Rules, even though a statement not involving an identification would not have been admissible as a prior inconsistent statement, since the pool hall transaction was not a sufficiently formal "proceeding".

      ii. **Compare with consistent statement:** Furthermore, the prior ID is easier to get into evidence than any other prior *consistent* statement: unlike the prior consistent statement, the prior ID is admissible even though it is completely consistent with the at-trial testimony of the identifier, whose veracity has not been attacked.

   b. **Ability to cross-examine:** Statements of identification, like prior inconsistent and consistent statements, are only allowed if the declarant "testifies at the trial or hearing and is subject to cross-examination concerning the statement. . . ." (First sentence of 801(d)(1).) Thus a major part of the rationale for allowing such prior statements of identification is that the opponent has the opportunity to test the accuracy of the prior identification by *questioning the declarant at the trial.* However, the Supreme Court has recently interpreted the requirement that the declarant be "subject to cross-examination" in such a loose way that much of the protection given by this requirement of cross-examination will in some cases be illusory. In *U.S. v. Owens*, 484 U.S. 554 (1988), the Court held that so long as the opponent has the ability to ask questions to the declarant about his prior identification, the prior identification qualifies as non-hearsay under 801(d)(1)(C) even though declarant admits to having a ***total lack of memory*** about the event that gave rise to the identification.

    i. Facts: In *Owens*, declarant was a corrections officer who was beaten and almost killed by an inmate. During one of declarant's few days of lucidity following the attack, he told an FBI agent visiting his hospital room that the assailant had been D. By the time of D's trial, declarant could no longer say that D was his assailant, but he testified that he remembered having identified D during the previous interview. Declarant could not explain why he had previously identified D, and admitted that he did not actually see D attack him.

    ii. Holding: A majority of the Court held that declarant was "subject to cross-examination concerning the statement" despite this memory loss. Since declarant was placed on the stand, under oath, and responded to questions about his prior statement as well as he could, this was all that Rule 801(d)(1) required. (But two dissenters pointed out that declarant was clearly "unavailable as a witness" under FRE 804(a)(3), applicable when the witness "testifies to a lack of memory of the subject matter of his statement." The dissenters thought it absurd to hold that a witness who is "unavailable" under one Rule could be meaningfully cross-examined under another.)

c. Bias or suggestion: FRE 801(d)(1)(C) does not contain an explicit requirement that the identification have been "fair," i.e., not the product of unfair ***bias or suggestion***. For instance, suppose that W tells the police that his assailant is a black male around thirty years old, and the police then give him a four-man lineup in which D (whom W identifies) is the only black male between the ages of twenty and forty in the group. By its literal terms, 801(d)(1)(C) would allow W's identification into evidence.

    i. Constitutional problem: However, use of such out-of-court identifications against a criminal defendant may pose ***constitutional*** problems. For instance, the holding of a ***lineup*** by the police will generally violate the defendant's Sixth Amendment ***right to counsel*** if the defendant is not given the right to have a lawyer present. Similarly, unduly suggestive identification procedures — such as the facts in the prior paragraph — would probably violate the defendant's ***due process*** rights.

XV. THE RESIDUAL ("CATCH ALL") EXCEPTION

A. Generally: Suppose a piece of hearsay evidence does not fall neatly within any of the special exceptions cataloged above. If the facts surrounding it convince the court that the evidence is highly reliable and badly needed, must it nonetheless be excluded? Both common-law jurisdictions and statutory approaches (including the Federal Rules) seem to be increasingly willing to receive such evidence under a ***"residual"*** or "catch all" exception to the hearsay rule.

1. **Broad approach:** In its broadest form, the residual hearsay exception might be phrased this way: "If a particular item of hearsay evidence has circumstantial guarantees of trustworthiness equivalent to the guarantees which attach to the recognized exceptions, that item of evidence should be admitted whether or not it meets the requirements of an established hearsay exception [so long as there is little or no non-hearsay evidence that bears on the issue]." L&S, p. 499.

> **Example:** The tower of the Dallas County Courthouse, in Selma, Alabama, collapses in 1957. P (the County) claims that the collapse was due to the tower's being struck by lightning several days before (in which case insurance would cover the loss). D (the insurance company) contends that the collapse was due to structural weakness and deterioration (not covered). Investigation of the debris shows the presence of charcoal and charred timbers. D, in order to show that this charring may not have been due to lightning, offers an unsigned article from the local newspaper, dated in 1901, describing a fire in the courthouse while it was under construction.
>
> *Held*, the newspaper article is admissible, even though it is hearsay and falls within no recognized exception. (It does not satisfy the "ancient documents" exception because the declarant's identity is unknown, and there is no proof that he had first-hand knowledge of the matter asserted.) Two requirements must be met for hearsay evidence to be admitted: (1) necessity, and (2) trustworthiness. Requirement (1) is satisfied because, 58 years after the fact, it is very improbable that any eyewitness can be found to give accurate testimony, from first-hand knowledge, about whether the 1901 fire really occurred. Requirement (2) is satisfied because "it is inconceivable to us that a newspaper reporter in a small town would report that there was a fire in the dome of the new courthouse — if there had been no fire. He is without motive to falsify, and a false report would have subjected the newspaper and him to embarrassment in the community. The usual dangers inherent in hearsay evidence, such as lack of memory, faulty narration, intent to influence the court proceedings, and plain lack of truthfulness are not present here." Thus, even though the article does not fall within any "readily identifiable and happily tagged species of hearsay exception," it will be admitted because it is "necessary and trustworthy, relevant and material. . . ." *Dallas County v. Commercial Union Assurance Co.*, 286 F.2d 388 (5th Cir. 1961).

B. **Federal Rules:** The Federal Rules codify the residual or "catch all" exception, to pick up needed, trustworthy evidence that happens not to fall within any of the recognized exceptions.

1. **Text of Federal Rule:** The Federal Rules contain two identically-worded provisions establishing this residual exception, 803(24) and 804(b)(5). (The former applies without regard to whether the declarant is available; the latter requires declarant unavailability.) Each gives a hearsay exception for:

   "A statement not specifically covered by any of the foregoing exceptions but having equivalent circumstantial guarantees of trustworthiness, if the court determines that (A) the statement is offered as evidence of a material fact; (B) the statement is more probative on the point for which it is offered than any other evidence which the proponent can procure through reasonable efforts; and (C) the general purposes of these rules and the interests of justice will best be served by admission of the statement into evidence. However, a statement may not be admitted under this exception unless the proponent of it makes known to the adverse party sufficiently in advance of the trial or hearing to provide the adverse party with a fair opportunity to prepare to meet it, his intention to offer the statement and the particulars of it, including the name and address of the declarant."

2. **Five requirements:** Taking apart the language of 803(24) and 804(b)(5), we see that there are five distinct requirements that must be met before the evidence may be admitted:

   a. **Circumstantial guarantees of trustworthiness:** Most important, the statement must have ***"circumstantial guarantees of trustworthiness"*** that are "equivalent" to those inherent in the remainder of the Rule 803 and 804(b) exceptions. (This all-important element is examined in detail *infra,* p. 261.)

   b. **Material fact:** The statement must be "offered as evidence of a material fact."

   c. **More probative:** The statement must be ***"more probative on the point*** for which it is offered than any other evidence which the proponent can procure through reasonable efforts." This is the other requirement that has some "bite" — if there is some other witness (or indeed, the declarant himself) who can give live testimony at the trial that is of equal probative value, the residual exception does not apply.

      i. **Unavailability:** For this reason, most of the time the residual exception has been successfully invoked only where the declarant is ***unavailable,*** since if he were available, his at-trial testimony would normally be more probative. (But observe that 803(24) is part of FRE 803, the "availability of declarant immaterial" set of exceptions. Nonetheless, most successful applications of the residual exception come under 804(b)(5), the version of the residual exception that applies where the declarant is unavailable.)

   d. **Interests of justice:** Use of the evidence must be consistent with "the general purposes of these rules and the interests of justice." This requirement has little practical significance.

   e. **Notice:** The person offering the evidence must give ***notice*** of his intention to offer the statement "sufficiently in advance of the trial or hearing to provide . . . a fair opportunity to prepare to meet it. . . ." The notice must include the ***particulars*** of the statement, including the declarant's name and address. This notice requirement, which is of considerable importance, is discussed *infra,* p. 265.

   f. **Illustration:** The case set forth in the following Example illustrates the operation of the federal residual exception.

      Example: The estate of P, a construction worker, sues D, the owner of an apartment building, for negligence leading to P's death. The main issue is whether D or its employees knew that a gate on the roof was dangerous, but nonetheless told P and other workers that they could not remove the gate.

The estate offers testimony by W (a fellow worker) that P told him prior to the accident that D's Superintendent had forbidden the crew to remove the gate because the Super used the roof area as a pen for his dog; it also offers W's statement that P said that the Super refused to let the crew reach the garage roof through his apartment window rather than by climbing the gate, because he did not want his rugs soiled.

Held, W's testimony about what P said the Super said is admissible under the residual hearsay exception, FRE 804(b)(5). The evidence was clearly material. The statement was certainly "more probative on the point for which it was offered" than any other reasonably available evidence (since the Super was out of the jurisdiction and did not testify at trial, and P was dead). The notice of the estate's intent to use this testimony was adequate. The testimony bore "equivalent circumstantial guarantees of trustworthiness" because: (1) P had little motive to lie, since he gave his account of what the Super said before the accident, and following the Super's instructions made the job much more difficult; and (2) The condition of the roof revealed that the area was frequently used by a dog, thus corroborating P's explanation of why the Super would not allow the gate to be removed. Finally, admission of the evidence served the interests of justice, because of the importance and apparent truthfulness of the evidence, the estate's good faith (but unsuccessful) efforts to discover the Super's whereabouts, and D's lack of diligence in helping the estate locate the Super. *Robinson v. Shapiro*, 646 F.2d 734 (2d Cir. 1981).

Note: Observe that, at first glance, this looks like a "hearsay within hearsay" problem, since W testified about what P said about what the Super had said. However, the trial court treated the Super's statement as being a non-hearsay "verbal act," i.e., an "event" that established the "conditions" under which the men were to work. The Court of Appeals did not have to decide whether this ruling was correct, since it found that the residual exception covered the entire chain of statements. But remember that you must always be on the lookout for "hearsay within hearsay" — under FRE 805, "hearsay included within hearsay" is admissible only if "each part of the combined statements conforms with an exception to the hearsay rule. . . ." See *supra*, p. 145.

3. **How used:** Here are some contexts in which the federal residual exception has been applied:

   a. **Grand jury testimony:** To allow use of ***grand jury testimony*** where the witness is not available to testify at trial. See, e.g., *U.S. v. Garner, infra*, p. 263. (The "former testimony" exception of 804(b)(1) does not apply to such testimony, because the opponent did not have the opportunity to cross-examine.)

   b. **Notes by observer:** To admit ***handwritten notes*** taken by an observer of an event, where the observer is not available to testify at trial. (Such a document cannot constitute Past Recollection Recorded, under FRE 803(5), because the author is, by hypothesis, not present as a witness to authenticate it.) See *Turbyfill v. International Harvester, infra*, p. 264.

c. **Oral statement:** To admit an ***oral statement*** by the declarant, where the declarant is now unavailable, the evidence is badly needed, and there are circumstantial guarantees of reliability. (See, e.g., *Robinson v. Shapiro, supra.*)

4. **Grand jury testimony:** Most of the controversy concerning the use of the Federal Rules' residual exception has concerned the use of ***grand jury testimony*** in circumstances where the grand jury witness is unavailable at trial. The issue is especially likely to arise where the grand jury witness either: (1) has been murdered prior to the trial (as not infrequently occurs in drug and organized crime cases); or (2) refuses to testify at trial, either by explicitly relying on his privilege against self-incrimination or by merely being uncooperative (perhaps because he is in fear of the defendant). Most, but not all, federal courts have been reasonably ***receptive*** to the use of the residual exception in this situation. See, e.g., *U.S. v. Garner, infra*, p. 263.

   a. **Waiver theory:** In those cases where the court believes that the witness' "unavailability" at trial is ***due to the defendant***, the court may, instead of, or in addition to, using the residual exception, apply a ***"waiver"*** theory. Under this theory, the defendant's act of making the witness unavailable is deemed to waive his objection to the grand jury testimony (as well as any Confrontation Clause constitutional right he might have had to not have uncross-examined evidence used against him.) See, e.g., *U.S. v. Thevis*, 665 F.2d 616 (5th Cir. 1982), where the Court of Appeals agreed with the trial court's finding that D was responsible for the murder of the declarant, who had testified before the grand jury. Even though the Court of Appeals doubted that the grand jury evidence could be reliable enough to satisfy the reliability requirement of the residual exception, it concluded that "under the circumstances of this case, [D's] waiver of his confrontation rights [by killing declarant] also acted as a waiver of the right to raise a hearsay objection once the prosecution demonstrated a need for the evidence."

C. **Circumstantial guarantees of trustworthiness:** The most important issue that arises in most residual exception cases is whether the statement has ***"circumstantial guarantees of trustworthiness"*** equivalent to those inhering in the specific exceptions (Rules 803(1)-(23), and 804(b)(1)-(4)).

1. **"Average" of other exceptions:** The requirement of "equivalent" circumstantial guarantees means guarantees equivalent to those inhering in the other, enumerated, exceptions. But there is tremendous variation in trustworthiness among the exceptions — for instance, an excited utterance (FRE 803(2)) is much less likely to be reliable than, say, former testimony subjected to cross-examination when given (FRE 804(b)(1)). Therefore, the question becomes: Should the standard for "equivalent trustworthiness" be that of the highest, lowest, or average other exception? "When the question has been asked, the answer seems to have been, 'not necessarily the highest.' " M, p. 908. Most courts have implicitly assumed some sort of ***"average."*** *Id.*

2. **Factors bearing on declarant:** How should the court go about determining whether there are "equivalent circumstantial guarantees of trustworthiness"? The

strongest case can be made for looking at factors that bore upon the ***declarant at the time he made the statement***, since these are the kinds of indicia of reliability that common-law courts use to derive the recognized hearsay exceptions. Such factors would include:

    a. Oath: Whether the statement was ***under oath.*** (So sworn grand jury testimony would be more reliable than, say, an unsworn statement to a police officer.)

    b. Time lapse: The ***length of time*** that elapsed between the event and the statement (the longer the time gap, the less reliable).

    c. Motive for truth: The declarant's ***motive*** for telling the truth. (So a co-defendant who is in custody at the time he implicates D will be viewed as having a motive to lie, since he may well believe that falsely implicating another may get him a lighter sentence.)

    d. First-hand knowledge: Whether the declarant had ***first-hand knowledge,*** or was merely repeating what someone else said.

    e. Written vs. oral: Whether the statement is ***written*** or oral. (Written, whether written out by the declarant or transcribed stenographically as in a confession to police, is presumed to be more reliable than oral).

    See generally W&B, Par. 803(24)[01]; M, p. 908.

3. Corroboration by other evidence: The major controversy is whether reliability can be demonstrated by the fact that the statement is ***corroborated*** by ***other evidence in the case***.

    a. Against corroboration: Some courts and commentators have argued that the other, corroborating, evidence in the case should be treated as ***irrelevant*** for this purpose. They point out that Congress intended the residual exception to be applied in a manner analogous to the other hearsay exceptions. Yet the other hearsay exceptions ***never*** look at the presence of other corroborating evidence in the case; they focus solely on whether, looking at the circumstances of the declaration itself, the evidence is likely to be reliable. L&S, p. 503.

    b. In favor of corroboration: Other courts and commentators have argued, in contrast, that consistency with the other evidence in the case is indeed a good way of measuring the reliability of a particular statement. A strong match-up between the statement and the other evidence at least indicates that the declarant had first-hand knowledge of the facts, and was not engaging in wholesale lying.

    c. Grand jury testimony by co-defendant: This approach of looking to the consistency between the statement and other evidence has been very heavily relied upon by courts seeking to use the ***grand jury testimony*** of witnesses (especially prospective co-defendants) who are unavailable to testify at trial. Without the corroboration-by-other-evidence approach, these courts would often be forced to exclude the evidence, since the circumstances surrounding the declaration itself usually do not inspire confidence in the declaration's reliability (e.g., the grand jury testimony is never cross-examined by the defense, and the witness is often one who is implicated in the crime, with a motive to give the testimony that the prosecution wants in return for more favorable treatment).

Example: The Ds are charged with importing heroin from Europe. The prosecution offers the grand jury testimony of one Robinson, implicating the Ds in the crimes. At trial, Robinson repudiates his grand jury testimony, and says he doesn't know anything about drug trafficking by the Ds. At the time of the trial, Robinson has plea bargained to an earlier drug charge and is in prison.

Held, Robinson's grand jury testimony is admissible under FRE 804(b)(5)'s residual exception. Such testimony may be admitted "when there are substantial guarantees of trustworthiness equivalent to those which warrant recognized exceptions to the hearsay rule." Here, there are "strong indicators of reliability." In particular, Robinson's account to the grand jury about a trip to Europe with one of the Ds matches airline tickets, hotel registrations, and other detailed travel records. (The Ds do not deny these travels, but claim that they were not for purposes of drug smuggling.) This other, corroborative, evidence satisfies not only the requirements of FRE 804(b)(5) but also the requirements of the Confrontation Clause. The fact that Robinson has since repudiated his grand jury testimony does not mean that the testimony is unreliable; he may have been the victim of threats by the Ds, or he may be, as a current prisoner, "the victim of the code that condemns a conspirator for testifying against his former associates." *U.S. v. Garner*, 574 F.2d 1141 (4th Cir. 1978).

i. **Criticism:** *Garner* represents probably about as far as federal courts have gone in allowing the residual exception to cover out-of-court declarations that no common-law court would have conceived of admitting. One commentator has criticized the case as representing "the best of all possible worlds for the prosecution: when a witness is sufficiently available to convey to the jury that he is in mortal fear of the defendant, but is technically unavailable so that his cross-examination is excused [see FRE 801(d)(1)(A)] his Grand Jury testimony becomes admissible." W&B, Par. 804(b)(5)[01].

ii. **Prior inconsistent statement:** The court in *Garner* could have analyzed Robinson's grand jury testimony as a ***prior inconsistent statement*** under FRE 801(d)(1)(A) (see *supra*, p. 252). That subsection allows use of grand jury testimony so long as it is inconsistent with the story that the witness is telling at trial. The problem is that had the court pursued this approach, it probably would have been forced to recognize that Robinson's lack of cooperation at trial was so extreme that he wasn't really "subject to cross-examination" (as 801(d)(1) requires). Use of the residual exception, and the emphasis on corroboration by other evidence, thus enabled the court to do an end-run around 801(d)(1)(A) (as well as to avoid problems that may have been posed by the Confrontation Clause).

4. **Other post-declaration factors:** In addition to corroboration by other evidence, courts have looked at two additional factors not existing at the time of the declaration, in determining whether the statement is sufficiently reliable: (1) whether the declarant has *recanted* (or, in contrast, reaffirmed) his out-of-court statement; and (2) whether the declarant is available at trial for cross-examination. M, pp. 908-09. Obviously, a recanted statement is of somewhat suspect reliability, and a declaration whose maker cannot now be cross-examined is also of lesser reliability than one where such examination can take place. (Observe, however, that availability for cross-examination cuts both ways — if the declarant is now available, then there is a lesser need for hearsay evidence.) These factors are clearly not dispositive — for instance, the declarant in *Garner* had recanted, and he was not in any real sense available for cross-examination.

D. **Near miss problem:** Suppose a particular fact pattern comes very close to matching the requirements for a recognized hearsay exception. Should the residual exception be available used in this kind of *"near miss"* situation?

1. **Policy decision:** Against such use, it can be argued that when Congress created the relevant narrow exception, it was making an explicit policy determination that unless the requirements were satisfied, the evidence should not be admitted. See *Zenith Radio Corp. v. Matsushita Electric Industrial Co., Ltd.*, 505 F.Supp. 1190 (E.D.Pa. 1980), making this argument. As the *Zenith* court put it, the draftsmen never "intended that the residual exceptions be used to qualify for admission evidence which is of a type covered by a specific exception, but which narrowly fails to meet the standards of the specific rule. Instead, they intended that the residual exceptions be used in *exceptional* and *unanticipated* situations which are not specifically covered by the specific exceptions."

2. **Contrary view:** But most courts have *not agreed.* Indeed, the residual exception has probably been used in "near miss" situations more often than for truly unanticipated novel fact patterns.

> **Example:** P, shopping on D's used car lot, is interested in a truck. P, together with Anderson (D's mechanic) try to start the engine; because one of P's companions is trying to pour gas into the carburetor at the time, the gas can catches fire and P is badly burned. At trial, D offers a handwritten, unsworn memo written by Anderson at the request of his supervisor three hours after the accident. (Anderson has died before trial.)
>
> *Held*, the handwritten statement is admissible under FRE 804(b)(5)'s residual exception. Had Anderson been available at trial, the handwritten account would have been admissible under FRE 803(5)'s exception for past recollection recorded. This shows that such almost-contemporaneous written accounts are recognized by the Federal Rules as having circumstantial guarantees of trustworthiness. *Turbyfill v. International Harvester Co.*, 486 F.Supp. 232 (E.D.Mich. 1981).

a. **Criticism:** Observe that if Anderson's statement is admissible, "so is any other uncoerced statement written or uttered while an event is fresh in the declarant's mind and not duplicable by other reasonably accessible evidence."

L&S, p. 502. Yet, Congress, in setting forth the requirements for past recollection recorded, explicitly required that the writer be available to testify at trial (and also provided that the record may not be admitted as an exhibit). The court in *Turbyfill* has, therefore, arguably contravened an express congressional judgment by using the residual exception to admit this "near miss" evidence. *Id.* (In fact, Anderson's statement is even more dubious than most narratives, since he wrote the statement at his supervisor's request, and had a clear incentive to minimize his own negligence. *Id.*)

3. **Grand jury testimony:** The use of ***grand jury testimony*** where the witness is unavailable is another "near miss" situation. Since Congress has explicitly provided that former testimony should be admitted only where the criminal defendant had an opportunity to cross-examine the prior testimony (something that almost never happens for grand jury testimony), a court's use of such testimony arguably contravenes an express congressional policy.

E. **Notice:** The biggest innovation in the Federal Rules' residual exception is the requirement of ***advance notice*** that the residual exception will be used. The last sentence of both FRE 803(24) and 804(b)(5) makes the statement inadmissible "unless the proponent of it makes known to the adverse party sufficiently ***in advance of the trial*** or hearing to provide the adverse party with a ***fair opportunity to prepare to meet it***, the proponent's intention to offer the statement and the particulars of it. . . ."

1. **Some discretion given:** This language seems, on its face, to allow very little judicial discretion. For instance, it does not seem to contemplate that a notice given ***after*** commencement of the trial will ever be sufficient. But most courts have been willing to allow notice to be given after the trial starts, if it is only then that the need to use the exception becomes clear; the court will then often give a ***continuance*** to allow the opponent time to combat the testimony.

> **Example:** D is charged with armed robbery. W, who has already made a plea bargain with the government as a co-defendant, has agreed to testify against D. But at trial, W suddenly refuses to testify. The government, in the middle of the trial, now seeks to introduce W's prior written confession under 804(b)(5)'s residual exception.
>
> *Held* (on appeal), the advance notice requirement is "satisfied when, as here, the proponent of the evidence is without fault in failing to notify his adversary prior to the trial and the trial judge has offered sufficient time, by means of granting a continuance, for the party against whom the evidence is to be offered to prepare to meet and contest its admission." Here, the government could not have known that W would refuse to testify, and a continuance adequately protects D's rights. (But the confession itself must be excluded, because it was made during plea-bargaining sessions, was not under oath, was not tested by cross-examination, and thus was not reliable enough to satisfy the "circumstantial guarantees of trustworthiness" requirement of 804(b)(5).) *U.S. v. Bailey*, 581 F.2d 341 (3d Cir. 1978).

a. **Criticism:** Courts that have allowed notice to be given after the start of trial (as the court did in *Bailey*) are ignoring the clear choice Congress made in putting an explicit pre-trial notice requirement into the rules. Furthermore, these courts' frequent assumption that a continuance is all that is needed to protect the opponent's rights assumes that allowing the opponent to avoid unfair surprise and rebut the hearsay is the only function of the notice requirement. Yet, the pre-trial notice requirement has at least two other plausible functions: (1) A party who has not received notice of his adversary's intent to use the residual exception by the beginning of trial may decide to *litigate* rather than settle; and (2) Without such a requirement, the proponent gets an unfair "second bite at the apple," i.e., he can try to prove a point by other evidence and then attempt to use the residual exception only when these earlier efforts fail. See L&S, p. 504.

XVI. THE FUTURE OF HEARSAY

A. Generally: What is the future of hearsay? Before we make some predictions, it might be useful to give a brief list of the pros and cons of the hearsay rule:

 1. **Pros:** Here are some of the virtues of the hearsay rule:

    a. **Reliability:** First, it excludes evidence which, in the aggregate, probably is less *reliable* than live testimony. Of the various reasons to believe that this is the case, the most important is probably that "cross-examination is less likely to be effective in testing reports of statements than in testing reports of more complex events." L&S, p. 520. Also, "small mistakes in overhearing statements may completely change the meaning of what is reported[, whereas] since most witnessed events are more complex than statements, small mistakes in perceiving them are less likely to distort their meaning." *Id.*

    b. **Balance of advantage:** Second, the hearsay rule has a net effect of *protecting criminal defendants* and *individual civil plaintiffs*. Repeal of the rule would allow prosecutors, as well as wealthy organizations involved in civil suits, to generate lots of hearsay evidence (especially files "recorded selectively by agents who elicited information by leading questions or who included only what they thought their superiors most wanted hear . . . "). This would have the arguably undesirable effect of rendering the currently-powerful still more powerful. L&S, pp. 521-22.

    c. **Trust of trial judges:** Third, since much hearsay is quite clearly unreliable, most proposals for "reforming" the hearsay rules turn on giving judges *greater discretion* in determining what hearsay evidence is sufficiently reliable to be admitted. (The Federal Rules' "residual" exception is a first step in this direction.) To the extent that one believes that many trial judges are biased, dishonest, or unscholarly, giving them greater discretion is not a good idea. L&S, p. 523.

    d. **It works:** Finally, the current system seems to *work.* For instance, there are few, if any, reported instances of the "wrong" result being reached because hearsay evidence was excluded. "One should be wary of changing a system which apparently delivers justice, however neat and attractive the suggested alternative." *Id.*

2. **In favor of reform:** Here are some countervailing arguments in favor of "reforming" the hearsay rules by making them less rigid (and thus allowing more hearsay in):

   a. **Too complex:** The hearsay system, with all of its exceptions, is ***too complex.*** (For instance, the Federal Rules contain 31 exceptions.) Requiring judges and lawyers to master this complex system is not worth whatever small incremental "truth value" it may produce.

      i. **Contra:** However, observe that "probably less than 10, and possibly no more than a half dozen, of the exceptions are encountered with any frequency in the trial of cases. . . ." M, p. 913.

   b. **Reliability not increased:** The rule and its exceptions are not very good at ***keeping the less reliable evidence out*** and the ***more reliable evidence in.*** For instance, "a series of independent letters written by disinterested ministers who are eyewitnesses to an event and who are shown to have acute vision, sound memories, and clear powers of communication [should] be given more weight than many dying declarations or implied admissions which may be made by a party having no knowledge of the event or may have been made many years before by a predecessor in interest who had every motive to lie." L&S, p. 528 (quoting Weinstein, 46 Iowa L. Rev. 331 (1961)). A better way to make sure that good evidence gets in and bad evidence doesn't is to give the trial judge discretion to admit or exclude hearsay depending on the particular item's indicia of reliability.

   c. **Witness demeanor:** While it is true that the jury's ability to observe the witness' ***demeanor*** is useful, there are better ways than the traditional hearsay rule to make this happen. If the declarant is available, his out-of-court declaration should be admissible, but only upon the proponent's making him available for cross-examination. If he is not available, then (assuming the trial judge finds the out-of-court declaration to have indicia of reliability) it is better to have the evidence without the jury's ability to observe the declarant's demeanor than not to have the evidence at all.

   d. **Other proceedings:** The hearsay rule is currently not applied in a large number of ***other fact-finding systems,*** including: continental systems, arbitrations, workers' compensation cases, grand jury proceedings, and small claims courts. There is no evidence that the truth-finding capacities of these other types of proceedings are materially harmed by absence of the hearsay rule. L&S, p. 531 (quoting Weinstein, *op. cit.*)

   e. **Jurors' sophistication:** The hearsay rule developed out of fear that naive jurors would be misled by unreliable evidence. But today, "there is little reason to believe that jurors — a much more highly educated and sophisticated group than their English Seventeenth and Eighteenth Century predecessors — are not . . . capable of assessing hearsay's force without giving it undue weight." L&S, p. 532 (quoting Weinstein, *op. cit.*) Furthermore, any lingering danger of juror naivete can be overcome by giving the trial judge the right to comment freely on the weight of hearsay evidence, so that the jury is warned of its pitfalls. L&S, p. 529 (quoting Weinstein, *op. cit.*)

B. The future of hearsay: What, then, is the future of hearsay? It is, of course, impossible to say with any confidence. Here are some likely developments:

1. **Greater liberalization:** Probably, in the aggregate, less and less evidence will be excluded on account of the hearsay rule. That is, the trend toward *"liberalization"* will probably continue.

2. **Judge's discretion:** This "liberalization" will probably happen not by formal abolition of the rule against hearsay, but by increasing reliance upon *"residual"* exceptions like that of FRE 803(24) and 804(b)(5), whereby the judge may admit hearsay if he finds good "circumstantial guarantees of trustworthiness" and the opponent is given notice so that unfair surprise is avoided. Not only are more and more states likely to enact such a "residual" exception (about half the states already have, by enacting the Federal Rules), but the residual exception in any jurisdiction is likely to become more and more frequently used.

3. **Criminal cases:** The use of hearsay will increase more in *civil* cases than against defendants in criminal cases. The reason is that constitutional constraints (principally the Confrontation Clause; see *infra*, p. 270) are an impediment to the unrestrained use of hearsay against criminal defendants. However, even in criminal cases, where the hearsay is sought to be used against the defendant, the Confrontation Clause will probably end up meaning little more than that: (1) the out-of-court declarant must be produced for *cross-examination* if reasonably possible; and (2) the declaration may not be used unless it has at least reasonable indicia of *reliability.* See, e.g., *Ohio v. Roberts*, 448 U.S. 56 (1980) (discussed *infra*, p. 273).

    a. **Classic exceptions:** One factor that, in criminal cases, will tend to maintain the classical structure of a general ban on hearsay accompanied by defined class exceptions, is that reliability for Confrontation Clause purposes "can be inferred without more in a case where the evidence falls within a firmly rooted hearsay exception." *Ohio v. Roberts, supra.*

CONFRONTATION AND COMPULSORY PROCESS

I. INTRODUCTION

A. Constitutional limits: In most contexts, there are no meaningful federal constitutional limits on the rules of evidence — the states are free to admit or exclude whatever evidence they wish, subject only to the requirement that they not violate a party's right to a fair trial, as guaranteed by the Fourteenth Amendment's Due Process Clause. In *criminal* trials, however, evidentiary rules that *disadvantage the defendant* may run afoul of two quite specific constitutional provisions, both part of the Sixth Amendment: the Confrontation Clause and the Compulsory Process Clause.

   1. Confrontation Clause: The Confrontation Clause, which guarantees a criminal defendant the right "to be confronted with the witnesses against him," to some extent "constitutionalizes" the hearsay rule. Thus if a state were to completely abolish the rule against hearsay, at least some types of out-of-court declarations could still not be introduced against a criminal defendant.

      a. Reliability: Furthermore, an out-of-court declaration may be so *unreliable* (or its use so unnecessary) that even though the evidence is admissible under a traditional exception to the hearsay rule, the Confrontation Clause bars it.

      b. Joint trial: Also, the Confrontation Clause poses problems where two co-defendants are *tried jointly*. An item of evidence that is completely admissible against one of the defendants (e.g., his own voluntary confession) may violate the other defendant's Confrontation Clause rights even if that evidence is never formally admitted against him.

      c. Exclusionary tool: The Confrontation Clause is mainly an *exclusionary* tool — when applicable, it operates mainly to allow the defendant to keep out certain types of damaging evidence (though occasionally it may entitle him to cross-examine a witness on a point that would otherwise be off-limits, or to produce extrinsic evidence to impeach a witness).

   2. Compulsory Process Clause: The Compulsory Process Clause, by contrast, is an *inclusionary* tool, i.e., one that may allow the defendant to gain admission of otherwise-inadmissible evidence. The clause (which guarantees the defendant's right to "have compulsory process for obtaining Witnesses in his favor") has been interpreted not only to mean that the defendant may subpoena witnesses, but also that he may have the right to ask questions, offer documents, and offer testimony, even though these would normally be inadmissible under the jurisdiction's rules of evidence.

B. Organization: This chapter is organized as follows: (1) a discussion of the general constitutional theory behind the Confrontation Clause, including a discussion of what factors the Supreme Court looks to in determining whether the state's rule of inclusion violates the clause; (2) a discussion of specific types of evidence (usually offered under hearsay exceptions), and the confrontation problems such evidence raises; and (3) the Compulsory Process Clause.

II. CONFRONTATION — GENERAL THEORY

A. History: At the very least, the drafters of the Confrontation Clause intended to assure a criminal defendant's right to *be present* at his trial, to *learn* what evidence is being introduced against him, and to *question* those who give live testimony. Probably the drafters also intended to exclude some types of hearsay evidence. For instance, they probably wished to prevent abuses like the trial of Sir Walter Raleigh, who was convicted principally based on the out-of-court confession (later recanted) of an alleged co-conspirator.

   1. Contrasting views: A few scholars — most notably Wigmore — have contended that the Confrontation Clause *only* guarantees the right to be present and to cross-examine live witnesses, and that the clause should *never* be interpreted to require exclusion of evidence because of its hearsay nature.

   2. Modern view: But a majority of the Supreme Court has never accepted this limited view. Today, the precise scope of the Confrontation Clause remains very blurry. But it is at least clear that *hearsay evidence that does not fall within a recognized traditional exception will be allowed only if it possesses "indicia of reliability."* See *Ohio v. Roberts*, discussed *infra*, p. 273.

   a. Raleigh trial: For instance, the alleged co-conspirator's confession in the Raleigh case would almost certainly be inadmissible today on Confrontation Clause grounds, since a co-defendant's confession is not within a narrow traditional hearsay exception, is presumptively unreliable, and only rarely will have particular "indicia of reliability" sufficient to overcome this presumption; see *Lee v. Illinois*, discussed *infra*, pp. 273-74 (roughly similar to the fact pattern of the Raleigh case).

   3. Application to states: The Confrontation Clause applies to *state* trials as well as federal trials. *Pointer v. Texas*, 380 U.S. 400 (1965).

B. Declarant produced at trial: A literal reading of the Confrontation Clause might suggest that no out-of-court declaration could ever be used against a criminal defendant unless the defendant had been given a right of *cross-examination at the time of the statement.* But the Supreme Court has *not* taken such an extreme view. So long as the declarant is *available at trial* to be cross-examined about his earlier declaration, the fact that the defendant did not cross-examine him at the time of the statement (or even have the opportunity to do so) will not by itself mean that the statement is barred by the Confrontation Clause.

   Example: In a preliminary hearing on drug sale charges against D, W identifies D as his drug supplier. D's lawyer briefly cross-examines W, but in a much less searching way than he would probably do at trial. At trial, W is called as a witness by the prosecution, but is evasive; the prosecutor "refreshes his recollection" by reading W's preliminary hearing testimony. D claims that this use of the prior testimony violates his Confrontation Clause rights.

Held, D's Confrontation Clause rights were not violated by the prosecution's use of W's preliminary hearing testimony (even though that testimony was admitted substantively, not merely for impeachment, under a rule allowing a witness' prior inconsistent statement to be used for the truth of the matter asserted). Even in those situations where the prior testimony was not subject to cross-examination at all, and was thus perhaps unreliable, "If the declarant is present and testifying at trial, the out-of-court statement for all practical purposes regains much of the lost protections." (In any event, here D had such a good chance to cross-examine W at the preliminary hearing that even if W were *not* present at the trial, the prior testimony could be used.) *California v. Green*, 399 U.S. 149 (1970).

1. **Evasive witness:** As *California v. Green* indicates, an uncross-examined out-of-court declaration will generally be admissible notwithstanding the Confrontation Clause, so long as the declarant is available in court to be cross-examined. However, the witness' "availability to be cross-examined" is not as simple a matter as it sounds. For instance, if the declarant takes the witness stand, but repeatedly asserts the Fifth Amendment when the defense tries to cross-examine him, or denies any recollection of the underlying event, the court might conclude that the defense is not really getting a fair chance to cross-examine the witness, in which case it could exclude the statement on Confrontation Clause grounds. (But it will not be easy for D to win with this argument, if D is able to impeach the declarant's testimony by getting across to the jury that W is being evasive now and, therefore, may well have been untruthful when he made the prior out-of-court declaration. See the further discussion of what constitutes a fair opportunity to cross-examine declarant *infra*, p. 279.)

C. **Preference for live testimony:** The Confrontation Clause clearly reflects the drafters' *preference for live testimony* in lieu of out-of-court declarations wherever possible. This preference, of course, does not mean that out-of-court declarations will never be admissible against a criminal defendant. But it does mean that an out-of-court declaration is much more likely to be found violative of the Confrontation Clause if the same evidence could be furnished by live testimony from an available witness, than where this is not the case. In other words, the Confrontation Clause, like the basic set of hearsay exceptions, dictates in most situations that live testimony *must* be used when it is feasible to do so.

1. **Observation of demeanor:** A key reason for the Confrontation Clause's preference for live testimony is that only where there is live testimony does the jury have a chance to observe and weigh the *demeanor* of the witness. Even if the prior out-of-court declaration was subjected to cross-examination, and even if a transcript was made of it, the criminal jury is deprived of the opportunity to conclude, for instance, that the declarant's nervous mannerisms (e.g., shifting in his seat, failing to look at the jury or examiner, etc.) make his testimony suspect. See, e.g., *Barber v. Page*, 390 U.S. 719 (1968) ("The right to confrontation is basically a trial right. It includes both the opportunity to cross-examine and the occasion for the jury to

weigh the demeanor of the witness.")

2. **Unavailability required:** In fact, the Supreme Court has on one occasion stated the following black-letter rule: "[W]hen a hearsay declarant is not present for cross-examination at trial, the Confrontation Clause ***normally requires a showing that he is unavailable.***" *Ohio v. Roberts*, 448 U.S. 56 (1980).

3. **Not to be taken literally:** If this statement were taken literally, it would mean that none of the "declarant's unavailability immaterial" exceptions to the hearsay rule could ever be used against a criminal defendant, unless the declarant was in fact unavailable. For instance, the many exceptions in FRE 803 — including present sense impression, excited utterance, recorded recollection, and business records — would all be unusable unless the declarant was in fact unavailable (and the distinction between Rule 803's exceptions, applicable regardless of whether the declarant is available, and 804's exceptions, which require declarant's unavailability, would be meaningless as to evidence offered by the prosecution). However, cases after *Roberts* indicate that the Supreme Court did not mean to lay down a hard and fast rule requiring unavailability, but merely to suggest that the use of hearsay is more likely to run afoul of the Confrontation Clause if the declarant is available to present the same evidence at trial.

   a. **Right to subpoena:** The most important weakening of *Robert*'s "declarant must be unavailable" rule came in a recent case involving a co-conspirator's statement made during the course of a conspiracy (as opposed to the former testimony at issue in *Roberts*). In *U.S. v. Inadi*, 475 U.S. 387 (1986), the Supreme Court held that *Roberts* means at most that no ***former testimony*** may be admitted against a criminal defendant if the declarant is not shown to be unavailable; other types of out-of-court statements (such as the co-conspirator's statement at issue in *Inadi*) may be admitted even if the declarant is available to testify at trial.

      i. **Rationale:** In the co-conspirator's statement situation, the defendant is (the Court asserted) adequately protected by his right to ***subpoena*** the declarant, to call him as a hostile witness, and to cross-examine him about his out-of-court statement (see FRE 806).

   b. **Confrontation of "remote utility":** Also, the prosecution does not have to call an available witness if the defendant's right of cross-examination at trial would be of ***"remote utility."*** For instance, in *Dutton v. Evans*, 400 U.S. 74 (1970), W was an alleged co-conspirator who, in a conversation with a cell mate, made a remark incriminating D as well as himself in the crime for which D was later charged. A plurality of the Supreme Court allowed the prosecution to introduce this remark against D without putting W on the stand (even though W was available), because due to the circumstances surrounding the statement it was (in the plurality's view) highly unlikely that even cross-examination of W would have allowed D to convince the jury either that the statement was not made or that it was unreliable.

D. **"Indicia of reliability":** Probably the most important principle under the Confrontation Clause is that even where the declarant is unavailable, his out-of-court declaration will not be allowed into evidence unless it contains *"indicia of reliability." Ohio v. Roberts*, 448 U.S. 56 (1980). How the court determines whether a statement has the requisite "indicia of reliability" depends on whether a traditional hearsay exception is involved.

1. **Traditional exception:** Where the out-of-court declaration is sought to be introduced under a *"firmly rooted hearsay exception,"* this will *by itself* be enough to allow reliability to be inferred. *Ohio v. Roberts, supra.* In this situation, the court will not look at the facts surrounding the particular declaration in question, and even if these facts suggest unreliability the declaration may be admitted without violating the Confrontation Clause.

   Example: In D's trial for possessing and conspiring to distribute cocaine, the prosecution introduces a tape recorded telephone conversation between one Lonardo and a government informant, in which Lonardo tells the informant the details of how his "friend" will participate in distributing the cocaine to be supplied by the informant. Lonardo refuses to testify at D's trial (he pleads the Fifth Amendment), so he is unavailable to be cross-examined by D. The prosecution offers Lonardo's out-of-court declaration under the hearsay exception for co-conspirators' statements; the statement suggests that D is the "friend." D argues that the statement violates his Confrontation Clause rights (and also that the statement cannot be considered in deciding the threshold question of whether a conspiracy has been shown to exist).

   Held, the statement was admissible and did not violate D's Confrontation Clause rights. "[T]he co-conspirator exception to the hearsay rule is firmly enough rooted in our jurisprudence that, under [*Roberts*], a court need not independently inquire into the reliability of such statements." Therefore, regardless of whether the facts surrounding this particular statement show it to be reliable, the statement is admissible. (Also, the statement may itself be considered by the court in determining whether a conspiracy exists; see *supra*, p. 167.) *Bourjaily v. U.S.*, 483 U.S. 171 (1987).

2. **Particularized facts:** If the out-of-court statement does *not* fall within a "firmly rooted hearsay exception," the prosecution must show that the *particularized facts* surrounding it demonstrate that it is probably reliable. That is, there must be *"particular guarantees of trustworthiness."*

   Example: D1 and D2 are charged with two murders. They agree to be tried jointly. The prosecution introduces confessions by each of them, which agree on some details, but not on other details (including details relevant to whether D1 had the necessary premeditation). The trial judge relies on D2's confession in finding D1 guilty. D1 argues on appeal that the use of D2's confession against her violated her Confrontation Clause rights.

   Held, for D. A co-defendant's confession, given while in custody, does not fall within any firmly rooted hearsay exception. (Although the confession may be a "declaration against penal interest," that exception "defines too large a class for meaningful Confrontation Clause analysis" and is thus irrelevant.) Therefore, the statement is "presumptively unreliable," and will be admitted only if the prosecution shows that it contains ***"particular guarantees of trustworthiness."***

Here, the circumstances surrounding D2's confession do not supply such trustworthiness guarantees — the statement was given while D2 was in custody and after the police told him that D1 had already implicated him, was made without any cross-examination, and was given when D2 was already considering turning state's evidence against D1 (and thus had a motive to maximize D1's culpability and minimize his own.) The fact that D2's confession "interlocked" with D1's on some details did not furnish the requisite guarantees of trustworthiness, since the two confessions contained major discrepancies on key points (e.g., D1's premeditation). (But the four dissenters contended that D2's confession did bear the requisite guarantees of trustworthiness, since it was clearly adverse to his penal interest, and was corroborated by other details, including many of the details of D1's confession.) *Lee v. Illinois*, 476 U.S. 530 (1986).

a. **Can't use corroborating evidence:** What facts may the prosecution rely on to show that there are "particular guarantees of trustworthiness" for the out-of-court statement? Most important, only the facts surrounding ***the particular statement***, not ***other evidence*** that corroborates the statement's ***truth***, may be considered. In other words, the prosecutor might show reliability by showing, say, that the declarant had no conceivable reason to lie, or had a strong incentive to tell the truth, but the prosecutor may not demonstrate reliability by showing that evidence unrelated to the statement (e.g., physical evidence) establishes the statement's truth. *Idaho v. Wright*, 110 S.Ct. 3139 (1990).

   i. **Illustration:** The facts of *Wright* show how this rule works. *Wright* was a sex abuse case in which the declarants were two young children who told a pediatrician that their mother (D) and the mother's husband had sexually abused them. The Supreme Court restated the general rule that where an out-of-court statement does not fall within a firmly rooted hearsay exception, its use will violate the Confrontation Clause unless the statement was supported by "particularized guarantees of trustworthiness." The Court then held that in making this showing, "the relevant circumstances include only those that surround the ***making of the statement*** and that render the declarant particularly worthy of belief." Thus the trial court properly considered whether each child had a motive to make up a story of this nature, and whether, given the child's age, the statements were of a type that one would expect a child to fabricate. But the trial court should not have relied on corroborative evidence such as physical evidence of abuse, D's opportunity to commit the abuse, and the other child's corroborating declarations. After the wrongly-considered evidence was thrown out, the Supreme Court found that each child's declaration was not particularly trustworthy, and should not have been admitted.

3. **What exceptions are "firmly rooted":** The Supreme Court has, since *Roberts*, considered only a few types of statements to determine whether they are ones falling within a "firmly rooted" hearsay exception and thus do not need to be supported by "particularized guarantees of trustworthiness." Here is what can be said so far: (1) Statements made in **custody** do **not** fall within a firmly rooted exception (*Lee*), even though they are arguably against the declarant's penal interest; (2) Statements by a **co-conspirator** during the course of the conspiracy and in furtherance of it, **do** fall within a firmly rooted exception (*Bourjaily*); and (3) **former testimony** given at a prior proceeding, with a right of cross-examination, introduced when the declarant is unavailable at trial, almost certainly **does** fall within a sufficiently firmly rooted exception (see FRE 804(b)(1); see also numerous pre-*Roberts* cases allowing such testimony with no particularized guarantees of trustworthiness, e.g., *Mattox v. U.S.*, 156 U.S. 237 (1895)).

   a. **Other narrow exceptions:** Other **narrowly-defined** exceptions, such as those for excited utterances, recorded recollections, business records and dying declarations, probably will be found to be sufficiently firmly rooted that no particularized guarantees will be required; however, this is not certain. See the treatment of these and other specific hearsay exceptions *infra*, pp. 279-84.

4. **Opportunity to cross-examine:** Recall that a central rationale for the rule against hearsay is that uncross-examined out-of-court declarations are less likely to be reliable than in-court testimony that is subject to cross-examination. (See *supra*, p. 120.) The presence or lack of an opportunity to cross-examine the out-of-court declaration will probably be important in determining whether the statement has sufficient "indicia of reliability" under *Roberts*; however, the precise importance of cross-examination as an "indicium of reliability" is unclear.

   a. **Actual cross-examination:** It is clear that an out-of-court statement can be perfectly reliable (either because it qualifies under a "firmly rooted exception" to the hearsay rule, or because it has "particularized guarantees of trustworthiness") even if there was **no actual cross-examination**. For instance, statements made by co-conspirators during the course of the conspiracy (e.g., the taped telephone conversation in *Bourjaily*, referring to D's expected participation) will rarely be cross-examined; nonetheless, since such statements are within a "firmly rooted exception" to the hearsay rule, the absence of actual cross-examination is irrelevant.

   b. **Opportunity to cross-examine:** If there is not only no actual cross-examination but not even an **opportunity** to cross-examine the statement, this is somewhat more likely to lead the court to hold that admission of the statement would violate the defendant's Confrontation Clause rights.

      i. **Former testimony:** For instance, suppose that the out-of-court declaration is made by W at a preliminary hearing charging D with burglary, and that testimony is later sought to be used against D in a murder case arising out of separate but related facts. A court might well hold that this testimony does not come within the "former testimony" exception, because D did not have the same motive to cross-examine at a hearing on a burglary charge that he would have had if he had known that the statement would be used in a murder prosecution. The court might also conclude that the absence of a motive to perform searching cross-examination made this prior testimony sufficiently unreliable that the Confrontation Clause dictates its exclusion.

ii. **Co-conspirator's statement:** But where a traditional hearsay exception has evolved that applies irrespective of whether there has been an opportunity for cross-examination, absence of cross-examination in a particular case will probably not trouble the court. Thus a co-conspirator's statement made in furtherance of the conspiracy will generally be admissible (because it falls within the "firmly rooted" co-conspirator's exception) even though the defendant not only did not engage in actual cross-examination at the time, but had absolutely no opportunity to do so.

5. **Criticism of *Roberts'* two-step test:** Observe that under the *Roberts* approach to reliability, if an out-of-court statement falls within a traditional, "firmly rooted" hearsay exception, the statement can be admitted without violating the defendant's Confrontation Clause rights *even if the facts surrounding the particular statement make its reliability extremely suspect*. This seems to be an unwise narrowing of the Confrontation Clause principle, since some types of traditional exceptions result more from historical practice than from a belief that statements falling within them are highly reliable.

> **Example:** Suppose that X, thinking he is about to die, names his old enemy D as the murderer. X dies, and in the autopsy trace amounts of LSD are found in his blood. Under the *Roberts* approach, X's statement will be automatically admitted because it falls within the "firmly rooted" dying declaration exception. Yet, the presence of LSD suggests that X may well have been hallucinating, in which case the statement's reliability is suspect. True, D can introduce the LSD findings to the jury and argue that X may have been hallucinating; but this is not nearly as good a way of determining whether X's statement was really accurate as would cross-examination of X. Therefore, on these facts, L&S (p. 595) argue that "the statement should be excluded because the only way to clarify the matter is by cross-examination, which, given the declarant's unavailability, is impossible."

E. **Right to confront testifying witnesses:** As we have seen from the above discussion, the Confrontation Clause's usual function is to allow a defendant to exclude a hearsay statement. There is another function that the Clause serves, however: it guarantees certain *procedures* at trial. In particular, it guarantees that the accused may be *present* at the trial, and that he may *test the testimony* of live witnesses by *cross-examining* them.

1. **W's refusal to answer:** For instance, if W gives testimony against D as part of the prosecution's direct case, and then wilfully refuses to answer the defense's questions on cross-examination, the Confrontation Clause generally requires that W's direct testimony be *stricken* at D's request. L&S, p. 605. (But if W makes a genuine effort to answer the defense's questions on cross-examination, and is unable to do so because he has suffered a severe loss of memory about the underlying event, this

will ***not*** violate the Confrontation Clause. See the discussion of *U.S. v. Owens*, *infra*, p. 280.)

2. **Restrictions on cross-examination:** Difficult questions can arise when the trial judge or the state has a sound ***policy reason*** for restricting certain lines of cross-examination.

    a. **Rules of relevance:** State rules of evidence, as applied by the trial judge, may constitutionally limit cross-examination to relevant matters, and may prevent the defense from unduly repetitive or argumentative questioning or the harassment of witnesses. L&S, p. 606. However, if the judge takes an unduly restrictive view of what should be allowed on cross-examination, this may violate the defendant's Confrontation Clause rights. *Id.*

    b. **State policies:** Occasionally, the state may limit cross-examination into admittedly relevant matters because the state is pursuing what everyone would agree is a sound policy. In this situation, the policy being pursued by the state and the defendant's Confrontation Clause rights come into direct conflict. The court must decide whether the defendant's Confrontation Clause rights should outweigh the state policy, but there is little consensus about how this weighing process should take place. What does seem clear is that if the state policy materially impairs the defendant's ability to present exculpatory evidence, the state must choose between its desire to convict and its desire to pursue its policy — ***it may not make the defendant pay the costs of that state policy.***

        Example: D is charged with stealing a safe from a bar. A key witness against him is one Green, who led the police to D, and whose trial testimony ties D to the place where the safe was found. D tries to bring out on the cross-examination of Green that at the time Green was assisting the police, he was on probation for burglary. However, Green was a juvenile at the time, and a state statute prevents D from bringing out Green's juvenile conviction and probationary status. Consequently, D is prevented from suggesting to the jury that Green had a strong motive for covering up any involvement he may himself have had with the safe burglary and for pinning the blame on someone else.

        Held, D's inability to bring out the fact of Green's prior juvenile conviction violated D's Confrontation Clause rights. "[T]he exposure of a witness' motivation in testifying is a proper and important function of the constitutionally protected right of cross-examination." Furthermore, "the right of confrontation is paramount to the State's policy of protecting a juvenile offender. . . . The State cannot, consistent with the right of confrontation, require [D] to bear the full burden of vindicating the State's interest in the secrecy of juvenile criminal records." *Davis v. Alaska*, 415 U.S. 308 (1974).

    c. **Witness' name or residence:** A similar conflict is posed when the state's evidence rules (or the trial judge in his own discretion) prevent the defense from asking a prosecution witness his ***true name*** or ***true address***. This often happens where there is reason to believe that the defendant (especially an organized crime member) may use the information to threaten or even murder the witness. So far, the Supreme Court has not dealt with this conflict, but lower courts have held that it is not unconstitutional to prevent the asking of such questions where there is reason to fear that the information may indeed endanger the witness. See, e.g., *U.S. v. Battaglia*, 432 F.2d 1115 (7th Cir. 1970).

    d. Rape shield laws: Similarly, the defendant's Confrontation Clause rights may be impaired by so-called ***rape shield*** laws, which limit a rape defendant's right to cross-examine the victim about her prior sexual conduct. For instance, if a state passed a shield law that flatly prohibited any inquiry into the victim's past sexual conduct, no matter how relevant such conduct was to the defendant's defense, a Confrontation Clause violation might well result.

        Example: D denies having had intercourse with V at all. The prosecution produces evidence that V contracted gonorrhea, and that D had the disease prior to the episode. A shield law that prevents D from showing that V had had intercourse with X shortly before the alleged D-V encounter, and that X had gonorrhea, would probably violate D's Confrontation Clause rights.

        By contrast, there is probably no Confrontation Clause violation from a shield law where the prosecution shows that D and V were strangers, and that D had sex with V in a parking lot. In this situation, D almost certainly does not have a Confrontation Clause right to inquire into V's past promiscuity in order to show consent. Here the direct evidence of consent is so small, and the link between past promiscuity and present consent so attenuated, that no constitutional Confrontation interest of D is really being impaired. See L&S, p. 639.

        i. Federal Rule: FRE 412 (the federal rape shield provision) largely avoids the Confrontation Clause problem by expressly allowing any evidence of the victim's past sexual behavior if it is "constitutionally required to be admitted." See FRE 412(b)(1); see also *supra*, pp. 44-47.

3. Right to be face-to-face with W: There is an additional, recently recognized, aspect to the defendant's Confrontation Clause right: the defendant has the right to be ***within the view*** of witnesses testifying against him at trial. The Clause "guarantees the defendant a ***face-to-face meeting*** with witnesses. . . ." *Coy v. Iowa*, 487 U.S. 1012 (1988). However, this guarantee is not absolute — it may be outweighed by a showing that the particular witness needs special protection.

    a. Child-abuse cases: The defendant's right to be face-to-face with his accusers is most often relevant in ***child-abuse*** cases. Many states have procedures whereby the child victim is permitted to give trial testimony without having to look at the defendant. (For instance, in *Coy*, *supra*, a screen was placed between the witness stand and the defendant, so that the child victims could not see the defendant while testifying, although he could see them.) *Coy* establishes that the state may not make a blanket declaration that in certain broad categories of cases (e.g., child-abuse cases), the defendant's right to be face-to-face with his accusers is outweighed by the state's interest in protecting witnesses. Only if there is an ***individualized*** finding that the particular witness in question needs special protection, may the defendant be deprived of his right to be viewed by the witness. (No such individualized findings existed in *Coy* itself.)

b. Individualized findings made: A post-*Coy* case shows that in some circumstances a court will in fact find that a particular witness needs special protection, so that the defendant's right to be faced by the witness can be taken from him. In *Maryland v. Craig*, 110 S.Ct. 3157 (1990), the trial judge in a state sexual assault case found that each of two child witnesses, if she were required to testify in front of D in open court, would suffer serious emotional distress that would prevent her from reasonably communicating. Therefore, the judge approved the taking of each child's testimony in a separate room, at which only the witness, prosecutor and defense counsel were present; the child's testimony was simultaneously displayed to the courtroom via closed-circuit TV. This arrangement preserved D's right to cross-examine the witness and to make objections (via an electronic link with defense counsel), but prevented the witnesses from seeing D. The Supreme Court held that this procedure did ***not*** deprive the defendant of his Confrontation Clause rights.

i. Rationale: In *Craig*, the individualized findings — that these ***particular*** child witnesses, not child witnesses in general, needed special protection — were held to be sufficient to validate the procedure. (The majority cautioned that there must be a finding that it is the ***presence of the defendant***, not the mere prospect of giving testimony in court, that would cause the trauma to the child witness.)

III. CONFRONTATION — SPECIFIC CONTEXTS

A. Introduction: We turn now to a brief discussion of the Confrontation Clause as it may apply to specific contexts and specific hearsay exceptions.

B. W present and available for cross-examination: First, suppose that the out-of-court declarant is present at the trial, testifies, and is available for cross-examination about his prior statement. (In federal trials, his prior statement would be admissible as a prior inconsistent statement under FRE 801(d)(1)(A), or as a prior consistent statement to rebut a charge of untruthfulness under 801(d)(1)(B).)

1. Effective cross-examination: If W is apparently candid in cross-examination and admits making the prior statement (even though he now says that it was erroneous), the prior statement may clearly be used substantively against D without violating D's Confrontation Clause rights. This is essentially the holding of *California v. Green, supra*, pp. 270-71.

2. Denies recollection of underlying event: If W claims that he ***cannot recall*** the underlying event, D may be able to argue that his Confrontation Clause rights are violated by use of W's prior statement, because he cannot effectively cross-examine W about that prior statement. Such an argument is suggested by the Court's dictum in *California v. Green* that "whether [W's] apparent lapse of memory so affected [D's] right to cross-examine as to make a critical difference in the application of the

Confrontation Clause in this case is an issue which is not ripe for decision at this juncture. . . ."

   a. W is honest: Where circumstances indicate that W is **honest** in stating that he cannot remember the underlying event, the defendant's Confrontation Clause argument will probably always fail, as a result of *U.S. v. Owens*, 484 U.S. 554 (1988). In *Owens*, the Supreme Court held that so long as D has the right to ask questions of W, and the right to impeach his credibility by pointing out that W has a bad memory, W's honest lack of recollection about the underlying event will not make D's cross-examination so ineffective that D's Confrontation Clause rights are violated.

      i. Illustration: Thus in *Owens*, W was a corrections officer who was so viciously attacked by an inmate that by the time of trial he had lost almost all memory of the attack, and could no longer identify his assailant; yet W was permitted to testify that he had previously identified D as the assailant, though he could no longer remember his basis for doing so. Despite the fact that this lack of memory of the underlying event made D's task of cross-examining W somewhat more difficult, D was nonetheless able to conduct a sufficiently "effective" cross-examination (by casting doubt on the overall reliability of W's prior identification) that D's Confrontation Clause rights were not violated.

   b. W is lying: If the circumstances indicate that W is **lying** when he says he can't recollect the underlying event, D probably has a slightly better chance of establishing a Confrontation Clause violation. For instance, he may be able to show that the prosecution is cooperating with the witness in a subterfuge to get the prior statement admitted without risk of cross-examination concerning its specifics. But even in this situation, D will find it difficult to succeed with his confrontation argument, in light of *Owens'* suggestion that so long as D has the right to impeach W by emphasizing his poor memory and consequent unreliability, there is no Confrontation Clause violation.

3. Denies underlying event: If W simply **denies** that the underlying event **ever happened**, and therefore gives no details that could be tested under cross-examination at trial, it is not clear whether D has a valid Confrontation Clause claim when W's prior statement is used against him. However, since the jury can see W's demeanor as he testifies about the actual underlying event (i.e., denies that the underlying event occurred), and since the discrepancy between the prior statement and the present denial of the underlying event can be probed (e.g., "If you weren't there to witness the shooting, why did you tell the grand jury that you were?"), the damage to D's Confrontation Clause rights does not seem substantial.

4. Identification of person: Suppose that W's prior statement is one *identifying the defendant* as the perpetrator of the crime (e.g., by picking him out of a police lineup). D could argue that use of this prior out-of-court statement violates his Confrontation Clause rights. However, such an argument is very **unlikely to succeed,** since: (1) this is a fairly well-rooted exception to the hearsay rule, or else non-hearsay (see FRE 801(d)(1)(C)); and (2) W is available at trial to explain, and be cross-examined about, this prior identification. However, if the facts surrounding the identification make it unduly suggestive and unreliable, under a series of Supreme Court decisions decided on right-to-counsel and due process grounds (see, e.g., *U.S. v. Wade*, 388 U.S. 218 (1967) and *Stovall v. Denno*, 388 U.S. 293 (1967)), D will have the right to have the identification results excluded.

C. **Co-conspirator's statement in furtherance of conspiracy:** Where the out-of-court declaration is a statement made by a *co-conspirator* made during the course of a conspiracy and in furtherance of it, it is very *unlikely* that any Confrontation claim by D will succeed.

1. **Unavailability unimportant:** First, the co-conspirator's unavailability is *not important* — the statement may be admitted even though the co-conspirator is available and is not called by the prosecution. *U.S. v. Inadi, supra*, p. 272.

2. **Indicia of reliability:** Second, since the exception for co-conspirator's statements is "firmly rooted," the court will not even look into the particular facts surrounding the statement to see whether it contains "indicia of reliability" — the mere fact that the statement was made during the conspiracy by a member is thought to supply enough evidence of reliability. *Bourjaily v. U.S., supra*, p. 273.

D. **Declarant's availability immaterial:** Now let us consider the group of hearsay exceptions which, traditionally, permit substantive use of a prior out-of-court statement even if the declarant is *available* but is not produced at trial. These include the exceptions for *excited utterances*, statements of *existing mental or physical condition, recorded recollections, business records,* and a number of others. See FRE 803.

1. **Unavailability:** *Ohio v. Roberts* (*supra*, p. 272) suggested that even statements falling under these "availability immaterial" exceptions may not be admitted unless the prosecution shows that the declarant is truly unavailable: "[W]hen a hearsay declarant is not present for cross-examination at trial, the Confrontation Clause normally requires a showing that he is unavailable." But later cases suggest that the court probably did not mean what it said. See *supra*, p. 272 for a further discussion.

   a. **Consequence:** Consequently, it is probably the case that as long as the statement does fall within one of these "availability immaterial" exceptions, there is no Confrontation Clause requirement that W be produced at trial, so long as the prosecution cooperates with D's right to *subpoena* W if he so desires. (Thus if the prosecution hides W's whereabouts, or discourages him from honoring the subpoena, this misconduct when combined with use of the prior out-of-court statement would probably be a violation of D's Confrontation Clause rights.)

2. **"Indicia of reliability":** Regardless of whether W is available to testify, his prior statement probably must have some "indicia of reliability." *Ohio v. Roberts, supra*, p. 273. But if, as we are hypothesizing, the statement falls within one of the traditional "availability immaterial" exceptions, this fact by itself is probably enough under *Roberts* to satisfy the requirement of reliability.

E. Declarant unavailable: Now let us consider those hearsay exceptions that *require* the *unavailability* of the declarant. (These include the *former testimony*, *dying declaration*, and *statement against interest* exceptions, among others; see FRE 804.)

    1 General rule: In general, D will not be able to raise a successful Confrontation Clause claim if the following are both true: (1) the prosecution shows that W really *is* unavailable, through no fault of its own; and (2) the out-of-court statement falls within a narrow, "firmly rooted" exception to the hearsay rule, or else has "particularized guarantees of trustworthiness." *Ohio v. Roberts, supra.*

    2. Former testimony: Thus *former testimony* given at a prior proceeding or deposition where D had an opportunity and similar motive to cross-examine W, may be admitted at D's trial without Confrontation Clause problems, if W is now unavailable. See, e.g., *Mattox v. U.S., supra*, p. 275 (testimony from D's previous trial admissible, because W died before new trial); see also *Ohio v. Roberts, supra* (W's preliminary hearing testimony admissible at D's trial given W's unavailability; fact that D's lawyer questioned W at the hearing provided sufficient "indicia of reliability"). But if the prior proceeding or deposition was on a *different charge*, so that D's motive or opportunity concerning cross-examination was different, use of that prior testimony may violate D's Confrontation Clause rights.

    3. Dying declaration: Since the Supreme Court set out what appears to be the modern Confrontation Clause test in *Ohio v. Roberts*, the Supreme Court has not decided any case involving use of a *dying declaration*. However, prior to *Roberts*, the Court allowed dying declarations into evidence. W&B, Par. 800[04]. Probably the Court would apply the *Roberts* approach to the dying declaration, and would allow it into evidence over a Confrontation Clause claim so long as W was truly unavailable and his dying statement met the traditional requirements for the dying declaration exception (e.g., W believed he was dying, and the statement concerned the cause of his impending death).

    4. Statement against interest: A *statement against interest* is the one hearsay exception where the Court has *not* strictly followed the *Ohio v. Roberts* two-step approach. When a co-defendant gives a *confession* implicating D, the confession will generally be admissible (as a matter of state evidence rules) under the "statement against interest" rules (at least in those states that recognize an exception for statements against penal, as opposed to pecuniary, interest; see *supra*, p. 237). Yet because of the special unreliability of confessions, the Supreme Court has refused to treat confessions as falling within a "firmly rooted" hearsay exception (which would make the particular facts irrelevant), and has insisted on looking to whether the particular facts show trustworthiness. See *infra*, p. 284.

    5. Meaning of "unavailable": When is the declarant "unavailable"? Until the early 1970's, it appeared that she would not be deemed "unavailable" for Confrontation Clause purposes until the prosecution had made all reasonable efforts to procure her attendance at trial. But more recent cases seem to have *watered down* the effort the prosecution must make to obtain the witness.

Example: In *Ohio v. Roberts, supra*, pp. 281-82, W was found to be "unavailable" based on the service of five subpoenas at W's mother's residence, even though there was clearly much else the prosecution could have done in trying to procure her appearance (e.g., contacting the social worker with whom she had previously been in contact).

    a. Federal definition: It is very probable that if the prosecution shows that W is "unavailable" within the definition of FRE 804(a), this will suffice to make W unavailable for Confrontation Clause purposes as well.

F. Co-defendant's statement: The overwhelmingly most important function of the Confrontation Clause is to limit the prosecution's ability to introduce **confessions by accomplices and co-defendants**. During the last 20 years, these are practically the only kinds of out-of-court declarations that have been held inadmissible on Confrontation Clause grounds.

    1. How arises: The prosecution rarely will try to introduce an accomplice's confession as substantive evidence against the accused. Rather, the confession can get heard by the jury in two common ways: (1) The accomplice who made the confession takes the stand (perhaps as a defense witness) and the confession is brought out by the prosecution on **cross-examination**, where it is theoretically used for impeachment rather than substantive purposes; or (2) The accomplice who made the confession and the defendant are tried in a **joint trial**, and the confession is used as substantive evidence against the accomplice, but is heard by the same jury that is trying the defendant.

    2. Reliability: The Supreme Court has consistently held that confessions given by persons in custody are **inherently unreliable**. Therefore, the Confrontation Clause prevents their use against a defendant (other than the person confessing) unless two requirements are satisfied: (1) the confessor is unavailable to give trial testimony; and (2) more importantly, the **facts surrounding the particular confession** give such **"particularized guarantees of trustworthiness"** that the presumption of unreliability is overcome.

        Example: D is charged with intent to commit murder. One Loyd, who was charged at the same time as D, has previously confessed, been tried separately, and been convicted. At D's trial, the prosecution calls Loyd as its principal witness, but Loyd pleads the Fifth Amendment. (The trial judge tells Loyd that this privilege does not apply once the witness has been convicted, but Loyd still refuses to answer.) The prosecution then, purporting to refresh Loyd's recollection on cross-examination, reads a document which it claims is Loyd's confession, and asks periodically, "Did you make that statement?" The document is never formally admitted into evidence.

        Held, the reading to the jury of Loyd's confession (including the parts that implicated D) violated D's Confrontation Clause rights. Even though the confession was never formally in evidence, the jury might reasonably have treated it as evidence, and treated Loyd's refusal to comment on the confession as being an implicit confirmation of its accuracy. *Douglas v. Alabama*, 380 U.S. 415 (1965).

3. **Joint trials:** So deeply does the Supreme Court mistrust the reliability of confessions that even a stringent *limiting instruction* will not be enough to allow a jury jointly trying D1 and D2 to hear D1's confession if D1 does not take the stand. Thus in *Bruton v. U.S.*, 391 U.S. 123 (1968), D1 and D2 were jointly tried for robbery. D1 had orally confessed that he and D2 had committed the robbery. At the joint trial, D1's confession was admitted only against him, and the judge told the jury that it was not to consider the confession as evidence against D2. D1 never took the stand, so D2 never got to cross-examine him about his confession. The Court held that D2's Confrontation Clause rights were violated by the jury's mere hearing of D1's confession (even though it was not technically evidence against him), because the jury could not be expected to follow the judge's limiting instruction.

   a. **The "two jury" technique:** One way around the problem of *Bruton* is to use *two juries* when co-conspirators are being tried. The trial court empanels a separate jury for each defendant. Then, D1 is allowed to withdraw his jury during presentation of evidence that D2 confessed and implicated D1. This saves the necessity of conducting two entirely separate trials. See *People v. Ricardo B.*, 535 N.E.2d 1336 (N.Y. 1989), approving this technique.

4. **Particularized facts showing reliability:** A third person's confession can be introduced against the defendant if the prosecution shows that the *particular facts* surrounding the confession provide enough signs of trustworthiness as to overcome the general presumption against the reliability of confessions. For instance, if D1 and D2 have given *"interlocking"* confessions, which dovetail to a very great extent on important points, a court might hold that a jury trying D1 can hear D2's confession, on the theory that the reliability of D2's particular confession is established by the great overlap between it and D1's confession.

   a. **Overlap must be substantial on key points:** However, the overlap must be very great, and must cover the key points — even where the two confessions overlap significantly, if they diverge on key points one defendant's confession will not be usable against the other. See, e.g., *Lee v. Illinois* (discussed *supra*, pp. 273-74), where D1's and D2's confessions overlapped on many details, but diverged on the key issue of D1's premeditation; this divergence was enough to prevent the requisite showing of particularized reliability, and the court therefore held that D1's Confrontation Clause rights had been violated when the trial judge heard and used D2's confession in convicting D1.

IV. COMPULSORY PROCESS

A. **General meaning:** A criminal defendant's ability to present an effective defense is buttressed by a second Sixth Amendment clause, the Compulsory Process Clause. That clause provides, "[I]n all criminal prosecutions, the accused shall enjoy the right . . . to have *compulsory process* for *obtaining witnesses* in his favor."

   1. **Interpretation:** The Clause thus on its face gives the defendant the right to *subpoena* defense witnesses; a witness who fails to honor the subpoena may be imprisoned by the trial judge for contempt of court. But the Clause has been

interpreted even more broadly, to entitle the defendant to **obtain and present all evidence** helpful to his defense.

   a. **Subpoena of documents:** For instance, in an early case, Chief Justice Marshall (sitting as a circuit judge) held that the Clause entitles a criminal defendant to **subpoena documents** necessary for his defense; Marshall rejected the argument that the Clause gives a right of process only to witnesses and not to their papers. *U.S. v. Burr*, 25 F. Cas. 30, 35 (C.C.D.Va. 1807, No. 14, 692d).

B. State rules restricting evidence: The main relevance of the Compulsory Process Clause to us here, however, is that it may render unconstitutional state or federal evidence rules that would **restrict the defense's ability to present exculpatory evidence.** Even a well-established rule of exclusion may run afoul of the Clause, if its effect is to prevent the defendant from presenting relevant and material evidence. Two Supreme Court cases illustrate how this may occur:

   1. **Ban on accomplice's testimony:** In one of these cases, *Washington v. Texas*, 388 U.S. 14 (1967), a Texas evidence statute provided that persons charged or convicted as co-participants in the same crime could not testify for one another (though one could testify for the state against the other). D was charged with murdering V; W (his companion during the shooting) had previously been convicted of murder for the same shooting. The statute prevented D from offering W's testimony that W, not D, fired the fatal shot, and that D had tried to dissuade W from doing so.

      a. **Holding:** The Supreme Court held that the state's no-testimony-by-accomplices rule violated D's Compulsory Process rights. The clause protects "the right to present a defense," and this right must be construed broadly enough to protect not only the right to have witnesses compelled to be present, but the right to present their testimony. Texas justified its rule on the theory that "if two persons charged with the same crime were allowed to testify on behalf of each other, 'each would try to swear the other out of the charge.' " But (the Court held), the rule was irrational as an attempt to prevent perjury, since Texas allowed one co-defendant to testify **against** another, and perjury is at least as likely in this setting (where the witness has a motive to curry favor with the authorities) as where the witness testifies for the defendant.

   2. **Restrictive hearsay rule:** The second Supreme Court case illustrating compulsory process principles is *Chambers v. Mississippi*, 410 U.S. 284 (1973). The case was decided on Due Process rather than Compulsory Process Clause grounds, but the Court was clearly trying to protect the same values that are protected by the Compulsory Process Clause, namely, the defendant's right to present all relevant and material exculpatory evidence.

      a. **Facts:** D was charged with murdering V, a policeman, while both were in a crowd. Another man who was in the crowd, W, later gave a sworn confession to D's lawyers that he, not D, had shot V. But W later repudiated this confession. At D's trial, he was allowed to call W, and to read W's confession to the jury, but was not permitted to examine W as a hostile witness (because

Mississippi, like many jurisdictions, still followed the common-law rule that a party who calls a witness "vouches for his credibility" and thus may not impeach him; see *supra*, p. 78). During cross-examination by the prosecution, W said that he had recanted this confession, and that he had made it only to gain part of a tort recovery. D then tried to present testimony of three witnesses to whom W had confessed at various times; the judge rejected this testimony as hearsay. (Again, Mississippi followed the common-law rule recognizing an exception for declarations against pecuniary interest but not an exception for statements against penal interest.)

    b. Holding: The Supreme Court held that the combination of these two common-law rules — the rule against impeaching one's own witness and the standard hearsay rule — violated D's due process right to present a fair defense. The "no impeachment of own witness" rule was irrational as applied here, since W's interests were clearly adverse to D's (even though in his testimony W did not accuse D of the crime). Similarly, it was unreasonable for Mississippi to reject the hearsay testimony of those who observed W's confession, since there were numerous assurances that this testimony would be reliable: the confessions were sharply against W's penal interest, there were several confessions that corroborated each other, and each was made spontaneously to a close acquaintance shortly after the murder. In summary, D was prevented from developing critical and reliable evidence in support of his defense.

    c. Significance: *Chambers* is even more significant than *Washington*, because it demonstrates that even ***traditional rules of evidence*** may violate the defendant's Compulsory Process rights, if they have the effect of preventing him from presenting important, and apparently reliable, evidence. L&S, p. 624. (In fact, even under the Federal Rules, testimony by the witnesses to W's confession would have been inadmissible, because although it was against W's penal interest, W was not unavailable, as required by FRE 804(b)(3)'s "statement against interest" exception. *Id.*)

3. Rules to promote orderly trials: On the other hand, exclusionary rules that rationally promote ***orderly trials*** will rarely violate the Compulsory Process Clause, even if they result in some curtailment of the defendant's ability to present exculpatory evidence. For instance, many jurisdictions require the defense to notify the prosecution before trial of the ***names of all witnesses*** it plans to present; the defendant is typically precluded from offering the testimony of any witness not so named, unless he has a valid excuse (e.g., the witness was not identified until after the trial started). The Supreme Court recently held that barring a witness' testimony under such a rule does ***not*** violate the defendant's Compulsory Process rights, if the defense's failure to comply with the rule is willful. *Taylor v. Illinois*, 484 U.S. 400 (1988).

C. Equality principle: The Supreme Court is probably especially likely to hold that a state rule of evidence violates the defendant's Compulsory Process rights if the rule in general ***favors the prosecution***. That is, there is probably a core value supported by the Compulsory Process Clause, the value of ***"equality in the right to produce***

evidence in court." L&S, p. 627.

Example 1: The "no testimony for defense by an accomplice" rule struck down in *Washington v. Texas, supra,* p. 285, was clearly one which always benefits the prosecution at the defense's expense: an accomplice or co-defendant could always testify for the prosecution, but never for the defense. This tilting of the scales probably contributed to the Court's decision to strike down the rule on Compulsory Process grounds, even though the rule was not wholly illogical (an accomplice who has already been convicted and sentenced might indeed have an incentive to help his colleague out of a jam at no cost to himself).

Example 2: D1 and D2 are charged with the rape and murder of a woman, and are tried separately. At D1's trial, W, a witness for the prosecution, testifies that D1 told him that D1 killed the woman after telling D2 to run an errand. At D2's trial, D2 calls W to give the same testimony, but it is excluded as inadmissible hearsay.

Held, exclusion of W's testimony in D2's trial violated D2's right to a fair trial, especially given that the prosecution thought that the testimony was reliable enough to be used against D1. "The hearsay rule may not be applied mechanistically to defeat the ends of justice." *Green v. Georgia,* 442 U.S. 95 (1979).

1. **Not the only principle:** However, "equality" between prosecution and defense is not the only value served by the Compulsory Process Clause. For instance, in *Chambers v. Mississippi, supra,* pp. 285-86, both of the exclusionary evidence rules at issue there — the rule against impeaching one's own witness and the rule that statements against penal interest are not exceptions to the ban on hearsay — probably do not over the long run benefit prosecutors over defendants. Nonetheless, the impact of these rules *in that particular case* was so severe that D's right to present an effective defense was compromised.

D. **Due process:** A defendant's right to present all material and reliable evidence in his own defense is protected not only by the Compulsory Process Clause but also by the Fourteenth Amendment's general *Due Process* Clause. That is, if a state rule of evidence prevents the defendant from presenting material and reliable exculpatory evidence, the effect may be so great as to constitute a violation of a defendant's right to a fair trial. Indeed, where a rule of evidence is overall neutral as between prosecutor and defense, but is highly unfair in its application in the particular case, the Supreme Court seems to prefer to decide the case on due process rather than compulsory process grounds — this is what happened in *Chambers, supra,* pp. 285-86. L&S, pp. 628-29.

PRIVILEGES

I. PRIVILEGES GENERALLY

A. Introduction: A privilege is the *right of an individual not to disclose information about a particular event*. L&S, p. 645. The best-known privileges are the privilege against self-incrimination, and the privileges for confidences exchanged between husband and wife, attorney and client, physician and patient, and clergyman and penitent.

1. **Rationale:** All of the exclusionary evidence rules we have considered so far are motivated by society's interest in having *more accurate adjudication*. Hearsay evidence, for instance, is generally excluded because it is thought to be unreliable and, therefore, not helpful to the truth-seeking process. The rationale behind the privilege rules, by contrast, is not a truth-seeking rationale at all. Giving a person the right to withhold information that is relevant (and probably highly reliable) does not aid the accuracy of verdicts; "rather than facilitating the illumination of truth, [privileges] shut out the light." M, p. 171.

2. **Other values:** Instead, the privilege rules promote broader social goals that have little, if anything, to do with truth-seeking. There are two main interests promoted by the privilege rules: (1) the encouragement of certain *professional advisory relationships*; and (2) the maintenance of certain *zones of privacy*.

   a. **Professional relationships:** Three of the most important generally-recognized privileges — attorney-client, physician-patient, and clergyman-penitent — are designed to facilitate *professional advisory relationships.* Each involves a non-professional who seeks advice about a difficult technical subject from a person whose profession it is to give that advice. Confidences exchanged pursuant to that relationship are protected because society has made the judgment that without such protection against disclosure, many people would not use these professionals, and those who did would find their utility severely reduced.

   Example: Suppose that client-lawyer confidences were not privileged against disclosure. Suppose also that Mary has been involved in an automobile accident with another driver. She thinks she may have a valid claim of her own, but she also worries that the other driver may have a valid claim against her. Without the safety net of a ban on the disclosure of lawyer-client confidences, Mary may decide not to go to a lawyer at all, on the theory that the disclosures she makes about the accident are likely to come back to hurt her (in the event of a suit by the other driver against her, at which suit Mary's lawyer could be forced to testify about confidences by Mary that would be damaging to her defense). In that event, justice may be ill-served, since Mary will never find out that she has a meritorious claim (if that is indeed the case).

   Alternatively, Mary may consult a lawyer but conceal those facts about the accident that she thinks put her in a bad light. Here, too, justice may be ill-served, since the lawyer may give inaccurate advice (e.g., by telling Mary to bring a suit that, had he known the facts, he would have told her was merit-less).

b. **Privacy:** Two of the other major privileges — the spousal privilege and the privilege against self-incrimination — are motivated mainly by *privacy* concerns. Especially in today's times, when government and "big business" appear to have limitless capacity to gather information about the individual, most people feel that the individual needs a "zone of privacy" which cannot be penetrated.

3. **Usually not constitutionally-based:** Most privileges are *not constitutionally-based*. (The privilege against self-incrimination is the only exception). Therefore, each state is free to establish whatever privileges it wishes, and to define the contours of those privileges as it wishes. See *infra*, p. 291.

4. **List of major privileges:** Here is a list of the major privileges, which we will be considering one at a time in this chapter:

   a. The *attorney-client* privilege;

   b. The *physician-patient* privilege;

   c. The *clergyman-penitent* privilege;

   d. The *spousal* (i.e., husband and wife) privilege;

   e. The privilege against *self-incrimination*;

   f. The *government secrets* privilege (including the privilege against disclosing the identity of *informants*); and

   g. A miscellaneous group of occasionally-recognized privileges (journalist-source, parent-child, business trade secrets, and accountant-client).

5. **Groupings:** These privileges fall into three main categories: (1) "Professional counseling"; (2) "Zone of privacy"; and (3) "Institutional."

   a. **Professional counseling:** The commonly-recognized *"professional counseling"* privileges, which protect confidential communications given in the course of a professional relationship, are: lawyer-client, physician-patient, and clergyman-penitent. Additionally, the accountant-client privilege, recognized in a few jurisdictions, falls within this category.

   b. **"Zone of privacy":** As noted, two major privileges reflect the need for a *"zone of privacy"* around certain key human relationships or around the individual: the spousal privilege and the privilege against self-incrimination. Additionally, the parent-child privilege (recognized in a few states) falls within this class.

   c. **"Institutional":** Finally, several privileges can be thought of as being *"institutional,"* in the sense that they are motivated by the need to protect some of society's major institutions rather than to protect the individual who asserts them. The "government secrets" privilege (including the government's right not disclose the identities of confidential informants in criminal cases) is motivated by the need to protect the institution of government. Similarly, those jurisdictions that have recognized a journalist-source privilege have done so not so much to protect the journalist as to protect the institution of the free press, thought to be of key importance to society.

B. Where applicable: Where a privilege not to disclose certain information exists, that privilege applies ***regardless of the proceeding***. That is, if W is privileged not to disclose fact or communication A, he will be protected against having to disclose A in a trial (whether by judge or jury), administrative hearing, deposition or other discovery proceeding, or any other proceeding. L&S, p. 650.

C. Who may assert: The privilege belongs to the ***person whose interest or relationship is intended to be fostered by that privilege.*** Therefore, he is the ***only one*** who may assert it. M, p. 173.

    1. Significance: The practical significance of this rule is that if P and D are the only parties to a lawsuit, and W is the person whom the privilege protects, the choice whether to assert or waive the privilege belongs solely to W, not to either of the litigants.

        Example: D is charged with murder. X is a co-defendant who is being separately tried. The prosecution calls L, X's lawyer, to testify about statements X has made to L that implicate D in the crime. The privilege to prevent L from disclosing these statements belongs *solely to X*. Therefore, it is solely up to him whether to assert the privilege or waive it. If X waives the privilege, D is powerless to stop L's testimony on attorney-client privilege grounds. (The testimony may violate D's Sixth Amendment Confrontation Clause rights, if X is not available for cross-examination at the trial — see *supra*, p. 270 — but this has nothing to do with privilege law.)

    2. Complete discretion of trial judge: Where the owner of the privilege is not a litigant, and one of the parties objects to evidence on the grounds that that non-litigant's privilege would be violated, the judge may use his discretion to exclude the evidence on the grounds that the absent owner of the privilege would want it that way. However, if the judge lets the evidence in anyway, the party who opposed the evidence may, in most jurisdictions, ***not complain on appeal***, since the privilege was not his in the first place. M, p. 174.

D. Risk of eavesdropping: Most privileges protect communications between two parties to a specified relationship (e.g., attorney and client). Suppose a ***third person*** learns of the content of the confidential communication. May this third person disclose the communication?

    1. Older view: The older view is that only the parties to the protected relationship may refuse to testify, and the third party may (and may be compelled to) testify. This is true even where the third party learns of the communication by ***eavesdropping*** or other unforeseeable, even illegal, means. M, p. 175.

        Example: D speaks to his lawyer by telephone; the call is placed through a phone company operator, W. Contrary to phone company rules, W eavesdrops on the conversation, and hears D confess to a murder. The prosecution puts W on the stand to testify to this confession. D asserts that it falls within his attorney-client privilege.

Held, W's testimony is admissible. "Since the means of preserving secrecy of communication are entirely in the client's hands, and since the privilege is a derogation from the general testimonial duty and should be strictly construed, it would be improper to extend its prohibition to third persons who obtain knowledge of the communications" (quoting Wigmore). *Clark v. State*, 261 S.W.2d 339 (Ct. Cr. App. Tex. 1953) (other aspects of which are discussed *infra*, p. 302).

2. **Modern view:** This traditional view was the product of a time in which methods of eavesdropping were far less sophisticated than they are today. Modern courts generally hold that the communication is ***protected even if intercepted,*** so long as the interception was ***not reasonably to be anticipated.*** M, p. 176. Thus most modern courts would decide *Clark v. State, supra*, differently.

   a. **Interception reasonably anticipated:** However, if the party protected by the privilege should reasonably have anticipated the interception, he will ***not*** be protected. For instance, "if . . . the communication takes place in a crowded elevator the client should expect that there will be persons listening and he will be taken not to have intended the statements to be in confidence." W&B, Par. 503(a)(4)[01] (referring to attorney-client privilege, but the result would presumably be the same for other privileges).

E. **Sources of privileges:** As noted, privileges (except for that against self-incrimination) are not constitutionally mandated. Therefore, each state, and the federal system, is free to develop whatever privileges it wants. It may do so by statute, by "common law" development (i.e., case law), or both.

   1. **State development:** All states recognize, in some form, the husband-wife and attorney-client privileges. M, p. 183. Most states do so by statute. M, p. 180. Additionally, all recognize a privilege for certain government information. M, pp. 183-84. All but ten recognize some kind of physician-patient privilege. M, p. 244. All but three have a clergyman-penitent privilege. M, p. 184. After that, coverage drops off rapidly: journalist-source, parent-child, and accountant-client are all recognized only by a minority of jurisdictions.

      a. **No Federal Rules:** The proposed Federal Rules on privilege were never enacted (see *infra*, p. 292). Therefore, in the privilege area, states have been left without the simple alternative that they have had in other evidence areas of simply enacting the Federal Rules. However, some states have enacted the proposed-but-never-enacted Federal Rules on privileges; others have enacted the similar (but not identical) Revised Uniform Rules of Evidence privilege provisions, drafted in 1974.

   2. **Federal courts:** The Federal Rules of Evidence, as originally proposed, approved by the Supreme Court, and presented to Congress, would have completely codified the federal law of privilege into nine non-constitutional privileges (required reports,

attorney-client, psychotherapist-patient, husband-wife, clergyman-communicant, political vote, trade secrets, secrets of state and other official information, and identity of informer; Proposed Federal Rules 502-510). But this package was so controversial that ***Congress rejected it.***

    a. Actual treatment: Instead, Congress deleted all of the specific rules of privilege from the Federal Rules as they were finally enacted, and left FRE 501 as the ***sole Federal Rule governing privileges.*** FRE 501 provides:

"Except as otherwise required by the Constitution of the United States or provided by Act of Congress or in rules prescribed by the Supreme Court pursuant to statutory authority, the privilege of a witness, person, government, state, or political subdivision thereof shall be governed by the principles of the common law as they may be interpreted by the courts of the United States in the light of reason and experience. However, in civil actions and proceedings, with respect to an element of a claim or defense as to which state law supplies the rule of decision, the privilege of a witness, person, government, state, or political subdivision thereof shall be determined in accordance with state law."

    b. Meaning: FRE 501 sets up a two-part system of privilege law in the federal courts:

      i. Diversity cases: In civil cases where "state law supplies the rule of decision," state law of privilege applies. The main significance of this provision is that in ***diversity cases***, the federal court must usually ***follow state law of privilege.***

      ii. Federal question cases: In criminal cases, and in civil "federal question" cases, the federal courts are free to ***use their own judgment*** — they are not bound by the privilege law of the state in which they sit. In making this ***"federal common law"*** of privilege for federal question cases, the federal courts often look to the Proposed Federal Rules of Evidence (PFRE 502-510), though they are not bound by these provisions. We, too, will often be considering the Proposed Federal Rules as we go through the various privileges.

II. THE ATTORNEY-CLIENT PRIVILEGE

    A. Introduction: The essence of the attorney-client privilege is that a client has the ***right not to disclose*** (and the right to prevent his lawyer from disclosing) ***any confidential communication between the two of them relating to the professional relationship.***

      1. Proposed Federal Rule: The Proposed Federal Rule of Evidence on the attorney-client privilege, like the rest of the specific privilege rules, was never enacted. However, because PFRE 503 codifies the prevailing common-law approach in most respects, it is worth reproducing here:

"(a) **Definitions.** As used in this rule:

    (1) A "client" is a person, public officer, or corporation, association, or other organization or entity, either public or private, who is rendered professional legal services by a lawyer, or

who consults a lawyer with a view to obtaining professional legal services from him.

(2) A "lawyer" is a person authorized, or reasonably believed by the client to be authorized, to practice law in any state or nation.

(3) A "representative of the lawyer" is one employed to assist the lawyer in the rendition of professional legal services.

(4) A communication is "confidential" if not intended to be disclosed to third persons other than those to whom disclosure is in furtherance of the rendition of professional legal services to the client or those reasonably necessary for the transmission of the communication.

(b) **General rule of privilege.** A client has a privilege to refuse to disclose and to prevent any other person from disclosing confidential communications made for the purpose of facilitating the rendition of professional legal services to the client, (1) between himself or his representative and his lawyer or his lawyer's representative, or (2) between his lawyer and the lawyer's representative, or (3) by him or his lawyer to a lawyer representing another in a matter of common interest, or (4) between representatives of the client or between the client and a representative of the client, or (5) between lawyers representing the client.

(c) **Who may claim the privilege.** The privilege may be claimed by the client, his guardian or conservator, the personal representative of a deceased client, or the successor, trustee, or similar representative of a corporation, association, or other organization, whether or not in existence. The person who was the lawyer at the time of the communication may claim the privilege but only on behalf of the client. His authority to do so is presumed in the absence of evidence to the contrary.

(d) **Exceptions.** There is no privilege under this rule:

(1) *Furtherance of crime or fraud.* If the services of the lawyer were sought or obtained to enable or aid anyone to commit or plan to commit what the client knew or reasonably should have known to be a crime or fraud; or

(2) *Claimants through same deceased client.* As to a communication relevant to an issue between parties who claim through the same deceased client, regardless of whether the claims are by testate or intestate succession or by inter vivos transaction; or

(3) *Breach of duty by lawyer or client.* As to a communication relevant to an issue of breach of duty by the lawyer to his client or by the client to his lawyer; or

(4) *Document attested by lawyer.* As to a communication relevant to an issue concerning an attested document to which the lawyer is an attesting witness; or

(5) *Joint clients.* As to a communication relevant to matter of common interest between two or more clients if the communication was made by any of them to a lawyer retained or consulted in common, when offered in an action between any of the clients."

2. **State approach:** The attorney-client privilege exists in *every state*. In most states, the privilege is controlled by statute. M, p. 180. Some, but probably not most, are modeled on the Proposed Federal Rule quoted above.

3. **Summary of requirements:** The provisions of the attorney-client privilege are intricate, and are discussed in detail below. Here, as a starting point, are some of

the key aspects of the privilege, as it applies in most states:

a. **"Client":** The "client" can be a *corporation* as well as an individual;

b. **Belongs to client:** The privilege belongs to the *client*, not to the lawyer or any third persons. The lawyer may assert it, but only if he is acting on behalf of the client in doing so.

c. **Professional relationship:** The privilege applies only to communications "made for the purpose of facilitating the rendition of *professional legal services* to the client." For instance, if the lawyer is giving business advice, or advice as a friend, the privilege does not apply.

d. **Confidential:** The privilege applies only to communications which are intended to be *"confidential."* Thus, if the client discloses the content of the communication to a third person not associated with the lawyer-client relationship (e.g., a friend), the privilege will be lost.

e. **Fact of employment and client's identity:** The fact that the lawyer-client relationship *exists*, and the *identity* of the client, are normally *not* privileged. Only the substance of the confidences exchanged between them is privileged. (But there are exceptions; see *infra*, p. 300.)

f. **Physical evidence:** Normally, the privilege does not permit the lawyer to conceal *physical evidence* or documents given to him by the client (other than documents written for the purpose of communicating from client to lawyer).

g. **Crime or fraud exception:** The privilege does not apply where the confidence relates to the commission of a *future crime* or *fraud*.

B. Rationale: As with most privileges, plausible arguments can be made against allowing the privilege as well as in favor of it:

1. **Against:** Against allowing the privilege, two main arguments can be made:

   a. **Suppresses evidence:** It suppresses evidence that is likely to be highly relevant, very probative, and, in some cases, not replaceable by any other evidence.

   b. **Bentham's "protection of the guilty" argument:** In criminal cases, the client will either be guilty or innocent. If the client is innocent, compelling his attorney to disclose any confidences from the client will not injure the client, because the client will be acquitted anyway. If the client is guilty, then permitting the lawyer to remain silent about what he has learned from the client merely aids the client in preparing a false defense or otherwise escaping punishment. To Jeremy Bentham, the Nineteenth Century utilitarian lawyer-philosopher who articulated this argument, any rule that helped the guilty sometimes go free was necessarily bad, not good.

2. **In favor:** But a number of arguments are often made in support of the privilege. These arguments, in the aggregate, are quite convincing:

a. Won't consult: If there were no privilege, many people (including some with good defenses or claims) would simply **not consult lawyers** at all. For instance, suppose that there was no privilege, and each lawyer felt the need to give the equivalent of *Miranda* warnings to any new client — "Anything you say to me may be used against you in a court of law by the other side." Many, if not most, clients would decide that it is better not to say anything at all to a lawyer than to run this risk. L&S, pp. 655-56.

b. Partial disclosure: Those clients who did decide to consult a lawyer at all would be loathe to make full disclosure to her. A client would probably omit mention of any fact that the client believed was unhelpful to his claim or defense. Yet, knowledge of *all* the relevant facts will be needed for the lawyer to give proper advice — the client doesn't necessarily know what facts seem damaging but are not, or what facts are damaging but are likely to come out anyway in the case. The net result is likely to be that, because of the less-than-full disclosure by the client, the lawyer gives bad advice. L&S, p. 656. For instance, the lawyer may conclude that the client should litigate, when full disclosure would have made it clear that there is no claim or defense worth litigating. L&S, p. 706.

c. Procedural problems: If there were no privilege, there would be extremely difficult **procedural problems** at trial. If the lawyer was required to take the witness stand, who would represent the client for purposes of cross-examination? How would that second lawyer (let's call him Lawyer 2) learn enough about the case to cross-examine Lawyer 1 — if Lawyer 2 knew enough to be useful as a cross-examiner, couldn't he, too, be put on the stand to be questioned about what his client told him? Would statements on the witness stand by Lawyer 1 "bind" the client? See L&S, p. 707. In sum, absence of a privilege would probably produce a procedural nightmare.

d. Little information suppressed: The privilege really **suppresses** very **little** information. If Client tells Lawyer that Fact A exists, the privilege does not prevent the other side from proving Fact A, it merely prevents proof that Client told Lawyer that Fact A was so. Other ways of proving Fact A (e.g., by evidence existing before the communication between Client and Lawyer) may be used to prove Fact A in exactly the same way as if Client had never told Lawyer about Fact A. If there were no privilege, Client would probably not have told Lawyer about Fact A in the first place. Therefore, the granting of the privilege is unlikely to result in the suppression of any evidence that would have existed in the absence of the privilege. L&S, pp. 705-06.

e. Unscrupulous lawyers: If there were no privilege, unscrupulous lawyers would receive an advantage. That is, lawyers with ostensibly "poor memories" when called at trial would have an advantage over scrupulous ones who testify truthfully. Similarly, the lazy lawyer who asks his client few questions would receive an advantage over the diligent one who quizzes his client extensively. L&S, p. 656.

f. Privacy of relationship: More broadly, it is socially beneficial to allow the lawyer-client relationship to be one of absolute confidence and trust. Especially in a society that seems more "Big Brother"-like every day, the individual needs "zones of privacy" free from government scrutiny. The attorney-client relationship should be one such zone. L&S, p. 707.

C. The professional relationship: The privilege applies only in the context of a professional lawyer-client relationship. As PFRE 503(b) puts it, the privilege applies only to communications "made for the purpose of facilitating the rendition of ***professional legal services*** to the client. . . ."

  1. No retainer needed: The required lawyer-client privilege can exist even though the client ***does not pay a fee.*** For instance, if the client receives a ***free initial consultation*** from the lawyer, the privilege applies even though, at the end of the consultation, either the client or the lawyer decides that the lawyer should not handle the case. M, p. 208.

  2. Non-legal advice: But the mere fact that the person giving the advice is a lawyer is not enough — the relationship must involve the giving of ***legal*** advice. "When lawyers are consulted as ***family friends***, ***business advisors***, or political consultants, the privilege is inapplicable." L&S, pp. 659-60. See, e.g., *Prichard v. U.S.*, 181 F.2d 326 (6th Cir. 1950), aff'd 339 U.S. 974 (1950) (privilege did not apply to communications between judge and attorney seeking legal advice about his own conduct in stuffing ballot boxes; judge had already called a grand jury to investigate election fraud, so no lawyer-client relationship could properly have existed between them at the time).

  3. Reasonable belief: Suppose the "lawyer" being consulted is in fact a charlatan who has never been admitted to the bar. So long as the client ***reasonably believes*** that the person he is talking to is a lawyer, this is all that is required. M, p. 210. Similarly, so long as the lawyer is admitted (or believed by the client to be admitted) in ***any*** state, the fact that he is not (and is known by the client not to be) admitted in the state where the advice takes place is irrelevant. *Id.*

  4. Client holds the privilege: The privilege ***belongs to the client***, not to the lawyer or anyone else. (See the discussion of who may claim a privilege, *supra*, p. 290, in the context of privileges generally.)

    a. Waiver: Like any privilege, the attorney-client privilege may be ***waived*** by the client's words or actions. For instance, if the client ***discloses*** to a third person (e.g., a friend) the substance of what he told the lawyer, this will be considered a waiver, and the privilege will no longer apply. M, p. 223.

D. Confidential communications: Only *"confidential"* communications are protected by the privilege. A disclosure is "confidential" if the client intends that it not be disclosed to persons other than the lawyer and those working with the lawyer. The client need not expressly state that he wants the communication to be held confidential; it is enough if, under the circumstances, he could reasonably assume that there would not be disclosure to others. M, p. 217.

1. **Client-to-lawyer:** Most importantly, disclosures by the ***client to the lawyer*** are protected if they are intended to be confidential.

   a. **Non-verbal communication:** When the client communicates orally or in writing to the lawyer, this is obviously covered. But what if the communication is ***non-verbal?*** For instance, suppose that the client rolls up his sleeve to show a scar. This should be treated as a confidential (and therefore protected) communication, since it was intended as a disclosure, and was intended to remain secret.

   b. **Lawyer's observation:** However, where the lawyer makes an observation that ***third parties*** could also have made, this will not be a confidential communication.

   Example: Shortly after Wife is found dead with stab wounds, Husband visits Lawyer to seek advice. Lawyer notices scratch marks on Husband's hands and face. Since these scratch marks could be viewed by anyone who happens to see Husband at that time, Lawyer's observations will not be protected by the attorney-client privilege, and he can be forced to testify about seeing them. (But if Husband had covered them with a bandage, and then removed the bandage to show them to Lawyer, Lawyer could not be forced to testify that he saw the scratches underneath the bandages, though he could be forced to testify that he saw the bandages.) L&S, p. 660.

   c. **Mental state:** When a criminal defendant asserts an insanity defense, the prosecutor may try to question the lawyer about the client's mental state around the time of the crime. Courts are split on whether the lawyer can be forced to testify in this situation. The better view seems to be that the lawyer should not be forced to testify, since his conclusions about the client's mental state in all probability derive from their conversations about privileged matters. *Id.*

2. **Lawyer-to-client statements:** The privilege also applies to statements made ***by the lawyer*** to the client. M, p. 212.

3. **Information involving third parties:** Suppose the communication is not between client and lawyer, but between client and some ***third party***. Whether the privilege applies depends on whether the third party is ***assisting the lawyer*** in rendering legal services.

   a. **Representative of lawyer:** Thus if the third party is assisting the lawyer, this party is in essence a ***representative*** of the lawyer, and communications involving him are treated the same way as if he were himself a lawyer. For instance, if an ***expert*** is retained by the lawyer to help investigate the case and to give tactical advice, any communication between the client and the expert will be privileged.

   Example: P brings a personal injury action against D, claiming that he has suffered a brain concussion and other medical injuries. At the request of P's lawyers, X, a physician, gives P a psychiatric and neurological examination.

D attempts to force X to testify about the examination. No physician-patient privilege applies in the case, so X claims that he was acting as a representative of P's lawyers, and that the attorney-client privilege applies.

Held, the attorney-client privilege applies. X was acting as P's lawyer's agent in examining P. (Had X been giving P medical treatment, the privilege would not apply; but the examination here was solely for purposes of conducting the litigation.) *City and County of San Francisco v. Superior Court*, 231 P.2d 26 (Cal. 1951). See also *People v. Lines*, 531 P.2d 793 (Cal. 1975), to the same effect.

b. Not assisting lawyer: But where the third person is ***not*** assisting the lawyer, there is no privilege for communications between that third person and the lawyer or client, even if these communications relate to the lawyer's providing of legal services. M, pp. 212-13.

Example: D is charged with murder. L, D's lawyer, while investigating the case to prepare D's defense, interviews X. X tells L, "I saw D near the scene of the murder moments before it happened." Because X is not acting as L's agent at the time he makes the statement to L, the statement is not privileged. Therefore, L can be required to testify about the statement. (However, the work-product immunity rule, discussed briefly *infra*, p. 313, may protect L from having to disclose the substance of X's oral statement. But that rule is quite distinct from the attorney-client privilege, which does not apply here.)

i. Lead generated by client: Suppose that, on the facts of the above example, the only way that L ever knew to interview X was because D told him that X might have some information. In this instance, D can make a strong argument that L's interview with X is a direct by-product of the earlier privileged communication between D and L, and that the interview should therefore also be privileged. D might well prevail with this argument — just as he might prevail if he had told L where the body was buried, and the prosecution then tried to force L to testify about how and where he found the body. (As to this discovery-of-evidence situation, see discussion, *infra*, p. 304.)

4. Tangible evidence and documents: Suppose the lawyer receives ***tangible evidence*** or ***documents*** from his client. May he be forced to disclose the existence of these items, or how he came into their possession? Generally, the attorney-client privilege adds nothing to the situation: if the client would have been required to disclose or turn over the items had they remained in his possession (e.g., because they are evidence in a criminal case), the lawyer must do the same. But the lawyer may be privileged to withhold information about how he came to possess the item. The matter is discussed more extensively *infra*, p. 304.

5. Miscellaneous issues: Here are some miscellaneous issues concerning whether a communication is "confidential" and thus privileged:

a. **Presence of third persons:** The *presence* of a ***third person*** when the communication takes place, or its later disclosure to such a person, may indicate that the communication was not intended to be "confidential." If so, the privilege will be treated as having been ***waived***.

> **Example:** If the communication takes place on a crowded elevator, where it is overheard by third persons, this setting will indicate that the client could not reasonably have expected confidentiality. Similarly, if the client, following the conference with the lawyer, tells a friend all about the conference, this is likely to be held to be an implied waiver of confidentiality.

> i. **Clerks or relatives:** However, if the third party's presence is reasonably helpful to the conference, that presence will not destroy the confidentiality. Thus if the lawyer's ***secretary*** or ***clerk*** is present, this will make no difference. Similarly, if the client's friend or relative attends the meeting in order to help (e.g., the friend interprets for the client, who cannot speak English very well), this too will not waive the privilege. M, pp. 218-19.

> ii. **Inadvertent eavesdropping:** If the client and lawyer take reasonable precautions to protect confidentiality, the fact that, unbeknownst to them, ***eavesdropping*** occurs will not cause the privilege to be waived, under modern decisions. (But see *Clark v. State, supra*, pp. 290-91, an older decision in which a telephone operator who eavesdropped on the lawyer-client conversation was ordered to testify about what she heard, even though her eavesdropping was against phone company regulations and ought not to have been foreseen by the lawyer or client; the case would almost certainly turn out differently today.)

> iii. **Multiple clients:** Where ***multiple clients*** (either with separate counsel or sharing the same counsel) are present during an otherwise-confidential disclosure, special issues arise. See *infra*, p. 311.

b. **Identity, fact of retention:** Only communications ***relating to the provision of legal services*** are protected. Thus the client's identity, or the fact that the lawyer has been retained, usually are not protected. (This is discussed further *infra*, p. 300.) Similarly, communications from lawyer to client about ***ministerial*** matters are probably not protected.

> **Example:** D, who is free on bail pending trial, does not appear at trial. In support of its case for bail jumping, the prosecution demands that D's lawyer, L, testify about whether he told D the time and place of the trial. L refuses to give this information on the grounds of attorney-client privilege.
>
> *Held*, the privilege does not apply. Communication between lawyer and client about the trial date does not involve "the subject matter of defendant's legal problem. . . . Such communications are non-legal in nature. Counsel is simply performing a notice function." *U.S. v. Woodruff*, 383 F.Supp. 696 (E.D.Pa. 1974).

c. **Underlying fact:** It is the ***communication*** that is privileged, ***not*** the ***underlying facts*** that are communicated. Therefore, the client can be required to disclose the underlying fact even though he has communicated it to his lawyer.

> **Example:** P, a pedestrian injured in a collision with D's car, brings a personal injury action against D. In preparing for trial, P tells L, a lawyer, that she (P) was crossing the street against the light at the time of the accident. L may not be required to testify or otherwise disclose the fact that P has made this statement (since this is a privileged communication). However, P may be called to the stand and required to testify about whether the light was green, even though that fact was the subject of a communication from her to her lawyer. (But P cannot be required to say whether she told this to the lawyer.) See W&B, Par. 503(b)[03].

E. Fact of employment; client's identity: Sometimes a client will want to keep secret the *mere existence* of the attorney-client relationship, including the client's identity, address, fee arrangements, and other information about the terms of the lawyer's employment.

   1. General rule: The general rule is that the *fact* that the attorney has been hired, and the *identity* of the client, are *not* privileged. M, p. 215.

   2. Exception: But at least some courts have recognized exceptions to this general rule of non-privilege:

   a. Anonymous restitution: For instance, where the client wishes to make *anonymous restitution* of some sort, courts have sometimes allowed him to do so through his lawyer.

   > **Example:** Two taxpayers have their lawyer mail the IRS a check for delinquent taxes, without revealing the taxpayers' identities. (The taxpayers are afraid of a criminal investigation, and decide that if one occurs, they will be in better shape if they can show that they have already paid the taxes, albeit anonymously. They realize that if they give the IRS their names, the very investigation they fear will be made more likely.) The IRS responds by demanding that the lawyer disclose the taxpayers' identities.
   >
   > *Held*, the identities are protected by the attorney-client privilege and need not be released. *Baird v. Koerner*, 279 F.2d 623 (9th Cir. 1960).

   i. Criticism: Cases like *Baird*, allowing the attorney to handle payments on behalf of an anonymous client, are criticized on the grounds that this approach allows the client to do with impunity through a lawyer what he could not do directly or through some other kind of agent. For instance, the taxpayers in *Baird* would not have been able to send the money into the IRS directly without disclosing their identities; why should they be able to "launder" their payment by use of a lawyer?

   b. "Missing link": Courts also sometimes allow the identity of the client to remain secret where so much other information is already public that disclosure of the client's identity would have the effective result of disclosing a privileged communication, or violating the client's privilege against self-incrimination.

Example: The Ls are lawyers who have appeared on behalf of various named defendants in drug prosecutions. The Ls are asked to disclose to a grand jury whether their representation of these named defendants has been arranged by unknown third parties, and whether such third parties have paid their fees. One reason the prosecution wants this information is to show that these third persons have paid more in legal fees alone than they show on their tax returns as having received in total income.

Held, the identity of the third persons who retained the Ls and paid their fees is privileged. The attorney-client privilege will be protected "when so much of the substance of the communications is already in the government's possession that additional disclosures would yield substantially probative links in an existing chain of inculpatory events or transactions." Here, disclosure of the third party clients' identities and fees would be directly tied to their motive in retaining counsel, and might lead them to be indicted. *In re Grand Jury Proceedings*, 517 F.2d 666 (5th Cir. 1975). (But see the older case of *U.S. v. Pape*, 144 F.2d 778 (2d Cir. 1944), where the fact that D had hired a lawyer to represent X was required to be disclosed, even though that fact was evidence of D's guilt.)

F. Physical evidence and documents: Suppose the client turns over to the lawyer *physical evidence* or *documents*. Is the fact that the lawyer now has these items in his possession privileged? Can he be required to disclose not only that he has them, but how he got them? These and related issues are probably the most difficult ones in all of attorney-client privilege law. Courts are frequently in disagreement on how to resolve these issues.

> **Example:** D, charged with murder, hands a gun to L, his lawyer. L has reason to believe that the gun was the murder weapon. (1) May L keep silent and decline to turn the gun over to the prosecution, on the grounds that he obtained it through his client's exercise of the attorney-client privilege? (2) If L must or does turn the gun over, can he refuse to say how he got it or what D told him about it, on privilege grounds? The issues are complicated, and courts may disagree on some aspects.

1. Can't assist in ongoing fraud: We must begin by keeping in mind the overarching principle that the attorney-client privilege does not apply where the lawyer's assistance is sought to enable the client to *commit a future crime or fraud*. (See *infra*, p. 310.)

2. Concealment of evidence: All states have statutes prohibiting the intentional concealment or destruction of *evidence* in pending proceedings. Therefore, the lawyer who helps his client conceal or destroy evidence is a co-conspirator to a *new crime*, and their actions and discussions together concerning the concealment or destruction are therefore *not privileged*.

a. Contraband and crime fruits or instrumentalities: This rule is especially clear where the item is *contraband*, *stolen money*, or a *fruit* or *instrumentality* of crime. In this situation, the nature of the item, and the illegality of possessing or concealing it, are so clear that the courts will not hesitate to hold the attorney-client privilege inapplicable.

Example: The Bank of Virginia is robbed of $7,500 by a man with a sawed-off shotgun. Two days later, Client tells Lawyer that he has put cash into a safe deposit box that he has just rented at the Richmond National Bank. At the time, Client is already under suspicion of the robbery (and Lawyer knows that he is). Lawyer goes to the Richmond National Bank, rents his own safe deposit box, takes the cash from Client's box (as well as a sawed-off shotgun he finds there) and puts them in his own box. Lawyer intends to keep the contents of his own box secret for as long as possible, preferably until the end of Client's trial; if Lawyer's possession of the money and gun is discovered, he intends to argue that his possession of them cannot be disclosed to the jury during Client's trial. Before the trial, however, the FBI searches Lawyer's box and discovers the money and gun.

Held, Lawyer's conduct was not encompassed by the attorney-client privilege. (Indeed, Lawyer must be suspended from practice.) By keeping possession of the money, even temporarily, Lawyer was knowingly receiving stolen property, thus participating in a crime or fraud as to which the privilege does not apply. Similarly, possession of a sawed-off shotgun was illegal, and thus barred from privilege by the crime/fraud exception. Lawyer has also violated Canon 15 of the state Canons of Ethics, whereby "the office of attorney does not permit, much less does it demand of him for any client, violation of law or any manner of fraud or chicane." *In re Ryder*, 263 F.Supp. 360 (E.D.Va. 1967).

b. **Destruction advice to client:** Similarly, the lawyer may not *advise his client* to *destroy* contraband, stolen goods, or other clear evidence of crime. If he does give such advice, the giving of that advice is not privileged.

Example: Client telephones his lawyer, and confesses to just having murdered his ex-wife. Lawyer asks, "Did you get rid of the weapon?" Client says, "No, I still got the weapon." Lawyer says, "Get rid of the weapon and sit tight and don't talk to anyone, and I will fly down in the morning." Unbeknownst to them, a telephone company operator has been eavesdropping on the call. Client, charged with murder, claims that this conversation may not be disclosed because it comes within the attorney-client privilege.

Held, the privilege does not apply to this conversation. The rule making the privilege inapplicable to advice on how to commit a crime "must extend to one who, having committed a crime, seeks or takes counsel as to how he shall escape arrest and punishment, such as advice regarding the destruction or disposition of the murder weapon or of the body following a murder." Lawyer's advice here was "not in the legitimate course of professional employment in making or preparing a defense at law." *Clark v. State*, 261 S.W.2d 339 (Crim.App.Tex. 1953) (the eavesdropping aspect of which is discussed *supra*, pp. 290-91).

c. **Ambiguous evidence:** Suppose that the lawyer receives, or learns about, a tangible item that is not contraband, stolen money, or some other fruit or instrumentality of a known crime. For instance, the item may be one which would be *evidence in a civil suit*; or it may be a "neutral" item (i.e., not a fruit or instrumentality of crime) that would nonetheless be admissible in a criminal prosecution that has not yet commenced but is likely. In this situation, the outcome is less clear; most courts, however, would nonetheless apply the general rule that so long as the item is likely to be evidence in a civil or criminal case, the lawyer may not conceal it or advise his client to conceal it, and if he does so, his conduct is not privileged.

> **Example:** Client is the defendant in a messy divorce case, in which Client's fidelity to his wife will be a material issue. Client asserts that he has always been faithful. During one of his conferences with Lawyer, Client leaves on the desk a ring inscribed (with a recent date), "To Client, with all my lust and love. [signed] Alice." Client's wife is not named Alice. May Lawyer keep the ring and conceal its existence during the suit? Most courts would probably say "no," since the item is relevant evidence in the pending suit. (But Lawyer may probably turn it over to Client with an admonition that it may have to be produced as part of discovery. See *infra*.)

3. **Attorney's choices:** If the client comes to the lawyer with a tangible item that is clear evidence, what the lawyer may not do, as noted, is to conceal or advise the client to conceal it. The lawyer does, however, have several choices:

   a. **Decline to take:** The wisest may well be for him to *decline to take possession of the evidence* at all, leaving it with the client. He should advise the client against destroying the evidence. (If he has reason to believe that the client will not listen to this advice, it is not clear what his obligations are. This issue is discussed further *infra*, p. 304.)

      i. **Lawyer's obligation:** If the lawyer follows this course, declining to take possession of the item, does he then have any obligation to *notify the prosecution* that the evidence exists? L&S (p. 679) suggest that so long as the client has not left the item with the lawyer, and has taken it away at the conclusion of their meeting, the lawyer has no obligation of disclosure.

   b. **Hold for reasonable time:** Alternatively, the lawyer may take the evidence for a *reasonable time*. This is especially true if evaluation of the item's value as evidence depends on some kind of *inspection* or *testing*. For instance, if the client is charged with murder by shooting, and the item is a gun that the lawyer suspects (but does not know) to be the murder weapon, the lawyer may keep the gun for long enough to have ballistics tests performed on it to determine whether it is the murder weapon. See, e.g., *State v. Olwell*, 394 P.2d 681 (Wash. 1964) (lawyer may withhold knife from prosecution "for a reasonable period of time").

      i. **After reasonable inspection:** Once the lawyer has held the item for the period of reasonable inspection or testing, he may normally *return the item* to the client. If he does so, he must certainly advise the client that destruction or concealment of evidence is a crime. (But if he believes the client will destroy or conceal it, he probably cannot return it. See *infra*.)

    ii. Stolen property: If the lawyer knows that the property has been **stolen**, he has an obligation to **return it** to its **rightful owner** once the time for reasonable inspection has passed. If the lawyer does not do this, he is a receiver of stolen goods, and is thus participating in an ongoing crime, so that the privilege does not apply. Thus, the lawyer in *Ryder*, *supra*, p. 302, should have returned the money to the bank (or perhaps to the FBI with instructions that it belongs to the bank). As noted below, some courts may permit him to return it without disclosing how he got it, or at least to conceal his source from the eventual jury.

  c. Turn over to prosecution: If the lawyer believes that the client will **destroy or conceal** the evidence, most courts would probably require the lawyer to **turn the item over** to the other side (usually the prosecution). Thus, in *Hitch v. Pima Superior Court*, 708 P.2d 72 (Ariz. 1985), the item was neither contraband nor dangerous (it was a watch owned by the deceased, whose evidentiary value derived solely from the fact that the defendant came into possession of it). Nonetheless, the court held that the defense lawyer **must** turn it over to the prosecution, because of the likelihood that it would otherwise be destroyed. (But the court barred the prosecution from showing at trial how it got the watch; see *infra*, p. 304.)

4. Evidence of source: Suppose that the other side does discover the evidence (whether through its own efforts or because the lawyer discloses and/or returns it). Can the lawyer be forced to testify about his **source**, i.e., that he got it from the client, or discovered it on the basis of information supplied by the client? The answer depends in part on whether the lawyer ever actually had possession of the item.

  a. No possession: First, consider the situation in which the lawyer never really gets custody of the item. For instance, he may merely have learned from the client that the item exists; or, the client may have shown it to him during their meeting, then taken it away. In this situation, the lawyer probably does *not* have to disclose what he has learned about the item — he has not participated in the concealment of evidence (assuming that he has not encouraged the client to conceal or destroy the item). L&S, p. 679.

  b. Custody: If, however, the lawyer has taken possession of the item, courts are in dispute.

    i. Need not disclose source: Some courts have held that the lawyer **need not disclose** (or at least testify about) his source, even though he may be obligated to turn the item over to the prosecution.

    Example: D is charged with the murder of X. L, D's lawyer, is served with a subpoena to "bring all knives in your possession and under your control relating to [D]." L is in possession of a knife relating to the crime.

Held, assuming that L got the knife based on a communication from D, the transaction is privileged. Therefore, although L must turn over the knife to the prosecution because it is evidence, the state, when attempting to introduce that evidence at trial, "should take extreme precautions to make certain that the source of the evidence is not disclosed in the presence of the jury. . . ." *State v. Olwell*, 394 P.2d 681 (Wash. 1964). See also *Hitch v. Pima, supra*, p. 304 ("prosecutor may not mention in front of the jury the fact that the evidence came from the defendant or his attorney. . . .")

   ii. Better view: However, other courts have held that the lawyer may be forced not only to turn over the evidence to the prosecution, but also to ***disclose its source*** at trial. This is probably the better view in most situations, since the approach in *Olwell* — allowing the lawyer to refuse to testify about how he got the item — lets the client "launder the evidence." That is, under the *Olwell* approach, the client is able to "remove [the evidence] from her possession and place it in the hands of the government without having the government connect it up with its source." Salzburg, 66 Iowa L. Rev. 811, 838 (1981).

Example: D, charged with murdering and robbing X, meets with Lawyer while in jail. D tells Lawyer that he saw a wallet near X's body after the crime, picked it up, tried to burn it, and threw it into the garbage behind his (D's) house. Lawyer sends an investigator to find the wallet from the garbage. Lawyer then turns the wallet over to the police, tells them that he believes the wallet belonged to X, but refuses to say how he came into possession of it.

   Held, Lawyer must reveal how he got the wallet. Had Lawyer left the wallet in its original position and condition (so that the police could have found it in D's trash can), Lawyer would have no obligation to disclose the fact that he knew its whereabouts. But once he chose to remove or alter it, he necessarily deprived the prosecution of its opportunity to observe the evidence in its original condition or location. Once this happened, the original location and condition of the evidence "loses the protection of the privilege," and Lawyer must disclose that location and condition. A contrary rule would "permit the defense in effect to 'destroy' critical information; it is as if . . . the wallet in this case bore a tag bearing the words 'located in the trash can by [D's] residence,' and the defense, by taking the wallet, destroyed this tag." Allowing the lawyer to refuse to disclose how and where he found the evidence "might encourage defense counsel to race the police to seize critical evidence." *People v. Meredith*, 631 P.2d 46 (Cal. 1981).

5. Information from third parties: The above discussion of physical evidence that comes into the attorney's possession assumes that the attorney got possession directly from the client, or that at least he learned where to find the item directly or indirectly from the client. If the lawyer discovers the item through an entirely ***independent investigation***, or it is given to him by a ***third person*** who is not working for the lawyer, remember that the attorney-client privilege ***simply does not apply***.

Example: Consider the facts of *State v. Olwell, supra,* pp. 304-05. Suppose that Lawyer had not gotten the knife from, or on account of information provided by, D. Instead, suppose that the knife or the information leading to it came from D's ex-wife. As the court in *Olwell* noted, in this situation, there would simply be no attorney-client privilege a t all regarding the knife. Therefore, Lawyer would have been required not only to turn the knife over, but could have been forced to testify at trial how he came into possession of the knife. This would be so even though Lawyer's possession of the knife occurred during the course of his representation of D. This result stems from the general rule (see *supra,* p. 305) that communications by an unaffiliated third party to the lawyer are simply not covered by the attorney-client privilege.

6. **Writings:** Sometimes the tangible item received by the lawyer will be a ***document***; for instance, a letter, receipt, or other writing. The lawyer's obligation to turn over that document is likely to depend on whether the document was ***prepared by the client***.

    a. **Not prepared by client:** If the document was not prepared by the client, the document is no different from any other kind of tangible evidence, and the rules discussed extensively above apply.

        Example: D is charged with murdering and robbing X in X's apartment. D denies ever having been to the apartment. D gives Lawyer a receipt showing X's purchase of a stereo system. This receipt is no different from the stereo system itself — it is stolen property and Lawyer must turn it over to the police.

    b. **Self-incrimination:** But if the writing was ***prepared by the client***, the client might be protected from having to disclose it by his privilege against self-incrimination (see *infra,* p. 320). If so, the lawyer ***stands in the client's shoes***, and need not disclose it either.

        i. *Fisher* **case:** This rule — that the lawyer may not be compelled to produce documents which the client could refuse to produce on self-incrimination grounds — is ***constitutionally required***, the Supreme Court has held. In *Fisher v. U.S.,* 425 U.S. 391 (1976), the IRS subpoenaed documents that taxpayers had given their attorneys in connection with legal services being performed by the latter. The Court held that if the taxpayers would have been protected by their self-incrimination privilege against turning the documents over to the IRS, the documents would remain immune from discovery in the lawyer's hands. The Court reasoned that "if the client knows that damaging information could more readily be obtained from the attorney following disclosure than from himself in the absence of disclosure, the client would be reluctant to confide in his lawyer and it would be difficult to obtain fully informed legal advice." (But the Court held that on the facts of this case, the taxpayers would *not* have had the right to refuse to turn over the papers on self-incrimination grounds; therefore, the lawyers did not have the right to refuse to disclose either, since "preexisting documents which could have been obtained by court process from the client when he was in possession may also be obtained from the attorney by similar process following transfer by the client in order to obtain more informed legal advice. . . .")

    ii. Work product immunity: Where the item sought to be disclosed is a document, you should also keep in mind the ***work product immunity*** doctrine. This doctrine (discussed *infra*, p. 313) prevents certain documents prepared by or on behalf of attorneys, in connection with a pending litigation, from being the subject of a discovery order.

G. Corporate clients: Up until now, our discussion of attorney-client privilege has assumed that the client is an ***individual***. To what extent does the privilege also protect clients that are ***corporations***? The short answer is that corporations ***are*** protected by the privilege. However, several of the ways in which corporations differ from individuals raise special problems when determining what is privileged: (1) for the privilege to apply at all, the client must be the corporation, yet the communication necessarily comes from an individual employee of the corporation, who is not speaking to "his" lawyer; (2) the lawyer may be an "in-house" lawyer, i.e., an employee of the very corporation he is representing; and (3) lawyers, especially in-house lawyers, often give business advice, and often receive a broad range of corporate reports and records that go far beyond the typical communications between an individual and his lawyer.

    1. Corporations have privilege: It is clear that, at least in the abstract, a corporation may take advantage of the attorney-client privilege. The only significant case to have held that the privilege does not apply to corporations, *Radiant Burners v. American Gas Assoc.*, 207 F.Supp. 771 (N.D.Ill. 1962), was reversed on appeal (320 F.2d 314, 7th Cir. 1963). (The court in *Radiant Burner* reasoned that "if an individual is not permitted to make an agent of still another individual, or more accurately of large groups of individuals, and thus increase the scope of the protection afforded to him through the attorney-client privilege . . . why permit a corporation to do the same thing through normal corporate operations?") With the Supreme Court's opinion in the *Upjohn* case, discussed below, it is clear that the application of the attorney-client privilege to corporations is here to stay.

    2. Who may communicate: When the client is an individual, it is very clear that the communications must come from or to the client in order for the privilege to apply. Yet, in the corporate setting, the "client" is the corporation, and the corporation as such cannot communicate — only its employees can do so. It has never been clear whether statements by or to even low-level, non-managerial employees will be deemed to be by (or to) the corporation.

        a. "Control group" test: Prior to 1981, a major approach was the ***"control group"*** test. By this test, only if the employee who dealt with the corporation's lawyer was a member of the corporate "control group" (i.e., one who is "in a position to control or . . . to take a substantial part in a decision about any action which the corporation may take upon the advice of the attorney") could the communication be deemed to be between lawyer and client, because only in that situation did the employee "personify" the corporation. (The quoted language is from *City of Philadelphia v. Westinghouse Electric Corp.*, 210

F.Supp. 483 (E.D.Pa. 1962), in which the test was first articulated.)

b. Supreme Court's *Upjohn* case: In 1981, the Supreme Court rejected the "control group" test, in *Upjohn v. U.S.*, 449 U.S. 383 (1981). Unfortunately for students, the Court did not say what the correct standard is, merely that the control group test is not it.

    i. Facts: In *Upjohn*, the corporation learned that officials of one of its subsidiaries had made possibly illegal payments to foreign government officials in order to get business. The corporation thereupon sent a questionnaire to all of its foreign managers above a certain rank, asking for detailed information about such payments. The letter was signed by the Chairman of the company, and told the recipients that the answers would be treated as "highly confidential"; responses were to be sent to the company's General Counsel. The IRS learned of the questionnaires, and attempted to obtain them via subpoena. The company argued that the responses were protected by the attorney-client privilege (and also by the work product immunity doctrine).

    ii. Privilege claim upheld: The Court held that the lower court was wrong in using the "control group" test (under which the questionnaire responses would not be privileged because the foreign managers were not of sufficiently high rank to "personify" the corporation). Use of the control group test, the Court held, would frustrate the purposes of the attorney-client privilege because it would discourage the communication of relevant information by the corporation's employees to attorneys seeking to render legal advice to the client corporation. Often, quite low-level employees will have the information that the lawyers need, and the fact that these employees are not part of the control group is irrelevant. Similarly, it will often be low-level employees who need to carry out the lawyer's advice. (The Court also held that, to the extent that some of the foreign managers responded orally instead of by written questionnaire, the lawyer's notes and recollections of the conversations were protected by work product immunity; see *infra*, p. 313.)

c. Who may communicate: *Upjohn* leaves it unclear whether absolutely every employee will be deemed to be speaking "for" the corporation, so that the privilege applies. For instance, it is not clear whether the privilege would apply if a low-level employee, completely on his own, called one of the company's in-house lawyers to ask a question relating to company business. It is possible that only communications authorized by a member of management will be deemed to be sufficiently "on behalf of" the corporation so as to make the privilege apply. See *Harper & Row Publishers, Inc. v. Decker*, 423 F.2d 487 (7th Cir. 1970), *aff'd* (equally divided court), 400 U.S. 955 (1971), holding that if the employee is not part of the corporation's control group, he must make the communication "at the direction of his superiors in the corporation." (The Supreme Court in *Upjohn* neither adopted nor repudiated this requirement.)

3. **Must concern employee's employment:** The mere fact that one party to the communication is an employee is *not* sufficient — the communication must relate to the employee's *performance of corporate duties*.

> **Example:** Driver, an employee of Bus Company, happens to see an accident involving one of Bus Company's buses on his way to work one morning. If Driver tells the company's lawyer the details of what he saw, this communication will *not* be privileged, because Driver was not acting on company business at the time he witnessed the accident. W&B, Par. 503(b)[04].

4. **Reports and other routine communications:** The communication must be *primarily* for the purpose of obtaining *legal services*. Thus, if the communication is a *routine report* generated in the ordinary course of the corporation's business, and happens to be received by one of the corporation's attorneys, the privilege will not apply. For instance, accident reports, personnel records, and financial documents are all items which may be circulated to the company's lawyers, but which are not privileged because they are not created primarily for the purpose of obtaining legal services.

5. **Confidentiality:** The privilege will apply only if the communication is treated *confidentially*. This does not mean that no one but the originator of the communication and the lawyer may learn of it. But it does mean that the corporation must handle the communication on a *"need to know"* basis — disclosure should be limited to "those persons who, because of the structure of the corporation, must know of the communication in order to ensure that the attorney is obtaining both full and accurate information." 69 Mich. L. Rev. 360 (1970).

6. **Potential for abuse:** These requirements are all needed to make sure that the privilege is not abused, something that can happen more readily in the corporate setting than in the individual-client setting. For instance, without the requirements that the communication be primarily for purposes of securing legal advice, and treated confidentially, routine business records could be "immunized" against discovery by merely forwarding one copy to the corporation's lawyer. Furthermore, the burden on the adversary stemming from the privilege is greater in the corporate setting — the adversary may have to track down large numbers of far-flung employees to get the same information that he would otherwise be able to get from a single lawyer who had already gathered the information on behalf of the corporation. (For instance, in *Upjohn* the IRS would probably have had to subpoena each foreign manager to get the information that the Supreme Court held it could not get through subpoena of the company's general counsel.) L&S, p. 708.

   a. **Qualified privilege:** For this reason, L&S argue that only a "qualified" privilege — one that "should give way upon a substantial showing of need in much the same way as 'work product' protection" — should apply in a corporate setting, unless the communication is "elicited under circumstances, including potential liability, virtually identical to those facing natural persons." *Id.* But the Supreme Court has clearly not taken this approach — even in the corporate setting, if the attorney-client privilege applies at all, it is absolute, in the sense that no matter how great the adversary's need, the privilege applies.

H. Exceptions to the privilege: We briefly consider now several exceptions to the attorney-client privilege, situations in which the privilege is deemed not to exist even though the standard requirements discussed above are met.

    1. Crime or fraud: When the client asks for help in defending against charges of a crime or wrong that he has already committed, the privilege of course applies — assisting even avowed criminals in preparing their defense is one of the functions of the privilege. But when the client asks for assistance in carrying out or defending against *future crimes* or wrongs, the privilege does *not* apply. The privilege's main goal — promoting justice — would be undermined if it could be used as a "cloak or shield for the perpetration of a crime or fraudulent wrongdoing." *U.S. v. Gordon-Nikkar,* 518 F.2d 972 (5th Cir. 1975).

> **Example:** Client says to Lawyer, "If X and I were to rob the First National Bank, and X were then to get caught and give a confession saying that I was with him on the job, could the police use that confession against me?" Circumstances subsequently make it clear that at the time of this conversation, Client has not yet pulled the bank job, but he does so thereafter. Even though this conversation clearly relates to the obtaining of legal services, it is not privileged, because it really seeks the lawyer's help in carrying out a future crime. Therefore, at Client's trial, Lawyer could be forced to testify about the conversation.

    a. Cover-up of past crime: The dividing line between seeking advice about past crimes or wrongs (privileged) and seeking such advice about future crimes or wrongs (not privileged) is usually clear. But, one situation can cause trouble: where the client seeks advice about how to *avoid discovery* of his *prior wrongdoing.* Here, the rule is as discussed above (*supra,* p. 301) in the treatment of physical evidence: if the discussions relate to the fraudulent concealment or destruction of evidence, or other obstruction of justice, the communications involve perpetration of a *new future crime or fraud,* and are thus *unprivileged.* See, e.g., *In re Ryder, supra,* p. 302 (holding unprivileged the lawyer's concealment of a weapon and money associated with a past bank robbery).

    b. Knowledge: The "crime or fraud" exception applies only where the client *knew* or should reasonably have known that his contemplated act would be wrongful. W&B, Par. 503(d)(1)[01]. Thus, if the lawyer tells the client that his proposed action is legal, and the client's belief in this advice is reasonable, the privilege applies even though the lawyer was wrong. See PFRE 503(d)(1).

    c. *In camera* examination: When one party asserts the privilege, but the opponent argues that the communication falls within the future-crime-or-fraud exception, how should the court *determine* whether the privilege applies? If the court examines the communication, some of the value of the privilege is lost. But without an examination of the communication itself, it will be hard — sometimes impossible — to determine whether a crime or fraud was in fact being planned. In cases arising under the Federal Rules, the trial judge is now authorized to conduct an *in camera examination* of the communication to determine its admissibility. The Supreme Court so held in *U.S. v. Zolin*, 491 U.S. 554 (1989).

  i. Rationale: The Court in *Zolin* reasoned that "the costs of imposing an absolute bar to consideration of the communications in camera . . . are intolerably high." There are simply too many abuses of the privilege which could never be demonstrated except by considering the communication itself.

  ii. Threshold showing: On the other hand, the Court held in *Zolin*, the party asserting the crime-or-fraud exception must make a ***threshold showing*** before the *in camera* examination may be made: that party must show "a factual basis adequate to support a ***good faith belief*** by a ***reasonable person***" that *in camera* review of the materials may reveal evidence establishing the crime-or-fraud exception. This will prevent "fishing expeditions." (Thus in *Zolin* itself, this threshhold showing was satisfied by lawfully-obtained, unprivileged, partial transcripts of the lawyer-client conversation, suggesting that an *in camera* examination of the full tapes of the conversation might well reveal evidence that the crime-fraud exception applied.)

2. **Through same deceased client:** In general, the privilege ***survives*** the ***death*** of the client. But there is one exception, which almost swallows this whole rule: if the suit is a ***will contest*** or other case in which the issue is who receives the deceased client's property, the privilege does ***not*** apply. See, e.g., PFRE 503(d)(2) (no privilege where issue is "between parties who claim through the same deceased client, regardless of whether the claims are by testate or intestate succession or by *inter vivos* transaction").

   Example: Client dies, leaving an ostensibly valid will that gives his entire estate to Son and that completely disinherits Daughter. Daughter sues to have the will declared invalid on the grounds that Client was incompetent when he made it. Son may call Lawyer (who prepared the will) to testify as to the conversations between Client and Lawyer leading up to the will, to show that Client was in control of his faculties. Daughter may also call Lawyer to testify as to these Client-Lawyer communications.

3. **Attorney-client dispute:** If the lawyer and client become involved in a ***dispute*** between themselves concerning the services provided by the lawyer, the privilege does ***not*** apply to their dispute. For instance, if the lawyer sues the client for a fee, the lawyer may testify as to communications between them that would otherwise be privileged. The lawyer may similarly disclose otherwise-privileged confidences as part of his defense of a malpractice action brought by the client. M, p. 220; PFRE 503(d)(3).

4. **Joint clients:** The privilege may be inapplicable to a dispute between ***multiple clients*** who were originally on the same side of a transaction.

  a. Same lawyer: If two clients ***retain a single lawyer***, and a dispute later breaks out between the two, the privilege does ***not*** apply. This is true whether or not the other client was privy to the communication in question. See discussion of PFRE 503(d)(5).

    i. Insurer-insured: This principle has been applied to disputes between an insured and his insurance company.

    Example: Driver is sued by Passenger for injuries arising out of an automobile accident. Insurer, who insures Driver, hires Lawyer for the case. Driver makes confidential communications to Lawyer. Later, Driver and Insurer have a dispute about the policy limits. In that dispute, most courts would probably hold that Insurer may compel Lawyer to testify about otherwise-privileged communications between Driver and Lawyer, since Lawyer represented both Driver and Insurer. W&B, Par. 503(b)[07].

  b. Different lawyers: Now suppose that the two clients retain *separate lawyers*. If both lawyers and both clients meet together to discuss common legal issues, the privilege *applies*, even in the event of a later dispute between clients. That is, the privilege exists in the "multiple client, multiple lawyer" setting but not the "multiple client, one lawyer" setting, a result some have criticized as being anomalous.

  c. Action vs. the world: If the eventual lawsuit is between the multiple clients and *some third party*, the privilege *applies,* whether there was one lawyer or more. For instance, in *U.S. v. McPartlin*, 595 F.2d 1321 (7th Cir. 1979), D1, D2, and their respective attorneys met to discuss strategy for the Ds' upcoming criminal trial. The prosecution was not permitted to force either D2 or the lawyers to testify about things D1 said at the meeting: "Uninhibited communication among joint parties and their counsel about matters of common concern is often important to the protection of their interests . . . Therefore, waiver is not to be inferred from the disclosure in confidence to a co-party's attorney for a common purpose." This was true even though the interests of the two Ds were not exactly identical. The same result would presumably have occurred had there been one lawyer for both defendants — the government couldn't have forced either D2 or the lawyer to testify about what D1 had said at their three-person conference (even though any of the three could be forced to testify in a subsequent dispute between D1 and D2).

I. Other constraints and ethical issues: So far, we have focused strictly on the attorney-client privilege. However, there are several other bodies of law which may be relevant to a situation in which the attorney-client privilege is invoked. These include: (1) the Code of Professional Responsibility and related ethical constraints upon lawyers; (2) the work product immunity doctrine; and (3) in criminal cases, the Sixth Amendment right to counsel. We will touch very briefly upon these as they relate to situations where the attorney-client privilege is at issue.

  1. Code of Professional Responsibility: Virtually all states have adopted either the American Bar Association's 1969 Code of Professional Responsibility (CPR) or the ABA's 1983 Model Rules of Professional Conduct (MRPC). We will refer to these two sets of rules, collectively, as "professional ethics."

a. Confidentiality: Professional ethics give the lawyer a right and duty not to *disclose confidential information*. In one sense this right/duty is broader than the attorney-client evidentiary privilege. For instance, MRPC 1.6(a) imposes on the lawyer the duty not to disclose any "information relating to representation of a client."

i. Covers nonprivileged information: This ethical duty of confidentiality covers much information that is not covered by the attorney-client evidentiary privilege. For instance, if the lawyer learns information about the client *from a third party* who is not affiliated with the lawyer, the lawyer is required by professional ethics not to disclose that information, even though it is not covered by the evidentiary attorney-client privilege (see *supra*, p. 305). Similarly, if the client gives information both to the lawyer and to other persons (thus destroying the confidentiality required for the evidentiary privilege; see *supra*, p. 299), this is nonetheless information which, as a matter of professional ethics, the lawyer may not divulge.

ii. Not applicable where disclosure required by law: Conversely, however, in a *litigation* context (either discovery or at trial), the professional ethics rules against disclosure must *give way* if the communication is not privileged.

Example: Lawyer, defending Client on a murder charge, learns from Client's ex-wife that, prior to the killing, Client owned a gun much like the one used in the killing. This knowledge is not covered by the attorney-client privilege, since it comes from a person other than the Client. However, professional ethics prevent Lawyer from disclosing this fact to, say, his best friend. But if the prosecution, at trial, calls Lawyer to testify about his conversation with the ex-wife, Lawyer must do so — the evidentiary rule that there is no privilege takes precedence over the professional ethics obligation not to disclose. However, the attorney should wait until the court has *ordered* him to disclose the information before doing so.

2. Work product immunity: The doctrine of *work product immunity* prevents the attorney from being required to disclose certain information that he obtains *while preparing for a lawsuit*. Most states have followed the approach laid down by Federal Rule of Civil Procedure 26(b)(3).

a. Qualified protection: Under FRCP 26(b)(3), a party may obtain discovery of a document that was "prepared in anticipation of litigation or for trial" by the other party or that party's lawyer "only upon a showing that the party seeking discovery has *substantial need* of the materials in the preparation of his case and that he is unable without undue hardship to obtain the substantial equivalent of the materials by other means." This form of the work product immunity supplies *"qualified"* immunity (i.e., immunity that is capable of being overridden.)

Example: Recall the questionnaires filled out by the foreign managers in the *Upjohn* case, and returned to Upjohn's general counsel. Assume for the moment that these questionnaire responses had been held by the Supreme Court not to be privileged (perhaps because they were disclosed to too many other non-lawyer employees within the corporation, thus waiving confidentiality). Because these documents were prepared in anticipation of possible litigation, the IRS could obtain discovery of them, under FRCP 26(b)(3), only by showing that it had a "substantial need of the materials" to prepare its case, and couldn't get the substantial equivalent without "undue hardship." Because the managers are spread all over the earth, the IRS might be able to make such a showing of need, in which case it could get discovery of the questionnaires. Thus the questionnaires would only be subject to a "qualified" work product immunity.

b. Absolute immunity for "mental impressions, conclusions, etc.": Some materials are so much the product of the *lawyer's own thinking,* that they receive what is essentially an *absolute* work product immunity. The last sentence of FRCP 26(b)(3) states that "in ordering discovery of such materials when the required showing has been made, the court shall protect against disclosure of the *mental impressions, conclusions, opinions*, or *legal theories* of an attorney or other representative of a party concerning the litigation." Probably there is no showing of need that will be enough to compel disclosure of this kind of material, although the Supreme Court explicitly declined to decide this issue in *Upjohn* (or since).

> **Example:** Recall that Upjohn's general counsel also conducted oral interviews of some managers, and made notes of what they were saying and his conclusions from what they were saying. The Supreme Court in *Upjohn* held that this information received more than the basic "qualified" privilege, and that the IRS had not shown sufficiently compelling need for this information. (The Court declined to hold that such information could *never* be compelled to be disclosed, but it did say that the showing of need by the IRS was not even close to enough.)

c. Significance: The important point to remember is that the work product immunity doctrine provides a *second, independent basis* for a lawyer's refusal to disclose certain documents during the trial preparation phase. Even though the document could be admissible at trial if the other side obtained it, the lawyer can refuse to give it over in discovery. (If the other side happens to get it anyhow, perhaps first from some non-lawyer source, the document then can be admitted at trial if the attorney-client privilege does not apply. If the attorney-client privilege *does* apply, the work product immunity rule never springs into action, because discovery is only allowed of "unprivileged" material; see FRCP 26(b)(1).)

3. Perjury on the stand, and the right to counsel: There is one other body of law that may bear upon the lawyer's right or duty to disclose information that he learns in confidence from the client. Every criminal defendant has a Sixth Amendment *right to counsel*, which has been interpreted to mean the right to the *effective* assistance of counsel. Suppose that the lawyer learns, from confidential talks with his client, that the client intends to **perjure himself** on the witness stand at trial, or to **present false evidence.**   As noted, no attorney-client privilege applies in this situation (since the use of perjured testimony or false evidence would be an ongoing crime or fraud, as to which no privilege applies; see *supra*, p. 310).   Yet, the client may argue that the lawyer's refusal to cooperate in this situation violates his Sixth Amendment right to counsel.

    a. Claim rejected: However, as a result of a recent Supreme Court decision, the client's Sixth Amendment claim will fail.   In *Nix v. Whiteside*, 475 U.S. 157 (1986), the Court held that an attorney's refusal to allow his client to take the stand and tell what the lawyer believed to be a false (and exculpating) story did not violate the client's right to counsel.   The Court observed that rules of professional ethics enacted in virtually all states **require** that the lawyer decline to put on testimony that he knows to be false; insistence on compliance with professional ethics cannot constitute a violation of the defendant's right to effective assistance of counsel.

III. PHYSICIAN-PATIENT PRIVILEGE

  A. Generally: All but ten states have by statute enacted some form of **physician-patient** privilege.   M, p. 244.   In general, these statutes give a patient a privilege against the disclosure of: (1) **confidential communications** (2) made to a **physician** (including **psychiatrist**) (3) if made for the purpose of obtaining **treatment**, or diagnosis looking toward treatment.

    1. History: There is **no** common-law physician-patient privilege analogous to the attorney-client privilege.   Thus, in those ten states that have not enacted a statute granting the privilege, the privilege does not exist.

    2. Rationale: The rationale for the physician-patient privilege is similar to that often given for the attorney-client privilege: unless the patient can rely upon confidentiality, she will not disclose all relevant matter (including embarrassing private details about health and bodily condition), and will thus not receive the best diagnosis and treatment.   *Id.*

      a. Criticism: However, the analogy to the attorney-client privilege is probably flawed.   When a client discusses a particular matter with a lawyer, the possibility of litigation, and thus disclosure, is much on his mind, and the existence of the privilege is likely to make a real difference in his willingness to disclose details.   When a patient consults a doctor, on the other hand, the patient is probably worried about getting cured, and is likely to be totally unconcerned about possible disclosure in court (indeed, the patient probably doesn't even know whether a statutory privilege exists).   Therefore, it is hard to see how the privilege really has the effect of encouraging confidential disclosures that would not otherwise be made.   *Id.*

      b. Constitutional underpinning: A second rationale for the privilege has begun to emerge: some aspects of the physician-patient privilege may be protected against government-compelled disclosure by virtue of the federal

Constitution's implied **right of privacy**. The Supreme Court has not yet spoken directly on this subject, but it has recognized a right of privacy concerning a number of highly personal areas (e.g., those relating to the decision whether to have a child). Several lower courts have held that governmentally-compelled disclosure of confidences between patient and doctor may in some instances violate that right.

    i. *Lifschutz***:** Thus the California Supreme Court has held that the "confidentiality of the psychotherapeutic session" falls within one of the "zones of privacy" created by the federal Constitution. *In re Lifschutz*, 467 P.2d 557 (Cal. 1970). (But the court held that this right belonged exclusively to the patient, not the psychotherapist, and that the California statute, even with its many exceptions including one covering the patient-litigant situation, was nonetheless "carefully tailored to serve the historically important state interest of facilitating the ascertainment of truth in connection with legal proceedings," and was thus constitutional.)

3. Psychiatrist-patient: The case for recognizing a **psychiatrist-patient** privilege is at least as strong as that for recognizing a general physician-patient privilege, if not stronger. When a patient consults a physician for a physical ailment, much of what the physician needs to know can be determined by visual examination and testing, as to which the patient's need to make "full disclosure" is not necessarily all-important. But the utility of psychotherapy rests almost entirely on complete and candid disclosure by the patient of highly personal, and perhaps embarrassing, details. Therefore, a few states have given even **greater** protection to the psychiatrist-patient relationship than to the general physician-patient one.

    a. Federal Rule: Furthermore, the drafters of the Federal Rules of Evidence declined to provide a general physician-patient privilege at all, but proposed a fairly broad psychiatrist-patient privilege. See Proposed FRE 504. (This rule, like the other specific privilege rules, was never enacted. See *supra*, p. 292.)

    b. Psychologist-patient: The general physician-patient statutory privilege applies only where the physician is a licensed M.D. A psychiatrist falls under this definition. However, a **psychologist** does not. Therefore, a number of states have enacted a separate psychologist-patient privilege, giving the same (occasionally greater) protection to disclosures by a patient to a psychologist than are given for disclosures from patient to physician.

B. Special issues: Here is a brief discussion of some of the special issues that arise in construing statutes granting a physician-patient privilege:

    1. Relationship: Under most statutes, the privilege applies only where the patient is consulting a **physician**, and is doing so with a purpose of obtaining **treatment**, or a **diagnosis** that will lead to treatment.

        a. Other professionals: Thus under most statutes, disclosures to other health professionals, such as dentists, druggists, or social workers, will **not** be covered. M, p. 246, n. 1. (But if the state has a separate psychologist-patient privilege, the definition of "psychologist" may be broad enough to include social workers, family counselors, and the like.)

 b. Consulted for litigation: The requirement that the consultation be for treatment, or diagnosis leading to treatment, means that some other kinds of common consultations are **not covered** by the statute. For instance, if the **court appoints** a physician to make a physical or mental examination of the party, or if the party hires a doctor to review his condition for the sole purpose of testifying as an **expert witness** on the party's behalf at trial, the privilege will not apply. M, p. 247.

2. Confidentiality: Most, but not all, statutes have been interpreted to include a requirement that the disclosure be intended by the patient to be **confidential.** (Recall that a similar requirement of confidentiality applies to the common-law attorney-client privilege; see *supra*, p. 296.) M, pp. 250-51. Thus if the patient later discloses to, say, a friend the substance of the communication to the doctor, the privilege would not apply in these states.

 a. Public records: State and municipal laws often impose upon the physician the duty to **report** certain types of health information (e.g., gunshot wounds and venereal disease) to the authorities. Generally, the privilege statutes have been held not to bar the physician from complying with the public recording statute. When the physician is required to report a particular piece of information to authorities under such a statute, he will generally be held to be required to disclose it to the **court** as well — that is, most physician-patient privilege statutes have been interpreted not to apply to material required to be reported to health or other public officials. M, pp. 251-52.

3. Who holds privilege: The privilege belongs to the **patient, not the doctor.**

 a. *Lifschutz:* For instance, in *In re Lifschutz, supra*, p. 316, the court refused to recognize any right on the part of a psychiatrist to decline to disclose his records, where there was no evidence that the patient in question was asserting any privilege. (The physician may attempt to exercise the privilege on the part of the patient, in which case it is generally up to the judge's discretion whether to accept this exercise without evidence of the patient's actual wishes. But if the patient waives the privilege, the doctor then has no right to refuse to disclose the information.)

4. Waiver: The physician-patient privilege, like any privilege, may be **waived** by its holder.

 a. Patient-litigant exception: Probably the majority of physician-patient privilege cases are ones in which the patient is a **party** and his physical or mental condition is in issue. (For instance, he may be the plaintiff in a tort suit in which his physical condition is at issue, or he may be the decedent insured under a life insurance policy as to which the cause of death makes a difference.) Nearly all physician-patient statutes have some kind of **exception** for the **"patient-litigant"** situation, under which a patient-litigant who puts his medical condition in issue is deemed to have in effect waived the privilege.

i. **California statute:** For instance, California's statute removes the privilege for any communication relating to "an issue concerning the condition of the patient if such issue has been tendered by: (a) the patient; (b) any party claiming through or under the patient; (c) any party claiming as a beneficiary of the patient through a contract to which the patient is or was a party; or (d) the plaintiff in an action . . . for damages for the injury or death of the patient." Cal. Evid. Code, §996. Thus, if P claims to have suffered paralysis as the result of D's negligence, D may require P's physician to disclose any communications between P and the doctor relating to the alleged paralysis, under the California statute.

ii. **Insurance suit:** Similarly, where the suit is against an ***insurance*** company under a life insurance policy, medical information concerning the ***cause of death*** is not privileged, under California's and nearly all other statutes.

Example: P is the wife of, and administratrix of the estate of, the deceased insured. P sues D, an insurance company, to recover on the policy; D claims that the death was an uncovered suicide. It is clear that the decedent — an associate at a New York City law firm! — either fell from or jumped from a thirty-sixth floor window in his office. D seeks to obtain information about the insured's treatment for depression by his psychiatrist.

Held, for D. "By bringing or defending [a] personal injury action in which mental or physical condition is affirmatively put in issue, a party waives the privilege." Because of the "unfairness of mulcting a defendant in damages without affording him an opportunity to prove his lack of culpability . . . [the insured] as plaintiff could not assert . . . the physician-patient privilege . . . to foreclose inquiry concerning whether his injury was the result of an attempt at suicide." Since the insured would be held to have waived the privilege had he survived, P as administratrix must also be bound by that waiver. *Prink v. Rockefeller Center, Inc.*, 398 N.E.2d 517 (N.Y. 1979),

Note: Observe that the privilege is not automatically extinguished by the death of the patient. For instance, in *Prink, supra*, had X been charged with murdering Mr. Prink, Mr. Prink would have had a privilege even in death not to have the communications from his prior psychiatric examinations disclosed (though the privilege might have had to give way to X's constitutional right to compulsory process; see *supra*, p. 285, including the discussion of *Chambers v. Mississippi*). But in the *Prink* case itself, his estate, by bringing the suit, was held to have tendered the issue of Mr. Prink's mental condition and thus to have waived the privilege.

iii. **What constitutes "putting in issue":** It will not always be clear when a patient-litigant has put his mental or physical condition "in issue." The mere fact of bringing suit is not enough to justify compelling the plaintiff to disclose all facts of his personal medical history.

Example: Suppose that P suffers what is indisputably a broken leg which he alleges to be the result of D's negligence. Suppose further that D believes that

P is a chronic liar, and that the broken leg has nothing to do with D's conduct. Even though D has good reason to believe that P has a history of lying, and that that history might be disclosed in the records of P's psychiatrist, these psychiatric records will probably not be required to be disclosed over P's objection — P has not placed his mental condition in issue merely by bringing suit for physical injuries.

iv. **Limited waiver:** Furthermore, the fact that the patient-litigant has implicitly waived some aspect of the privilege merely by bringing the suit (or by disclosing partial information) does not mean that **all** aspects of medical condition are covered by the waiver. In general, the courts construe the waiver as **narrowly** as they can, consonant with the need to protect the right of the other party (generally the defendant) to present his case.

Example: P sues D, a drug company, claiming that she was injured as the result of her mother's taking the drug DES while P was *in utero*. Petitioner, P's mother, discloses in a deposition taken by D many facts about her medical condition up to the birth of P, including otherwise-privileged conversations with her physician. When asked questions about her medical history after P's birth, Petitioner asserts the privilege. D claims that Petitioner, by giving the information she has already given, has waived her privilege with respect to her later medical history.

Held, mostly for Petitioner. Petitioner may indeed have waived the privilege with respect to communications concerning prescriptions for DES for subsequent pregnancies. But she has certainly not waived the privilege with respect to her entire subsequent medical history, most of which has nothing to do with the questions she has already answered. (Nor does the patient-litigant exception apply to Petitioner, since she is not the litigant, and her daughter does not stand in Petitioner's shoes.) *Jones v. Superior Court*, 174 Cal. Rptr. 148 (Cal. Dist. Ct. App. 1981).

v. **Waiver as to related issues:** Although courts attempt to narrow the scope of implied waivers, a party or non-party witness may nonetheless be held to have unintentionally waived the privilege with respect to some information by disclosing other, **related information.** "A patient, for example, who has disclosed her conversation with a physician on Monday ought not to be permitted to claim the privilege with respect to a conversation with the same physician and relating to the same subject matter on Tuesday." *Jones, supra.* Similarly, if the patient consults **more than one** doctor as to a particular condition, and then discloses in court the substance of his conversations with one of the doctors, most courts would probably hold that the privilege is waived with respect to the other doctors. M, p. 255. "It is not consonant with justice and fairness to permit the patient to reveal his secrets to several doctors and then when his condition comes in issue to limit the witnesses to the consultants favorable to his claims." M., pp. 255-56. But a substantial minority of courts would not find a waiver in this situation. M, p. 256.

5. **"Public safety"**: Another exception to the privilege, recognized by some courts in recent years, might be called the *"public safety"* exception. If a physician (usually a psychiatrist) believes that his patient may be *dangerous* to others, many states allow him to disregard the patient's privilege and give a *warning* to the authorities or to any person he identifies as a likely *victim*.

   a. **Tort liability**: In fact, some courts have allowed the victim of violence by a patient to sue the psychiatrist if the psychiatrist's failure to give a warning was unreasonable. The classic case is *Tarasoff v. Regents of University of California*, 551 P.2d 334 (Cal. 1976).

   b. **Discovery**: The more interesting development, for our purposes, is that when a victim of patient-violence brings a *Tarasoff*-like suit against the psychiatrist, some courts allow the plaintiff to obtain *discovery* of communications between the defendant-psychiatrist and the patient-assailant. This permits the plaintiff to establish whether the psychiatrist knew or should have known of the danger to plaintiff. See, e.g., *Mavroudis v. Superior Court*, 162 Cal.Rptr. 724 (Cal. Dist. Ct. App. 1980), holding in this situation that the court should first examine the medical records *in camera* to determine whether P is readily identifiable as a potential victim of the patient; if so, the court should then appoint an expert to give *in camera* testimony as to whether the records disclose that D realized, or should have realized, that the patient posed a serious danger of violence to P. If the *in camera* testimony establishes this, the judge should then rule that the patient's privilege does not apply (in which case, presumably, the treatment records may then be presented to the jury in open court).

IV. THE PRIVILEGE AGAINST SELF-INCRIMINATION

A. **Introduction**: We turn now to the privilege against self-incrimination. At the outset, two important things about this privilege, in contrast to the other ones discussed above, should be noted: (1) it is the only privilege that is explicitly required by the federal *Constitution*; and (2) it is, and has always been, a very *controversial* privilege, one which large segments of the population would prefer to see abolished or at least drastically curtailed.

   1. **History**: A detailed treatment of the historical development of the privilege against self-incrimination is beyond the scope of this outline. See generally M, pp. 279-84. In brief, the privilege developed as a response by the English Parliament and common-law courts to abuses by ecclesiastical and political courts. During the Fifteenth through Seventeenth Centuries, two courts in particular — the notorious Star Chamber and High Commission — forced those accused of religious or political crimes to testify under oath, to undergo rigorous questioning, and often to be physically tortured.

   2. **Two branches**: The privilege has two distinct branches:

      a. **Witness**: The first provides that a *witness* (defined here as any person giving testimony other than a defendant testifying at his own criminal trial) may refuse to answer any question put to him on the grounds that it may tend to incriminate him. But the witness must ***take the stand***, listen to each question, and assert the privilege question-by-question.

    b. Accused: The second branch provides that the ***accused*** in a criminal trial ***need not take the stand at all***. That is, the accused gets complete immunity from even being questioned, let alone being forced to answer.

3. Arguments: There are arguments that can be made both against and in favor of the privilege as it now exists.

    a. Against: Some of the arguments that have been made ***against*** the privilege (most often against the second branch above, the criminal defendant's right not to take the witness stand at all) are:

        i. Torture rationale nonexistent: The main danger that the privilege was developed to protect against — physical torture to compel incriminating answers — no longer is prevalent, and in any event can be controlled by a much narrower rule barring the use of coerced confessions;

        ii. Valuable information: The privilege deprives the government of one of the most valuable sources of ***reliable information*** — the subject himself — and this cost to society outweighs any benefits, especially in hard-to-prove cases such as "white collar" crimes;

        iii. Inferences: The privilege is ***ineffective,*** since the jury will probably assume that a defendant who does not take the stand must be guilty (otherwise he would proclaim his innocence); instructions by the judge that such an inference of guilt is not justified are rarely followed by the jury, so this argument goes. (See *infra*, p. 333, for a discussion of the rules on comment and inference.)

        iv. Protection of guilty: Finally, the privilege (especially branch (2), giving the criminal defendant the right not to step onto the witness stand) by its nature ***protects the guilty only***, since the innocent will virtually always take the stand to proclaim their innocence.

    See generally M, p. 286; K&W, pp. 610-13.

    b. Arguments in favor: *Supporters* of the privilege make these arguments:

        i. Protection of innocent: The privilege sometimes protects the ***innocent*** as well as the guilty. An innocent defendant might have physical traits or mannerisms that might make him appear guilty while on the stand (e.g., shifty eyes or a nervous tick). Similarly, a defendant under the strain of interrogation might, even though innocent, contradict himself in some small way and thus appear to be guilty.

        ii. Good police practices: The rule helps encourage ***good police investigative practices.*** Without the privilege (including the privilege as it applies to police interrogation — see the brief discussion of *Miranda*, *infra*, p. 325), the police will lean too heavily on confessions, including coerced ones. As one person put it in explaining why prisoners are sometimes tortured,

"There is a great deal of laziness in it. It is far pleasanter to sit comfortably in the shade rubbing red pepper into a poor devil's eyes than to go about in the hot sun hunting up evidence." (Quoted at M, p. 287.)

   iii. **Respect for human dignity:** The privilege assures that "even guilty individuals are treated in a manner consistent with *basic respect for human dignity*." M, p. 287. If there were no privilege, the guilty person would be faced with "a dilemma too cruel to be justifiable. To place an individual in a position in which his natural instincts and personal interests dictate that he should lie and then to punish him for lying, or for refusing to lie or violate his natural instincts, is an intolerable invasion of his personal dignity." *Id.*

   iv. **Equalizing the game:** The privilege helps to *level the playing field* — the government's huge investigative and prosecutorial advantage over the lone individual is at least slightly reduced.

   See generally M, pp. 286-88.

   Note: Observe that all of these pro-privilege rationales are less applicable when the subject of the criminal investigation is a *business organization*. Perhaps for this reason, the privilege protects only human beings, not organizations. See *infra*, p. 323.

4. **Constitutional language:** The privilege derives, as noted, from the U.S. Constitution. The Fifth Amendment provides that *"no person . . . shall be compelled in any criminal case to be a witness against himself. . . ."*

   a. **Protects witnesses also:** This language, on its face, looks as though it applies only to a defendant in a criminal proceeding. However, since 1892 the Supreme Court has interpreted the provision as also applying to persons other than criminal defendants, that is, to witnesses in grand jury proceedings, congressional investigations, other people's criminal trials, etc.

5. **Applied to states:** Until 1964, the Fifth Amendment privilege was *not binding on the states*. But in that year, the Supreme Court held in *Malloy v. Hogan*, 378 U.S. 1, that the Fourteenth Amendment's Due Process Clause incorporates the Fifth Amendment's privilege against self-incrimination. Since the Fourteenth Amendment binds the states, they must honor the Fifth Amendment privilege.

   a. **Rationale:** The Court in *Malloy* relied mainly on the rationale that the use of coerced confessions violates due process, and on the theory that where a person is forced to choose between answering incriminating questions or being imprisoned for contempt, his answers are effectively coerced.

   b. **Emphasis on federal privilege:** Because the Fifth Amendment is now binding on the states as a result of *Malloy*, our discussion below of the privilege focuses exclusively on the Fifth Amendment. Bear in mind, however, that nearly all *state constitutions* contain a privilege against self-incrimination, and state courts are free to interpret these state constitutional provisions in a way that creates a broader privilege than what exists under the Fifth

Amendment.

B. General rules: We consider now the general parameters of the privilege, including four issues: (1) Who may assert the privilege? (2) In what kinds of proceedings does it apply? (3) To what types of information does it apply? and (4) How may it be invoked?

1. **Who may assert:** The privilege is a *"personal"* one.

    a. **May not assert another's privilege:** This means, first of all, that a person may not assert *another's* privilege.

    > **Example:** D is on trial for robbery. The prosecution presents testimony by X, an unindicted co-conspirator, in which X says that he and D did the robbery together. D may not exclude this testimony by arguing that it violates X's privilege against self-incrimination — since it is X who is testifying, only he may assert (or, as in this case, waive) his privilege against self-incrimination.

    b. **Business organization:** The "personal" nature of the privilege also means that *business organizations* do *not* have the privilege. "No artificial organization may utilize the personal privilege against compulsory self-incrimination." *Bellis v. U.S.*, 417 U.S. 85 (1974).

        i. **Corporations, partnerships, and associations:** Thus neither *corporations, partnerships*, nor labor unions may claim the privilege. For instance, in *Bellis, supra*, a three-partner law firm was not allowed to assert the privilege as to its financial records.

        ii. **Sole proprietorship:** But where a person does business as a *sole proprietorship*, he may assert the privilege. In other words, it is not the fact of doing business that removes the privilege, it is the use of an "artificial organization" (e.g., a corporation or partnership) that causes the privilege not to apply. See *U.S. v. Doe*, 465 U.S. 605 (1984), implicitly recognizing that a person does not forfeit protection he would otherwise have merely by doing business as a sole proprietor.

    c. **Use by agent:** The rules just discussed mean that an *agent* of a corporation or other artificial entity may not claim the privilege on the entity's behalf. But suppose the agent claims that answering questions about the entity's affairs will incriminate *him* personally, or that producing the business' records will do so.

        i. **Records:** The individual may *not* refuse to produce the entity's *records*. One who associates himself with a corporation or other artificial business entity is deemed to give up the right to assert the privilege, with respect to the entity's business records. M, p. 313.

        ii. **Pre-existing documents:** In any event, a person who attempts to use the privilege to avoid surrendering business records faces a second problem: since the documents are pre-existing and were generally kept voluntarily, the documents themselves are not "compelled" and the privilege does not apply to them. See *infra*, p. 331. (However, the *act of production* is compelled, and if that act would be incriminating, there may be a privilege to refuse to do so. See *infra*, p. 331.)

   iii. Answering questions: The agent of the corporation or partnership may also probably be required to ***identify*** the records he has produced, even though that identification may incriminate him (e.g., by showing that he probably had at least some knowledge of their contents).

   iv. Additional questions: But the agent may not be required to do more than this simple identification. For instance, he may not be required to disclose the ***whereabouts*** of books and records not in his possession, since this might pose a significant additional risk of incriminating him. *Curcio v. U.S.*, 354 U.S. 118 (1957).

   v. Personal business documents: Keep in mind that even the rule making the privilege inapplicable to production of a business entity's documents applies only to documents that properly belong to the ***organization*** rather than to the individual. For instance, even a person who works for a corporation could probably assert the privilege not to produce his personal ***pocket calendar***, despite the fact that it contained information about work done for the company, if the employee bought it, maintained it, and only he had access to it. M, p. 315.

2. Proceedings where applicable: In what ***kinds of proceedings*** does the privilege apply? It of course applies when asserted by the defendant in a criminal trial. But it also applies when asserted by a ***witness*** who is not currently on trial. It does not matter ***what kind of proceeding*** is involved.

   a. Various contexts: Some of the contexts in which a person may assert the privilege are:

      i. When he is a witness in a ***grand jury investigation*** (regardless of whether he is the "target" of the investigation);

      ii. When he is a witness in ***another person's criminal trial***;

      iii. When he is a party or a witness in a ***civil*** proceeding;

      iv. When he is a party or a witness in pre-trial ***discovery*** proceedings (e.g., he is a party or non-party whose deposition is being taken in a civil suit);

      v. When he is being ***questioned by the police***, regardless of whether the questioning takes place in "custody."

      See generally M, p. 334.

   b. Different manner of invoking: Remember that the privilege applies quite differently when the person asserting it is a defendant in a criminal trial than in all other situations — the criminal defendant may refuse to undergo questioning at all (by refusing to take the witness stand); all other persons asserting the privilege must take the stand, listen to the question, and then assert the privilege. This distinction is discussed more extensively *infra*, p. 326.

c. **Confessions:** The relationship between the privilege against self-incrimination and *confessions* that take place in police custody is a complicated one, usually covered extensively in Criminal Procedure courses. For present purposes, all you need to keep in mind is this: under *Miranda v. Arizona,* 384 U.S. 436 (1966), the police must, prior to custodial interrogation of a suspect, warn him that he has a right to remain silent, that any statement he does make may be used as evidence against him, and that he has the right to the presence of an attorney during questioning. If the police do not follow these rules, any statement made by the suspect is not admissible. The decision relied essentially on a Fifth Amendment rationale — that a custodial interrogation is inherently coercive, and that without these procedural safeguards, therefore, no confession can truly be regarded as being the product of the suspect's free will.

3. **Information must be "testimonial":** Not all activity that might incriminate a person is protected — only "testimonial" activity is covered by the privilege. This limitation essentially means that only products of an individual's *thoughts* are covered by the privilege. L&S, p. 757. Or, as the notion is sometimes put, the activity must be *"communicative."*

   a. **Samples:** Thus taking a *blood sample* from an individual does not violate his Fifth Amendment rights, because a blood sample is not evidence of a "testimonial or communicative nature." *Schmerber v. California,* 384 U.S. 757 (1966). Similarly, the suspect may be required to give *fingerprints,* *handwriting samples,* or even to *speak* so that his voice may be compared with a previously intercepted conversation. (The speaking is not "testimonial," because, even though it involves the speaking of words, its effect is not to communicate the suspect's thoughts, merely to give a sample of one of his physical characteristics, namely his voice.) Similarly, a suspect may be required to appear in a *lineup* for identification. And a drunk driving suspect's slurred response to routine booking questions (e.g., name, address, date of birth, etc.) is not testimonial; *Pennsylvania v. Muniz,* 110 S.Ct. 2638 (1990).

   b. **Gestures and other non-verbal but testimonial acts:** Conversely, some *non-verbal* actions are nonetheless communicative, and, therefore, covered by the privilege. For instance, a person's gesture (e.g., nodding or shaking his head in response to a question) is clearly testimonial. Similarly, other actions may have an implicit communicative dimension. For instance, if the state demands that a person produce certain *records,* his doing so contains an implicit communication that "these are the records you asked for," as well as "I had these records in my possession or was able to get them." For this reason, the privilege may sometimes be used to prevent compulsory production of documents; this subject is discussed further *infra,* p. 331.

4. **Testimony must be "compulsory":** The communication must be not only "testimonial" but also *"compulsory."*

   a. **Voluntarily-written documents:** The main impact of this requirement of compulsion is that where a person voluntarily puts information in *written form,* the document is *not privileged* even though it is incriminating and testimonial. (But the person may have a privilege against **producing** the document for the government; see *infra*, p. 331.)

5. **Must be incriminatory:** The response must have a tendency to **incriminate** the person.

   a. **Ridicule or disgrace:** The possibility that answering a question may subject a person to **ridicule**, **disgrace**, or other non-criminal sanctions, is **not sufficient**. L&S, p. 756.

   b. **No possibility of criminal prosecution:** Similarly, the privilege does not apply if there are **procedural reasons** why the witness could not be prosecuted. For instance, if the statute of limitations has run, or the witness has already been either convicted or acquitted, or the witness has been granted immunity (see *infra*, p. 336), the privilege will not apply because there is no possibility of subsequent prosecution.

C. **Procedure for invoking:** The procedure for claiming the privilege varies depending on whether the person asserting it is doing so as a criminal defendant.

   1. **Criminal defendant:** When the assertion is made by the defendant in a criminal trial, he may invoke the privilege by **declining to testify**, and declining even to be questioned.

      Example: D is on trial for murder. The prosecutor knows that D is guilty as sin, and knows that if he could just get D on the witness stand, D would, by his demeanor and his refusal to answer questions, signal his guilt to the jury. However, D's privilege against self-incrimination means that he **need not take the witness stand at all**, so that he will not even have to listen to the prosecution's questions, let alone respond to them. (If D does take the witness stand in his own defense, he will be deemed to have waived his privilege with respect to at least some questions on cross-examination; see *infra*, p. 328.)

      a. **Suspect in custody:** A similar right to **refuse all cooperation** is given to a **suspect** who is in **police custody** — under *Miranda*, the accused has the right to refuse to speak to the police at all. That is, he is not required to listen to question after question, and each time to respond "I refuse to answer on the grounds that it may tend to incriminate me."

   2. **Non-defendant witness:** But where the privilege is being claimed by a **witness**, i.e., a person other than the defendant in a criminal trial, the rule allowing total non-cooperation does **not** apply. The witness must take the stand, be sworn, listen to the question, and then assert the privilege.

      a. **Grand jury or other investigative body:** Suppose that a person is already a suspect at the time he is called before a **grand jury**, congressional committee, or other investigative body. May he claim to be a "defendant" and thus decline to take the witness stand at all? The answer is **"no"** — even though the investigation may have focused on that person, he must still take the stand, be sworn, listen to the questions, and then assert the privilege. L&S, p. 759. (But the suspect at a **preliminary hearing** probably does have the right to refuse even to be subjected to questioning. M, p. 317.)

b. Court must decide: When the privilege is asserted by a criminal defendant, he himself is the sole determiner of his right to claim the privilege — no judge may rule on whether his taking the stand would tend to incriminate him. But this is not true of witnesses other than criminal defendants — such a witness must assert the privilege, but it is up to the *court* to decide whether there is some basis for his assertion.

   i. "Incriminatory" response: Recall that the basic notion behind the privilege is that it is a right not to incriminate oneself. Therefore, the privilege may only be invoked where the response might be *"incriminatory."*

   ii. Link in chain: However, the requirement of an "incriminatory" response has been very loosely interpreted by the courts. The response need not be one which, by itself, would support a conviction. It is enough that the response would *"furnish a link in the chain of evidence* needed to prosecute. . . ." *Hoffman v. U.S.*, 341 U.S. 479 (1951).

   iii. Burden of proof: Furthermore, courts realize that if the witness is required to "prove" that the response might be incriminatory, the witness will be forced to divulge some or all of the very information that is privileged. Therefore, if there is no evidence either way on the issue of whether the response would really be incriminatory, the privilege must be allowed. As the Supreme Court put it in *Hoffman, supra,* the court may only deny the claim of privilege if it is " '*perfectly clear*, from a careful consideration of all the circumstances in the case, that the witness is mistaken, and that the answer[s] *cannot possibly* have such tendency' to incriminate." (Emphasis in original.)

   iv. Burden of proof shifted: Thus it is the party who seeks the testimony who bears the *burden of proving* that responding to the questions cannot possibly tend to incriminate the witness. As a practical matter, the person seeking the testimony (generally the government) generally cannot make this showing — it is very hard to prove a negative — so the "assertion of the privilege is usually sufficient to forestall further questioning." L&S, p. 757.

D. Waiver: When a person takes the stand and gives some testimony, to what extent has she *waived* her right to then assert the privilege in response to further questions? The answer depends in significant part on whether the person is a criminal defendant or an ordinary witness — the criminal defendant forfeits a major part of the Fifth Amendment privilege just by taking the stand at all, whereas an ordinary witness does not.

   1. Criminal defendant: The defendant in a criminal trial, as noted, has the privilege not to take the witness stand at all. If he does take the stand and testifies in his own defense, he has *waived a significant portion* of his Fifth Amendment privilege.

a. **Cross-examination regarding direct testimony:** At the very least, all courts agreed that he has waived the privilege with respect to those questions that are ***necessary for an effective cross-examination***. L&S, p. 759. As the Supreme Court has put it, the accused has waived the privilege at least with respect to matters "reasonably related to the subject matter of [the] direct examination." *McGautha v. California*, 402 U.S. 183 (1971).

> **Example:** D (heiress Patty Hearst) is prosecuted for a robbery that took place in April 1974. D takes the stand and testifies that she was kidnapped in February 1974, by members of the Symbionese Liberation Army (SLA), and compelled under threat of death to participate in the April robbery. She describes ongoing coercion by her captors through September of 1974. Her testimony then jumps ahead a year to her arrest in September 1975. On cross-examination, the prosecutor attempts to ask questions about the year not covered in her direct testimony. D claims that answering these questions might incriminate her with respect to crimes for which she is not on trial.
>
> *Held*, for the prosecution. By testifying on her own behalf, a criminal defendant "waives [the] privilege against self-incrimination with respect to the relevant matters covered by [her] direct testimony and subjects [herself] to cross-examination by the government." D's direct testimony implied that her conduct was completely coerced by her captors, from her kidnapping until her arrest. Since this direct testimony placed in issue D's behavior during the entire kidnapping, questions about the "lost year" were reasonably related to D's testimony on direct. Nor was the prosecution blocked from asking questions as to which it knew D would plead the Fifth Amendment; the prosecution was entitled to impeach D's credibility by asking questions which she refused to answer — "If the refusals could not be put before the jury, the defendant would have the unusual and grossly unfair ability to insulate himself from challenges merely by declining to answer embarrassing questions. He alone could control the presentation of evidence to the jury." *U.S. v. Hearst*, 563 F.2d 1331 (9th Cir. 1978).

b. **State cross-examination rules:** As noted, all courts hold that the defendant, by taking the stand at all, has waived the privilege at least with respect to those cross-examination questions that are "reasonably related" to the subject of the direct testimony. Some courts have gone even further, holding that there is a waiver as to ***any*** questions that, according to the state's rules of procedure, are properly within the scope of cross-examination. (See *supra*, p. 70, for a summary of the various rules on the scope of cross-examination.) Since some states allow cross-examination on subjects not covered on direct, this rule can have the effect of causing the defendant to make a virtually complete waiver of self-incrimination rights.

> i. **Criticism:** However, this is a ***minority*** position, and has been criticized on the grounds that it "base[s] a determination of the degree to which a federal constitutional right is waived on local rules of procedure concerned not with fundamental constitutional values but rather with the promotion of orderly trials." L&S, p. 759.

2. **Witness:** In contrast to a criminal defendant, an ordinary witness does not have the right to decline to take the witness stand at all. As noted, the ordinary witness must take the stand, be sworn, listen to the question(s), and plead the Fifth Amendment. Therefore, it would be unfair to hold that the witness, by merely taking the stand and answering truly non-incriminatory questions (which he is compelled to answer) has waived the privilege with respect to incriminatory ones.

   a. **Disclosure of details:** On the other hand, if the witness makes a general and incriminatory statement about a matter, he may not then refuse to answer *follow-up questions eliciting the details*, at least where the details would not add significantly to the incrimination.

      i. *Rogers* **case:** Thus in the leading case on witness waiver, *Rogers v. U.S.*, 340 U.S. 367 (1951), Rogers testified before a Grand Jury that she had once been the Treasurer of the Communist Party of Denver, and that she had at one time been in possession of its membership lists and books, but had subsequently turned them over to another. However, she asserted the privilege when asked to identify that other person. The Supreme Court held that since Rogers had already incriminated herself as being a member and officer in the Party and as being the one-time holder of its records, disclosure of the identity of the new holder would not pose any "real danger" to her of additional incrimination. Along the way, the Court observed that "disclosure of a fact waives the privilege as to details."

      ii. **Significance:** Most courts have interpreted *Rogers* as being merely a specialized application of the rule requiring that the response be "incriminatory" — if, because of what the witness has already revealed, a response to the next question would not increase the danger to the witness, the witness must answer. This majority view regards the *Rogers* Court's statement that "disclosure of a fact waives the privilege as to details" as being merely dictum; if disclosure of details would subject the witness to additional danger, the witness need not answer.

   b. **Perjury:** One setting in which a waiver will generally be found *not* to have occurred is where the witness gives non-incriminating testimony relating to a matter under questioning by one party, and his story is then forcefully *challenged on cross-examination* by the other party. If the witness realizes that truthful answers to the cross-examination questions will make it clear that the witness lied on direct, the possibility that the witness will open himself up to perjury charges by answering on cross will be sufficient to justify assertion of the privilege. For instance, in *People v. Bagby*, 482 N.E.2d 41 (N.Y. 1985), W testified for the prosecution in a drug case, implicating the defendant (but not implicating herself). She was later re-called as a defense witness, but the prosecutor threatened to charge her with perjury if she changed her story. The court held that even though the new testimony would relate to the same subject matter as the former testimony, W had not waived the privilege, because she now ran the risk of incriminating herself for perjury, something she had not done in the original testimony.

c. Other proceedings: If the witness does waive the privilege, this waiver is effective *throughout the proceeding* in which it occurs, but *not* for *subsequent* proceedings. Thus it would apply to later appearances in the same trial. But a waiver during *grand jury* proceedings would not prevent the witness from asserting the privilege when called as a witness at a subsequent trial on the indictment returned by the grand jury. M, p. 348.

d. Use of waived testimony: If a witness has the right to assert the privilege, but declines to do so and answers the questions, the answers may be *used against the witness* in a later criminal proceeding.

> **Example:** D files federal tax returns reporting certain income from "gambling" and "wagering." Under applicable tax laws, instead of completing the return and identifying his illegal sources of income, D could have claimed the privilege against self-incrimination (in which case the IRS could have completed his return based on its own best information).
>
> *Held*, the government may now use D's returns as evidence against D in a non-tax prosecution for illegal gambling. Because D could have claimed the privilege instead of answering the incriminating questions on the tax return, his responses on the return were not "compelled," so no Fifth Amendment protection now applies to them in the later prosecution. "Only the witness knows whether the apparently innocent disclosure sought may incriminate him, and the burden appropriately lies with him to make a timely assertion of the privilege. If, instead, he discloses the information sought, any incriminations properly are viewed as not compelled. . . ." *Garner v. U.S.*, 424 U.S. 648 (1976).

> **i. No "waiver" theory:** Observe that in *Garner*, the Supreme Court did not find that D "waived" the privilege, merely that he had the chance to assert it, did not do so, and thus was not "compelled" to give the testimony. Since a "waiver," in traditional analysis, is the "knowing and intelligent relinquishment of a known right," the Court's decision not to ask whether a waiver took place is significant — even though D may *not have known* that he had a right to assert the Fifth Amendment privilege on his tax return, the fact that he did have such a right stops his disclosures from being "compelled," and those disclosures can therefore be used against him in the later criminal prosecution.

E. Documentary evidence: The government sometimes issues a subpoena for the *production of documents*; this is called a subpoena *duces tecum*. To understand how compliance with such a subpoena might cause the recipient of the subpoena to be forced to incriminate himself, we must first distinguish between: (1) the *contents* of the subpoenaed documents; and (2) the *act of complying with the subpoena* for those documents, i.e., the act of handing the documents over to the government.

> **Example:** The IRS suspects Taxpayer of tax fraud. It issues a subpoena *duces tecum* to him, ordering him to produce all of his personal financial records for the last three years. To understand how Taxpayer's Fifth Amendment rights may be implicated, we must look at first, the self-incrimination

interest he may have with respect to the documents themselves, and second, the interest he may have in resisting production of those documents.

1. **Contents:** The *contents* of the subpoenaed documents will virtually never be protected by the Fifth Amendment. Even though Taxpayer, in our above example, created the documents himself, and even though those documents may incriminate Taxpayer, his claim that government use of those documents to convict him would violate his Fifth Amendment rights fails for one simple reason: he was not *compelled* to create the documents in the first place. That is, at the time he created these documents, he did so voluntarily, not pursuant to any governmental order.

    a. **Private documents:** A few courts have held that some papers are *so private* that, even though their author was not compelled to write them, the Fifth Amendment protects their author from having them used against him. See, e.g., *In re Grand Jury Proceedings*, 632 F.2d 1033 (3rd Cir. 1980), holding that pocket-sized appointment books, containing only items written by the owner and not disclosed to anyone else, were so private that the owner had Fifth Amendment protection against having the books used against him. However, the majority view now seems to be that there are *no "privacy" aspects to the Fifth Amendment at all*, so that if the document was created voluntarily, it may be used against its author no matter how private it is (putting aside the issue of whether the author may be compelled to turn the document over to the government, an issue discussed immediately below).

2. **Production:** A person's act of *producing* the documents in response to a subpoena, by contrast, may indeed constitute implicit compelled self-incrimination. For instance, if Taxpayer hands documents over in response to the IRS's subpoena in our above tax fraud hypothetical, he is implicitly saying three things that may be incriminating: (1) that the records exist; (2) that the records were within his possession or control; and (3) that taxpayer believes that these are indeed what the government has asked for, i.e., his personal financial records for the last three years. At the very least, this implicit "testimony" by Taxpayer might be later used by the IRS to *authenticate* the records in a criminal prosecution of Taxpayer; it may prevent Taxpayer from claiming these are not his records, or that he had no idea what was in them.

    a. **Status of law:** May the recipient of the subpoena, therefore, refuse to produce the documents because of the risk of this implicit incriminating "testimony"? The law in this area is unclear. However, it seems that if the court concludes that there is indeed a risk of implicit authentication or other incrimination from the act of production, the court must relieve the person of the obligation to produce the records.

        i. *Doe* **case:** The Supreme Court upheld this kind of "implied authentication" claim in *U.S. v. Doe*, 465 U.S. 605 (1984). The sole proprietor of several businesses argued that if he were to produce the subpoenaed business records (including telephone records), he would be implicitly admitting that the records existed, that they were in his possession, and that they were genuine. The Court upheld a lower court finding that these allegations were "sufficient to establish a ***valid claim of the privilege. . . .***" The Court indicated that the government could then ***rebut*** this claim by producing evidence that possession, existence, and authentication could later be proved by means ***independent*** of the proprietor's implied authentication. However, the government had not made such a showing, so the claim of privilege stood. (But the Court stressed that the documents themselves were not privileged; if the government could get them by some other means, it would be able to introduce them against the proprietor at trial, since he was not compelled to create them in the first place.)

    ii. Independent authentication: As *Doe* suggests, if the government can show that it will be able to authenticate the requested documents by ***other means,*** the possessor's claim of privilege will not be upheld. For instance, in *Fisher v. U.S.*, 425 U.S. 391 (1976) (other aspects of which are discussed *supra*, p. 306), the documents had been prepared not by the subpoenaed taxpayers but by their accountants, and belonged to the accountants. In that situation, the Court held, the government would be able to (and would have to) authenticate the papers by testimony other than that of the taxpayers, so the taxpayers' compliance with the subpoena was not a "substantial threat of self-incrimination," and the taxpayers were therefore required to produce the documents.

3. The "required records" exception: In our highly regulated economy, many records are ***required*** by the government to be kept, especially the records of businesses in closely-regulated industries. A person who keeps such ***"required records"*** could plausibly argue that, if they are incriminating and he is forced to turn them over to the government, his Fifth Amendment rights have been violated.

    a. The "required records" doctrine: But this is, in general, a ***losing argument.*** The Supreme Court has held that no violation of the Fifth Amendment occurs where: (1) the law requiring the keeping and turning over of the records is "essentially regulatory"; (2) the records are of a kind which the regulated party has customarily kept; and (3) the records are analogous to "public documents." The rule making the Fifth Amendment inapplicable to such records has come to be known as the ***"required records"*** exception.

    Example: In *Shapiro v. U.S.*, 335 U.S. 1 (1948), in which the Court articulated these three requirements for the exception, the defendant was charged with violating the Emergency Price Control Act of 1942. The Court held that records that the defendant was required to keep, and turn over to the government, under that Act could nonetheless be admitted against him at his criminal trial, because the three requirements were met.

    b. Penal statutes: But if the statute is essentially ***penal*** rather than regulatory, the "required records" exception will not apply. Thus the Court has held that individuals may not be required to register or pay an occupational tax as required by federal wagering tax statutes, nor be required to register a regulated firearm under another federal statute. See, e.g., *Grosso v. U.S.*, 390 U.S. 62 (1968) (the wagering tax and firearm registration provisions are not "essentially regulatory" like the price control regulations in *Shapiro*; rather, they are directed at a narrow group suspected of criminal activities, and do not involve records that the individual would otherwise customarily keep).

   c. **Production:** If the documents do fall within the "public records" exception, the person required to have filed them has *no* Fifth Amendment privilege concerning them: not only may he not argue that their content is privileged, but he also may not refuse to *produce them* on the theory that doing so would amount to an implied authentication (see *supra*, p. 331). M, p. 353.

4. **Other kinds of production:** The "required records" doctrine discussed above is part of a more general rule: a person who has assumed custodial duties relating to documents, things or people, may be required to produce them where the production is part of a *non-criminal regulatory regime*. This is true even if the act of production does have some testimonial effects.

   Example: D has long been suspected of abusing her young child, Maurice. While D has custody of Maurice pursuant to a court order, additional evidence of abuse arises. The court orders D to produce Maurice. D argues that if she were to produce him, this would be evidence that she had control and possession of him, which might incriminate her on the abuse charge.

   Held (by the U.S. Supreme Court), D may not claim the Fifth Amendment to resist the production order, "because she has assumed custodial duties related to production and because production is required as part of a non criminal regulatory regime." (But the trial court may decide to limit the prosecution's use of this production as evidence in D's abuse trial.) *Baltimore City Dep't of Social Services v. Bouknight*, 493 U.S. 549 (1990).

5. **Consent to production by another:** A person may be required to *consent* to the production of documents by *another*. In this kind of situation, the court is likely to find that the mere giving of consent is not really "testimonial" and thus is not protected by the Fifth Amendment. For instance, a taxpayer suspected of tax fraud can be required to consent to a court order directing a foreign bank to disclose records of the taxpayer's accounts to the government — by consenting, the taxpayer is not testifying that there are such accounts or what their contents are; he is merely saying, "If there are any accounts, you may furnish the information to the government." This is not testimonial within the meaning of the Fifth Amendment. *Doe v. U.S.*, 487 U.S. 201 (1988).

F. **Inferences and comment:** When a criminal defendant or ordinary witness pleads the Fifth Amendment, the public's reaction is likely to be, "He must have something to hide" or "He must be guilty." Of course, people's tendency to react in this way limits the usefulness of the privilege itself. While no procedural safeguards can completely remove this natural human reaction, the Supreme Court has held that two procedural safeguards are *constitutionally required* to protect the usefulness of the privilege: (1) neither the judge nor participants may make an *adverse comment* on a criminal defendant's failure to testify; and (2) the criminal defendant is entitled to have the jury *instructed* that his failure to testify is not to be held against him.

1. **"No comment" rule:** Neither the judge nor the prosecution may encourage the jury to draw an *inference of guilt* from a criminal defendant's failure to testify. The Supreme Court so held in *Griffin v. California,* 380 U.S. 609 (1965).

    a. **Arguments by prosecution:** The requirement that the prosecution not comment on the defendant's silence is not always easy to apply. Probably the key distinction is between talking about what the "defendant" has done and what the "defense" has done: if the prosecution says, "The defendant has not seen fit to explain away this evidence, and if anyone should know, he should," there is clearly a violation of the *Griffin* no-comment rule. But if the prosecutor points out that certain evidence has been left uncontradicted "by the defense," this will usually be permissible. M, pp. 320-21. However, even comments about what "the defense" has not done may violate *Griffin* if the facts are such that the jury would reasonably conclude that only the defendant himself could have controverted the evidence, by taking the stand. *Id.*

2. **Right to instruction:** The criminal defendant has an affirmative right to have the judge *instruct the jury* that they are not to draw any adverse inference from the defendant's failure to testify. *Carter v. Kentucky,* 450 U.S. 288 (1981). The jury may make a negative inference from the defendant's silence anyway, but the judge has the obligation, upon request, to use the "unique power of the jury instruction" to reduce such inferences to a minimum.

3. **Silence at other proceedings:** Suppose the criminal defendant has remained silent at *prior proceedings.* May this silence be commented upon at the later criminal trial? In some kinds of situations, the prior silence may not be commented upon.

    a. ***Doyle:*** One situation in which the defendant's prior silence may ***not*** be commented upon at the later criminal trial is where the defendant has exercised his *Miranda* right to remain silent during a *custodial police interrogation.* In *Doyle v. Ohio,* 426 U.S. 610 (1976), the defendant remained silent under police questioning, and then claimed at trial that he had been framed. On cross-examination, the prosecutor impeached D's credibility by asking, in effect, "Why didn't you speak up and tell that story to the police?" The Court held that because the defendant had had an affirmative constitutional (*Miranda*) right to remain silent under police questioning, his due process rights would be violated if the prosecution were allowed to capitalize at trial upon this exercise of a constitutionally-protected privilege.

    b. **Other silence not protected:** But the defendant's prior silence in some other contexts may be commented upon.

        i. **Pre-arrest silence:** For instance, the defendant's *pre-arrest silence* may be commented upon. That is, if the defendant has not been placed in custody, the fact that he has not voluntarily gone to the police to tell them his story may be commented upon to impeach his trial testimony. Thus in *Jenkins v. Anderson,* 447 U.S. 231 (1980), D defended against a murder charge by claiming self-defense. On cross-examination, the prosecutor brought out the fact that D had left the scene of the crime, and during the two weeks between the crime and his arrest, did not go to the police to tell them his story. Since this pre-arrest silence was not induced by governmental action (unlike the defendant's silence in *Doyle*, which was induced by the *Miranda* warnings the police gave him), the prosecution's comments were not "fundamentally unfair."

ii. **Defendant does not take stand:** In *Jenkins, supra,* the defendant took the stand, and the prosecutor used his pre-arrest silence to impeach his credibility. *Jenkins* does not make clear what happens if the defendant does not take the stand, and the prosecution comments (perhaps in summation) on the defendant's pre-arrest silence. The fact that the prosecutor used the silence for impeachment purposes seems to have been important to the Court's reasoning in *Jenkins*; the Court noted that "impeachment follows the defendant's own decision to cast aside his cloak of silence and advances the truth finding function of the criminal trial." Thus it is possible that the Court would hold that, where the defendant never takes the stand, the prosecution may not comment upon his pre-arrest silence. But it seems more likely that so long as the defendant's failure to tell his story to the police was not induced by governmental action (e.g., the giving of *Miranda* warnings), that silence may be commented upon even when the defendant does not take the stand.

iii. **Grand jury:** Suppose the defendant is called to testify before a ***grand jury*** or at a ***preliminary hearing***, but asserts his Fifth Amendment right to remain silent. The logic of *Jenkins* indicates that the prosecution should ***not*** be allowed to comment on this silence at the defendant's later criminal trial — in this situation, the defendant's silence stems from the exercise of a clear constitutional privilege, and should thus not be able to be commented upon any more than the silence of the defendant who asserted his *Miranda* rights in *Doyle*.

4. **Civil suits:** When the suit is a *civil* one, there is apparently no rule against commenting upon a party's failure to testify or a witness' assertion of a Fifth Amendment privilege.

   a. **Party:** Thus if a party fails to testify at a civil proceeding, the other party may ask the trier of fact to draw an adverse inference from this failure. This is probably true even if the non-testifying party has failed to do so because he is afraid of incriminating himself. See *Baxter v. Palmigiano*, 425 U.S. 308 (1976) (prison disciplinary hearing is a civil proceeding, and adverse inferences may thus be drawn against an inmate who declines to testify).

   b. **Silence by non-party witnesses:** Similarly, a ***non-party witness'*** assertion of the Fifth Amendment may probably be commented upon. For instance, in *Brink's, Inc. v. New York*, 717 F.2d 700 (2d Cir. 1983), one issue was whether Brink's had adequately supervised its employees who collected coins from New York City's parking meters. The city called past and present Brink's employees as witnesses and questioned them about pilferage from the meters, but the employees declined to answer on Fifth Amendment grounds. The Court of Appeals held that the trial judge was entitled to instruct the jury that it could infer from the employees' refusal to answer "that the answers would have been adverse to the witness' interest." (But a dissenter contended that this holding was very unfair to Brink's, since it let New York City pose damaging questions safe in the knowledge that the witness would not attempt any explanation; it also effectively deprived Brink's of its ability to cross-examine each witness, since the witness could not be forced even to explain why he invoked the privilege let alone to contradict the city's inference of criminality.)

G. Immunity: The Fifth Amendment privilege applies only where the person asserting it faces some danger of having his testimony used against him in a criminal prosecution. (See *supra*, p. 326.) Therefore, one way to nullify a person's Fifth Amendment privilege is to grant him ***immunity*** from prosecution.

    1. "Transactional" vs. "use" immunity: There are two types of immunity that may be granted: ***transactional*** immunity and ***use*** immunity.

        a. Transactional immunity: Transactional immunity protects the witness against any prosecution for the transactions about which he has testified. For instance, if a witness testifies under a grant of transactional immunity to having robbed the First National Bank on April 14, 1974, he cannot be prosecuted for that robbery — even if the prosecution does not directly or indirectly make use of his testimony in the prosecution.

        b. Use immunity: Use immunity, by contrast, is much narrower — it merely protects against the direct or indirect use of the testimony in a subsequent prosecution. Thus if the witness testifies under a grant of use immunity that he robbed the First National Bank on April 14, 1974, the prosecution may not use that testimony as part of the prosecution, but it may nonetheless prosecute him for the robbery if it can prove its case without making any use whatsoever of his testimony.

    2. Use immunity sufficient: For years, it was thought that a person's Fifth Amendment privilege would be nullified only by the grant of transactional, not use, immunity. But in *Kastigar v. U.S.*, 406 U.S. 441 (1972), the Supreme Court held that ***use immunity is sufficient*** to nullify the witness' Fifth Amendment privilege. In so holding, the Court reasoned that the Fifth Amendment merely protects the witness against being compelled to give testimony that may be used to incriminate him; so long as the immunity statute prevents any such use (direct or indirect), the witness is left in "substantially the same position" as if he had claimed his Fifth Amendment privilege.

        a. Burden on prosecution: However, the witness must indeed be protected against even ***indirect*** use of his testimony. The burden of proving that there has been no use is placed upon the prosecution at the subsequent trial. The prosecution must prove that it did not use the testimony to obtain ***leads*** to information or witnesses, focus the subsequent investigation, interpret the independently-derived evidence, plan cross-examination, or in any other way.

U.S. v. McDaniel, 482 F.2d 305 (8th Cir. 1973).

    i. Don't use transcript: As a practical matter, the only way the prosecutor will be able to bear this burden is if he has *not witnessed* the testimony, nor read a transcript of it. For instance, in the Iran-Contra affair, Special Prosecutor Walsh instructed his entire staff not to watch or read the testimony of potential defendants before congressional committees investigating the affair.

3. **Procedural issues:** Here are a few procedural aspects of immunity:

    a. By statute: Prosecutors normally do not have inherent authority to grant immunity. Instead, prosecutorial authority to grant immunity is generally conferred by *statute*; the statute describes the situations in which immunity may be granted, and the scope (use versus transactional) of that immunity. Immunity from federal prosecution is covered by a single statute (the Witness Immunity Act, 18 U.S.C. §§6001-6005), which allows only use immunity. Many states, however, retain transactional immunity.

    b. Procedure for granting: The prosecution must initially decide that immunity is justified. It must then *apply to the court* for the grant; the court generally has the right to refuse the request if the grant would not be in the public interest. M, p. 357.

    c. Perjury not covered: A grant of immunity generally does not immunize the witness from use of his immunized testimony as part of a subsequent *perjury* prosecution. Thus if the witness gives immunized testimony that is false, that testimony may be introduced against him at a subsequent perjury prosecution.

    d. Other jurisdictions: If immunity is granted by jurisdiction A, can jurisdiction B nonetheless use the immunized testimony in a subsequent prosecution? The answer seems to be "no." Thus if a state grants immunity, the federal government may not use the immunized testimony (or its fruits) in a subsequent federal prosecution. *Cf. Murphy v. Waterfront Commission of New York Harbor*, 378 U.S. 52 (1964). Conversely, if a witness is given federal immunity, the supremacy clause of the U.S. Constitution should prevent use of that testimony in a subsequent state prosecution. L&S, p. 757. Finally, if one state gives immunity, other states should be barred from using that testimony in their own prosecutions. *Id.* The latter result could be based on due process or self-incrimination grounds.

4. **Defense witness immunity:** Suppose that a criminal defendant would like to be able to offer what he thinks will be the favorable testimony of a witness, W, but that W refuses to testify on self-incrimination grounds. May the defense require the prosecution to grant use immunity to W so that the defense will get the benefit of his testimony? Such a grant is known as *"defense witness immunity."* Since immunity is normally granted at the wishes of the prosecution, for government purposes, it can be argued that fair play requires that defense witness immunity be awarded under at least some circumstances.

a. **General rule:** However, the vast majority of courts that have considered the issue have ***refused to grant*** defense witness immunity. For instance, the court in *U.S. v. Turkish*, 623 F.2d 769 (2d Cir. 1980), held that "trial judges should summarily reject claims for defense witness immunity whenever the witness for whom immunity is sought is an actual or potential target of prosecution."

   i. **Rationale:** The court in *Turkish* advanced several reasons for denying defense witness immunity: (1) the "fair play" rationale does not make sense, since "accuser and accused have inherently different roles, with entirely different powers and rights . . . "; (2) even use immunity is likely to cripple the prosecution's efforts to prosecute the witness subsequently, because of the prosecution's heavy burden of proving that its evidence was not obtained as the indirect result of the immunized testimony; (3) if defense witness use immunity is granted, the prosecution will be so worried about losing its practical ability to subsequently prosecute the witness that it may be forced to curtail the scope of its cross-examination of that witness; and (4) such immunity "could create opportunities for undermining the administration of justice by inviting cooperative perjury among law violators. Co-defendants could secure use immunity for each other, and each immunized witness could exonerate his co-defendant at a separate trial by falsely accepting sole responsibility for the crime, secure in the knowledge that his admission could not be used at his own trial for the substantive offense."

b. **Special situations:** However, a few cases have granted defense witness immunity, generally in special circumstances. The leading such case is *Government of Virgin Islands v. Smith*, 615 F.2d 964 (3d Cir. 1980), in which the court suggested that defense witness immunity should be granted where either: (1) the witness can offer testimony clearly exculpating the defendant, and the prosecution gives no strong reasons for withholding immunity; or (2) there is prosecutorial misconduct involving a deliberate attempt to distort the truth-seeking process by withholding immunity.

H. **Prosecutorial discovery:** Criminal defendants are usually given extensive ***discovery*** rights. Many jurisdictions have tried to even out this advantage by giving some pretrial discovery rights to the prosecution. Under some circumstances, compelling the defendant to release information to the prosecution may violate the defendant's privilege against self-incrimination. However, as a result of two Supreme Court decisions, only in rare situations will compulsory prosecutorial discovery violate the defendant's Fifth Amendment rights.

1. **Disclosed at trial:** First, if the information will be ***disclosed at trial*** by the defendant anyway, his Fifth Amendment rights are not violated by being required to give the prosecutor the information before the trial begins. Thus in *Williams v. Florida*, 399 U.S. 78 (1970), the Court concluded that D's Fifth Amendment rights were not violated by a requirement that he disclose to the prosecution, before the start of the trial, notice of his intent to claim an ***alibi*** defense, and the place he would claim to

have been, as well as the names and addresses of witnesses who would support the alibi. The Court argued that "nothing in the Fifth Amendment privilege entitles a defendant . . . to await the end of the State's case before announcing the nature of his defense. . . ." Similarly, a rule requiring D to disclose before trial the names of **all witnesses** he will be presenting at trial, and barring the testimony of any witness not so named, does not violate D's Fifth Amendment rights. *Taylor v. Illinois*, 484 U.S. 400 (1988) (discussed more extensively *supra*, p. 286).

    a. Summary: *Williams* and *Owens* thus seem to mean that there is no privilege against the forced disclosure of **any matter** that will be part of the defense's case at trial. M, p. 327.

2. **Material from third persons:** Second, information which comes from **persons other than the defendant** is not protected against prosecutorial discovery. In *U.S. v. Nobles*, 422 U.S. 225 (1975), the trial judge ordered the defense to reveal a report by a defense investigator that contained statements the investigator had obtained from witnesses, so that the prosecution could effectively cross-examine the investigator (who was called as a defense witness). The Court held that this order did not violate the defendant's Fifth Amendment rights: since the information given to the investigator was given by third parties rather than by the defendant, ordering that these statements be given to the prosecutor "would not in any sense compel [D] to be a witness against himself or extort communications from him."

3. **Application of privilege:** Thus there is only a narrow area left as to which prosecutorial discovery might violate the defendant's Fifth Amendment rights. The defendant would have to show two things in order to resist such discovery: (1) that the information will **not be disclosed by him at trial**; and (2) that the information **came from him**, not from some third party. For instance, the defendant might be able to refuse to release incriminating statements he made to a private investigator retained by him to aid in the defense. (If the investigator was hired by the lawyer rather than by the client, this information would presumably also be protected by the extension of the attorney-client privilege to cover "attorney's representatives"; see *supra*, p. 297.)

V. THE MARITAL PRIVILEGES

A. Two privileges: Two distinct privileges protect the marital relationship in most states: (1) the privilege against adverse spousal testimony; and (2) the privilege protecting confidential communications.

1. **Nature of the two provisions:** Although the two privileges overlap to some extent, there are significant differences between them. Here is a "thumbnail sketch" of the two:

    a. Adverse testimony: The *adverse testimony* privilege (sometimes called the *"spousal immunity"*) gives a spouse **complete** protection from **adverse testimony** by the other spouse. Thus if Husband is on trial for a crime, this privilege protects Husband from having Wife take the witness stand to testify against him, regardless of the subject matter of her testimony.

b. Confidential communication: The ***confidential communications*** privilege protects only against the disclosure of confidential communications made by one spouse to the other during the marriage. For instance, if Husband tells Wife during their marriage, "I just shot X," Wife cannot be forced to disclose this communication at Husband's subsequent trial. However, if Wife ***witnessed*** Husband kill X, most states would probably hold the confidential communications privilege inapplicable, so that Wife could be forced to tell what she saw.

2. **Rationale:** Both privileges have historically been justified on the grounds that they ***promote marital harmony***. The adverse testimony privilege is said to do so on the theory that requiring one spouse to testify against the other will tend to break up the marriage. The confidential communications privilege arguably promotes marital harmony by encouraging the exchange of confidences between spouses.

   a. Criticism: This "marital harmony" justification is often criticized as it applies to each of the privileges. In the case of adverse spousal testimony, critics contend that the rationale certainly does not justify giving a defendant spouse the right to block *voluntary* testimony by the witness spouse, since if the witness is willing to testify against the spouse, there is probably very little marital harmony left. (This was the basis for the Supreme Court's decision in *Trammel v. U.S., infra*, p. 342, to vest the adverse testimony privilege solely in the witness-spouse.) Similarly, critics contend that the confidential communications privilege does not promote marital harmony by encouraging confidences, because most couples don't know that the privilege exists (and even if they did, the likelihood of disclosure in court is generally so small that the privilege is unlikely to alter their conduct.)

   b. Alternate rationale: However, an alternate rationale supports both privileges. It has been argued that they should be based on "the concept of ***human dignity*** in connection with an especially confidential relationship, one incidentally packed with 'emotional dynamite' and one which the state has a strong interest in protecting and fostering. . . . [S]omething in the spirit is shocked and hurt at the betrayal of former confidences, at the revelation of the secrets of the bedchamber, and perhaps at the vindictiveness of alienated ex-spouses, in some cases to the point of perjury. . . ." Gardner, 8 Vill. L.R. 489-90, quoted in L&S, p. 725. The rationale behind the privilege against self-incrimination — the cruelty of forcing a person to choose between contempt, perjury, and self-condemnation — seems equally applicable to the spousal situation, in which a witness-spouse who is deprived of both privileges would have to choose between contempt, perjury, and betraying his or her loved one. L&S, p. 725.

3. **Distinctions:** In many situations, both privileges will apply. However, there are a number of situations in which only one will apply. Here are some of the situations in which one but not the other will apply:

   a. End of marriage: The adverse testimony privilege applies only if the parties are still married ***at the time of the trial***. The confidential communications privilege, by contrast, applies so long as the parties were married at the time of the communication, even if the marriage has **subsequently ended**.

> **Example:** H and W are married. H tells W, "I've just shot X." Before H is tried for the crime, he and W are divorced. H cannot assert the adverse testimony privilege at trial, because he and W are no longer married. He may, however, assert the confidential communications privilege to prevent W from testifying about the statement H made to her.

b. **Pre-marital communication:** Conversely, if the communication took place **before** the parties were married, the confidential communication privilege will not apply. But if the parties to the conversation have married by the time of trial, the adverse testimony privilege will apply. Thus, "individuals are allowed to and, indeed, have married to prevent testimony against them." L&S, p. 721. (But see Proposed FRE 505(c)(2), never enacted, which would have made the adverse testimony privilege inapplicable to "matters occurring prior the marriage.")

c. **Civil vs. criminal:** The adverse testimony privilege is usually allowed only in **criminal** cases. The confidential communications privilege, by contrast, is available in civil as well as criminal cases. L&S, p. 722.

d. **Party vs. non-party:** The adverse testimony privilege may be invoked only by **a party**. The confidential communications privilege, by contrast, may be invoked by a non-party **witness**. *Id.*

e. **Acts:** The adverse testimony privilege will prevent the non-party spouse from testifying even as to **acts** committed by his/her spouse; by contrast, the confidential communications privilege will generally not bar such testimony, since it applies only to communications (though the term "communication" is sometimes read broadly enough to cover certain communicative acts; see *infra*, p. 343).

> **Example:** W watches H shoot X to death in a public park. The adverse testimony privilege will prevent the prosecution from calling on W to describe what she has seen. The confidential communications privilege will not (since even those states giving a loose reading to the requirement of a "communication" will hold that a shooting that takes place in a public park is not intended to be "confidential" and is thus not covered by the privilege).

4. **Variety of state statutes:** States vary as to whether both or just one of the privileges apply:

a. **Adverse testimony:** Only a slight majority of states recognize the adverse testimony privilege. 98 Harv. L. Rev. 1567 (1985).

b. **Confidential communications:** By contrast, virtually all states recognize the confidential communications privilege (including those that recognize the adverse testimony privilege). M, p. 189.

c. **Federal Rule:** In federal courts, **both** privileges are recognized. The confidential communications privilege is deemed part of the common law and thus generally applicable under FRE 501 (see discussion *supra*, p. 292); it is generally held to belong to the spouse who **makes** the communication. 98 Harv. L. Rev. 1571-72. The adverse testimony privilege belongs only to the **testifying spouse**, as the result of the Supreme Court's holding in *Trammel v. U.S.*, discussed further *infra*.

B. Adverse testimony privilege: Here are some of the details of the adverse testimony privilege:

1. **Who holds:** Courts and statutes are not in agreement about **who holds** the adverse testimony privilege.

   a. **Federal practice:** In federal cases, the adverse testimony privilege belongs to the **testifying spouse**, not the party spouse. That is, the defendant in a federal criminal trial may not block his or her spouse's testimony; only the witness-spouse may assert or waive the right. The Supreme Court so concluded in *Trammel v. U.S.*, 445 U.S. 40 (1980).

      i. **Rationale:** The Court in *Trammel* concluded that the main rationale for the adverse testimony privilege — preventing marital discord — does not justify giving the defendant spouse the right to block the voluntary testimony of the witness spouse. The Court reasoned that if one spouse is willing to testify against the other, "their relationship is almost certainly in disrepair; there is probably little in the way of marital harmony for the privilege to preserve." There is a strong countervailing interest, the Court noted, in making available to the trier of fact all relevant information.

      ii. **Application to facts:** The facts of *Trammel* illustrate how the adverse testimony privilege will now be used, and limited, in federal criminal cases. W, D's wife, was arrested for narcotics smuggling during a routine airport customs search. In return for not being prosecuted, she agreed to cooperate with the government in its case against D. She then testified in detail about the roles she and D played in a heroin distribution conspiracy. Since the Court held in *Trammel* that only the witness-spouse could assert the adverse testimony privilege, D was out of luck. Furthermore, although the federal courts recognized the independent privilege for confidential marital communications (see *infra*, p. 343), that privilege was inapplicable to most of W's testimony, since she was describing her and her husband's actions, not their confidential communications to each other.

      iii. **Criticism:** Some commentators have criticized the Court's decision in *Trammel* to vest the privilege solely in the testifying spouse. L&S (pp. 720-21) assert that the opinion "ignores the role that the government may play in setting one spouse against the other," and gives the government "strong incentives to break up those marriages it can." For instance, on the facts of *Trammel* itself, the rule giving the privilege exclusively to W gave the federal prosecutors strong incentive to use whatever pressure they could (including the threat of criminal prosecution) to induce W to testify against D; the marriage was unlikely to have survived the resulting testimony. By contrast, the marriage would have had a better chance of surviving had the privilege been found to belong to D — the prosecution would probably not have bothered trying to convince W to testify, since it would have known that D could then block the testimony.

   b. States: Those thirty or so states that recognize the adverse testimony privilege vary about whom the privilege belongs to. Fourteen allow the party to prevent his/her spouse from giving adverse testimony; another four treat the non-party spouse as being "incompetent" to testify. The remaining states follow the federal approach of vesting the privilege in the witness spouse. 98 Harv. L. Rev. 1567.

2. **Criminal vs. civil:** Most jurisdictions, including the federal courts, limit the adverse testimony privilege to *criminal* cases. 98 Harv. L. Rev. 1570. States vary as to whether the privilege applies in grand jury proceedings; the privilege does apply in *federal* grand jury proceedings. *Id.*, n. 55.

3. **"Testimony" required:** The privilege applies only to *"testimony"* by the spouse. Thus the spouse may be required to give non-testimonial evidence such as a handwriting sample or a fingerprint. *Id.*

   a. Out-of-court statements: However, the privilege is often held to apply to *out-of-court statements* by the spouse, not just in-court testimony.

      Example: W tells X that she has just watched her husband, H shoot Joe Smith. Many states, and the federal courts, will hold the adverse testimony privilege applicable to prevent X from repeating W's statement in court (even if that statement satisfies some hearsay exception).

4. **Divorce:** As noted, the witness and the defendant must be married *at the time of the testimony* for the privilege to apply. Thus, a defendant has no privilege to keep his ex-spouse off the stand. (But conversely, in most states he may prevent his current spouse from testifying against him, even as to matters that occurred before the marriage. However, courts will not apply the privilege if they find the marriage is a "sham," and some exclude pre-marital events. See, e.g., Proposed FRE 505(c)(2), never enacted by Congress, which excludes pre-marital events.)

C. **Confidential communications:** We turn now to the second privilege, that for *confidential communications* between spouses.

1. **Where applied:** This privilege is much more widely recognized than that for adverse spousal testimony: virtually every state recognizes it.

   a. Federal: In federal courts, nothing in the Federal Rules explicitly grants the privilege. In fact, the Rules as drafted explicitly declined to give the privilege, instead giving a narrowly-tailored adverse testimony privilege (see *supra*, p. 342). However, because Congress deleted all of the proposed privilege rules, the confidential communications privilege remains applicable in federal courts because of FRE 501's direction that privileges be determined "by the principles of the common law as they may be interpreted by [federal] courts . . . in the light of reason and experience." Since federal courts prior to the enactment of the Federal Rules of Evidence had always recognized the confidential communications privilege, that privilege has been carried forward under the Rules.

2. **Who holds:** As with the adverse testimony privilege, there is disagreement about *who holds* the confidential communications privilege.

   a. **Traditional view:** The traditional common law view, probably accepted by the majority of states, is that *either spouse* may assert the privilege. But some critics have argued that only the spouse who *made the communication* should be protected, since the purpose of the privilege is to foster confidences between spouses. 98 Harv. L. Rev. 1571.

   b. **Federal:** There is no clear rule in federal cases. Most federal courts give the privilege only to the spouse who made the communication. *Id.* at 1571-72.

3. **"Communication" required:** Only *"communications"* are privileged. An oral or written statement obviously is covered. Most courts also include *gestures*. M, p. 191.

   a. **Acts not intended to communicate:** A number of courts have gone even further, and have applied the privilege to *acts* that are not intended to convey information at all, but that are done privately in the other spouse's presence. These courts effectively remove the requirement of a "communication."

      Example: H is charged with theft. The prosecution offers W's testimony that H brought home loot from the theft and hid it under the bed.
      Held, the privilege applies. The privilege applies only to "communications," but the term "communication" includes "knowledge derived from the observance of disclosive acts done in the presence or view of one spouse by the other because of the confidence existing between them by reason of the marital relation and which would not have been performed except for the confidence so existing." *People v. Daghita*, 86 N.E.2d 172 (N.Y. 1949).

   b. **Criticism:** The rationale behind the communications privilege is presumably to encourage the making of confidences between spouses. Where a person does not intend to convey information, and simply performs a private act witnessed by the other spouse (as in *Daghita*), there is no "confidence" being exchanged, so it is hard to see why the privilege should apply. M, p. 192.

4. **Confidentiality:** The communications privilege applies only where the communication is *"confidential."*

   a. **Presence of third persons:** Thus the *presence of a third person* at the time the communication was made will generally show that it was not intended to be confidential. This is true even where the third person is a *child* of the couple, if the child is old enough to understand what is said. L&S, p. 722.

5. **Marital status:** The parties to the communication must be *married at the time of the communication*. If this requirement is met, it does not matter that the parties have gotten divorced between the time of the communication and the time of the trial. Most courts apply the privilege even where the spouses are *legally*

separated at the time of the communication. M, p. 196.

6. **Exceptions:** The states have carved out various *exceptions* to the communications privilege. Here are some common ones:

   a. **Crime against other spouse:** Prosecution for crimes *committed by one spouse against the other* or against the children of either. M, p. 199.

   b. **Suit between spouses:** Suits by *one spouse against the other*. The most common illustration is a *divorce* suit.

   c. **Justification:** A criminal prosecution in which disclosure of the communication would justify the accused spouse's action or reduce the severity of his offense. (E.g., W tells H that V has raped her; H kills V. Most states would hold the privilege inapplicable to W's statement, since it would show that H committed manslaughter rather than murder). This exception is important where the non-defendant spouse would otherwise assert the privilege over the defendant's objection.

   d. **Facilitating crime:** Communications made for the purpose of *planning* or *committing* a crime, or helping someone else do so. (E.g., H brings home loot from a robbery and asks W to help him hide it; since H is seeking W's help in committing an additional crime — possession of stolen goods — many states would find the privilege inapplicable to H's statement.)

VI. MISCELLANEOUS PRIVILEGES

A. **Priest-penitent privilege:** The *priest-penitent* privilege probably did not exist at common law. M, p. 184. However, all states except West Virginia now have statutes granting some form of privilege for confidential communications between a clergyman and penitent. 98 Harv. L. Rev. 1556.

   1. **Federal practice:** A privilege for clergymen-penitent confidences was included in the Proposed Federal Rules of Evidence privilege provisions, but was deleted by Congress together with all of the other specific privileges. See PFRE 506. However, a federal court in a federal question case would probably recognize some form of the privilege as a matter of common-law interpretation, under FRE 501 (see *supra*, p. 292.)

   2. **Scope of privilege:** In most states, the privilege covers all confidential communications made by a person to a clergyman in his professional character as *spiritual advisor*.

      a. **Narrow view:** Some statutes, particularly older ones, are narrowly drawn to cover only confidences the taking of which are *mandated by church doctrine* (e.g., Roman Catholic confessions). These statutes would apparently deny the privilege if the taking of confidences, and the duty not to disclose them, are not formal requirements imposed by the religion on the spiritual advisor. Such a statute, if interpreted to exclude less highly-structured communications, would probably be unconstitutional as preferring Catholicism over other religions, but most courts would probably interpret it liberally to cover non-mandated confidences. 98 Harv.L.Rev. 1558. M, p. 184.

3. Mail order and fringe cults: Self-designated ministers (including those who obtain their certification by "mail order"), and ministers of *fringe* cults, will probably not be regarded as clergymen for purposes of most statutes. See W&B, Par. 506[02] (concerning federal practice).

B. Journalist's privilege: The most dramatically growing privilege in recent years has been the privilege given to *journalists* to decline to divulge the *identities* of their confidential *news sources*.

1. Rationale: Reporters have forcefully argued that they must be able to promise confidentiality to their sources, and that those sources will *"dry up"* if their identities may be subject to compulsory disclosure. M, p. 184. Since the use of confidential sources lets reporters be more effective, and since more effective reporting is in the public's interest, journalists contend that the grant of at least a limited privilege is socially desirable. Journalists are most concerned about disclosure of the identity of their sources, but are also concerned about being forced to disclose the *contents* of the communications when those contents are intended as "background" information rather than for publication (especially where the information would itself identify the source). L&S, p. 767.

2. Statutes: The journalist-source privilege has evolved mostly by the enactment of state statutes. A little over half the states have enacted *"shield laws"* that give journalists various degrees of protection against being forced by legal process to testify about their confidential sources. 98 Harv. L. Rev. 1602, n. 57. Even the narrow statutes generally protect the journalist from having to disclose the identity of his sources; some give him protection against forced disclosure of his notes and records about what he has learned from the source. *Id.*

3. Constitutional argument: Reporters have frequently argued that a privilege against compelled disclosure of sources is not only socially desirable but *constitutionally required*. They contend that since the First Amendment protects freedom of the press, compulsory disclosure of sources interferes with proper functioning of the press and thus violates the First Amendment.

a. Claim rejected in *Branzburg*: The Supreme Court *rejected* such a constitutionally-based journalist source privilege in *Branzburg v. Hayes*, 408 U.S. 665 (1972). However, because the vote was 5-4, and the critical vote was supplied by Justice Powell's somewhat equivocal concurrence, *Branzburg* does not eliminate the possibility that in some situations, forcing a journalist to reveal his sources might violate the First Amendment.

i. Facts: *Branzburg* involved three cases in which journalists asserted a privilege to refuse to testify before grand juries investigating possible crimes as to which the journalists may have received information from confidential sources. (One, for instance, published an article in which he said he had spent weeks interviewing local drug users and had seen some of them smoking marijuana; the grand jury subpoenaed him to answer questions about any crimes actually observed by him, but he refused to divulge either the identities of the informants or any information given to him in confidence, on the grounds that his effectiveness as a reporter would be damaged if he did so.)

   ii. Holding: Four members of the Court saw no need at all to recognize a constitutional privilege to protect news sources. But Justice Powell, in his key concurrence supplying the fifth vote, said that such a constitutionally-based privilege might exist in some cases even though it did not in the instant case — the Court should, on a case-by-case basis, balance freedom of the press against "the obligation of all citizens to give relevant testimony with respect to criminal conduct." The four dissenters would have granted journalists a qualified privilege to refuse to reveal confidences to a grand jury.

   b. Present law: *Branzburg* thus leaves five members of the Court willing to recognize a constitutionally-based journalist's privilege in some situations. Post-*Branzburg* decisions by the lower federal courts have, indeed, often recognized such a privilege, sometimes on First Amendment grounds. 98 Harv. L. Rev. 1603-04. For instance, if the information being sought is not very central to the case of the litigant who is seeking it, or can be gotten from other sources, post-*Branzburg* courts have often given the journalist a privilege to refuse to disclose the information. See, e.g., *U.S. v. Cuthbertson*, 631 F.2d 139 (3d Cir. 1980) (party seeking disclosure must demonstrate that he has been unable to obtain the information from other sources, and that the information is "crucial" to his case).

   c. Common-law basis: Some federal courts have recognized a qualified journalist source privilege on **common-law**, rather than constitutional, grounds. L&S, p. 782. They have relied on FRE 501, which requires federal courts in criminal cases and federal question civil cases to apply "the principles of the common law as they may be interpreted . . . in the light of reason and experience."

4. Conflict between privilege and defendant's rights: Suppose that it is a criminal defendant who seeks information, including identification of sources, from a journalist. In this situation, any privilege the journalist has (whether from a state shield statute, from the Constitution or from the common law) may **conflict** with the defendant's Sixth Amendment right to **compulsory process** and to **confront witnesses** against him.

   a. *Farber* case: At least one court has held that where such a conflict exists, the journalist's privilege must **give way** to the defendant's Sixth Amendment rights. *Matter of Farber*, 394 A.2d 330 (N.J. 1978).

   i. Facts: Farber, a New York Times reporter, investigated a series of unsolved hospital deaths, and then wrote a series of articles that led to the prosecution of one Dr. Jascalevich for murder. The defense subpoenaed Farber's records of his investigation, but Farber asserted both the First Amendment and New Jersey's broadly worded shield law in refusing to comply. (He went to jail on contempt charges rather than comply.)

    ii. Holding: The New Jersey Supreme Court conceded that Farber's refusal was covered by the New Jersey shield law. But the information sought was so central to Jascalevich's defense, and so completely unavailable from other sources, that granting a privilege to Farber would amount to denying Jascalevich his federal and state constitutional right to have "compulsory process for obtaining witnesses in his favor."

    iii. Procedure: Therefore, the court held, if Jascalevich could convince the trial judge that there was a reasonable probability that the information sought was material and relevant, and not obtainable by other means, the judge should inspect the materials *in camera*. The trial judge would then decide which information was so vital and otherwise unavailable that it should be turned over to the defense. (For a more extensive discussion of *in camera* inspection and other procedures designed to safeguard privileges, see *infra*, p. 350.)

C. Government information: Litigants will often need information that is in the ***possession of the government.*** This may be the case both where the government is a party to the litigation (e.g., a criminal prosecution in which the accused, to prepare his defense, needs information from law enforcement files) and where it is not a party (e.g., a routine civil suit between two private litigants, as to which government-held information is relevant). Yet government will often have a strong countervailing interest in not disclosing the material.

    1. Organization of discussion: A number of distinct privileges for government-held information have evolved. Our discussion below first focuses on general problems of "government secrets," with distinct treatment for: (1) military and state secrets; (2) Executive-branch deliberations (including Presidential privilege); and (3) law enforcement investigative files. Then, we give a separate and more detailed treatment to the problem of government informants.

    2. Government secrets generally: When a litigant has a legitimate need for secret information held by the government, courts generally apply a ***balancing test*** to determine whether to treat the information as privileged or require it to be disclosed: the litigant's need for the information is balanced against society's (i.e., the government's) need to keep the information secret. However, the way this balancing test gets applied varies depending on the context; in one instance (military and state secrets), the privilege is usually held to be absolute so that there is no balancing at all.

    3. Military and diplomatic secrets: An ***absolute privilege*** exists as to ***military*** and ***diplomatic*** secrets. No matter how badly a litigant needs a document or other information held by the government, the government is privileged not to disclose it if it can show a reasonable chance that without the privilege, a secret relating to ***national defense*** or international relations would be disclosed.

        Example: An Air Force B-29 aircraft crashes, killing many of those aboard. The families of three civilian observers killed in the crash sue the U.S. under the Federal Tort Claims Act. The Ps demand production of the Air Force's official accident investigation report and statements made by surviving crew members. The Air Force asserts that the purpose of the flight was to test secret electronic equipment of military importance, and that disclosure of the materials sought would reveal military secrets.

Held, the information is privileged and need not be released. "[E]ven the most compelling necessity cannot overcome the claim of privilege if the court is ultimately satisfied that military secrets are at stake." Here, the undisputed fact that the accident occurred to a military plane that had gone aloft to test secret electronic equipment, was sufficient to establish a "reasonable danger" that the investigation report would contain references to that secret equipment. Therefore, the court should uphold the government's claim of privilege without even inspecting the report. This is especially true where, as here, the person seeking the information has been offered a reasonable alternative by the government (namely, the right to depose the crash survivors). *U.S. v. Reynolds,* 345 U.S. 1 (1953).

   a. Federal Rules: This "absolute privilege" approach is followed by the Proposed Federal Rule of Evidence on the subject (which was, of course, dropped by Congress with all the other specific privilege rules). PFRE 509 grants an absolute privilege to a "secret of state," defined as a "governmental secret relating to the national defense or the international relations of the United States." Whereas other types of "official information" are given only a qualified privilege by PFRE 509 (so that the government must show that disclosure would be "contrary to the public interest"), the privilege for state secrets applies even though the government makes no showing that the secret would actually damage national security or diplomacy, or that this damage outweighs the litigant's need to know the information. While PFRE 509 is not binding on the federal courts, they are likely to consider it in interpreting the "common law" in criminal and federal question civil cases; see FRE 501 (*supra,* p. 292).

4. Other government information: Two other types of government information are generally given a *qualified* privilege, one which will apply only where the damage to the public welfare from disclosure outweighs the litigant's need for the information. These two areas are: (1) internal governmental policy-making deliberations; and (2) law enforcement investigatory files.

   a. Internal deliberations and policy making: When government officials, especially members of the ***Executive Branch,*** make policy decisions, they need to be able to discuss the various options candidly with each other. To encourage such candor in the exchange of views, a privilege has generally been recognized for intragovernmental opinions and recommendations concerning ***policies to be adopted.***

      i. Factual reports not covered: But the privilege applies only to opinions and policy deliberations, not to ***factual reports.*** For instance, in *Reynolds, supra,* the Air Force's report investigating the crash of the military plane would not fall within the privilege, since it did not involve policy deliberations, and merely reported facts.

ii. **Presidential privilege:** This privilege for intragovernmental deliberations is probably based on the common law, not the Constitution. But one subset of it does seem to have a constitutional dimension: deliberations between the *President* and his advisors are protected by a qualified privilege that derives from the constitutional principle of *separation of powers*. In *U.S. v. Nixon*, 418 U.S. 683 (1974), the Supreme Court seemed to hold that President Nixon's claim of executive privilege concerning his deliberations with his top advisors was supported by constitutional separation-of-powers principles. But, the Court held, the privilege was not absolute: it must yield to a "demonstrated, specific need for evidence in a pending criminal trial."

b. **Law enforcement investigatory files:** A similar qualified privilege is recognized for *investigative files* compiled by *law enforcement* agencies. For instance, a criminal defendant has no general right to make the government turn over to him the files it compiled in investigating and preparing the case (though under criminal discovery rules he may have the right to certain items, such as statements by witnesses and the results of scientific tests). See PFRE 509(a)(2)(B).

c. **Effect of Freedom of Information Act:** When information is held by the *federal* government, the *Freedom of Information Act* (FOIA) may come into play. FOIA makes most kinds of governmental information available to any citizen (even a non-litigant) upon request. If particular information would be available under FOIA, a court is very unlikely to recognize a claim of privilege to prevent it from being introduced into evidence at a proceeding. (But FOIA has special exemptions that match most of the government-secrets privileges; for instance, law enforcement investigatory files and military secrets are specifically exempted from FOIA.)

5. **Procedures and consequences:** There are two important procedural issues that arise when the government makes a claim that particular material is privileged against disclosure: (1) how does the judge go about determining the merits of the government's claims?; and (2) if the judge upholds the claim, what are the consequences?

a. **How judge decides:** The procedure which the judge is to follow in deciding the merits of the government's privilege claim depends on whether "state secrets" are involved.

i. **State secrets:** Where the claim is that secrets of state (military and diplomatic secrets) are involved, the judge is relatively powerless to go behind the government's assertion. So long as the head of the government department makes the claim upon personal knowledge, the judge must uphold the claim of privilege so long as he finds, from the surrounding circumstances, that there is a reasonable possibility that state secrets are indeed involved. The judge is *not* authorized to examine the material itself, even *in camera*. See *Reynolds, supra*, pp. 348-49.

ii. **Other information:** Where other information falling within the other government secrets privileges is involved, the judge has much more authority. Most importantly, he may *examine the materials in camera* (that is, alone in his chambers). M, p. 270. Furthermore, he may then engage in a *balancing process*: if he finds that the damage to the government from disclosure would be outweighed by the damage to the litigant in not having the material, he may order disclosure even though the material falls into one of the privileged categories (e.g., it contains opinions or recommendations about policy, or consists of law enforcement investigatory materials). The judge may also *separate* privileged from non-privileged material, and release to the litigant the non-privileged portion.

b. **Consequences of upholding claim:** What happens when the court upholds the government's claim of privilege? The answer depends on whether the government is a party to the suit:

i. **Government not a party:** When the government is *not* a party, its successful privilege claim merely makes the evidence *unavailable*, just as if a witness had died. There are no other consequences from the claim of privilege. M, p. 268.

ii. **Government a party:** But where the government *is* a party, it may have to *pay a price* for its assertion of privilege. Most dramatically, if the case is a *criminal* prosecution brought by the same government unit that is asserting the privilege, and the court concludes that the material would be materially helpful to the defense, the court will generally offer the government a *choice*: it must either disclose the material or *dismiss the prosecution*. *Id.*. Similarly, if the government is a plaintiff in a civil action, it may have to choose between releasing the material or having its claim dismissed. *Id.*

iii. **Government is defendant:** Where the government is a *defendant* in a civil action brought by a private litigant, the government usually will *not* be put to this painful choice. Instead, the government will usually be allowed to have its cake and eat it too — it can decline to release the material, yet assert a defense which might be disproved by release of the material. For instance, where the government is sued under the Federal Tort Claims Act (as in *Reynolds, supra*, pp. 348-49), the government can claim that it was non-negligent, yet at the same time refuse to release privileged materials which, if they were released, might show governmental negligence (e.g., the Air Force's investigative report in *Reynolds*).

6. **Government informers:** The government has a special privilege to decline to disclose the *identity* of *informants* who give it information about crimes. M, pp. 270-71.

a. **Rationale:** Use of informants is necessary for the prosecution of many types of crimes, especially so-called "victimless" ones (e.g., narcotics crimes). Yet if an informant could not rely on the government's ability to keep his identity secret, this kind of information might dry up — even with the privilege, many an informant has been murdered or tortured when his identity became known to those he implicated in crime.

b. Protects identity only: Most courts have held that the government informant privilege protects only the ***identity*** of the informant, not the substance of the ***information*** that he gives to the government. However, if the content would effectively reveal the informant's identity, the content, too, is privileged.

c. Qualified privilege: The privilege is not an absolute one. Most importantly, if disclosure of the informant's identity is likely to be of material assistance to a criminal defendant in preparing his ***defense***, the government must disclose that identity (or drop the case; see discussion *infra*, p. 353). *Roviaro v. U.S.*, 353 U.S. 53 (1957).

   i. Illustration: The facts of *Roviaro* illustrate how disclosure of an informant's identity may be so important to the defendant's ability to defend himself that the privilege is overridden. In *Roviaro*, D was charged with selling and transporting narcotics. The informer was not only present at the alleged crime, but had been an active participant in it. The government refused to disclose the informer's identity or put him on as a witness. The Court held that the informant's testimony could have aided D at trial in a number of ways; for instance, he could have rebutted the prosecution's claim that D knew that the substance was narcotics, he might have helped D establish an entrapment defense, and cross-examination of him would have certainly been more valuable to D than was cross-examination of the only other person who witnessed the transaction (a government agent who was secretly present). Therefore, the government had to disclose the informant's identity or drop the case.

d. Tipster/participant distinction: Most lower courts, in applying *Roviaro's* holding that the privilege must give way when the informer's identity is necessary to the defense, have distinguished between informants who are ***"participants"*** and informants who are mere ***"tipsters."*** An informant who participates in the crime (like the informant in *Roviaro*) will almost always be so central to the defense that his identity must be disclosed. Similarly, an informant who is also a crucial ***eyewitness*** usually must be identified. But an informant who merely learns about a past crime and passes the police a "tip" that leads them to the defendant, generally need not be identified. 98 Harv. L. Rev. 1598.

e. Probable cause: Frequently the police rely (or claim to rely) on information from a confidential informant in obtaining ***probable cause*** to make an arrest or to obtain a search warrant. Under the exclusionary rule, evidence that results from an illegal search or arrest will be ***excluded*** under the "exclusionary rule." (See *infra*, p. 355.) Therefore, a criminal defendant will often want to obtain the identity of a government informant to show that the police unreasonably relied on the informant's information, or lied when they said they relied on an informant.

i. ***McCray* case:** However, the government will usually be able to avoid disclosing the informant's identity in this suppression hearing context. In *McCray v. Illinois*, 386 U.S. 300 (1967), the Supreme Court held that police officers need not reveal the informant's identity if the officers testify as to the reasonableness of their reliance on the informant. *McCray's* actual holding is merely that the defendant has no constitutional **due process** right to disclosure of the informant's identity in this situation. As a practical matter, however, the case means that courts will in general uphold the government's claim of privilege if the officers testify to the details of their reliance on the informant, even though the result is that the police testimony is taken on blind faith, often impairing the defendant's right not to be convicted based upon illegally-seized evidence.

f. **Exceptions:** There are two important *exceptions* to the government's privilege not to disclose the identity of an informant:

i. **Voluntary disclosure:** First, if the informant's identity has already previously been disclosed to "those who would have cause to resent the communication," the privilege ceases. *Roviaro, supra*, p. 352. For instance, if the defendant has already learned the informant's identity, the government may not refuse to acknowledge that identity at trial.

ii. **Witness:** Second, if the government calls the informant as a **witness**, it must disclose his identity. See PFRE 510(c)(1). For instance, the government may not put an informant on the stand wearing a mask to conceal his identity.

g. **Procedure:** The trial judge need not accept the government's claim of informant privilege without scrutiny.

i. **Needed for defense:** For instance, if the defense contends that disclosure of the informant's identity is necessary to the defense, the judge may order the government to disclose in an *in camera* proceeding (at which defense counsel is not present) facts that would show whether the informant would indeed be able to give testimony useful to the defense. See PFRE 510(c)(2). See also *U.S. v. Strange*, 52 F.R.D. 542 (E.D.Tenn. 1970) (judge will examine the informant *in camera*, with only a court reporter and without either prosecution or defense counsel present, to determine whether disclosure of informant's identity is helpful or essential to D's defense; transcript will then be sealed and made available only to appellate court in the event of an appeal).

ii. **Dismissal:** Furthermore, if the judge concludes that disclosure of the informant's identity would indeed be materially helpful to the defense, the judge may require the government to choose between making that disclosure or **dropping the prosecution**. PFRE 510(c)(2).

7. **Required reports and returns:** There is one last category of government-held information that may in some circumstances be privileged. Many statutes require individuals to make **reports** to, or file **returns** with, government agencies. **Traffic**

accident reports and ***tax returns*** are two examples. The government has **no** general privilege to decline to disclose such reports. However, if the statute that imposes the duty to report also includes a provision prohibiting the government from disclosing the information, then courts will generally **honor** that specific statutory prohibition, treating it as a privilege. M, pp. 273-74.

   a. Rationale: Often, such specific statutory privileges for a given kind of report are motivated by the theory that the state's promise of confidentiality is needed to ***encourage*** private citizens to make the report. For instance, state statutes requiring doctors to report cases of ***venereal disease*** to public health officials generally include such a confidentiality provision on the theory that without one, doctors will often not comply.

D. Trade secrets: Some courts have recognized a privilege for ***trade secrets***. A trade secret may be a secret process, information about the marketplace, or any other knowledge which a business has that aids it in competing. There are several common situations where the trade secret privilege may be invoked: (1) ***antitrust*** actions in which the government or a private litigant tries to force the defendant to disclose information about the defendant's marketplace position that would show that the defendant is a monopoly; (2) patent or unfair competition suits in which the plaintiff tries to get the defendant to disclose secret information about a device or process that is the subject of the suit; and (3) tort and breach-of-warranty suits in which the plaintiff, usually an individual, tries to get the defendant to give detailed manufacturing information about a product that is claimed to be defective and/or dangerous.

   1. Qualified privilege: Most courts have treated the trade secrets privilege as being ***qualified*** rather than absolute. That is, the holder's need to keep business information from leaking out into competitors' hands is weighed against the litigant's need to develop information for his case. Thus PFRE 508 (never enacted) grants the privilege, but only "if the allowance of the privilege will not tend to conceal fraud or otherwise work injustice."

   2. Protective order: If the judge does partly override the privilege because of a litigant's great need for the material, he may issue a ***protective order*** limiting the use to which the information may be put. For instance, the litigant receiving the information may be ordered not to disclose it to anyone else. See the last sentence of PFRE 508, and the Advisory Committee's Note thereto.

E. Newly-emerging privileges: We now consider briefly a few privileges that are "emerging," in the sense that a few courts have recognized them in recent years, or commentators have urged that they be adopted. None of these privileges has so far been enacted in anything close to a majority of states.

   1. Parent-child communications: Because of society's interest in seeing families remain intact, many commentators have argued that there should be a privilege for ***parent-child communications***, analogous to the privilege for spousal communications. See 98 Harv. L. Rev. 1575-76.

      a. Limited success: Three states have so far recognized the privilege: New York by case law, and Idaho and Minnesota by statute. *Id.* An occasional federal court has also recognized the privilege. *Id.*

    b. One-way only: In general, those cases and statutes recognizing the privilege have protected only communications from **child to parent**, not from parent to child. *Id.* at 1576. Also, most courts and statutes limit the privilege to situations in which the child is a **minor**. *Id.* at 1577.

2. Other professional-client relationships: Because lawyers, doctors and clergymen have persuaded legislatures to give them privileges covering communications they receive during the practice of their professions, **other professionals** have urged that they, too, receive such beneficial treatment. These claims have been relatively unsuccessful.

    a. Accountants: About one-third of the states have granted a privilege for communications to **accountants**. M, p. 185. This privilege has been justified by its relatively strong resemblance to communications made to one's lawyer, especially where the subject matter is the client's financial and tax dealings. One court has also granted a qualified **work product immunity** against the discovery of certain tax-related work papers prepared by accountants doing tax planning for their client. See *U.S. v. Arthur Young & Co.*, 677 F.2d 211 (1982).

    b. Counselor-counselee: Since clergymen and doctors generally receive a privilege for communications made during the course of their counseling of individuals, other professional counselors — school counselors, social workers, marriage counselors, etc. — have urged a privilege. Occasionally, this has been granted. M, p. 185.

3. Academic researchers: *Academic researchers* have argued that in order for them to induce research subjects to cooperate with them, they must offer confidentiality similar to that given by journalists to their sources. Only rarely has such a researcher-subject privilege been recognized. 98 Harv. L. Rev. 1609-11. Some special federal and state statutes recognize a special limited privilege for confidential facts disclosed pursuant to research on **drugs**. *Id.* at 1611.

F. Exclusionary rule: Before we leave the subject of privileges, we mention in passing one rule that is sometimes thought of as a privilege. This is the rule, formulated by the Supreme Court, that evidence obtained in violation of the Constitution (usually the Fourth Amendment) may not be admitted in a criminal prosecution of the person whose rights were violated. This so-called "exclusionary rule" is not really a rule of privilege, however, since privilege rules prevent the acquisition of evidence as well as its use at trial, whereas the exclusionary rule prevents only use at trial. L&S, p. 766. In any event, treatment of the exclusionary rule is beyond the scope of this outline, since the subject is usually covered in Criminal Procedure courses. See *Emanuel on Criminal Procedure*.

REAL AND DEMONSTRATIVE EVIDENCE, INCLUDING WRITINGS

I. INTRODUCTION

A. Real and demonstrative evidence: So far, we have focused almost exclusively upon "testimonial" evidence. That is, we have concentrated on evidence consisting of testimony by a live witness in which the witness makes assertions about facts — with such evidence, the jury does not have a first-hand sense impression of the ultimate fact, and must rely on the witness' own observation, memory, and narration. In this chapter, we consider evidence that the trier of fact can *perceive first-hand*, without a witness as intermediary.

1. **Consequence of distinction:** The most important consequence of this distinction is that testimonial evidence always requires the trier of fact to assess the *credibility* of the witness, whereas the kind of evidence considered in this chapter — "real" and "demonstrative" evidence — may be evaluated without considerations of credibility. (However, often the real or demonstrative evidence will need to be "sponsored" by a live witness, whose credibility is important in determining whether the evidence is what its proponent says it is).

   Example 1: The issue is whether D acted reasonably when he shot V in response to V's brandishing a knife at him. W testifies that he witnessed the event, and that V's knife was a large, lethal-looking switchblade. This is testimonial evidence, and the jury can only decide the nature of the knife (and therefore the nature of the threat apparently posed by it) by evaluating W's credibility (including his ability to perceive accurately, remember what he saw, and describe it accurately).

   Example 2: Same facts. Now, however, the prosecution produces the actual knife brandished by V. Here, the jury perceives first-hand this "real" evidence, and is therefore able to see for itself that the knife is really an obviously-fake plastic prop, not a dangerous switchblade. No judgment of credibility is needed for the jury to evaluate this evidence (except the credibility of the "sponsoring" witness produced by the prosecution, who states that the knife produced by the prosecution is indeed the one brandished by V).

2. **"Real" distinguished from "demonstrative" evidence:** We consider two distinct types of evidence in this chapter: *"real"* and *"demonstrative"* evidence.

   a. **"Real":** As we will use the term, "real" evidence is a tangible object that *played some actual role* in the matter that gave rise to the litigation. L&S, p. 988.

      Example: The knife in Example 2, above, is "real," since it is the very knife that was used in the altercation that forms the basis for the lawsuit.

i. Other examples: Other examples of "real" evidence would be: (1) the actual ransom demand letter written by D to V, introduced by the prosecution in a kidnapping prosecution of D; (2) a wiretap recording of D soliciting a bribe from an undercover operator, introduced in the bribery prosecution of D; and (3) an automatic photo taken by equipment at a bank, showing D cashing a check, introduced in a forgery prosecution of D. In each of these three instances, the object is the very one used in the underlying controversy.

b. "Demonstrative": "Demonstrative" evidence, by contrast, is tangible evidence that merely *illustrates* a matter of importance in the litigation. L&S, p. 988. Common types of demonstrative evidence include maps, diagrams, models, summaries, and other materials created especially for the litigation.

Example: Same facts as Examples 1 and 2 on p. 356, *supra*. The prosecution is unable to recover the knife allegedly brandished by V. From circumstantial evidence, the prosecution is convinced that what was really waved was an obviously-fake Halloween knife. The prosecution buys such a knife from a costume store, and has the knife marked as People's Exhibit 1 for Identification. It then presents a witness to the original event, W, who testifies that this Exhibit closely resembles the "knife" actually used by V. Exhibit 1 is "demonstrative" evidence, rather than "real" evidence, because it is not the very knife used in the underlying event, and merely illustrates some point of interest (namely, the type of knife used by V).

c. Note on terminology: Some courts and commentators use the term "demonstrative" more broadly, to refer to *all* kinds of tangible evidence (i.e., to refer to both what we are calling "real" as well as what we are calling "demonstrative"). This is the usage made by McCormick, for instance; see M, p. 664.

d. Significance of distinction: The distinction between "real" and "demonstrative" evidence is important because it helps determine the standards that the evidence must meet to be admissible. In particular, the *"foundation"* that must be laid for real evidence is generally somewhat different from that needed for demonstrative evidence.

i. Foundation for real evidence: For real evidence, the required foundation relates to proving that the evidence is indeed the object used in the underlying event. Thus suppose that in a prosecution for selling heroin to an undercover agent, the state presents white powder that it says was sold by D to the agent; the foundation consists of evidence tending to prove that this powder was indeed the powder sold by D to the agent.

ii. Demonstrative evidence: The foundation for demonstrative evidence, by contrast, does not involve showing that the object was the one used in the underlying event. Rather, the foundation generally involves showing that the demonstrative object *fairly represents* or illustrates what it is alleged to illustrate. For instance, where a drawing is presented to illustrate the relative positions of the protagonists and witnesses to a killing, the foundation will normally consist of testimony by one or more eyewitnesses or investigators stating that the drawing does indeed fairly represent the positions of those present at the event.

3. **General rule for real and demonstrative evidence:** In the broad sense, the standards for admitting real and demonstrative evidence are no different than for admitting testimonial evidence. Tangible evidence (whether real or demonstrative) will be admitted if: (1) it is ***relevant***, in the sense that it makes some consequential and contested proposition of fact more or less likely, or aids the jury in understanding some issue (see *supra*, p. 10); unless (2) its ***probative value*** is ***outweighed*** by prejudice, confusion, delay, or other ***countervailing consideration*** (see *supra*, p. 14).

   a. **What chapter is about:** Therefore, most of this chapter is not about the broad requirements for admissibility of tangible objects. Rather, it is concerned with three main questions: (1) What foundation must be laid before the object may be introduced (especially, what ***"authentication"*** must be supplied)?; (2) When do the especially dramatic properties of real and demonstrative evidence — including the fact that the jury perceives such evidence directly, rather than through impressions derived from an intermediary's testimony — make the evidence ***so prejudicial***, confusing, or so much more important-seeming than it really is, that it should be excluded even though relevant and properly-authenticated?; and (3) In the case of writings and other recorded communications, when is the proponent required to offer the ***"original"*** rather than a mere "copy"?

B. **Direct vs. circumstantial:** When analyzing real evidence, it is often useful to distinguish between "direct" and "circumstantial" evidence. A given tangible object can be direct proof of some facts, and circumstantial proof of other facts.

   Example: Suppose that the real evidence in question is a three-year-old child, and the child's appearance. If the case is a personal injury action in which the claim is that the child's face has been disfigured by loss of an eye, the child's face, when shown to the jury, is direct evidence of the loss of an eye. If, by contrast, the suit is a paternity proceeding, the child's face (and its similarity or dissimilarity to the face of the defendant who is alleged to be the father) is merely circumstantial evidence that he and the defendant are related.

1. **Significance:** Why is the distinction between direct and circumstantial real evidence significant? Direct evidence, when properly authenticated, will almost always be admitted unless admission would involve substantial prejudice or other strong countervailing consideration. When circumstantial evidence is offered, by contrast, the trial judge generally has ***broader discretion*** to conclude that waste of time, confusion, or mild prejudice outweigh the item's probative value. M, p. 666.

   a. **Appearance of person:** For example, where the ***physical appearance*** of a person is sought to be introduced for circumstantial purposes, courts will often conclude that the inference sought to be established is so weak, and the possibility of prejudicing one side or confusing the jury so great, that the evidence should be suppressed.

> **Example:** In ***paternity proceedings***, the plaintiff will often attempt to display the baby or child to the jury, to establish that there is a ***resemblance*** to the defendant. While courts traditionally have allowed such evidence, the modern trend seems to be to hold that the possibility of prejudice to the defendant is great, and that a lay jury cannot properly determine whether the degree of resemblance is enough to make it more probable than it would otherwise be that a father-child relationship exists. See, e.g., *Almeida v. Correa*, 465 P.2d 564 (Haw. 1970) ("Any evidence concerning resemblance or non-resemblance must be given by the testimony of a qualified expert and not by an exhibition of the child to the jury.")

> **i. Age:** Similarly, if a person's ***age*** is in question, some courts will not allow this to be proved by mere display of the person to the jury without expert testimony. See, e.g., *Watson v. State*, 140 N.E.2d 109 (Ind. 1957), holding that the prosecution could not meet its burden of proving that the defendant was over the statutorily-required age of sixteen merely by having the jury view his appearance.

II. AUTHENTICATION

A. Authentication generally: All real and demonstrative evidence must be ***"authenticated"*** before it is admitted. That is, it must be shown to be ***"genuine."*** What does it mean for a tangible object to be "genuine"? In general, it means that the object must be ***what its proponent claims it to be***. See FRE 901(a).

1. Real evidence: Where the object is ***real*** evidence, authentication normally consists of showing that the object is ***the*** object that was involved in the underlying event.

> **Examples:** (1) Proof that this object is the gun that was actually used by the defendant in robbing the bank; (2) Proof that this document is the contract actually signed by plaintiff and defendant; (3) Proof that this tape accurately reproduces a conversation in which D tried to bribe a public official.

2. Demonstrative: Where the evidence is ***demonstrative,*** authentication basically involves a showing that the object ***fairly represents or illustrates*** what it is claimed to represent or illustrate.

> **Examples:** (1) Proof that this diagram really shows the position of the parties and witnesses at the time of the murder; (2) Proof that this experiment on brake failures in a car accurately reproduced the conditions existing when P's car malfunctioned; (3) Proof that this summary of evidence already introduced at the trial accurately reflects that evidence.

3. No assumption of authenticity: The key rule of authentication is that, with few exceptions, an object offered in evidence will ***not be presumed to be authentic***. That is, the proponent bears the burden of establishing that the object is what he says it is; he may not merely offer the object and put his adversary to the burden of showing that the object is not genuine.

> **Example:** D is charged with sexual assault. The prosecution offers what appears to be a blood-stained bedspread from D's bed, on which the prosecution claims the attack took place. No scientific proof that the stains are blood is ever presented by the state, but a police officer testifies that the spread came from D's bedroom, and that the stains are blood (a scientific issue on which he is not qualified). The spread is finally held inadmissible, but only after the jury has heard this damaging information.
>
> *Held* (on appeal), permitting the jury to see the spread, and to hear that it was from D's bed and contained blood, was highly prejudicial, and reversible, error. The spread was not admissible except upon testimony by a chemist who had tested and analyzed the stains on it that these were blood. *State v. Scarlett*, 395 A.2d 1244 (N.H. 1978).

4. **Applies to all evidence:** Historically, the requirement of authentication has generally applied only to writings and other tangible evidence. However, modern courts recognize that *all* evidence must be authenticated, including conversations and other *intangible evidence.* This approach is codified in the Federal Rules — FRE 901(a) implicitly applies to all evidence, and at least some of the illustrative authentication methods given in 901(b) cover intangible evidence (e.g., 901(b)(6), which deals with "telephone conversations").

5. **Relevance:** The requirement of authentication is a special case of the requirement that all evidence be *relevant.* For instance, suppose that in a murder prosecution, the prosecution offers into evidence a gun. Without a showing that the gun has at least some connection to the crime (e.g., that it was found at the scene), the gun is simply irrelevant — it does not make any proposition of fact more or less probable than it would be without the gun. Thus, the requirement of authentication is a requirement that there be "a logical nexus between the evidence and the point on which it is offered." L&S, p. 997.

B. **Methods of authentication:** As we noted above, authentication consists of showing that an item of evidence *is what the proponent claims it is*. Techniques for doing this vary depending on whether the evidence is real, demonstrable, a writing, etc.

1. **Real evidence:** Recall that we used the term "real" evidence to describe an object that played some actual role in the events leading up to the lawsuit. Authenticating an item of real evidence consists of showing that the item really *is* the item that was actually used in the underlying transaction (e.g., that the gun being presented at trial really was the gun used to kill the victim). There are two general methods of authenticating an item of real evidence:

a. **Ready identifiability:** The first method is sometimes called *"ready identifiability"* or "unique identifiability." If the item has a *unique, one-of-a-kind* characteristic, this method can be used. The sponsoring witness merely testifies that the object he originally saw has a specified unique characteristic, and that the item shown to him in court bears that same unique identifier. This testimony is all that is needed for identification of the object, i.e., for authenticating it. Imwinkelried, p. 66.

Example: D is charged with stabbing V to death. W is a police officer who inspected the crime scene shortly after the killing occurred. After W testifies about beginning the inspection of the crime scene, the following testimony would authenticate the knife as the murder weapon:

Prosecutor: What did you do during this inspection?

Witness: I looked for any evidence of what had killed the deceased.

Prosecutor: What did you find?

Witness: I found a knife next to the body, which was a pearl-handled switchblade about ten inches long, coated with a sticky red substance.

Prosecutor: What did you do then?

Witness: In the case of a comparatively inexpensive object like this one, I mark it for identification by scratching my initials and the date into the handle.

Prosecutor: I show you People's Exhibit No. 1 for identification. What is it?

Witness: It's the knife I found.

Prosecutor: How can you tell that that's what it is?

Witness: As I said, I marked my initials and the date on the handle. They're right there.

Prosecutor: Has the Exhibit changed since you found it?

Witness: No, it seems to be in the same condition I found it.

Prosecutor: Your honor, I now offer People's Exhibit No. 1 for identification into evidence as People's Exhibit No. 1.

Court: It will be received.

See Imwinkelried, pp. 67-68.

b. **Chain of custody:** The second method for authenticating real evidence is by showing its *"chain of custody."* This method is used when one of the elements for ready identifiability is absent. For instance, the object may not have any uniquely identifying characteristic, or the witness may not previously have observed that unique identifier, or the key issue may not be the identification of the object itself but rather, its chemical composition or other condition. The chain of custody method of authentication requires that every "link" in the chain of custody — every person who has handled or possessed the object since it was first recognized as being relevant to the case — must explain what he did with it.

Example: D is charged with selling cocaine to an undercover agent. Before the prosecution may introduce a bag of white substance as being the cocaine sold by D, it would need to call the undercover agent, the person to whom he turned over the bag, the chemist who performed the test, the person to whom the chemist gave the drug, and anyone else who had custody of the drug up until the appearance of the packet in court. Each witness would testify how he handled the item (e.g., "I put the glassine envelope into a large gray envelope, which I sealed and marked with the name of the case and the date, and placed it in the police safe used for evidence"). Each witness would also be asked: (1) whether the condition of the object appears to be the same as when he or she had custody of it; and (2) whether anyone else had access to the evidence during the time the witness had custody (e.g., **Q:** Did anyone else have the combination to the lock on the property storage safe? **A:** Only the head of the property storage section and myself).

    i. Prevention of tampering: A key reason for the elaborate chain-of-custody method is to prevent (or at least discourage) *tampering* with evidence. The chain-of-custody method will need to be used most often by the prosecution in a criminal case, probably the situation in which innocent and not-so-innocent switching of evidence is most likely. The chain-of-custody method is discussed further *infra*, p. 373.

2. Demonstrative evidence: Where the evidence is "demonstrative" (i.e., used merely to *illustrate* some fact or evidence in the case), the function of authentication is quite different. Here, the object is authenticated not by showing that it is one that was actually used in the underlying events (since it was not), but rather, by showing that it *fairly represents* some aspect of the case.

    Example: In a complicated multi-defendant bank-robbery case, the prosecution offers into evidence a diagram showing the positions of the witnesses, victims, and defendants during the robbery. This diagram will have to be authenticated by a sponsoring witness who can testify that it fairly represents the actual positions of those involved. In this case, that will have to be someone who personally witnessed the robbery (rather than, for instance, the person who drew the diagram).

3. Writing: Special techniques exist for authenticating a *writing* or other recorded communication. These are discussed in detail beginning *infra*, p. 364.

4. Federal Rules: The Federal Rules state a simple principle of authentication. FRE 901(a) provides that "the requirement of authentication or identification as a condition precedent to admissibility is satisfied by evidence *sufficient to support a finding* that the matter in question is *what its proponent claims.*" This general principle controls *all* authentications and identifications, including those involving real evidence, demonstrative evidence, writings, and even intangible events (e.g., telephone conversations).

    a. Illustrations: The Federal Rules do not purport to give detailed standards for authenticating each of the many special types of evidence. Instead, FRE 901(b) gives 10 "illustrations," i.e., examples of authentication that satisfy 901(a)'s general provision:

"(1) *Testimony of witness with knowledge.* Testimony that a matter is what it is claimed to be.

(2) *Nonexpert opinion on handwriting.* Nonexpert opinion as to the genuineness of handwriting, based upon familiarity not acquired for purposes of the litigation.

(3) *Comparison by trier or expert witness.* Comparison by the trier of fact or by expert witnesses with specimens which have been authenticated.

(4) *Distinctive characteristics and the like.* Appearance, contents, substance, internal patterns, or other distinctive characteristics, taken in conjunction with circumstances.

(5) *Voice identification.* Identification of a voice, whether heard firsthand or through mechanical or electronic transmission or recording, by opinion based upon hearing the voice at any time under circumstances connecting it with the alleged speaker.

(6) *Telephone conversations.* Telephone conversations, by evidence that a call was made to the number assigned at the time by the telephone company to a particular person or business, if (A) in the case of a person, circumstances, including self-identification, show the person answering to be the one called, or (B) in the case of a business, the call was made to a place of business and the conversation related to business reasonably transacted over the telephone.

(7) *Public records or reports.* Evidence that a writing authorized by law to be recorded or filed and in fact recorded or filed in a public office, or a purported public record, report, statement, or data compilation, in any form, is from the public office where items of this nature are kept.

(8) *Ancient documents or data compilation.* Evidence that a document or data compilation, in any form, (A) is in such condition as to create no suspicion concerning its authenticity, (B) was in a place where it, if authentic, would likely be, and (C) has been in existence 20 years or more at the time it is offered.

(9) *Process or system.* Evidence describing a process or system used to produce a result and showing that the process or system produces an accurate result.

(10) *Methods provided by statute or rule.* Any method of authentication or identification provided by act of Congress or by other rules prescribed by the Supreme Court pursuant to statutory authority."

    i. Discussed elsewhere: Most of these illustrative types of authentication are discussed at various places below. See, e.g., the treatment of handwriting (*infra*, p. 366), voice identification in telephone conversations (*infra*, p. 367), public records (*infra*, p. 371), ancient documents (*infra*, p. 370), and processes or systems (*infra*, p. 391).

b. Testimony of witness with knowledge: Illustration (1) above (FRE 901(b)(1)) covers the most basic method of authentication: a witness may authenticate an item by giving "***testimony*** that [it] is what it is claimed to be."

Example: Recall the example on p. 361, *supra*, involving the knife found at the murder scene. W's testimony that this is the knife he found, and that he can recognize it because he carved his initials into it, is what 901(b)(1) refers to as "testimony that a matter is what it is claimed to be."

5. **Judge-jury allocation:** In determining the authenticity of an item of evidence, both the judge and the jury play a role. It is not up to the judge to decide whether the item *is* what its proponent claims it to be; that job is for the jury. But it is up to the judge to decide whether there is **some evidence** from which a jury could reasonably find that the item is what it is claimed to be. See W&B, Par. 901(a)[01] (The judge must admit the evidence "once a prima facie case has been made on the issue [of authenticity]. . . . [FRE 901(a)] requires only that the court admit evidence if sufficient proof has been introduced so that a reasonable juror could find in favor of authenticity or identification. The rest is up to the jury.")

Example: In a complicated antitrust case, the Ps seek introduction of certain diaries by Mr. Yajima, an employee of one of the Ds, who is now dead. The Ps claim that the diaries are authentic accounts of what took place at the meetings of an industry trade group at which the Ds conspired in restraint of trade.

Held, it is not up to the trial judge to decide whether the diaries really are accounts of what took place at these meetings. Rather, all the judge must determine is whether there is "substantial evidence from which the [jury] might conclude that [the] document is authentic." Here, various aspects of the diaries and the surrounding circumstances (e.g., testimony by Mr. Yajima in a prior suit; the fact that the diaries have been produced by one of the Ds in discovery; the logo of one of the Ds on the diaries; their similarity to other authenticated documents) are, taken together, sufficient to let the court reach this conclusion that there is a *prima facie* case for authenticity. (The court should determine only whether there is substantial *admissible* evidence that the diaries are authentic; inadmissible evidence of authenticity may not be taken into account by the trial judge, since it may not be taken into account by the jury.) At trial, it will be up to the jury to determine whether the diaries really are what the plaintiffs claim them to be, and to determine how much weight to give them. *Zenith Radio Corp. v. Matsushita Electric Industrial Co., Ltd.,* 505 F.Supp. 1190 (E.D.Pa. 1980).

a. **Conditional relevancy:** This rule about the role of the judge in determining matters of authenticity — that the judge merely makes a preliminary determination of whether a jury *could* reasonably find that the item is authentic — is an illustration of the principle of *"conditional relevance."* There are many other contexts in which the judge must similarly make a conditional determination of admissibility, subject to later proof of a fact to the satisfaction of the jury. See FRE 104(b). The topic is discussed more generally *infra*, p. 456.

C. **Authentication of writings and other recorded communications:** Most authentication problems arise with respect to **writings** and other **communications**. Special rules have developed to handle some recurring issues in this area.

1. **Authorship:** Usually, authentication of a writing will consist of showing **who its author is.**

2. **No presumption of authenticity:** The general requirement of authentication applies to writings and other communications every bit as much as it applies to non-assertive evidence like a knife or a bloodstained bedspread: there is **no presumption of authenticity.** Instead, the proponent bears the burden of making an affirmative showing that the writing or communication is authentic.

    a. **Signature:** Most dramatically, this requirement means that a writing's own recital regarding its authorship (e.g., a **signature**) will **not** be automatically believed.

       Example: P, an individual, sues D, a shoe retailer, for invasion of privacy. P claims that D published a newspaper advertisement using P's name without permission. P offers the advertisement, which features the name of D's store repeatedly and urges people to shop there. P claims that the advertisement, because of its frequent mentions of D, is authenticated as having been taken out by D.

       Held, the references to D in the advertisement are not sufficient authentication, and the advertisement may not be admitted into evidence. "The mere presence in printed material of a particular person constitutes no substantial evidence that that person caused such material to be written or published." (But a dissent argued that the identification of D's name in the advertisement was sufficient circumstantial evidence of D's involvement that the advertisement should have been admitted and the burden placed upon D to come forward with evidence that it did not take out the ad.) *Mancari v. Frank P. Smith, Inc.,* 114 F.2d 824 (D.C.Cir. 1940).

       Note: Although all courts today agree with the general proposition that a document's proclamation of its source will generally not be sufficient authentication, most modern courts would probably hold that the *Mancari* case goes too far. Given the costliness of newspaper advertising, it was very unlikely that anyone other than D would have taken out a newspaper advertisement urging people to shop in D's store. Under the Federal Rules, P could probably get the newspaper advertisement into evidence without extrinsic proof that D took it out — FRE 901(b)(4) allows a document to be authenticated based upon "appearance, contents, substance, internal patterns, or other distinctive characteristics, taken in conjunction with circumstances." A court applying FRE 901(b)(4) would be justified in concluding that the advertisement's appearance and contents, taken together with the circumstance that newspaper advertisements cost money, made it sufficiently likely that the advertisement had been taken out by the firm that would most benefit from it (D) as to constitute authentication.

3. **Direct testimony:** A writing or communication may, of course, be authenticated by **direct testimony** that the document is what its proponent claims it to be.

Example: Consider the newspaper advertisement in *Mancari, supra.* P could have authenticated the ad by calling a representative of D to the stand, and asking him whether his company had taken out the ad. Alternatively, he could have put the advertising manager of the newspaper on the stand, to testify that a person he knew to be the authorized representative of D had taken out the ad.

4. **Distinctive characteristics; circumstances:** There is an increasing trend to allow a writing's ***distinctive characteristics***, and the ***circumstances*** surrounding it, to suffice for authentication. FRE 901(b)(4) allows use of "appearance, contents, substance, internal patterns, or other distinctive characteristics, taken in conjunction with circumstances."

   Example: Recall the diaries at issue in *Zenith, supra,* p. 364, which were claimed by the plaintiffs to be accounts by Mr. Yajima of meetings he attended with representatives of other defendants. In concluding that the plaintiffs had made a *prima facie* case for the diaries to be considered "authentic" (i.e., written by Mr. Yajima, and dealing with the meetings they purport to deal with), the court relied on a wide variety of internal and extrinsic clues, including: (1) a logo of D's corporate employer, found on the diaries; (2) testimony given by Mr. Yajima in a prior proceeding; (3) the fact that Yajima's employer produced the diaries during discovery, and referred to them in its interrogatory answers; and (4) the diaries' similarity to other documents that had previously been authenticated.

5. **Signature or other handwriting:** Often, a document's author can be established by showing that it was ***signed*** or written in the hand of a particular person. One way to do this, of course, is by testimony of the witness that he actually observed the document being signed or written. But another common method is to have the witness ***identify*** the ***signature or handwriting*** on the document as belonging to a particular person.

   a. **Weak credentials:** Courts do not require the witness to have any special abilities or training at handwriting analysis for this purpose. It will be sufficient if the witness has ***seen*** the writing of the person in question at some time previously (even if a decade ago). In fact, it will suffice that the witness has previously seen documents ***purporting*** to have been written by the person (e.g., W has received correspondence purporting to be from X in the past, and now testifies that he recognizes the current document to be in X's handwriting). M, p. 690.

   b. **No real impediment:** The nearly total lack of credentials required for handwriting identification by non-experts probably is a tacit recognition by the courts that the vast majority of documents are authored by the person they purport to be authored by. If the opponent of a document casts serious doubt on whether the person who purported to write it really did, the proponent should offer expert handwriting testimony, even though this is not required for authentication.

c. Federal Rules: The Federal Rules recognize the general rule that non-experts may identify handwriting; FRE 901(b)(2) allows "nonexpert opinion as to the genuineness of handwriting, based upon *familiarity not acquired for purposes of the litigation*." Thus if W is not a handwriting expert, he may give testimony that X wrote the document in question if he has had occasion to see X's handwriting before the litigation began (e.g., because he has had correspondence with X). But he may not give such testimony based solely upon a study of handwriting specimens from X in preparation for his trial testimony. (If handwriting testimony is to be given based upon a study of specimens made in preparation for the testimony, it must be given by an expert.)

d. Exemplars: Handwriting may also be proved by the use of *exemplars*, i.e., specimens of the handwriting of the person claimed to be the author of the document in question. Courts differ as to the strength of proof that must be offered that X really wrote the exemplar; see, e.g., *U. of Illinois v. Spalding*, 51 A. 731 (N.H. 1901), holding that the exemplar must be proven to have been authored by X "upon clear and undoubted evidence" as found by the trial judge. (Other courts would allow the exemplar to be admitted on a less strong showing.)

  i. Jury may compare: Once the exemplar has been admitted, most courts hold that it is up to the jury to compare the exemplar with the offered writing, to conclude whether the latter was written by the same person. The jury can be helped to do this by expert testimony offered by the proponent, but such expert testimony is *not required*. M, p. 691.

6. Reply letters and telegrams: A *letter* or *telegram* can sometimes be authenticated by the circumstantial fact that it appears to be a *reply* to a prior communication, and the prior communication is proved. For instance, if P can prove that he wrote a letter to D on January 1, a letter that purports to have been written by D to P on January 15, and that alludes to the contents of the earlier P-to-D letter, will generally be held to be authenticated by these circumstantial facts. See, e.g., *Whelton v. Daly*, 37 A.2d 1 (N.H. 1944) ("It is a fair inference, considering the habitual accuracy of the mails, that the letter addressed to B reached the real B and that an answer, referring to the tenor of A's letter and coming back in due course of mail, leaves only a negligible chance that anyone other than B has become acquainted with the contents of A's letter so as to forge a reply").

  a. Proving first communication: But observe that for this technique to be used, the proponent must *prove* the first communication. If the first communication was in writing, probably the original must be produced, if available, because of the Best Evidence rule (see *infra*, p. 375). But oral testimony about the first letter will generally suffice if that letter has been lost or destroyed.

7. Telephone conversations: Recall that the requirement of authentication now is generally held to apply to intangible as well as tangible evidence. One illustration is that when the contents of a *telephone conversation* are sought to be proved, the proponent must authenticate the conversation by *establishing the parties to it*.

a. Recognition of voice: Often, this can be done by presenting testimony from a witness who can *identify the voice* at the other end of the phone.

Example: Prosecution of D for making telephone death threats to V, D's ex-wife. V will be permitted to testify that she received such a telephone death threat from D on a particular date only if the prosecution authenticates the conversation by showing that it was indeed D who made the call. But the prosecution can meet this burden by having V testify that as the result of her long familiarity with the sound of D's voice over the phone, she recognized his voice on the occasion in question.

b. Surrounding circumstances: The party to a telephone conversation can also be identified (and the conversation thus authenticated) by *circumstantial evidence*, i.e., by the surrounding circumstances. For instance, the fact that the caller *knew certain facts* that only X would have known will generally be enough to authenticate the conversation as having involved X.

Example: Longo, a detective, is trying to contact D, whom he knows of by the name "Speedy." He meets a man who says that he is Speedy's brother, and who states that Speedy's real name is Julius Lynes. Longo leaves a request that D call him at his office. A few hours later, Longo answers his office phone, and the caller announces himself as "Speedy-Julius Lynes," then asks, "What are you looking for me for?" The caller then makes incriminating remarks. The prosecution offers this conversation against D at trial, but the defense argues that since Longo never met D personally, he cannot testify that he knew the voice on the phone to be that of D.

Held, the conversation was admissible, because there was a sufficient foundation for a jury to be able to find that D was indeed the caller. There were numerous "alternative indices of reliability," including the fact that the caller asked for Longo by name, used his own formal name as well as the nickname "Speedy," and knew that Longo had been looking for him. *People v. Lynes*, 401 N.E.2d 405 (N.Y. 1980).

c. Conditional admission: It is not necessary that the identity of the caller be ascertainable solely from the facts immediately surrounding the conversation. In fact, a conversation may be *conditionally admitted* into evidence, subject to later admission of evidence that would show that the conversation really was with the person that the proponent claims. See FRE 104(b) ("When the relevancy of evidence depends upon the fulfillment of a condition of fact, the court shall admit it upon, or subject to, the introduction of evidence sufficient to support a finding of the fulfillment of the condition.")

Example: D is charged with transporting "kiddie porn" in interstate commerce. The prosecution offers the testimony of W, who states that he called J-E Enterprises on several occasions to order kiddie porn, and that he spoke with a person named "Joe" to place the order. W concedes that he never met "Joe" and cannot say that the person at the other end of the line was D.

Held, the trial judge correctly admitted this testimony conditionally. Later evidence was sufficient to link D to this conversation — for instance, the invoice received by W for the goods bore a fingerprint identified as belonging to D, and FBI and police agents testified that D was active in the business; these facts, combined with the detailed knowledge that "Joe" seemed to have of the business, were enough to identify D as the "Joe" who participated in the conversation, and thus to authenticate W's testimony about that conversation. *U.S. v. Espinoza*, 641 F.2d 153 (4th Cir. 1981).

8. **Sound recordings:** Some courts have imposed especially tough authentication requirements where a *sound recording* is sought to be admitted, perhaps because they fear that such recordings are especially susceptible to tampering or distortion. See, e.g., *U.S. v. McKeever*, 169 F.Supp. 426 (S.D.N.Y. 1958), requiring that before a sound recording is admitted into evidence, a foundation for it must be established by showing all of the following: (1) that the recording device was *capable* of recording the conversation; (2) that the *operator* of the machine was *competent* to operate it; (3) that the recording is *authentic* and *correct*; (4) that *changes, additions, or deletions* have *not* been made in the recording; (5) that the recording has been preserved in a manner shown to the court; (6) that the speakers are *identified*; and (7) that the conversation elicited was made *voluntarily* and in good faith.

> **Example:** Thus in *McKeever*, the court held that the recorded conversation between D and W could not be introduced, even though W testified that he remembered the conversation. The recording failed the authenticity requirements because, *inter alia*, W couldn't recognize his own voice on the recording, he couldn't remember how D was dressed during the conversation, and he couldn't recall whether the recording contained the entire conversation or just a part. Other courts, however, would be less strict on the foundation issue.

9. **Attesting witnesses:** Documents are often *attested to* or *subscribed to* by "witnesses." This is most commonly the case with *wills*. A special rule for authentication of such documents has evolved: at common law, before the document may be authenticated, at least one *attesting witness* must be called to the stand (unless all attesters are shown to be unavailable). M, p. 688.

a. **Anomaly:** This does not mean that the document must be *authenticated* by an attesting witness. It merely means that before the document can be authenticated by non-attesting witnesses, at least one attesting witness must be called to testify. For instance, if a will has been attested to or subscribed to by one or more witnesses, at common law one of them must be called — even if, on the stand, he denies having attested to the document — before non-attesting witnesses (e.g., a handwriting expert, or a beneficiary with direct knowledge of the will) may testify that the will is genuine. M, p. 689.

b. **Federal Rule:** The Federal Rules cut back sharply on this common law requirement concerning attested-to documents. FRE 903 provides that "the testimony of a subscribing witness is not necessary to authenticate a writing unless required by the laws of the jurisdiction whose laws govern the validity of the writing." Thus so long as *state law* does not impose a requirement that a subscribing or attesting witness be called, no subscribing or attesting witness need be called in the federal proceeding. (But if the state whose law governs the validity of the document would require such testimony, as some states still require in the case of wills, the federal court must follow suit.)

    i. Attestation not required: The Federal Rule, like most state statutes today, drops the requirement of testimony by the subscribing witness in those situations where the document was not *required* by local law to be attested to, but the attestation took place anyway.

10. **Ancient documents:** A document that is very *old* generally carries with it some assurance of reliability by that fact alone. For instance, it is not likely that even a dishonest person would take the trouble to forge a document where the forgery does not bear fruit (in the sense of being used as evidence in a proceeding) until many years have passed. M, p. 692. Furthermore, direct authentication of an old document is often difficult; for instance, there are unlikely to be witnesses who can testify that they saw it executed. Therefore, special rules have been developed to make authentication of so-called *"ancient documents"* easier.

    a. Common law: At common law, a writing is automatically deemed authenticated as an ancient document if it meets three requirements:

        i. Thirty years old: It is at least *thirty years old*;

        ii. Unsuspicious: It is *unsuspicious* in appearance;

        iii. "Produced from": It has been "produced from" (i.e., found in) a place of custody *natural* for such a document.

        M, pp. 692-93.

    b. Attesting witnesses: Where a document is authenticated by showing that it is an "ancient document," another benefit to the proponent is that he is *not required* to produce *attesting witnesses* (as he would be, under the common law rule, if the document were not ancient; see *supra*, p. 369). See, e.g., *Jarboe v. The Home Bank & Trust Co.*, 99 A. 563 (Conn. 1917) (signature of attesting witness need not be proved, nor the witness called, where will was more than thirty years old, was produced from the proper custody, and was otherwise free from suspicion.)

    c. Federal Rules: The Federal Rules broaden the ancient document exception in two ways. FRE 901(b)(8) keeps the three basic requirements, except that: (1) the document needs to be only *twenty years old*, not thirty; and (2) the exception covers not only "documents," but also *"data compilations"* in any form. This clearly includes *electronically stored data* (e.g., a computer tape). Furthermore, it should probably be interpreted to include still photographs, X-ray films, movies, and sound recordings. See W&B, Par. 901(b)(8)[01], arguing for such a broad interpretation.

    d. Not guarantee of admissibility: Keep in mind that a showing that a document meets the three requirements for an "ancient document" merely overcomes the "authentication" hurdle, and *does not automatically guarantee admissibility.* For instance, a document that meets these requirements may nonetheless be inadmissible for a particular purpose because it is **hearsay**. M, p. 693. (Also, be careful of the distinction between the ancient document rule that covers authenticity, discussed here, and the ancient document rule which has been recognized in some jurisdictions as an exception to hearsay rule, discussed *supra*, p. 217.)

D. Self-authentication: There are a few categories of documents that are deemed so likely to be what they seem to be that no testimony or other extrinsic evidence of their genuineness need be produced. Such documents are said to be *"self-authenticating."* The categories of self-authenticating documents vary from state to state, and are almost always set by statute rather than case law.

   1. **State statutes:** Here are the kinds of documents most likely to be made self-authenticating by state statutes: (1) **deeds** and other instruments that are duly **notarized**; (2) **certified** copies of **public records** (e.g., a certified copy of a death certificate); and (3) books of **statutes** which appear to be printed by a government body (most commonly used to establish the laws of a **sister state** or **foreign country**). M, p. 700.

      a. **Seal:** Observe that the first two of these categories apply only where a notary or public official in some sense **vouches** for the genuineness of the document. (In the case of a notarized document — category (1) above — this certification is the notary's certification that the document was executed by the person whose signature appears on it; in the case of a certified copy of a public record — category (2) above — it is the public official's certification that the attached document indeed comes from the public records). But how can the court know that the notary or public official who purports to have made the certification really did so? The answer is that this certification is done by a **seal** (a notary's seal or the seal of the public official); separate statutes then provide for such seals to be treated as sufficient evidence of the genuineness of the official's certification. *Id.*

   2. **Federal Rules:** The Federal Rules establish an even broader set of self-authenticating documents. These are listed in FRE 902. In addition to the common categories listed above, Rule 902 makes self-authenticating these new categories:

      a. **Official publications:** All "books, pamphlets, or other publications purporting to be issued by public authority" (not just statutes); see FRE 902(5);

      b. **Newspapers and periodicals:** "Printed materials purporting to be **newspapers** or **periodicals**"; see FRE 902(6); and

      c. **Trade inscriptions:** "Inscriptions, signs, tags, or labels purporting to have been affixed in the course of business and indicating **ownership, control,** or **origin**"; see FRE 902(7).

      Example: In a personal injury action against Green Giant Co., P seeks to introduce a can of peas bearing the label "Green Giant Brand . . . Distributed by Green Giant Company. . . ." At common law, P was unable to get the label into evidence because it was not self-authenticating, and there was no independent proof that Green Giant Co. really "wrote" the label and, therefore, distributed the peas. *Keegan v. Green Giant Co.*, 110 A.2d 599 (Me. 1954). But under the Federal Rules, the label (and consequently the can to which it was attached) would be admissible as a label "purporting to have been affixed in the course of business and indicating ownership, control, or origin" as provided in FRE 902(7).

3. **Attack on genuineness:** The fact that a document is "self-authenticating" does *not* mean that it is irrebuttably presumed to be genuine. Self-authentication merely means that the proponent does not have to produce extrinsic evidence of authenticity. The opponent is always free to come forward with evidence showing that the document is not genuine (e.g., that a document purporting to be executed by X, and certified by a notary to have been executed by X, really was not signed by X). M, pp. 701-02. Where this happens, the evidence will be received, but the trier of fact will be free to conclude that the document is not genuine and should therefore be disregarded. L&S, p. 995.

E. **Ways of avoiding authentication:** The process of authentication often wastes a lot of time, given how seldom a document is other than what it purports to be. Therefore, modern courts have developed several other ways in which the proponent of evidence may avoid the need to authenticate it. Two are worth noting here:

1. **Request for admission:** In the federal courts, and in many states, a party may serve upon his opponent a written *request for admission* of the genuineness of any relevant document described in the request. See Fed. R. Civ. Proc. 36; M, p. 699. For instance, in a contract dispute P might submit a copy of the alleged contract to D, and request that D admit the document's authenticity. If D unreasonably refuses to make the admission, a statute usually makes him liable for P's expenses in proving authenticity.

2. **Stipulation:** Similarly, the parties may jointly *stipulate* to the genuineness of a particular document, object, or fact. This is especially likely to occur during a *pretrial conference* run by the judge. M, p. 699. See Fed. R. Civ. Proc. 16.

III. OTHER FOUNDATION REQUIREMENTS AND OBJECTIONS

A. **Introduction:** A party who has authenticated an object or document has merely passed the first hurdle to getting it into evidence. Depending on the nature of the item, he must then overcome one or more additional hurdles: (1) in the case of "real" evidence, he may have to prove the "chain of custody"; (2) in the case of "demonstrative" evidence, he must show that the evidence is useful and fairly representative of the fact or thing it purports to illustrate; and (3) in either case, he must avoid a finding that the evidence is unduly prejudicial. We consider each of these obstacles in turn.

B. **Mere relevance not enough:** Recall that in our discussion of authentication, we said that the authentication requirement is really an aspect of relevance — if the gun, bedspread, etc. offered in evidence is not really the very one used in the underlying event, it is probably not relevant to the action. Yet the stringency of requirements for the admission of real evidence goes beyond what would be required if mere relevance were all that had to be shown.

> **Example:** Suppose that, in a drug prosecution of A, W, the police chemist, is shown a sample of white powder, and testifies, "I tested this substance and found it to be cocaine; because of a lack of labeling, I know that the substance was taken from either A or B, but I'm not sure which." If admissibility turned solely upon logical relevance, the court would admit the sample, since the sample and the supporting testimony by W make it more likely (a 50% chance) that A really possessed cocaine, than would be the case in the absence of this evidence. Yet no judge would admit the sample, because of the prosecution's utter failure to trace the sample directly to A. See L&S, p. 997.

1. **Chain of custody:** Therefore, a requirement has evolved that calls for the *"special handling"* of real evidence, a requirement motivated more by a concern for fairness and prevention of official misconduct than by mere concerns of logical relevance: the requirement that a *"chain of custody"* be proved where the item is *not uniquely identifiable.*

   a. **Criminal cases:** Proof of a chain of custody is *always* required in criminal cases if the object is not uniquely identifiable. The chain is only occasionally required in civil cases. L&S, p. 998. The difference is probably that when the police or prosecution come into possession of an item of evidence, they are likely to *know* that the item will need to be admitted, and are institutionally capable of documenting the chain as it develops; a private person, by contrast, will often not know that the object will ever be needed as evidence, and would be substantially more burdened by having to account for each change in the custody of the item. L&S, p. 998.

   b. **Links:** Proving the chain of custody usually requires that *each person* who had custody of the item after it came into police or prosecution hands must testify as to three things: (1) how and when he came into possession; (2) how he stored the object while he had possession (and who else had access to it during that time); and (3) how he disposed of it and to whom and when.

   c. **Break:** A "break" in the chain of custody is not necessarily fatal. For instance, the fact that others may have had the opportunity for brief access to the object will almost never lead it to be excluded — thus, the fact that the gun allegedly used in the murder lay on police officer W's desk for ten minutes while he was out of the room (during which time someone could have switched weapons) will virtually never lead the court to exclude the item. Generally, the court will only require "reasonable care and a reasonable showing that there was no realistic opportunity for tampering. . . ." L&S, p. 999.

2. **Condition unchanged:** Similarly, if the object's *condition* is important, the proponent will have to show that that condition has not substantially *changed* between the time the object was acquired and some later time (e.g., the time it was tested or the time it is being introduced into evidence). Here, the problem tends to be strictly one of relevance — if the change makes the object no longer relevant for the purposes for which the proponent offers it, it will be excluded.

Example: P slips and falls on the floor of a building owned by D. P claims that the fall was due to the fact that D negligently placed a heavy accumulation of wax on the floor. At the jury's request, the judge lets it examine a sample of the floor wax used, so the jury can see how thick or thin the wax was (apparently on the theory that if the wax is thin, excess build-up is less likely).

Held (on appeal), admission of the wax was reversible error, since the wax should have been admitted only upon a showing that there had been no substantial change in its thickness during the four and one-half years between when it was obtained by D and when it was shown to the jury. *Anderson v. Berg*, 451 P.2d 248 (Kan. 1969).

   a. Change irrelevant: Conversely, sometimes even a substantial change in condition will be irrelevant to the point for which the object is offered. In that event, the change will not bar admission. For instance, if D in *Anderson* had offered the wax bottle not for purposes of showing fitness but rather to show that it was a commercial product available in any store, then the age and thickness of the wax would have been irrelevant.

C. Demonstrative evidence: There are no "special handling" requirements for ***demonstrative*** evidence. For instance, the proponent of a map or model will almost never be required to prove its chain of custody, because it is irrelevant who has had possession of the document since its creation. Instead, other issues commonly arise concerning the admissibility of demonstrative evidence:

   1. "Essential" vs. merely useful: Opponents of an item of demonstrative evidence sometimes argue that it should not be admitted because it is not ***"essential"*** to the case. However, there is no requirement that evidence created for illustrative purposes be essential. L&S, p. 1000. All that is required is that the evidence be ***useful*** to the jury in understanding testimony or real evidence in the case. *Id.* If the illustrative material meets this requirement, it will almost always be admitted unless there is some countervailing consideration. *Id.*

   2. Not a fair representation: The most telling objection to evidence prepared for illustrative purposes is that the item does ***not fairly represent*** what it is supposed to illustrate. The trial judge generally has a great deal of discretion (which will rarely be reversed on appeal) in determining whether the illustration is indeed a sufficiently fair representation that it should be admitted. M, pp. 668-69.

     Example: D, prosecuted for the murder of V, claims that V pulled a knife on him and that the killing was in self-defense. The original switchblade is never recovered, but the prosecution concedes that one was used. The prosecution procures, as a model, a different type of switchblade that is two-thirds the size of the type believed used by V, but of similar shape and material. If this illustrative knife is offered into evidence, the trial judge may well conclude that its differing scale makes it so likely to mislead the jury that it should be excluded.

D. Undue prejudice: Whether the evidence is real or demonstrative, it may, like any other evidence, be excluded on the grounds that it is likely to lead to **unfair prejudice** to the other side.

   1. **Gruesome photos:** For instance, in a murder case, the defendant may object to admission of photos of the victim's body, on the grounds that this will unfairly inflame the jury against the defendant. Most such objections are unsuccessful, since the photo often shows the nature of the victim's injuries, something relevant to the case. But the court will generally weigh the probative value against the prejudicial effect, and if the latter is substantially greater than the former, the court may exclude certain photos. For instance, the court might exclude life-sized blowups in favor of smaller prints, or might exclude a photo taken after an autopsy (showing mutilation from the autopsy), requiring a pre-autopsy photo instead.

   2. **"Day in the life" films:** Plaintiffs in personal injury actions often try to introduce so-called **"day in the life" films**, i.e., short films depicting the plaintiff's daily life since the accident, and demonstrating the impact that the injury has had on the plaintiff. Such films are generally admissible. See, e.g., *Bannister v. Town of Noble, OK*, 812 F.2d 1265 (10th Cir. 1987) (film properly admitted). However, the court may exclude a particular film as being unduly prejudicial to the defendant. More commonly, the court will screen the film in chambers before it is shown to the jury, and will order sequences evoking undue sympathy to be edited out. See, e.g., *Grimes v. Employers' Mutual Liability Ins. Co.*, 73 F.R.D. 607 (D.Alas. 1977) (Film of P's life post-accident, including segments of P performing a standard test to show hand function, generally admissible; however, scenes of P hugging his daughter and putting a cigarette in the mouth of his quadriplegic brother "serve little purpose other than to create sympathy" for P, and must be excised before film is shown to the jury).

   3. **Bodily demonstration:** An injured plaintiff in a personal injury action may seek to **demonstrate his injuries** before the jury (e.g., by displaying his prosthetic device). Although this is likely to cause some prejudice to the defendant, the mere illustration of the injury or prosthesis will generally be allowed. If the plaintiff attempts to **perform** some activity, however, the court is more likely to bar the demonstration on the grounds that it will be prejudicial (and perhaps misleading as well). For instance, suppose that P claims that he is unable to bend his injured arm more than 90 degrees; a demonstration in which P's doctor tries to manipulate the arm into a greater bend, likely to be accompanied by a grimace of pain or scream by P, may be excluded by the judge on the grounds of undue prejudice. M, pp. 676-77.

IV. THE "BEST EVIDENCE" RULE FOR RECORDED COMMUNICATIONS

   A. Best Evidence rule generally: The Best Evidence rule might be better called the Original Document rule. The rule is this: ***"In proving the terms of a writing, where the terms are material, the original writing must be produced unless it is shown to be unavailable for some reason other than the serious fault of the proponent."*** M, p. 704.

Example: P claims that D has defrauded her by selling her, as new, a car that has really been driven over 7,000 miles. W (P's husband) testifies that shortly after the car was delivered, he discovered a sticker on the inside of the car door, showing the current mileage as 7,244.

Held (on appeal), W's testimony about what the sticker said should not have been admitted, because the Best Evidence rule required that the contents of a writing (the sticker) must be proved by introducing the writing itself, not by oral testimony about what the writing said, unless it was shown that the original sticker could not be produced in evidence. Here, P made no showing that the sticker could not be detached and brought into the court. *Davenport v. Ourisman-Mandell Chevrolet, Inc.*, 195 A.2d 743 (D.C.Ct.App. 1963).

1. **Requirements:** Taking the Best Evidence rule apart, we see that it has three main components:

   a. **Original document:** The ***original document*** must be produced, rather than using a copy or oral testimony about the document;

   b. **Prove terms of writing:** The rule applies only where what is to be proved is the ***terms*** of a ***writing*** (or under the modern approach, an equivalent recorded communication such as an audio tape of a conversation); and

   c. **Excuse:** The rule does not apply if the original is ***unavailable*** because it has been destroyed, is in the possession of a third party, or cannot be conveniently obtained, and the unavailability is not due to the serious fault of the proponent.

2. **Only writings and equivalents:** Probably the most important thing to remember about the Best Evidence rule is that it applies ***only to writings*** (and, today, equivalent recorded communications). It does ***not apply to evidence generally***.

   Example: Suppose that D, a karate expert, is charged with killing V by a direct blow to the neck. The prosecution asks the pathologist who did the autopsy to illustrate on a plastic skeleton where the injury occurred. If D objects to use of the skeleton on the theory that it is not the "Best Evidence" (which would be the actual bones of V), this objection will *not* be sustained, because the Best Evidence rule only applies where what is being proved is the contents of a writing or other recorded communication.

3. **Rationale for rule:** The purpose of the Best Evidence rule is to make sure that the ***exact terms*** of the writing are brought before the trier of fact. If the original is not used for proving the terms, there are several reasons to fear that the trier of fact may be misled about what the writing says: (1) ***distortion*** may inadvertently occur when a copy (especially a handwritten copy) of the writing is produced, or an oral account of its contents is given; (2) ***fraud*** is easier where the original need not be produced; and (3) if the original need not be produced, the proponent has a better opportunity to mislead by taking a small portion of a larger document out of context. L&S, p. 1007.

4. **Federal Rules:** The Federal Rules in general carry forward the Best Evidence rule, in some ways broadening it and in other ways narrowing it:

   a. **Statement of Rule:** The federal version of the Best Evidence rule is stated in FRE 1002: "To prove the content of a writing, recording, or photograph, the original writing, recording, or photograph is required, except as otherwise provided in these rules or by Act of Congress."

   b. **Broadened to include other recordations:** In one sense, the Federal Rules broaden the class of items covered by the Best Evidence rule. Some common-law courts included only conventional writings within the rule. But the Federal Rules cover any "writing, *recording*, or *photograph*" whose contents are sought to be proved. "Writings" and "recordings" are in turn defined in FRE 1001(1) as "letters, words, or numbers, or their equivalent, set down by handwriting, typewriting, printing, photostating, photographing, magnetic impulse, mechanical or electronic recording, or other form of data compilation."

      i. **Illustrations:** So under the Federal Rules, an *audio tape* of a conversation, or a *computer tape* of data, would be covered by the rule, and if available their contents could not be proved by, say, oral testimony. This aspect is discussed further *infra*, p. 378.

   c. **Duplicate:** But the Federal Rules also make it easier than it was at common law to satisfy the Best Evidence rule. Most notably, FRE 1003 provides that "a *duplicate* is admissible to the same extent as an original unless (1) a genuine question is raised as to the authenticity of the original or (2) in the circumstances it would be unfair to admit the duplicate in lieu of the original." "Duplicate" is defined in FRE 1001(4) as "a counterpart produced by the same impression as the original, or from the same matrix, or by means of photography, including enlargements and miniatures, or by mechanical or electronic re-recording, or by chemical reproduction, or by other equivalent technique which accurately reproduces the original."

      i. **Photocopies:** Most significantly, *photocopies* are included in the definition. Therefore, a party may offer a photocopy instead of the original without any showing that the original is unavailable, and it is up to the adversary to raise a "genuine question" as to the authenticity of the original or the unfairness of using the duplicate. In view of the reliability and mechanical nature of photocopying, the adversary will generally be unable to bear this burden, and the photocopy will be admitted. This aspect is discussed further *infra*, p. 384.

B. **What is a "writing" or other recorded communication:** It will not always be clear what constitutes a "writing" (or, under the modern approach, an equivalent recorded communication). Here are some of the special issues that arise:

   1. **Short inscription:** An object may have an *inscription* on it. For instance, a watch may be inscribed, "To Joe From Maryjane, With Love, December 12, 1982." Does this inscription turn the watch into a "writing," so that the "contents" of the inscription may only be proved by producing the watch itself? Courts have treated

the inscription issue on a case-by-case basis: the Best Evidence rule is more likely to be held applicable if the inscription is complicated, if its precise (rather approximate) content is important to the litigation, or if it is easily produced. M, p. 706.

2. **Photographic evidence:** Photographs, X-rays, and similar products of the photographic process are generally not offered to prove their contents, so the Best Evidence rule usually does not apply regardless of whether the item is deemed to be a "writing." But occasionally, a photograph, X-ray, movie, etc. is offered to prove its contents; in this situation, it is not clear whether the common-law approach would treat them as "writings." Probably the majority rule, and clearly the trend, is to broaden the meaning of "writing" to include such items within the rule.

> **Example:** P brings a personal injury action against D. To prove her damages, she calls as a witness W, a radiologist, who has taken X-rays of P's spine and studied them. W does not bring the X-rays with him, and seeks to testify about their content.
>
> *Held*, the X-rays are, for purposes of the Best Evidence rule, a "document," i.e., a "physical embodiment of information or ideas." Therefore, P may not prove the contents of the X-rays by having W testify about them; instead, the X-rays themselves must be introduced in evidence if available. *Sirico v. Cotto*, 324 N.Y.S.2d 483 (Civ. Ct. N.Y. City 1971).

a. **Federal Rules:** The Federal Rules explicitly expand the Best Evidence Rule to include all "photographs" whose contents are to be proved. FRE 1002. "Photographs" is defined in FRE 1001(2) to include "still photographs, X-ray films, video tapes, and motion pictures." (But remember that most times when such materials are introduced, it will not be for the purpose of "proving the contents" of the item. See *infra*, p. 380.)

3. **Sound recordings:** When a ***sound recording*** is introduced for the purpose of proving the recording's contents, the Rule applies even according to most common-law courts. Again, however, remember that this occurs only when the recording is offered for the purpose of proving its contents.

> **Example:** D is charged with kidnapping. The prosecution offers testimony by W, a policeman, that the voice on a ransom tape delivered to the victim's parents resembles the voice of D. Since by this testimony W is trying to prove the contents of the tape, the court will probably hold that the prosecution must produce and introduce into evidence the tape itself if it is available. (But if W had personally received a telephone demand for ransom, he could testify to the contents of the call, without producing a tape he made of the call contemporaneously; in this situation, the tape would be incidental, and he would be proving the contents of the call, not of the tape.) See M, p. 706, n. 8.

C. **What constitutes "proving the terms":** As noted frequently above, the Best Evidence rule applies only where what is sought to be proved are the ***"terms"*** or ***"contents"*** of the writing or other communication.

1. **Existence, execution, etc.:** This limitation means that if all that is proved is that a writing ***exists***, was ***executed***, or was ***delivered***, the Best Evidence rule does not

apply.

> **Example:** Prosecution of D for kidnapping. A prosecution witness, W, mentions that a ransom note was received, but does not testify as to the note's contents. This proof that the ransom note was delivered does not constitute proof of its terms, so that note need not be introduced in evidence. (But if W goes on to testify to the details of what the note said, the note would have to be produced.)

2. **Incidental record:** Frequently an event occurs which is *memorialized* or evidenced by a writing. In general, the fact that there happens to be a writing memorializing a transaction does *not* mean that the transaction can only be proved by introduction of the writing. In this situation, the writing is treated as an *incidental by-product* of the transaction. For instance, the earnings of a business may be proved without putting the books and records into evidence; similarly, the fact that a payment was made may be proved without producing a receipt, and the fact of marriage may be proved without producing the marriage certificate. M, pp. 707-08.

> **Example:** In a wrongful death action, P (the estate of the decedent) wants to prove the decedent's earnings. P puts on testimony by one of the other partners in a business in which P was a partner, concerning the earnings of the partnership and the decedent's share. D contends that the best evidence of these earnings is the partnership books and records, and that oral testimony as to the earnings must therefore be excluded.
>
> *Held,* P was not attempting to prove the contents of the books and records. Rather, P was attempting to prove the earnings of the partnership, and the books and records were merely incidental recordations of those earnings. Therefore, the partner's oral testimony should have been admitted. *Herzig v. Swift & Co.,* 146 F.2d 444 (2d Cir. 1945).

Note: But remember that if the proponent *does* try to prove the contents of a writing that happens to record a fact, the Best Evidence rule applies. For instance, W in *Herzig* would not have been permitted to testify, "The books and records of the partnership show that P's share for last year would have been $30,000," without producing the books and records themselves — in this situation, the terms of the writing *are* being proved.

a. **Transcript:** A person's prior *testimony* can generally be proved by an oral account of a witness who heard the testimony, *even if a transcript exists*. In this situation, courts generally reason that what is being proved is the prior oral testimony, and that the transcript is merely an incidental recordation whose contents are not being proved.

> **Example:** D is charged with perjuring himself in testimony before a congressional committee. The prosecution calls W, who was a lawyer for the committee, to testify about what D said under oath to the committee. D objects, arguing that the best evidence of what D said is contained in the available transcript, and that W must therefore not be permitted to give oral testimony

about what D previously said.

Held, the oral testimony is admissible. "Here there was no attempt to prove the contents of a writing; the issue was what [D] had said, not what the transcript contained." (But a dissent forcefully argued that the majority's approach "appl[ies] a meaningless formula and ignore[s] crystal-clear actualities. The transcript is, as a matter of simple indisputable fact, the best evidence. The principle and not the rule of law ought to be applied.") *Meyers v. U.S.*, 171 F.2d 800 (D.C.Cir. 1948).

i. Confessions: But where a criminal defendant has made a *confession* that has been both heard by a person and reduced to a written transcript, many if not most courts would rule that the transcript, not the testimony of the person who heard the confession, must be introduced. M, p. 709. There is no logical reason for treating this confession situation differently from general testimony of the sort involved in *Meyers, supra*; probably the difference stems from courts' strong desire to protect against false or misleading evidence of confessions.

b. Photos and other non-testimonial items: Suppose that a *photograph*, x-ray, audio recording, video tape, etc., has been made of an object or event. Is live testimony about the object or event allowed in lieu of introducing the photograph, etc.? In general, the answer is *"yes,"* since the photograph or other recordation is merely an *incidental* record, and its "contents" are therefore not really being proved.

Example: Suppose Lee Harvey Oswald had been brought to trial on a charge of assassinating President Kennedy. The famous Zapruder film shows the President during the moments when the bullets were hitting him. Assume the prosecution offers the testimony of W, who was watching the President at the moment the bullets hit, about the President's movements at that moment. The prosecution would be permitted to use this oral evidence from W, and would not be required to introduce the film instead. The prosecution is not trying to prove that the film had certain contents; instead, the film is an incidental recording of an actual event, and it is the actual event that is being proved. Thus the fact that the film may in some sense be the "best evidence" of the President's motions at the moment of impact would be irrelevant, and the Best Evidence rule would not apply.

i. Proof of contents of photograph: But contrast this with other situations in which the contents of the photograph, x-ray, etc., really *are* being proved. For instance, suppose a prosecution is brought for distributing or showing an *obscene* still photo or movie, or for selling a photograph that *infringes a copyright*. In this situation, the contents of the photo or film really *are* what is being proved, and therefore the photo or film must be introduced rather than be described by oral testimony. See, e.g., *People v. Enskat*, 98 Cal.Rptr. 646 (Cal. 1971) (prosecution for showing obscene film; prosecution may not present oral testimony about the contents of the film, but must instead introduce the film itself into evidence and show it — "Just as it is better for the trier of fact to read a document than have it described, it is better for the trier of fact to see a movie than have it described.")

   3. **Contract, deed, or other key document:** There are some transactions in which the role played by a document is so key that the document really *embodies* the transaction. In this case, the Best Evidence rule requires introduction of the document rather than mere testimony about it. For instance, if P brings a *contract* action against D, all courts hold that the written contract must be introduced, and that its contents cannot be proved by oral testimony, other documents referring to it, etc. One might argue that the contract is just the incidental written record of the intangible agreement between the parties, and that the written document should not be required any more than the books and records of account in *Herzig*, *supra*, p. 379. But courts have rarely if ever accepted this argument. Thus not only contracts, but also *deeds and judgments,* are always required to be produced. M, p. 707.

D. Collateral writings: During testimony, a witness may refer to some writings which have only the most tangential connection to the litigation. Even though the contents of the writing are in some sense being "proved," courts do not require production of the original, on the theory that it is not worth the time and effort that this will take. This willingness to dispense with the Best Evidence rule if the document is of only tangential importance is known as the *"collateral writings"* exception.

> **Example:** W, who witnesses the arrest of his neighbor, D, testifies that he knows the arrest took place on the day after the killing of V. He tells the court that he knows this because he witnessed the arrest on the same day he read about the killing in the newspaper, and the newspaper article referred to the crime as having taken place "yesterday." Here, W is proving the contents of a writing (the article). Yet the writing is so tangentially related to the case that nearly all courts would dispense with the requirement that the article itself be produced, and would allow oral testimony about its contents under the "collateral writings" exception. See M, p. 709.

   1. **Factors:** Trial judges are given a great deal of discretion in determining what writings are sufficiently collateral as to fall within the exception. Factors that the court takes into account include: (1) the *"centrality* of the writing to the principal issues of the litigation"; (2) the *complexity* of the relevant features of the writing; and (3) the "existence of genuine *dispute*" about the writing's contents. M, p. 710.

   2. **Federal Rule:** The "collateral writings" exception is codified in FRE 1004(4). That provision, captioned "Collateral Matters," dispenses with the need for the original writing if "the writing, recording, or photograph is not *closely related* to a *controlling issue*."

E. Which is the "original": Recall that the Best Evidence rule requires that the "writing itself" be produced. That is, an *"original,"* rather than a "copy," must be produced. In some instances there will be two versions of a document — one created first, and the other some kind of reproduction of it — and it will not be so clear which is the "original."

1. **Not necessarily earliest:** It is *not* the case that the earlier-created document is always the "original." The court must look at what is really being proved, and may conclude that it is the contents of the *second* writing that are being proved, so that the second writing is the one that must be produced. In that case, the fact that the later-created document happens to be a copy of an earlier one is irrelevant, and the earlier one need not be produced.

   Example: Document 1 is a handwritten letter written by D, addressed to Y, that libels P. D hands this manuscript to his secretary, who types it up as Document 2, and sends it to Y. If P sues D for libel, P will have to produce the original of Document 2, since by the substantive law of libel, it is the receipt of the libelous document by the addressee that completes that act of libel. D will not be permitted to bar introduction of Document 2 by the argument that it is a copy of Document 1, and that Document 1 thus must be produced — the fact that Document 2 happens to be a transcript of an earlier document is irrelevant, since it is Document 2 which has the legal consequences and whose contents are therefore being proved. M, p. 711.

2. **Duplicate originals:** In some situations there may be *"duplicate originals."* For instance, there may be multiple copies of a contract, each executed by all parties. Or, there may be multiple copies of a contract, each executed by one party, with a statement in the contract providing that "so long as each party has signed at least one copy of this contract, any copy signed by any party shall be deemed an original executed copy." In this situation, any of these originals will meet the requirement of the Best Evidence rule (but secondary evidence, such as testimony about what the contract said, would not be admissible unless *all* of the duplicate originals were shown to be unavailable). M, pp. 711-12.

3. **Original destroyed:** If the court focuses carefully on which of two documents is the one whose contents are being proved, and that document turns out to be unavailable, the queer result may be that oral testimony is allowed in lieu of presentation of the other, closely related, document.

   Example: P (an oil company) sues D (the U.S.) to quiet title to some mineral rights in a particular property. D seeks to prove that its predecessor in title (the Federal Farm Mortgage Corp. or FFMC, a federal agency) always reserved a one-half mineral interest in any property it transferred, and that it must therefore have reserved such an interest before transferring to P's predecessor in interest. The original deed and all copies appear lost, except for a recorded version kept in the local land records office. D offers oral and written evidence that since this was the FFMC's practice, the original deed must have contained such a reservation. P argues that the Best Evidence rule requires that the recorded version from the local land records be introduced by certified copy (as provided in FRE 1005, providing for proof by certified copy of "the contents of an official record, or of a document authorized to be recorded or filed and actually recorded or filed . . . ") P argues that D's attempt to show the routine practice of the FFMC amounts to proving the contents of the deed by extrinsic evidence rather than by use of the available certified copy of the recorded version of the deed.

Held, for D. What D is trying to prove is the contents of the original deed, not the contents of the recorded copy. D's claim is that the original deed had a reservation of mineral interests that was not correctly transcribed onto the recorded copy. Since the original deed is not available, any probative evidence of what it contained (including evidence that it was the FFMC's routine practice to reserve mineral interests) may be admitted, notwithstanding the existence of a recorded copy of the original. (For instance, oral testimony, and documents from the working files of the FFMC's sister agency, could be introduced to show that it was the routine practice of the FFMC to reserve such an interest during the time in question.) *Amoco Production Co. v. U.S.,* 619 F.2d 1383 (10th Cir. 1980).

Note: *Amoco Production* also illustrates the federal rule (adopted in some states as well) that there are "no preferences among items of secondary evidence." That is, once it became clear that the original deed, whose contents were being proved, was not available, the proponent was not required to use the "next best" secondary evidence, i.e., the recorded deed; he could use *any* kind of probative evidence of what the original contained, including oral testimony and evidence of general agency practice. The "preferences among secondary evidence" issue is discussed further *infra,* p. 388.

F. **Reproductions:** Today, there exist many techniques for making a very accurate copy of an original document, most notably the photocopier. However, when the Best Evidence rule developed at common law, copying was done by hand, and was notoriously inaccurate. Therefore, the rules on whether and when a "copy" may be used in lieu of the original have changed in recent times.

   1. **Common law:** At common law, the general principle was that ***no subsequently-created copy was the equivalent of the original,*** and that only the original could be used, if available. M, p. 712. Most notably, this meant that a ***hand-transcribed*** copy could not be admitted in lieu of the original.

      a. **Carbon paper:** When ***carbon paper*** was developed, courts perceived that carbon copies were more reliable than copies made by prior techniques, since the same hand or typed impression that made the original also made the carbon copy. Therefore, most courts accepted carbon copies as being "duplicate originals" (even if the parties never signed or otherwise legally executed the copies).

   2. **Photocopying and other modern techniques:** Today, of course, the main method of copying is by ***photocopying.*** The right to use a photocopy in lieu of the original varies from state to state:

      a. **Statutes:** Most states have a ***statute,*** modeled on the Uniform Photographic Copies of Business and Public Records as Evidence Act, by which regularly-kept photographic copies of business and public records are ***admissible,*** even if the original is available. Thus in such states, a party may introduce a photocopy without showing the unavailability of the original. L&S, p. 1009.

b. No statute: But in the minority of jurisdictions that do not have such a statute, courts generally hold that photocopies are *not* the equivalent of the original, even though carbon copies are. M, p. 713. This view seems to derive from the fact that the carbon is made as part of the same impression as the original, whereas the photocopy is made after the fact. (But this distinction is illogical, since "a person bent on creating a false copy can do so with carbon paper almost as easily as with a Xerox machine." L&S, p. 1009.)

3. Federal Rules: The Federal Rules make copies produced by *any reliable modern method* (including photocopying) "duplicates" that are *presumptively admissible.* This result is reached by the combination of FRE 1001(4) and 1003:

a. Special treatment for "duplicate": FRE 1003 makes "duplicates" admissible even if the original is available, under ordinary circumstances: "A duplicate is admissible to the same extent as an original unless (1) a *genuine question* is raised as to the authenticity of the original or (2) in the circumstances it would be *unfair* to admit the duplicate in lieu of the original."

b. "Duplicate" defined: FRE 1001(4) defines "duplicate" to include all copies made by highly accurate reproduction techniques: "A 'duplicate' is a counterpart produced by the same impression as the original, or from the same matrix, or by means of photography, including enlargements and miniatures, or by mechanical or electronic re-recording, or by chemical reproduction, or by other equivalent technique which accurately reproduces the original."

c. Rationale: The rationale behind this broad federal rule is that these modern reproduction methods are sufficiently accurate that the burden of proof should be placed upon the opponent to show inaccuracy, not upon the proponent to show accuracy.

d. Scope: Here are some kinds of copies that would be presumptively admissible "duplicates" under the Federal Rules: photocopies, mimeograph copies, carbon copies, images of a document scanned into a computer and then printed out on paper, copies of an original video or audio tape made by a re-recording, etc.

i. Handwritten or typed copies not covered: But copies produced *manually*, whether *typed* or *hand-written*, are *not* "duplicates" under the Federal Rules. FRE 1001(4), Advisory Committee's Note. These methods of reproduction are so prone to inadvertent error or fraud that the principles behind the Best Evidence rule dictate their exclusion if the original is available.

G. Excuses for non-production: Recall that the Best Evidence rule does not inflexibly bar the use of secondary evidence — it bars such evidence only if the original is available, or is unavailable due to the serious fault of the proponent. In other words, the basic rationale for the rule is that the best *obtainable* evidence must be used. M, pp. 714-15. Therefore, there are several kinds of "excuses" for non-production of the document that will allow the proponent to use an otherwise-inadmissible copy of the document or oral testimony about the document:

1. **Loss or destruction:** If the proponent can show that the original has been ***destroyed*** or ***lost***, he may use a copy.

   a. **Burden of proof:** Courts generally do not hold that the proponent must spend huge amounts of time and money searching for the original. He merely has to show that he has explored "all reasonable avenues of search . . . to the extent that reasonable diligence under the circumstances would dictate." M, p. 716.

   b. **Bad faith loss:** On the other hand, the proponent cannot intentionally destroy the original because he thinks a copy would be more favorable. If the document was lost or destroyed due to the ***bad faith*** of the proponent — sometimes referred to as the "serious fault of the proponent" (M, p. 704) — the proponent will not be allowed to use a copy, and will thus be stuck with no evidence at all.

   c. **Federal Rules:** The Federal Rules codify this "lost or destroyed" exception. FRE 1004(1) dispenses with the need for the original if "all originals are lost or have been destroyed, unless the proponent lost or destroyed them in bad faith."

      Example: P claims that the creators of the movie "The Empire Strikes Back" have infringed on P's copyright in certain science fiction creatures, called "Garthian Striders." P claims to have created the characters before 1980, the year in which the movie appeared. P seeks to introduce drawings made after 1980, which he says are "recreations" of the original characters. P claims there were pre-1980 drawings, but that he has not been able to find them. The defendants object, citing the Best Evidence Rule.

      Held, for the defendants. The drawings were "writings" within the meaning of FRE 1001(1), and are therefore subject to the Best Evidence Rule. Since (the trial judge found) P lost or destroyed the originals in bad faith, FRE 1004(1) renders the recreated drawings inadmissible. *Seiler v. Lucasfilm, Ltd.*, 797 F.2d 1504 (9th Cir. 1986).

2. **Inconvenience:** Some courts have recognized extreme ***inconvenience*** as an excuse for non-production of the original. For instance, "one does not have to uproot a tombstone to prove in court the inscriptions which it bears. . . ." W,M,A&B, p. 229 (noting that in this situation, a good lawyer will, for psychological reasons, use a photograph rather than mere oral testimony about what the tombstone says). The "inconvenience" rationale could also have been used in *Davenport, supra*, p. 376, to excuse the proponent's failure to pry off the automobile mileage sticker. Similarly, a showing that an original writing is in a foreign country, and cannot be obtained without major effort, might be sufficient to excuse a failure to produce the original. *Id.*

3. **Possession by third person:** If the original is ***in the possession of a third person***, and cannot be obtained by either informal or formal efforts (e.g., a subpoena duces tecum), this will excuse non-production. M, pp. 716-17. (Some but not all courts require merely a showing that the person holding the original is beyond the subpoena power of the court; others require an additional showing that informal efforts have either been tried and failed or are unlikely to work under the circumstances. *Id.*) FRE 1004(2) incorporates this exception: copies may be used if

"no original can be obtained by any available judicial process or procedure."

4. **Original in opponent's possession:** The proponent is excused from producing the original if he can show that: (1) the original is in the hands of his **adversary** or under the latter's control; and (2) the proponent has **notified him** to produce it at the trial, and the adversary has **failed** to do so. M, p. 718.

   a. **Significance of notice:** The notice referred to in (2) above does not have to be one that **compels** the adversary to supply the document (e.g., a subpoena duces tecum or a request to produce). Instead, the notice merely allows the proponent to force the adversary to **choose:** the adversary can supply the original, or he can waive his objection to use of a copy or oral testimony, but he must do one or the other. *Id.*

   b. **Federal Rules:** The Federal Rules embody this exception in FRE 1004(3), which excuses the failure to produce the original if "at a time when an original was under the control of the party against whom offered, that party was put on notice, by the pleadings or otherwise, that the contents would be a subject of proof at the hearing, and that party does not produce the original at the hearing."

5. **Public records:** **Public records** and **public documents** need not be produced in their original form, since the originals are generally required to be kept in a public depository (e.g., the originally-filed copy of a real estate deed must remain in the land records). Instead, a **certified copy** may be used. See, e.g., FRE 1005, allowing use of a certified copy to prove the contents of "an official record, or of a document authorized to be recorded or filed and actually recorded or filed, including data compilations in any form. . . ."

H. Summaries: If original writings are so **voluminous** that they cannot be conveniently be introduced into evidence and examined in court, most courts permit a **summary** to be introduced instead. M, p. 708. This summary must be sponsored by a witness (usually an expert) who has reviewed the underlying writings and the summary, and who can testify that the summary is an accurate reflection of the underlying documents; often, the witness is the person who prepared the summary.

> **Example:** D, a union official, is charged with 16 counts of misuse of union funds, as manifested by 21 overt acts. The government introduces 161 exhibits consisting of thousands of pages of documents, as well as the testimony of 8 co-conspirators who have previously pleaded guilty. The government then introduces a series of large charts, each of which summarizes a count or an overt act and lists some of the documentary proof already in evidence in support of that charge or act. The FBI agent who compiled the chart testifies that he is familiar with the underlying documents, and that the chart is a fair summary.
>
> *Held*, the chart is admissible. FRE 1006 allows use of a summary of "the contents of voluminous writings . . . which cannot conveniently be examined in court. . . ." The presence of 161 exhibits, covering 16 counts and 21 overt acts, qualified. *U.S. v. Scales*, 594 F.2d 558 (6th Cir. 1979).

1. **Underlying originals:** Before a summary may be used, courts generally require that the underlying documents be made available for examination by the opponent. Also, since the summary actually becomes *evidence* (in contrast to the "demonstrative" use of charts, see *infra*, p. 392, where the chart is non-evidence that merely helps the jury understand previously-admitted evidence), the proponent must at least in a general sense establish the *admissibility* of the *underlying evidence*. For instance, a summary of documents would not be admissible if the underlying documents were inadmissible hearsay. M, pp. 708-09.

2. **Federal Rules:** The Federal Rules allow liberal use of summaries. FRE 1006 provides that "the contents of voluminous writings, recordings, or photographs which cannot conveniently be examined in court may be presented in the form of a chart, summary, or calculation. The originals, or duplicates, shall be made available for examination or copying, or both, by other parties at reasonable time and place. The court may order that they be produced in court."

   a. **Recordings and photographs:** Observe that this rule allows summaries not only of writings, but also of *recordings* and *photographs*.

I. **Admission by adversary:** Sometimes a party makes an *admission* about the terms of a writing. All courts allow at least some such admissions to be used by the other party as evidence of what the writing says, in lieu of producing the original. M, p. 722.

   1. **Written admission or transcript:** If the admission is made in *writing*, or in sworn testimony (e.g., in a deposition or at a prior trial), nearly all courts will allow the opponent to prove the contents of the writing by use of the admission rather than by production of the original.

      Example: P sues D for negligence arising out of an automobile accident. In a deposition, D is asked, "Didn't you write to P saying you were sorry you went through a red light?" D responds, "Yes, I wrote the letter, but I now realize that I didn't go through a red light." At trial, virtually all courts would allow P to introduce this deposition testimony (rather than the letter itself) to prove that D wrote the letter and that it contained a statement by D that he went through the red light.

   2. **Oral admission:** Where a party made (or is claimed to have made) an *unsworn oral* admission about the contents of a writing, courts are split. Some allow a witness to testify at the trial that he heard the party make the oral admission; others reject such evidence, on the grounds that it is likely to be unreliable. M, p. 722.

   3. **Federal Rules:** The Federal Rules allow use of some but not all types of party admissions to prove the contents of a writing. FRE 1007 provides that "contents of writings, recordings, or photographs may be proved by the *testimony* or *deposition* of the party against whom offered or by that party's *written* admission, without accounting for the non-production of the original." Thus this rule does *not* allow proof of an unsworn *oral* admission by a party. "Since one of the strong policies underlying the Best Evidence rule is obtaining an accurate version of the contents of writings and the other items covered by the rule, if all oral admissions sufficed to prove the contents of writings, accuracy would be jeopardized." S&R, p. 1076.

    a. Not exclusive means: Even if FRE 1007 does not apply, there may be other opportunities to use oral evidence of a party's admission to prove the contents of a writing. For instance, suppose on the facts of the above example that D conceded having written the letter to P not in sworn deposition testimony, but in a casual conversation to a friend, W. If P can show that the letter has been lost or destroyed without his fault (thus meeting the terms of FRE 1004(1)), P may prove the contents of the letter by having W testify at trial as to what D told him. The difference is that this type of proof under Rule 1004 requires accounting for the original, whereas Rule 1007, if applicable, may be used *even if the original is perfectly available. Id.*

J. Preferences among secondary evidence: Recall that the purpose of the Best Evidence rule is to make sure that the best available evidence of a writing's contents is used. If the original is not available, so that some kind of secondary evidence (e.g., a copy or oral testimony) must be used, does the same rationale apply? That is, must the proponent use the *"next best evidence"* available? The courts are split.

    1. Minority ("English") rule: A *minority* of American courts have adopted the position taken by the English courts, that *"there are no degrees of substantive evidence."* M, p. 721. Under this view, if there exists a handwritten copy of a document, as well as a witness who remembers reading the original, the proponent may offer the oral testimony even though the handwritten copy would almost certainly be "better" evidence than the testimony.

        a. Rationale: This minority approach has the advantage of *simplicity:* courts do not get dragged into disputes about whether one type of secondary evidence is indeed better than another.

    2. Majority rule: Most American courts, by contrast, *do* recognize "degrees of substantive evidence." M, p. 721. These courts hold that when there is a choice between a written copy and oral testimony, the *written copy must be used*. This approach has the virtue of carrying forward the general rationale behind the Best Evidence rule, that of making sure that the best available evidence is used.

    3. Federal Rules: The Federal Rules adopt the *minority* approach. See Advisory Committee's Note to FRE 1004, which states: "The rule recognizes no 'degrees' of secondary evidence. While strict logic might call for extending the principle of preference beyond simply preferring the original, the formulation of a hierarchy of preferences and a procedure for making it effective is believed to involve unwarranted complexities." The Note also observes that even without a formal requirement, the "next best available" evidence will generally be produced because of a party's normal motivation to "present the most convincing evidence possible and the arguments and procedures available to his opponent if he does not."

K. Judge-jury allocation: There are many factual issues that may need to be determined in order to apply the Best Evidence rule. Most are to be decided by the judge as "preliminary questions of fact" (see *infra,* p. 454). But some are so central to the major issues in the case that they must be decided by the *jury.*

1. **Federal Rules:** The Federal Rules explicitly allocate the division of responsibility between judge and jury for Best Evidence rule issues. Most states would probably follow roughly the same allocation. FRE 1008 provides:

   "When the admissibility of other evidence of contents of writings, recordings, or photographs under these rules depends upon the fulfillment of a condition of fact, the question whether the condition has been fulfilled is ordinarily for the court to determine in accordance with the provisions of Rule 104. However, when an issue is raised (a) whether the asserted writing ever existed, or (b) whether another writing, recording, or photograph produced at the trial is the original, or (c) whether other evidence of contents correctly reflects the contents, the issue is for the trier of fact to determine as in the case of other issues of fact."

   a. **Decided by judge:** Thus a variety of preliminary questions in applying the Best Evidence rule are to be decided by the judge, not the jury. For instance, it is the judge who must decide such matters as: (1) whether a particular item of evidence is an "original"; (2) whether a particular item is a "duplicate" under FRE 1001, and therefore presumptively admissible under FRE 1003; (3) whether the original has been lost or destroyed (and if so, whether this occurred due to the proponent's bad faith), as provided in FRE 1004(1); and (4) whether the evidence relates to a "collateral matter" (in which case the Rule does not apply) or rather to a controlling issue (see FRE 1004(4)). See S&R, p. 1078.

V. SPECIAL TYPES OF REAL AND DEMONSTRATIVE EVIDENCE

A. **Pictorial evidence (photographs, x-rays, and movies):** Pictorial evidence — including still photographs, x-rays, movies, and video tapes — presents some special issues.

   1. **Authentication of pictures:** Most importantly, how does one *authenticate* such pictorial evidence? All courts recognize one method; most also now recognize a second.

      a. **"Illustrative of what witness saw" method:** Traditionally, most photographic evidence is admitted on the theory that it is merely a "graphic portrayal of oral testimony." M, p. 671. That is, a witness testifies to facts, and then says that the photograph, movie, etc., accurately reflects what the witness saw. If X and W see P stab D, and X happens to make a movie of the stabbing, the movie could be authenticated by W's testimony: "I saw P stab D, and this movie accurately reflects the stabbing as I saw it."

         i. **Not necessarily by taker:** Observe that this method of authentication does *not* require that the sponsoring testimony be by the person who *took* the photograph or movie, or even that the sponsoring witness know anything whatsoever about the conditions under which the photograph was taken. Thus in the above stabbing hypothetical, W could authenticate the movie as being an accurate portrayal of what he witnessed even if W was not aware that X was shooting the movie, has no idea who X is, has no idea the type of camera used, etc.

ii. Relevant evidence excluded: Old cases often took, and some courts still take, the position that this is the *only* type of authentication allowed for a photograph or movie. Under this view, if there is no witness who testifies to having personally observed the scene or event shown in the photo, the photo cannot be admitted no matter how much testimony there is that the photograph was taken by a reliable method.

Example: D, a tavern operator, is charged with murdering V at the tavern. The prosecution offers several photographs taken by W; W testifies that the photos were taken within an hour after the shooting of V, and that they accurately portray the objects intended to be photographed. One photo appears to be of D standing at the bar, the other seems to be of V lying on the floor. No one testifies about what the pictures show.

Held, the photos should not have been admitted. "Photographs are generally inadmissible as original or substantive evidence. They must be sponsored by a witness or witnesses whose testimony they serve to explain and illustrate." Since no witness testified as to what these photos portrayed, they were inadmissible. *Knihal v. State*, 36 N.W.2d 109 (Neb. 1949).

b. "Silent witness" method: But most modern decisions recognize a **second method** of authenticating a photograph, movie, etc. Under this method, the photo is verified not by the testimony of any witness who has actually witnessed the scene or event portrayed, but rather from testimony about the **reliability of the process** by which the photo was produced. M, p. 672. This is sometimes called the **"silent witness"** theory of admission, because once the process is shown to be reliable, the picture or movie "speaks for itself" as to its contents.

i. X-rays: This is generally the basis on which **x-rays** are introduced, for instance. After all, an x-ray can never be authenticated by the testimony of a human being that he has witnessed the scene shown in the x-ray, and knows the x-ray to be an accurate depiction of that scene. Instead, the x-ray is authenticated by the following kind of testimony: "I, a radiologist, took this x-ray, by commonly used techniques of proven scientific validity, and I therefore believe that it accurately represents the bones of the patient's hand."

ii. Automatic devices: This method is similarly used to authenticate photos taken by **automatic** devices. For instance, banks have automatic cameras which record each teller transaction. A photograph taken by such a camera could be introduced even without a witness to testify that he personally observed the transaction and that the photograph is a true representation; instead, testimony about how the automatic camera system works, and testimony showing that the particular photo was taken at the appropriate time or in connection with the appropriate transaction, would suffice. See, e.g., *State v. Tatum*, 360 P.2d 754 (Wash. 1961) (dual photograph of person cashing check and the check itself, taken by "Regiscope" machine, admissible based on testimony about how machine worked and how store used it in every transaction).

    iii. Foundation requirement: When a photograph or movie taken by an automatic device is introduced, with no testimony by one who witnessed the scene or event, courts impose a fairly heavy *foundation* requirement: the proponent must show in some detail how the machine works, how it was employed in the particular application, and, perhaps, that there was no editing or tampering. L&S, p. 1026.

2. Movies: *Motion pictures* are now generally treated like photographs. That is, if a foundation is laid so that there is reason to believe that the motion picture accurately portrays what it purports to portray, the film will be admitted.

    a. Inflammatory: Keep in mind, however, that a movie is perhaps even more likely to be *unduly prejudicial* than a photograph. Therefore, the judge has discretion to exclude it if its prejudicial effect substantially outweighs its probative value. See, for instance, the discussion of "day in the life" films, *supra*, p. 375.

    a. Context: Also, the judge has discretion to prevent the showing of just a part of a film, if failure to show the entire film would be misleading. L&S, p. 1026.

B. Computer print-outs: *Computer print-outs* present two special problems, one of authentication and one as to the Best Evidence rule:

1. Authentication: When a computer print-out is offered as evidence of the facts contained in the print-out (typically financial or numerical facts), the print-out must be *authenticated*. Generally this is done by a witness who can testify as to the methods used to input the data into the computer and the methods used to produce a print-out of that data, as well as testimony showing why the result that appears on the print-out is an accurate reflection of the original transactions being recorded.

    a. Federal Rules: Under the Federal Rules, this kind of authentication would come under FRE 901(b)(9), which allows authentication by "evidence describing a process or system used to produce a result and showing that the process or system produces an accurate result."

2. Best Evidence rule: Where a computer print-out is offered to prove the facts recorded in the document, the opponent may raise a Best Evidence argument. First, he may contend that the record on the computer (e.g., the hard disk or magnetic tape) is the "best evidence," not the print-out. Alternatively, he may argue that the original paper records of the transaction, not the computer records, are the "original" and thus the best evidence (e.g., that to prove that a check was received from a customer, the original is the check itself, not the computer entry showing receipt of the check).

    a. Unsuccessful: In general, such objections will be *unsuccessful*. For instance, in federal courts the proponent may make use of FRE 1001(3), which provides that "if data are stored in a computer or similar device, any printout or other output readable by sight, shown to reflect the data accurately, is an 'original.'" This at least means that the printout, if shown to reflect the computer's data accurately, is an "original" of the computer-stored data, so that the magnetic tape or hard disk need not be used.

  i. Printout is duplicate: Where the claim is that the original pre-computer paper document is the "original," the proponent can make use of FRE 1001(4) to have the printout treated as a "duplicate," since it is at least arguably a "mechanical or electronic re-recording, or . . . other equivalent technique which accurately reproduces the original." The burden will then be upon the opponent to show that the computer record is not an accurate reproduction of the original paper record. See generally W&B, Par. 1001(4)[07].

C. Maps, models, diagrams, and summaries: Recall that "demonstrative" evidence, as we use the term here, consists of items that were not involved in the underlying event, but *illustrate* events or testimony. Common examples of such demonstrative evidence are *maps*, *models*, *diagrams*, and *summaries*.

  1. **Authentication:** These items must, of course, be authenticated. Here, authentication generally consists of showing that the map, model, etc., is an *accurate representation* of what it purports to portray. In the case of a model of an allegedly defective truck, for instance, the witness would testify that the model is an accurate portrayal (at a small scale) of the truck actually involved in the crash.

  2. **Generally admissible:** So long as the object is properly authenticated and would be helpful to the jury in understanding other evidence or testimony, the judge will generally admit it. Trial judges have a wide discretion to determine whether the value of such illustrative items is sufficient to justify their admission.

  3. **Charts and summaries:** Increasingly, lawyers try to help the jury understand previously-admitted evidence or testimony by the use of *charts* or *summaries.* (This use of charts and summaries to help the jury understand previously-admitted evidence is different from the use of such items to summarize writings that are too voluminous to be individually admitted; as to the latter, see *supra*, p. 386.) So long as the judge feels that the chart or summary will be helpful to the jury, and not be misleading, he will generally admit it. But again, trial judges have broad discretion about whether to admit such charts and summaries, and that discretion will rarely be reversed on appeal. See, e.g., *Crocker v. Lee*, 74 So.2d 429 (Ala. 1954) (not abuse of discretion to prohibit use of blackboard with diagram of accident to help witness illustrate his testimony, especially since use of a blackboard would make it hard for the appellate court on review to understand the witness' testimony).

  4. **Evidentiary status:** The evidentiary status of a map, model, chart, etc., is often unclear. Whenever possible, courts will treat such items as being *incorporated into the witness' testimony*, and thus part of the record on appeal. For instance, the court might ask the witness to draw a diagram on a large piece of paper attached to an easel, rather than on a blackboard, so that the drawing can be made part of the record on appeal. Otherwise, the appellate court may have trouble understanding the witness' testimony (as the court in *Crocker, supra*, apparently feared). M, pp. 669-70, including n. 8.

D. Views: Some events cannot be fully explained to the jury by testimony or by tangible evidence that can be brought into the courtroom. Where this is the case, the jury and/or judge may journey outside the courtroom to visit and observe a particular place. This excursion is called a *"view."*

> **Example:** D is accused of stabbing V in front of 523 Main Street. W, the sole eyewitness, testifies that she was just turning onto Main Street from First Avenue when she saw the stabbing and saw D's face; she says that D then turned and ran, and she never got any closer to him. The stabbing took place after dark, but W says that the street lights were bright enough for her to be able to see D's face.
>
> At the request of D's lawyer, the trial judge might allow the jury to take a view of the crime scene. In particular, he might let them stand after dark at the corner of First and Main, to see whether the face of a person standing at 523 Main could be visible and identifiable from First and Main under the street lights.

1. **Discretion of judge:** In nearly all courts, it is within the trial judge's *discretion* whether to allow the jury to take a view (or, in a bench trial, whether to take a view himself). Some of the factors that the judge is likely to consider in reaching his decision are: (1) How important to the case is the information which would be gained from the view? (2) Can the information be gained instead from maps, photographs, diagrams, or other in-court evidence? and (3) Has the place or object to be viewed *changed its appearance* materially since the event? M, p. 679.

2. **Presence of judge:** Must the judge be *present* at the view? The answer varies, depending mostly on whether the case is civil or criminal.

   a. **Civil:** In civil cases, the judge need normally *not* be present. Instead, "showers" are hired to chaperone the jurors to the site of the view. Counsel and the parties are usually allowed to attend, although the judge generally has discretion about this. M, p. 679.

   b. **Criminal cases:** In criminal cases, by contrast, many states have statutes *requiring* the judge to be present at the view. This way, the jury will not be exposed to inadmissible hearsay during the view, and will not be permitted to carry out unauthorized experiments that might be unfair to the defendant.

      i. **Unauthorized view:** In fact, if members of the jury take a view without the permission or presence of the trial judge in a criminal case, this will often be grounds for granting the defendant's motion for a new trial. See, e.g., *People v. Crimmins*, 258 N.E.2d 708 (N.Y. 1970) (notorious trial of Alice Crimmins for murder of her small daughter; W testified to having watched Crimmins and a man carry a small bundle thought to be the victim's corpse; three jurors took unauthorized view of place where W said this happened, to see whether it was "well lit" as W asserted. *Held*, visit without presence of judge violated statute and was *per se* prejudicial to D, so new trial ordered).

3. **Defendant's right to be present:** Statutes usually provide that the criminal defendant has the right to be *present* at the view. Furthermore, the defendant's

constitutional right of confrontation (see *supra*, p. 270) may well include the right to be present at a view (although this is less clear in states in which, as discussed *infra*, the view is deemed not to be evidence). M, p. 679.

4. **Evidentiary status of view:** Many (probably most) courts hold that a view is in itself **not evidence**, and is merely a way of helping the jury understand previously-admitted evidence. M, p. 680.

   a. **Rationale:** Courts following this "view is not evidence" approach generally do so on the theory that a contrary rule would deprive the appellate court of the ability to judge the **sufficiency** of the evidence. After all, the appellate court cannot know what the jury saw, and therefore cannot take what they saw into consideration in determining whether the evidence was sufficient to support the verdict. (This problem is similar to the problem of witness' demeanor — a witness' demeanor may have a major impact on the jury's opinion of his testimony, yet this demeanor is invisible to the reviewing court.)

      i. **Significance:** Courts holding the "view is not evidence" standard, therefore, take the position that if there is no evidence apart from the view in support of an essential element of a claim or defense, the claim or defense must fail.

   b. **Better view:** But a substantial minority of courts treat a view as having evidentiary status. These courts observe that the jurors are unlikely to make a mental distinction between admissible evidence and facts learned during a view, so that treating the view as being non-evidentiary for appellate review purposes would be at odds with how the jury really functions. This seem to be the more sensible approach. M, p. 680.

E. **Demonstrations and experiments:** *Demonstrations* and *experiments* will generally be admissible, if the trial judge concludes that their relevance outweighs any prejudice, waste of time, confusion, etc., that might result.

   1. **Demonstrations:** The most frequent kind of demonstration in the courtroom is that in which an injured plaintiff **displays** the **body part** that has been injured. Courts nearly always permit a simple display of the injury, on the theory that its relevance is greater than any prejudice that might result.

      a. **Actions or manipulations:** But if the injured plaintiff wants to go beyond a mere display of his injury, and wants to **perform actions** or undergo **manipulation** to show the practical impact of the injury, courts are more hesitant. See *supra*, p. 375.

      b. **Similarity of conditions:** Courts insist that the demonstration be relevant, in the sense that the matters demonstrated are **similar** to the matter in issue.

         Example: D is on trial for murdering his wife, W, by shooting her in the head with his revolver. D's defense is that W shot herself with the revolver. The prosecution puts on an expert witness who testifies that based on powder burns, the gun was 18 inches from W's head when it was fired. The prosecution then offers demonstrative evidence, by having a woman of slightly longer arm-length than W hold the revolver and point it toward her head. The muzzle of the gun is less than four inches from the witness's face when this is done. D objects to this demonstration as being irrelevant and prejudicial.

Held, the demonstration was properly admitted. The prosecution had the burden of demonstrating "substantial similarity of conditions." But this burden was carried here by the showing that the witness was a woman of approximately the same arm-length as W. *U.S. v. Wanoskia*, 800 F.2d 235 (10th Cir. 1986).

2. **Experiments:** A party will often want to make an *experiment* to determine whether an event is possible, or to determine the causes of a prior event. This experiment may take place either in court or out of court prior to trial.

   a. **In-court experiment:** Where a party proposes an in-court experiment, the trial judge has the same broad discretion as in determining whether to allow a demonstration. The court will pay special attention to whether there is a sufficient *similarity of conditions* between the original event and the test. M, p. 677. For instance, if P, who has been injured by a defective cigarette lighter, wants to use a copy of the same brand to show how a jet of flame can erupt, the trial judge will want to be sure that the lighter to be used in the experiment is indeed the same model, and has not been doctored.

   b. **Out-of-court experiment:** In-court experiments have two big drawbacks from the proponent's point of view: (1) It is often very hard to assure similarity of conditions if the experiment must take place in the courtroom; and (2) Since there is no way to be sure how the experiment will turn out, the proponent risks embarrassment and damage to his case if the experiment does not go as planned. Therefore, most experiments are carried out *before the trial*, out of court. The evidence issue that arises is: May the results of the out-of-court experiment be communicated to the jury?

      i. **Generally admissible:** Again, such experiments may be admissible as evidence "if their probative value is not substantially outweighed by the usual counterweights of prejudice, confusion of the issues, and time consumption." M, p. 601. As with in-court experiments, similarity of conditions is especially important.

   Example: P, while driving a car made by D (General Motors), has a terrible accident when the car leaves the highway and crashes into a tree. P's theory is that the car had a defective drive shaft, which exploded and forced the car off the highway. D seeks to introduce the results of a pre-trial experiment, in which a car with a comparably-defective drive shaft did not veer off the road.

   Held, the trial judge correctly used her discretion to exclude the test, because the conditions surrounding the experiment were not sufficiently similar to the circumstances of the accident. In GM's experiment, the drive shaft was taped, not bolted as in P's car and the test car was pushed, not driven, to its speed of 50 mph. A trial judge's determination about similarity of circumstances will not be upset unless it is clearly erroneous, which the judge's decision here was not. *Hall v. General Motors Corp.*, 647 F.2d 175 (D.C. 1980).

F. Exhibits in the jury room: When may the jury be given tangible exhibits to inspect *in the jury room*?

1. **Tangible evidence including writings:** In most states, the jury is ***allowed*** to take tangible exhibits (including writings) into the jury room, if the exhibit was admitted into evidence. Sometimes this is required by statute. If not required by statute, the trial judge usually has ***discretion*** about whether to allow it in a particular case. Lilly, p. 534.

2. **Substitute for testimony:** However, if the writing is in effect a ***substitute for testimony***, the jury will usually ***not*** be allowed to inspect it in the jury room. This is the case, for instance, if the exhibit is a ***deposition transcript*** or a report that was admitted under the past recollection recorded doctrine (*supra*, p. 189). In this situation, there is a danger that if this "written testimony" is allowed in the jury room, the jury will give it more attention than it deserves, and more attention than live testimony. *Id.*

    a. **Confession:** In criminal cases, a transcript of the defendant's ***confession*** is usually allowed in the jury room, even though the confession is testimonial. M, p. 681. Apparently, this exception is based on the theory that the confession is so central to the case that the risk of the jury's paying extra attention to it is worth running. *Id.*

OPINIONS, EXPERTS, AND SCIENTIFIC EVIDENCE

Introductory Note: This chapter discusses three related but distinct areas: (1) the requirement that ordinary witnesses have *first-hand knowledge* of the facts they testify to, and that they state "facts," not "opinions"; (2) the rules governing testimony by *expert* witnesses; and (3) the use of *scientific evidence*.

I. FIRST-HAND KNOWLEDGE AND LAY OPINIONS

A. Generally: Courts have a preference for the best available evidence on any given point. The hearsay rule and the Best Evidence rule are illustrations of this preference. Two other rules arising from the preference for the best available evidence are the rule requiring that a witness have first-hand knowledge of the facts about which he testifies, and the rule purporting to forbid ordinary witnesses from expressing their opinions.

B. First-hand knowledge required: An ordinary (non-expert) witness must limit his testimony to facts of which he has *first-hand knowledge.* That is, if the witness testifies about a fact that could have been perceived by the senses, the witness must have perceived it himself, not learned of it from someone else. M, p. 23.

> **Example:** W, a passenger in P's car, testifies that D drove through a red light. On cross-examination, W admits that he didn't actually see what color the light was when D drove through, and that he is relying on what P told him shortly after the two cars collided. Since W is not testifying from personal knowledge about the color of the light, his testimony on that subject will be stricken.

1. Distinguished from hearsay: An objection to testimony on the grounds that it is not based on the witness' personal knowledge can sometimes be confused with an objection based on *hearsay*. The distinction is this: if the witness' statement on its face makes it clear that the witness is merely repeating what someone else said, the objection is to hearsay; if the witness purports to be stating matters which he personally observed, but he is actually repeating statements by others, the objection is to lack of first-hand knowledge. M, p. 24. See *supra*, p. 143, for a more complete discussion of the distinction.

2. Experts: *Experts* are generally not limited to testifying about facts of which they have personal knowledge. For instance, an expert will often be asked to give an opinion based upon hypothetical facts listed by the questioner, in which case the expert may state what inference he would make, even though he has no first-hand knowledge of the facts used in the hypothetical. (See *infra*, p. 408.)

3. Federal Rules: The federal courts, like all state courts, prohibit lay witnesses from testifying on matters as to which they lack personal knowledge. FRE 602 provides:

"A witness may not testify to a matter unless evidence is introduced sufficient to support a finding that the witness has personal knowledge of the matter. Evidence to prove personal knowledge may, but need not, consist of the witness' own testimony. This rule is subject to the provisions of Rule 703, relating to opinion testimony by expert witnesses."

C. Lay opinions: It is often said that the witness must confine herself to reciting the "facts," and that she may not state her *"opinions"* or *"conclusions."* However, in contrast to the rule just described above requiring first-hand knowledge, the rule barring opinions has never really been strictly applied, and is today often largely abandoned.

1. **Traditional formulation:** Traditionally, the courts have stated the rule against opinion testimony as if it were a black-letter prohibition to be strictly enforced: the witness must confine himself to stating the "facts," and may not state his opinions, conclusions, or inferences relating to those facts.

   Example: W, a bystander, testifies that when D hit P (a pedestrian) with his car, D was driving "very carelessly." Many courts traditionally (and some today) would strike this testimony, on the grounds that W was giving his opinion about D's conduct, rather than confining himself to stating the "facts."

2. **Rationale:** The rationale behind the rule barring opinion testimony is that the process of *making inferences* from the underlying facts properly belongs to the *trier of fact*, not to the witness. Thus in our above example, W should confine himself to stating how fast D was driving, what side of the street he was on, whether he stopped for the traffic light, etc. It is the jury, not W, who should then infer from these basic facts whether D was indeed "careless."

   a. **Preference for specificity:** To put it another way, the rule barring opinions and conclusions is really a rule preferring the *most specific available evidence.* Again using our above example, if W testifies merely that D drove "carelessly," the jury is being deprived of the most specific possible information about D's conduct (e.g., whether he ran a stop light, how fast he was going, etc.) Since W has knowledge of these more specific aspects, he should limit his testimony to these specifics.

3. **Exception for "short-hand renditions":** Courts have always recognized an exception to the rule against opinions where the "opinion" is really a *"short-hand rendition."* That is, if the witness has perceived a number of small facts that cannot each be easily stated, he will be permitted to summarize the collective facts with a "short-hand" formulation. M, p. 28.

   Example: D is on trial for murder, and raises an insanity defense. W, his mother, testifies that he was "in such a terrible shape," and was "mentally and physically ill." The trial judge strikes these remarks as opinions.

   Held, W's statements should have been admitted. W was not capable of describing D's condition in facts more specific than this, and the jury understood what W meant. *State v. Garver*, 225 P.2d 771 (Ore. 1950).

   a. **Other examples:** Here are some other situations in which W will often be allowed to speak in a somewhat conclusory, short-hand manner: (1) The car "passed at high speed"; (2) X "looked like he was no more than thirty years old"; and (possibly) (3) "Z looked like he was drunk." In each of these situations, it is somewhat hard for W to articulate the precise underlying facts that have led him to the conclusion (though in the case of (3), W might have been able to say that Z wasn't able to walk straight, had slurred speech, smelled of liquor, etc.) Lilly, p. 108. In general, trial judges have a wide degree of ***discretion*** in determining when to allow in a witness' conclusion or opinion under the "short-hand rendition" exception.

4. **Criticism of general rule:** More generally, many courts and commentators have criticized the entire attempt to distinguish between opinions and facts and to allow only the latter. These critics argue that even what appears to be a statement of facts always contains some inference or conclusion. What is important, these critics say, is that the jury be given as many of the underlying facts as is feasible; the fact that the witness also includes his opinion or inference is rarely damaging.

5. **Modern view:** Reflecting these criticisms, modern courts are generally much more willing to allow witnesses to state their opinions than the traditional no-opinions rule would imply. Many, if not most, take the view that "opinions of laymen should be rejected only when they are superfluous in the sense that they will be of no value to the jury." M, p. 28.

6. **Federal Rules:** The Federal Rules embody this liberal modern view. FRE 701 provides that "if the witness is not testifying as an expert, his testimony in the form of opinions or inferences is limited to those opinions or inferences which are (a) ***rationally based*** on the perception of the witness and (b) ***helpful*** to a ***clear understanding*** of his testimony or the determination of a fact in issue."

   a. **Perception of witness:** Thus FRE 701(a) merely codifies the universal requirement (see *supra*, p. 397) that the witness have first-hand knowledge of the matter.

   b. **Helpful:** FRE 701(b) allows much more liberal introduction of a witness' opinions than the traditional common-law formulation does. Even if the witness' testimony is quite clearly an opinion, the judge should ***allow*** it in if it will be ***helpful to the jury*** in its fact-finding.

      Example: D is charged with bank robbery. The prosecution's principal evidence consists of surveillance photos taken by the bank's automatic cameras. D offers testimony by W, a corrections officer, that the person in the photos strongly resembles X, a suspect in two other robberies who is still at large. The trial judge excludes W's testimony on the grounds that it is merely W's opinion about whom the photos do or do not resemble.

      Held (on appeal), the trial judge should have admitted W's testimony. W's testimony would have been helpful to the jury in deciding whether the person in the photo was D, since the jury could not see X and therefore could not tell whether he looked more like the man in the photos than D did. Therefore, the evidence qualified under FRE 701. (Conversely, the testimony by W that the person in the photo did or did not resemble *D* would *not* have been admissible under FRE 701, since the jury could have reached this conclusion just as accurately by itself.) *U.S. v. Robinson*, 544 F.2d 110 (2d Cir. 1976).

7. **Specifics still preferable:** Under the modern and federal approach, as under the traditional common-law rule, ***specific testimony*** is still preferable. If the matter is an important one, and the judge feels that the witness could be more specific than he is being, he will often require the greater specificity. For instance, in a negligence action, if W testifies, "D was going very, very fast," the judge might well ask W to estimate more precisely the speed of the vehicle.

    a. **Cross-examination:** Furthermore, even if the witness' opinion or conclusory statement is allowed on direct testimony, the adversary always has the right, during ***cross-examination***, to ferret out the specifics. Thus if W is allowed to testify on direct that "D seemed intoxicated," D's lawyer can ask on cross questions like, "Did you smell liquor on his breath?," "Did he enunciate his words clearly?" etc.

8. **Expert opinions:** The rule against opinions, even in its straight common-law version, applies only to ***lay*** opinions, not to the opinions of experts. Indeed, the principal function of expert testimony is to draw inferences and state opinions from the facts. The nature of expert testimony is discussed extensively *infra*, p. 402.

D. **Opinion on "ultimate issue":** In any case, some issues are more important than others. Some are ***"ultimate issues,"*** in the sense that the trier's decision on these issues necessarily decides the outcome of the case. For instance, in a prosecution for speeding, the rate of speed of the vehicle is an "ultimate issue."

    1. **Rule barring opinions on ultimate issues:** Even those courts that generally allow witnesses to state their opinions may impose a rule barring "opinions on ultimate issues." Courts adhering to this view often apply it not only to lay testimony, but to expert testimony as well. This prohibition is justified on the theory that if a witness is permitted to express his opinion on an ultimate fact in issue, this "usurps the function of the jury." M, p. 30.

    2. **Modern view:** But most courts today have ***abandoned*** the rule barring opinion testimony on ultimate issues. *Id.*

      a. **Federal:** The federal courts have done so as well. FRE 704(a) provides that "except as provided in subdivision (b) [dealing with the mental state of criminal defendants], testimony in the form of an opinion or inference otherwise admissible is not objectionable because it embraces an ultimate issue to be decided by the trier of fact." Under this rule, both lay witnesses and experts may give their opinions or inferences on ultimate issues (provided that they satisfy the requirements of other Rules; for instance, if the witness is not an expert, his testimony must satisfy the two parts of FRE 701, *supra*, p. 399. S&R, p. 688.)

    3. **Exceptions:** Even in courts following the modern and federal view allowing testimony on ultimate facts, some types of ultimate issues may ***not*** be the subject of opinions:

a. **How case should be decided:** For instance, a witness will generally not be permitted to give an opinion that amounts to an assertion of *how the case should be decided*. Thus in a negligence action by P versus D, no witness (not even an expert on safety) should be permitted to testify that "D should be liable for damages," because the whole case is about whether D should indeed be found liable. M, p. 30. Some courts might similarly prevent any witness from saying that "D was careless" in this situation.

b. **Questions of law:** Witnesses will not be permitted to express their opinion as to *questions of law* (except foreign law). M, p. 31. The reason is that in our system, the *trial judge* should be the sole source of instruction to the jury about what the law is.

> **Example:** P claims that D has violated a contractual provision requiring D to make "best efforts" to make a securities law registration of shares owned by P. W, a securities law expert appearing as a witness for P, testifies as to the actions by D that were necessary to fulfill this clause (e.g., the clause imposed on D "an absolute, unconditional responsibility, to set to work promptly and diligently to do everything that would have to be done to make the registration statement effective. . . .")
>
> *Held*, W's testimony should have been excluded, because it consisted of legal opinions about the meaning of the contract terms. "It is not for witnesses to instruct the jury as to applicable principles of law, but for the judge." (W might have been entitled to explain to the jury common *practice* in the securities industry, since that would have been an opinion as to facts; what W actually said, however, went much beyond the facts to incorporate an opinion about the law.) *Marx & Co., Inc. v. Diners Club, Inc.*, 550 F.2d 505 (2d Cir. 1977).

i. **Related facts:** But a law expert or law enforcement expert may help the jury understand *facts*, even if these facts are very closely related to a rule of law. For instance, had W in *Marx* testified as to how the securities industry generally interprets a "best efforts" obligation to register shares, this testimony would probably have been allowed. Similarly, in a criminal prosecution for an uncommon and complicated crime, experts will generally be permitted to explain to the jury the *"modus operandi"* of a particular crime — this is allowed on the theory that the expert is merely describing a factual pattern, not instructing the jury as to the legal definition of the crime.

> **Example:** D1 and D2 are charged with burglary. The prosecution asserts that they engaged in "till tapping," a form of theft in which one person distracts a store clerk while the cash register is open, and the other takes money from the register. The prosecution puts on a policeman who is an expert on till tapping. The expert is asked a hypothetical question corresponding to the facts of the case, and then testifies that those facts reveal the "usual procedure of till tappers."

Held, W's testimony is admissible. W did not attempt to define a statutory term — only the court may do this. Rather than testifying what constitutes the crime charged, W "merely described the *modus operandi* of a certain class of criminals. His expert testimony was not directed to a question of law but towards assisting the jury in determining a factual issue, namely that of defendant's **intent** at the time he diverted [the clerk's] attention." *People v. Clay*, 38 Cal.Rptr. 431 (D.C.App. 1964).

    c. **Legal criteria:** Some courts prevent questions and answers that use a **legal term** or **label** that has not been defined for the jury. For instance, even under the liberal federal rules, a judge would not allow the question, "Did T have capacity to make a will?" since the phrase "capacity to make a will" is a legal rather than everyday term; instead, the questioner would have to ask, "Did T have sufficient mental capacity to know the nature and extent of his property and the natural objects of his bounty and to formulate a rational scheme of distribution?" or some similar formulation using non-legal terms. See Advisory Committee's Note to FRE 704.

II. EXPERT WITNESSES

    A. **Reasons for using experts:** An expert witness is, in brief, one whose **specialized knowledge** will be helpful to the jury in deciding the case correctly. See FRE 702.

      1. **Opinions:** Most of the time, the way an expert witness helps the trier of fact is by furnishing an **opinion** about **inferences that should be drawn** from a set of complex facts that the trier would not otherwise be capable of interpreting easily and correctly. Often, the underlying facts are placed into evidence through witnesses other than the expert.

        Example: The prosecution wishes to prove that a bullet found in the body of V was fired from a gun recovered from D's apartment. Through the use of lay witnesses, the prosecution could introduce the bullet recovered from V's body, as well as a bullet fired on a test range from the gun in question. It could then present testimony by W, a ballistics expert, in which W points out to the jury the identical grooves and other firing marks made on the two bullets. W would then give his opinion that, from these identical marks, it can be inferred that the two bullets were fired from the same gun.

      a. **Contrast to lay opinions:** Recall that courts are generally not sympathetic to opinions by lay witnesses, on the theory that it should be up to the jury, not the witness, to make inferences from facts in evidence. But the rule regarding opinions by experts is exactly opposite: the main purpose of expert testimony is to have the expert draw an inference from facts that the jury is not capable of easily interpreting on its own. Thus, in our above example, the jury might be able to inspect the bullets and notice that the firing marks appear to be the same on the two bullets, but it would have no way of inferring from this similarity the likelihood that the two bullets were fired by the same gun.

2. Statements of fact: While the giving of opinions and inferences is the main function of expert testimony, experts also frequently testify as to facts. Often, for instance, the expert will be called upon to state the **general scientific principles** of his specialty. For example, when, in the above example, W stated that no two guns produce exactly the same marks on bullets that they fire, he was stating a scientific fact, not an opinion (though when he went on to say that the markings on the two bullets were so nearly identical that they must have been fired from the same gun, he was giving what would probably be viewed as an opinion). Most of the difficulties with expert testimony — and the main focus of our discussion of experts here — concern the use of expert opinions.

B. When expert testimony allowed: There are two requirements that expert testimony must meet in order to be admissible: (1) the expert must be **"qualified"**; and (2) the subject matter of his testimony must be **suitable**, which generally means helpful or essential to the jury in deciding the case correctly. We consider each of these requirements in turn.

    1. Qualifications: What qualifies a person to be treated as an expert? She must have **knowledge and/or skill in a particular area** that distinguishes her from an ordinary person.

        a. Source of expertise: The expertise may come from either **education** or **experience**. Most experts derive their expertise from both of these factors, but **either** will suffice if it makes the witness more knowledgeable about a specialized field than a lay person would be.

            Example: D is charge with conspiracy to import marijuana. The prosecution offers testimony by W that the marijuana in question came from Colombia. W has no special training or education in identifying marijuana, but has smoked it over 1,000 times, has dealt in it 20 times, and has identified its origin on over 100 past occasions.

            Held (on appeal), the trial judge's decision treating W as an expert will not be overturned. FRE 702 provides that expertise may be obtained by experience as well as from formal training or education, and the prosecution showed that W had ample practical experience in marijuana identification. *U.S. v. Johnson*, 575 F.2d 1347 (5th Cir. 1978).

        b. Need for sub-specialist: Generally, a specialist in a particular field will be treated as an expert even though he is not a specialist in the particular **subfield** or **branch** of that field. For instance, if a medical condition involves brain damage or kidney failure, a doctor would probably be found to be a qualified expert even though he was a general practitioner rather than a neurologist or nephrologist. See M, p. 34, n. 11. See also *Knight v. Otis Elevator Co.*, 596 F.2d 84 (3d Cir. 1979) (where issue was dangerous defect in elevator button panel, an engineer who is expert in "machine guarding" could give expert testimony, even though he had no training in the sub-specialty of elevator guarding; his lack of experience with elevators went to the weight of his testimony rather than its admissibility, and could be brought out on cross-examination).

   i. Discretion of court: Keep in mind, however, that the ***trial judge*** has a great deal of ***discretion*** about whether to treat a witness as being an expert. Thus in a case involving intricate issues relating to the proper technique for open heart surgery, a court might well hold that a general practitioner M.D. who had never done an open heart operation did not have expertise that would be helpful to the jury. See L&S, p. 863.

2. Subject matter: The second requirement is that the expert's testimony concern a topic that is ***so specialized*** that without the testimony, the jury would be unable (or at least less able) to reach an accurate conclusion. Courts vary in the strictness with which they apply this requirement.

   a. Traditional "beyond ken" rule: Some cases, usually older ones, state that the subject matter of the expert testimony must be one that is so specialized that it is ***"beyond the ken"*** of laymen. M, p. 33.

   b. Modern and federal rule: But the modern trend is to impose a less strict requirement, that the expert's testimony merely be ***"helpful"*** to the jury's understanding of the case. This is the approach of the Federal Rules; FRE 702 provides that "if scientific, technical, or other specialized knowledge will ***assist*** the trier of fact to understand the evidence or to determine a fact in issue, a witness qualified as an expert by knowledge, skill, experience, training, or education, may testify thereto in the form of an opinion or otherwise."

   Example: P sues D for injuries suffered when P's car collides with D's truck. D calls as an expert W, a sheriff, who has many years of experience investigating and analyzing accidents. W testifies that from the position of the vehicles as he found them shortly after the crash, W believes that the accident took place on D's side of the highway.

   Held, this testimony was properly admitted. It is true that from other testimony and evidence of the location of the cars, the jury might without expert testimony be able to make inferences about where the crash took place. But determining the site of the crash was sufficiently difficult that W's testimony might well have assisted the jurors, so it was properly admitted. *Een v. Consolidated Freightways,* 120 F.Supp. 289 (D.N.D. 1954), *aff'd,* 220 F.2d 82 (8th Cir. 1955).

   c. Ordinary evidence: Courts are quickest to find the subject of expert testimony to be appropriate where it involves the interpretation of facts of a sort that lay persons are ***not usually called upon to evaluate.*** Thus testimony on such issues as whether two bullets were fired from the same gun, whether two fingerprints match or whether proper medical practice was followed, would all be appropriate subjects for expert testimony because a lay person is never called upon in real life to evaluate such evidence. By contrast, courts are much more reluctant to allow expert testimony (or scientific tests) to aid the jury in making the kinds of evaluations that juries, and lay people outside of a courtroom, customarily make. L&S, p. 167.

i. Eyewitness reliability: For instance, courts presume that lay jurors can intelligently evaluate the reliability of an *eyewitness identification* (e.g., "The man sitting at the defendant's table is the one who attacked me"). Therefore, judges will often refuse to allow an expert on human memory and perception to testify as to the frequent unreliability of such eyewitness identifications. This topic is discussed further *infra*, p. 423.

ii. Credibility of witness: Similarly, most judges believe that lay jurors are capable of intelligently evaluating the *truthfulness* of witnesses, based on demeanor, content of testimony, etc. Therefore, they will usually resist testimony by experts that purports to help the jury decide whether a particular witness is telling the truth. For instance, most courts have refused to allow the prosecution in rape cases to produce an expert to testify that V exhibits the symptoms of "rape trauma syndrome," and is thus probably telling the truth about whether the attack occurred. See *infra*, p. 426.

3. **Role of trial judge:** It is up to the trial judge, not the jury, to decide whether the proposed witness should be allowed to testify as an expert. That is, the trial judge decides as a preliminary matter both: (1) whether the witness has the requisite qualifications to be treated as an expert; and (2) whether the subject of the expert's testimony will be necessary or helpful to the jury.

   a. *Voir dire* **in front of jury:** Generally, the proponent of the expert will draw out the witness' qualifications *in front of the jury*. This saves time, since if the judge concludes that the witness should be allowed to give testimony, the jury has now heard the facts about the witness' expertise, and can decide how much weight to give to his testimony. L&S, p. 863.

   b. **Discretion:** On both of the requirements (credentials and subject matter), the trial judge has *wide discretion* about whether to admit or exclude. Thus whichever way the trial judge decides, reversals on appeal are relatively rare. Lilly, p. 485.

C. **Basis for expert's opinion:** Occasionally, the expert is called upon merely to state general scientific or technical principles, leaving it to the jury to decide how to apply these principles to the facts the jury has heard. Generally, however, the expert testifies concerning the facts of the case, either by stating some fact himself (e.g., the pathologist who did an autopsy of V testifies, "I found a puncture wound through the carotid artery") or by stating an inference about facts that have come from some other source (e.g., "Based on the facts you have stated in your hypothetical, counselor, I would say that the cause of death was . . . ") There are a number of a different ways in which an expert can learn about the facts of the present controversy, each of which we will consider in turn.

   1. **Personal knowledge:** The simplest situation occurs when the expert has *first-hand knowledge* of the facts. Where this happens, he may testify to his observations just as any non-expert would, and he may then go on to give his inferences from those facts. M, p. 35.

Example: A police ballistics officer might testify that he personally fired a gun found in D's apartment, retrieved the bullet, and noticed a high degree of similarity between the markings on that bullet and the markings on a bullet found in V's body. He could then go on to state that based on the high level of similarity, and based upon his knowledge of ballistics, he believes that it is overwhelmingly probable that both bullets were fired from the same gun.

2. **Observation of prior evidence:** The expert may gain information about the case by *listening to other witnesses* who testify before he does.

    a. **Use with hypothetical:** The expert cannot say that he "knows" a certain fact merely because a prior witness has testified to it. Instead, the way the prior testimony enters into the expert's testimony is by use of a *hypothetical question*: the questioner asks the expert to assume that the prior testimony is true, and then to give an inference or opinion.

    b. **Difficulties:** Courts freely accept expert opinions based on testimony by prior witnesses, where the prior testimony is *clear* and the prior witnesses agree with each other. But if the prior witnesses disagree, or give ambiguous testimony, the court will be less quick to allow the expert to give an opinion based on this prior testimony. At the least, the court will require the expert to state exactly which testimony, and which facts, he is assuming to be true. Also, if the prior testimony itself is an opinion, the court may refuse to allow the expert to rely on it, on the theory that "opinions based on opinions" should be excluded. (But under FRE 703, an expert may rely on any facts or data "reasonably relied upon by experts in the particular field in forming opinions or inferences upon the subject. . . ." If an expert might reasonably rely on another person's opinion in forming a conclusion, the expert's reliance on the prior opinion would be allowable under FRE 703. M, p. 37, n. 15.)

3. **Hypothetical questions:** A third source of information for the expert is the *hypothetical question* itself. That is, even if the expert knows virtually nothing about the facts of the particular case, he may be given factual assumptions in the form of a hypothetical question, and may then express his opinion about the conclusion to be drawn from these assumed facts. Hypothetical questions are discussed extensively *infra*, p. 408.

4. **Otherwise inadmissible evidence:** Each of the three sources of information listed above (personal knowledge, observation of prior evidence, and presentation of assumed facts through a hypothetical) typically consists of admissible evidence. But what if the expert's opinion is based upon "facts" that could *not* otherwise be *admitted* into evidence?

    a. **Traditional rule:** Traditionally, many courts have *refused* to allow an expert to give an opinion that is based in part upon "facts" that are not supported by admissible evidence. Indeed, some courts have gone so far as to say that each fact relied on by the expert must be supported by *evidence actually admitted* at the trial, not just theoretically admissible; these courts would, for instance, prevent a doctor from expressing a medical opinion based upon a presumably accurate hospital record that was not formally introduced at the trial, even though the record could have been introduced as a business record (*supra*, p. 200). Lilly, p. 487.

b. **Modern and federal trend:** But the modern trend, as exemplified by the Federal Rules, *removes* entirely the requirement that the expert's opinion be based solely upon admissible evidence. Thus FRE 703 states: "The facts or data in the particular case upon which an expert bases an opinion or inference may be those perceived by or made known to the expert at or before the hearing. If of a type *reasonably relied upon by experts* in the particular field in forming opinions or inferences upon the subject, the facts or data *need not be admissible in evidence.*"

   i. **Hearsay:** Thus FRE 703 means that an expert may base an opinion upon clearly inadmissible *hearsay*, if the type of hearsay is one that would be reasonably relied upon by experts in that situation. For instance, suppose that Doctor treats Patient for a cut foot, is told by Patient, "I cut it on my lawn mower," and makes a notation to that effect on the hospital record. Suppose then that Expert, another doctor (who has not treated Patient) is asked at trial to express an opinion as to what caused Patient's injury. If a medical expert in Expert's position would reasonably rely on what the patient told another doctor, Expert may base his opinion on Patient's statement, even though that statement is an out-of-court declaration that would not otherwise be directly admissible.

   ii. **Not reasonably relied on:** Conversely, if a reasonable expert would *not* reasonably rely on a fact or data, that fact or data may not be relied upon by the expert in giving his opinion, if the fact or data is not admissible. (For instance, the Advisory Committee's Note to FRE 703 asserts that an "accidentologist" could not give an opinion about the point of impact in an automobile collision based on the statements of bystanders, since the "reasonably relied upon by experts in the particular field" requirement is not satisfied. The Note does not state how the Advisory Committee knew this.)

Example: P's estate sues several chemical companies for illnesses (especially cancer) and death he allegedly suffered as a result of being exposed to Agent Orange manufactured by the Ds. He offers testimony by a medical expert, W, who never examined P, and who has gotten most of his information regarding P's symptoms, personal habits, and medical background from P's widow.

Held, W's expert opinion is not admissible. Physicians do not customarily rely upon second-hand information from persons other than the patient in diagnosing illness. This is especially true where the information is clearly sketchy and often inaccurate (e.g., the widow's assertion that P never smoked is clearly contradicted by other evidence). Therefore, W's opinion is not based upon facts that qualify under FRE 703, and his opinion that Agent Orange caused P's injuries and death will not be admitted at trial. *In re Agent Orange Product Liability Litigation (Lilley)*, 611 F.Supp. 1267 (D.C.N.Y. 1985).

c. **Disclosure to jury:** In courts, such as the federal courts, that allow an expert to base his opinion upon otherwise-inadmissible facts or data, may these under-lying facts or data be **revealed** to the jury? The Federal Rules do not expressly say whether the expert may disclose this underlying factual basis for his opin-ion. Probably he may, however. One commentator argues that the expert should be allowed to "give a full account to the jury, which is necessary to ensure that the jury has a basis for properly assessing the testimony. Evidence not otherwise admissible is not admitted under this Rule for its truth; it is admitted to explain the basis of the expert opinion." S&R, p. 671

5. **Mandatory disclosure to jury:** The converse question is whether the expert is **required** to disclose to the jury the factual basis for his opinion.

a. **Disclosure on direct:** The courts are split as to whether the expert must dis-close during direct examination the factual basis for his opinion or conclusion. Some require the underlying facts to be brought out before the expert gives his opinion, some merely require that the underlying facts be disclosed at some point during the direct examination, and some do not require disclosure at all on direct (though in these courts the adversary always has the right to inquire on **cross-examination** as to the underlying facts and assumptions). L&S, p. 866.

b. **Federal Rules:** The Federal Rules do not impose any requirement that the expert disclose during direct examination the data and assumptions he is rely-ing on. FRE 705 provides that "the expert may testify in terms of opinion or inference and give reasons therefor without prior disclosure of the underlying facts or data, unless the court requires otherwise. The expert may in any event be required to disclose the underlying facts or data on cross-examination."

i. **Rationale:** Recall that FRE 703 allows the expert to base his opinion upon otherwise inadmissible facts, if other experts in the field could reasonably rely on such evidence. That being the case, the drafters of the Rules reasoned, there is no need for a blanket rule requiring the expert to state the underlying facts he is relying on. (Those common-law jurisdictions that required such disclosure on direct were generally ones that would not allow opinions based on inadmissible evidence, so the requirement of disclosure of the underlying facts might give the court the chance to prevent the expert from giving his opinion if the underlying facts were inadmissible.)

ii. **Court has discretion:** Observe, however, that the phrase "unless the court requires otherwise" in Rule 705 gives the court **discretion,** in a particular instance, to require that the expert disclose on direct his factual basis. And keep in mind that the adversary always has the right to **cross-examine** the expert about the underlying data on which his conclusion is based. S&R, p. 701.

D. **The hypothetical question:** The **hypothetical question** is still probably the most common way of presenting the expert with facts about the case from which to draw a conclusion. Therefore, we examine the law concerning hypothetical questions in some detail.

1. **General technique:** When a direct examiner asks the expert a hypothetical question, he generally does so by presenting the relevant facts to the expert in a fairly lengthy and specific manner.

    > **Example:** P is trying to prove that the lung cancer he suffers from was caused by cigarettes he smoked, manufactured by D. P offers the testimony of W, an expert in lung disease, who has never personally examined P or P's medical records. P's lawyer might ask the following hypothetical question: "Assume, doctor, that a person has smoked one pack of cigarettes per day for the last twenty years. Assume further that the patient has not had substantial occupational or other exposure to asbestos. Assume that the patient has had a cough and emphysema for the last fifteen years. Assume that the patient's parents did not suffer from cancer. Assume finally that the patient is diagnosed as having cancer of the left lung at the age of 47, and that there is no other sign of cancer in the patient's body. On these facts, doctor, what if anything can you tell us about the likely cause of the lung cancer?"

2. **Evidentiary basis required:** Most skirmishing about hypothetical questions involves the extent to which there must be an *evidentiary basis* for the assumptions listed in the question. Thus, in terms of our example above, the issue is the extent to which there must be evidence in the record that the patient has really been diagnosed as having lung cancer, that the patient really smoked one pack of cigarettes a day, etc. There are a number of sub-issues:

    a. **In record at time of question:** First, must evidence of each of the assumed facts be *in the record* at the time the question is asked? Some courts impose such a requirement, but the modern, and probably majority, trend, is to hold that there is *not* such a requirement. That is, most courts allow the question if the questioner assures the court that supporting evidence will be introduced later in the case. M, p. 37.

    b. **Inadmissible evidence:** Second, must the underlying evidence be *admissible* (even if not yet admitted)? In courts that follow the federal rule that otherwise inadmissible evidence may be relied on by an expert if similar experts reasonably rely on this type of information, the data that supports the hypothetical may fall into this otherwise-inadmissible category. *Id.*

        i. **Illustration:** For instance, consider our lung cancer example above: Assume that P's medical records are not admitted into evidence, and that the only source for the assumption that P has had a persistent cough for 15 years is P's statement to a doctor, who entered this information into those medical records. Since doctors generally can reasonably rely upon information placed in medical records by other physicians who have examined the patient, information from those records can form the factual basis for the hypothetical (even if those records might be otherwise-inadmissible hearsay). M, p. 37, n. 17.

c. Based on opinion of another: Third, may the hypothetical be based on *another witness' opinion?* Some cases, usually older ones, say "no". See, e.g., *State v. David*, 22 S.E.2d 633 (N.C. 1942) (toxicologist's opinion that V died of carbon monoxide poisoning, given in response to hypothetical question, should not have been admitted where his opinion was based upon a pathologist's opinion that there was no other plausible cause of death. "[I]t is uniformly held that the opinion of one expert based upon that of another is incompetent and inadmissible as evidence. . . .")

   i. Modern and federal approach: But the modern trend, as exemplified by FRE 703, is as noted that an expert opinion may be based upon any data reasonably relied on by similar experts. If an expert could reasonably rely on another person's opinion, under the federal approach presumably that other opinion could be part of a hypothetical question and answer. Thus, *David, supra*, would probably be decided differently under the Federal Rules.

d. Far-fetched assumptions: However, even under the modern and federal approach, the factual assumptions made in the hypothetical question *cannot be totally far-fetched.* There must be some evidence at some point in the trial to support, either directly or by inference, each of the facts hypothesized in the question. "The opinion will be stricken if the jury cannot possibly find that its factual underpinnings are true." L&S, p. 868.

3. Advantage of hypothetical: The main advantage of the hypothetical question is that the party calling the expert *need not pay* for the expert's time in becoming personally acquainted with the facts of the case. In our lung cancer example, for instance, the plaintiff might not have been able to afford the medical expert if he had been required to pay for the expert's time in examining P and studying P's medical records. Also, the hypothetical approach has the merit of telling the jury exactly what factual assumptions the expert is making in arriving at his opinion. *Id.*

a. Criticism: However, most commentators and many courts heavily criticize the hypothetical question technique. The main criticism is that the questioner generally gives a highly partisan *slanting* in listing the facts, one which often amounts to an early summation of the case for the benefit of the jury. M, p. 41. A second criticism is that if the questioner conscientiously tries to include all of the material facts, the question can become so long — often dozens of pages of trial transcript — that the jury gets confused or loses attention. See, e.g., *Rabata v. Dohner*, 172 N.W.2d 409 (Wisc. 1969), announcing the new rule that the expert may be asked to give his opinion without the underlying facts being presented in a hypothetical; the court termed the hypothetical question "a dangerous device which can lead to slanted questions, jury fatigue, and obfuscation of the facts."

4. Federal approach: The Federal Rules respond to these criticisms by attempting to reduce practitioners' reliance on the technique. The Rules do *not* forbid the use of hypotheticals. But they take several steps to make the need for hypothetical questions less pressing than at common law. The Rules do this mainly by the first sentence of FRE 705: "The expert may testify in terms of opinion or inference and give his reasons therefor without prior disclosure of the underlying facts or data, unless the court requires otherwise."

    a. Remains useful: Even under the liberal federal approach, a practitioner may occasionally find it wise to use the hypothetical technique. For instance, he may want to use a "super expert" who testifies about how general scientific principles would be applied to particular facts, but as to whom there is not enough time (or money) for him to familiarize himself directly with the facts. Also, in a case where the underlying facts are sharply disputed, the questioner may find it helpful to state just his version of the facts to form the basis of the expert's opinion. L&S, p. 869, n. 17.

E. Procedural issues: Here are some procedural issues that often arise in connection with expert testimony:

    1. Cross-examination: Cross-examining an expert witness is likely to be more difficult than examining a lay witness. The expert is often a knowledgeable — sometimes almost "professional" — witness; also, he is likely to be fiercely loyal to the side that called him. Most importantly, he has spent his career mastering a particular technical specialty, and knows far more about it than the lawyer who must cross-examine him. Nonetheless, there are several ways in which experts can often be effectively cross-examined:

        a. Bias: The examiner can attempt to show that the witness is *biased*. Most frequently, the examiner will do this by showing that the witness is being *paid* by the side that called him. Similarly, the examiner may bring out the fact that the expert has testified in many similar cases in the past, and has always allied himself with the same side (e.g., the plaintiff in asbestos cases).

        b. Different assumptions: The examiner may probe the *factual data* on which the expert's opinion is based. He may then try to vary this underlying base, perhaps by alluding to other, conflicting evidence.

            i. Hypothetical: This technique is especially useful where the expert's opinion on direct was made in response to a hypothetical question; the cross-examiner can merely vary the facts of the hypothetical (e.g., "Would your conclusion that the plaintiff's lung cancer was caused by smoking be changed, doctor, if it were assumed that the plaintiff came in daily contact with asbestos during his job as shipbuilder over a thirty-year period?")

        c. Learned treatises: The examiner will sometimes be able to use *treatises*, *articles*, or other professional texts written by other experts to impeach the witness. Normally, the examiner must first get the witness to acknowledge that the text in question is a *standard authority* in the field. In most jurisdictions, the examiner may then impeach the expert by reading a portion of the text that contradicts the expert's testimony, and thus implying that the jury should disregard the expert's view.

i. **Reliance unnecessary:** A few courts allow the examiner to read the text during cross-examination only if the expert admits that he ***relied*** on the text in his training or in forming his present opinion. Lilly, p. 492, n. 4. But most courts allow use of the treatise as impeaching evidence so long as the expert concedes that it is authoritative, regardless of whether the expert has read it or relied on it. See, e.g., *Ruth v. Fenchel*, 121 A.2d 373 (N.J. 1956) (where W, a doctor called by D, testified that whiplash symptoms always appear within hours after an accident, P could impeach him by reading from a treatise that says otherwise, even though W had not relied on the treatise but conceded that it was well-respected in the field).

ii. **Treatise as substantive evidence:** Many courts that allow the treatise to be read from allow it only as ***impeachment*** evidence, not as substantive evidence proving the truth of the facts stated in the treatise. But the Federal Rules, and some state courts, have a hearsay exception for learned treatises, whereby the treatise's contents are admissible as substantive evidence as long as the contents are brought out during direct or cross-examination of the expert. See FRE 803(18), discussed *supra*, p. 215.

iii. **Use of treatise in examination of defendant expert:** Suppose D is herself an expert. A clever lawyer for P could call D to the stand as a witness, direct her attention to a treatise, and thereby argue that the treatise should be admissible as substantive evidence under FRE 803(18). However, 803(18) allows substantive use of the treatise only to the extent that it is "called to the attention of an expert witness upon cross-examination or relied upon him in direct examination. . . ." L&S (p. 867) suggest that when P has called D as a hostile witness and referred to the treatise, "it is not clear that this should qualify as cross-examination under FRE 803(18)."

2. **Court-appointed experts:** When a lawyer retains an expert to testify on behalf of the client, the lawyer of course usually looks for a witness who will express an opinion clearly favorable to that party. In most instances, each party will present an expert favorable to that party, leading to the much-criticized "battle of the experts." In criminal cases involving an insanity defense, for instance, it is almost universally the case that the defendant will produce one or more psychiatrists testifying that the defendant does not know right from wrong (or whatever the applicable test is), and the prosecution will inevitably produce one or more who testify that he does. The jury is likely to be confused more than enlightened by the conflicting expert testimony, especially where the field of expertise is highly technical and/or there is a lot of jargon. Many commentators have proposed that this unhelpful battle can be avoided by the use of a ***court-appointed expert***. The theory is that such an expert would be ***"neutral,"*** and his non-partisan testimony would therefore be more useful to the jury.

a. **Federal Rule:** The Federal Rules facilitate the appointment of an expert by the court. FRE 706 (too long to be worth reproducing in full here) codifies a number of aspects of court appointment of experts, including:

    i. Court chooses own: The court may ask the parties to submit their own nominations or to agree upon a selection, but the court may also make a selection of its ***own***;

    ii. Costs: In most civil cases, the court can order the ***cost*** of the expert to be borne by either or both parties as if these expenses were court costs. (In criminal cases a statute often provides that the government must pay);

  iii. No compulsion: The rule does not allow the court to ***compel*** the expert to accept the appointment; the court may appoint only if the expert consents. (But the rule applies only where the expert will have to ***specially prepare*** for trial; if a person with expertise happens to have knowledge of the facts of a particular case — e.g., a treating physician — the expert may be subpoenaed like any other person with personal knowledge and required to testify, willingly or not. L&S, p. 708.)

    iv. Deposition: The expert's ***deposition*** may be taken by either party;

    v. Cross-examination: The expert may be called to testify at trial by either party (or by the court), and each party — including the party calling him — may ***cross-examine*** him;

    vi. Disclosure to jury: Under 706(c), the court has discretion to ***disclose*** to the jury the fact that the witness has been appointed by the court.

  b. Criticism: Federal courts have been slow to make use of this power to appoint expert witnesses. This is due in part to the fact that most lawyers distrust the whole notion of a court-appointed expert. This lack of trust stems, in turn, from the fact that most experts tend to be ***inevitably "partisan,"*** in the sense that they believe in a particular school of thought about the subject. Thus the fact that an expert has been appointed by the court rather than retained by a party does not mean that the expert will necessarily be open-minded or willing to tell the jury that there are other experts who do not agree with him. Furthermore, the jury may infer from the fact of court-appointment that the expert is more neutral than he really is; the jury may therefore give his testimony more weight than it deserves. See L&S, pp. 979-83.

3. Discovery: One key to effectively cross-examining an expert is to have had adequate ***pre-trial discovery*** of that expert, including discovery of his findings and conclusions.

  a. Federal approach: In federal courts, a party may obtain reasonably broad pre-trial discovery of experts that the other side expects to call at trial. Federal Rule of Civil Procedure 26(b)(4)(A)(i) lets a party send interrogatories to his adversary requiring the latter to "identify each person whom the other party expects to call as an expert witness at trial, to state the subject matter on which the expert is expected to testify, and to state the substance of the facts and opinions to which the expert is expected to testify and a summary of the grounds for each opinion."

     i. Deposition: But a party may not ***depose*** the other party's expected trial witnesses without a court order, and even then will generally have to pay for that expert's time in preparing for and attending the deposition. FRCP 26(b)(4)(A)(ii); 26(b)(4)(B). (If the expert is ***not*** expected to be called at trial, the other side will only under "exceptional circumstances" be able to obtain discovery about the expert's opinions on facts known to him. FRCP 26(b)(4)(B).)

4. Calling at trial: At trial, a party may call any expert witness with knowledge of the facts of the case. This probably even means that if D has retained W as an expert, familiarized him with the facts of the case, and then decided not to call him at trial (perhaps because W has formed an opinion unfavorable to D's position), P may call W to the stand. This is true even though P could probably not obtain ***discovery*** of W's factual information or opinions except under "exceptional circumstances" (as discussed in the prior paragraph). See, e.g., *Rancourt v. Waterville Urban Renewal Authority*, 223 A.2d 303 (Me. 1966) (eminent domain action; D, the government, retained W, a valuation expert, to form an opinion about the fair value of P's property; *held*, P may call W to the stand at trial and elicit his opinion on valuation — "there is no privilege on the part of the employer of the witness. . . .")

III. SCIENTIFIC EVIDENCE — THE *FRYE* STANDARD

A. Special rule for scientific evidence: As we have seen (*supra*, p. 404), an expert's testimony must be helpful — and in some courts, necessary — to the jury's understanding of the case. This is basically a requirement of relevance. But where the expert's testimony concerns a ***scientific*** test or principle, many courts impose an ***additional*** requirement: The proponent must show that the test or principle has been ***generally accepted in the scientific community***. M, p. 605.

1. *Frye* case: The idea that there should be a special rule for scientific evidence derives from *Frye v. U.S.*, 293 F. 1013 (D.C.Cir. 1923). The court in that case upheld a lower court's refusal to admit the results of a lie detector test offered by the defendant in a murder case. The appeals court reasoned, "[W]hile courts will go a long way in admitting expert testimony deduced from a well-recognized scientific principle or discovery, the thing from which the deduction is made must be sufficiently established to have gained general acceptance in the particular field in which it belongs." The polygraph was simply too new a technique to have attained such acceptance "among physiological and psychological authorities."

2. Spotty adherence: Courts have varied sharply on whether and when they are willing to follow *Frye's* requirement that the test or technique have attained "general acceptance."

     a. Lie detector tests: Most courts follow *Frye's* "general acceptance" requirement where the results of ***lie detector*** tests are sought to be introduced. L&S, p. 861. This is not surprising, since it was this very sort of evidence that was at issue in *Frye* itself.

b. Other areas: But outside the polygraph area, the "general acceptance" test has been less frequently applied. Many new scientific techniques have come into widespread judicial acceptance seemingly without ever having had to prove that they were "generally accepted" in scientific quarters. See, e.g., neutron activation analysis (discussed *infra*, p. 421), which was accepted even while in its infancy by most courts that considered it.

    i. Excuse: Of the courts that purport to apply the "general acceptance" standard outside the polygraph area, many seem to be doing so on a very selective basis to reach a pre-conceived result. L&S (p. 862, n. 11) state that *Frye* "is often the precedent that is used by courts that want to reject expert evidence but have difficulty in writing an opinion in relevance language." Thus courts seem to use *Frye* to reject such scientific techniques as *hypnosis*, *truth serums*, *psychological stress evaluators*, and *voice prints*, more because the court feels the techniques are unreliable or misleading than because they lack scientific acceptance.

3. Pros and cons: Courts and commentators make conflicting arguments about whether the "general acceptance" standard of *Frye* is worthwhile.

    a. In favor: Here are some arguments commonly made in support of the general acceptance standard: (1) It promotes **uniformity** of decision-making (since admissibility will turn on a scientific consensus, rather than the opinions of individual judges); (2) It leaves the decision about the validity of a scientific technique with the people **most qualified** to make it, the scientific community; (3) Use of a novel scientific test, especially one invented by one or two people, is **unfair** to the opponent because there may be few if any experts who can evaluate it from the opponent's perspective; and (4) The standard reduces the risk that the jury will be **unduly swayed** by the "misleading aura of certainty which often envelopes a new scientific process. . . ." *People v. Kelly*, 549 P.2d 1240 (Cal. 1976) (applying the *Frye* test to bar voice prints).

    b. Criticisms: But critics of the general acceptance standard have forceful arguments of their own: (1) Every scientific technique must at some point be comparatively new, yet newness alone does not equal unreliability; (2) The rule is **hard to apply**, since it requires the court to define how "general" the general acceptance must be, exactly what principle it is that must be accepted, and what the "particular field" is to which the evidence belongs and in which it must be accepted; and (3) The dangers cited by proponents can be combatted by a less drastic rule, such as by focusing on the technique's **reliability**, of which general acceptance is just one indicator. See generally M, pp. 608-09.

4. Federal Rules: The Federal Rules neither explicitly accept nor reject the general acceptance standard. The basic rule on expert testimony (FRE 702) lumps scientific testimony together with testimony concerning "technical or other specialized knowledge," and says nothing about the importance of general acceptance in the relevant scientific community.

a. Status unclear: At this writing, it is unclear whether the Federal Rules should be interpreted as having overruled the *Frye* general acceptance standard. Both cases and commentators seem split on this issue. For instance, W&B (Par. 702[03]) assert that "the silence of the rule and its drafters should be regarded as tantamount to an abandonment of the general acceptance standard," whereas S&R (p. 633) suggest that at least some types of scientific evidence should be rejected in the absence of general scientific acceptance ("It would be odd if the Advisory Committee and the Congress intended to overrule the vast majority of cases excluding such evidence as lie detectors without explicitly stating so.")

IV. SCIENTIFIC EVIDENCE AND EXPERTISE — PARTICULAR TYPES

A. Overview: An analysis of the hundreds of types of scientific evidence is obviously beyond the scope of this outline. However, we touch briefly upon a few of the more important and controversial types of scientific evidence.

B. Probabilities: A branch of mathematics called ***probability theory*** helps calculate the probability that a certain event has occurred. Courts disagree about whether computations made by use of probability theory may be presented to the jury to help them conclude whether a particular event took place.

> **Example:** P is negligently knocked down by a blue bus. P is unable to directly identify the bus as belonging to D, one of two local bus companies. He can establish, however, that D owns 85 of the 100 blue buses in town. Courts are in dispute about whether P may present this fact — perhaps accompanied by testimony by a probabilities expert — and then argue to the jury that this fact shows an 85% probability that the bus that hit him was owned by D.

1. Foundation: All courts agree that if probability evidence is to be introduced at all, a ***proper foundation*** for it must be laid. In particular, solid evidence of the numerator and denominator used to compute the probabilities must be presented to the jury.

a. *Collins* case: Failure to comply with the foundation requirements was the main reason why probability evidence was rejected in the leading case on the subject, *People v. Collins*, 438 P.2d 33 (Cal. 1968).

i. Facts: In *Collins*, D and his wife were charged with robbery. There were no complete eyewitness identifications of either D or his wife. However, the prosecution apparently produced at least some evidence of six facts about the robbers: (1) they had a partly yellow automobile; (2) the man had a mustache; (3) the girl had a ponytail; (4) the girl had blond hair; and (5) the man was a black man with a beard; and (6) the robbers were an interracial couple in a car. The prosecution then called a mathematics professor, who was instructed to assume certain probabilities for each of these events (e.g., 1/10 for partly yellow automobile, 1/4 for man with mustache, etc.) The mathematician then testified that the probability that any given couple would possess these six factors by chance was to be computed by using the "product rule" (i.e., one multiplies each probability by the next). Applying this rule, the professor concluded that there was only one chance in 12 million that any given couple would possess these six factors. The prosecutor then argued to the jury that the individual probabilities he had assigned were "conservative," and that the chance of any couple other than D and his wife having these same characteristics was probably more like "one in a billion." D and his wife were convicted.

   ii. **Holding:** The California Supreme Court reversed the conviction. The court seemed to rely most heavily on the fact that there was no evidence in the record relating to any of the six individual probability factors used by the prosecutor (e.g., that only 1 in 10 automobiles is partly yellow). The court was also troubled by two other considerations: (1) There was no showing that the factors were "independent" of each other, a requirement for the "product" method of computing probabilities. (For instance, once a man is assumed to have a mustache, the chance that he would also have a beard is much higher than if he does not have a mustache, and much higher than the 1/10th the prosecutor assumed.) (2) The jury would be tempted to "accord disproportionate weight" to the resulting figure, instead of concentrating on the critical issue: "Of the admittedly few such couples [having all six factors], which one, if any, was guilty of committing this robbery?" (The court attached an Appendix in which, using sophisticated mathematics, it demonstrated that there was about a 40% chance that at least one **other** couple in the Los Angeles area had the same characteristics.)

2. **Arguments against use:** The *Collins* court was clearly troubled by what it saw as the prosecutor's inaccurate, mathematically-unsound application of probability principles. But the court also seemed troubled by the basic idea of using probability to assess guilt. Many other courts and commentators have expressed similar misgivings about giving the jury even mathematically-sound probability estimates. For instance, Tribe (84 Harv. L. Rev. 1329 *et seq.*) raises several arguments against such use: (1) Probability proof is so seemingly precise and methodical that it "may dwarf all efforts to put it into perspective with more impressionistic sorts of evidence." (2) Such proof may "shift the focus away from such elements as volition, knowledge, and intent, and toward such elements as identity and occurrence [thus producing] a tendency to emphasize the wrong questions." (3) Probability proof would "make the legal system seem even more alien and inhuman than it already does to distressingly many," by intimidating the jury and making their role appear to be "largely mechanical and automatic."

3. **Supporters:** But other commentators argue that probability proof, when wisely used, enhances the accuracy of fact-finding and is thus desirable. For instance, Saks and Kidd (15 Law & Assoc. Rev. 123) argue that, contrary to Tribe's assertion, studies indicate that fact-finders give **too little** weight to quantitative evidence in the face of "anecdotal" information, not too much. They give the following example:

Example: Two groups of respondents were given the following the description: "John is a 39 year old man. He is married and has two children. He is active in local politics. The hobby that he most enjoys is rare book collecting. He is competitive, argumentative, and articulate." Group 1 was told that John was selected at random from a group composed of 70 lawyers and thirty engineers. Group 2 was told that John was selected from a group composed of 30 lawyers and 70 engineers. Each group was asked to estimate the probability that John was a lawyer rather than an engineer. Both groups came up with the same median probability estimate: that the chances are 95% that John is a lawyer rather than an engineer.

a. Conclusion: Saks and Kidd conclude from this that "when descriptive case-specific information is added, [respondents] tend to ignore the numerical base rate and rely instead on the degree to which the description of John is representative of their stereotype of lawyers." Respondents ignore the fact that, statistically, John is much more likely (5.44 times as likely) to be a lawyer if he is drawn from a pool consisting of 70% lawyers than from a pool consisting of 30% lawyers. Since juries will apply their anecdotal and stereotypical reasoning anyway, Saks and Kidd argue, they will hardly be overwhelmed by probability evidence (e.g., the composition of the overall pool from which John is drawn).

4. Modern trend: The modern trend is probably towards ***increased acceptance*** of probability evidence, when a careful scientific and mathematical basis for it is laid.

a. Paternity testing: Courts have been especially willing to accept such evidence in ***paternity*** cases. New, more sophisticated blood and tissue analysis techniques allow scientists to exclude a quite high percentage of the male population from being the possible father of any given child. Whereas older tests were generally allowed into evidence only if they ***excluded*** the possibility of the defendant's paternity, modern tests are often allowed to express not only the fact that the defendant is ***not*** excluded from paternity, but also the "probability" that he *is* the father.

Example: Suppose that D is claimed to be the father of C. Tests for "genetic markers" may now be performed that, typically, will allow the geneticist to state, "Not only are C's genetic markers consistent with D being C's father, but only one in several thousand males of the same race as D would have markers consistent with being the father of C." Nearly all courts will allow the geneticist to phrase her findings in this way, and to testify further that there is thus a "percentage of exclusion" of, say, 2,999 out of 3,000. Some but not all courts would also permit the geneticist to say that there was a "99.9% chance" that D was the father. (However, this latter probability estimate is misleading: it merely means that the genetic marker is 1,000 times more likely to be found in a person who is the real father than in one who is chosen at random, not that the jury is 99.9% likely to be correct if they determine that D is the father. For this reason, M, p. 661, argues that "testimony as to the 'probability of paternity' as it typically is calculated, should not be allowed.")

b. Other contexts: Outside of paternity cases, courts have been somewhat more reluctant to allow statistical evidence.

  i. Sexual assault cases: However, courts have recently begun to allow serological and other biological tests in *rape* and other sexual assault cases, where the test indicates the likelihood that the defendant is or is not the assailant.

  Example: A few courts have admitted the results of so-called DNA "fingerprints" of the defendant's blood and his semen. As with the paternity test described above, such DNA tests typically come into evidence with two components: (1) a statement by the tester that the DNA "fingerprint" of D is the same as the DNA found in the blood or semen left on or in the victim; and (2) a statement that only some small percentage (e.g., 1 in 7,000) of persons chosen at random from the population would have this same fingerprint. See N. Y. Times, Feb. 7, 1988, at A1, col. 1 (defendant convicted based principally on DNA "fingerprints.") As with the results of paternity tests, most courts are more likely to admit this testimony about frequency of occurrence within the population than they are to allow additional testimony purporting to be the "probability that D is guilty."

  ii. Identification of body: Similarly, biological markers may be used for purposes other than identifying the defendant. See, e.g., *State v. Klindt*, 389 N.W.2d 670 (Iowa 1986) (issue is whether body is that of V; testimony about genetic markers allowed to demonstrate that it is 107 times as likely that the body found is the child of V's parents than that it is the child of some random couple).

C. Speed detection: The police commonly use two methods of ***speed detection*** to determine whether a motorist has been speeding.

  1. Radar: Most commonly, the police use ***radar***. Like all scientific tests, radar cannot be used unless the court is satisfied both that the general theory behind it is sound and that the application of theory to fact in the particular case was reliable.

  a. General theory: The general theory behind the use of radar to measure the speed of moving objects is now so generally accepted that not only is the relatively stringent *Frye* test (*supra*, p. 414) satisfied, but courts will usually take ***judicial notice*** of radar's theoretical reliability. (See *infra*, p. 463 for a discussion of judicial notice.) Therefore, the prosecution generally does not have to put in any expert evidence as to the general reliability of radar as a speed detection technique. M, p. 613.

  b. Accuracy in particular case: On the other hand, the accuracy of radar depends very much on how carefully it is used in the particular case. Courts vary in how they handle the possibility that the particular equipment or its use may have been inaccurate: some require the prosecution to make at least some showing that the equipment was accurate when used (e.g., proof that its accuracy was confirmed both shortly before and after the arrest); others merely give the defendant the right to challenge the accuracy, and treat any showing of inaccuracy as going merely to weight rather than admissibility.

2. **VASCAR:** A second speed measuring technique is known as VASCAR (Visual Average Speed Computer and Recorder). This is a relatively simple technique that relies on the time the car takes to cover a fixed distance to compute its speed. As with radar, many courts now take judicial notice of the general soundness of the technique, but allow the defendant to show that its application in the particular case was not accurate (though this generally, as with radar, goes only to weight, not admissibility). M, p. 611.

D. **Intoxication:** Several scientific techniques for determining whether a person is *intoxicated* exist.

   1. **Breathalyzer:** The most important is the ***Breathalyzer***, which measures the amount of alcohol in the breath, and then extrapolates this to estimate the amount in the blood stream. In most states, a statutory scheme makes breathalyzer results automatically admissible if a proper foundation is laid. (To lay the foundation, the prosecution must produce a witness — usually the person who administered the test — who can testify that the device was one covered by the statute, and was correctly used in the particular case.) Many states also have enacted ***statutory presumptions*** that flow from particular findings; for instance, a level of .05% or less of blood alcohol generally raises a rebuttable presumption that the defendant was not drunk, and a level of .10% or higher raises a rebuttable presumption that he was drunk. M, p. 617.

E. **Voice prints:** The *"voice print"* technique has been developed in recent years as a method of determining whether two voice samples — generally recordings — were made by the same person. Typically, the voice of an unidentified suspect on a taped telephone call (e.g., a ransom demand in a kidnap case, or an attempt to arrange a drug purchase) is compared with a sample given by the defendant after his arrest. The voice print expert examines a *"spectrograph"* of the two voices, i.e., a graph showing the various frequencies in each of the voices. The theory behind voice prints is that individuals have differently-shaped oral cavities, and manipulate their lips, tongue, etc. in a unique way; therefore, proponents claim, no two speakers will produce an identical or even very similar voice print on a single word. M, p. 639. Proponents frequently analogize voice prints to fingerprints, and assert that no two persons have identical voice prints any more than fingerprints.

   1. **Criticisms:** But the voice print technique has achieved nowhere near the same level of general scientific acceptance as fingerprinting. The technique has many critics in scientific circles, and a number of studies report very high misidentification rates (e.g., 80% misidentification rate, with 42% of the sample being false positives. M, p. 640.)

   2. **Courts split:** Courts are badly split as to the admissibility of voice prints.

      a. *Frye* **test:** Courts frequently apply the *Frye* "general scientific acceptance" test to voice print evidence, even where they do not apply *Frye* to other kinds of tests. Most courts that have applied *Frye* have **excluded** the evidence. *Id.* A particular problem with voice prints is that the technique was designed expressly for forensic purposes; therefore, its proponents are generally law enforcement officials who by their very occupation tend to have a bias in favor of the device. See, e.g., *People v. Kelly*, 549 P.2d 1240 (Cal. 1976), in which the California Supreme Court held voice prints inadmissible, in part because the prosecution's only "expert" supporting the technique was a police officer who was a "technician" rather than a "scientist"; the court suggested that only testimony by a scientist could establish that the technique had achieved the general acceptance in the scientific community required by *Frye*.

    b. Admitted: But other major jurisdictions have admitted voice prints. See, e.g., *U.S. v. Williams*, 583 F.2d 1194 (2d Cir. 1978), citing: (1) a recent study with a false identification rate of only 6.3%; and (2) the fact that the tapes themselves can be, and usually are, played for the jury, thus eliminating the risk that all judgment on similarity will be delegated to the expert.

F. Blood tests and other biological tests: There are a number or tests that can be performed on **blood**, tissues, or other biological specimens, to determine the identity of the person who supplied it or something else about that person. These tests range from conventional blood grouping (e.g., a specimen is shown to be type AB blood) to much newer and more arcane techniques (e.g., "genetic markers," now identifiable in blood or tissue, that are claimed to uniquely identify an individual). These techniques are described *supra*, p. 418, as part of the analysis of probability.

G. Neutron Activation Analysis: Where a small sample of material must be **identified**, the technique of **Neutron Activation Analysis (NAA)** is now frequently used. NAA is a technique for making the object artificially radioactive, and then measuring the resulting radiation to determine the amount of each chemical element in the sample. By this method, a laboratory can determine, for instance, whether a hair found near a crime scene belongs to the defendant, whether a piece of rope comes from a particular batch produced by a manufacturer, whether a speck of paint came from a particular car, etc.

    1. Generally receptive: Courts have generally **admitted** NAA evidence when a proper foundation is laid. Lilly, p. 505. In doing so, courts are probably influenced by the fact that the technique seems to be relatively objective, and exceptionally accurate in the sense that it can measure even minute trace amounts of each element in a sample. The technique also has the advantage that it does **not destroy** the sample, which thus remains available for re-testing or for admission into evidence.

        Example: D is charged with sending a letter bomb that kills V. The prosecution tries to prove that the packing materials in which the bomb was enclosed (cardboard, tape, gummed label, etc.) were from the same manufacturer and the same batches as similar items found at D's place of employment. To do this, the prosecution puts on testimony by W, an expert trained in NAA, who testifies that based on NAA performed by him, the mailing label and cardboard tube fragments are of the "same type and same manufacturer" as those found at D's employer, and the metal cap and vinyl tape fragments are not only of the same manufacture but from the same "batch" (i.e., same single day's manufacturing production) as those found at the employer.

    Held, the trial judge properly admitted this NAA testimony. The trial judge could properly have found that NAA has gained "general acceptance in the particular field in which it belongs" (the test of *Frye, supra*, p. 414). However, in view of the time-consuming and expensive nature of NAA, the government in a criminal case must give the defendant the chance to make his own NAA test, and if the defendant is indigent the government must pay for those tests. *U.S. v. Stifel*, 433 F.2d 431 (6th Cir. 1970).

H. Psychology and psychiatry: Expert scientific testimony is often offered on issues of *psychology* and *psychiatry*. Most frequently, such evidence relates to the mental condition of a criminal defendant, but it can also be relevant to a wide variety of other contexts (e.g., the reliability of eyewitness testimony, the truthfulness of a sexual assault victim, etc.)

    1. Mental condition of defendant: Whenever the *mental condition* of a *criminal defendant* is at issue, one or both sides is likely to try to use expert testimony bearing on this condition, usually in the form of a psychiatrist's opinion. This happens most often where the defendant raises an *insanity* defense, in which case both the defense and prosecution are likely to offer expert psychiatric testimony.

        a. Battle of the experts: Traditionally, the use of psychiatric testimony in insanity cases has led to a confusing "battle of the experts" — the defendant's psychiatrist almost invariably recites his opinion that the defendant is insane by whatever legal test is applied in the jurisdiction, and the prosecution's expert psychiatrist asserts that he is sane by this test. Each expert's opinion is often phrased in conclusory terms, so that the effect is frequently to entrust to the experts, rather than to the jury, the duty of making the ultimate legal conclusion as to sanity.

        b. Judicial response: Courts have struggled to restrict psychiatric testimony on the defendant's mental condition to medical diagnosis, and to leave the drawing of legal conclusions for the jury. For instance, in *Washington v. U.S.*, 390 F.2d 444 (D.C.Cir. 1967), the Court of Appeals drafted a tight set of instructions to expert witnesses in insanity defense cases, under which the expert is told: (1) "You may not state conclusions or opinions as an expert unless you also tell the jury what investigations, observations, reasoning and medical theory led to your opinion"; (2) You may not "express an opinion on whether the alleged crime was a 'product' of a mental disease or defect" (the relevant test at the time); (3) If you give an opinion as to whether the defendant suffered from a "mental disease or defect," you should concern yourself only with the clinical diagnostic meaning of this term, not its legal meaning; and (4) You should not consider or state whether you think the defendant should be found guilty or responsible for the alleged crime, since this is a question for the court and jury.

        c. Amendment to Federal Rules: Fear that psychiatric testimony in insanity cases was usurping the role of the jury also led Congress to amend the Federal Rules of Evidence. In the aftermath of John Hinkley's insanity acquittal when charged with attempting to assassinate President Reagan, Congress not only made the insanity defense more difficult to establish as a matter of substantive law (e.g., by shifting the burden of persuasion to the defendant), but also added a new subsection (b) to FRE 704.

   i. **Text of 704(b):** FRE 704(a) continues to state the general rule that testimony (whether by an expert or lay witness) is not objectionable because it embraces an "ultimate issue" to be decided by the trier of fact. But 704(b), added in 1984, provides that "no expert witness testifying with respect to the mental state or condition of a defendant in a criminal case may state an opinion or inference as to whether the defendant did or did not have the mental state or condition constituting an element of the crime charged or of a defense thereto. Such ultimate issues are matters for the trier of fact alone."

  ii. **Significance:** FRE 704(b) will probably make it somewhat more difficult for a defendant to successfully assert an insanity defense. The defendant can no longer present an expert to testify as to his opinion that the defendant is insane. Presumably, the psychiatrist will also not be permitted to state that the defendant "was unable to appreciate the wrongfulness of his conduct, due to his mental disease" (now the substantive standard for insanity in federal cases). However, the expert will probably still be able to give a medical diagnosis of the defendant, and perhaps to discuss the symptoms that this diagnosed condition might produce.

Example: Murder case; insanity defense. The defense psychiatrist expert will probably be permitted to state that D is, in his opinion, a schizophrenic with low impulse control. He will probably be permitted to state the reasons that led him to this conclusion. He might be permitted to say that this condition may have contributed to the particular homicidal act charged. He will not, however, be permitted to say that D's condition prevented him from appreciating the wrongfulness of the killing — this will be held to be an ultimate legal issue, properly left to the jury.

 iii. **Other conditions:** FRE 704(b) applies not only to insanity questions, but to any other "ultimate issue" relating to a criminal defendant's mental state. For instance, if D is charged with murder (so defined as to require proof of premeditation), neither the defense nor the prosecution psychiatrist expert will be permitted to express his opinion as to whether D premeditated, or was capable of premeditating, the killing. W&B, Par. 704[03].

2. **Reliability of eyewitness testimony:** Scientists have consistently shown, over many years, that *eyewitness identifications* are notoriously unreliable. Yet, juries are constantly required to reach verdicts based on such identifications, especially in criminal cases. Consequently, many defense lawyers have attempted to introduce expert testimony, usually by psychologists, to persuade the jury that eyewitness identifications in general, and especially identifications of the type involved in the present case, are less likely to be accurate than the jury might otherwise suppose. For instance, the defense might seek to have a psychologist tell the jury that: (1)

witnesses are particularly bad at identifying persons of the opposite race; (2) a witness' subjective degree of certainty about the correctness of his identification bears no relation to its actual likelihood of being correct; (3) when a witness gives present (in-court) testimony that he recognizes the defendant as the perpetrator, this identification is quite likely to stem not from the witness' perception at the crime scene, but rather from his identification of the suspect from photos, in a line-up, or some other later episode; or (4) the longer the gap between the perception and the identification, the less likely it is to be correct, yet the more likely the witness is to supply lots of convincing (but inadvertently false) details. See L&S, pp. 168-76.

   a. Traditional judicial resistance: Traditionally, courts have been relatively ***unwilling*** to accept such psychological testimony about the weaknesses of human perception and memory. This unwillingness seems to stem mostly from judges' belief that lay persons have a basic ability to judge the reliability of identifications, and a reluctance to allow experts to help the jury do what it can do adequately without the expert.

   b. Increasing willingness: But trial courts seem to be growing increasingly willing to allow expert testimony about the unreliability of eyewitness identifications, at least in situations where: (1) the expert confines herself to stating general principles, and does not purport to give an opinion about whether the witness in the particular case is accurate; and (2) the expert testimony relates to particular aspect of the case (e.g., the fact that the witness is identifying a person of another race), rather than being about the general fallibility of eyewitness identifications. L&S (p. 167) state that "an acknowledged expert in this area [told us] that about half the time her testimony is allowed [by the trial judge]."

   c. Appellate court: However, if the trial judge excludes such testimony, it is very difficult for the defendant to convince the appeals court to reverse. That is, the decision to admit or exclude such testimony is generally held to be within the trial court's ***discretion***, and that discretion is very rarely found to be abused. See, e.g., *U.S. v. Fosher*, 590 F.2d 381 (1st Cir. 1979) (expert testimony relating to perception and memory of eyewitnesses could properly be excluded by the trial judge on the grounds that it was neither sufficiently directly related to the issues in the case nor "sufficiently beyond the ken of lay jurors" to satisfy FRE 702).

   d. Appellate case overturns exclusion: One of the very few (perhaps the only) appellate cases overturning a trial court's refusal to allow expert testimony on the reliability of eyewitness identifications is *State v. Chapple*, 660 P.2d 1208 (Ariz. 1983).

      i. Facts: Scott and his sister, Buck, agreed by phone to help find someone who would sell drugs to Coley. Coley arrived in town with two assistants whom Scott and Buck had never seen before, one of whom was introduced to them as "Dee." During the actual sale, Coley and his assistants murdered two of the sellers, then left town. Nothing ever tied D to the crime, except that Scott and Buck picked D's photograph out of a line-up, as being

Dee, more than one year after the date of the crime. At trial, the prosecution offered Scott and Buck's testimony that they recognized D as being Dee.

ii. Offer of testimony: At trial, D denied that he was Dee. He offered testimony by Dr. Elizabeth Loftus, perhaps the most famous expert on the reliability of eyewitness identifications, to testify as to several factors that make identifications like the one in this case relatively unreliable. (For instance, Loftus would have pointed to: (1) the long lapse of time between the crime and the initial photo ID; (2) Scott's initial failure to identify D's photo when it was shown to him only four months after the crime; (4) the effect of stress on perception; (4) the problem of "unconscious transfer," whereby "a witness who takes part in a photo identification session without identifying any of the photographs and who then later sees a photograph of one of those persons may relate his or her familiarity with the picture to the crime rather than to the previous identification session"; (5) the problem of "feedback factor," whereby two witness to the same event — here, Scott and Buck — may have reinforced each other's mistaken identification; and (6) the lack of any relationship between a witness' confidence in his identification and the actual accuracy of that identification, relevant because both Scott and Buck asserted their absolute certainty that their identification of D was correct). The trial judge refused to allow this testimony.

iii. Holding: The appellate court held that the trial court's refusal to allow this testimony was ***reversible error.*** It found that because of the closeness of the issues, and the fact that Dr. Loftus' testimony would be limited to an exposition of the general factors affecting reliability (rather than an opinion on the actual credibility or accuracy of Scott and Buck's testimony) the probative value of Dr. Loftus' expertise would outweigh any prejudice to the state. The court was apparently impressed by the number of relevant respects in which a lay juror's ***expectation*** would be ***different*** from what experimentation had proved. For instance, the court believed that most lay jurors might well assume that the more certain a witness is that his identification is correct, the more likely it is to be correct; therefore, the jury would have been assisted by Dr. Loftus' testimony that this is absolutely not the case. (A dissent argued that such expert testimony, with its "scientific aura of trustworthiness," would "permit academia to take over the fact-finding function of the jury.")

iv. Significance: Even in Arizona, reversals of a trial court's decision to exclude expert testimony about the reliability of eyewitness identifications will be rare. The *Chapple* court stressed that only because of the unusual facts of that case was expert testimony so likely to assist the jury in overcoming its incorrect assumptions about the way memory works that exclusion of the testimony amounted to an abuse of discretion.

3. Lie detectors, truth serums, and hypnosis: A number of other scientific techniques rely on psychology to determine the credibility of witnesses, or to help witnesses become more accurate. These include the **lie detector**, **truth serums**, and **hypnosis.** All of these are discussed *supra*, pp. 112-16.

4. **Rape trauma syndrome:** Another instance in which a party may try to introduce expert testimony bearing on the credibility of a witness concerns evidence of so-called *"rape trauma syndrome."* To rebut defense assertions that the rape victim is distorting or making up the episode, prosecutors sometimes try to introduce testimony by a psychologist or social worker that the victim exhibits the symptoms of rape trauma syndrome, and therefore probably actually experienced the events she claims to have experienced.

   a. **Judicial reluctance:** Courts are likely to be reluctant to admit such expert testimony, because of the extreme danger of unfair prejudice to the defendant. See, e.g., *State v. Saldana*, 324 N.W.2d 227 (Minn. 1982), holding that testimony by W (a counselor for sexual assault victims), to the effect that W believed that V was not making her story up, and that it was common for victims not to report the incident until the following day, should not have been admitted; the jurors were quite capable of determining whether a rape had occurred, and W's testimony was merely a useless legal conclusion whose danger of unfair prejudice outweighed any probative value. "Credibility is the sole province of the jury," the *Saldana* court asserted.

BURDENS OF PROOF, PRESUMPTIONS, AND OTHER PROCEDURAL ISSUES

Introductory note: In this chapter, we consider four procedural areas: (1) burdens of proof; (2) presumptions; (3) allocation of functions between judge and jury; and (4) appellate review as it relates to evidence.

I. BURDENS OF PROOF

A. Two burdens: Courts frequently refer to "the burden of proof." However, there are in reality two distinct burdens: (1) the burden of ***production***; and (2) the burden of ***persuasion***. In our discussion of each of these burdens, we will assume that plaintiff has both burdens with respect to an issue which we shall call A.

    1. Burden of production: When we say that P bears the burden of ***production*** with respect to issue A, we mean that P has the obligation to come forward with ***some evidence*** that A exists. This burden is sometimes referred to as the burden of ***"going forward."***

        a. Consequence of failure to carry burden: If a party does not satisfy this burden of production, the court will ***decide the issue against him*** as a matter of law. If A is part of P's *prima facie* case (e.g., a showing that the defendant was negligent in a negligence case), the consequence of P's failure to discharge his burden of production is that the judge will ***direct a verdict*** against P, without the case ever going to the jury. If A is not part of P's *prima facie* case, the court will direct the jury to ***find against P*** on issue A.

    2. Burden of persuasion: The burden of ***persuasion*** is quite different. When we say that P has the burden of persuasion on issue A, we mean that if at the close of the evidence the jury cannot decide whether A has been established with the relevant level of certainty (usually "preponderance of the evidence" in civil cases), the jury must find against P on issue A. The phrase ***"risk of nonpersuasion"*** is often used to describe this burden — if neither P nor D have persuaded the jury about whether A exists, to say that P bears the burden of persuasion or the risk of nonpersuasion means that he is the one who will lose on this issue.

    3. One burden shifts, other does not: The burden of production as to issue A can, and often does, ***shift*** throughout the trial. The burden of persuasion, by contrast, always remains on the party on whom it first rests. The operation of both burdens can be better understood by use of the following drawing:

Figure 11-1

(Adapted from Lilly, p. 50)

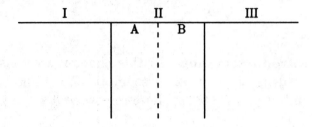

a.   **Application of drawing:** Let's assume that P sues D in a negligence action, and that the only issue in dispute is whether D was in fact negligent. (That is, assume D concedes that P was harmed by D's act and that P was not contributorily negligent.) In all jurisdictions, negligence is part of P's *prima facie* case — that is, he has the burden of production as to it; also, in virtually every jurisdiction, P will have the burden of persuasion on the negligence issue. We will now add a "ball" to the drawing to show the location of the burden of production on the issue of D's negligence.

b.   **Initial burden of production:** Since P bears the initial burden of producing evidence of negligence, at the start of the case the "ball" is in Zone I (literally, in P's court):

Figure 11-2

Initial burden of production on D

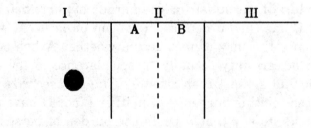

   If P does not come up with enough evidence of D's negligence to allow a reasonable jury to find that D was negligent (i.e., P doesn't move the ball out of Zone I), at the conclusion of P's case, the judge will direct a verdict for D.

c.   **Burden sustained:** Now, let's assume that P presents a witness, W, who testifies that he was in the car with D at the time of the accident, and that D was glancing at a blond model on a billboard by the side of the road rather than at the road when the accident occurred. Since this is evidence which, if believed by the jury, would allow a reasonable jury to find that D was negligent, P has moved the ball into at least Zone II.

Figure 11-3

*P satisfies initial burden of production;
neither party bears it now*

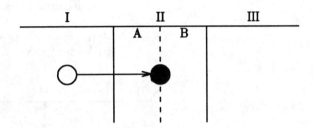

i. **Cross-examination:** Now, assume (as would almost certainly be the case) that D is able to cast some doubt on W's testimony by a reasonably effective cross-examination. If D does not come up with any other evidence of his non-negligence, the judge will probably conclude that the case remains in Zone II at the end of the evidence. If so, he will send the case to the jury on the issue of whether D was negligent — that is, he will let the jury decide this issue.

d. **Shifting of burden:** Now, let's change our assumption about what P proved in his direct case — let's now assume that W testified about D's looking at the billboard, and that D chose not to cross-examine W. At the close of P's case, the judge would probably find that the ball was in Zone III — based solely on the evidence heard so far, a reasonable jury **must** find that D was negligent. Therefore by the close of P's case, **the burden of production has shifted** to D — if D were to rest without putting on a defense, D would lose.

Figure 11-4

*P shifts burden of production
onto D*

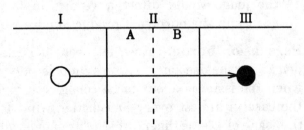

e. **Rebuttal evidence:** Finally, let us assume that D puts on rebuttal evidence of non-negligence, in the form of D's own testimony that he did not look at the billboard, and watched the road at all times. This testimony will probably be sufficient to move the ball back to Zone II. That is, the judge will probably conclude that a reasonable jury could believe either W or D. If so, the judge will let the case go to the jury.

Figure 11-5

D satisfies burden of production;
neither party bears it now

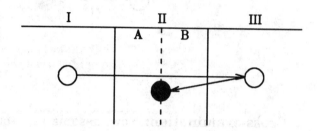

i. **Incredible testimony:** Alternatively, if the judge finds that D's testimony is so totally unconvincing that no reasonable jury could believe it, he will conclude that D has not moved the ball back out of Zone III, in which case he will direct a verdict in favor of P at the close of D's case. (But judges will rarely take the case away from the jury based solely upon the judge's belief that a party's witnesses are not credible; therefore, the judge will probably let the case go to the jury, i.e., he will treat it as falling within Zone II.)

ii. **Back to Zone I:** It is even conceivable that D's case as to his own non-negligence will be so compelling that the ball will be moved all the way from Zone III back to Zone I. This might be the case, for instance, if D gave convincing evidence by another passenger in the car contradicting W's billboard story, plus impeached W's evidence by showing that W was not in the car at all at the time in question. In this event, at the close of the evidence the judge would direct a verdict in favor of D. However, such extreme swings in the burden of production are rare.

f. **Persuasion burden:** Now, let's consider the burden of ***persuasion:*** The burden of persuasion only matters (and is only measured) at the end of the case, when the issue is about to be considered by the jury. Assuming (as would be the case in almost every jurisdiction) that P has the burden of persuasion on the issue of D's negligence by a "preponderance of the evidence" (*infra*, p. 439), here's what would happen:

i. **Significance of persuasion burden:** If the jury finds that the ball is in Zone IIA (non-negligence more probable than negligence), it will decide for D without the burden of persuasion's having any significance. If it finds that the ball is in Zone IIB (negligence more probable than non-negligence), it will decide for P, again without reference to the burden of persuasion.

But if it finds that the ball is *exactly on the dotted line* that divides IIA from IIB (negligence exactly as probable as non-negligence), it will decide for D *based on the burden of persuasion*.

    ii. **Tie-breaker:** In other words, with respect to the usual civil issue (A or non-A) that is to be decided according to the preponderance of the evidence standard, the *only time the burden of persuasion makes a difference* is when the jury finds A and non-A to be *equally probable*.

Figure 11-6

*Only in this situation does the
burden of persuasion make a difference*

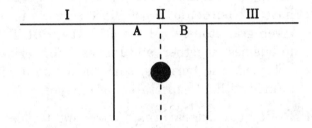

B. **Allocating the burdens in civil cases:** In civil cases, there is no simple formula for determining which side will bear the burden of production, or the burden of persuasion, as to a given issue. Here are some general guidelines:

    1. **Usually on plaintiff:** On most civil issues, both the burden of production and the burden of persuasion are on the *plaintiff*. M, p. 949. For instance, in a typical negligence case, the plaintiff bears both burdens — production and persuasion — with respect to showing the defendant's negligence, the plaintiff's harm, and the causal link between the two. (But the defendant bears both burdens with respect to contributory negligence, in most jurisdictions.)

    2. **Pleading burden:** The burden of production and the burden of persuasion are both usually on the *same party*. Furthermore, this is usually the same party who has the burden of *pleading* on the issue. For instance, the plaintiff in a negligence case generally has the burden of pleading all three elements, as well as the burdens of production and persuasion as to those issues. Likewise, it is generally the defendant who bears the burden of pleading contributory negligence, as well as the burdens of production and persuasion.

    3. **Substantive law:** The burdens are allocated by the jurisdiction's *substantive law*. That is, for every type of claim or defense, the jurisdiction has either a statutory or case-law precedent allocating the burdens. L&S, p. 794. The trial judge has little discretion about who bears the burdens, unless the issue happens to be one of first impression in the jurisdiction.

4. **Factors:** Courts and legislatures generally consider a number of factors in determining which party should bear the burdens on a given issue. Some of these factors are as follows:

    a. **Change of status quo:** The party who is attempting to **change the status quo** is more likely to have to bear the burdens. For instance, since the plaintiff in a negligence action is the one trying to change the status quo — trying to shift the financial loss from himself to the defendant — this is a reason for imposing most of the burdens on him.

    b. **Unusual event:** The party who is contending that the more **unusual** event has occurred will be more likely to have the burdens of proof. For instance, suppose P and D are in a business relationship, and P sues for services rendered; if D claims that the services were intended as a gift he will probably have the burden of proof, since services in a business context generally are not given gratuitously. M, pp. 950-51. (But if P and D are father and son, are not in business together, and P sues D for services performed, it is P who will probably bear the burdens, since in a family situation services are generally performed without expectation of repayment. *Id.*)

    c. **Policy considerations:** Courts and legislatures often use the allocation of burdens as a means of pursuing **social policy**, including the **disfavoring** of certain defenses. This, more than anything else, probably accounts for most jurisdictions' decision to require the defendant to bear both burdens with respect to contributory negligence.

        i. **"Alternative liability" theory:** Pursuit of social policy also explains the California Supreme Court's landmark decision in *Sindell v. Abbott Laboratories*, 607 P.2d 924 (Cal. 1980), in which the court shifted to the Ds (drug companies) the burden of proving that they were *not* the suppliers of the drug (DES) that harmed P. It was P's mother, not P, who had taken the drug some 20 years before; neither P nor the Ds could determine which manufacturer (out of 200 that manufactured the drug) produced the actual DES that P's mother took. The court decided to shift to each of the Ds the burden of proving that it could not have produced the DES that P's mother took (by showing that it was not selling the drug at the relevant time); any defendant who could not discharge this burden would be required to pay a portion of the award equal to its portion of the DES market. The court relied explicitly on policy considerations: "As between an innocent plaintiff and negligent defendants, the latter should bear the cost of the injury. . . . [D]efendants are better able to bear the cost of injury resulting from the manufacture of a defective product."

    d. **Peculiar knowledge of one party:** When knowledge of the facts required to prove a particular claim or defense lies **peculiarly within the knowledge** of one party, the burdens of proof are more likely to be placed on that party. For instance, a defendant in a contract action who claims that he has already paid for the goods or services generally bears the burdens of proving payment, on the theory that his records are a better source of information about the defense than are the plaintiff's. M, p. 950. However, this "peculiarly within the knowledge of one party" doctrine is frequently **ignored**; for instance, a defendant must generally prove contributory negligence even though the facts surrounding the alleged negligence are probably better known to the plaintiff than to the defendant. *Id.*

5. **"*Prima facie* case":** The term **"*prima facie* case"** is often used to describe the collection of issues on which the plaintiff has the burden of **production**. W,M,A&B, p. 1181. According to the most common use of the term *"prima facie,"* the plaintiff has established a *prima facie* case for, say, negligence when he has produced enough evidence of defendant's negligence, his own harm, and a causal link, to permit the case to go to the jury.

C. Allocation of burdens of proof in criminal cases: The allocation of the burdens of proof in **criminal** cases is subject to constitutional (due process) limits.

1. **Element distinguished from affirmative defense:** Before we can understand these constitutional limits on how the state may allocate the burdens of proof in a criminal case, we must first understand a key distinction which the Supreme Court has drawn between **"*elements of the crime*"** and **"*affirmative defenses.*"**

   a. **Elements of the crime:** When the legislature defines a particular crime, those factors which the definition lists as part of the crime are the "elements" of that crime. For instance, if the state has defined murder to be the premeditated taking of another person's life, the two elements of the crime are: (1) the taking of another person's life; and (2) the mental state of premeditation.

   b. **Affirmative defense:** The state may choose to recognize certain factors as being **excuses** or **justifications** that prevent otherwise culpable conduct from being criminal, or at least reduce the severity of the crime. These excuses and justifications are commonly made **"*affirmative defenses,*"** as distinguished from being elements of the crime. The state might, for instance, define murder in the simple way summarized in the prior paragraph, and then add a clause: "However, if the accused demonstrates that, at the time of the killing, he could not tell the difference between right and wrong, this shall constitute an affirmative defense."

   c. **Significance:** The key significance of the distinction is that the **state has the burdens of production and persuasion with respect to all elements** of the crime, whereas the **defendant always has the burden of production**, and often the burden of persuasion, with respect to an **affirmative defense**. (This distinction is explored further below, in connection with the discussion of constitutional limits on allocating burdens to the defendant.)

   d. **Discretion:** The state has a considerable amount of discretion in deciding whether to define a factor as being an element of the crime or, rather, an affirmative defense. For instance, a state could obviously choose to make absence of insanity an element of the crime of murder (in which case the prosecution would have the burden not only of producing evidence of sanity but of persuading the jury beyond a reasonable doubt that the defendant was sane), rather than making insanity an affirmative defense. The state is always free to make a given factor an element of the crime (since this works to the defendant's advantage).

   i. Limits on affirmative defenses: But there may be constitutional limits on the state's ability to make a factor an affirmative defense. For instance, the Supreme Court would probably hold that a state was violating the defendant's due process and Eighth Amendment rights if it authorized the death sentence for murder, and then defined murder as "the taking of another's life," while making absence of premeditation an affirmative defense as to which the defendant has the burdens of both production and persuasion.

   ii. Allowable affirmative defenses: It seems quite clear that the state may constitutionally make the following factors affirmative defenses, as to which the defendant bears the burden of both production and persuasion: ***insanity, self-defense, duress, voluntary intoxication,*** and ***extreme emotional disturbance.*** Most of these are discussed below in the context of burden of persuasion.

2. Elements of crime: If the state has made a factor an ***element of the crime***, the state must bear both the burden of ***production*** and ***persuasion*** with respect to that element. In fact, the Due Process Clause requires that the state not only bear the burden of persuasion on each element, but that it do so according to a ***"beyond a reasonable doubt"*** standard. The Supreme Court so held in *In re Winship*, 397 U.S. 358 (1970).

3. Allocation for affirmative defense: By contrast, the state has far more leeway with respect to allocating the burdens concerning an ***affirmative defense***:

4. Production burden: Apparently the state may impose on the defendant the ***burden of production*** on ***any affirmative defense***. M, p. 991. Even if there is an overlap between conduct or a mental state the absence of which is an element of the crime, and conduct or a mental state which has been defined as an affirmative defense, the state may impose upon the defendant the burden of coming forward with at least some evidence in support of the affirmative defense.

   Example: Suppose the state defines murder to include only those killings in which the defendant acts "with premeditation and without fear for his own life or safety." Suppose further that the state defines self-defense as an affirmative defense. The state may constitutionally place the burden of production on D, in the sense that he must come forward with at least some evidence of self-defense before the jury will be given an instruction that self-defense can negate the crime. This is true even though the state has defined the crime in such a way that an aspect of the affirmative defense (fear for one's own safety) is also a factor the absence of which is an element of the crime. M, p. 991.

5. Burden of persuasion: But the state is more limited when it comes to allocating the burden of ***persuasion***. If the defense is a "true" affirmative defense, in the sense that it does not overlap with an element of the crime, the state may place upon the defendant the burden of persuasion by a preponderance of the evidence. But if there is a **substantial overlap** between an act or mental state needed to show an affirmative defense, and the absence of that act or mental state needed as an element of the crime, the **state** must bear the burden of persuasion (and, in fact, persuasion beyond a reasonable doubt). Determining when such an overlap exists can be difficult, as shown by a series of recent Supreme Court cases:

a. **Heat of passion (*Mullaney*):** In *Mullaney v. Wilbur*, 421 U.S. 684 (1975), the Court held it unconstitutional for Maine to place on the defendant the burden of persuasion with respect to the affirmative defense of **"heat of passion."** Maine defined murder in such a way that "malice aforethought" was an essential element, which could be implied from the fact that the killing was both intentional and unlawful. It then made "heat of passion" an affirmative defense (which if proved downgrades the offense from murder to manslaughter). The Supreme Court held that requiring D to bear the burden of persuasion on heat of passion was tantamount to requiring him to negate the existence of malice aforethought. This requirement, in turn, ran afoul of the principle established in *In re Winship* (*supra*, p. 434) that the prosecution must prove each element of the crime beyond a reasonable doubt.

b. **Extreme emotional disturbance (*Patterson*):** But one year after *Mullaney*, the Court held that a murder defendant could be constitutionally required to bear the burden of persuading the jury that he acted under **"extreme emotional disturbance."** *Patterson v. New York*, 432 U.S. 197 (1977). In ***Patterson***, New York defined second degree murder to include the element of "intent to cause the death of another person," and made it an affirmative defense that the defendant "acted under the influence of extreme emotional disturbance for which there was a reasonable explanation or excuse." The Court concluded that the defendant, to succeed with the affirmative defense here, was **not required to negative any element of the crime**: a showing by the defendant that he acted under extreme emotional disturbance was not necessarily inconsistent with his having had the basic mental state for the crime (an intent to kill). (Three dissenters in *Patterson* contended that the defense of "extreme emotional disturbance" was a direct descendant of the "heat of passion" defense at issue in *Mullaney*, and that the prosecution should have the burden of persuasion on the emotional disturbance defense.)

c. **Insanity:** So long as the state defines murder in such a way that sanity is not an element of the crime, the defendant may constitutionally be required to bear the burden of persuasion on **insanity**. *Leland v. Oregon*, 343 U.S. 790 (1952). (The *Patterson* Court indicated that it believed *Leland* was still good law).

d. **Self-defense:** The defendant can ordinarily be required to bear the persuasion burden with respect to the affirmative defense of **self-defense**. In *Martin v. Ohio*, 480 U.S. 228 (1987), the Court upheld an Ohio statute that placed the persuasion burden for a self-defense defense upon the defendant. Ohio defined the crime of aggravated murder as requiring the defendant to have "purposely, and with prior calculation and design, caus[ed] the death of another." The affirmative defense of self-defense required the defendant to show, by a preponderance of the evidence, that he was not at fault in creating the situation, that he had an honest belief that he was in imminent danger of death or great harm which could be escaped only by use of deadly force, and that he did not violate any duty to retreat or avoid danger.

    i. Rationale: The majority concluded that there was no necessary overlap between the two definitions. The Court conceded that "it may be that most encounters in which self-defense is claimed arise suddenly and involve no prior plan or specific purpose to take life." Nonetheless, Ohio had not shifted to D the burden of proving any of the basic elements of aggravated murder, including the "prior calculation or design" requirement. For instance, the jury was still free to consider D's evidence relating to self-defense and to determine that it created a ***reasonable doubt*** about whether D had the requisite mental state for the crime, even if it found that D had not established by a preponderance of the evidence all three of the elements for the affirmative defense.

    ii. Dissent: Four justices dissented in *Martin*. They contended that there was such overlap between the basic mental state and the defense that evidence on self-defense necessarily tended to negate the mental state for murder. Furthermore, by instructing the jury that D bore the burden of establishing self-defense (the dissenters argued), the trial judge produced a great risk that the jury would mistakenly believe that D had the burden of negating an element of the crime (prior calculation and design).

e. Summary: Following the string of cases ending in *Martin*, the state's right to assign the persuasion burden to the defendant on an affirmative defense is confused. However, some things seem clear:

    i. Great leeway: The state has substantial leeway to define affirmative defenses as it wishes, and to assign the burden of persuasion to the defendant as to those defenses. So long as there is not a ***virtual identity*** between the act or mental state defined as an element of the crime, and the act or mental state whose absence is an element of the affirmative defense, the state may define affirmative defenses as it wishes and impose on the defendant the persuasion burden as to those defenses.

    ii. Valid defenses: If the state is at all careful in defining the crimes and the defenses, it may impose upon the defendant the burden of persuasion concerning the common affirmative defenses of ***extreme emotional disturbance***, ***insanity***, and ***self-defense***; probably by careful drafting, the state can even make the defendant prove ***heat of passion*** (despite the fact that Maine, due to its clumsy drafting, failed to do this constitutionally in *Mullaney*).

D. Satisfying the burden of production: When a party bears the burden of production on an issue, ***how much evidence*** must he produce in order to discharge that burden? The answer varies depending on whether the case is civil or criminal.

1. **Civil case:** In a civil case, the party bearing the burden of **persuasion** as to fact A will generally have to prove that A exists "by a preponderance of the evidence." (This preponderance-of-the-evidence test is discussed more extensively *infra*, p. 439.) If P has this persuasion burden concerning issue A, and also has the production burden on A, he will discharge his production burden if he comes forward with enough evidence *so that a reasonable jury could conclude, by a preponderance of the evidence, that A exists*.

   a. **Judge decides:** It is the *judge*, not the jury, who decides whether the party bearing the production burden has satisfied that burden. The judge's only function is to decide whether a reasonable jury could reach either conclusion — if not, he will take the case away from the jury in response to a motion for directed verdict.

      Example: Suppose that P, in a negligence case, has the burden both of persuasion and production as to D's negligence. (Assume there are no other issues in the case.) At the close of D's evidence, D moves for a directed verdict. The trial judge does *not* attempt to determine whether, in the judge's personal opinion, P has established D's negligence by a preponderance of the evidence. (That is the function of the jury.) Instead, he merely determines whether P has **met his production burden**. To do this, the judge will ask himself, "Regardless of what I personally think about D's negligence, has P produced at least enough evidence so that a reasonable jury could find that D was negligent?" If the answer is "yes," the judge will deny (and if "no," the judge will grant) D's motion for a directed verdict. (Putting the matter in terms of our chart on p. 484, *supra*, the judge must decide whether the "ball" is in Zone I — in which case he must direct a verdict for D, or is rather in Zone II or III, in which case he will tell D to put on his case.)

   b. **Single witness:** A party will often be able to satisfy his burden of production by presenting just a *single witness*, even though his adversary presents many more witnesses on the issue. Unless the single witness is patently unbelievable, the judge will ordinarily conclude that a reasonable jury might believe his testimony instead of the testimony of the greater number of witnesses on the other side, and will allow the case to go to the jury.

   c. **Disbelief of adversary's denials:** But now, suppose that P, having the burden of proof on issue A, doesn't call any witnesses who testify to A, but does call his **adversary** (or witnesses favorable to the adversary), who testify to non-A. Suppose further that A cross-examines these witnesses, in a way that casts doubt on whether they are correct in asserting non-A. Has P, by this cross-examination, discharged his burden of producing some evidence of A? After all, P can claim that a reasonable jury might *disbelieve* the defense witness' assertions of non-A.

      i. **Unsuccessful:** Generally, P will be held *not* to have carried his production burden no matter how withering his cross-examination of D or D's witnesses. See, e.g., *Dyer v. MacDougall*, 201 F.2d 265 (2d Cir. 1952), so indicating. The reason is that if P were held to have carried his production burden here, then there is no situation in which D could ever successfully **appeal** the judge's **refusal to direct a verdict for him**. For, as the court pointed out in *Dyer*, no matter how overwhelming in the trial record was the evidence for the defendant who seeks a directed verdict, and no matter how non-existent the evidence for the plaintiff, an appeals court would still have to conclude that "a reasonable jury might have disbelieved all the witnesses, based on their demeanor, which we cannot evaluate on appeal. Therefore, the trial judge rightly sent the case to the jury." Therefore, to meet the production burden, a plaintiff must come up with **some affirmative evidence** for the proposition on which he bears the burden.

d. **Burden on defendant:** Recall that the production burden may **shift** during the trial. For instance, if P begins by having the burden of producing evidence of D's negligence, the evidence that P presents during his case may be so overwhelming that the production burden now shifts to D. (That is, in terms of our chart *supra*, p. 428, the ball shifts not just into Zone II, but all the way to Zone III, as shown in Drawing 11-4.) Now, unless D comes forward with some evidence that he was not negligent, at the close of D's case the judge will have to direct a verdict in *P's* favor (assuming there are no other issues in the case).

   i. **Easy to satisfy:** Here, however, D generally does not have the burden of producing direct evidence of his own non-negligence; he can probably carry his production burden by an effective **cross-examination** of P's witnesses, or by calling hostile witnesses in his own case and using leading questions to impeach their testimony. "Unless [D's] challenge to the plaintiff's case is incredible or does not dispute the central issues, the judge must let the case go to the jury." L&S, p. 795, n. 4.

2. **Criminal case:** In a **criminal** case, the prosecution bears the burden of persuasion on all issues. Furthermore, it must discharge this burden according to a "beyond a reasonable doubt" standard (see *infra*, p. 440). This tougher standard has an important effect on the burden of **production**.

   a. **Production burden on defendant:** Recall that a criminal defendant will only be required to bear the production burden if the issue constitutes an **affirmative defense**. That is, when an issue is an element of the crime, it is the prosecution who will bear the production (as well as persuasion) burden. (See *supra*, p. 434.) If the defendant bears the production burden on a given affirmative defense — e.g., insanity or self-defense — the amount of evidence he must produce to get to the jury on that affirmative defense will generally **depend on the persuasion burden**.

      i. **Illustration:** For instance, if the legislature has said that a defendant must prove insanity by a preponderance of the evidence, then to meet the production burden the defendant must come forward with enough evidence of insanity so that a reasonable jury could conclude that the defendant was more likely insane than not. If he does not, the judge will instruct the jury that it must find the defendant to have been sane. If, by contrast, the legislature has said that although insanity is an affirmative defense, once properly raised the prosecution bears the burden of disproving it beyond a reasonable doubt (this is the practice in most states), then it is easier for the defendant to discharge his production burden. He must merely come forward with enough evidence of insanity so that a reasonable jury could have a reasonable doubt about his sanity.

b. Burden on prosecution: With respect to *elements of the crime*, it is the prosecution which must (as a constitutional matter) bear the burden of production as well as persuasion. Recall that according to *Winship* (*supra*, p. 434), the prosecution has the burden of persuading the jury "beyond a reasonable doubt" as to each of these elements. The vast majority of courts have held that this tough standard *also applies to the production burden*. That is, in order to even have the case go to the jury, the prosecution must come forward with enough evidence on each element that a reasonable jury could find that the element has been proved beyond a reasonable doubt. M, p. 953. Under this majority view, if at the close of the prosecution's case the judge believes that a reasonable jury must have a doubt about one of the elements, he must direct a verdict of acquittal, *even though he believes that it is more probable than not that the defendant committed the crime*.

> **i. Historical dispute:** Judge Learned Hand held that, even in criminal cases, the prosecution should have the burden only of coming forward with enough evidence to establish the elements of the crime by a preponderance of the evidence; *U.S. v. Feinberg*, 140 F.2d 592 (2d Cir. 1944). But this view was later rejected even in Hand's own circuit; see *U.S. v. Taylor*, 464 F.2d 240 (2d Cir. 1972), where the court stated that if at the close of the prosecution's case, "there is no evidence upon which a reasonable mind might fairly conclude guilt beyond a reasonable doubt, the motion [for a directed verdict of acquittal] must be granted."

E. Satisfying the burden of persuasion: We turn now to a different but related issue: What must a party do to satisfy the burden of *persuasion* on an issue? Again, the answer varies depending on whether the case is civil or criminal.

1. Civil cases: In civil cases, a party who bears the burden of persuasion on an issue, A, must generally show that A exists "by a *preponderance of the evidence*." This standard is usually interpreted to mean that the party bearing the persuasion burden must persuade the jury "that the existence of the contested fact is *more probable than its non-existence*." M, p. 957.

> **a. Sheer statistics:** There is an important practical exception to the principle that the civil burden of persuasion is carried by proof that the event is "more probable than not." Courts generally *refuse* to accept evidence that is *purely statistical* as sufficient to carry this burden, even though the evidence produces a likelihood of greater than 50%. Instead, courts generally require that the jury end up with an *"actual belief"* in the truth of the fact, not merely a probabilistic estimate of its truth. M, p. 958.

Example: Suppose that a jet plane "buzzes" Farmer's field, frightening a mule, which then kicks Farmer in the head. Farmer sues the Air Force, but the only evidence he can come up with that the plane belonged to the Air Force rather than to a civilian airline is that according to air traffic control records, 70% of the planes flying over Farmer's farm that day belonged to the Air Force.

Probably no court would find that Farmer had carried his burden of persuasion here, even though, on a purely statistical basis, there was a 70% chance that the offending plane belonged to the Air Force. Yet, had Farmer testified that he got just a fleeting glimpse of the plane, and he thought he identified a five-pointed star on the tail, the court would probably accept this as sufficient. In the latter situation, the trier could reasonably have an "actual belief" that the plane was an Air Force plane, rather than a mere statistical hunch. Yet, probably the traffic control records are a better predictor of whether the plane actually belonged to the Air Force than Farmer's weak testimony. See K&W, p. 767.

See also *Smith v. Rapid Transit, Inc.*, 58 N.E.2d 754 (Mass. 1945) (P claimed that bus that hit her was owned by D, although she did not see any marking. Evidence that D was the only licensed bus company to be operating in the city was not sufficient to get case to jury, because of possibility that bus was private or chartered — it is "not enough that mathematically the chances somewhat favor a proposition to be proved. . . . A proposition is proved by a preponderance of the evidence if it is made to appear more likely or probable in the sense that ***actual belief in its truth***, derived from the evidence, exists in the mind or minds of the tribunal. . . .")

b. "Clear and convincing" standard: For the vast bulk of civil issues, the party bearing the burden of persuasion must show the fact by a "preponderance of the evidence." But for a few types of issues, a stricter standard is used: the fact must be proved by ***"clear and convincing"*** evidence. Examples of claims requiring proof by clear and convincing evidence are: (1) suits to rescind a contract on account of ***fraud***; (2) suits on oral contracts to make a will; and (3) suits for the specific performance of an oral contract. M, p. 960. In general, claims based on equity rather than law are more likely to be subject to this more stringent standard.

 i. "Highly probable": It has been argued that to meet the burden of persuading by "clear and convincing" evidence, the proponent must show that the fact is ***"highly probable."*** *Id.* One court has suggested that the probabilities must be "in the order of above 70%" to satisfy the "clear and convincing" burden. *U.S. v. Fatico*, 458 F.Supp. 388 (E.D.N.Y. 1978).

2. Criminal cases ("beyond reasonable doubt"): In criminal cases, the prosecution's burden of persuasion on all elements of the case means that these elements must be proved ***"beyond a reasonable doubt."*** This requirement is constitutionally mandated, and stems from *In re Winship, supra,* p. 434. Some jurisdictions do not attempt to define "reasonable doubt" for the jury, while others do. M, p. 963.

a. **Voluntariness of confession:** Suppose the prosecution wants to introduce a *confession* that it claims was given by the defendant, and the defendant asserts that the confession was *involuntary*. There is no constitutional requirement that the prosecution prove the voluntariness of the confession beyond a reasonable doubt. Instead, the dictates of due process are satisfied so long as the trial judge determines that the confession was voluntary by a *preponderance of the evidence*. *Lego v. Twomey*, 404 U.S. 477 (1972).

b. **Sentencing facts:** In *sentencing* a defendant who has just been convicted of a crime, the judge will often need to take into account facts and allegations that were not elements of the crime, and thus not proved beyond a reasonable doubt by the mere fact of conviction. Proof of these facts relied on in sentencing probably does *not* have to be made beyond a reasonable doubt. However, some judges have required that such facts be established by a "clear and convincing evidence" standard. See, e.g., *U.S. v. Fatico, supra,* p. 440, holding that for D to receive a longer sentence because he is a member of organized crime, the fact of his membership in organized crime must be proven by the "clear and convincing" standard.

II. PRESUMPTIONS

A. **Presumptions generally:** The term "presumption" refers to a relationship between a "basic" fact (which we'll call B) and a "presumed" fact (which we'll call P). When we say that fact P can be presumed from fact B, we mean that once B is established, P is established or at least rendered more likely.

1. **Four meanings:** However, the precise meaning of "presumption" is uncertain. When courts and legislatures say that P is to be presumed from B, they may mean any of at least four quite distinct things. In order from weakest to strongest link between P and B, these possibilities are as follows:

    a. **Permissible inference:** The court or legislature may mean merely that once B is established (and in the absence of any direct proof about whether P does or does not exist), the jury *may* (but need not) conclude that P exists. This is the weakest link between B and P that is ever contemplated by the term "presumption." More commonly, this weak link is referred to as a *"permissible inference"* rather than a presumption.

    b. **Shifts production but not persuasion burden:** The presumption may mean that if a party who has the burden of production on P establishes B, his adversary has the *burden of production* on non-P. That is, the existence of the presumption, according to this view, shifts the production burden to the person who does not benefit from the presumption. However, under this view, the burden of *persuasion* is *not shifted* — if the burden of persuasion on fact P would have been on a party in the absence of that presumption, that burden is still upon him even though he is the beneficiary of the presumption.

    c. **Shifts both production and persuasion burdens:** Another view of presumptions is that once the beneficiary proves B, both the burden of production and the burden of ***persuasion*** shift to his adversary with respect to fact P. Under this view, if plaintiff would in the absence of a presumption have the burden both of production and persuasion as to P, once he establishes B it is up to defendant not only to produce some evidence of non-P, but to persuade the jury of P's non-existence.

d. Conclusive presumption: Finally, the term presumption may mean that once B is established, P is ***conclusively (irrebuttably) presumed*** to exist. Such a "conclusive presumption" really amounts to a ***substantive rule of law***.

> **Example:** Suppose that the legislature enacts a statute providing that when a letter is shown to have been properly addressed and mailed, it shall be presumed to have been received by the addressee. Assume further that plaintiff is trying to prove that a letter he sent to defendant was received by defendant, that defendant denies having received the letter, and that in the absence of the presumption, plaintiff would have both the burden of producing evidence of defendant's receipt of the letter as well as the burden of persuading the jury, by a preponderance of the evidence, that defendant received the letter. Here is what would happen under each of the four above meanings of "presumption":
>
> Under definition (a) — permissive inference — even if P proved conclusively that he properly addressed and mailed the letter, and even if D came forward with no evidence at all that he never received it, the presumption's only result would be that the judge would instruct the jury, "If you find that plaintiff properly addressed and mailed the letter, you may, but need not, find that defendant received it."
>
> Under definition (b) — shift of production but not persuasion burden — once P produced evidence of the basic fact (that he properly addressed and mailed the letter), this would be enough to shift to D the burden of coming forward with some evidence that he did not receive the letter. If D came forward with such evidence (e.g., his own testimony that he examines his mail every day, and knows that he did not receive the letter), this would probably be enough to discharge D's production burden. Since under this meaning of "presumption" the persuasion burden is not shifted, P would still have the burden of persuading the jury that D actually received the letter, and P would lose if the jury thought it was as likely that D did not receive the letter as that he did. (Probably the judge would not mention the presumption in instructing the jury, if the judge concluded that D had met his production burden by coming forward with some evidence of non-receipt.)
>
> Under definition (c) — burden of persuasion, as well as production, shifted — once P produced evidence of proper addressing and mailing, D would not only have to produce some evidence of non-receipt, but would also now bear the burden of persuading the jury, by a preponderance of the evidence, that he never received the letter. If D came forward with some evidence of non-receipt (e.g., his testimony of non-receipt), the judge would then instruct the jury, "If you find that P properly addressed and mailed the letter, then you must find that D actually received it, unless you find it more

probable than not that D never in fact received the letter." (The judge might also inform the jury of the presumption's existence.)

Under definition (d) — conclusive presumption — if P shows that the letter was properly addressed and mailed, the judge will conclude as a matter of law that D is deemed to have received the letter. The jury will not even get to decide this issue.

2. **Presumptions are rebuttable:** Most courts and commentators agree that only those relations between facts B and P summarized by definitions (b) and (c) are properly classified as presumptions in *civil* cases. That is, for a relationship to be a presumption in a civil case, it: (1) must at least shift the burden of *production* to the party opposing the presumption; and (2) must be *rebuttable*.

3. **Reasons for creating:** Presumptions may be created either by the legislature or by judges. Here are some of the many reasons why a judge or legislature might create a presumption:

   a. **Probability:** To reflect the judge's or legislature's belief that if the basic fact (B) is proved, it is so highly probable that the presumed fact (P) also exists that it is sensible and *time-saving* to assume the truth of P unless the adversary disproves it. M, p. 969.

      Example: When a properly stamped and addressed letter is mailed, it is so probable that the addressee received it that it is sensible and time-saving to presume receipt unless the addressee shows otherwise.

   b. **Social and economic policy:** To carry out some *social* or *economic policy* by benefiting one contention over another.

      Example: Statutes commonly create a presumption that when a woman gives birth to a child while married, the husband is presumed to be the father. This presumption furthers the social policy of not needlessly burdening children with the label of illegitimacy.

   c. **Superior access to proof:** To counteract the opponent's *superior access* to proof.

      Example: When a bailor turns goods over to a bailee in good condition, and they are returned in damaged condition, it is commonly presumed that the damage was due to the bailee's negligence. The bailee has better knowledge of what happened than the bailor, so it is only fair to shift to him the burden of showing what happened once the bailor demonstrates that the damage occurred while the goods were in bailee's custody.

B. **Effect of presumption in civil cases:** We turn now to a more detailed consideration of the effect of a presumption in a civil case. Our discussion focuses on what are usually thought of as "true" presumptions, i.e., definitions (b) and (c) above (presumption at least shifts the burden of production, and is rebuttable).

1. **Debate between Thayer and Morgan:** Probably the most famous intellectual disagreement in evidence history concerned the effects to be given to presumptions

in civil cases.

    a. Thayer ("bursting bubble") majority view: Professor Thayer believed that presumptions should be given the effect of definition (b), that is, that they should shift the burden of production but not the burden of persuasion. Under the Thayer approach, once the opponent discharges his production burden by coming up with some evidence showing the non-existence of the presumed fact, the presumption **disappears from the case**, and the jury decides the issue as if the presumption had never existed. For this reason, the Thayer approach is often referred to as the **"bursting bubble"** approach. The Thayer approach has been adopted by a **majority** of jurisdictions.

    b. Morgan (minority) view: Professor Morgan argued that the Thayer approach gives too little weight to presumptions, and that a presumption should ordinarily be given the effect described in definition (c). That is, he contended that the presumption should shift not only the burden of production, but **also the burden of persuasion**, to the presumption's opponent. He contended that presumptions normally reflect well-reasoned and deeply held beliefs about policy or probability on the part of the legislature, and that these beliefs should not be disregarded merely because the opponent has managed to come up with just enough evidence of the non-existence of the presumed fact to take that issue to the jury. Nonetheless, only a minority of jurisdictions have adopted Professor Morgan's approach.

        i. Partial adoption: Some states have given a Thayer effect to some presumptions and a Morgan effect to others. For instance, the California Evidence Code divides presumptions into two categories: (1) Presumptions based on public policy place the burden of persuasion, not just production, on the presumption's opponent (a Morgan effect); but (2) Presumptions that do not implement any public policy other than facilitating correct adjudication do not shift the burden of persuasion (a bursting bubble or Thayer effect). See Cal. Evid. Code §600 et seq.

    c. Chart: Observe that the Thayer and Morgan positions differ from each other only when the presumption's opponent comes up with evidence of the non-existence of the presumed fact. Table 11-1 on p. 445, *infra*, shows the effect of the presumption, under various states of the evidence, for both the Thayer and Morgan approaches:

2. Defense of "bursting bubble" view: Why is it that despite Morgan's apparently persuasive arguments, only a few jurisdictions have adopted his view that the presumption should shift the burden of persuasion? There are a couple of reasons:

    a. Probative force remains: First, even though under the "bursting bubble" view the presumption itself disappears when the opponent comes forward with some evidence of the non-existence of the presumed fact, this does not mean that the **logical relationship** between the basic fact and the presumed fact disappears. The jury always has the power to infer that where the basic fact exists, the presumed fact is likely to exist. In fact, the judge will often **tell** the

Table 11-1

Rebuttable Presumptions — Thayer/"Bursting Bubble" vs. Morgan

Presumption is that a properly addressed and mailed letter (basic fact) was received by the addressee (presumed fact). *B* is the beneficiary of the presumption and *O* is the opponent. Without the presumption, *B* would have the burden of persuasion (and production) that addressee received the letter. Presumption enters the case when *B* introduces some evidence of the proper addressing and mailing of the letter. This is the only issue in the case.

Type of Presumption	O introduces:	The jury will be instructed that:
Thayer / "Bursting Bubble" (Burden of production, but not of persuasion, shifted to *O*)	No evidence of whether letter was either mailed properly (basic fact) or received (presumed fact)	If they find proper mailing, they must find receipt. [If reasonable jury must find proper mailing, judge will direct verdict for *B*.]
	Some evidence that letter was not properly mailed,* but no evidence regarding receipt	If they find proper mailing, they must find receipt.
	Some evidence that letter was never received (with or without evidence regarding proper mailing)	[No jury instruction requiring the jury to find receipt if they find mailing.] If *B* convinces jury by a preponderance of the evidence that letter was received, they shall decide for *B*; otherwise they must decide for *O*. [In some states (and possibly under the Federal Rules), judge will tell jury that the presumption exists, but he will tell them that they may, not must, infer receipt from proper mailing.]
Morgan (Burden of persuasion, as well as production, shifted to *O*)	No evidence of whether letter was either mailed properly or received	[Same as for Thayer]
	Some evidence that letter was not properly mailed,* but no evidence regarding receipt	[Same as for Thayer]
	Some evidence that letter was never received (with or without evidence regarding proper mailing)	If they find proper mailing, they must find receipt (and thus decide for *B*), unless *O* convinces them by a preponderance of the evidence that letter was not received. [The jury thus learns of the presumption.]

*If *O*'s evidence of improper addressing or mailing is so convincing that no jury could reasonably find proper addressing and mailing, court will order the jury to find improper addressing or mailing, and presumption will not help B. This is true for Morgan-type presumption as well.

[Adapted from L&S, Table IX-1 (p. 805)]

jury that it may make this permissive inference — the only effect of the presumption's "disappearance" is that the inference is **not mandatory**.

> **Example:** In our letter presumption, let's call the beneficiary of the presumption (the one who mailed the letter) B, and the opponent of the presumption O. Even under the "bursting bubble" view, once O has come forward with some evidence that he never received the letter, if the jury believes that B properly addressed and mailed it, the jury is free to conclude (as a matter of logic and permissive inference, not mandatory presumption) that this proper mailing makes it more likely than not that O actually received the letter. And the judge may well instruct the jury that it may make this permissive inference of receipt by O if it finds proper mailing by B. The "bursting bubble" approach, therefore, does not gut the presumption as totally as might be thought.

   b. **Greater proof required before presumption disappears:** Second, some jurisdictions (though probably only a minority), while adhering to the "bursting bubble" approach, have **increased the amount of evidence** that O must come up with in order to have the presumption disappear from the case. Under the traditional "bursting bubble" approach, so long as the opponent came up with **just enough evidence** of the non-existence of the presumed fact to allow a reasonable jury to find that the presumed fact did not exist, the presumption disappears. But the courts taking this "middle ground" require more evidence than this before the presumption disappears — some of these jurisdictions require **"substantial"** evidence of the presumed fact's non-existence before the presumption disappears, and others make the presumption disappear only if O's rebuttal evidence makes the non-existence of the presumed fact **at least as probable** as its existence. Lilly, pp. 63-64. See, e.g., *Hinds v. John Hancock Mutual Life Ins. Co.*, 155 A.2d 721 (Me. 1959), taking the latter hybrid approach.

3. **Federal Rules:** The choice between the "bursting bubble" and Morgan approaches is so difficult that when it came time to enact the Federal Rules, the Supreme Court and Congress disagreed. FRE 301, as originally approved by the Supreme Court, enacted the Morgan approach of having the presumption shift the burden of persuasion as well as production. But Congress rejected the Morgan approach, and by modifying FRE 301 instead enacted what is really the "bursting bubble" approach to presumptions:

> "In all civil actions and proceedings not otherwise provided for by Act of Congress or by these rules, a presumption imposes on the party against whom it is directed the burden of going forward with evidence to rebut or meet the presumption, but does not shift to such party the burden of proof in the sense of the risk of nonpersuasion, which remains throughout the trial upon the party on whom it was originally cast."

   a. **Illustration:** The workings of FRE 301 are illustrated by *Texas Dept. of Community Affairs v. Burdine*, 450 U.S. 248 (1981).

      i. **Facts:** P claimed that D, a public agency, had refused to promote her and had then fired her, because she was a woman. She sued under Title VII of the 1964 Civil Rights Act. Under prior decisions interpreting Title VII, the burdens of proof and the benefits of presumptions were distributed as follows: P had the burden of producing evidence that D intentionally discriminated against her. She also had the burden of persuading the trier of fact that such discrimination occurred. However, she had the benefit of a presumption: upon showing the basic fact (that she was qualified, that she was rejected, and that the position remained open for some time after the rejection, until it was filled by a male), she gained the benefit of a presumption that there had been unlawful discrimination against her.

ii. **Court of Appeals:** The Court of Appeals had held that D should lose unless it came forward with evidence that would ***persuade*** the trier of fact that D had acted for lawful motives. In other words, the Court of Appeals held that the existence of the presumption shifted to D the burden of persuading the trier of fact as to D's motives.

iii. **Supreme Court:** But the Supreme Court reversed. Although it referred to FRE 301 only in passing, it followed that Rule's approach to presumptions. As the Supreme Court held, the existence of the presumption affected only the initial burden of production, not the burden of persuasion — the burden of persuasion remained on P, not D. Therefore, D was not required to "persuade" the trier of fact that its motives were proper. Instead, D was required "only [to] produce admissible evidence which would allow the trier of fact rationally to conclude" that the presumed fact (improper motives by D) did not exist.

b. **Instructions to jury:** Under FRE 301, once the opponent of the presumption comes up with enough evidence of the presumed fact's non-existence that a jury could reasonably find that the presumed fact does not exist, the presumption clearly disappears from the case in the sense that there is no effect on the burden of persuasion. This is a consequence of the fact that FRE 301 adopts the "bursting bubble" view. But it is not so clear whether the trial judge may ***tell the jury*** that a presumption exists. Probably, the judge may tell the jury that it ***"may"*** infer the existence of the presumed fact from the basic fact, but the jury is not required to make this inference. S&R, p. 86.

c. **Criminal cases:** Observe that FRE 301 deals only with ***civil*** cases. Presumptions in ***criminal*** cases were to have been dealt with by FRE 303, but this Rule was not passed by Congress, which instead intended to deal with the subject in the complete recodification of federal criminal law which it was working on at the time. This recodification has not yet occurred. Therefore, presumptions in federal criminal cases are not governed by any general statute; the matter is left to case law, except that some particular federal statutes establish the effect of particular presumptions, and except that the constitution limits the use of presumptions against criminal defendants. These constitutional issues are discussed *infra*, p. 449.

4. **Conflicting presumptions:** Occasionally, two ***conflicting presumptions*** may be present in a case. If neither presumption is rebutted by its opponent, does either

one survive to influence the jury?

   a. **Social policy:** When one or both of the presumptions reflects a ***social policy***, courts frequently hold that the one reflecting the social policy (or, if both do, the one reflecting the ***weightier*** policy) should control. M, p. 977.

   b. **Probabilities:** If both presumptions merely reflect an estimate of probabilities, or concerns for trial convenience, neither will generally predominate, and ***both*** will generally be held to have ***dropped*** from the case. M, p. 977. See, e.g., *Legille v. Dann*, 544 F.2d 1 (D.C.Cir. 1976) (P, a patent applicant, relied on the presumption that a properly addressed and mailed letter was received by addressee; D, the patent office, relied on the conflicting presumption that the Office has regular practices; *held*, there was no justification for preferring either of the two presumptions over the other, and the case should have been permitted to go to trial).

   c. **Rebutted:** If each presumption is ***rebutted*** by its adversary, then under the majority "bursting bubble" (and Federal Rules) approach, both presumptions ***drop out*** of the case and become at most permissible inferences. S&R, p. 89.

5. Constitutional questions: Normally the use of presumptions in a civil case will not raise any ***constitutional*** issue.

   a. **Rebuttable presumptions:** When "presumption" is used in its normal sense — a rebuttable presumption, under either the bursting bubble or Morgan view — it seems very unlikely that there are now significant constitutional limits on the effect that may be given to presumptions. Even if the legislature uses a presumption to shift the burden of persuasion (i.e., gives the presumption a Morgan effect), and even if there is little if any rational relation between the basic fact and the presumed fact, the presumption will probably withstand constitutional attack. M, p. 987. So long as the presumption is rebuttable, its effect is merely to allocate the burden of production (and perhaps of persuasion), something that states are pretty much free to do as they wish.

   b. **Conclusive presumption:** But a ***conclusive*** or irrebuttable presumption has a quite different constitutional status. Since the irrebuttable presumption is really a rule of substantive law, it is subject to the same due process and equal protection standards as any other substantive rule. For instance, if there is no rational relation between the basic fact and the presumed fact, the irrebuttable presumption may be held to violate the opponent's right to substantive due process or equal protection.

      i. **Stricter test:** At one time, the Supreme Court appeared to be subjecting irrebuttable presumptions to an even stronger test. For instance, in *Vlandis v. Kline*, 412 U.S. 441 (1973), the Court struck down two irrebuttable presumptions in connection with Connecticut's higher charges for non-residents at state universities than for residents (e.g., the presumption that a married student was not a resident if, at the time of his application, he had a legal address outside the state). The Court held that when a "presumption is not necessarily or universally true in fact, and when the state has reasonable alternative means of making the crucial determination," an individual must be given an ***opportunity to rebut the presumption***.

    ii. No independent force: But post-*Vlandis* cases indicate that irrebuttable presumptions are now to be judged merely by the ***same constitutional standards as any other substantive rule of law***, not by stricter ones. So long as the legislature had a ***rational reason*** for linking the basic fact to the presumed fact, the presumption will not be overturned. See, e.g., *Weinberger v. Salfi*, 422 U.S. 749 (1975); see also L&S, p. 820.

C. Effect in criminal cases: In ***criminal*** cases, the main issues involving presumptions are ***constitutional***: To what extent may the state impose a presumption that operates to the defendant's detriment?

    1. Terminology: Before we can get into the constitutional issues, we must first revise our terminology. Recall that in the context of civil presumptions, we treated only "rebuttable presumptions" as being true presumptions — irrebuttable presumptions on the one hand, and permissive inferences on the other, were treated as being something other than presumptions. But in the criminal context, recent Supreme Court cases unfortunately use the term "presumption" to describe links between the basic and presumed facts that, in a civil context, would not be presumptions. The Supreme Court's terminology now seems to be as follows:

        a. Permissive presumptions: *"Permissive"* presumptions are those that never require the jury to do anything. A permissive presumption merely authorizes the judge to instruct the jury that it "may" infer the presumed fact if it finds the basic fact. (This is what, in the civil context, we referred to as a "permissive inference.")

        Example: The legislature, in defining the crime of stolen property, requires that the defendant be shown to have had knowledge that the property was stolen, but also provides that knowledge that the property was stolen may be inferred from the fact that it was stolen. If the judge merely instructs the jury, "If you find that the property was stolen, you may — but need not — infer that D knew it was stolen," this is a "permissive presumption."

        b. Mandatory presumption: Conversely, the Supreme Court now recognizes two types of *"mandatory"* presumptions (corresponding to the "bursting bubble" and Morgan presumptions in the civil context):

            i. Burden of production only: Some mandatory presumptions shift to the defendant the burden of producing some evidence on an issue, but do not shift the burden of persuasion. (This corresponds to the "bursting bubble," presumption on the civil side.)

            ii. Shift of persuasion burden: Alternatively, a mandatory presumption might also shift the burden of persuasion as well as production. (This corresponds to the Morgan view on the civil side.)

        iii. Affirmative defense: There is a very close practical relationship between a mandatory presumption and an *affirmative defense*. An affirmative defense always has the effect of shifting to the defendant the burden of producing evidence on the defense; sometimes (but not always) it also has the effect of shifting the burden of persuasion to him (in which case it is comparable to a "bursting bubble" presumption). Yet, as we shall see, the Supreme Court has imposed greater constitutional limitations on the use of mandatory presumptions in criminal cases than on the use of affirmative defenses.

2. Constitutionality of affirmative defenses: Before we consider the constitutionality of presumptions, let's briefly recap the constitutional rules on *affirmative defenses*: Recall that the state may treat any defense as an affirmative defense, and place both burden of production and persuasion on the defendant, so long as there is not a total overlap between the facts relevant to the affirmative defense and those relevant to an essential element to the offense. (See *supra*, pp. 434-36, especially the discussion of the *Mullaney*, *Patterson*, and *Martin* cases.) Consequently, statutes treating self-defense, insanity, and extreme emotional distress as affirmative defenses, as to which the defendant bears the burdens both of production and persuasion, have been upheld against constitutional attack by the Court.

3. Presumptions: Now, we turn to the constitutionality of presumptions. A presumption's constitutionality in criminal cases depends heavily on whether the presumption is found to be "permissive" or "mandatory."

      a. Permissive: If the presumption is *"permissive,"* apparently all that is required is that the fact-finder could *"rationally"* have inferred the presumed fact from the basic fact.

          Example: In the case which gave rise to the new "permissive" versus "mandatory" terminology, a New York statute provided that the presence of a firearm in an automobile is (with certain exceptions) presumptive evidence of the weapon's illegal possession by all persons then occupying the vehicle. The three Ds (all adult males) were charged with illegal possession of guns that were found in the purse of a 16-year-old girl who was travelling with them in a car. The jury was told of the presumption, and told that "upon proof of the presence of the [guns], you may infer and draw a conclusion that [the prohibited weapons were] possessed by each of the defendants who occupied the automobile at the time when such instruments were found."

          By a 5-4 vote, the Supreme Court held that the presumption here did not violate the Ds' due process rights. The presumption here — as expressed to the jury — was "permissive," since the jury was told that it "need not be rebutted by affirmative proof. . . ." On all the facts in the record — including the fact that the guns were found in the handbag of a 16-year-old girl accompanied by three adult men — it was rational to infer from the presence of the guns in the car that they were possessed by the men. *County Court of Ulster County v. Allen*, 442 U.S. 140 (1979).

Note: The four dissenters in *Allen* contended that the presumption here was irrational — the mere fact that guns are found in a car cannot give rise to the rational inference that all occupants possessed the guns. Furthermore, the dissenters were not convinced that this was a truly "permissive" inference; they thought the jury might in fact not have relied on all the facts of the case or on logic, and may have relied solely on the presumption to find possession. The dissenters would have required that the presumed fact be "more likely than not" to flow from the basic fact, and that this determination be made abstractly, rather than by considering the particular facts of the case.

b. **Mandatory:** By contrast, if the presumption is found to be *"mandatory,"* it will be subjected to much more stringent constitutional scrutiny:

   i. **Shift of persuasion burden:** If the presumption shifts the burden of *persuasion* to the defendant, it will normally be unconstitutional if the *presumed fact* is an *element of the crime*. The reason for this rule is that such a presumption runs afoul of the principle of *In re Winship* (*supra*, p. 434) that the prosecution must prove each element of the crime beyond a reasonable doubt.

   Example 1: In a murder case, D concedes having killed V, but contends that he did not do so "purposely or knowingly," so that he is not guilty of the crime of "deliberate homicide." The judge instructs the jury that "the law presumes that a person intends the ordinary consequences of his voluntary acts."

   Held, this presumption violated D's due process rights. The presumption, as carried out in the judge's instruction, could have been interpreted by a reasonable jury as being "mandatory," and in fact as shifting to D the burden of persuasion on the issue of intent. For instance, the jury was not told that the presumption could be rebutted; furthermore, even if the jury understood that rebuttal was possible, it might have assumed that in the absence of rebuttal by D the mere fact of the slaying was enough to constitute proof of intent. An instruction that might be interpreted as shifting to D the burden of persuasion on any element of the crime is unconstitutional under *Winship*. *Sandstrom v. Montana*, 442 U.S. 510 (1979).

   Example 2: D, a dealer in second-hand goods, is charged with knowingly receiving stolen goods. The applicable statute provides that a second-hand dealer who buys goods that are in fact stolen, and who does not make reasonable inquiries as to whether the seller has the right to sell the goods, shall be presumed to have known the property was stolen. The judge instructs the jury that it is to presume knowledge on D's part "unless from all the evidence you have reasonable doubt that [D] knew the property was stolen." The judge also tells the jury that despite the presumption, D "can go forward and raise a reasonable doubt that [he] actually knew that."

   Held, this instruction, and the underlying statutory language, created a mandatory presumption that violated D's due process rights under *Winship*. The jury could reasonably have understood the law to be (especially in light of the judge's comment that D could "go forward and raise a reasonable doubt

. . . ") that once the prosecution proved that the goods were stolen, the burden shifted to D to persuade the jury that there was at least a reasonable doubt that D knew the goods to be stolen. Instead, the judge should have carefully instructed the jury that it was permitted, but not required, to infer guilty knowledge when a dealer does not make reasonable inquiries; the jury must also be explicitly instructed that the prosecution retains the burden of persuading the jury that the defendant had guilty knowledge beyond a reasonable doubt. (In other words, the statutory language should be reinterpreted in future jury instructions to create a "permissive" presumption.) *People v. Roder*, 658 P.2d 1302 (Cal. 1983).

    ii. Shift of production burden only: Where the presumption is "mandatory" but shifts only the burden of production, not the burden of persuasion, the presumption may be constitutionally valid. The Supreme Court in *Sandstrom* attached great importance to the fact that the burden of persuasion was shifted under the presumption there, and hinted that had the presumption merely shifted the burden of production and not of persuasion, the result might have been different.

    iii. Beyond reasonable doubt: Even a mandatory presumption relating to an essential element of the crime (and even one which shifts the burden of persuasion to the defendant) would probably be constitutional if the prosecution showed that: (1) the presumed fact *flows from the basic fact beyond a reasonable doubt*; and (2) the basic fact is *true beyond a reasonable doubt.* M, p. 999. But because there are very few presumptions that have this tight a link between basic fact and presumed fact, almost all presumptions used in criminal cases will have to be permissive ones.

4. Reconciling affirmative defenses and presumptions: It is hard to reconcile the Supreme Court's standard for evaluating affirmative defenses with its standard for evaluating mandatory presumptions. Consider two statutes, A and B. Under statute A, all possession of stolen property is made a crime, but the defendant is given an affirmative defense that he did not know the goods were stolen; he must establish this affirmative defense by a preponderance of the evidence. Under statute B, the crime is defined as the "knowing" possession of stolen property, and there is a presumption that a person who buys stolen property without making inquiries into the seller's title knows the goods to be stolen; the presumption may be rebutted, but in the absence of rebuttal evidence the presumption is binding on the jury. Statute A would probably be constitutional — under *Patterson* (*supra*, p. 435), D is not required to bear the burden of persuasion on any element of the crime (since guilty knowledge is not an element of the crime). Statute B, by contrast, is clearly unconstitutional under *Sandstrom* — it is a mandatory presumption, shifting the burden of persuasion on an element of the crime. Yet it is hard to see why statute B is less fair to defendants.

D. Choice of law: In federal cases (especially diversity cases), the well-known case of *Erie v. Tompkins*, 304 U.S. 54 (1938) requires that the federal courts use state substantive law if state law is the source of the right sued upon. *Erie* has always been applied to questions of burden of proof. Consequently, Congress, in enacting the Federal Rules, has decided that the federal courts should generally apply the state's law regarding *presumptions* (and the *effect* to be given to presumptions) in any case in which state substantive law has to be looked to.

1. **FRE 302:** Thus FRE 302 provides that "in civil actions and proceedings, the effect of a presumption respecting a fact which is an element of a claim or defense as to which State law supplies the rule of decision is determined in accordance with State law."

> **Example:** P brings a diversity action against D, claiming that D was negligent in driving a car. Under *Erie v. Tompkins*, New Jersey law controls on the substantive issue of whether P has a claim for negligence, since the accident took place in New Jersey and the case is brought in New Jersey federal district court. A New Jersey statute establishes a rebuttable presumption that a person whose blood alcohol is more than .1% is legally drunk. New Jersey substantive law of negligence establishes the doctrine of negligence *per se*, by which violation of a statute (including the drunk driving statute) is *prima facie* evidence that the act that violated the statute is negligent. New Jersey law applies a Morgan approach to presumptions, so a presumption shifts to the opponent the burden of persuasion (as it would not under FRE 301).
>
> The federal court will have to follow New Jersey's approach to presumptions. That is, once P shows that D's blood alcohol level was higher than .1%, then even if D comes up with some other evidence that he was not drunk, the judge will have to instruct the jury that if it finds D's blood alcohol to have been higher than .1%, it must find D to have been drunk (and therefore, negligent under the negligence *per se* doctrine) unless D convinces the jury by a preponderance of the evidence that he was not drunk. In other words, the federal court must apply New Jersey's Morgan-style law of presumptions, rather than FRE 301's "bursting bubble" treatment.

2. **"Tactical" presumptions:** However, some presumptions may have so little importance to the particular case that a federal court will be justified in treating them as *"tactical"* presumptions as to which it may apply the federal approach rather than state law. See Advisory Committee's Note to FRE 302 ("the rule does not apply state law when the presumption operates upon a lesser aspect of the case, i.e., 'tactical' presumptions"). For instance, if it was an incidental issue in the case whether someone gave notice to someone else, the effect of the presumption that a properly addressed and mailed letter was received by the addressee would be as specified in FRE 301's general federal rule, not by looking to how state law treats the presumption.

III. JUDGE-JURY ALLOCATION

A. Introduction: We now examine the division of responsibility between the judge and the jury as it concerns decisions about the admissibility of evidence. In general, the judge decides issues of law, and the jury decides issues of fact. However, drawing this line is not always so easy. Furthermore, even where an issue is one of fact, and thus within the jury's province, the judge has a role to play (by instructing the jury, and perhaps by summarizing or commenting on the evidence).

B. Issues of law: All American courts follow the general principle that *issues of law* are to be decided by the *judge*, not the jury. Consequently, when the admission of a particular piece of evidence turns on an issue of law, it is up to the judge, not the jury, to decide whether the item should be admitted.

> **Example:** D calls P to the stand, and asks a question regarding statements made by P to L. P asserts that he need not answer because the communication was protected by the attorney-client privilege. D demonstrates that L, although he is a law school graduate, has not yet taken the bar exam in any state and is therefore not admitted anywhere. The resulting issue of law — whether the attorney-client privilege applies to a communication made to a law school graduate who is not yet admitted — will be decided solely by the judge. Therefore, it is the judge who will have sole control over whether P must answer. See L&S, p. 1056.

C. Issues of fact: The division of responsibility between judge and jury is more complicated when admissibility of a piece of evidence turns on an issue of *fact* rather than law.

1. Generally: In general, the roles of judge and jury turn on whether the objection to admission raises a technical exclusionary rule, or rather goes merely to relevance.

2. Competence: When an objection to admissibility is based on a *technical exclusionary rule* (e.g., hearsay), any factual question needed to decide that objection belongs solely to the *judge*. Thus when factual issues arise in connection with a *hearsay* objection, an objection based on *privilege*, an objection based on the alleged *incompetency* of the witness (e.g., a child), or most issues regarding the *Best Evidence* rule, the *judge must decide* the issue.

  a. Federal Rules: This rule is codified in FRE 104(a): "Preliminary questions concerning the qualification of a person to be a witness, the existence of a privilege, or the admissibility of evidence shall be determined by the court, subject to the provisions of subdivision (b). . . ."

   i. Rules of evidence not binding: FRE 104(a) then goes on to say, "In making its determination [the court] is *not bound by the rules of evidence* except those with respect to privileges."

  Example: Suppose that the judge has to decide whether V's out-of-court statement, "X shot me," is admissible under the "dying declaration" exception to the hearsay rule (see *supra*, p. 231.) In determining this factual issue, the court could consider another out-of-court statement made by V just before to someone else, in which he said, "It seems like only a flesh wound" — the fact that this latter statement would not be admissible does not prevent the judge from considering it in determining whether the main statement qualifies as a dying declaration.

b. Some illustrations: Here are some illustrations of objections that would be treated as technical exclusionary ones, whose related factual issues will be decided by the judge:

Example 1: Whether a witness' notes were made when the matter in question was fresh in his mind, and thus qualify under the "past recollection recorded" exception to the hearsay rule (*supra*, p. 189).

Example 2: Whether H and W were really married at the time of a statement by H to W, so as to make the communication protected by the privilege for marital communications (*supra*, p. 343).

Example 3: Whether an original of a writing has really been lost (as alleged by the proponent), so as to give rise to an exception under the Best Evidence rule (*supra*, p. 377). (But see FRE 1008, discussed *supra*, p. 389, which provides that some factual issues related to the Best Evidence rule are to be given to the jury; see *supra*, p. 388.)

c. Preponderance of the evidence: Most courts hold that the judge should decide such factual issues by a ***preponderance of the evidence*** standard. M, p. 136, n. 8.

Example: In a federal conspiracy case, the prosecution offers an out-of-court statement by an alleged co-conspirator. Under the co-conspirator's statement exception to the hearsay rule, a co-conspirator's statement is only admissible if it was made "during the course and in furtherance of the conspiracy." (FRE 801(d)(2)(E)). D asserts that the statement should only be admitted if the trial judge first concludes, beyond a reasonable doubt, that a conspiracy existed.

Held, for the prosecution. In federal cases, the issue of whether a conspiracy existed should be decided by a preponderance-of-the-evidence standard, not a "beyond-a-reasonable-doubt standard." (Also, the judge may consider the alleged statement itself in deciding whether the conspiracy has been proved by a preponderance of the evidence.) *Bourjaily v. U.S.*, 483 U.S. 171 (1987) (discussed more fully *supra*, p. 273.)

i. Voluntariness of confession: A *confession* may, of course, only be introduced against a criminal defendant if it was voluntarily made. In most states, it is solely up to the judge to determine whether the confession was voluntary. In such states, it is constitutional for the judge to decide this issue by a preponderance-of-the-evidence rather than a "beyond-a-reasonable-doubt" standard; *Lego v. Twomey*, 404 U.S. 477 (1972). (Other states follow a two-step rule, in which the judge will exclude the confession only if its involuntariness is very clear, and the jury gets an additional chance to disregard the confession if it finds it to be involuntary. M, p. 430.)

3. Relevance: Now let us consider evidence to which the sole objection is that it is ***irrelevant***.

a. Ordinary relevance problem: Ordinarily, the judge may decide an objection based on relevance grounds without making any findings of fact. That is, if the proponent offers proof of fact A, and the opponent argues that the proof is irrelevant, the judge merely has to decide, "Does the proof tend to establish the existence of fact A?" and "Does establishment of fact A make some material issue in the case more (or less) likely than it would be without fact A?" The judge can answer both of these questions without making any findings of fact.

b. Conditional relevance: There are some pieces of proffered evidence, however, which are logically relevant *only if some other fact exists*. That is, evidence of fact B may be relevant only if fact A also exists. In this situation, evidence of fact B is said to be *"conditionally relevant,"* that is, conditioned upon fact A. This leads to the question, Who decides whether fact A has been established, the judge or the jury?

> **Example:** P borrows D's car, and is injured when a tire blows out. D seeks to prove that as P drove away, D shouted, "The left tire's bad, so keep it under 55." (D claims that this statement made P assume the risk of the kind of accident that occurred.) P asserts that she never heard this warning, and points out that if she didn't, she cannot be held to have assumed the risk because she didn't know about it.
>
> Evidence of fact B (that D made the warning) is not logically relevant unless fact A (that P heard the warning) is first established. The issue thus becomes, who should decide whether P heard the warning, judge or jury?

  i. Jury decides: Nearly all courts, and the Federal Rules, hold that it is the *jury*, not the judge, who should decide such issues of conditional relevance. Thus it is the jury who would decide whether P heard D's warning.

  ii. Role of judge: But the judge still has a role to play on the preliminary fact question. He must decide *whether a reasonable jury could find that the preliminary fact exists*: if the answer is "no," he will not allow the conditionally relevant evidence; if the answer is "yes," he will allow it (even if he believes that it is less likely than not that the preliminary fact exists). As FRE 104(b) puts it, "When the relevancy of evidence depends upon the fulfillment of a condition of fact, the court shall admit it upon, or subject to, the introduction of evidence sufficient to support a finding of the fulfillment of the condition."

> **Example:** Let's return to our tire blowout example. Before D will be permitted to give detailed testimony about the warning he shouted to P, the judge will first decide whether a reasonable jury could conclude that P heard the warning (whatever its contents). If he concludes that a reasonable jury could not so find, he will prevent D from stating the contents of the warning. If he determines that a reasonable jury could find that P heard the warning, he will then allow D's testimony about the contents of the warning (even if he thinks that there is less than a 50-50 chance that P in fact heard the warning). If he decides to allow the jury to hear the testimony about the warning's contents, he might instruct the jury to consider those contents only if it first decides, by

a preponderance of the evidence, that P heard the warning.

   iii. **Subject to "connecting up":** Sometimes the proponent will want to show the conditionally relevant fact *before showing the preliminary fact*. To allow this, the judge will frequently admit the conditionally relevant evidence *"subject to connecting up,"* i.e., subject to the later introduction of evidence proving the preliminary fact. L&S, p. 1059, n. 4. For instance, in our tire blowout example the judge might allow the contents of D's warning to P to come in, subject to the later presentation of evidence that P in fact heard the warning. For this to happen, D's lawyer will have to assure the court that he will subsequently introduce evidence that P really heard the warning. If D does not come up with this evidence sometime in the case, the judge will order the testimony about the warning's contents to be *stricken*. (In federal courts, the judge's authority to accept the conditionally relevant evidence in advance of evidence of the preliminary fact is indicated by FRE 104(b)'s reference to admission of the former "subject to" introduction of evidence of the preliminary fact.)

4. Presence of jury: When the judge has to decide a preliminary issue of fact, he will often receive evidence on that preliminary issue *outside the presence of the jury*. Otherwise, the jury may hear prejudicial or privileged information that it will probably not be able to put out of its mind if the ultimate evidence is found inadmissible.

   a. Confessions: In fact, where the preliminary issue is whether a criminal defendant's *confession* was voluntary, the defendant probably has a *constitutional right* to have his evidence concerning the voluntariness of his confession heard outside the presence of the jury. In any event, in federal trials this is required by FRE 104(c): "Hearings on the admissibility of confessions shall in all cases be conducted out of the hearing of the jury. Hearings on other preliminary matters shall be so conducted when the interests of justice require, or when an accused is a witness and so requests."

D. Instructions: The subject of *jury instructions* is generally beyond the scope of this book. However, two kinds of instructions relate directly to evidence, and are worth discussing briefly:

1. Limiting instructions: First, when evidence has been admitted that should properly be considered only on some issues, the judge will on request give a *limiting instruction*, which tells the jury for what issues the evidence can and cannot be considered.

   Example: P, a golfer, is injured while riding a cart that he has rented from D, a golf course. P offers evidence that X, who had rented the cart before P did, had told D, "The brakes are bad." This evidence is not admissible to prove that brakes really were bad (since it is hearsay not within any exception), but is admissible to show that D was on notice of a possible defect. If the judge admits the evidence for this latter purpose, on P's request, the judge will issue a limiting instruction, telling the jury to consider the statement only on the issue of notice, not on the issue of whether the brakes really were bad. See Lilly, pp. 189-90.

    a. Confession of co-defendant: Limiting instructions are often of doubtful utility — the jury is usually unwilling or unable to refrain from using the evidence for the forbidden purpose. In one situation, a limiting instruction is ***constitutionally inadequate***: in a joint trial, the Confrontation Clause sometimes prevents one co-defendant's confession from being used against the other (see *supra*, p. 283), and the Supreme Court has held that a limiting instruction does not provide constitutionally sufficient protection. *Bruton v. U.S.*, 391 U.S. 123 (1968) (discussed *supra*, p. 284).

  2. Cautionary instruction: Another type of instruction relating to the evidence is the so-called ***"cautionary instruction."*** This is an instruction designed to alert the jury to the dubious value of a certain type of evidence. For instance, where the prosecution uses testimony by an accomplice against a criminal defendant, the judge may warn the jury to weigh carefully the significance to be attached to the accomplice's testimony, because of the latter's incentive to curry favor with the authorities. L&S, p. 1070.

E. Summary and comment: Depending on the jurisdiction, the judge may ***summarize*** the evidence, ***comment*** upon it, or both.

  1. Common-law rule: At common law, the judge could ***both*** summarize the evidence and comment on it. L&S, p. 1078.

  2. Federal Rule: Today, the federal courts and a minority of state courts preserve this power to both summarize and comment. *Id.*

  3. Majority rule: But in most states today, the judge may ***not comment*** on the evidence. This restriction is due to fears that if comment were allowed, the judge would in practice usurp the jury's role as fact-finder. *Id.* However, many of the states that forbid judicial comment allow, or even encourage, judicial summation. *Id.*

  4. Warning to the jury: Where the judge does comment on the evidence, she must also instruct the jurors that it is up to them to make the final decision as to the weight of the evidence and the credibility of the witnesses, and that they are in no way bound by her comments. *Id.*

F. Nonjury trials: Nearly everything we have said in this book so far assumes that the trial is to a jury. When the trial is a ***"bench"*** trial (i.e., one without a jury), the rationale behind many of the procedures and rules of exclusion changes: the trial judge is presumably better able to disregard inadmissible evidence whose contents he hears than would a lay jury; yet at the same time, he will often not be able to shield himself from hearing those contents as he would be able to shield the jury. (For instance, in a nonjury trial there is no analog to the practice of hearing an offer of proof outside the presence of the jury.)

  1. Same rules of evidence: Nonetheless, in general ***all rules of evidence applicable to jury trials also apply to bench trials.*** M, p. 153. Most importantly, if an item of evidence would be inadmissible in a jury trial, it is inadmissible in a bench trial.

2. **Practical relaxation:** On the other hand, appellate courts are understandably much more reluctant to reverse the trial court for an error of evidence law when a bench trial is involved. Therefore, appellate courts are generally *less strict in reviewing* evidentiary rulings made in a bench trial. *Id.*

   a. **"Sufficient competent evidence" rule:** The most important way in which appellate courts do this is by applying the following rule: in a bench trial "the admission of incompetent evidence over objection will not ordinarily be a ground of reversal if there was *competent evidence* received *sufficient to support the findings*. The judge will be *presumed* to have *disregarded the inadmissible* and relied on the competent evidence." M, p. 153.

   b. **Erroneous exclusion:** But if the judge in a bench trial erroneously *excludes* evidence, the appellate court will *not* bend over backwards to uphold the verdict: the appellate court will reverse if the exclusion was "substantially harmful to the losing party." *Id.*

   c. **Provisional admission:** These two contrasting appellate practices, turning on whether the mistake is to admit or to exclude evidence, have led many trial judges to protect themselves from reversal by the following tactic: When an item of evidence is objected to and the judge believes the evidentiary point is debatable, he will frequently *admit the evidence provisionally*, while telling the parties that he will reserve his evidentiary ruling until the evidence is all in. M, p. 154. When the evidence is all in, he may not issue the ruling at all unless one or the other parties makes a motion to strike. If he does have to rule at the end of the case, he will err on the side of admitting rather than excluding debatable evidence. *Id.*

      i. **Criticism:** This practice of reserving rulings until all evidence is in has the merit of saving time and of making sure that the appellate court has all available evidence in the record. But it is often criticized on the grounds that it reduces the importance of the exclusionary rules of evidence. *Id.*

IV. APPEALS AND THE "HARMLESS ERROR" DOCTRINE

A. **"Harmless error" generally:** If an appellate court were to order a new trial every time it concluded that the trial judge had made an error in excluding or admitting a particular piece of evidence, the cost in judicial resources would be enormous. Therefore, appellate courts universally apply the *"harmless error"* standard: the verdict below will be reversed, or a new trial ordered, only if the appellate court believes that the error may have made a *difference to the outcome*; an error that is "harmless" (i.e., that probably did not affect the outcome) is disregarded.

1. **Federal Rules:** The Federal Rules of Evidence obliquely impose the harmless error doctrine: FRE 103 begins by providing that "error may not be predicated upon a ruling which admits or excludes evidence unless a *substantial right* of a party is affected. . . ." Presumably, a ruling admitting or excluding evidence only affects a

party's "substantial right" if it may have affected the outcome. M, p. 134.

2. **Different standards:** How *likely* must it be that the error affected the outcome, for a new trial or reversal to be ordered on appeal? The answer depends on whether the defendant's constitutional rights have been violated:

   a. **Constitutional issue in criminal case:** In a *criminal* case, where the error is the admission of evidence in violation of the defendant's *constitutional* rights, it is fairly easy for the defendant to convince the appellate court that the error was not "harmless." "[B]efore a federal constitutional error can be held harmless, the court must be able to declare a belief that it was harmless *beyond a reasonable doubt*." *Chapman v. California*, 386 U.S. 18 (1967). For instance, the error in *Chapman* was that the prosecution was allowed to comment on the defendant's failure to take the stand; this comment was in violation of the defendant's Fifth and Fourteenth Amendment rights. The Supreme Court concluded that there were at least reasonable doubts about the error's harmlessness (i.e., there was at least a reasonable chance that without the prosecutor's comment, the jury might have concluded that the defendant's guilt had not been shown beyond a reasonable doubt). Therefore, the defendant was entitled to a new trial.

   b. **Civil cases and non-constitutional criminal errors:** In a *civil* case, and in a criminal case where the error does *not* affect the defendant's constitutional rights, it is harder for the appellant to avoid a finding of harmless error. Usually the error will be ignored as harmless unless the appellate court believes it *"more probable than not"* that the error affected the outcome.

      i. **Criticism:** Affirming a defendant's criminal conviction merely because it is not "more probable than not" that the non-constitutional error affected the outcome, has been frequently criticized. Thus, Professor Saltzburg argues that in order to be consistent with *In re Winship*'s requirement that all elements of the crime be proved beyond a reasonable doubt, appellate courts should reverse trial court verdicts "if there is a reasonable possibility that the error affected the judgment," whether the error is constitutional or not. L&S, pp. 856-57.)

B. **"Plain" error:** Recall that a party's failure to respond promptly to the erroneous admission or exclusion of evidence may result in a *waiver* of that party's right to complain about the error on appeal. Thus the opponent's failure to object to the improper inclusion of evidence, or the proponent's failure to make a timely offer of proof in the face of an erroneous exclusion of evidence, will cause the error to be waived. But there is a key exception to this rule of waiver: if the appellate court concludes that the error was *"plain,"* it may treat the error as grounds for a new trial *even if no objection or offer of proof was made*.

   1. **Civil cases:** Reversals for plain error are *rare* in *civil* cases, perhaps because liberty and life are not involved. M, p. 134, n. 74.

   2. **Criminal cases:** In criminal cases, where by definition the error must have been to the defendant's detriment (since the prosecution cannot appeal an acquittal), courts

are ***more willing*** to find plain error. M, p. 134. This is especially likely to be the case if the defendant was represented by court-appointed counsel not of his own choosing. W&B, Par. 103[07].

3. **Standard:** There is no precise standard for determining how prejudicial the error must be to be "plain." Most courts state or assume that the error must be more prejudicial to be "plain" than is required for an error that was pointed out at the trial level to avoid being "harmless."

   a. **Federal standard:** In federal trials, the plain error doctrine is imposed by FRE 103(d): "Nothing in this rule precludes taking notice of plain errors affecting substantial rights although they were not brought to the attention of the court."

   b. **Ambiguity:** Observe that this federal definition of "plain error" includes the same phrase, "substantial rights," as does FRE 103(a)'s definition of "harmless" error. Thus if one merely looks at the two rules, it looks as though an error that does not affect "substantial rights" is automatically "harmless," and one that does affect "substantial rights" is automatically "plain." If this were the case, a party would never gain any advantage by making a timely objection or offer of proof at trial. S&R, p. 17. However, since the two concepts are not defined very precisely in the Federal Rules, federal courts are free to require a larger showing of prejudice before they will deem an error to be "plain" than before they will find an error that was pointed out below to be "non-harmless." (But if the error affects the constitutional rights of a criminal defendant, the court will generally find it to be "plain" unless the prosecution shows beyond a reasonable doubt that it did not affect the verdict, whether or not the error was pointed out below. This is probably required by the Supreme Court's *Chapman* holding, *supra*, p. 460.)

C. **Sufficiency of evidence:** Appellate courts serve another function when they review the evidence from the trial below: they will often need to determine whether there was ***sufficient evidence*** to support the decision of the trier of fact.

   1. **Procedural context:** The appellate court's duty to judge the sufficiency of the evidence can arise in a variety of procedural contexts. For instance, in a civil case a sufficiency issue arises from the trial judge's handling of a motion for a directed verdict or a motion for judgment notwithstanding the verdict (j.n.o.v.) — if the judge directs the verdict or grants the j.n.o.v. motion, the party who didn't get to the jury or who lost the benefit of the jury verdict will raise the sufficiency issue; if the judge denies the motion, the movant will raise sufficiency. In a criminal case, it is always the defendant who argues that the evidence was insufficient to support the verdict (since if there is an acquittal, the prosecution cannot appeal). L&S, p. 852.

   2. **Standard:** In deciding whether the evidence was sufficient to support the fact-finder's decision, the appellate court does ***not*** attempt to determine how it would have decided the case. Its task is "only to determine whether the evidence was such that a ***reasonable trier of fact*** might have reached the decision below." *Id.* This determination in turn depends on whether the case is civil or criminal:

a. **Civil:** In a civil case, the appellate court's determination mirrors the "preponderance of the evidence" standard. Thus if the plaintiff wins at trial, the appellate court will ask itself: ***Could a reasonable jury have concluded that plaintiff proved all elements of his case by a preponderance of the evidence?*** In making this determination, the appellate court "gives the winning party the benefit of all doubts and assumes that the proof properly offered was accepted for all that it was worth, since the judge or jury might reasonably have given it the maximum possible weight." *Id.*

b. **Criminal:** In a criminal case, by contrast, the appellate court takes the "reasonable doubt" standard into account in determining sufficiency. Thus it will order a new trial (or, occasionally, dismiss the charge entirely) if it concludes that a ***reasonable jury could not have found the defendant guilty beyond a reasonable doubt*** (even if the appeals court finds the evidence sufficient to allow a jury to have found the defendant guilty "by a preponderance of the evidence").

c. **Summary:** In other words, the standard for review of sufficiency mirrors the standard of proof used at the trial level, except that the question is always whether the trier of fact could "reasonably" have decided the case as it did. *Id.*

d. **Rare:** In general, appellate courts *rarely* reverse the lower court outcome based on a conclusion that the evidence was not sufficient to support that outcome. L&S, p. 853.

JUDICIAL NOTICE

I. JUDICIAL NOTICE GENERALLY

A. Function: Normally, a party who seeks to have the trier find that a fact exists must introduce evidence of that fact. However, our system provides a number of ways in which a party's obligation to produce evidence proving a fact may be relieved. Presumptions (*supra*, p. 441) are one such method. Another is the doctrine of *judicial notice*, whereby the *judge* accepts a fact as true even though no evidence to prove it has been offered. If the case is a civil one being tried to a jury, the judge, after taking judicial notice, will instruct the jury that it must find the fact.

> **Example:** In a civil jury trial, P needs to establish that March 10, 1982 was a Tuesday. He can ask the judge to take judicial notice of this fact. Probably he will have to give the judge some assistance in verifying the fact (e.g., by showing the judge an almanac or calendar). But he will not have to introduce any evidence before the jury to establish this fact. Once the judge is convinced that March 10, 1982 was indeed a Tuesday, she will instruct the jury that they must treat that date as being a Tuesday in their deliberations. L&S, p. 838.

1. Rationale: The principal rationale for judicial notice is the *saving of time and money*. Litigants would have to spend more money proving their cases if they had to prove even incontrovertible facts; trials would be needlessly long.

2. Correction after close of evidence or on appeal: Another important function of the judicial notice doctrine is to allow a court to *correct a party's inadvertent failure* to provide evidence on a key, but indisputable, fact. For instance, if the losing party raises on appeal for the first time the argument that his adversary did not come up with evidence at trial of some indisputable fact necessary to the verdict, the appellate court may take judicial notice of that fact, thus saving the verdict below. Similarly, the trial court may, after the close of evidence at the trial, take judicial notice of a fact necessary to the verdict, rather than reopening the evidence for the party to supply that fact. See L&S, p. 842.

B. Two types of facts: The doctrine of judicial notice has evolved to recognize two distinct types of facts: (1) *"adjudicative"* facts; and (2) *"legislative"* facts.

1. Adjudicative facts: *Adjudicative* facts are those facts which relate to the *particular event*. "[T]hey help . . . explain who did what, when, where, how, and with what motive and intent." M, p. 920.

2. Legislative facts: *Legislative* facts are "more general facts that do not concern the immediate parties." L&S, p. 838. They are facts which the judge considers as part of his law-making function. Any non-evidentiary fact which the judge considers in determining whether a statute is constitutional, how a statute should be interpreted, or how the common law should treat a particular issue, will be a legislative fact. For instance, a judge who is deciding whether the implied warranty of habitability should, as a common-law matter, be extended to apartment rentals, may take judicial notice of legislative facts concerning the nature of apartment rentals in big cities (e.g., that tenants generally are not capable of making structural repairs); see *Javins v. First National Realty Corp.*, discussed *infra*, p. 470.

3. **Significance of distinction:** The Federal Rules, and many states, recognize this distinction between adjudicative and legislative facts.

    a. **Main difference:** The main consequence of the distinction is that judicial notice of adjudicative facts is much more circumscribed: in most courts, the judge may take notice of an adjudicative fact only if the fact is *indisputable*, whereas he may take notice of a legislative fact much more liberally (in most situations, the fact merely needs to be more probable than not).

    b. **Covered by statute:** A second consequence is that judicial notice of adjudicative facts is more likely to be covered by a precise statute than is notice of legislative facts. For instance, the federal rules deal only with adjudicative facts (in FRE 201), not with legislative facts.

C. **Judicial notice of law:** A third situation in which something may be established without the submission of formal evidence is so-called "judicial notice of *law*." This phrase refers to the doctrine that a party will in some situations not be required to "prove" what the law is by a formal submission of evidence; instead, the judge may research the relevant law himself, or the party may merely assist the judge's research (say, by submitting a non-evidentiary photocopy of the relevant provision). See *infra*, p. 471.

D. **Federal Rules:** The only Federal Rule dealing with judicial notice is FRE 201. FRE 201 deals only with notice of adjudicative facts; that is, it does not cover either notice of legislative facts or notice of law. FRE 201 largely mirrors the common-law treatment of judicial notice of adjudicative facts:

> "(a) *Scope of rule.* This rule governs only judicial notice of adjudicative facts.
>
> (b) *Kinds of facts.* A judicially noticed fact must be one not subject to reasonable dispute in that it is either (1) generally known within the territorial jurisdiction of the trial court or (2) capable of accurate and ready determination by resort to sources whose accuracy cannot reasonably be questioned.
>
> (c) *When discretionary.* A court may take judicial notice, whether requested or not.
>
> (d) *When mandatory.* A court shall take judicial notice if requested by a party and supplied with the necessary information.
>
> (e) *Opportunity to be heard.* A party is entitled upon timely request to an opportunity to be heard as to the propriety of taking judicial notice and the tenor of the matter noticed. In the absence of prior notification, the request may be made after judicial notice has been taken.
>
> (f) *Time of taking notice.* Judicial notice may be taken at any stage of the proceeding.
>
> (g) *Instructing the jury.* In a civil action or proceeding, the court shall instruct the jury to

accept as conclusive any fact judicially noticed. In a criminal case, the court shall instruct the jury that it may, but is not required to, accept as conclusive any fact judicially noticed."

II. ADJUDICATIVE FACTS

A. Definition: As noted, adjudicative facts are those specific facts relating to the particular parties in the action, and to their particular controversy. Examples would include: (1) whether a particular accident, which took place on March 10, 1980, took place on a Tuesday; (2) whether a particular street is part of the general business district of the town it is located in, where the issue is whether the speed limit is that for business districts; or (3) whether the local phone company is an interstate common carrier, for purposes of determining whether D has illegally intercepted communications on such a carrier. M, p. 920.

    1. Application of doctrine: Most modern cases hold that there are *two* different types of adjudicative facts that may be judicially noticed: (1) those that are *"generally known"* in the community; and (2) those that are "capable of *immediate* and *accurate verification*" by use of easily-available sources that are indisputably accurate. M, pp. 922-24. Regardless of which category the fact falls into, the court will not take judicial notice of it unless it is convinced that that fact is virtually *indisputable*.

B. Common knowledge: The first of these categories — "common" or "general" knowledge in the community — gives rise to judicial notice only relatively rarely.

        Example: P sues D for personal injuries resulting from an automobile accident at the corner of Mission Street and Twenty-first Street in San Francisco. P contends that D was speeding at the time. The judge tells the jury that the statutory speed limit for any "business district" is 15 mph, and that a business district is one that is "mainly built up with structures devoted to business." No evidence is offered as to whether Mission Street at Twenty-first is a business district; however, the judge instructs the jury that this is so.

        Held (on appeal), the business character of Mission at Twenty-first Street is so well known, and so indisputable, that the trial court could correctly take judicial notice of it and, therefore, so instruct the jury. *Varcoe v. Lee*, 181 P. 223 (Cal. 1919).

    1. Judge's own knowledge insufficient: Suppose the *judge himself* knows a fact to be so because of his past experiences. May he take judicial notice of that fact even though it is not "common knowledge"? The answer is *"no."* M, p. 923.

        Example: The case is a child custody dispute between H and W. W plans to move to another town in the same state so that she can attend law school. H argues that this will render W unable to take care of their children, ages nine and eleven. No evidence is presented about the rigors of law school, but the trial judge takes judicial notice, from his own personal experience, that law school is extremely time-consuming and will interfere with W's ability to care for her children.

        Held (on appeal), the trial judge should not have taken judicial notice of the time-consuming nature of law school. Judicial notice "is limited to what a judge may properly know in his judicial capacity, and he is not authorized to make his personal knowledge of a fact not generally or professionally known the basis of his action." *In re Marriage of Tresnak*, 297 N.W.2d 109 (Iowa 1980).

C. Certain verification: Most adjudicative facts that are suitable for judicial notice are of the second category: facts capable of ***immediate verification*** by consulting sources of ***indisputable accuracy***.

   1. History and geography: For instance, facts of ***history*** and ***geography*** are often judicially noticed because they fall into this category. Thus the day of the week on which a certain date fell is judicially noticed because it can be verified in an indisputably accurate almanac; the boundaries of a city or state can be verified by consulting an indisputably accurate map, etc.

   2. Scientific tests and principles: *Scientific principles*, including testing methods, are often subject to judicial notice of this type. Thus courts frequently take judicial notice of the general validity of such scientific methods as ***blood tests*** for paternity, ***fingerprint*** identifications, and ***radar*** tests for detecting speed. See, e.g., *State v. Finkle*, 319 A.2d 733 (Super. Ct. N.J. 1974) (court may properly take judicial notice of the general reliability of the VASCAR method of speed detection, since this reliability is established in various authoritative scientific studies).

      a. Change over time: Observe that the scientific principles of which a court may take judicial notice will ***vary*** with the passage of time, as new techniques become generally accepted. (See the discussion of various scientific methods *supra*, p. 416). Also, remember that judicial notice will only allow the court to assume the ***general*** reliability of a technique, not its correct application in a particular case; for instance, the trial judge in *Finkle*, even after taking judicial notice of VASCAR's general reliability, would still have insisted on a showing that the particular device used in that case had been correctly calibrated and correctly used.

   3. Court records: Courts frequently take judicial notice of ***their own records*** of things that happened earlier in the litigation. M, p. 927. For instance, if a case is re-tried, the judge might take judicial notice of the fact that a particular witness had not testified at the prior trial. Some, but not all, courts take judicial notice of court records in ***other cases*** from the ***same court***. *Id.* Most courts ***do not*** take judicial notice of court records from ***other courts***, though it is hard to see why. *Id.*

D. Federal Rule 201: Recall that FRE 201, the sole Federal Rule to deal with judicial notice, deals exclusively with adjudicative facts. In determining what facts are sufficiently indisputable, FRE 201 basically follows the common-law approach — the fact must be beyond ***"reasonable dispute,"*** and may achieve this status in one of two ways: (1) by being "generally known" within the community; or (2) by being "capable of accurate and ready determination" by the use of "sources whose accuracy cannot reasonably be questioned."

E. Jury's right to disregard: When the judge takes judicial notice of an adjudicative fact, is that fact conclusively determined, or may the jury choose to find otherwise? In most courts, the answer varies depending on whether the case is civil or criminal:

1. **Civil:** In *civil* cases, most courts treat judicial notice as being **conclusive** on the issue. These courts, therefore, **instruct the jury** that they **must** treat the fact as being so. Courts are especially likely to make the judicial notice conclusive if they follow the majority view that judicial notice may be taken only of facts that are "indisputable." Thus FRE 201, after providing in section (b) that the noticed fact must be one that is "not subject to reasonable dispute," provides in section (g) that "in a civil action or proceeding, the court shall instruct the jury to accept as **conclusive** any fact judicially noticed." (Commentators who argue that judicial notice should also be taken of a fact that is merely "very likely" to be true as long as it is much more convenient to notice the fact than to require it to be proved, also tend to argue that the jury should not be bound by the judicial notice. See M, p. 932, n. 10.)

2. **Criminal:** In a *criminal* case, courts generally hold that the noticed fact is **not conclusive** upon the jury. The reason for this difference from the civil context is that courts are afraid that to take away the jury's right to make their own determination of the fact would violate the defendant's **constitutional right** to a **jury trial**.

> **Example:** D is charged with grand larceny, for the theft of a three-year-old automobile. The statute defines "grand larceny" to require that the property have a value of greater than $50. The prosecutor offers no evidence of the car's value. The trial judge charges the jury that it must treat the value of the property as being greater than $50. D is convicted.
>
> *Held* (on appeal) for D. The trial judge should not have told the jury that they were bound to treat the car as being worth more than $50. Even though the jury almost certainly would have assumed the car to be worth more than $50 as a matter of common sense, D had the right to have the jury make an actual determination of any element of the crime, under his state constitutional right to jury trial. "If a court can take one important element of an offense from the jury and determine the facts for them because such fact seems plain enough to him, then which element cannot be similarly taken away, and where would the process stop?" *State v. Lawrence*, 234 P.2d 600 (Utah 1951).

a. **Criticism:** Remember that, in the vast majority of courts, judicial notice will only be taken of those facts that are truly "beyond dispute." As a dissent pointed out in *State v. Lawrence*, why should the jury be given a chance to contradict an indisputable fact? It is hard to see how the constitutional right to a jury trial includes a right to have a jury behave irrationally.

b. **Federal Rules:** The Federal Rules follow the standard approach of not binding the jury in a criminal case. FRE 201(g) provides that "in a criminal case, the court shall instruct the jury that it may, but is not required to, accept as conclusive any fact judicially noticed."

   c. On appeal: One consequence of the rule that the jury is not bound to accept the judicially-noticed fact in a criminal case, is that the prosecution's failure to supply evidence of an element of the crime ***cannot be corrected on appeal***, even if the missing fact is one which would otherwise be the proper subject of judicial notice. For instance, in *U.S. v. Jones*, 580 F.2d 219 (6th Cir. 1978), D was charged with illegally intercepting telephone conversations from an interstate common carrier. The prosecutor inadvertently failed to show that the telephone company in question provided interstate lines. Even though this fact may well have been appropriate for judicial notice at the trial level, the appellate court refused to take judicial notice of it — to do so would deprive D of his right, embodied in FRE 201(g), to have the jury disregard even a judicially noticed fact if it chooses to do so. Therefore, the court directed that D be acquitted.

F. Procedure: We now take a brief look at some other procedural aspects of judicial notice:

   1. Advance notice to parties: Must the judge give ***advance notice*** to the parties that he plans to take judicial notice of a fact? Generally, the answer is ***"no."*** M, p. 934.

   a. Motion by party: In most situations, the question does not even arise — one party makes a motion asking the judge to take judicial notice of a fact, and this motion itself effectively gives advance notice to the other party.

   b. On judge's own motion: However, virtually all courts also allow the judge to take judicial notice of a fact on his ***own*** initiative. In this situation, advance notice to the parties would enable the one who would be disadvantaged to explain why judicial notice would be inappropriate. Nonetheless, few if any courts require this to be done.

   c. Right to argue under Federal Rules: The Federal Rules do not require the judge to give advance notice of his intent to take judicial notice. But FRE 201(e) does require the judge to give a party who so requests "an ***opportunity to be heard*** as to the propriety of taking judicial notice and the tenor of the matter noticed. In the absence of prior notification, the request may be made after judicial notice has been taken." In other words, the judge may take judicial notice without giving the parties advance notice of his intent to do so; once he has taken the notice, however, the disadvantaged party may ask for a hearing, which must be granted. See *Soley v. Star & Herald Co.*, 390 F.2d 364 (5th Cir. 1968) (trial judge took notice of a prior case he had tried, but did not offer parties the chance to be heard on the propriety of his doing so; reversed, on the grounds that "litigants should have the opportunity to challenge even a judge's recollections").

   2. Contradictory evidence: Once the judge has judicially noticed a fact, may the disadvantaged party introduce ***contradictory evidence*** on that issue? The answer seems to depend on whether the taking of judicial notice is ***conclusive*** upon the jury, and thus probably depends in turn on whether the case is civil or criminal.

a. Civil: If the case is civil, recall that most courts (and the Federal Rules) make the judicial notice conclusive upon the jury. In this situation, most courts have held that contradictory evidence is ***not admissible***. M, p. 931. After all, judicial notice is only being allowed of facts that are deemed to be "indisputable," so little would be gained (and trial efficiency would be lost) if a party were to be permitted to try to rebut the irrebuttable. This seems to be true under the Federal Rules; see S&R, p. 60.

b. Criminal: In criminal cases, recall that most courts do ***not*** make the judicially noticed fact conclusive upon the jury, mostly because of concerns about infringing the defendant's right to a jury trial. Most courts would probably also let the defendant introduce evidence to ***rebut*** the judicially noticed fact. Federal courts would probably follow this approach. S&R, p. 61.

3. When taken: Most courts hold that judicial notice of an appropriate adjudicative fact may be taken ***at any time*** during the proceeding.

a. Before trial: For instance, notice may be taken ***before trial*** if the noticed fact relates to pre-trial proceedings. Thus a trial judge might take notice of a fact relating to ***jurisdiction*** even before the trial begins, if the defendant argues that the court has no jurisdiction over him or the subject matter. See, e.g., *Bulova Watch Co., Inc. v. K. Hattori & Co., Ltd.*, 508 F.Supp. 1322 (E.D.N.Y. 1981) (judicial notice taken of methods of Japanese multinational companies, in deciding to deny D's pre-trial motion to dismiss for lack of personal jurisdiction).

b. On appeal: Similarly, in most states judicial notice may be taken even ***on appeal***. Thus at least in civil cases, if the trial judge has not taken judicial notice of a fact, the appellate court may do so on its own. M, p. 935. (But most courts do not permit this in a criminal case tried to a jury; see *supra*, p. 468.)

c. Federal Rules: The Federal Rules apparently allow an appellate court to take judicial notice in a civil case; FRE 201(f) provides that "judicial notice may be taken at any stage of the proceeding."

III. LEGISLATIVE FACTS

A. Notice of legislative facts: Judges take constant notice of so-called ***"legislative"*** facts. The most important distinction between judicial notice of administrative facts and legislative facts is that whereas an adjudicative fact must be "indisputable" before it can be judicially noticed, this is not the case for a legislative fact. Most courts would probably say that the judge has the right to judicially notice any legislative fact so long as the judge ***believes it to be true***, even though it is not indisputable. L&S, p. 847.

1. Types of legislative facts: Recall that a legislative fact is one that does not pertain directly to the particular parties and their controversy; rather, it is a more general fact that relates to whether a statute is constitutional, whether a common-law principle should be modified, how a statute should be interpreted, or some other aspect of a judge's law-making process.

a. **Constitutionality:** For instance, judges often have to consider a wide variety of legislative facts in determining the ***constitutionality*** of a statute.

   i. **Due process and equal protection:** Thus in substantive due process cases, the judge will generally have to decide whether there is a rational relation between the objective sought by the legislature and the means it chose to achieve that objective. Similarly, consideration of non-evidentiary legislative facts will often be necessary to decide an equal protection challenge, especially one in which there is no special scrutiny and the court must thus decide whether there is a rational basis for the legislative classification.

   ii. **Desegregation:** Thus when the Supreme Court had to decide whether separate-but-equal segregated schools violated black children's equal protection rights, the Court relied on a large volume of non-evidentiary legislative facts about the effect of segregation on black children. For instance, the Court relied on non-evidentiary studies by psychologist Kenneth B. Clark showing the psychological impact of segregation. *Brown v. Board of Education*, 347 U.S. 483 (1954).

   iii. **Abortion:** Perhaps the most dramatic instance of a court's taking judicial notice of legislative facts came in the Supreme Court's ***abortion*** decision, *Roe v. Wade*, 410 U.S. 113 (1973). The Court's "trimester" approach to abortion (e.g., that the state may not impose barriers to abortion during the first trimester) was heavily based upon asserted medical facts that were not introduced into evidence (e.g., that a fetus generally does not become viable until 28 weeks after conception).

b. **Non-constitutional cases:** In cases not involving the constitution, the judge will similarly often have to resort to legislative facts to interpret a statute, or to decide whether to extend or modify a common law principle. For instance, in the landmark case imposing an implied warranty of habitability for apartment rentals, the court relied on many legislative facts not introduced into evidence (e.g., that tenants have very little leverage to enforce demands for better housing, so that they are in a take-it-or-leave-it situation). *Javins v. First National Realty Corp.*, 428 F.2d 1071 (D.C.Cir. 1970).

B. **Not usually codified:** Unlike judicial notice of adjudicative facts, judicial notice of legislative facts is usually ***not handled by statute***. There are so many different contexts in which the need to take notice of legislative facts may arise that it is difficult or impossible to specify a single set of standards for when notice is appropriate. Instead, the judge is left pretty much on her own in deciding what facts should be taken notice of, and what the consequence of that notice should be.

   1. **Federal Rules silent:** Thus the Federal Rules are completely ***silent*** on the issue of judicial notice of legislative facts. S&R, p. 58. As in most state courts, the federal judge is left largely on his own (but under the supervision of the appellate court) in deciding what legislative facts to take notice of, and what procedures to follow in doing so.

C. **Binding on jury even in criminal case:** Recall that in criminal cases, judicial notice of an adjudicative fact is not binding on the jury. This rule does *not* apply to legislative facts: if the judge takes judicial notice of a legislative fact, this notice is ***binding on the jury*** even though the noticed fact operates to the detriment of the criminal defendant. Consequently, it will often be quite important to determine whether a particular fact is legislative or adjudicative.

> **Example:** The Ds are charged with illegally importing cocaine. The statute under which they are charged prohibits the importation of "cocoa leaves and any . . . derivative or preparation of cocoa leaves. . . ." The prosecution proves that the Ds imported cocaine hydrochloride, but does not introduce evidence to show that cocaine hydrochloride is a derivative of cocoa leaves. The trial judge instructs the jury that if it finds that what the Ds imported was cocaine hydrochloride, it must find that the substance was a proscribed cocoa leaf derivative. The Ds argue that the jury should have been permitted to disregard this factual conclusion.
>
> *Held* (on appeal), the trial judge was correct in telling the jury that it must treat cocaine hydrochloride as being a cocoa leaf derivative. This fact was a legislative, not adjudicative, fact — legislative facts are "established truths, facts, or pronouncements that do not change from case to case but apply universally . . . " and the question whether cocaine hydrochloride is a derivative of the cocoa leaf is a question of scientific fact applicable to all enforcement proceedings under federal drug laws. Since FRE 201 does not apply to legislative facts, Rule 201(g)'s provision that the jury is not bound in a criminal case is inapplicable. It was up to the judge, not the jury, to make this factual determination, since allowing juries to make that determination would produce the "preposterous" result that juries could make "conflicting findings on what constitutes controlled substances under federal law. . . ." *U.S. v. Gould*, 536 F.2d 216 (8th Cir. 1976).

IV. NOTICE OF LAW

A. **Notice of law generally:** Recall that under our system, questions of law are to be decided by the judge, not the jury. (*Supra*, p. 454.) This concept is often expressed by saying that the judge may take "judicial notice of law." Most importantly, this means that at least as to some types of law, when the judge determines what the law is he is ***not restricted*** to materials given to him by the parties; he may conduct his ***own investigation***, into whatever materials he wishes, in determining what the law is. For instance, he is free to locate, read, and cite cases that he believes to be on point, even if neither party has called these cases to his attention.

1. **Restriction:** However, some types of law have historically been viewed as being so difficult to locate and verify that: (1) they must be "proved" by a party's formal submission of evidence; (2) they must be explicitly *pleaded*. Therefore, a judge's ability to take judicial notice of law (i.e., to dispense with the need for formal evidence or pleadings about what the law is) exists for some sources of law but not others.

B. Domestic law: Let us first consider ***"domestic"*** law, i.e., the law of the jurisdiction in which the court sits. A judge may always take ***judicial notice*** of domestic law; by corollary, a party need not "prove" domestic law. M, pp. 938-39.

    1. State courts: For a state court, "domestic" law is the ***law of that state***, plus federal law (since federal law is controlling in every state). M, p. 939. Thus a state judge has the right (and in fact the obligation) to take judicial notice of some controlling provision of federal law, even if neither party makes any showing of what that law is, or even calls it to the judge's attention.

        a. Administrative regulations and municipal codes: A state's own law, for judicial notice purposes, also includes ***administrative regulations***, so long as these are published in a way that makes them readily accessible. L&S, p. 850. By contrast, ***municipal ordinances*** are usually ***not*** judicially noticeable, because they are often compiled in a haphazard way that makes them hard to research. M, p. 939. Therefore, such ordinances must be proved.

    2. Federal courts: In federal courts, "domestic" law is usually held to include not only federal law, and not merely the law of the state where the federal court sits, but also the law of ***all states*** if relevant. *Id.*

C. Laws of sister states: By contrast, the common-law rule has been that one state may ***not*** judicially notice the laws of a ***sister state***; instead, this must be "proved" by the submission of evidence as to what that sister state's law really is. M, p. 940. Thus if a case is being tried in state A and the law of state B is relevant (under conflict of laws principles), the party seeking to benefit from state B's law will probably literally have to introduce into evidence a certified copy of state B's statutes, court opinions, etc, if state A has not modified the common law's unwillingness to permit judicial notice of a sister state's law.

    1. Change by statute: However, most states have adopted the Uniform Judicial Notice of Foreign Law Act. L&S, p. 850. That Act allows the judge to take judicial notice of the law (whether statutory or common law) of every sister state.

D. Law of other countries: The law of ***other countries*** may not be judicially noticed, according to most states. Therefore, a party must generally plead and prove such law. L&S, pp. 850-51.

    1. Federal Rules: But this is not the case in federal courts. Fed. R. Civ. Proc. 44.1 allows the federal judge to conduct his own research on an issue of foreign law, rather than limiting him to evidence supplied by a party. (But a party who intends to raise an issue concerning foreign law must nonetheless give notice of this fact in his pleadings, in contrast to the true "judicial notice of law" situation where no pleading concerning the law need be made.)

MULTISTATE BAR EXAM
QUESTIONS AND ANSWERS

These questions are from Multistate exams from the past several years, and have been released by the National Conference of Bar Examiners. They assume that the *Federal Rules of Evidence* are in force in the jurisdiction.

Questions (c) 1980, 1981, 1983, 1985, 1987 by National Conference of Bar Examiners. Reprinted by permission.

Questions 1-3 are based on the following fact situation.

Pemberton and three passengers, Able, Baker and Charley, were injured when their car was struck by a truck owned by Mammoth Corporation and driven by Edwards. Helper, also a Mammoth employee, was riding in the truck. The issues in *Pemberton v. Mammoth* include the negligence of Edwards in driving too fast and failing to wear glasses, and of Pemberton in failing to yield the right of way.

1. Pemberton's counsel proffers evidence showing that shortly after the accident Mammoth put a speed governor on the truck involved in the accident. The judge should rule the proffered evidence

    (A) admissible as an admission of a party

    (B) admissible as *res gestae*

    (C) inadmissible for public policy reasons

    (D) inadmissible, because it would lead to the drawing of an inference on an inference

2. Pemberton's counsel seeks to introduce Helper's written statement that Edwards, Mammoth's driver, had left his glasses (required by his operator's license) at the truck stop when they had left five minutes before the accident. The judge should rule the statement admissible only if

    (A) Pemberton first proves that Helper is an agent of Mammoth and that the statement concerned a matter within the scope of his agency

    (B) Pemberton produces independent evidence that Edwards was not wearing corrective lenses at the time of the accident

    (C) Helper is shown to be beyond the process of the court and unavailable to testify

    (D) the statement was under oath in affidavit form

3. Mammoth's counsel seeks to have Sheriff testify that while he was investigating the accident he was told by Pemberton, "This was probably our fault." The judge should rule the proffered evidence

    (A) admissible as an admission of a party

    (B) admissible, because it is a statement made to a police officer in the course of an official investigation

    (C) inadmissible, because it is a mixed conclusion of law and fact

    (D) inadmissible, because it is hearsay, not within any exception

4. Drew is charged with the murder of Pitt. The prosecutor introduced testimony of a police officer that Pitt told a priest, administering the last rites, "I was stabbed by Drew. Since I am dying, tell him I forgive him." Thereafter, Drew's attorney offers the testimony of Wall that the day before, when Pitt believe he would live, he stated that he had been stabbed by Jack, an old enemy. The testimony of Wall is

    (A) admissible under an exception to the hearsay rule

    (B) admissible to impeach the dead declarant

    (C) inadmissible because it goes to the ultimate issue in the case

    (D) inadmissible because irrelevant to any substantive issue in the case

substantive issue in the case

5. Jones offered to testify that he looked up Smith's telephone number in the directory, called that number, and that a voice answered "This is Smith speaking." At this Jones asked, "Was that your horse that tramped across my cornfield this afternoon?" The voice replied "Yes." The judge should rule the testimony

(A) admissible, because the answering speaker's identification of himself, together with the usual accuracy of the telephone directory and transmission system, furnishes sufficient authentication

(B) admissible, because judicial notice may be taken of the accuracy of telephone directories

(C) inadmissible unless Jones can further testify that he was familiar with Smith's voice and that it was in fact Smith to whom he spoke

(D) inadmissible unless Smith has first been asked whether or not the conversation took place and has been given the opportunity to admit, deny, or explain

6. Jones seeks to introduce in evidence a photograph of his cornfield in order to depict the nature and extent of the damage done. The judge should rule the photograph

(A) admissible if Jones testifies that it fairly and accurately portrays the condition of the cornfield after the damage was done

(B) admissible if Jones testifies that the photograph was taken within a week after the alleged occurrence

(C) inadmissible if Jones fails to call the photographer to testify concerning the circumstances under which the photograph was taken

(D) inadmissible if it is possible to describe the damage to the cornfield through direct oral testimony

7. Patty sues Mart Department Store for personal injuries, alleging that while shopping she was knocked to the floor by a merchandise cart being pushed by Handy, a stock clerk, and that as a consequence her back was injured.

Handy testified that Patty fell near the cart but was not struck by it. Thirty minutes after Patty's fall, Handy, in accordance with regular practice at Mart, had filled out a printed form, "Employee's Report of Accident — Mart Department Store," in which he stated that Patty had been leaning over to spank her young child and in so doing had fallen near his cart. Counsel for Mart offers in evidence the report, which had been given him by Handy's supervisor. The judge should rule the report offered by Mart

(A) admissible as *res gestae*

(B) admissible as a business record

(C) inadmissible, because its hearsay, not within an exception

(D) inadmissible, because Handy is available as a witness

Questions 8-10 are based on the following fact situation.

Dann, who was charged with the crime of assaulting Smith, admitted striking Smith but claimed to have acted in self-defense when he was attacked by Smith, who was drunk and belligerent after a football game.

8. Dann offered testimony of Employer, that he had known and employed Dann for twelve years and knew Dann's reputation among the people with whom he lived and worked to be that of a peaceful, law-abiding, nonviolent person. The trial judge should rule this testimony

(A) admissible, because relevant to show the improbability of Dann's having committed an unprovoked assault

(B) admissible, because relevant to a determination of the extent of punishment if Dann is convicted

(C) not admissible, because whether Dann is

normally a person of good character is irrelevant to the specific charge

(D) not admissible, because irrelevant without a showing that Employer was one of the persons among whom Dann lived and worked

9. On cross-examination of Employer (Dann's), the state's attorney asked Employer if he had heard that Dann often engaged in fights and brawls. The trial judge should rule the question

(A) not objectionable, because evidence of Dann's previous fights and brawls may be used to prove his guilt

(B) not objectionable, because it tests Employer's knowledge of Dann's reputation

(C) objectionable, because it seeks to put into evidence separate, unrelated offenses

(D) objectionable, because no specific time or incidents are specified and inquired about

10. Dann's friend Frank was called to testify that Smith had a reputation among the people with whom he lived and worked for lawbreaking and frequently engaging in brawls. The trial judge should rule the testimony

(A) admissible to support Dann's theory of self-defense, touching on whether Dann or Smith was the aggressor

(B) admissible if Frank testifies further as to specific acts of misconduct on Smith's part of which Frank has personal knowledge

(C) inadmissible on the question of Dann's guilt because Dann, not Smith, is on trial

(D) inadmissible, because Frank failed to lay a proper foundation

Questions 11-14 are based on the following fact situation.

Carr ran into and injured Pedersen, a pedestrian. With Carr in his car were Wanda and Walter Passenger. Passerby saw the accident and called the police department, which sent Sheriff to investigate.

All of these people were available as potential witnesses in the case of *Pedersen v. Carr*. Pedersen alleges that Carr, while drunk, struck Pedersen who was in a duly marked crosswalk.

11. Pedersen's counsel wants to introduce testimony of Sheriff that at the police station Carr told Sheriff, "I think this was probably my fault." The trial judge should rule this testimony

(A) admissible as a part of the *res gestae*

(B) admissible as an admission of a party

(C) inadmissible because it includes a conclusion of law which the declarant was not qualified to make

(D) inadmissible because it constitutes an opinion rather than an admission of specific facts

12. Pedersen's counsel wishes to prove that after the accident Carr went to Pedersen and offered $1,000 to settle Pedersen's claim. The trial judge should rule this evidence

(A) admissible as an admission of a party

(B) admissible as an admission to show Carr's liability, provided the court gives a cautionary instruction that the statement should not be considered as bearing on the issue of damages

(C) inadmissible since it is not relevant either to the question of liability or the question of damages

(D) inadmissible because even though irrelevant and an admission, the policy of the law is to encourage settlement negotiations

13. Pedersen's counsel wants to have Sheriff testify to the following statement made to him by Walter Passenger, out of the presence of Carr: "We were returning from a party at which we had all been drinking." The trial judge should rule this testimony

    (A) admissible as an admission of a party

    (B) admissible as a declaration against interest

    (C) inadmissible as hearsay not within any exception

    (D) inadmissible because it would lead the court into nonessential side issues

14. On the evening of the day of the accident, Walter Passenger wrote a letter to his sister in which he described the accident. When Walter says he cannot remember some details of the accident, Pedersen's counsel seeks to show him the letter to assist him in his testimony on direct examination. The trial judge should rule this

    (A) permissible under the doctrine of present recollection refreshed

    (B) permissible under the doctrine of past recollection recorded

    (C) objectionable because the letter was not a spontaneous utterance

    (D) objectionable because the letter is a self-serving declaration in so far as the witness, Walter, is concerned

15. Dever was indicted for the murder of Vickers by poison. At trial, the prosecutor calls the county coroner, Dr. Wolfe, who is a board-certified pathologist, to testify that, in accord with good practice in her specialty, she has studied microphotographic slides, made under her supervision by medical assistants, of tissue taken from Vickers' corpse and that it is Wolfe's opinion, based on that study, that Vickers died of poisoning. The slides have not been offered in evidence.

    Dr. Wolfe's opinion should be

    (A) excluded, because the cause of death is a critical issue to be decided by the trier of fact

    (B) excluded, because her opinion is based on facts not in evidence

    (C) admitted, because Wolfe followed accepted medical practice in arriving at her opinion

    (D) admitted because her opinion is based on matters observed pursuant to a duty imposed by law

16. At the trial of Davis for a murder that occurred in Newtown, the prosecution called Waite, who testified that she saw Davis kill the victim. Davis believed that Waite was 600 miles away in Old Town, engaged in the illegal sale of narcotics, on the day in question. On cross-examination by Davis, Waite was asked whether she had in fact sold narcotics in Old Town on that date. Waite refused to answer on the ground of self-incrimination.

    The judge, over the prosecutor's objection, ordered that if Waite did not testify, her direct testimony should be stricken. The order to testify or have the testimony stricken can best be supported on the basis that

    (A) Waite had not been charged with any crime and, thus, could claim no privilege against self-incrimination

    (B) Waite's proper invocation of the privilege prevented adequate cross-examination

    (C) the public interest in allowing an accused to defend himself and herself outweighs the interest of a non-party witness in the privilege

    (D) the trial record, independent of testimony, does not establish that Waite's answer could incriminate her

17. Cars driven by Pugh and Davidson collided, and Davidson was charged with driving while intoxicated in connection with the accident. She pleaded guilty and was merely fined, although under the statute the court could have sentenced her to two years in prison.

    Thereafter, Pugh, alleging that Davidson's intoxication had caused the collision, sued Davidson for damages. At trial, Pugh offers the properly authenticated record of Davidson's conviction. The record should be

(A) admitted as proof of Davidson's character

(B) admitted as proof of Davidson's intoxication

(C) excluded, because the conviction was not the result of a trial

(D) excluded, because it is hearsay not within any exception

18. Pitt sued Dow for damages for injuries that Pitt incurred when a badly rotted limb fell from a curbside tree in front of Dow's home and hit Pitt. Dow claimed that the tree was on city property and thus was the responsibility of the city. At trial, Pitt offered testimony that a week after the accident, Dow had cut the tree down with a chainsaw. The offered evidence is

(A) inadmissible, because there is a policy to encourage safety precautions

(B) inadmissible, because it is irrelevant to the condition of the tree at the time of the accident

(C) admissible to show the tree was on Dow's property

(D) admissible to show the tree was in a rotted condition

19. Dean, Charged with murder, was present with her attorney at a preliminary examination when White, who was the defendant in a separate prosecution for concealing the body of the murder victim, testified for the prosecution against Dean. When called to testify at Dean's trial, White refused to testify, though ordered to do so.

The prosecution offers evidence of White's testimony at the preliminary examination. The evidence is

(A) admissible as former testimony

(B) admissible as past recollection recorded

(C) inadmissible, because it would violate White's privilege against self- incrimination

(D) inadmissible, because it is hearsay not within any exception

20. Potts, a building contractor, sued Dennis for failure to pay on a small cost-plus construction contract. At trial, Potts, who personally supervised all of the work, seeks to testify to what he remembers about the amount of pipe used, the number of workers used on the job, and the number of hours spent grading.

Dennis objects on the ground that Potts had routinely recorded these facts in notebooks which are in Pott's possession.

Pott's testimony is

(A) admissible as a report of regularly conducted business activity

(B) admissible as based on first-hand knowledge

(C) inadmissible, because it violates the best evidence rule

(D) inadmissible, because a summary of writings cannot be made unless the originals are available for examination

21. Dryden is tried on a charge of driving while intoxicated. When Dryden was booked at the police station, a videotape was made that showed him unsteady, abusive, and speaking in a slurred manner. if the prosecutor lays a foundation properly identifying the tape, should the court admit it in evidence and permit it to be shown to the jury?

(A) Yes, because it is an admission.

(B) Yes, because its value is not substantially outweighted by unfair prejudice.

(C) No, because the privilege against self-incrimination is applicable.

(D) No, because specific instances of conduct cannot be proved by extrinsic evidence.

22. In Polk's negligence action against Dell arising out of a multiple-car collision. Witt testified for Polk that Dell went through a red light. On cross-examination, Dell seeks to question Witt about her statement that the light was yellow, made in a deposition that Witt gave in a separate action between Adams and Baker. The transcript of the deposition is self-authenticating. On proper objection, the court should rule the inquiry

(A) admissible for impeachment only

(B) admissible as substantive evidence only

(C) admissible for impeachment and as substantive evidence

(D) inadmissible, because it is hearsay not within any exception

23. Powers sued Debbs for battery. At trial, Powers' witness Wilson testified that Debbs had made an unprovoked attack on Powers.

On cross-examination, Debbs asks Wilson about a false claim that Wilson had once filed on an insurance policy. The question is

(A) proper, because the conduct involved untruthfulness

(B) proper provided that the conduct resulted in conviction of Wilson

(C) improper, because the impeachment involved a specific instance of misconduct

(D) improper, because the claim form would be the best evidence

24. While crossing Spruce Street, Pesko was hit by a car that she did not see. Pesko sued Dorry for her injuries.

At trial, Pesko calls Williams, a police officer, to testify that, ten minutes after the accident, a driver stopped him and said, "Officer, a few minutes ago I saw a hit-and-run accident on Spruce Street involving a blue convertible, which I followed to the drive-in restaurant at Oak and Third," and that a few seconds later Williams saw Dorry sitting alone in a blue convertible in the drive-in restaurant's parking lot.

Williams' testimony about the driver's statement should be

(A) admitted as a statement of recent perception

(B) admitted as a present sense impression

(C) excluded, because it is hearsay not within any exception

(D) excluded, because it is more prejudicial than probative

25. Post sued Dean for personal injury alleged to have been caused by Dean's negligence. A major issue at trial was whether Post's disability was caused solely by trauma or by a preexisting condition of osteoarthritis.

Post called Dr. Cox, who testified that the disability was caused by trauma. On cross-examination, Dr. Cox testified that a medical textbook entitled *Diseases of the Joints* was authoritative and that she agreed with the substance of passages from the textbook that she was directed to look at, but that the passages were inapplicable to Post's condition because they dealt with rheumatoid arthritis rather than with the osteoarthritis that Post was alleged to have.

Dean then called his expert, Dr. Freed, who testifies that, with reference to he issue being litigated, there is no difference between the two kinds of arthritis. Dean's counsel then asks permission to read to the jury the textbook passages earlier shown to Dr. Cox.

The judge should rule the textbook passages

(A) admissible only for the purpose of impeaching Cox

(B) admissible as substantive evidence if the judge determines that the passages are relevant

(C) inadmissible, because they are hearsay not within any exception

(D) inadmissible, because Cox contended that they are not relevant to Posts's condition.

26. Pratt sued Danvers for injuries suffered by Pratt when their automobiles collided. At trial Pratt offers into evidence a properly authenticated letter from Danvers that says, "your claim seems too high, but, because I might have been a little negligent, I'm prepared to offer you half of what you ask."

The letter is

(A) admissible as an admission by a party-opponent

(B) admissible as a statement against pecuniary interest

(C) inadmissible, because Danver's statement

is lay opinion on a legal issue

(D) inadmissible, because Danver's statement was made in an effort to settle the claim

27. Darden was prosecuted for armed robbery. At trial, Darden testified in his own behalf, denying that he had committed the robbery. On cross- examination, the prosecutor intends to ask Darden whether he had been convicted of burglary six years earlier.

The question concerning the burglary conviction is

(A) proper if the court finds that the probative value for impeachment outweighs the prejudice to Darden

(B) proper, because the prosecutor is entitled to make this inquiry as a matter of right

(C) improper, because burglary does not involve dishonesty or false statement

(D) improper, because the conviction must be proved by court record, not by question on cross-examination

28. In Peel's personal injury action, Wilson, a physician who had no previous knowledge of the matter, sat in court and heard all the evidence about Peel's symptoms and conditions.

Wilson is called to give her opinion whether Peel's injuries are permanent. May Wilson so testify?

(A) Yes, provided she first identifies the data on which her opinion is based

(B) Yes, because an expert may base her opinion on facts made known to her at the trial

(C) No, because she has no personal knowledge of Peel's condition

(D) No, because permanence of injury is an issue to be decided by the jury

29. In a tort action, Fisher testified against Dawes. Dawes then called Jones, who testified that Fisher had a bad reputation for veracity. Dawes then also called Weld to testify that Fisher once perpetrated a hoax on the police.

Weld's testimony is

(A) admissible, provided that the hoax involves untruthfulness

(B) admissible, provided that the hoax resulted in a conviction of Fisher

(C) inadmissible, because it is merely cumulative impeachment

(D) inadmissible, because it is extrinsic evidence of a specific instance of misconduct

30. David is being tried in federal court for criminal conspiracy with John to violate federal narcotics law. At trial, the prosecutor calls David's new wife, Wanda, and asks her to testify about a meeting between David and John that she observed before she married David.

Which of the following is the most accurate statement of the applicable rule concerning whether Wanda may testify?

(A) the choice is Wanda's

(B) the choice is David's

(C) Wanda is permitted to testify only if both Wanda and David agree

(D) Wanda is compelled to testify even if both Wanda and David object

31. In a civil suit by Pine against Decker, Decker called Wall, a chemist, as an expert witness and asked him a number of questions about his education and experience in chemistry. Over Pine's objection that Wall was not shown to be qualified in chemistry, the trial court permitted Wall to testify as to his opinion in response to a hypothetical question.

On cross-examination, Pine asked Wall if he had failed two chemistry courses while doing his graduate work. The answer should be

(A) admitted, because it is relevant to the weight to be given to Wall's testimony

(B) admitted, because specific acts bearing on truthfulness may be inquired about on cross-examination

(C) excluded, because the court has determined that Wall is qualified to testify as an expert

(D) excluded, because Wall's character has not

been put in issue

32. In a contract suit by Perez against Drake, each of the following is an accepted method of authenticating Drake's signature on a document offered by Perez EXCEPT:

(A) a non-expert who, in preparation for trial, has familiarized himself with Drake's usual signature testifies that, in his opinion, the questioned signature is genuine.

(B) the jury, without the assistance of an expert, compares the questioned signature with an admittedly authentic sample of Drake's handwriting.

(C) a witness offers proof that the signature is on a document that has been in existence for at least 20 years, that was in a place where it would be if it was authentic, and that it has no suspicious circumstances surrounding it

(D) a witness testifies that Drake admitted that the signature is his

33. Paulsen sued Daly for nonpayment of a personal loan to Daly, as evidenced by Daly's promissory note to Paulsen. Paulsen called Walters to testify that he knows Daly's handwriting and that the signature on the note is Daly's. On direct examination, to identify himself, Walters gave his name and address and testified that he had been employed by a roofing company for seven years

During presentation of Daly's case, Daly called Wilson to testify that she is the roofing company's personnel manager and that she had determined, by examining the company's employment records, that Walters had worked there only three years. The trial judge should rule that Wilson's testimony is

(A) inadmissible, because it is not the best evidence

(B) inadmissible, because it is impeachment on a collateral question

(C) admissible as evidence of a regularly conducted activity

(D) admissible as tending to impeach Walters' credibility

34. Parker sued Dodd over title to an island in a river. Daily variations in the water level were important

For many years Wells, a commercial fisherman, kept a daily log of the water level at his dock opposite the island in order to forecast fishing conditions. Parker employed Zee, an engineer, to prepare graphs from Wells's log.

Wells was called to testify to the manner in which he kept the log, which had been available for inspection. His testimony should be

(A) excluded on a general objection because it is not admissible for any purpose

(B) excluded on a specific objection that it calls for hearsay

(C) admitted to support the credibility of Wells and Zee as witnesses

(D) admitted as part of the foundation for admission of Zee's graphs

35. Dray was prosecuted for bank robbery. At trial, the bank teller, Wall, was unable to identify Dray, now bearded, as the bank robber. The prosecutor then showed Wall a group of photographs, and Wall testified that she had previously told the prosecutor that the middle picture (concededly a picture of Dray before he grew a beard) was a picture of the bank robber.

Wall's testimony is

(A) inadmissible, because it is hearsay not within any exception

(B) inadmissible, because it is a violation of Dray's right of confrontation

(C) admissible as prior identification by the witness

(D) admissible as past recollection recorded

36. Duncan was charged with aggravated assault. At trial, Duncan did not testify; however, he sought to offer opinion evidence of his good character for truth and veracity.

This testimony should be

(A) admitted, because a criminal defendant is entitled to offer evidence of his good character

(B) admitted, because a party's credibility is necessarily in issue

(C) excluded, because character is not admissible to prove conduct in conformity therewith

(D) excluded, because it is evidence of a trait not pertinent to the case

ANSWERS TO MULTISTATE QUESTIONS

1. **C**   The installation of a speed governor is a subsequent remedial measure, inadmissible under FRE 407 to prove negligence. This exclusion fulfills the public policy of encouraging the use of safety measures. [p. 56] (A) is wrong because the rule against showing subsequent remedial measures to prove negligence applies even where the statement is otherwise admissible as a party admission.

2. **A**   Under 801(d)(2)(D), a statement may be offered against a party if it was made "by the party's agent or servant concerning a matter within the scope of the agency or employment, made during the existence of the relationship." [p. 160] The facts hypothesized in (A) are enough to satisfy these requirements, so Helper's statement thereby avoids being hearsay. (B) is wrong because without a showing of agency the statement will be hearsay, and corroborated hearsay is generally no more admissible than uncorroborated hearsay. (C) is wrong because Helper's unavailability is by itself not enough to get his uncross-examined statement past the hearsay rule (but if he had made the statement in a "proceeding" where Mammoth had the right to question him about it, it would have been admissible under the "former testimony" exception). (D) is wrong because the fact that a statement is contained in an affidavit under oath is not enough to bring it within any hearsay exception.

3. **A**   Any statement by a party may be admitted against that party as an admission; admissions are made non-hearsay by FRE 801(d)(2). [p. 152] (B) is wrong because statements made *to* a police officer during an official investigation are not exempt from the hearsay rule (though a statement made *by* an officer in an investigative report may sometimes come within the "factual findings" part of the public records exception, FRE 803(8)(c)). (C) is wrong because an admission is admissible against a party even if it contains a conclusion of law. [p. 151]

4. **B**   Where an out-of-court declarant's statement is admitted under a hearsay exception (as was Pitt's statement to the police), the adversary may impeach this declarant just as if he were a live witness, by showing that he made a prior inconsistent statement. (A) is arguably also correct, since the court might hold that the statement to Wall should come within the residual or "catch all" exception of FRE 804(b)(5) (though the facts do not disclose any "circumstantial guarantees of trustworthiness" as that rule requires). (C) is wrong because there is no rule against admission of evidence on ultimate issues. (D) is wrong because the statement does go to the substantive issue of who murdered Pitt.

5. **A**   Under FRE 901(b)(6), a telephone conversation may be authenticated by showing that a call was made to the listed phone number of a particular person, and that "circumstances, including self-identification, show the person answering to be the one called. . . ." [p. 368] (B) is wrong because a given telephone directory listing is certainly not indisputable, as is required for judicial notice. [p. 465] (C) is wrong because although testimony that the caller recognized the voice of the person called is one way to authenticate the conversation, it is not the only way — circumstances, including self-identification by the person called, will also suffice. (D) is wrong because the only time the questioner must ask about a conversation and give the witness the opportunity to admit, deny, or explain is when the witness is to be impeached by a prior inconsistent statement (and in any event this may happen after introduction of the prior statement; see FRE 613(b)). [p. 96]

6. **A**   A photograph may always be authenticated by testimony from a witness that it fairly and accurately portrays the event or condition that the proponent claims it portrays. [p. 389] (B) is wrong because the authentication requirement is not satisfied where up to a whole week might have intervened to change the condition of the corn field before the photograph was taken. (C) is wrong because testimony by the photographer who took a photo is not necessary for authentication of the photo; anyone who can testify that the photograph accurately portrays what it is claimed to portray will suffice. (D) is wrong because there is no rule of evidence preferring direct oral testimony to a photograph of the thing described (and in fact under some circumstances a photo might be *required* instead of testimony about what the photo shows — the Best Evidence Rule would require this in situations where the contents of the photo are what is being proved, though this is not what is being proved here.)

7. **C**   The issue is whether this report falls within the "business records" exception of FRE 803(6). It was certainly the regular practice of Mart to have its employees make a report of such accidents. However, 803(6) does not apply if "the source of information or the method or circumstances of preparation indicate lack of trustworthiness." A court would probably hold that Handy's strong incentive to prepare a self-exonerating report made the report untrustworthy. Therefore, (B) is wrong. [pp. 196-97] (A) is wrong because the report was not an excited utterance or a present sense impression, which is what the term "*res gestae*" principally refers to. (D) is wrong because the declarant's availability as a witness is irrelevant in determining whether the business records exception applies.

8. **A**   There is a general rule preventing character evidence to show conformity with the character trait. But there is an exception permitting a criminal defendant to show that he possesses a favorable character trait that is relevant to the charge. Under FRE 405(a), this trait may be shown by testimony as to reputation, and is now interpreted to cover reputation at the defendant's place of business as well as where he lives. [p. 38] (C) is wrong because the evidence specifically shows that Dann is non-violent, not merely that he is of "good character" (and even general "good character" evidence may be presented by any criminal defendant).

9. **B**   When a witness testifies to the defendant's favorable reputation for a trait, the prosecution is entitled to ask whether the witness knows of specific past acts by the defendant that are at variance with the asserted favorable reputation; see FRE 405(a). [p. 39] (A) is wrong because prior problems or misdeeds by the defendant may not be used to prove that he acted similarly on this occasion. (C) is gibberish. (D) is wrong because the prosecution may ask questions either about the defendant's reputation or his specific past acts, once the defendant has raised this issue by putting in evidence of his favorable reputation.

10. **A**   FRE 404(a)(2) allows "evidence of a pertinent trait of character of the victim of the crime offered by an accused. . . ." Since Dann is claiming self-defense, this evidence was pertinent, since it made it more probable that Smith rather than Dann was the aggressor. (B) is wrong because this evidence may (and perhaps must) take the form of reputation evidence rather than evidence of specific past misdeeds; see FRE 405(a) and (b). (C) is wrong because (A) is right. (D) is wrong because the only foundation required is that the witness knows Smith's reputation, a requirement that appears to have been satisfied by the facts of the question.

11. **B**   A statement by a party, when offered against that party, falls within the party admission exception to the hearsay rule. This is true even though the statement contains an opinion or a conclusion of law. [p. 151] (A) is wrong because the exception for "*res gestae*" applies to excited utterances and statements of present sense impression, not to statements

regarding recent past events as were involved here. (C) and (D) are wrong because the hearsay exception for admissions covers conclusions of law and opinions even though other hearsay exceptions generally do not.

12. **D**   FRE 408 excludes all offers to compromise from being introduced to prove liability. [p. 61] This is true even though the statement might otherwise be admissible under the party-admissions exception to the hearsay rule.

13. **C**   The statement is being offered to prove the truth of the matter asserted (that they had all been drinking at the party). It does not fall within any hearsay exception. (A) is wrong because Passenger is not a party, and Carr did not implicitly adopt the statement since he was not present when it was made. (B) is wrong because no pecuniary or penal interest of Passenger was weakened by it (Passenger did not drive, so his confession to having had some drinks was not a confession to a criminal or even tortious act). (D) is wrong because the statement is relevant to a highly material issue.

14. **A**   The doctrine of present recollection refreshed permits the examiner to show virtually any item or document to the witness to aid him in giving his present testimony; the item shown does not become evidence. [p. 74] (B) is wrong because Walter has not testified that the letter was accurate when written, a requirement for past recollection recorded. [p. 191] (Had Walter given this testimony, the other requirements for the past recollection recorded exception probably would also have been met, and the letter could then have been read into evidence under FRE 803(5).) (C) is wrong because the spontaneous or excited utterance exception is merely one of many exceptions to the hearsay rule, and in any event the letter was not actually offered in evidence, merely used as a tool to stimulate the witness' recollection. (D) is wrong because, again, the letter is never being offered in evidence.

15. **C**   Even though the slides were not offered in evidence, Wolfe may state her conclusions based on them, if experts in that field would reasonably rely on such a source. FRE 703. [p. 407] (A) is wrong because experts may give opinions even upon "ultimate" or critical issues under the Federal Rules. (B) is wrong for the same reason that (C) is right. (D) is wrong because the only significance of a matter observed persuant to a duty is in the hearsay area (for the business records and public records exceptions) and no hearsay issue is presented here — there is no out-of-court "assertion" being made by the slides.

16. **B**   The defendant's constitutional right of confrontation includes the right to ask questions and have them answered to the best of the witness' ability; if the defendant is deprived of this, he is entitled to have the testimony stricken. [p. 276] (A) and (D) are wrong because a witness may assert the privilege against self-incrimination unless the answer ***could not possibly*** incriminate her. [pp. 326-27] (C) is wrong because it is the accused's constitutional right, not the nebulous "public interest," that is at issue.

17. **B**   A person's conviction for having committed an act can be used to show that that act occurred, if the conviction was for a felony (i.e., if the crime was such that the person could have been sent to jail for more than a year); such a conviction falls within a hearsay exception given by FRE 803(22). (It needs a hearsay exception because it is in effect a jury or judge's statement that the defendant did the act charged, offered to prove the fact stated.) The exception applies even if the actual punishment was less than a year. [p. 221] (A) is wrong because a conviction is not allowable as evidence of the defendant's character and therefore circumstantial evidence that he behaved in conformity with that character. (FRE 404(b)) [p. 24] (C) is wrong because FRE 803(22)'s exception applies to guilty pleas as well as trial verdicts. (D) is wrong for the same reasons (B) is right.

18. **C**   FRE 407 establishes the general rule that subsequent remedial measures are not admissible to show negligence. However, 407 also provides that such measures can be shown as evidence on other issues, including "proving ownership," as was done here.

19. **A**   FRE 804(b)(1) gives a hearsay exception for former testimony if the declarant is unavailable, the testimony was given as a witness in "another hearing," and the criminal defendant had an opportunity and similar motive to develop the testimony by cross or other examination at that prior hearing. All these requirements are satisfied here (since White's refusal to testify makes him "unavailable" under FRE 804(a)(1)). [pp. 223, 225] (B) is inapplicable because, among other reasons, there is no sponsoring witness to testify that the document is correct. (C) is wrong because White waived his self-incrimination privilege with respect to the preliminary hearing testimony by giving it in the first place. (D) is wrong because (A) is right.

20. **B**   A witness may always testify based on first-hand knowledge of the events being described; the fact that there happens to be an incidental written record of those events is irrelevant. (The Best Evidence Rule applies only where the contents of the writing are being directly proved, which is not what is happening here). [p. 379] (A) is wrong because the exception for records of a regularly conducted business activity merely furnishes a hearsay exception, and there is no hearsay problem here. (C) is wrong for the reason that (A) is right. (D) is wrong because Potts is not giving a summary of writings, he is testifying about events that happen to be described in writings.

21. **B**   Any evidence may be excluded under FRE 403 if its probative value is substantially outweighed by the danger of unfair prejudice. [p. 14] But it is very unlikely that any court would find that to be the case here, since only "unfair" prejudice is counted, and Dryden's appearance and behavior after arrest are fair evidence of whether he was intoxicated. (A) is wrong because his behavior is probably not an "admission," and in any event an admission is significant only as an exception to the hearsay rule, and no hearsay problem is presented here (Dryden's statements are not being offered for their truth). (C) is wrong because Dryden's statement is not being offered for its "testimonial" content (it is like a blood sample or voice sample). (D) is wrong because the rule against extrinsic evidence of specific instances of conduct applies only where the witness is being impeached on a collateral matter, and Dryden's behavior and speech after the arrest are material rather than collateral.

22. **C**   The statement is admissible as substantive evidence because under FRE 801(d)(1)(A), it is a prior inconsistent statement made under oath that occurred at a deposition, and is therefore not hearsay. (This is true even though Polk was not there to cross-examine her at the time she made the statement; Polk has his opportunity to do this cross-examination now at trial.) [p. 252] The statement is also admissible for impeachment, since a witness may always be impeached by showing, on cross-examination, that he made a prior inconsistent statement. [p. 94]

23. **A**   Even if Wilson was never convicted for the false insurance claim, the question was proper as a prior bad act under FRE 608(b), since it was raised on cross-examination (rather than through extrinsic evidence), and was relevant to the witness' character for truthfulness. [p. 88] (B) is wrong because although the question would have been proper had there been a conviction, the converse is not true — the question is proper even without a conviction under the "prior bad act" exception just discussed. (C) is wrong because the only rule restricting impeachment based on specific instances of misconduct limits the use of extrinsic evidence (FRE 608(b)). (D) is wrong because the Best Evidence Rule applies only where the proponent is trying to substantively establish the "contents" (i.e., the truthfulness) of

the writing; in any event, extrinsic evidence of prior bad acts to impeach the witness is expressly prohibited by FRE 608(b).

24.   **C**   Since the driver's statement is being offered to establish the truth of the matter asserted in it (that the driver saw a hit-and-run accident with a blue convertible that the driver followed to the restaurant parking lot), it must be excluded unless it falls within some hearsay exception. It is not a statement of present sense impression, because the driver's statement did not take place substantially contemporaneously with the sensing; hence (B) is wrong. [p. 187] (A) is wrong because there is no exception for a statement of "recent perception." (D) is wrong because this evidence is clearly not more prejudicial than probative (though if it were, this could be a ground of exclusion).

25.   **B**   A professional treatise is substantively admissible if it is: (1) relevant; (2) established as a reliable authority; and (3) introduced while an expert is on the stand to help interpret it. This met all the requirements. (It is not required that the expert on the stand be the one who helped establish the treatise's authoritativeness; therefore, Dr. Cox's concession on cross-examination that the book was authoritative sufficed, even though a different expert was on the stand at the time of the proposed second reading.) See FRE 803(18). [p. 215] (A) is wrong because substantive use is allowed here, as discussed above. (C) is wrong because the rule described above is an exception to the hearsay rule. (D) is wrong because the original witness' contention of irrelevance is not binding on the judge.

26.   **D**   Statements made in an effort to settle a claim (including collateral admissions or statements of fact) are inadmissible, under FRE 408. [p. 61] (A) is wrong because, although admissions by a party-opponent do not pose a hearsay problem, the rule against admitting settlement offers is a distinct hurdle apart from hearsay. (B) is wrong for the same kind of reason — the fact that a statement is against the maker's pecuniary interest merely solves the hearsay problem, and the rule against admitting settlement offers remains. (C) is wrong because the statement, "I might have been a little negligent," is probably more factual than legal, and in any event the rule against opinions or conclusions of law does not apply to admissions by a party-opponent. [p. 151]

27.   **A**   Since the burglary did not involve dishonesty or false statement, but is a felony, it is admissible, but only if the judge determines that its probative value outweighs its prejudicial effect on the defendant. FRE 609(a). [p. 81] (B) is wrong for the same reason that (A) is right. (C) is wrong because even crimes not involving dishonesty or false statement are admissible if the probative value outweighs the prejudicial effect, and the crime is a felony. (D) is wrong because FRE 609(a) allows the evidence of conviction to be admitted if it is either "elicited from the witness *or* established by public record. . . ."

28.   **B**   An expert may base her opinion on facts that she does not know first-hand, but has learned at trial (including facts learned through observing the prior witnesses). [p. 406] (A) is wrong because FRE 705 explicitly relieves the expert of the need to disclose the underlying facts or data, unless the court requires otherwise. (C) is wrong because experts are not limited to opinions based on facts they know first-hand; the hypothetical question, the use of hearsay evidence relied upon in similar situations by experts generally, and the use of other witness' trial testimony, are all illustrations of this principle. (D) is wrong because even if the permanence of the injury is an "ultimate" question," FRE 704(a) allows opinion testimony regarding such ultimate issues (except where the mental state of a criminal defendant is at issue).

29. **D** A witness' specific prior instance of misconduct (a "prior bad act") may not be shown by extrinsic evidence — the examiner must establish the specific instance by cross-examination of the witness who is being impeached, or not at all. FRE 608(b). [p. 88] (A) and (B) are wrong for this reason. (C) is wrong because the judge would be unlikely to hold that this evidence is merely cumulative of the prior bad-reputation evidence.

30. **A** In federal cases, the adverse testimony privilege belongs to the testifying spouse, not the party spouse. [p. 342] (The "confidential communications" privilege does not apply here because it applies only to communications that took place during the marriage.)

31. **A** Even after an expert has been permitted to testify on the merits, his credentials may be scrutinized under cross-examination so that the jury can know how much weight to give his opinion. (B) is wrong because Wall's failure of chemistry courses does not bear on his truthfulness. (C) is wrong because the fact that the court has determined that an expert is qualified does not end the opponent's right to establish that his testimony is entitled to little weight. (D) is wrong because Pine's attempt to impeach Wall has nothing to do with Wall's character, just his qualifications.

32. **A** (A) is the correct answer (i.e., the least accepted method of authentication) because FRE 901(b)(2) allows non-expert opinion as to the genuineness of handwriting only if it is "based upon familiarity not acquired for purposes of the litigation." [p. 367] (B) is wrong because the jury may compare exemplars with the challenged handwriting, even without participation of an expert. [*Id.*] (C) is wrong because the three showings by the witness do satisfy the requirements for authentication of an ancient document under FRE 901(b)(8). [p. 370] (D) is wrong because this testimony by the witness would be direct evidence of authenticity (i.e., if the witness is believed, no process of inference is required). Also, this testimony would not have hearsay problems because it is an admission (i.e., it is used against the defendant who made it.) [p. 150]

33. **B** The fact that a witness has made an incorrect statement during his direct testimony may not be shown by extrinsic evidence if the statement related to a collateral issue. [p. 104] The length of time the witness has worked at his present job is clearly collateral, if the witness' testimony has nothing to do with the witness' present job. (A) is wrong because the Best Evidence Rule relates only to proving the *contents* of the document, and here the issue is who signed the document, not what it says. (C) is wrong because "evidence of a regularly conducted activity" relates to the business records exception to the hearsay rule, and no hearsay issue is presented by the authentication of Daly's signature. (D) is wrong for the same reason that (A) is right — a witness' credibility cannot be impeached by showing that he made an incorrect statement in his direct testimony concerning a collateral issue.

34. **D** Before Parker may introduce Zee's graphs, he must establish a foundation for the graphs, i.e., show that they accurately represent the daily water-level variations; this will in turn require a showing that the log from which the numbers for the graph were taken was accurate. (C) is wrong because Wells' testimony has not been attacked yet, so evidence cannot be admitted to support that credibility (this would violate the rule against "bolstering"). [p. 106] (B) is wrong because the document falls within the business records exception to the hearsay rule, FRE 803(6). [p. 194]

35. **C** A statement by a witness that he has previously identified a person after perceiving him, is admissible as non-hearsay under FRE 801(d)(1)(C), if the witness is available for cross-examination. [p. 256] For this reason, (A) is wrong. (B) is wrong because the Supreme Court has interpreted the Confrontation Clause to require merely that the declarant (the

person who made the identification) be present at trial and available for cross-examination. [*Id.*] (D) is wrong because there is no written document whose contents are being offered for their truth, as required for past recollection recorded. [p. 189]

36.   **D**   Although a criminal defendant is generally entitled to introduce evidence of his good character even though that character has not been attacked by the prosecution, he may only do so where the evidence relates to a character trait that is in issue in the case; veracity is not in issue in a prosecution for assault. [pp. 36-37] (B) is wrong, because a party's credibility is normally in issue only when he takes the stand and his credibility is attacked. (C) is wrong because although it is true that generally "character is not admissible to prove conduct in conformity therewith," there is a special exception for proof by a criminal defendant of his favorable relevant character trait.

MULTISTATE-STYLE QUESTIONS

Here are 30 multiple-choice questions, in a Multistate-Bar-Exam style. The questions assume that the Federal Rules of Evidence are in force. These questions are taken from *"The Finz Multistate Method"*, a compendium of 1100 questions in the Multistate subjects (*Contracts*, *Torts*, *Property*, *Evidence*, *Criminal Law* and *Constitutional Law*) written by Professor Steven Finz of National University School of Law, San Diego, CA, and published by us. This book is available at your bookstore or from us, for $31.95.

1. Finney operated a chain of fast food restaurants which specialized in fried fish. Finney entered into a valid written contract with C-Foods, for the purchase of "six thousand pounds of frozen pinktail fish filets of frying quality," to be delivered by C-Foods over a period of six months. One week after C-Foods made its first delivery pursuant to the contract, however, Finney notified C-Foods that the product delivered was unacceptable because the filets delivered weighed only eight ounces each, and that they were cut from Grade B pinktail fish. Finney offered to return the unused portion of the delivery, and refused to make payment.

C-Foods subsequently brought an action against Finney for breach of contract. At the trial of that action C-Foods offered the testimony of Cooke. Cooke testified that he was the head chef at a leading hotel, and that he had been employed as a chef in fine restaurants for more than thirty years. He testified further that in that time he had purchased large quantities of fish on numerous occasions, and was familiar with the terminology used in the wholesale fish industry. Cooke stated that when the phrase "pinktail fish filets of frying quality" is used in the wholesale fish business, it means boneless pieces from six to nine ounces in weight and cut from Grade A or B pinktail fish. Upon proper objection by Finney's attorney, Cooke's testimony as to the meaning of the phrase should be

(A) admitted as evidence of trade terminology.

(B) admitted only if Cooke qualifies as an expert on the preparation of fried fish in fast food restaurants.

(C) excluded since it is an opinion.

(D) excluded unless the parties specifically agreed to be bound by the terminology of the wholesale fish industry.

2. Dr. Withey was hired by the defense to examine the plaintiff in a tort case. At trial, Dr. Withey stated that during the course of the examination the plaintiff said, "My arm hurts so much, I don't see how I'll ever be able to go back to work." Which of the following would be the defendant's strongest argument in support of a motion to strike the testimony?

(A) The plaintiff's statement was made in contemplation of litigation.

(B) The doctor was not examining the plaintiff for the purpose of treatment.

(C) The plaintiff's statement was self-serving.

(D) Evidence of the plaintiff's statement is more prejudicial than probative.

3. Dr. Withey then stated that during the course of the examination the plaintiff also said, "When I was struck by the car my right elbow struck the ground so hard that I heard a sound like a gunshot." If the defendant objects to this testimony, the court should

(A) sustain the objection, since the statement is hearsay.

(B) sustain the objection, since the examination was not performed for the purpose of diagnosis or treatment.

(C) overrule the objection, since the statement was part of a pertinent medical history.

(D) overrule the objection, since the statement described a former sense impression.

4. Fritz, a house painter, was charged with stealing three valuable figurines from the home of Valens while painting the interior of that home. At Fritz's trial, Valens testified that he first noticed that the figurines were missing about an hour after Fritz left his home. He stated that he looked Fritz's number up in the telephone book and properly dialed the number listed therein. Over objection by Fritz's attorney, Valens stated that a man answered the phone by saying, "Fritz speaking." Valens stated that he then said, "Fritz, where are the figurines?" and that the person at the other end of the line said, "I'm sorry. I took them." The objection by Fritz's attorney should be

(A) sustained, unless independent evidence establishes that Fritz was the person to whom Valens was speaking.

(B) sustained, since Valens did not actually see the person to whom he was speaking.

(C) sustained, since the statement is hearsay.

(D) overruled.

5. After his vehicle collided with Pringle's on March 1, Dicton retained Addie, an attorney, to represent him in any possible litigation which might develop. Addie hired Vesto, a private investigator, to interview Pringle regarding the facts of the accident. On March 5, Vesto followed Pringle into a bar, sat next to him, and engaged him in conversation. During the conversation, Pringle described the accident which he had with Dicton, and said, "Just between you and me, I drank a six-pack of beer just before the accident happened. It's a good thing nobody smelled my breath." Eventually Pringle commenced a personal injury action against Dicton. At the trial of the action, Pringle testified on direct examination that he had been driving at a slow rate of speed when Dicton's vehicle suddenly pulled out a driveway into his path.

On cross-examination, Dicton's attorney asked Pringle whether he had drunk alcohol during the hour prior to the accident. Pringle answered that he had not. Dicton's attorney then asked, "Didn't you tell an investigator from my office that you had consumed an entire six-pack of beer just before the accident?" If Pringle's attorney objects to the

question, the court should

(A) sustain the objection, since Pringle's prior statement was not made under oath.

(B) sustain the objection, since it was unethical for Dicton's attorney to make contract with Pringle through an investigator.

(C) sustain the objection, since the statement is hearsay not within any exception to the hearsay rule.

(D) overrule the objection.

6. Postum was crossing the street on foot when she was struck by a Daxco delivery van driven by Currier, a Daxco employee in the process of making a delivery for Daxco. Following the accident, Currier was charged with reckless driving and pleaded not guilty. At the trial on the charge of reckless driving, Currier testified in his own defense. He stated that at the time of the accident, he had taken his eyes off the road to look for the address of the place to which he was supposed to make his delivery, and that as a result he never saw Postum before striking her.

Postum subsequently brought an action against Daxco for personal injuries resulting from Currier's negligence under the theory of respondeat superior. At the trial of *Postum v. Daxco,* Postum proved that Currier remained in Daxco's employ until Currier died from causes not related to the accident. Postum then offered a transcript of Currier's testimony at the reckless driving trial. Upon objection by Daxco's attorney, the transcript should be

(A) admitted under the prior testimony exception to the hearsay rule.

(B) admitted under the past recollection recorded exception to the hearsay rule.

(C) admitted as a vicarious admission under the official written statement exception to the hearsay rule.

(D) excluded as hearsay not within any exception to the hearsay rule.

7. Vason was found dead in his garage, hanging by the neck from a rope tied to a roof beam. His widow Alma brought an action against Vason's psychiatrist Si under the state's wrongful death statute. In her complaint, Alma alleged that Si was negligent in his treatment of Vason, whom he knew or should have known to be suicidal. In his answer, Si denied that he knew Vason to be suicidal, denied that he had treated him negligently, and denied that Vason's death was a suicide. At the trial of the wrongful death action, Nina, a nurse employed by Si, testified that the day before Vason's death, she heard Vason say to Si, "I think suicide is the only way out." Upon objection by Si's counsel, which of the following statements is most correct?

   I. The statement should be admitted for the purpose of establishing that Vason's death was a suicide.

   II. The statement should be admitted for the purpose of establishing that Si knew or should have known that Vason was suicidal.

   (A) I only.

   (B) II only.

   (C) Both I and II.

   (D) Neither I nor II.

8. Angel was insured by Innco Insurance Company under a policy which required Innco to pay the total value of any damage to Angel's motorcycle resulting from collision. After Angel's motorcycle was totally destroyed in a highway accident, Angel submitted a claim to Innco as required by the terms of her policy. Innco offered only two thousand dollars, although Angel claimed that the motorcycle was worth twice that amount. Angel subsequently instituted an action against Innco for benefits under the policy. At the trial of Angel's action against Innco, which of the following is LEAST likely to be admitted as evidence of the motorcycle's value?

   (A) Angel's testimony that it was worth four thousand dollars.

   (B) Angel's testimony that two days before the accident she had received an offer of four thousand dollars from someone who

wanted to purchase the motorcycle.

   (C) The testimony of a used motorcycle dealer who had never seen Angel's motorcycle, but who, after examining a photograph of it, stated that motorcycles like it were regularly bought and sold for prices ranging from three thousand five hundred to four thousand two hundred dollars.

   (D) the testimony of an amateur motorcycle collector, who had bought and sold many motorcycles like Angel's, that two days before the accident he had looked at Angel's motorcycle because he was interested in buying it, and that in his opinion the motorcycle had been worth four thousand dollars.

Questions 9-10 are based on the following fact situation.

Lanham was the owner of a three-story professional building. The entire second floor of Lanham's building was rented to Dr. View, an optometrist. Persons visiting the office of Dr. View either rode in an elevator located inside the building or climbed a stairway which was fastened to the outside of the building and which led from the street level to the second floor only. Priller was a patient of Dr. View's. One day upon leaving Dr. View's office and descending the stairway on the outside of the building, Priller fell, sustaining serious injuries. She commenced an action against Lanham, alleging that the stairway was dangerous in that it was too steep, it lacked a handrail, and the stair treads were too narrow. Lanham denied that the stairway was dangerous. In addition, as an affirmative defense, he denied control over the stairway, asserting that it had been leased to Dr. View as part of the second-floor office.

9. At the trial, Priller called Walker, who had been employed by Lanham as building manager at the time of the accident, but who was presently unemployed. Walker testified that two days after the accident Lanham instructed him to install a handrail on the stairway, and to post a sign which read, "CAUTION: Steep and narrow stairway!" Lanham's attorney objected to the testimony and moved

that it be stricken. Which of the following would be Priller's most effective argument in response to the objection and in opposition to the motion to strike?

(A) Walker is no longer in Lanham's employ.

(B) The testimony is relevant to establish that the stairway was dangerous.

(C) The testimony is relevant to establish that Lanham was aware that the stairway was dangerous.

(D) The testimony is relevant to establish that Lanham was in control of the stairway.

10. On cross-examination by Lanham's attorney, Walker testified that he had been employed by Lanham as building manager for a period of three years prior to the accident. He stated that the condition of the stairway was substantially the same during that period as it was on the day of Priller's accident, and that although many people used the stairway every day, Walker had never before heard of anyone falling while using it. Priller's attorney objected to this testimony. Should the court sustain Priller's objection?

(A) Yes, since evidence that no accident had occurred in the past is not relevant to the issues on trial.

(B) Yes, unless there is evidence that Walker would have heard of such accidents had they occurred.

(C) No, if Lanham raised a defense of contributory negligence.

(D) No, since Walker was called as Priller's witness.

11. In an action by Pillow Products against Daphne, Pillow alleged that it had entered into a written contract with Daphne for the purchase of satin material which Pillow intended to use in manufacturing its products, and that Daphne failed to deliver the material as promised. At the trial, Legg testified that he worked in the Pillow Products legal department, and that he had negotiated the contract in question. He stated further that, although the original and all copies of the contract had been destroyed in an office fire, he knew the substance of its contents. When Pillow's attorney

began to question Legg about the contents of the contract, Daphne objected. The trial court should

(A) sustain the objection, since Legg's testimony would violate the parol evidence rule.

(B) sustain the objection, since Legg's testimony would violate the best evidence rule.

(C) overrule the objection, since the absence of the original document has been explained.

(D) overrule the objection, since the Statute of Frauds is satisfied by the fact that a written memorandum of agreement was made.

12. Rider, an investigative reporter for the *Daily Globe,* wrote a series of articles exposing corruption in city government. In the articles, he said that "a building permit can be obtained for just about anything in this town if bribes are given to the right city officials." As a result of the series, a grand jury began investigating the allegations of corruption. When Rider was called to testify, however, he refused to divulge the sources of his information, claiming reportorial privilege. Rider was charged with contempt. While his prosecution on that charge was pending, the grand jury continued with its investigation by causing the city's mayor, Mayo, to be served with a subpoena. When asked whether she knew of any city official accepting bribes for the issuance of building permits Mayo refused to answer, invoking her Fifth Amendment privilege against self-incrimination. After being granted use immunity, however, she testified that Cooms, the city's building commissioner, regularly accepted bribes for the issuance of permits, and that Cooms regularly shared the bribe money with Mayo. After Mayo's testimony, both Mayo and Cooms were indicted by the grand jury on charges of bribery. Because there was no other evidence against Mayo, prior to the trial, the prosecutor agreed to accept a plea to a lesser offense from Cooms if he would testify against Mayo. At Mayo's trial, if Mayo objects to the testimony of Cooms, the objection should be

(A) sustained, if the prosecutor had no evidence against Cooms other than Mayo's testimony.

(B) sustained, since a prosecutor may not bargain away the rights of one co-defendant in a deal with another.

(C) overruled, because the proceeding was instituted as a result of the statements made in the articles by Rider, not as a result of the testimony of Mayo at the grand jury hearing.

(D) overruled, if the testimony of Cooms was voluntary and not the result of coercion.

13. Pelton sued Transport Inc. for damage which resulted from a collision between Pelton's motorcycle and one of Transport's trucks. After receiving the summons, Thomas, the president and sole stockholder of Transport Inc., notified Lottie, the company attorney. Lottie said that she wanted to meet with Thomas and the driver of the truck. At Lottie's request, Thomas went to Lottie's office with Darla, who had been driving the truck at the time of the accident. While discussing the case with Lottie in the presence of Darla, Thomas said that on the day before the accident he was aware that the truck's brakes were not working properly, but that because of a heavy work load he postponed making the necessary repairs.

At the trial of Pelton's suit against Transport, Pelton attempted to have Darla testify to the statement which Thomas made to Lottie about the brakes. Transport's attorney objected on the ground of the attorney-client privilege. Should Darla be permitted to testify to Thomas's statement?

(A) Yes, because the attorney-client privilege does not apply to testimony by one who does not stand in a confidential relationship with the person against whom the evidence is offered.

(B) Yes, because it is presumed that a communication made in the presence of third persons is not confidential

(C) Yes, because communications made by or on behalf of corporations are not privileged.

(D) No.

14. At the trial of an automobile accident case, for the purpose of showing the relationship and directions of the streets involved, the plaintiff offered into evidence a photograph of the intersection where the accident occurred. The plaintiff testified that on the day of the accident the intersection looked exactly as depicted in the photograph, except that on the day of the accident some of the trees on the street had small Christmas ornaments on them. Upon objection, should the photograph be admitted in evidence?

(A) Yes, if the absence of Christmas tree ornaments did not prevent the photograph from being a fair representation of the intersection at the time of the accident.

(B) Yes, but only if the photograph was taken within a reasonable time following the accident.

(C) No, unless the photographer who made the photograph testifies to its authenticity.

(D) No, not under any circumstances.

15. Peterson was sitting in his car at a dead stop waiting for a traffic light to change color, when his vehicle was struck in the rear by a car operated by Dodge, rendering Peterson unconscious. Police were called to the accident scene and as a result of their investigation Dodge was charged with "operating an unregistered vehicle," a misdemeanor. The following day, Dodge pleaded guilty to the charge and was sentenced to five days in jail.

Peterson subsequently asserted a claim for damages resulting from Dodge's negligence. Because of admissions which were made in the pleadings, a hearing was held on the sole questions of whether Dodge was negligent. At the hearing, a transcript of Dodge's conviction for operating an unregistered vehicle should be

(A) admitted.

(B) excluded, because it is not relevant to the question of negligence.

(C) excluded, because it was not the result of a trial.

(D) excluded, because it is hearsay, not within any exception.

16. A state statute provides that the owner of any motor vehicle operated on the public roads of the state is liable for damage resulting from the negligence of any person driving the vehicle with the owner's permission. Pavlov was injured when a vehicle operated by Dawson struck her while she was walking across the street. At the scene of the accident, Dawson apologized to Pavlov, saying, "I'm sorry. It isn't my car. I didn't know that the brakes were bad." Pavlov subsequently instituted an action against Oster for her damages, asserting that Oster owned the vehicle. She alleged that Oster was negligent in permitting the vehicle to be driven while he knew that the brakes were in need of repair, and that he was vicariously liable under the statute for the negligence of Dawson. Oster denied ownership of the vehicle. At the trial, Pavlov offered testimony by Mecco, a mechanic, that on the day after the accident Oster hired him to completely overhaul the brakes. Upon objection by Oster, the evidence is

(A) admissible, to show that Oster was the owner of the vehicle.

(B) admissible, to show that the brakes were in need of repair on the day of the accident.

(C) inadmissible, because the condition of the vehicle on any day other than that of the accident is irrelevant to show its condition at the time the accident occurred.

(D) inadmissible, under a policy which encourages safety precautions.

17. Keller had been a member of a professional crime organization for twenty years, and had participated in many crimes during that period of time. Because Keller's testimony was crucial to the district attorney's attempt to break the crime organization, he was offered immunity if he would testify against other members of the organization. He did so, and his testimony resulted in several convictions. Keller subsequently wrote and published a book entitled *Contract Killer,* in which he described in detail many of the crimes which he committed, including the shotgun murder of Vicuna. Following the publication of *Contract Killer,* Vicuna's wife commenced an action against Keller for damages resulting from the wrongful death of her husband. At the trial, a police officer who had been called to the scene of Vicuna's shooting testified that just before Vicuna died he heard him say, "I saw Keller pull the trigger on me." If Keller moves to strike the police officer's testimony, his motion should be

(A) granted, since a dying declaration is admissible only in a trial for criminal homicide.

(B) granted, if Keller received transactional immunity.

(C) denied, if Vicuna believed himself to be dying when he made the statement.

(D) denied, if the jurisdiction has a "dead man's statute."

Questions 18-19 are based on the following fact situation.

After the crash of Wing Airlines Flight 123, an action for wrongful death was brought by the husband of a passenger killed in the crash. During the trial, the plaintiff called Weston, an employee of the State Aviation Agency which investigated the circumstances surrounding the crash.

18. Weston testified that during the course of his investigation he questioned a mechanic named Marshall on the day of the crash. He said that Marshall stated that he and a mechanic named Stevens had been assigned by the Wing Airlines airport supervisor to inspect Flight 123 before take-off, but that they did not inspect the plane as directed. If Weston's testimony is objected to, the judge should rule it admissible

(A) if Weston testifies that Marshall claimed to be an employee of Wing.

(B) only if independent evidence indicates that Marshall was employed by Wing at the time the statement was made.

(C) only if independent evidence indicates that at the time the statement was made, Marshall was authorized to speak for Wing.

(D) if Marshall is unavailable to testify.

19. Weston also read aloud from an investigation report which quoted an unidentified witness to the crash as stating that she heard an explosion several seconds before she saw the plane burst into flames. He testified that the report from which he was reading was one kept in the regular course of business by the State Aviation Agency, that the entry from which he was reading had been made by another investigator who worked for the Agency, that the investigator who made the entry was sworn to investigate airplane crashes and to keep honest and accurate records of the results of those investigations, and that the investigator who made the entry was now dead. Upon appropriate objection, the evidence should be ruled

(A) admissible as a business record.

(B) admissible as an official written statement.

(C) admissible as past recollection recorded.

(D) inadmissible as hearsay not within any exception.

Questions 20-21 are based on the following fact situation.

Kane's dog frequently dug holes in the lawn of Kane's neighbor Nixon, who had telephoned Kane to complain in a loud voice on several occasions. One day, after the dog dug up Nixon's prize rosebush, Nixon ran to Kane's house and banged on Kane's front door. When Kane opened the door, Nixon shouted, "You dirty son of a bitch." Kane struck him in the face with his fist, and closed the door. Nixon later sued Kane for battery, and Kane asserted the privilege of self-defense. At the trial Kane offered the testimony of a local shopkeeper who stated that he knew Nixon's reputation in the neighborhood, and that Nixon was known as "a bad actor who will fight at the drop of a hat." He also offered the testimony of the local parish priest who stated that he had known Kane for years, and that everyone in the community thought of him as a peaceable man who would never resort to violence except in self-protection.

20. If Nixon's attorney objects to the testimony of the shopkeeper, the objection should be

(A) sustained, since evidence of Nixon's character is not relevant to his action for battery.

(B) sustained, since Nixon is not the defendant.

(C) overruled, since the testimony is relevant to Kane's assertion of the privilege of self-defense.

(D) overruled, since Nixon placed his character in issue by bringing the lawsuit.

21. If Nixon's attorney objects to the testimony of the parish priest, the testimony should be

(A) excluded, if it is offered as circumstantial evidence to prove that Kane did not strike Nixon without justification.

(B) excluded, unless the priest testified that his own opinion of Kane coincided with what the community thought about him.

(C) admitted, because Kane is the defendant.

(D) admitted, for the limited purpose of establishing Kane's state of mind at the time of the occurrence.

22. After receiving a tip, police officers stopped a car being driven by Davidson, and forced him to open the trunk. In it, the officers discovered a canvas bag containing seven pounds of cocaine. They seized the car and the cocaine as evidence, and placed Davidson under arrest. Without advising him of his rights to remain silent and to consult with an attorney, they questioned him about the cocaine. During the questioning, Davidson said, "I don't know anything about it. It isn't even my car."

Davidson was charged with illegal possession of a controlled substance. Subsequently, Davidson's motion to suppress the use of the cocaine as evidence was granted, and the charges against him were dismissed. Davidson thereupon commenced an appropriate proceeding against the police department for recovery of his automobile. On presentation of his direct case, Davidson testified that he owned the seized automobile, but had registered it to a friend for purposes of convenience. On cross-examination, the attorney representing the police department asked, "After your arrest, did you tell the arresting officers that it wasn't your car?"

If Davidson's attorney objects to this question, the objection should be

(A) sustained, because Davidson's interrogation was in violation of his *Miranda* rights.

(B) sustained, because Davidson's motion to suppress was granted.

(C) overruled, because the automobile in which the cocaine was transported is "fruit of the poisonous tree."

(D) overruled, because his denial that he owned the car was a prior inconsistent statement.

23. In the trial of a tort action in a United States District Court, if the substantive law of the state is being applied, which of the following statements is correct regarding confidential communications between psychotherapist and patient?

   I. The United States District Court MUST recognize the psychotherapist-patient privilege if it is recognized by the law of the state.

   II. The United States District Court MAY recognize the psychotherapist-patient privilege even if it is not recognized by the law of the state.

   (A) I only.

   (B) II only.

   (C) I and II.

   (D) Neither I nor II.

24. Derringer was charged with violating a federal law which prohibits the unlicensed transportation of specified toxic wastes across a state line. At his trial in a federal district court, the prosecution proved that Derringer had transported certain toxic wastes from Detroit, Michigan to Chicago, Illinois. The prosecuting attorney then moved that the court take judicial notice that it is impossible to travel

between those two cities without crossing a state line. Upon proper objection by Derringer's attorney, the prosecution's motion should be

(A) granted, if it is generally known within the territorial jurisdiction of the court that it is impossible to travel from Detroit to Chicago without crossing a state line.

(B) granted, but only if the prosecution presents the court with a reputable map or other reference work indicating that a state line lies between the cities of Detroit and Chicago.

(C) denied, but only if Derringer's attorney demands an offer of proof for the record.

(D) denied, if the fact that Derringer traveled across a state line concerns an ultimate issue of fact.

25. Draper was charged with the second degree murder of Valle under a statute which defined that crime as "the unlawful killing of a human being with malice aforethought, but without premeditation." Draper's attorney asserted a defense of insanity, and called Draper as a witness in his own behalf. After Draper testified on direct and cross-examination, his attorney called Dr. Wendell to the witness stand. Dr. Wendell stated that he was a psychiatrist, had practiced for thirty years, had treated thousands of patients with illnesses like Draper's, and had testified as an expert in hundreds of criminal homicide trials. He testified, "After listening to Draper's testimony, I am of the opinion that Draper did not have malice aforethought as our law defines it on the day of Valle's death." On cross-examination, Dr. Wendell admitted that he had never spoken to or seen Draper before, and that his opinion was based entirely on his observations of Draper's testimony.

Which of the following would be the prosecuting attorney's most effective argument in support of a motion to exclude Dr. Wendell's statement?

(A) Dr. Wendell's testimony embraces the ultimate issue.

(B) Dr. Wendell's opinions were based entirely upon courtroom observations.

(C) Dr. Wendell had insufficient opportunity to examine Draper.

(D) Whether Draper had "malice aforethought" is a question to be decided by the jury.

26. Dempsey was charged in a state court with third degree arson on the allegation that he set fire to his own house for the purpose of collecting benefits under a fire insurance policy. At his trial, Dempsey called Wrangler as a witness in his favor. On direct examination by Dempsey's attorney, Wrangler testified that at the time of the fire he and Dempsey were together at a baseball game fifty miles away from Dempsey's home.

On rebuttal the prosecuting attorney offered evidence that two years earlier Wrangler was released from custody after serving a five year sentence in a federal prison following his conviction for perjury. If Dempsey's attorney objects to the introduction of this evidence, the objection should be

(A) overruled, but only if Wrangler is given a subsequent opportunity to explain the conviction.

(B) overruled, because perjury is a crime involving dishonesty.

(C) sustained, because the conviction was not more than ten years old.

(D) sustained, unless the prosecuting attorney asked Wrangler on cross-examination whether he had ever been convicted of a crime.

27. At the trial of a personal injury action, Dr. Watson testified that she examined the plaintiff on the day of trial, and that at that time the plaintiff told her that she felt pain in her knee. On cross-examination, the defendant's attorney asked Dr. Watson whether she had ever met the plaintiff before the day of trial. Dr. Watson responded that she had not, and that her sole purpose in examining the plaintiff was to prepare for testifying at the trial. The defendant's attorney then moved to strike that portion of Dr. Watson's testimony which referred to the plaintiff's complaint of pain. In a jurisdiction which applies the common-law rule regarding confidential communications

between patient and physician, should the defendant's motion be granted?

(A) Yes, because the examination was solely for the purpose of litigation.

(B) Yes, because the probative value of the statement is outweighed by the possibility of prejudice.

(C) Yes, because statements made to a physician are privileged.

(D) No, because the statement described what the plaintiff was feeling at the time.

28. During the presentation of plaintiff's direct case in a personal injury action, the plaintiff's attorney called Dr. Wallace to the stand for the purpose of establishing that the plaintiff had sustained an injury to her epiglammis gland.

When the plaintiff's attorney began to question Dr. Wallace about her qualifications, the defendant's attorney conceded on the record and in the presence of the jury that Dr. Wallace was an expert on injuries of the epiglammis gland and objected to any further questions regarding the qualifications of Dr. Wallace. Should the plaintiff's attorney be permitted to continue questioning Dr. Wallace regarding her qualifications?

(A) No, because the qualifications of Dr. Wallace are no longer in issue.

(B) No, if the court is satisfied that Dr. Wallace qualifies as an expert on diseases and injuries of the epiglammis gland.

(C) Yes, because the court must determine for itself whether a witness qualifies as an expert, and cannot allow the matter to be determined by stipulation of the parties.

(D) Yes, because the jury may consider an expert's qualifications in determining her credibility.

Questions 29-30 are based on the following fact situation.

Handel, a federal officer, had been informed that a person arriving from Europe on a particular airline flight would be carrying cocaine in his baggage. Handel went to the airport and stood at the arrival gate with Findo, a dog which had been specially trained to recognize the scent of cocaine. When Dodd walked by carrying his bag, Findo began barking and scratching the floor in front of him with his right paw. Handel stopped Dodd and searched his bag. In it, he found a small brass statue with a false bottom. Upon removing the false bottom, Handel found one ounce of cocaine. Dodd, who was arrested and charged with the illegal importation of a controlled substance, claimed he had purchased the statue as a souvenir and was unaware that there was cocaine hidden it its base.

29. Assume for the purpose of this question only that Dodd's attorney moved for an order excluding the use of the cocaine as evidence at Dodd's trial. At a hearing on that motion, Handel testified that he was an expert dog trainer and handler, that he had personally trained Findo to signal by barking and scratching the floor in front of him with his right paw whenever he sniffed cocaine, that Findo had successfully found and signaled the presence of cocaine on several previous occasions, and that Findo had given the signal when Dodd walked away. If Dodd's attorney moves to exclude Handel's testimony regarding the way Findo acted when Dodd walked by, that testimony should be

   (A) excluded, because the sounds and movements made by Findo are hearsay and not within any exception.

   (B) excluded, unless Findo is dead or otherwise unavailable.

   (C) admitted, but only if Findo's effectiveness is established by an in-court demonstration.

   (D) admitted, because a proper foundation has been laid.

30. Assume for the purpose of this question only that at Dodd's trial the prosecution offers to prove that Dodd had been convicted fifteen years earlier of illegally importing cocaine by hiding it in the base of a brass statue. If Dodd's attorney objects, the court should rule that proof of Dodd's prior conviction is

   (A) admissible, as evidence of habit.

   (B) admissible, because it is evidence of a

distinctive method of operation.

   (C) inadmissible, because evidence of previous conduct by a defendant may not be used against him.

   (D) inadmissible, because the prior conviction occurred more than ten years before the trial.

ANSWERS TO
MULTISTATE-STYLE QUESTIONS

1. **A**   Under both common law and the UCC, evidence of trade terminology is admissible for the purpose of establishing the meaning of a particular term in a contract between parties in the trade. Since the contract calls for the sale of fish at wholesale, evidence of trade terminology used in the wholesale fish industry is relevant to establish the meaning of the term in question.

    Ordinarily, a witness is not permitted to testify to her opinion. A witness who qualifies as an expert in a particular field, however, may be permitted to testify to an opinion regarding her field of expertise. Since Cooke is not offering an opinion regarding the preparation of fried fish in fast food restaurants, he need not qualify as an expert in that particular field. **B** is, therefore, incorrect. **C** is incorrect because an expert may offer an opinion regarding her field of expertise. **D** is incorrect because even if parties have not specifically agreed to be bound by the terminology of a particular industry, that terminology may be relevant in determining the meaning of unexplained terms in a contract so long as both parties are likely to have been aware of the meaning of the trade terminology.

2. **D**   Hearsay is an out of court assertion offered for the purpose of proving the truth of the matter asserted. Thus, if the plaintiff's statement to Dr. Withey is being offered to prove that the plaintiff was experiencing pain in his arm, the statement would be hearsay. An exception to the hearsay rule, however, permits the admission of statements made as part of a medical history given in connection with a medical examination made for the purpose of treatment or diagnosis. Since Dr. Withey's examination was being made for the purpose of diagnosis, the patient's statement should be admissible. Under the FRE, the circumstances surrounding the medical examination in which a patient's statement was made go to the weight rather than to the admissibility of that statement. Thus the fact that the examination was not made for the purpose of treatment or that it was made in contemplation of litigation is not, alone, sufficient to prevent admission unless the prejudicial effect of the statement is likely to outweigh its probative value. While a court might not come to that conclusion, the argument in **D** is the only one listed which could possibly support the motion to strike.

    A and **B** are incorrect because, unless the probative value is likely to be outweighed by the prejudicial effect, the fact that the examination was not being made for the purpose of treatment or that it was being made in contemplation of litigation would not be sufficient to result in its exclusion. **C** is incorrect because there is no rule which prevents the admission of self-serving statements.

3. **C**   Under FRE 803(4), statements purporting to describe the way in which a physical condition came about are admissible as part of a medical history if made for the purpose of diagnosis, and if pertinent to diagnosis. "Diagnosis" refers to the nature and origin of an injury. Even though Dr. Withey's examination was performed to enable her to testify, she was attempting to form a diagnosis. Since the sound made by the plaintiff's elbow striking the pavement might be pertinent to a determination of the nature and origin of plaintiff's injury, (i.e., diagnosis) the statement is admissible.

    A is incorrect. A statement made as part of a medical history is admissible as an exception to the hearsay rule. **B** is incorrect because even though the examination was performed in contemplation of Dr. Withey's testimony, one of its purposes was to allow Dr. Withey to diagnose (i.e., determine the nature of) the plaintiff's injury. Although a witness might be permitted to testify to his own former sense impression, there is no exception to the hearsay rule for a witness's repetition of a declarant's former sense impression. **D** is, therefore, incorrect.

4.   **D**   Under the FRE, voice identification can be made by a witness who testifies that he properly dialed a number listed in the telephone book, and that circumstances including self-identification show that the person listed was the one who answered.

A and **B** are, therefore, incorrect. Since Fritz's statement is contrary to his interests, it is an admission, which is not hearsay under the FRE and is admissible as an exception to the hearsay rule under common law. **C** is, therefore, incorrect.

5.   **D**   Since a person who makes statements which contradict each other might not be worthy of belief, a witness may be impeached on cross-examination by inquiry regarding prior inconsistent statements. See FRE 613.

A is, therefore, incorrect. Although it may be unethical for an attorney to make contact directly with an adversary known to be represented by counsel, information obtained by such a contact is not necessarily inadmissible. In any event, **B** is incorrect because there is no reason to believe that Pringle was represented by counsel at the time of his conversation with Vesto, or, if he was, that Addie knew him to be. A statement of a party offered against that party is admissible as an admission. Under the FRE, an admission is not hearsay. (Under the common law, an admission is an exception to the hearsay rule.) **C** is, therefore, incorrect.

6.   **C**   Since an employer is vicariously liable for the negligence of an employee committed within the scope of employment, statements tending to establish that the accident resulted from Currier's negligence are relevant in Postum's action against Daxco. The evidence should, thus, be admitted unless excluded under the hearsay rule. Hearsay is an out of court statement offered to prove the truth of the matter asserted. These facts raise what is sometimes called a multiple level hearsay problem (i.e., a problem involving an out of court statement which contains another out of court statement). This is so because Currier's testimony at the reckless driving trial was not made during the negligence trial and so is an "out of court" statement, and because the evidence of his statement is contained in a transcript which was also not made as part of the negligence trial and so is an "out of court" statement. In order for multiple level hearsay (i.e., the transcript containing Currier's statement) to be admissible each level must be separately admissible. The first level of hearsay is the testimony by Currier at the reckless driving trial. Under the common law, statements by an employee are admissible against the employer only if the employee had the authority to make them. But FRE 801(d)(2)(D) requires only that the employee's statement concerned a matter within the scope of his employment, and was made while the employment relationship existed. Currier's statement is therefore a vicarious admission which is an exception to the hearsay rule at common law, and is not hearsay at all under the FRE. The second level of hearsay is the transcript. Since it was made by a public official (the reporter), regarding matters in his own knowledge (that Currier made the admission), in the course of his public duties and at the time the matter recorded (Currier's statement) occurred, the transcript qualifies as an official written statement. **C** is, therefore, correct.

Under FRE 804(b)(1), prior testimony is admissible as an exception to the hearsay rule only if the party against whom it is offered had an incentive and an opportunity to cross-examine when the testimony was first given. Since Doxco was not a party to the proceeding at which Currier's testimony was given, the testimony does not qualify for admission under this exception. **A** is, therefore, incorrect. The past recollection recorded exception requires that the record was made from the recorder's own knowledge and requires the recorder to authenticate the record in court. **B** is incorrect because Currier's statement was not authenticated or recorded by Currier. **D** is incorrect for the reasons stated above.

7. **C**   Under FRE 803(3), statements of a declarant's then-existing state of mind are admissible as an exception to the hearsay rule. Since it is likely that a suicidal state of mind such as that indicated by Vason's statement to Si would continue until the following day, and since it is likely that a person with that state of mind would commit suicide, the fact that Vason was of a suicidal state of mind on the day before his death is relevant to the question of whether his death was a suicide. **I** is, therefore a correct statement. Hearsay is an out-of-court statement offered to prove the truth of the matter asserted in that statement. If Vason's statement to Si is offered for the purpose of establishing that Si knew or should have known that Vason was suicidal, it is not hearsay, since it is not offered to prove the truth of the matter asserted (i.e., that suicide is the only way out). **II** is, therefore, a correct statement.

8. **B**   Since a statement as to the value of a chattel is a statement of opinion, and since lay opinions are not usually admissible, some qualification is necessary to demonstrate the competence of a person stating an opinion regarding the value of a chattel. Since an unaccepted offer to purchase a chattel suggests the offeror's opinion as to its value, an unaccepted offer to purchase is not usually admissible to establish the value of the subject chattel because the offeror is not necessarily an expert in the value of such chattels, and because even if the expert were an expert, his out of court statement as to its value would be hearsay. For this reason, evidence of an offer to purchase the motorcycle is probably inadmissible, and **B** is the correct answer.

In the belief that the owner of a chattel has some special knowledge about his property, courts usually allow a chattel's owner to give an opinion regarding its value. **A** is, therefore, likely to be admitted. In **C**, the motorcycle dealer would probably qualify as an expert on the value of motorcycles. An expert may testify to an opinion in response to a hypothetical question, even though he has no personal knowledge of the facts in a particular case. Thus, if the photograph can be shown to be a fair and accurate representation of the motorcycle immediately prior to the accident, the motorcycle dealer's opinion of its value may be admissible. **D** would be admissible since an expert's qualifications may be based on experience with the matter in issue, and the amateur motorcycle collector's previous purchases and sales might qualify him as such.

9. **D**   Although evidence of subsequent repairs is inadmissible to establish that a condition was dangerous or that the defendant was negligent, it may be admitted if relevant to some other issue. Since it is not likely that Lanham would have taken the action indicated if he were not in control of the stairway, the evidence may be admitted for the purpose of establishing control.

A is incorrect because it suggests that some rule of privilege prevents testimony by the defendant's employee, when no such rule exists. The admissibility of Walker's testimony does not, therefore, depend on his employment status. **B** and **C** are incorrect because of the rule of policy which prohibits evidence of subsequent repairs to establish fault.

10. **B**   Testimony that a witness never heard of similar accidents in the past may be admitted as circumstantial evidence that the condition was not dangerous if a proper foundation is laid. This requires showing that the condition was substantially the same on the day of plaintiff's accident as it was during the period described by defendant, that there was sufficient traffic over the condition and sufficient time to provide an opportunity for such accidents to have occurred, and that the witness was likely to have heard of such accidents had they occurred. Since Walker testified that the stairs were in substantially the same condition throughout the period described, that many people used them every day for three years, and that he never heard of such an accident, the only element of the necessary foundation which is lacking is evidence that he probably would have heard of such an accident

if it had occurred. His testimony is thus admissible if this can be shown, but is not admissible otherwise. **B** is, therefore, correct.

A is incorrect because the fact would tend to establish that the condition was not a dangerous one. Evidence of the non-occurrence of similar accidents in the past might tend to prove that the plaintiff did not use the care exercised by ordinary persons in encountering the situation. **C** is incorrect, however, because without evidence that Walker would have heard of such accidents had they occurred, the assertion of contributory negligence is not, alone, sufficient to make Walker's statement probative. **D** is incorrect because there is no rule which prevents a party from objecting to improper testimony elicited by cross-examination of its own witness.

11.   **C**   Under the best evidence rule, where the terms of a writing are in issue, the writing itself must be offered into evidence unless the writing is shown to be unavailable through no action in bad faith. See FRE 1002, 1004. Since the original and all copies of the contract were destroyed in a fire, oral testimony as to its contents is admissible.

The parol evidence rule prohibits oral testimony of prior or contemporaneous agreements to alter the terms of a contract intended to be a complete integration of the parties, but does not prevent oral testimony regarding the contents of a written agreement. **A** is, therefore, incorrect. **B** is incorrect because the writing has been shown to be unavailable. The Statute of Frauds provides that certain contracts are unenforceable unless in writing, but does not relate to the evidence used to establish the existence of a contract. **D** is, therefore, incorrect.

12.   **A**   Although use immunity does not prevent prosecution relating to the transaction which was the subject of the testimony for which the immunity was granted, it does prevent the subsequent use of that testimony *or its fruits. The "fruits" include all evidence gained as a direct or indirect result of the testimony.* If the prosecutor had no evidence against Cooms other than Mayo's testimony, then Cooms' testimony was one of the "fruits" of Mayo's, and should be excluded.

B is incorrect because it is based on a distorted view of the facts. By making a deal for the testimony of Cooms, the prosecutor has not bargained away any "rights" of Mayo. **C** is incorrect because the articles by Rider did not identify Cooms. Cooms's evidence must, therefore, be seen as one of the fruits of Mayo's testimony. **D** is incorrect because the use immunity granted Mayo makes Cooms' testimony inadmissible. The fact that it was given voluntarily and without coercion is not, alone, enough to make it admissible.

13.   **D**   A client is privileged to prevent another from disclosing the contents of a confidential communication with his attorney. Although the presence of third persons usually results in a finding that the communication was not intended to be confidential, this is not so if the presence of those persons was essential to the communications with the attorney. Darla's presence does not have that effect, since, as the driver of the truck, she was essential to the conference between Thomas and Lottie.

A is incorrect since, if the communication was confidential, the client's privilege applies to any attempt to disclose it. **B** is incorrect because Darla's presence was essential to the purpose of the conference. **C** is incorrect because corporations are entitled to the privilege, which clearly applies to communications between lawyers and high-ranking officers of the corporation.

14.   **A**   If relevant, a photograph or pictorial representation is admissible if a witness identifies it as a fair and accurate representation of what it purports to be. Since the directions and relationship of the streets which were the scene of an accident are relevant to the way in which the accident occurred, a photograph which fairly and accurately depicts them is admissible. Thus, even though the absence of Christmas tree ornaments in the photograph prevents it from showing all aspects of the accident scene exactly as they appeared on the day of the accident, it is admissible if it fairly and accurately represents the directions and relationship of the streets. Since the plaintiff testified that it does, the photograph should be admitted.

B is incorrect because a photograph which fairly and accurately represents what it purports to represent is admissible without regard to when it was taken. C is incorrect because the authentification of a photograph may be made by any competent witness who is familiar with what the photograph purports to represent, and need not be made by the photographer herself. D is incorrect for the reasons stated above.

15.   **B**   Evidence is relevant if it tends to prove or disprove a fact of consequence. Since the hearing is being held on the sole question of whether Dodge was driving negligently, the only facts of consequence relate to that question. Dodge was driving negligently if he was driving in a way in which the reasonable person would not. Since the fact that the vehicle was unregistered is not related to how it was being driven, the conviction for operating an unregistered vehicle is not relevant to the question of negligence.

A is, therefore, incorrect. An admission is a statement made by a party and offered against that party. C is incorrect because, if it is relevant, a guilty plea may be admissible as an admission. At common law, admissions fall under an exception to the hearsay rule. Under FRE 801(d)(2), an admission is not hearsay. Either way, D is incorrect.

16.   **A**   The law seeks to encourage safety precautions by prohibiting evidence of subsequent remedial measures from being used for the purpose of showing fault. See FRE 407. Such evidence may be admissible for other purposes, however. Here, Oster had denied ownership of the vehicle. Since it is unlikely that anyone other than the owner would arrange to have the brakes overhauled, the testimony of Mecco is relevant to establish Oster's ownership and should, therefore, be admitted.

B is incorrect because of the above stated rule of policy. C is incorrect because the evidence is being used to establish that Oster was the owner of the vehicle, not to establish the condition of the brakes. D is incorrect since the evidence is admissible to establish ownership.

17.   **C**   Under FRE 804(b)(2), a statement is admissible as a dying declaration in a civil or criminal case if it was made by a person now unavailable, about the cause of his death, upon personal knowledge, and under a sense of immediately impending death. Since Vicuna is presently unavailable and said that he saw Keller shoot him, his statement is admissible if he made it with a sense of impending death.

Although the common law made such statements admissible in cases of criminal homicide only, A is incorrect because FRE 804(b)(2) extends the exception to civil litigation as well. Transactional immunity prevents criminal prosecution, but does not prevent civil litigation. B is, therefore, incorrect. Where it exists, the effect of the "dead man's statute" is to exclude certain evidence, not to make it admissible. D is, therefore, incorrect.

18. **B**   Hearsay is an out of court statement offered to prove the truth of the matter asserted in that statement. An admission is an out of court statement made by a party which is offered against that party. Under the common law, admissions are admissible as exceptions to the hearsay rule. Under FRE 801(d)(2), admissions are admissible because they are not hearsay. If an employee of a party makes a statement which is offered against the employer, the statement may be admissible as a vicarious admission of the employer if it was made while the employment relationship existed and concerned a matter within the scope of the declarant's employment. If Marshall was employed by Wing as a mechanic, his statement that he failed to inspect Flight 123 does concern a matter within the scope of his employment. It would not be admissible as a vicarious admission of Wing, however, unless it can be established that Marshall was so employed. If Marshall made an out of court statement that he was so employed, it would be hearsay if offered to prove his employment by Wing. For this reason, independent evidence of the employment relationship is required.

A is, therefore, incorrect. Although the common law requires that the declarant be one authorized to speak for the party, **C** is incorrect because the FRE has abolished that requirement. **D** is incorrect because the unavailability of a declarant is not, alone, sufficient to make his out-of-court assertion admissible.

19. **D**   Hearsay is defined as an out-of-court assertion offered for the purpose of proving the truth of the matter asserted. FRE 801(c). Since there appears to be no reason for offering the statement of the unidentified witness except to prove the truth of the matter which asserts, it is hearsay. A business record may be admitted under an exception to the hearsay rule only if it was made by one who had personal knowledge of the information recorded or received it from an inherently reliable source. Since the investigator did not have personal knowledge and there is no indication that the witness interviewed by the deceased investigator was an inherently reliable source, **A** is incorrect. An official written statement may be admitted as an exception to the hearsay rule only as to information which the public official who recorded it knew of his own knowledge. Since the quote from the unidentified witness concerns information which the investigator did not know of his own knowledge, **B** is incorrect. Past recollection recorded is also admissible only if the record was made from the recorder's own knowledge and if the recorder is present in court to authenticate it. **C** is incorrect for these reasons, and because even if it were admissible, past recollection recorded can be read to the jury but not physically introduced into evidence.

20. **C**   Evidence is relevant if it tends to prove or disprove a fact of consequence. Relevant evidence is ordinarily admissible. Self-defense is a privilege to use force which the reasonable person in Kane's shoes would have considered necessary to prevent an attack upon himself. Evidence of Nixon's reputation for unprovoked violence is relevant because it tends to establish whether the reasonable person in Kane's shoes would have believed himself to be under attack.

A and **B** are incorrect because the evidence is relevant to the reasonableness of Kane's fear. **D** is incorrect because the plaintiff's character is not related to the essential elements of a battery action.

21. **A**   Character evidence is not ordinarily admissible for the purpose of proving a person's conduct on a particular occasion. Thus, if evidence of Kane's character is offered to prove anything about his conduct on the occasion of the incident in question, it is not admissible.

B is incorrect because a witness who testifies to a person's reputation is not required to know that person or to have any personal opinion about him. The "mercy" rule which permits a defendant to offer evidence of his own character as circumstantial evidence of his innocence applies only to criminal prosecutions. **C** is, therefore, incorrect. If the evidence were allowed for the purpose stated in **D** , it would be to prove that Kane did not strike Nixon without justification. **D** is, therefore, incorrect for the same reasons that make **A** correct.

22.　**D**　The fact that a witness made prior statements which were inconsistent with his testimony indicates that he is not a credible witness, or at least that his testimony is not worthy of belief. Thus, for the purpose of impeachment, a witness may be cross-examined about prior inconsistent statements. Since Davidson's statement to the arresting officers was inconsistent with his statement on the witness stand, he may be cross-examined about it.

The purpose of the exclusionary rule which prohibits the use of illegally obtained evidence or confessions is to remove police incentive for violating the constitutional rights of suspects. For this reason, statements obtained in violation of a prisoner's *Miranda* rights cannot be used against him in a criminal prosecution. Because use of such statements for impeachment in a civil proceeding is not ordinarily contemplated by the police, prohibiting such use is not likely to affect police conduct. For this reason, it has been held that statements obtained in violation of a prisoner's *Miranda* rights may be used for purposes of impeachment in civil proceedings. **A** is, therefore, incorrect. **B** is incorrect for two reasons: first, Davidson's motion was to suppress the use of the physical evidence, rather than the use of statements made during the interrogation; and, second, even an order suppressing the use of his statements in the criminal prosecution would not prevent their use in this civil proceeding. If statements are obtained from a prisoner in violation of his constitutional rights, the same policy which prohibits their use as evidence prohibits also the use of leads obtained as a result of those statements. This is the "fruit of the poisonous tree" doctrine. Although this doctrine may result in the exclusion of evidence, it never is used to justify the admission of evidence. **C** is, therefore, incorrect.

23.　**A**　FRE 501 provides that in the trial of a civil proceeding in which state law provides the rule of decision, the rules of privilege shall be determined in accordance with state law. Thus, if a civil action is being tried in a federal court under the substantive law of a state, the federal court must apply the state law of privilege. If the state law recognizes a psychotherapist-patient privilege, the federal court must recognize it as well. **I** is, therefore, correct. If the state law does not recognize a psychotherapist-patient privilege, the federal law may not. **II** is, therefore, incorrect.

24.　**A**　To save time and expense in proving facts which cannot reasonably be disputed, and to avoid the embarrassment which might result from a judicial finding which is contrary to well-known fact, a court may take judicial notice of certain facts without requiring evidence to establish them. Courts will take judicial notice of facts which are either generally known within the territorial jurisdiction of the trial court or capable of accurate and ready determination by resort to sources whose accuracy cannot reasonably be questioned. FRE 201(b). Thus, if it is generally known within the territorial jurisdiction of the court that it is impossible to travel from Detroit to Chicago without crossing a state line, the court may judicially notice that fact, making proof of it unnecessary.

Although the presentation of a map or other reputable reference would permit the court to take judicial notice, **B** is incorrect because this is not the only way; in the case of facts which are generally known, such references are not required. If the fact in question is one which qualifies for judicial notice, the objection of a party or the fact that it bears on an ultimate issue in the case will not prevent the court from judicially noticing it. **C** and **D** are, therefore, incorrect.

25.   **D**   It is the jury's job to determine whether the evidence proves facts sufficient to satisfy the requirements of law as charged by the court. Expert opinion may be admitted to *assist* the trier of fact to understand the evidence or to determine a fact in issue, but it may not be stated in a way which would deprive the jury of its power to determine facts. Since the jury must decide whether Draper had malice aforethought, expert testimony regarding Draper's mental capacity would be admissible. Dr. Wendell's statement, however, did not express an opinion regarding Draper's mental condition, but rather his opinion whether Draper had malice aforethought.

Although the common law once prohibited expert testimony which "embraced the ultimate issue," **A** is incorrect because FRE 704(a) (and many states) have eliminated this restriction. The opinions of an expert may be based solely on courtroom observations (or may even be based on assumed facts contained in a hypothetical question). The fact that a testifying psychiatrist has never spoken to the subject or even seen him outside a courtroom may reflect on the weight (i.e., persuasive value) of his testimony, but not on its admissibility. **B** and **C** are, therefore, incorrect.

26.   **B**   Under FRE 609(a), conviction for a crime punishable by imprisonment for one year or more or by death is admissible for the purpose of impeaching a witness. If either the conviction or the termination of incarceration occurred within the past ten years, the trial judge has discretion to exclude such a conviction only if it was not for a crime involving dishonesty. Since Wrangler's perjury was punished by five years in prison, since his period of incarceration terminated within the past ten years, and since perjury is obviously a crime involving dishonesty, the trial judge is without discretion to exclude evidence of Wrangler's conviction.

Although the common law requires confrontation prior to the use of certain evidence offered for the purpose of impeachment, **A** is incorrect because the FRE completely dispense with that requirement. FRE 609(b) provides that if more than ten years have elapsed since the conviction or termination of incarceration (whichever is *later*), the conviction is inadmissible unless the trial court finds that its probative value substantially outweighs its prejudicial effect. **C** is incorrect because if, as here, fewer than ten years elapsed, the conviction is admissible. Under the FRE, extrinsic evidence of prior inconsistent statements by a witness is admissible for the purpose of impeachment, but only if the witness is given a subsequent opportunity to explain the inconsistency. **D** is incorrect, however, because no such requirement exists regarding the use of convictions.

27.   **D**   Under FRE 803(3), an assertion of the declarant's then-existing physical sensation is admissible as an exception to the hearsay rule. The common law makes a distinction which prohibits the admission of such statements if they were made in contemplation of litigation. The FRE does not make such a distinction, however, allowing the circumstances under which the statement was made to go to the weight rather than the admissibility of the evidence.

A and **B** are, therefore, incorrect. Where it is recognized, the physician-patient privilege may prevent the admission of testimony by a doctor regarding confidential communications with the patient over objection by the *patient*. **C** is incorrect because an objection based on the privilege would not be available to anyone but the patient.

28.   **D**   Although the court decides whether evidence is admissible and whether a witness is competent to testify, it is for the jury to decide what weight to give testimony which the court has admitted. In doing so, the jury must determine how credible it finds a particular witness to be. If that witness is an expert testifying to her opinions, it would be impossible for the jury to make that determination without knowing the witness' qualifications. The

concession by the defendant's attorney is not sufficient, since it is very likely that the jury will hear contrary opinions given by other experts. To decide which of the experts it believes, the jury must be able to compare their qualifications. For this reason, the details of Dr. Wallace's qualifications remain an issue even though the defendant's attorney concedes that she is sufficiently qualified to testify to her opinions.

A and **B** are, therefore, incorrect. If all parties agree to a fact, a court may accept it as true without requiring further proof. Thus, if all parties agree that a particular witness qualifies as an expert, the court may — on the basis of that stipulation — dispense with the *requirement* of further proof (although it may not prevent the party offering the testimony of that witness from questioning her about her qualifications). **C** is, therefore, incorrect.

29. **D**   Ordinarily, evidence of the behavior of a trained dog is admissible if a foundation is laid similar to the foundation required for any other kind of scientific evidence. This means that it must be shown that the dog was competent to do the job which it was doing and that its handler was competent to interpret the result. Since Handel was an expert dog trainer and handler, and since Findo successfully detected cocaine on several prior occasions, the proper foundation has been laid, and the evidence is admissible.

Hearsay is an out of court statement offered for the purpose of proving the truth of the matter asserted in that statement. Although our society tends to personify dogs, dogs are not persons and are not capable of making statements. For this reason, the behavior of a dog cannot be hearsay (Since a primary reason for the hearsay rule is that out of court declarants are not subject to cross examination and since a dog could not be cross examined in any event, it would not be logical to apply the hearsay rule to a dog's behavior.) **A** is therefore, incorrect. **B** is incorrect because, since the dog could not testify, its availability is irrelevant to the admissibility of its behavior. Although a court might permit demonstration of a scientific method, there is no requirement that it do so. **C** is, therefore, incorrect.

30. **B**   In general, evidence of a defendant's character or disposition is inadmissable for the purpose of proving that he acted in a particular way on a particular occasion. See FRE 404(b), first sentence. An exception is made, however, for evidence which shows a definite, particular, and strong inference that the defendant did the precise act charged. Included in this exception is evidence tending to establish that the defendant uses a distinctive *modus operandi* (MO), or method of operation. For this reason, the fact that Dodd previously smuggled cocaine using a brass statue with a false bottom could be admissible. Although it is not certain that a court would admit the evidence for this purpose, **B** is the only answer listed which could possibly be correct.

FRE 406 permits evidence of habit to be used as circumstantial evidence that on a particular occasion the defendant's conduct was consistent with his habit. **A** is incorrect, however, because habit evidence requires a showing that the actor in question consistently acts in a particular way, and one prior experience is not sufficient to establish a habit. Although evidence of a defendant's previous conduct is inadmissible if offered against him for some purposes, it may be admissible if offered against him for others. **C** is thus incorrect because it is overinclusive. Evidence of a prior conviction is not usually admissible for the purpose of impeaching a witness if the conviction occurred more than ten years prior to the trial at which it is offered. **D** is incorrect, however, because Dodd's prior conviction is not being offered to impeach his credibility, but rather to establish a distinctive MO.

508

TABLE OF CASES

Abel, U.S. v. 99-100
Adkins v. Bret 173
Agent Orange Product Liability Litigation
   (Lilley), In re.................................. 407
Alcade, People v.................................... 179
Alker, U.S. v..................................... 157-58
Almeida v. Correa.................................. 359
Amoco Production Co. v. U.S..................... 382-83
Anderson v. Berg 374
Annunziato, U.S. v................................. 183
Arkansas Power & Light Co. v. Johnson 51
Arthur Young & Co., U.S. v. 355
Ault v. International Harvester Co. 58

Bagby, People v. 329
Bailey, U.S. v. 265
Baird v. Koerner 300
Baker v. Elcona Homes Corp. 212-13
Baker v. State 192-93
Ball, State v. 15
Ballou v. Henri Studios, Inc........................ 14
Baltimore City Dep't of Soc. Serv. v. Bouknight 333
Bannister v. Town of Noble 375
Barber v. Page 224, 271
Barmore v. Safety Casualty Co. 109
Barrel of Fun, Inc. v. State Farm 116
Barrett, U.S. v. 241
Barrick, People v. 83
Battaglia, U.S. v. 277-78
Baxter v. Palmigiano 335
Beech Aircraft Corp. v. Rainey................. 210-11
Beechum, U.S. v. 26-28, 35-36
Bellis v. U.S. 323
Benn, U.S. v. 111
Betts v. Betts 133
Big Mack Trucking Co., Inc. v. Dickerson 159, 161
Bock, State v. 31
Bourjaily v. U.S. 166-67, 273, 275, 281, 455
Branzburg v. Hayes............................. 346-47
Bridges v. State................................... 132
Brink's, Inc. v. New York 335-36
Brown v. Board of Education.................... 470
Brown, U.S. v. 143-44, 182
Bruton v. U.S.............................. 284, 458
Buck v. State 147-48
Bulova Watch Co., Inc. v. K. Hattori & Co., Ltd. 469
Burr, U.S. v. 285

California v. Green 227, 249, 254, 270-71, 279
Carpenter v. Davis 237
Carter v. Kentucky 334
Central of Georgia Railway Co. v. Reeves 130-31
Cestero v. Ferrara 185
Chambers v. Mississippi 80, 115-16, 243, 285-86
                                             287, 318
Chapman v. California 460, 461
Chapple, State v. 424-25
City and County of San Francisco v.
   Superior Court................................. 297-98
City of Philadelphia v. Westinghouse
   Electric Corp. 307
City of Webster Groves v. Quick 146-47
Clark v. State 290-91, 299, 302

Clay, People v. 401-02
Cleghorn v. New York Central & H. River
   Railway Co..................................... 19
Coleman, Commonwealth v. 188
Coles v. Harsch 95-96
Collins, People v. 416-17
Collins, State ex rel. v. Superior Court 112-13
County Court of Ulster County v. Allen 450-51
Coy v. Iowa 278
Crimmins, People v. 393
Crocker v. Lee 392
Curcio v. U.S. 324
Cuthbertson, U.S. v. 347

Daggett v. Atchison, Topeka & Santa Fe
   Railway Co...................................... 57
Daghita, People v. 344
Dallas County v. Commercial Union
   Assurance Co. 258
Davenport v. Ourisman-Mandell
   Chevrolet, Inc. 376, 385
David, State v..................................... 410
Davis v. Alaska 100, 277
DiCarlo v. U.S. 248
Doe v. U.S. 333
Doe, U.S. v. 323, 331-32
Donnelly v. U.S. 238, 242
Dorsey, U.S. v. 82
Douglas v. Alabama 283
Dowling v. U.S. 33
Doyle v. Ohio 157, 334-35
Dutton v. Evans 272
Dyer v. MacDougall 437-38

Een v. Consolidated Freightways 404
Enskat, People v.............................. 380-81
Erie v. Tompkins............................. 452-53
Escobar, U.S. v. 131
Espinoza, U.S. v. 368-69

Farber, Matter of 347-48
Fatico, U.S. v. 440, 441
Feinberg, U.S. v.................................. 439
Fielding, U.S. v. 165-66
Figueroa, U.S. v. 34
Filesi v. U.S..................................... 241-42
Finch v. Weiner 70
Finkle, State v. 466
Fisher v. U.S. 306, 332
Fosher, U.S. v. 424
Frye v. U.S. 414-16, 419, 420-21

Gaines v. Thomas 228
Gardner, People v. 256
Garner v. U.S..................................... 330
Garner, U.S. v. 261, 261, 263
Garver, State v. 398
Gordon-Nikkar v. U.S. 310
Gould, U.S. v. 471
Government of Virgin Islands v. Smith 338
Government of Virgin Islands v. Carino........... 41
Grady, U.S. v..................................... 208
Grand Jury Proceedings, In re 301, 331

Green v. Georgia 287
Grenada-Steel Industries v. Alabama Oxygen Co. . 58-59
Griffin v. California 334
Grimes v. Employers' Mutual Liability
    Insurance Co. 375
Grosso v. U.S. 332-33

Hall v. General Motors Corp. 395
Halloran v. Virginia Chemicals, Inc. 47-48
Hansford v. U.S. 34-35
Harper & Row Publishers, Inc. v. Decker 308
Hearst, U.S. v. 34, 89, 328
Herzig v. Swift & Co. 379, 381
Hess v. Marinari 21
Hinds v. John Hancock Mutual Life Ins. Co. 446
Hiss, U.S. v. 111-12
Hitch v. Pima Superior Court 304, 305
Hoffman v. U.S. 327
Hoosier, U.S. v. 155
Houston Oxygen Co. v. Davis 187
Howard, U.S. v. 31-32
Huddleston v. U.S. 29, 32-33
Hurd, State v. 113

Idaho v. Wright 274
Inadi, U.S. v. 272, 281
Iron Shell, U.S. v. 170

Jarboe v. The Home Bank & Trust Co. 370
Javins v. First National Realty Corp. 463-64, 470
Jenkins v. Anderson 157, 334-35
Johnson v. Baltimore & Ohio Railroad Co. 78
Johnson v. Lutz 195-96, 201
Johnson v. Misericordia Community Hospital 130
Johnson, U.S. v. 403
Joice v. Missouri-Kansas-Texas Railway 62-63
Jones v. State 24-25, 26
Jones v. Superior Court 319
Jones, U.S. v. 468

Karsun v. Kelley 54
Kastigar v. U.S. 336
Keegan v. Green Giant Co. 371-72
Kelly, People v. 415, 421
Kirby v. U.S. 221-22
Klindt, State v. 419
Knapp v. State 13
Knight v. Otis Elevator Co. 403
Knihal v. State 390
Krulewitch v. U.S. 165

Lawrence, State v. 467
Leake v. Hagert 117-18
Lee v. Illinois 242, 270, 274, 275, 284
Legille v. Dann 448
Lego v. Twomey 441, 455
Leland v. Oregon 435
Leone, People v. 114
Lewis' Estate In re 244
Lifschultz, In Re 316, 317
Lines, People v. 298
Linthicum v. Richardson 53
Little, State v. 33
Litton Systems Inc. v. AT&T 211
Lloyd v. American Export Lines, Inc. 229-30

Los Robles Motor Lodge, Inc. v. Dept. of
    Alcoholic Beverage Control 128
Luce v. U.S. 85
Lungsford, State v. 216
Lynes, People v. 368

Mack, State v. 112-13
Mahlandt v. Wild Canid Survival &
    Research Center, Inc. 151-52
Mahone, U.S. v. 83-84
Malloy v. Hogan 322
Mancari v. Frank P. Smith, Inc. 365, 366
Mancusi v. Stubbs 224
Mandel, U.S. v. 183
Marriage of Tresnak In re 465-66
Martin v. Ohio 435-36, 450
Marx & Co., Inc. v. Diners Club, Inc. 401
Maryland v. Craig 279
Massey, People v. 33
Matthew v. State 154
Mattox v. U.S. 275, 282
Mavroudis v. Superior Court 320
McCray v. Illinois 353
McDaniel, U.S. v. 333
McGautha v. California 328
McKeever, U.S. v. 369
McKelvey Co. v. General Casualty Co.
    of America 234-35
McKinnon v. Skil Corp. 216
McPartlin, U.S. v. 312
McSloy, State v. 74
Meredith, People v. 305
Merkouris, People v. 182
Meyers v. U.S. 379-80
Michelson v. U.S. 40
Miles, U.S. v. 79
Miranda v. Arizona 321, 325, 326
Miranda, State v. 41
Monarch Federal Savings & Loan Assoc.
    v. Genser 203
Mosley v. Commonwealth 111
Mullaney v. Wilbur 435-36, 450
Murphy Automobile Parts Co. v. Ball 186
Murphy v. Waterfront Commission of New
    York Harbor 337
Mutual Life Insurance Co. v. Hillmon . . . 174-78, 181-83
Mutual Life Insurance Co. v. Kelly 22

Nehring v. Smith 60-61
Nelson v. O'Neil 253-54
Newton v. State 92
Nix v. Whiteside 315
Nixon, U.S. v. 350
Nobles, U.S. v. 339

Oates, U.S. v. 207, 208-10
Ohio v. Roberts . . 224-25, 268, 270, 272, 273-76, 281-83
Olden v. Kentucky 100
Olwell, State v. 303, 304-05, 306
194th St. Hotel Corp. v. Hopf 130
Oswalt, State v. 102-04
Owens, U.S. v. 72, 90, 256-57, 276-77, 280, 339

Palmer v. Hoffman 196-97, 212
Pape, U.S. v. 301

Parris, State v. 239-40
Patterson v. New York 435, 450, 452
Pawlowski v. Eskofski 156
Pennsylvania v. Muniz 325
Pheaster, U.S. v. 177-80
Poe, State v. 14-15
Pointer v. Texas 270
Pope, State ex rel. v. Superior Court 44
Prichard v. U.S. 296
Prink v. Rockefeller Center, Inc. 318

Queen's [Caroline's] Case 96-97

Rabata v. Dohner 410
Radiant Burners v. American Gas Associate 307
Rancourt v. Waterville Urban Renewal Authority .. 414
Reynolds, U.S. v. 348-49, 350, 351
Ricardo, People v. 284
Riccardi, U.S. v. 75
Robinson v. Shapiro 259-60, 261
Robinson, U.S. v. 399-400
Robitaille v. Netoco Committee Theaters 51
Rock v. Arkansas 113-14
Roder, People v. 451-52
Roe v. Wade 470
Rogers v. U.S. 329
Roviaro v. U.S. 352, 353
Rubin, U.S. v. 109
Ruhala v. Roby 252
Ruth v. Fenchel 412
Ryder, In re 302, 304, 310

Safeway Stores, Inc. v. Combs 117-18
Saldana, State v. 426
San Antonio Traction Co. v. Cox 54
Sandstrom v. Montana 451-52
Saporen, State v. 249
Scales, U.S. v. 386
Scarlett, State v. 360
Schmerber v. California 325
School District of Ferndale, U.S. v. 211
Segal, U.S. v. 71
Seiler v. Lucas-Film, Ltd. 385
Semler v. Psychiatric Institute of Washington 221
Shapiro v. U.S. 332, 333
Shepard v. U.S. 180-83
Shirley, People v. 112
Silver v. New York Central Railroad 136-37
Sindell v. Abbott Laboratories 432
Sirico v. Cotto 378
Smith v. Rapid Transit, Inc. 440
Smith, U.S. v. 207
Soles v. State 234
Soley v. Star & Herald Co. 468
Sollars v. State 132-33
Sorge, People v. 87-89
Spreigl, State v. 28-29, 35
Stifel, U.S. v. 421-22
Stovall v. Denno 281

Stover, U.S. v. 29-30
Strange, U.S. v. 353
Straub v. Reading Co. 69
Subramaniam v. Public Prosecutor 129

Tarasoff v. Regents of University of California 320
Tatum, State v. 390
Taylor v. Illinois 286, 339
Taylor, U.S. v. 439
Ternan, State v. 92
Texas Department of Community Affairs v.
  Burdine 446-47
Thevis, U.S. v. 261
Toney, U.S. v. 82
Town of Ninety-Six v. Southern Railway Co. 217
Trammel v. U.S. 340, 342-43
Travelers Fire Insurance Co. v. Wright 227-28
Tucker v. State 32
Turbyfill v. International Harvester Co. ... 260, 264-65
Turkish, U.S. v. 338

U. of Illinois v. Spalding 367
Upjohn v. U.S. 307, 308-09, 313-14

Valdez, State v. 115
Van Gaasbeck, People v. 36-37
Varcoe v. Lee 465
Vitello, Commonwealth v. 115
Vlandis v. Kline 448-49

Wade, U.S. v. 281
Wanoskia, U.S. v. 394-95
Washington v. Texas 285, 286, 287
Washington v. U.S. 422
Watson v. State 359
Weinberger v. Salfi 449
Werner v. Upjohn Co. Inc. 57
Whelton v. Daly 367
White v. State 76
Williams v. Alexander 200-01
Williams v. Florida 338-39
Williams, U.S. v. 421
Wilson County Board of Education v. Lamm 236
Wilson v. State 233-34
Winship, In re 434, 435, 439, 440, 451, 460
Wong, U.S. v. 82
Woodruff, U.S. v. 299
Woods, U.S. v. 32, 33
Wright v. Doe d. Tatham 125-26, 138-40, 141-42

Yates v. Bair Transport, Inc. 198

Zackowitz, People v. 23, 25
Zenith Radio Corp. v. Matsushita Electric
  Industrial Co., Ltd. 264, 364, 366
Zenni, U.S. v. 139, 140-41
Zippo Manufacturing Co. v. Rogers Imports, Inc. 134-35
Zolin, U.S. 310-11

REFERENCES TO THE
FEDERAL RULES OF EVIDENCE

101	1
103	459
103(a)	461
103(a)(1)	4
103(a)(2)	7
103(b)	7
103(c)	7
103(d)	461
104(a)	454
104(b)	234, 364, 368, 456-57
104(c)	457
201	464, 466-67, 471
201(b)	467
201(e)	468
201(f)	469
201(g)	467-68, 471
301	446-47
302	453
303	447
401	10, 13
402	10
403	14-15, 24, 27, 34, 63, 81-84, 98, 105-06, 244, 254
404(a)	20, 219
404(a)(1)	43
404(a)(2)	42, 44
404(b)	24, 26, 31, 32
405(a)	19-20, 38, 39, 41, 45
405(b)	19-20
406	49-50
407	56-58
408	61-63
409	65
410	64, 154
410(2)	64, 87
410(4)	64-65
410(i)	65
411	59
412	42, 44-47, 278
412(a)	45, 46
412(b)	46
412(b)(1)	45, 46-47, 278
412(b)(2)	47
412(b)(2)(A)	45
412(b)(2)(B)	45
412(c)	46
412(c)(1)	45
412(c)(2)	45, 46
412(c)(3)	46
501	292, 342, 343, 345, 347, 349
502 (Prop.)	292
503 (Prop.)	292
503(b) (Prop.)	296
503(d)(1) (Prop.)	310
503(d)(2) (Prop.)	311
503(d)(3) (Prop.)	311
503(d)(5) (Prop.)	311-12
504 (Prop.)	292, 316
505 (Prop.)	292
505(c)(2) (Prop.)	341, 343
506 (Prop.)	292, 343
507 (Prop.)	292
508 (Prop.)	292, 354
509 (Prop.)	292, 349
509(a)(2)(B) (Prop.)	350
510 (Prop.)	292
510(c)(1) (Prop.)	353
510(c)(2) (Prop.)	353
601	8-9
602	8, 397-98
603	8
607	80, 90, 98
608	89, 90
608(a)	92-93
608(a)(1)	93
608(a)(2)	106
608(b)	88-90, 93
608(b)(2)	93
609	82-84, 87-90
609(a)	81, 84, 90
609(a)(1)	85
609(1)(2)	82
609(b)	84, 85
609(c)	86
609(d)	86
609(e)	86
610	106
611(a)	100
611(b)	71
611(c)	68, 70, 80
612	76
612(2)	75
613(a)	97
613(b)	95, 96
614(a)	76
614(b)	76
615	3
701	399, 400
701(a)	399
701(b)	399
702	402-04, 415, 424
703	398, 406-08, 410
704	402
704(a)	400, 423
704(b)	423
705	408, 410-11
706	412
706(c)	413
801	125, 141, 159, 247
801(a)	125, 135, 139, 141, 142
801(a)(2)	126, 137, 141
801(c)	125, 142
801(d)	125
801(d)(1)	94, 127, 256-57, 263
801(d)(1)(A)	126, 248, 252, 254, 263, 279
801(d)(1)(B)	109, 126, 213, 255, 279
801(d)(1)(C)	126, 248, 256-57, 280
801(d)(2)	96, 126, 150, 152
801(d)(2)(A)	152
801(d)(2)(B)	155
801(d)(2)(C)	158-59

801(d)(2)(D) 152, 158, 160
801(d)(2)(E) 158, 164, 166, 455
803 . . . . 206, 211, 218, 259, 272
803(1) 186-88, 261
803(2) 184, 186, 261
803(3) 169, 173, 176, 178, 182, 184, 261
803(4) 170-72, 261
803(5) 189-92, 208, 212, 260, 261, 264
803(6) 194-95, 197-99, 208-09, 261
803(7) 199, 261
803(8) 205-14, 261
803(8)(B) 197, 206-10, 212-14
803(8)(C) 206-12, 214
803(9) 220, 261
803(10) 221, 261
803(11) 220, 261
803(12) 220, 261
803(13) 219, 245, 261
803(15) 218, 261
803(16) 217-19, 261
803(17) 216, 261
803(18) 214-16, 261, 412
803(19) 218, 245, 261
803(20) 219, 261
803(21) 219, 261
803(22) 221-22, 261
803(24) 208, 258-59, 261, 265, 268
804 . . . . 272, 282
804(a) 223, 283
804(a)(3) 257
804(b) 259
804(b)(1) 225, 227, 229-30, 260, 261, 275
804(b)(2) 223, 231-33, 261
804(b)(3) 223, 235, 238, 240-42, 261, 286

804(b)(4) 223, 244, 261
804(b)(5) 258-60, 263-65, 268
805 . . . . 146, 260
806 272
901(a) 359, 360, 362, 364
901(b) 360, 362-63
901(b)(1) 363-64
901(b)(2) 367
901(b)(4) 365-66
901(b)(6) 360
901(b)(8) 217, 370
901(b)(9) 391
902 371
902(4) 204
902(5) 371
902(6) 371
902(7) 371-72
903 369
1001 389
1001(1) 377, 385
1001(2) 378
1001(3) 391
1001(4) 377, 384, 392
1002 . . . . 377, 378
1003 . . . . 377, 384, 389
1004 388
1004(1) 385, 388, 389
1004(2) 385
1004(3) 386
1004(4) 381, 389
1005 . . . . 204, 382, 386
1006 386-87
1007 387-88
1008 . . . . 389, 455

SUBJECT-MATTER INDEX

ADMISSIONS
Generally, 149-68
Adoptive admissions, 155-58
Agent, admission by, 159-61
Conduct as, 154
Conspirator, admission by co-, 161-67
    See also CONSPIRATORS
Criminal defendant, admission by, 154-55
Distinguished from declaration against
    interest, 150-51
Federal Rule on, 152
First-hand knowledge not required, 151-52
General rule, 150
Opinion or conclusion contained in, 151-52
Personal admissions, 152-55
Pleadings as, 153-54
Privity, persons in, 167-68
Representative admissions, 158-61
    Explicitly authorized, 158-59
    Vicarious admission by agent, 159-61
Silence as, 156-58

ANCIENT DOCUMENTS
Authentication of, 370-71
Hearsay exception for, 217-18

APPEAL
Sufficiency of evidence reviewed on, 461-62

ARGUMENTATIVE QUESTIONS, 76

ATTORNEY-CLIENT PRIVILEGE
Generally, 292-315
Confidential communication required, 296-300
    Client-to-lawyer statements, 297
    Lawyer-to-client statements, 297
    Third parties, 297-98, 305-06
Corporations as clients, 307-09
"Crime or fraud" exception to, 310-11
Death of client, 311
Dispute between attorney and client, 311
Federal Rule, proposed text of, 292-93
Identity of client, 300-01
Joint clients, 311-12
Physical evidence, 301-07
    Concealment of evidence, 301-03
    Destruction of evidence, 302
    Documents, 306-07
    Source, evidence of, 304-05
    Turning over to prosecution, 304
Professional relationship required, 296
Rationale for, 294-96
Work product immunity, 313-14

AUTHENTICATION
Generally, 359-72
Ancient documents, 370-71
Attesting witnesses, 369-70
Certified copies of public records, 371
Demonstrative evidence, 362
Federal Rules on, 362-64
Judge-jury allocation, 364

Movies, 391
Pictorial evidence, 389-91
Public records, 371
Real evidence, 360-62
Self-authentication, 371-72
Sound recordings, 369
Telephone conversations, 367-69
Writings, 364-71
    Direct testimony about, 365-66
    Distinctive characteristics of, 366
    Handwriting on, 366-67
    Labels, 371-72
    Newspaper articles, 371
    No presumption of authenticity of, 365
    Reply letters and telegrams, 367
    Signature on, 366-67

BENCH TRIALS
Rules for, 458-59

BEST EVIDENCE RULE
Generally, 375-89
Admission by adversary, 387-88
Collateral writings exception, 381
Computer print-outs, 391-92
Contract, 381
Definition of, 375
Excuses for non-production, 384-86
Federal Rule on, 375
Incidental record, 379-81
Judge-jury allocation, 388-89
Lost or destroyed original, 385
"Original" defined, 381-83
Photographs, 378, 380-81
Photocopies, 383-84
Public records, 386
Reproductions, 383-84
Requirements for, 376
Secondary evidence, preferences among, 388
Sound recordings, 378
Summaries, 386-87
Writing
    Applicable to, 376
    Definition of, 377-78
    Existence of writing, 378-79
    Incidental record, 379-81
    Inscription, 377-78
    Photograph as, 378
    Proving terms of, 378-81
    Sound recording as, 378
    Transcript, 379-80

BIAS
See also IMPEACHMENT OF WITNESS'
    CREDIBILITY
Impeachment by showing of, 98-100

BURDEN OF PROOF
Generally, 427-41
Allocating, 431-36
    In civil cases, 431-33
    In criminal cases, 433-36

"Beyond reasonable doubt" standard, 440-41
Persuasion, burden of
    Allocation of, in civil cases, 431-33
    "Clear and convincing" standard, 440
    Defined, 427
    In criminal cases, 434-36
    Satisfying, in civil case, 439-40
    Satisfying, in criminal case, 440-41
    Significance of, 430-31
"Preponderance of the evidence" standard, 439-40
Production, burden of
    Defined, 427
    In criminal cases, 434
    Satisfying in civil case, 437-38
    Satisfying in criminal case, 438-39
    Shifting of, 429
    Statistical evidence to satisfy, 439-40

BUSINESS RECORDS EXCEPTION
Generally, 193-204
Absence of entry in records, 198-99
Accident reports, 196-97
"Business" defined, 194
Business duty by person reporting, 195-96
Computer print-outs, 202-04
Federal Rule on, 194
First-hand information required, 195
History of, 193-94
Hospital records, 200-02
Opinions contained in record, 197-98
Oral reports, 199-200
Police reports, 197
Proving, procedure for, 200
Public record, use of against accused, 208-10
"Regular course of business" requirement, 196-97
Trustworthiness required, 198

CHAIN OF CUSTODY
Real evidence, use of to authenticate, 361-62, 373

CHARACTER
Generally, 17-47
Care, civil cases, 20-21
Civil cases, 20-22
Crimes
    See also OTHER CRIMES
    Civil cases, 21-22
    Criminal cases, 22-36
Criminal defendant, good character of, 36-40
    Cross-examination of witness to, 38-40
    Opinion not allowed as to, 37
    Rebuttal by prosecution, 38-40
    Relevance, requirement of, 37
    Reputation evidence, use of to prove, 37
    Specific incidents, proof of not allowed, 37
General rule regarding evidence of, 20
Impeachment by proof of bad, 91-93
In issue, 19-20
Other crimes, see OTHER CRIMES
Victim, bad character of, 40-47
    Federal Rules on, 42
    Murder victim's violent character, 41-43
    Prosecution, rebuttal by, 42-43
    Rape shield laws, 44-47
    Rape victim, 43-47

CIRCUMSTANTIAL EVIDENCE
Definition of, 11

COLLATERAL ISSUE RULE
Generally, 102-05
Bias, 104
Character for truthfulness, 93, 104
Contradiction of main witness' testimony, 104
Prior bad acts, 87, 104
Prior convictions, 81, 103-04
Sensory or mental defect, 104

COMMENT ON EVIDENCE
Judge's right to make, 458

COMPETENCY OF WITNESSES
Generally, 7-9
Common-law approach to, 7
Dead Man's Statutes, 8-9
Diversity cases, 8
Federal Rules on, 7-8
Meaning of, 7
Mental incapacity or immaturity, 8
Modern approach to, 7-9

**COMPROMISE AND OFFERS OF
COMPROMISE**
Generally, 60-63
Admissions of fact accompanying, 61-62
Exceptions to rule of exclusion, 61-63
Federal Rule on, 61-62
Medical expenses, offer to pay, 65

COMPULSORY PROCESS
Accomplice's testimony as violating, 284-85
Due Process clause, relation to, 287
Equality principle, 286-87
Hearsay rules as violating, 285

COMPUTER PRINT-OUTS
Authentication of, 391
Best Evidence rule and, 391

CONFRONTATION
Generally, 269-84
Co-conspirator's out-of-court statement, 281
Co-defendant's statement, 283-84
Cross-examination, opportunity for, 275-76
Declarant unavailable, 282-83
Dying declaration, 282
Face-to-face, right to, 278-79
Former testimony, 282
"Indicia of reliability" required, 273-76
Live testimony preferred, 271-72
Particularized facts showing reliability, 273-74
Rape Shield laws as violating, 278
Statement against interest, 282
Testifying witness, right to confront, 276-79
Traditional hearsay exceptions as satisfying, 273
Witness denies recollection of event, 279-80
Witness refuses to answer, 276-77

CONSPIRATORS
Admissions by, 161-67
    Charge of conspiracy not required, 166

"During course of" requirement, 164-65
General rule, 162
"In furtherance of" requirement, 165-66
Procedure for admitting statement by, 166-67
Rationale, 162-64

CRIMES
Proof of other crimes by D, *see* OTHER CRIMES

CROSS-EXAMINATION
See WITNESSES, EXAMINATION OF

CUSTOM
See HABIT AND CUSTOM

DEAD MAN'S STATUTES
See also COMPETENCY
Effect on competency of witnesses, 8-9

DECLARATIONS AGAINST INTEREST
Generally, 234-43
Admissions, distinguished from, 235
Collateral statements, 240-41
Confrontation, use of declaration violates, 282
Constitutional issues, 242-43
Federal Rule on, 235
Neutral statements, 240-41
Pecuniary interest, 236-37
Penal interest, 237-40
Corroboration of exculpatory
statement, 238-39
Inculpation of accused, 239-40
Tort liability, 237

DEMONSTRATIONS AND EXPERIMENTS
Generally, 394-95
Similarity of conditions, 394-95

DEMONSTRATIVE EVIDENCE
Authentication of, 359
Defined, 357
Diagrams, 392
Fair representation, requirement of, 374
Foundation for, 357, 359, 374
Maps and models, 392
Prejudice caused by, 375
Summaries, 392

DIRECT EVIDENCE
Definition of, 11

DYING DECLARATIONS
Generally, 231-34
Awareness of imminent death, 231-32
Confrontation, right of not violated, 282
Death, requirement of actual, 232
Homicide, requirement of, 232
Opinions contained in declaration, 233
Preliminary questions of fact, 234
Victim, requirement that declarant be, 232-33

EXPERTS
Court-appointed, 412-13
Cross-examination of, 411-12
Discovery of, 413-14

Hypothetical question, 408-411
Opinion of
Disclosure to jury of basis for, 408
Hypothetical question as basis for, 406
Inadmissible evidence as basis for, 406-08
Personal knowledge, based on, 405-06
Prior testimony observed as basis for, 406
Qualifications of, 403-04
Subject matter of testimony by, 404-05

EXCITED UTTERANCES
Generally, 184-87
Reference to exciting event, 186
Time lapse, 185-86

EXTRINSIC EVIDENCE
See also COLLATERAL ISSUE RULE;
IMPEACHMENT OF WITNESS' CREDIBILITY
Bias, 99-100
Prior bad acts, 87
Prior inconsistent statement, 97-98

FEDERAL RULES OF EVIDENCE
Adoption of, 1
States, adoption of by, 2

FIRST-HAND KNOWLEDGE
See KNOWLEDGE, FIRST-HAND

FORMER TESTIMONY
Generally, 225-31
Confrontation, right of not violated, 282
Cross-examination, opportunity for, 225-27
Issues, identity of, 227-28
Parties, identity of, 228-31
Preliminary hearing, 227

FOUNDATION
Bias, 99-100
Demonstrative evidence, 357
Prior inconsistent statement, 95-97
Real evidence, 356-57

GUILTY PLEAS
Inadmissibility of, 64-65

HABIT AND CUSTOM
Generally, 47-50
Business practice, 50
Character, distinguished from, 48
Federal Rule on, 49
Minority rule, 48-49

HARMLESS ERROR, 459-60

HEARSAY
See also individual exceptions
Absence of complaints as, 136
Admissions, see ADMISSIONS
Assertions not offered for truth of matter
asserted, 141-43
"Availability of declarant immaterial"
exceptions, 168-222
Business records exceptions, *see* BUSINESS
RECORDS

Conduct, 135-41
   Non-assertive conduct, 138-41
   Silence as, 136-38
Convictions, previous felony, 221-22
Cross-examination, lack of, 121
Dangers of, 118-21
Declarations against interest, see DECLARATIONS
   AGAINST INTEREST
Definition, 117, 122
Diagram illustrating, 118
Dying declarations, see DYING DECLARATIONS
Effect on hearer or reader, statement offered to
   show, 129-31
Exceptions, 149-268
   See also individual bold-faced entries for
      each exception
Excited utterances, see EXCITED UTTERANCES
Family records exception, 219
Federal Rule, 125
First-hand knowledge, distinguished from
   lack of, 143-45
Former testimony, see FORMER TESTIMONY
Future of, 266-68
History, exception for facts of, 219
Impeachment, 135
Intent of declarant, see Mental State
Learned writings, exception for, 214-16
Machine or animal, "statement" by, 146-48
Mental state, statements about declarant's, 172-84
   As proof of another's act, 177-80
   As proof of declarant's prior act, 180-84
   As proof of subsequent act, 175-76
   Present state as bearing on past or future
      state, 174
   State of mind directly in issue, 172-75
   Will, statement regarding declarant's, 184
Multiple hearsay, 145-46, 212-14
Notice, statement offered to show, 130
Opinion surveys, 134-35
Out-of-court statement, 126
Past recollection recorded, see PAST RECOL-
   LECTION RECORDED
Pedigree, see PEDIGREE, STATEMENTS OF
Personal or family history, exception for
   facts of, 218-19
Physical condition, statement as to, 168-72
   Lay person, made to, 169
   Physician who testifies but doesn't
      treat, 171-72
   Treating physician, made to, 170-71
Present sense impression, see PRESENT
   SENSE IMPRESSION
Prior statement by witness, see PRIOR
   STATEMENTS BY AVAILABLE WITNESS
Public records and reports, see PUBLIC
   RECORDS
Reputation, exception for statements
   showing, 134, 218-19
Res Gestae exceptions, 168, 188
Residual exception, 257-66
   Corroboration by other evidence, 262-63
   Federal Rule on, 258-61
   Grand jury testimony, 260
   "Near-miss" problem, 264-65
   Notice requirement, 265-66

Trustworthiness, circumstantial guarantees
   of required, 261-64
"Statement," meaning of, 135-38
State of mind of declarant, statement offered
   to show, 131-34
Title documents, exception for recitals in, 218
Treatises, exception for, 214-16
Truth of matter asserted, 127-35
"Unavailable" defined, 223-25
"Unavailability of declarant required"
   exception, generally, 222-25
Verbal acts, 128
Verbal parts of acts, 128-29
Vital statistics, exception for, 219-20
Will, execution or revocation of, 184
Written hearsay, 117
Written report of oral statement, 145

HYPNOSIS
Statements made under influence of, 112
Testimony of witness after, 112-14

HYPOTHETICAL QUESTION
Asked to expert, 408-11

IDENTIFICATION, STATEMENT OF
Common-law rule on use of, 247-48, 255-56
Cross-examination, requirement of, 256-57
Federal Rule on use of, 247-48, 256-57

IMPEACHMENT OF WITNESS' CREDIBILITY
   Generally, 77-106
Alcohol, 101
Bad acts, prior, 87-91
   Crime for which no conviction occurred, 90
   Extrinsic evidence of, 87
   Federal Rule on, 88
Bias, 98-100
Character, witness' reputation for, 91-93
Collateral issue rule, 102-05
   See also COLLATERAL ISSUE RULE
Contradiction, impeachment by, 102-05
Convictions, prior criminal, 80-87
   Civil case, use in, 84
   Crimen falsi, 82
   Federal Rule on, 82-85
   Felony not involving dishonesty, 82, 83-84
   In limine motions, 85
   Old convictions, 84-85
   Procedure for using, 86
   Witness other than accused, use against, 84
Drug addiction, 101
Opinion regarding witness' character, 91-93
Own witness, rule against impeaching, 78-80
Prior inconsistent statement by witness, 93-98
   Extrinsic evidence of, 94, 97-98
   Foundation required for, 94, 95-97
   Writing, 96-97
Psychiatric testimony, 101
Rehabilitation after impeachment, see REHAB-
   ILITATION OF WITNESS
Religious beliefs of witness, 105-06
Reputation as to character, 91-93
Sensory or mental defect in witness, 101

INSURANCE
Generally, 59-60
Liability insurance, proof of not admissible, 59-60

JUDGE-JURY ALLOCATION
Comment on evidence by judge, 458
Competence, 454-55
Conditional relevance, 456-57
Fact, issues of, 454-57
Federal Rule on, 454
Hearsay, 454
Instructions, 457-58
Jury, presence of, 457
Law, issues of, 454
Preliminary fact question, 456
Privilege, 454
Relevance, 455-57

JUDICIAL NOTICE
Generally, 463-72
Adjudicative facts
"Common knowledge," 465-66
Contradictory evidence as to noticed fact, 468-69
Defined, 463
Federal Rule on, 464-65
"Immediately verifiable," 466
Jury's right to disregard, 466-68
Time for taking notice of, 469
Function of, 463
Federal Rule on, 464-65
Law, notice of
Domestic law, 472
Foreign countries, 472
Sister state's law, 472
Legislative facts,
Binding on jury, 471
Defined, 463-64
Types of, 469-70
Federal Rules silent, 470

KNOWLEDGE, FIRST-HAND
Experts not required to have, 397
General requirement of, 397-98

LIABILITY INSURANCE
See INSURANCE

LIE DETECTOR TESTS
General rule excluding, 114
Psychological Stress Evaluation tests, 116
Stipulation regarding use of, 115

MATERIALITY
Relevance, requirement for, 10

MISLEADING QUESTIONS, 76

NEUTRON ACTIVATION ANALYSIS, 421-22

OBJECTIONS
Generally, 4-7
Exceptions, taking of, 5
Specificity, how much required, 4
Time for making, 4

OFFER OF PROOF
Generally, 6
Cross-examination, not needed on, 6
Federal Rule on, 7
Presence of jury during, 6

OPINIONS
Federal Rules on, 397-98, 399
Law, opinion of, 401-02
Lay opinions discouraged, 398-400
On ultimate issue, 400-02
"Short-hand rendition" exception to ban on, 398-99

OTHER CRIMES
See also CHARACTER
Proof of, in criminal cases, 22-36
Acquittal, effect of, 33
Certainty, degree of required, 32
Context, 24
Controversy, requirement of, 34
Conviction not required, 33
Identity, 30-31
Impeachment, 31
Intent, 26-28
Knowledge, 29
Larger plan or scheme, 24-25
Modus operandi, 25-26
Motive, 29-30
Notice, prosecution not required to give before using, 35
Opportunity, 30
Preparation, 25
Sex crimes, 28-29
Signature, 25
Subsequent crimes, 34

PAST RECOLLECTION RECORDED
Generally, 189-93
Accuracy when written, testimony as to, 191
Evidentiary status of, 191-92
First-hand knowledge, requirement of, 190
Fresh in writer's memory, requirement of, 190
Impaired recollection, requirement of, 190
Non-writings, 191
Present recollection refreshed, distinguished from, 192-93

PEDIGREE, STATEMENTS OF
Before controversy arose, 244-45
Family relationship, 244
Federal Rule on, 244

PHYSICIAN-PATIENT PRIVILEGE
Confidentiality required, 317
Patient as litigant, 317-19
Psychiatrist-patient, 316
"Public safety" exception, 320
Waiver of, 317-19
Who holds privilege, 317

PLAIN ERROR, 460-61

POLYGRAPH TEST
See LIE DETECTOR TESTS

PREJUDICE
Outweighing probative value, 14-16

PRELIMINARY QUESTION OF FACT
Generally, 456-57
Dying declarations, 234

PRESENT RECOLLECTION REFRESHED
Distinguished from past recollection recorded, 192-93
Document consulted before trial, 75-76
Traditional rule, 75

PRESENT SENSE IMPRESSIONS
Generally, 187-88
Description of event required, 188

PRESUMPTIONS
Generally, 441-53
"Bursting bubble" theory, 444-46
Choice of law, 452-53
Civil cases, effect of in, 443-49
Conflicting presumptions, 447-48
Criminal cases, effect of in, 449-52
    Mandatory, 449-50, 451-52
    Permissive, 449
    Persuasion burden shifted, 451-52
    Production burden shifted, 452
Federal Rules on, 446-47
Irrebuttable presumption, 448-49
Meanings of, 441-43
Morgan theory, 444

PRIOR CONSISTENT STATEMENT
Common-law rule on use of, 246, 255
Federal Rule on, 247, 255
Use of to rehabilitate impeached witness, 108-10

PRIOR INCONSISTENT STATEMENT
See also IMPEACHMENT OF WITNESS'
    CREDIBILITY
Common-law rule on use of, 245-46
Cross-examination not required, 252-53
Federal Rule on, 247, 252-55
Forgetful witness, 254
Impeachment by proof of, 93-98
Oath, requirement of, 252
Prior statement denied, 253-54
Prior statement repudiated, 253
Proceeding, requirement of, 252
Rationales for and against allowing, 248-52

PRIOR STATEMENTS BY AVAILABLE WITNESSES
Generally, 245-57
See also PRIOR CONSISTENT STATEMENT;
    PRIOR INCONSISTENT STATEMENT;
    IDENTIFICATION, STATEMENT OF

PRIVILEGES
See also bold-faced listings for individual
    privileges
Generally, 288-355
Accountant-client, 355
Attorney-client, see ATTORNEY-CLIENT
    PRIVILEGE

Counselor-counselee, 355
Eavesdropping as affecting, 290-91
Federal law governing, 291-92
Government information, 348-54
    Informers, 351-53
    Internal deliberations, 349-50
    Military and diplomatic secrets, 348-49
    Policy-making, 349-50
    Procedure for evaluating claim of, 350-51
    Required reports and returns, 353-54
Husband-wife
    Adverse testimony privilege, 342-43
    Confidential communications
        privilege, 343-45
    Divorce, 340-41
    Exceptions to, 345
    Federal law governing, 341-42
    Pre-marital communications, 341
    Who holds, 341, 342-43
Informers, 351-53
Journalist-source, 346-48
    Constitutional argument, 346-47
    Conflict with defendant's rights, 347-48
Military and diplomatic secrets, 348-49
Parent-child communications, 354-55
Physician-patient, see PHYSICIAN-
    PATIENT PRIVILEGE
Priest-penitent, 345-46
Self-incrimination, see SELF-INCRIM-
    INATION, PRIVILEGE AGAINST
State creation of, 291
Trade secrets, 354
Values protected by, 288-89
Who may assert, 290

PROBABILITIES
As evidence, 416-19
Foundation for, 416-17

PROBATIVE VALUE
See also RELEVANCE
Requirement of, 10

PSYCHIATRIC TESTIMONY
Regarding credibility of witness, 110-12

PUBLIC RECORDS AND REPORTS
Generally, 204-214
Absence of entry in, 221
Activities of public office, 205-06
Criminal cases, 207-10
    Accused's use of, 207
    Business records exception, use of
        against accused, 208
    "Other law enforcement personnel,"
        reports by, 207
Common-law rule, 204-05
Evaluative reports, 210-11
Federal Rule on, 205
"Factual findings," 210-11
Investigative reports, 206-07
Matters observed under duty, 206
Multiple hearsay, 212-14
Trustworthiness, requirement of, 211-12, 214

RAPE SHIELD LAWS
Generally, 44-47
Confrontation, violation of right of, 278
Federal rape shield provision, 44-47

REAL EVIDENCE
Admission of, 358
Authentication of, 359, 360-62
Chain of custody, 361-62
"Ready identifiability" method, 360-61
Defined, 356
Foundation for, 357, 359
Jury room, taking of exhibits into, 396
Pictorial evidence, 389-91

RECROSS EXAMINATION
See WITNESSES, EXAMINATION OF

REDIRECT EXAMINATION
See WITNESSES, EXAMINATION OF

REHABILITATION OF WITNESS
After impeachment, 106-10
Good character for truthfulness, 107-08
Meeting the attack, requirement of, 107
Prior consistent statement, use of 108-10

RELEVANCE
Generally, 10-16
Credibility irrelevant, 14
Inference, chain of, 12
Probative relationship, requirement of, 10
Materiality, 10

REMEDIAL MEASURES
See REPAIRS

REPAIRS
Generally, 55-59
Federal Rule, 56, 57
General rule, 55
Impeachment, proof of to show, 57
Ownership, proof of to show, 56-57
Product liability suit, 58-59
Third persons, repair by, 58

SCIENTIFIC EVIDENCE
Eyewitness testimony, reliability of, 423-25
Frye standard for, 414-16
Intoxication, 420
Neutron Activation Analysis, 421-22
Paternity tests, 418
Probabilities, 416-419
Psychology and psychiatry, 422-26
Radar, 419-20
Speed detection, 419-20
Voice prints, 420-21

SELF-INCRIMINATION, PRIVILEGE AGAINST
Generally, 320-39
Burden of establishing, 326-27
Comment on exercise of, 333-36
Civil suits, 335-36
Exercise in prior proceedings, 334-35
Pre-arrest silence, 334-35
Compulsory, requirement that disclosure be, 325-26
Corporations, no use by, 323
Criminal defendant, invocation by, 326
Documents, application to, 330
Contents of, 331
Production of, 331-32
"Required records" exception, 332-33
Immunity, 336-38
Defense witnesses, 337
Perjury, not applicable to, 337
Transactional, 336
Use, 336
Prosecutorial discovery as violation of, 338-39
Rationale for and against, 321-22
"Required records" exception to, 332-33
States, applicable to, 322
Testimonial, information must be, 325
Waiver of, 327-30
Who may assert, 323-24
Witness, invocation by, 326

SETTLEMENTS
See COMPROMISE AND OFFERS OF COMPROMISE

SEQUESTRATION OF WITNESSES
Federal Rule allowing, 3-4

SIMILAR HAPPENINGS
Generally, 50-55
Accidents and injuries, 51
Accident-proneness, 54
Contracts, 52-53
Fraud, 54
General rule, 50-51
Past safety, evidence of, 51-52
Plaintiff, prior claims by same, 54

SUMMARY OF EVIDENCE
Judge's right to make, 458

TREATISES
Hearsay exception for, 214-16

ULTIMATE ISSUE
Opinions on disallowed, 400-02

VIEWS
Defendant's right to be present, 393-94
Evidentiary status of, 394
Presence of judge, 393

VOICE PRINTS, 420-21

WITNESSES, EXAMINATION OF
Generally, 66-116
Argumentative questions, 76
Court, questioning by, 77
Direct examination, 66-69
Cross-examination, 69-73
Art of, 72-73
Leading questions during, 70
Scope of, 70-72
Impeachment, see IMPEACHMENT OF

WITNESS' CREDIBILITY
Leading questions
   Definition of, 67
   Exceptions to ban on, 68-69, 70
Misleading questions, 76
Psychiatric testimony regarding witness, 110-12
Recross, 74
Redirect, 73-74

WRITINGS
See also AUTHENTICATION
Authentication of, 364-71

EMANUEL LAW OUTLINES
PRODUCTS FOR 1992-93 ACADEMIC YEAR

emanuel law outlines

Civil Procedure, *new* '92-93 Ed. $16.95

Constitutional Law, *new* '92-93 Ed 22.95

Contracts, '90-91 Ed 15.95

Corporations, *new* '92-93 Ed. 17.95

Criminal Law, *new* '92-93 Ed 14.95

Criminal Procedure, *new* '92-93 Ed 14.95

Evidence, '91-92 Ed 16.95

Property, '89-90 Ed. 16.95

Secured Transactions, '88-89 Ed 12.95

Torts (General Edition) '91-92 Ed. 16.95

Torts (Casebook Edition), '88-89 Ed 15.95
    Keyed to '88 Ed. Prosser, Wade & Schwartz

---

emanuel law tapes
Constitutional Law
New '92-93 Edition

(11 90-Minute Cassettes)

Each set is attractively displayed in a shrink-wrapped distinctive Emanuel box. Features:
- mnemonics
- songs
- skits
- Multi-State Bar Exam questions and answers
- a special night-before-the-exam review tape and
- a printed supplement.

$37.95

Steve Emanuel's
FIRST YEAR
Qs & As, '91 Ed.

1,143 Objective-style questions & answers in first-year subjects, as preparation for exams. A single volume covers Contracts, Torts, Civil Procedure, Property, Criminal Law & Procedure.

with
New '92-93 Civil Procedure Supplement

$17.95

SMITH'S REVIEW

All outlines in this series are written by law school professors for Emanuel Law Outlines. They all follow the Emanuel style and format. They have big, easy-to-read type, extensive citations and notes, and clear, crisp writing. Most have capsule summaries and sample exam Q & A's.

Agency & Partnership '88-89 Ed $11.95
Commercial Paper '90-91 Ed. 12.95
Family Law '88-89 Ed 14.95
Federal Income Taxation '90-91 Ed 14.95
Intellectual Property '90-91 Ed 15.95
Labor Law '88-89 Ed. 11.95
Products Liability '92-93 Ed. 12.95
Torts '91-92 Ed. 13.95
Wills, Trusts, Probate '88-89 Ed 13.95

SIEGEL'S Essay & Multiple-Choice Q & A's

Now published and distributed by Emanuel, each of these books contains 20-25 essay questions with model answers *plus* 50-100 Multistate-format Q & A's. The objective is to acquaint the student with the techniques needed to successfully handle law school exams.

Civil Procedure   Criminal Procedure
Constitutional Law   Evidence
Contracts   Real Property
Criminal Law   Torts

Wills & Trusts

each title . . .$14.95

Steve Finz's MULTISTATE METHOD

967 MBE (Multistate Bar Exam)-style multiple choice questions and answers covering all six Multistate subjects—**Plus** a complete 200-question model MBE practice exam—perfect for law school exam review and for the BAR EXAM in all states.

New '92-93 Title $31.95

SOCRATUTOR SOFTWARE

A specially condensed version of the corresponding Emanuel Outline on a computer disk for use on IBM-Compatible PCs. Lets you add your own comments and create your own outline.

Civil Procedure   *Criminal Law*
Constitutional Law   *Evidence*
Contracts   *Property*
Corporations   *Torts (Gen'l. Ed.)*

each title . . .$34.95